LINCOLN CHRISTIAN UNIVERSITY

 W9-BVH-054

THIRD EDITION

TEACHING *by* PRINCIPLES

An Interactive Approach

to Language Pedagogy

PEARSON
Longman

H. DOUGLAS BROWN
San Francisco State University

Teaching by Principles, An Interactive Approach to Language Pedagogy, Third Edition

Copyright © 2007 by Pearson Education, Inc.
All rights reserved.

No part of this publication may be reproduced,
stored in a retrieval system, or transmitted
in any form or by any means, electronic, mechanical,
photocopying, recording, or otherwise,
without the prior permission of the publisher.

Pearson Education, 10 Bank Street, White Plains, NY 10606

Staff credits: The people who made up the **Teaching by Principles, An Interactive Approach to Language Pedagogy, Third Edition** team, representing editorial, production, design, and manufacturing, are Danielle Belfiore, Dave Dickey, Christine Edmonds, Pam Fishman, Katherine Keyes, Tracey Munz Cataldo, and Paula Van Ells.

Cover design: Tracey Munz Cataldo
Cover image provided by: www.millworkforless.com
Text composition and text art: Laserwords Private Limited
Text font: 10.5/12.5 Garamond Book
Text credits: See p. xvi

Library of Congress Cataloging-in-Publication Data
Brown, H. Douglas
    Teaching by principles: an interactive approach to language pedagogy/
    H. Douglas Brown.—3rd ed.
        p. cm.
Includes bibliographical references and indexes.
ISBN 0-13-612711-8 (text)
    1. Language and languages—Study and teaching.   I. Title.

P51.B7754 2007
418.0071—dc22   2006037229

LONGMAN ON THE **WEB**

Longman.com offers online resources for teachers and students. Access our Companion Websites, our online catalog, and our local offices around the world.

Visit us at **longman.com**.

ISBN-10: 0-13-612711-8
ISBN-13: 978-0-13-612711-6

Printed in the United States of America
10 11 12 13 14 15 —V054—15 14 13 12 11

CONTENTS

Chapter 13   Initiating Interaction in the Classroom   **211**

Chapter 14   Sustaining Interaction through Group Work   **223**

Chapter 15   Classroom Management   **241**

Chapter 16   Strategies-Based Instruction   **257**

PREFACE

As I pulled together books, articles, chapters, abstracts, unpublished papers, notes, and electronic sources of information that spanned the seven years since the last edition of *Teaching by Principles*, I was repeatedly reminded of how complex this profession has become! Dozens of respected periodicals and hundreds of textbooks and anthologies currently offer ample evidence that language teachers must be technicians, well versed in the pedagogical options available to meet the specialized needs of the various ages, purposes, proficiency levels, skills, and contexts of language learners around the globe.

Such was not always the case. The first 40 years of the twentieth century saw little if any development of a field of language pedagogy. But by the middle of the century, language teachers witnessed the "birth" of a disciplined approach to second language learning and teaching: Methodological frameworks were the subject of applied linguistic research on the nature of language learning and the successful acquisition of languages in classrooms. Yet the nascent profession was hard put to come up with viable answers to questions about how to teach interactive skills in the classroom. By the 1970s, second language acquisition was establishing itself as a discipline in its own right, asserting its place not merely as an offshoot of linguistics or psychology. The resulting research of this adolescent profession was beginning to provide some profound observations about interactive language pedagogy. As the field gathered momentum, journals, professional organizations, university departments, and research studies grew with amazing speed.

PURPOSE AND AUDIENCE

And so today, with reams of accumulated data to sift through in order to examine our own craft, I hope that this third edition of *Teaching by Principles* will provide the kind of synthesis of the state of our art that will enlighten and challenge you. It is a book for prospective and new teachers who need to learn how to walk into a classroom and effectively accomplish communicative objectives. It primarily addresses the needs of those in teacher education programs who have never taught before, but it secondarily serves as a refresher course for those who have had some experience in the classroom. The book speaks both to those who are in English as a Second Language contexts (in English-speaking countries) and to those who are in English as a Foreign Language situations. And the book is designed to be read, studied, and enjoyed by those with little or no previous work in linguistics, psychology, or second language acquisition.

The use of the term *approach* in the subtitle of the book signals an important characteristic of current language-teaching pedagogy. For a significant part of the twentieth century, teacher education programs were expected to deliver a handful of prefabricated methods—relatively homogeneous sets of classroom practices that sprang from one particular theoretical perspective. In today's "postmethod" approach, we have graduated beyond such a restrictive concept of classroom practice. Our current and, I like to think, more *enlightened* foundations of language teaching are built on numerous principles of language learning and teaching about which we can be reasonably secure. A principled approach to interactive language pedagogy is one that is built on such foundation stones.

So, *Teaching By Principles (TBP)* is a book that helps teachers to build a repertoire of classroom techniques that are firmly embedded in well-established principles of second language acquisition. Most of these principles are treated comprehensively in my companion volume, *Principles of Language Learning and Teaching (PLLT)* (H.D. Brown, 2007), now in its fifth edition. Those who use *TBP* in their teacher-training program would benefit from (a) having first read *PLLT*, or (b) using *PLLT* as a companion text. However, *TBP* can be used effectively without its companion, since major principles on which current pedagogical practice are based are summarized here in the early chapters.

PRINCIPAL FEATURES

Most of the features of the first and second editions of *TBP* are retained:

- A practical focus grounded in fundamental principles of second language acquisition
- Reader-friendly prose that talks to teachers in plain, understandable language, with a minimum of distracting references to the dozens of potentially related research studies
- A step-by-step approach to teaching language interactively that helps the novice teacher to become confident in directing interactive, student-centered, cooperative classrooms
- Separate treatment of the four skills of listening, speaking, reading, and writing, but with special emphasis on the integration of skills

- End-of-chapter topics for discussion, action, and research, many of which model an interactive classroom by providing tasks for pairs or small groups
- Suggestions for further reading at the end of each chapter, annotated to facilitate judicious choices of extra reading

IMPROVEMENTS IN THE THIRD EDITION

A number of improvements have been made in this Third Edition, following the comments and suggestions of teachers, students, and reviewers who have used *TBP* in its Second Edition. Here are the major changes:

- **Advance organizers at the beginning of chapters.** Each chapter now begins with a brief list of objectives of the chapter, which serve as prereading organizers for students.
- **New chapters.** Three chapters have been added. Chapter 9, Curriculum Design, introduces Part III, offering readers the "big" picture into which lessons, materials, and management issues must fit. Chapter 12, Technology in the Classroom, is now a separate chapter that summarizes principles and pedagogical options for using technology to promote interactive language classrooms. Chapter 26, Teachers for Social Responsibility, the book's final chapter, underscores the importance of considering one's role as a socially responsible agent for change in today's world of global challenges.
- **New topics.** In the span of seven years of research and practice in the language-teaching profession, inevitably a number of new topics rise to the top of the assortment of "hot" issues. In this third edition of *TBP*, you will find treatment of the following areas of concern that may not have received as much attention in the last edition:

> Postmethod condition
> Lexical Approach
> Multiple intelligences
> Two new principles: Autonomy & Willingness to Communicate
> Nonnative English-speaking teachers (nonNESTS)
> Cultural issues
> Practical steps to course design
> Technological advances
> Microskills and macroskills
> Form-focused instruction
> Corpus linguistics and the place of vocabulary teaching
> Reorganized principles of assessment
> Completely reworked chapters on assessment
> Alternatives in assessment

Teacher development and reflective teaching
Social responsibility
Critical pedagogy

- **Updated references throughout.** In seven years, the field of language pedagogy has made some significant advances that are reflected in every chapter of the book. Especially noticeable are new and updated suggestions for further reading at the end of each chapter.

ACKNOWLEDGMENTS

Teaching by Principles is a product of several decades of instruction and research in teaching English as a Second/Foreign Language. During that time, it has been my pleasure and challenge to teach and to learn from thousands of students in my courses. I am grateful for all those inquisitive minds—now scattered around the world—whose insights are well represented here.

I am also indebted to teachers in many countries of the world, especially in those countries where I have had the honor of lecturing and teaching: Bolivia, Brazil, Canada, Chile, Costa Rica, Croatia, the Dominican Republic, Egypt, Guatemala, Hong Kong, Italy, Japan, Korea, Mexico, Panama, Peru, Portugal, Singapore, Spain, Taiwan, Thailand, Turkey, Uruguay, Yugoslavia, and of course the United States. I learn so much from the exchanges of ideas and issues and stories from these contacts!

I of course wish to acknowledge the feedback I received from my San Francisco State University faculty associates, Professors David Olsher, Tom Scovel, and May Shih, and from my colleagues at the American Language Institute, Kathy Sherak and Peg Sarosy. The nurture and camaraderie among these and other colleagues at SFSU and the ALI are a source of professional stimulation and of personal affirmation that what we are all collectively trying to do is most certainly worth the effort.

Last but by no means least, I am eternally grateful for the support that my wife, Mary, unswervingly offers as she tolerates my various episodes of crankiness and need for long hours of uninterrupted focus during these book-writing periods. This support and nurture on the home front is a wondrous affirmation of my work!

H. Douglas Brown
San Francisco, California

TEXT CREDITS

Grateful acknowledgment is made to the following publishers and authors for permission to reprint copyrighted material.

American Council on Teaching Foreign Languages (ACTFL), for material from: *ACTFL Proficiency Guidelines* (1986); G. Moskowitz, "Interaction analysis usage for supervisors," *Foreign Language Annals 5* (1971): 211–221.

Cambridge University Press, for material from J.C. Richards and T.S. Rodgers, *Approaches and Methods in Language Teaching* (1986); D. Nunan, *Designing Tasks for the Communicative Curriculum* (1989); G. Ellis and B. Sinclair, *Learning to Learn English* (1989).

Heinle & Heinle Publishers, for material from R. Mackay, "Teaching the information gathering skills," in M.H. Long and J.C. Richards, *Methodology in TESOL* (1987); A.F. Kruse, "Vocabulary in context," in Long and Richards (1987); G. Crookes and C. Chaudron, "Guidelines for classroom teaching," in M. Celce-Murcia (ed.), *Teaching English as a Second or Foreign Language* (1991); P.W. Peterson, "A synthesis of models for interactive listening," in Celce-Murcia (1991); A. Chamot, J. M. O'Malley, and L. Kupper, *Building Bridges* (1992); R. Oxford, *Language Learning Strategies: What Every Teacher Should Know* (1990).

Language Learning, for material from R. B. Kaplan, "Cultural thought patterns in intercultural education," *Language Learning 16* (1) (1966): 1–20.

Oxford University Press, for material from M. Finocchiaro and C. Brumfit, *The Functional-Notational Approach: From Theory to Practice* (1983); R. Nolasco and L. Arthur, *Conversation* (1987).

Pearson Education, for material from J. Saslow and A. Ascher, *Top Notch: English for Today's World,* Book 2, Unit 2 (2006); H.D. Brown, *Principles of Language Learning and Teaching*, Fifth Edition (2007); H.D. Brown, *Vistas: An Interactive Course in English* (Prentice-Hall Regents, 1992); H.D. Brown, D. Cohen, and J. O'Day, *Challenges: A Process Approach to Academic English* (Prentice-Hall Regents, 1991); I. Boone, J. Bennett, and L. Motai, *Basics in Reading: An Introduction to American Magazines* (Lateral Communications, 1988); R. Wong, *Teaching Pronunciation: Focus on English Rhythm and Stress* (Prentice-Hall, 1987); D.L.F. Nilsen and A.P. Nilsen, *Pronunciation Contrasts in English* (Regents, 1971).

Simon & Schuster International, for material from D. Nunan, *Language Teaching Methodology: A Textbook for Teachers* (Cassell, 1991); D. Cross, *A Practical Handbook of Language Teaching* (Prentice-Hall, 1991); S. McKay, *Teaching Grammar: Form, Function, and Technique* (Pergamon, 1985).

Teachers of English to Speakers of Other Languages (TESOL), for material from J.C. Richards, "Listening comprehension: Approach, design, procedure," *TESOL Quarterly 17* (2) (1983); M. Celce-Murcia, "Grammar pedagogy in second and foreign language teaching," *TESOL Quarterly 25* (3) (1991); S. Bassano and M.A. Christison, "Teacher self-observation," *TESOL Newsletter* (August, 1984).

University of Michigan Press, for material from S. Silberstein, B. Dobson, and M. Clarke, *Reader's Choice*, Fourth Edition (2002), Reading Selection 3.

University of Minnesota Press, for material from B.W. Robinett, *Teaching English to Speakers of Other Languages: Substance and Technique* (1978).

Donna Jurich, Kate Kinsella, Tim Murphey, Karen Tenney, and Lauren Vanett, for unpublished material.

Kelley Keith, Tamotsu Miyagi, and Karla Frizler Octavio, for comments on a draft of Chapter 12, Technology in the Classroom.

FOUNDATIONS FOR

CLASSROOM PRACTICE

The five chapters of this first part of *Teaching by Principles* are designed to provide the theoretical basis for the practical classroom pedagogy that will be addressed in the rest of the book. Part I serves to give each reader the same grounding—to put you on the same page, theoretically, as the rest of your classmates. It also serves to facilitate the comprehensibility of subsequent chapters by defining terms, concepts, and issues in the field.

Chapter 1 takes you into a language classroom as an observer and describes the process of one period of language instruction. It's intended to be a "warm-up" for you. If you have never observed an English language class, it will give you a reasonably good picture of a typical lesson. If you have observed such classes, it will perhaps stimulate you to think beneath the overt activity and to look at the choices that the teacher made in unfolding the planned events of the class hour. In either case, the questions posed in the section titled "Analyzing the Lesson" are intended to whet your appetite for the many questions about teaching that will be addressed in the book.

Chapters 2 and 3 offer a historical perspective of language teaching and a description of the current "postmethod" condition, respectively. By placing your understanding of language teaching in the context of a century or more of practice, and by becoming familiar with current approaches, you can begin to synthesize your own developing theory of language pedagogy.

The core of Part I is contained in Chapter 4, in which the 12 principles of language teaching are described in some detail. These principles will be used throughout the book to evaluate everything from general approaches to the details of minute-by-minute teacher and student behavior in the classroom. They form basic, fundamental building blocks for teaching. Then, the final chapter in this part, Chapter 5, is an elaboration on one of the 12 principles, Intrinsic Motivation. It serves to illustrate both the complexity of any one principle and the multiple possible uses such a principle serves in designing a lesson or in assessing its effectiveness.

CHAPTER 1

GETTING STARTED

OBJECTIVES After reading this chapter, you will be able to:

- understand what a typical English language lesson "looks" like

- identify transitions from one component to another in a language class

- observe a language class yourself and have some idea of what to look for

- ask questions about the choices that teachers must make, minute by minute, when delivering planned lessons

---

So you've decided to be a language teacher! Welcome to a profession that will guarantee you more than your fair share of challenges, growth, joy, and fulfillment. Challenges await you at every turn in your professional path because the discipline of language teaching has only begun to solve some of the perplexing questions about how people learn foreign languages successfully. Opportunities for growth abound because, for as long as you continue to teach, you will never run out of new questions, new possibilities, new ways of looking at your students, and new ways of looking at yourself. The joy of teaching lies in witnessing your students' attainment of broader and broader vistas of linguistic proficiency and in experiencing the communal bond that you have been instrumental in creating in your classroom. And, ultimately, few professions can offer the fulfillment of knowing that your seemingly insignificant work really can make a difference in a world in need of communication that transcends national borders and interests.

At present, all those lofty ideals notwithstanding, you may be a little apprehensive about what sort of a teacher you are going to be: What will it be like to be in front of a classroom full of expectant ears and eyes, hanging on my every word and action, ready and waiting to pounce on me if I make a false move? How will I develop the composure and poise that I've seen modeled by "master" teachers? Will I be able to take the sea of theoretical information about second language acquisition that I have studied and by some miracle transform it into practical classroom applications? How do I plan a lesson? What do I do if my lesson plan falls apart? Where do I begin?

Before you ask anymore questions, which might at this stage overwhelm you, sit back for a moment and tell yourself that you can indeed become a teacher who will fully meet the challenges ahead and who will grow in professional expertise, thereby opening the doors of joy and fulfillment. This textbook is designed to help you take that developmental journey one step at a time.

The first step in that journey is to come with me into a language classroom and observe what happens. As the lesson unfolds, take special note of each choice that the teacher makes: choices about how to begin the lesson, which activity will come next, how long to continue an activity, whom to call on, whether to correct a student, and so on. Everything a teacher says and does in the classroom is the result of conscious or subconscious choices among many alternatives. Many of these choices are—or should be—the result of a careful consideration of a host of underlying principles of second language learning and teaching.

A CLASSROOM OBSERVATION

The classroom we are about to enter is in a private language school in Seoul, Korea. Inside the classroom, a course in English as a Second Language (ESL)* is taking place. The 15 students in the course are young adults, most of whom are recent college graduates and now are working in businesses in Seoul. This is an intermediate level class; most of the students "graduated" into the class after completing the beginner's level. The goal of the course is for students to be able to use English in their local context (television, movies, pop culture, Internet) and for international travel. A few might eventually use English in job-related duties.

The course focuses on integrative skills (combining the four skills of speaking, listening, reading, and writing). The main textbook being used is *Top Notch: English for Today's World,* Level 2 (Saslow & Ascher, 2006). At this stage, two weeks into the course, the students are still not completely confident in their speaking ability but they can engage in simple social conversations and make some practical requests. Their listening ability varies but the course material seems to be appropriately pitched at their level. They are quite good readers, having had English in their university studies. Their writing is fairly accurate at the sentence level using basic grammar, but rhetorical factors involved in composing an essay remain a challenge.

The lesson we are about to observe covers Lesson 2 of Unit 2 of *Top Notch,* on the topic of "movies and entertainment." The functional focus of the lesson is to discuss preferences, likes, and dislikes. The formal objectives of the lesson are for students to comprehend and produce *would rather* in meaningful sentences and to use a number of terms to categorize types of movies.

---

* *ESL* is used in this book in two ways: (a) as a generic acronym to refer to instruction of English to speakers of other languages in any country under any circumstance, and (b) to refer to English as a Second Language taught in countries (such as the United States, the United Kingdom, or India) where English is a major language of commerce and education, a language that students often hear outside the walls of their classroom. Most instances of reference in this book to "ESL" are in the generic sense. *EFL* (English as a Foreign Language) always refers specifically to English taught in countries (such as Taiwan, Korea, or Brazil) where English is not a major language of commerce and education. See Chapter 8 for important pedagogical and curricular implications of each type of English language teaching.

The teacher, Ms. Lee, a native of Seoul, has about five years of teaching experience, and she holds a certificate in Teaching English to Speakers of Other Languages (TESOL) from a local university in Seoul. Her English is excellent, partly the result of spending two years in Canada as a high school student while her father was assigned work there for his electronics company. She is confident and poised, and shows a great deal of empathy for her students. They seem to appreciate her warmth.

The lesson is reasonably well planned and executed, and characteristic of current communicative language-teaching methodology. However, it is not necessarily "perfect" (are there ever any perfect lessons?), so what you are about to see may have a few elements that you or others could take issue with. Please remember this as you read on and, if you wish, take note of aspects of the lesson that you might question; then compare these notes with the comments following the lesson description.

We take our seats in the rear of the classroom and observe the following sequence of activities.

1. Ms. Lee (hereafter "T") begins the 50-minute class hour on this Monday evening with some small talk with the students (hereafter "Ss"), commenting on the weather, her own weekend's activity hosting a family friend from Canada, and a movie that several Ss saw (in English) over the weekend.
2. As she engages them in small talk, she marks attendance in her class roster.
3. She then asks the Ss to think of some movies they have seen recently, either in English or subtitled. She asks them *not* to name any movies that have been dubbed (into Korean). Ss volunteer names, somewhat hesitantly at first, but come up with a list that the T puts on the board:

> Harry Potter
> Pride and Prejudice
> March of the Penguins
> Mrs. Henderson Presents
> Pink Panther
> Chicago
> Ice Age
> Good Night and Good Luck
> War of the Worlds
> Da Vinci Code

4. At this point the T stops and writes "Categories" on the board and then writes the following movie types, or categories, on the board:

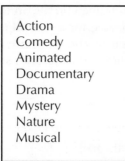

Action
Comedy
Animated
Documentary
Drama
Mystery
Nature
Musical

5. She then asks Ss to volunteer what each word means. One by one, Ss slowly venture "definitions" for *animated, comedy,* and *documentary* with synonyms such as "cartoon, Nemo, Disney" for the first, "funny, comic, makes me laugh" for the second, and "news, history" for the third. They seem hard-pressed to define others. One S says "Tom Cruise" for *action.* Ss eventually fall into silence.

6. Seeing that definitions may be too difficult for Ss to create, the T takes a different tack. She provides her own definitions verbally, and as some Ss nod their heads in apparent understanding, she says, "Okay, now, does everyone understand the meaning of each of these categories?" A few more heads nod, and the T moves on.

7. The T then says, "Now, take out a sheet of paper and write down the names of all the movies that are up on the board, and then with a partner, decide what kind of movie each one is and write the category beside the name of the movie." She quickly pairs up Ss, with one group of three. Ss write the movies down, and proceed to engage in the pair work. The T walks around listening and checking on the pairs.

8. Next, the T asks Ss to report the movie categories. There is a little disagreement among pairs in that some movies are thought to be in two or more categories (*Harry Potter,* for example, was thought to be action, drama, and mystery).

9. The T now says, "I want you to turn to page 18 in your books and listen to a dialogue on my CD player. Just listen this first time." The following dialogue is then presented on the CD:

A: What would you rather see—a comedy or a musical?
B: It doesn't matter to me.
A: Well, what do you think of Madonna?
B: Actually, not much.
A: For real? She's my favorite star.
B: Not mine.
A: Well, that's what makes the world go 'round.

10. Next, T asks Ss to listen again and repeat each line chorally in the pause provided on the CD. This procedure is repeated for a second time.

11. The T then asks Ss to turn to page 19 of their textbook, where examples are given for the grammatical construction *would rather* in both statements and questions:

Statements

I'd rather rent a movie than go to the theater.
He'd rather not see a comedy tonight.

Questions

Would you rather see, *Star Wars* or *Frida?*
Which would they rather see—a comedy or a drama?
Would you like to rent a movie?

---

12. The T engages in some explanation of the structure, pointing out, for example, that the phrase *would rather* is similar to saying "prefer." She also provides a rough Korean translation of the construction and gives a brief explanation in Korean before reverting back to English. Ss remain attentive but silent.

13. Next, the T says, "Now I want all of you to take your lists of the movies that we discussed (the ones on the board) and make a grid like this."

Movie	Category	Would you rather see it?
		YES
Harry Potter		
Pride and Prejudice		
March of the Penguins		
Mrs. Henderson Presents		
Pink Panther		
Chicago		
Ice Age		
Good Night & Good Luck		
War of the Worlds		
Da Vinci Code		

14. The T then directs Ss to write in the category or categories of each movie. Next she says, "Now, everyone stand up and move around the room and talk to as many people as you can. Choose two movies each time to compare, and ask them, 'Would you rather see _____ , or _____?' Then, write the name of the person you talk to in the 'yes' box beside the movie they would rather see. Okay? Make sure your partner answers you in a complete sentence! So, your partner must say 'Yes, I'd rather see _____' or something like 'Actually, I don't care.' Does everyone understand?" Ss look a little confused, so T translates the directions into Korean and then models in English as follows:

Student A: Would you rather see *Harry Potter* or *Chicago?*

Student B: I'd rather see *Harry Potter.*

Student A then writes the name of Student B in the box by *Harry Potter.*

Then Student B asks Student A a similar question and writes the answer down. Then you move on to a new partner.

But, listen carefully! If you don't have a preference, just answer, "It doesn't matter to me." And in that case pick another pair of movies to compare until your partner gives you a definite preference.

Okay, do you understand now?

15. Ss nod in agreement, and the T tells them to start their multiple interviews. This exercise lasts for about 15 minutes as Ss quite enthusiastically engage in the task.
16. When the T calls them back together, she tallies the number of students who responded affirmatively to each movie and in an unscientific poll, announces what appears to be their favorite movie. It's a tie between *Harry Potter* and *War of the Worlds*!
17. With the time that's left (about 5 minutes) T asks Ss to complete the exercise on page 19 in which they write responses to six questions or statements, such as "I'd love to see a movie tonight" and "Would you like to see a comedy?" Their responses range from "I'd rather not" and "It doesn't matter to me" to "Actually, I'd rather see an action movie."
18. As time runs out and students gather papers together to exit the classroom, the T tells Ss to complete their written exercise as homework, and to try to see an English movie sometime before the next class (on Wednesday evening).

ANALYZING THE LESSON

You've just observed a relatively effective class hour in which the teacher competently planned a lesson around a textbook lesson, managed most segments of the hour without major problems, and carried out the activities with some warmth and enthusiasm. Easy, right? Well, maybe not. What you have just witnessed is the product of a teacher's experience and intuition grounded in reasonably sound theoretical principles of learning and teaching. For every tiny moment of that classroom hour, certain choices were made, choices that can for the most part be justified by our collective knowledge of second language acquisition and teaching. Think about those choices as you contemplate the numerous pedagogical questions that arise out of each numbered "statement" that follows.

1. Why the small talk (versus just getting straight to the lesson)? What teaching principle justifies such an opening? How long should such chatter continue?
2. Why did the T mark attendance while engaging in the small talk? It apparently didn't interfere with the small talk—how did the T manage to do two things at once?
3. The textbook began with the dialogue (see #9) that this T chose to insert later. Why do you suppose she didn't start with that dialogue? Was her choice a better segue from the initial small talk that began the class? What purpose was served by asking Ss to come up with names of movies themselves at the outset? Why didn't the T just provide a list of her own? And if she simply wants names of movies, why restrict the list to movies in English? What purpose did that serve? She chose to write the names of movies on the board—what purpose did that list serve?
4. Here she initiated the names of the categories. Should she have asked the Ss to create that list? What you don't know is that the textbook referred to "genres" of movies—why did the T not use that same term?
5. Why did the T ask Ss for definitions? Wouldn't it be more efficient for the T to provide them? What purpose was served by forcing them to struggle with definitions? When Ss had some difficulty with defining, they tended to become more silent. Why was that?
6. At this point it was apparent that T felt the task was over Ss' heads—what led her to that determination? Was it a good idea to switch to providing definitions herself at that point? She then asked if everyone understood and seeing some heads nodding affirmatively, she assumed they understood. Is such a question appropriate in this situation? Are you sure the Ss understood? What alternatives might she have employed to carry out that informal assessment?

Before you move on, notice, that each question implies that a choice was exercised by the teacher. Among dozens of possibilities for teaching this lesson on movies, categories, and the *would rather* construction, Ms. Lee has chosen, either consciously or subconsciously, a particular set of activities, a particular order, and a particular tone for each. A relatively straightforward lesson is supported by a plethora of principles of learning and teaching. To further complicate matters, some of those principles are disputable. For example, the issue of when to simply give information to Ss (#6) and when to push for "discovery learning" by the Ss is not always clearly dictated by the context.

7. She now sets in motion some pair work for Ss. This exercise did not come from the textbook; it was her own innovation, only distantly resembling one in the textbook. Why didn't she just follow the book here? Were her pair work directions clear? Some teacher guidelines suggest modeling such pair work—why didn't she do so? What do you suppose she was listening for as she walked around the classroom during this pair work?

8. Why did the T have Ss report their results of such a noncontroversial exercise? What purpose did the reporting and processing serve?

9. The T chose at this point to play the opening dialogue for the lesson. Did the background of the first 10–15 minutes of class provide enough context and interest for the Ss? What advantages and disadvantages do professionally recorded audio sound bites offer in a classroom in this context? The dialogue isn't terribly exciting; is that okay for the purposes of this lesson?

10. Choral drilling is a commonly used technique in language teaching. Was it appropriate and useful here? How do you think the T mentally justified its use? Why didn't the drill continue for several more repetitions?

11. This is one of the moments in the lesson that the T turns Ss' focus to form— that is, grammatical structure. Does the textbook segment sufficiently explain the structure?

12. Is the T's explanation justified at this point? Or should Ss just intuitively get a "feel" for the *would rather* structure? And what do you think about providing some explanation, as the T did, in Korean? Why did she choose to do so then, and was the language switch justified? She seemed to be "lecturing" to Ss here. Should she have asked explicitly for some kind of response from the Ss? Or should they have had some more choral or quasi-communicative practice at this point?

13. The grid is an adaptation of a similar one in the textbook, but the T added the feature of using it in face-to-face interviews. Why did she choose to have another communicative activity here instead of following the textbook's suggestion of having Ss listen to some movie reviews on the CD and write in their recommendations?

14. The whole-class mingling activity seems simple enough, but Ss had a little difficulty figuring out the process. Were the T's directions sufficient and clear, once she was able to follow up after the looks of confusion? What could she have done to make this stage of the activity clearer?

15. What is the objective of this activity? It's clear what Ss are being asked to do: frame questions, respond to them, and record the responses. They seemed enthusiastic about the activity—why? Why was an activity with fairly routine grammatical practice met with enthusiasm? Were those 15 minutes put to good purpose?

16. Did the informal tally serve the objectives of the activity or simply offer a modicum of interest?

17. It's possible that this last activity was squeezed into too short a time frame. Was that okay? When a T runs out of time at the end of a lesson, should he or she hurry through an activity like this? Or provide an alternative wrap-up? What purpose did a writing activity (as opposed to the other three skills) serve here?

18. Sometimes these last-second comments are lost in the shuffle of students getting ready to leave the classroom. Was some purpose nevertheless accomplished? If they are being asked to see an English movie as "homework," would it help to give them some more advice on what to *do* while seeing the movie?

A final question: As you look back over the lesson you've just observed, do you think the initial objectives were accomplished? Is there anything you think you might have done differently? Remember, you're dropping in on a class that is ongoing, so it may not be possible to completely judge the effectiveness of this lesson without the context of preceding and following lessons.

You've now skimmed through some of the many questions that one could ask about why certain choices were made about how to teach this lesson. Some of the answers are relatively standard, with few disagreements. Other answers would find even the best of teachers arguing the merits and demerits of the teacher's choices. But the answers to all these questions can be found, in one form or another, in the huge stockpile of second language acquisition research and collective experience of language teachers around the world. And many of those answers will appear in the chapters ahead of you in this book.

☆   ☆   ☆   ☆   ☆

As you continue this journey, your job is to make the connections between research/theory/principles on the one hand, and classrooms/teaching/practice on the other. By making those connections as you learn to teach, you will perhaps avoid some of the pitfalls of haphazard guesswork and instead engage in teaching that is enlightened by research and theory, or put another way, teaching by principles.

TOPICS FOR DISCUSSION, ACTION, AND RESEARCH

[Note: (I) Individual work; (G) group or pair work; (C) whole-class discussion.]

1. (G) A good activity for the beginning of a course on teaching methodology is to ask the members of small groups of three or four to talk about who was the "best" teacher they ever had. In the process, each should specify *why* that teacher was the best. As each group reports back to the whole class, make a chalkboard list of such reasons, which should reveal some attributes for all to emulate. (This activity also serves the purpose of (a) getting students to talk early on and (b) giving students in the class a chance to get to know each other. To that end, group reports could include brief introductions of group members.)

2. (G/C) On page 3, it was noted that teachers are constantly making *choices* in the course of a class hour. Assign to pairs one or two of the numbered items through #18. They should talk about (a) what the teacher chose to do, (b) why she made that choice, and (c) what alternative choices she could have made. Make sure they refer to the second matched set of items in which certain questions were posed, and try to answer the questions. Pairs can then report their conclusions to the whole class. All should then begin to appreciate the complexity of teaching.

3. (I) As soon as possible, arrange to observe an ESL (or EFL) class somewhere near you. At this stage, don't go in with a checklist or agenda. Just try to sit back and get a feel for the dynamics of the classroom. As you observe, jot down any questions that occur to you about why the teacher made certain choices, and discuss them later in a small group or as a whole class.

4. (I/G) On your own or with a partner, find some currently popular textbooks in ESL and spend some time leafing through them without a specific agenda—just noting things that you like and don't like about each. Share those ideas later with the rest of the class.

FOR YOUR FURTHER READING

Brown, H. D. (2007). *Principles of language learning and teaching* (5th ed.). White Plains, NY: Pearson Education.

This book (PLLT) provides a comprehensive survey of issues in second language acquisition as they apply to language teaching. In PLLT you will find fuller explanations of the principles that are described in Chapter 4 of the present book (TBP). If you have not already read PLLT, it is recommended that you read it along with TBP.

Harmer, J. (2001). *The practice of English language teaching* (3rd ed.). Harlow, UK: Pearson Education Limited.

For a second perspective on language-teaching methodology, you may find it useful to consult Harmer's book. Many of the same topics are covered there, but with different supporting details and information.

Nunan, D. (Ed.). (2003). *Practical English language teaching.* New York: McGraw-Hill Contemporary.

Another source of summary information, this anthology features separate articles by a number of luminaries in the field. Kathleen Bailey, Neil Anderson, John Murphy, Michael McCarthy, Donna Brinton, Kathleen Graves, Mary Ann Christison, and David Nunan himself offer state-of-the-art summaries of subfields such as the four skills, form-focused instruction, content-based instruction, and computer-assisted language learning.

Richards, J. (Ed.). (1998). *Teaching in action: Case studies from second language classrooms.* Alexandria, VA: Teachers of English to Speakers of Other Languages.

This book offers 76 classroom scenarios: techniques, tasks, and innovative procedures (written by teachers around the world) of actual classes of various levels and skill areas. Each description is followed by a very brief commentary from an expert in the field. These scenarios provide glimpses of actual classroom activity with comments on why certain things worked or didn't work, thereby offering a bridge between theory and practice.

CHAPTER 2

A "METHODICAL" HISTORY

OF LANGUAGE TEACHING

OBJECTIVES After reading this chapter, you will be able to:

- develop a historical understanding of language-teaching methodology

- explain differences between approaches and methods

- understand how teaching methods borrow from and contribute to theoretical trends in linguistics, psychology, education, and other fields

- summarize major characteristics of a number of methods

- appreciate your need as a teacher to be cautiously eclectic in deriving insights about your classroom practices

The first step toward developing a principled approach to language teaching will be to turn back the clock about a century to learn from the historical cycles and trends that have brought us to the present day. After all, it is difficult to completely analyze the class session you just observed (Chapter 1) without the backdrop of history. In this chapter we focus on methods as the identifying characteristics of a century of "modern" language-teaching efforts. What do we mean by the term "method" by which we tend to characterize that history? How do methods reflect various trends of disciplinary thought? How does current research on language learning and teaching help us to distinguish, in our history, between passing fads and "the good stuff"? These are some of the questions we will address in this chapter.

In the next chapter, this historical overview culminates in a close look at the current state of the art in language teaching. Above all, you will come to see how our profession is now more aptly characterized by a relatively unified, comprehensive "approach" rather than by competing, restricted methods. That general approach will be described in detail, along with some of the current professional jargon associated with it.

As you read on, you will encounter references to concepts, constructs, issues, and models that are normally covered in a course in second language acquisition (SLA). I am assuming that you have already taken or are currently taking such a course. If not, may I recommend that you consult my *Principles of Language Learning and Teaching,* Fifth Edition (Brown, 2007), or a book like Mitchell and Myles's (2004) *Second Language Learning Theories* that summarizes current topics and issues in SLA. Throughout this book I will refer to specific chapters of my *Principles* book (*PLLT*) for background review or reading, should you need it.

APPROACH, METHOD, AND TECHNIQUE

For the century spanning the mid-1880s to the mid-1980s, the language-teaching profession may be aptly characterized by a series of methods that rose and declined in popularity. It appears that some practitioners in this time period hoped to define the ultimate method, one that would be generalizable across widely varying audiences, contexts, and languages. Historical accounts of the profession tend to describe a succession of methods, each of which was more or less discarded as a new method took its place (Larsen-Freeman, 2000; Richards & Rodgers, 2001). We will turn to that "methodical" history of language teaching in a moment, but first, we should try to understand what we mean by **method**.

What is a method? About four decades ago Edward Anthony (1963) gave us a definition that has admirably withstood the test of time. His concept of "method" was the second of three hierarchical elements, namely approach, method, and technique. An **approach**, according to Anthony, was a set of assumptions dealing with the nature of language, learning, and teaching. **Method** was described as an overall plan for systematic presentation of language based upon a selected approach. **Techniques** were the specific activities manifested in the classroom that were consistent with a method and therefore were in harmony with an approach as well.

To this day, for better or worse, Anthony's terms are still in common use among language teachers. For example, at the approach level, a teacher may affirm the ultimate importance of learning in a relaxed state of mental awareness just above the threshold of consciousness. The method that follows might resemble, say, Suggestopedia (a description follows in this chapter). Techniques could include playing baroque music while reading a passage in the foreign language, getting students to sit in a yoga position while listening to a list of words, or having learners adopt a new name in the classroom and role-play that new person.

A couple of decades later, Jack Richards and Theodore Rodgers (1982) proposed a reformulation of the concept of "method." Anthony's approach, method, and technique were renamed, respectively, **approach**, **design**, and **procedure**, with a superordinate term to describe this three-step process, now called "method." A method, according to Richards and Rodgers, was "an umbrella term for the specification and interrelation of theory and practice" (1982, p. 154). An approach defines assumptions, beliefs, and theories about the nature of language and language learning. Designs specify the relationship of those theories to classroom materials and activities. Procedures are the techniques and practices that are derived from one's approach and design.

Through their reformulation, Richards and Rodgers (1982, 2001) made two principal contributions to our understanding of the concept of method:

1. They specified the necessary elements of language-teaching designs that had heretofore been left somewhat vague. Their schematic representation of method (see Figure 2.1) described six important features of designs: objectives, syllabus (criteria for selection and organization of linguistic and subject-matter content), activities, learner roles, teacher roles, and the role of instructional materials. The latter three features have occupied a significant proportion of our collective attention in the profession for the last decade or so. Already in this book you may have noted how, for example, learner roles (styles, individual preferences for group or individual learning, student input in determining curricular content, etc.) are important considerations in your teaching.

2. Richards and Rodgers nudged us into relinquishing the notion that separate, definable, discrete methods are the essential building blocks of methodology. By helping us to think in terms of an approach that undergirds our language designs (curricula), which are realized by various procedures (techniques), we could see that method, as the term was historically understood over the last century, is a concept that is too restrictive, too preprogrammed, and too "prepackaged." Many of the methods that form our historical milestones make the oversimplified assumption that what teachers "do" in the classroom can be conventionalized into a set of procedures that fit all contexts. We are now all too aware that such is clearly not the case.

Richards and Rodgers's reformulation of the concept of method was soundly conceived. However, their attempt to give new meaning to an old term did not catch on in the pedagogical literature. What they wanted us to call "method" is more comfortably referred to, I think, as "methodology" in order to avoid confusion with what we will no doubt always think of as those separate entities (like the Audiolingual Method or Suggestopedia) that are no longer at the center of our teaching philosophy.

Another terminological problem lies in the use of the term **design**; instead, we more comfortably refer to **curriculum** or **syllabus** when we refer to design features of a language program.

What are we left with in this lexicographic confusion? It's interesting that the terminology of the pedagogical literature in the field appears to be more in line with Anthony's original terms, but with some important additions and refinements. Following is a set of definitions that as closely as possible reflect what appears to be a consensus on current usage (Harmer, 2001; Kumaravadivelu, 2006b; Richards & Renandya, 2002).

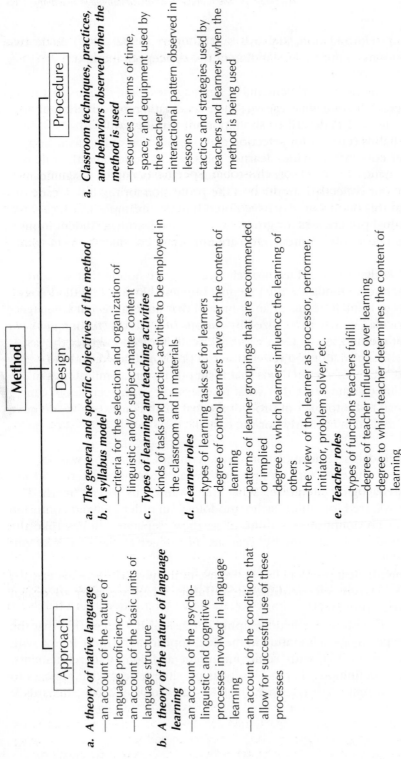

Method

Approach

a. *A theory of native language*
—an account of the nature of language proficiency
—an account of the basic units of language structure

b. *A theory of the nature of language learning*
—an account of the psycho-linguistic and cognitive processes involved in language learning
—an account of the conditions that allow for successful use of these processes

Design

a. *The general and specific objectives of the method*

b. *A syllabus model*
—criteria for the selection and organization of linguistic and/or subject-matter content

c. *Types of learning and teaching activities*
—kinds of tasks and practice activities to be employed in the classroom and in materials

d. *Learner roles*
—types of learning tasks set for learners
—degree of control learners have over the content of learning
—patterns of learner groupings that are recommended or implied
—degree to which learners influence the learning of others
—the view of the learner as processor, performer, initiator, problem solver, etc.

e. *Teacher roles*
—types of functions teachers fulfill
—degree of teacher influence over learning
—degree to which teacher determines the content of learning
—types of interaction between teachers and learners

f. *The role of instructional materials*
—primary function of materials
—the form materials take (e.g., textbook, audiovisual)
—relation of materials to other input
—assumptions made about teachers and other learners

Procedure

a. *Classroom techniques, practices, and behaviors observed when the method is used*
—resources in terms of time, space, and equipment used by the teacher
—interactional pattern observed in lessons
—tactics and strategies used by teachers and learners when the method is being used

Figure 2.1 Components of method (Richards & Rodgers, 2001, p. 33)

16

Methodology: Pedagogical practices in general (including theoretical underpinnings and related research). Whatever considerations are involved in "how to teach" are methodological.

Approach: Theoretically well-informed positions and beliefs about the nature of language, the nature of language learning, and the applicability of both to pedagogical settings.

Method: A generalized set of classroom specifications for accomplishing linguistic objectives. Methods tend to be concerned primarily with teacher and student roles and behaviors and secondarily with such features as linguistic and subject-matter objectives, sequencing, and materials. They are sometimes—but not always—thought of as being broadly applicable to a variety of audiences in a variety of contexts.

Curriculum/syllabus: Specifications—or in Richards and Rodgers's terminology, "designs"—for carrying out a particular language program. Features include a primary concern with the specification of linguistic and subject-matter objectives, sequencing, and materials to meet the needs of a designated group of learners in a defined context. (The term "syllabus" is used more customarily in the United Kingdom to refer to what is commonly called a "curriculum" in the United States.)

Technique (also commonly referred to by other terms*): Any of a wide variety of exercises, activities, or tasks used in the language classroom for realizing lesson objectives.

CHANGING WINDS AND SHIFTING SANDS

A glance through the past century or so of language teaching will give an interesting picture of how varied the interpretations have been of the best way to teach a foreign language. As disciplinary schools of thought—psychology, linguistics, and education, for example—have come and gone, so have language-teaching methods waxed and waned in popularity. Teaching methods, as "approaches in action," are of course the practical application of theoretical findings and positions. In a field such as ours that is relatively young, it should come as no surprise to discover a wide

---

* There is currently quite an intermingling of such terms as "technique," "task," "procedure," "activity," and "exercise." They are often used in somewhat free variation across the profession. Of these terms, *task* has received the most concerted attention, viewed by such scholars as Nunan (2004) and Ellis (2003) as incorporating specific communicative and pedagogical principles. Tasks, according to specialists in task-based instruction, should be thought of as a special kind of technique and, in fact, may actually include more than one technique. See Chapter 3 for a more thorough explanation.

variety of these applications over the last hundred years, some in total philosophical opposition to others.

Albert Marckwardt (1972, p. 5) saw these "changing winds and shifting sands" as a cyclical pattern in which a new method emerged about every quarter of a century. Each new method broke from the old but took with it some of the positive aspects of the previous practices. A good example of this cyclical nature of methods is found in the "revolutionary" Audiolingual Method (ALM) (a description follows) of the mid-twentieth century. The ALM borrowed tenets from its predecessor the Direct Method by almost half a century while breaking away entirely from the Grammar Translation Method. Within a short time, however, ALM critics were advocating more attention to thinking, to cognition, and to rule learning, which to some smacked of a return to Grammar Translation!

What follows is a sketch of the changing winds and shifting sands of language teaching over the years.

THE GRAMMAR TRANSLATION METHOD

A historical sketch of the last hundred years of language teaching must be set in the context of a prevailing, customary language-teaching "tradition." For centuries, there were few if any theoretical foundations of language learning upon which to base teaching methodology. In the Western world, "foreign" language learning in schools was synonymous with the learning of Latin or Greek. Latin, thought to promote intellectuality through "mental gymnastics," was until relatively recently held to be indispensable to an adequate higher education. Latin was taught by means of what has been called the **Classical Method:** focus on grammatical rules, memorization of vocabulary and of various declensions and conjugations, translations of texts, written exercises.

As other languages began to be taught in educational institutions in the eighteenth and nineteenth centuries, the Classical Method was adopted as the chief means for teaching foreign languages. Little thought was given to teaching someone how to speak the language; after all, languages were not being taught primarily to learn oral/aural communication, but to learn for the sake of being "scholarly" or, in some instances, for gaining a reading proficiency in a foreign language. Since there was little if any theoretical research on second language acquisition in general or on the acquisition of reading proficiency, foreign languages were taught as any other skill was taught.

In the nineteenth century the Classical Method came to be known as the **Grammar Translation Method**. There was little to distinguish Grammar Translation from what had gone on in foreign language classrooms for centuries beyond a focus on grammatical rules as the basis for translating from the second to the native language. Remarkably, the Grammar Translation Method withstood attempts at the turn of the twentieth century to "reform" language-teaching methodology (see Gouin's Series Method and the Direct Method, which follow), and to this day it is practiced in too many educational contexts. Prator and Celce-Murcia (1979, p. 3) listed the major characteristics of Grammar Translation:

1. Classes are taught in the mother tongue, with little active use of the target language.
2. Much vocabulary is taught in the form of lists of isolated words.
3. Long, elaborate explanations of the intricacies of grammar are given.
4. Grammar provides the rules for putting words together, and instruction often focuses on the form and inflection of words.
5. Reading of difficult classical texts is begun early.
6. Little attention is paid to the content of texts, which are treated as exercises in grammatical analysis.
7. Often the only drills are exercises in translating disconnected sentences from the target language into the mother tongue.
8. Little or no attention is given to pronunciation.

It's ironic that this method has until very recently been so stalwart among many competing models. It does virtually nothing to enhance a student's communicative ability in the language. It is "remembered with distaste by thousands of school learners, for whom foreign language learning meant a tedious experience of memorizing endless lists of unusable grammar rules and vocabulary and attempting to produce perfect translations of stilted or literary prose" (Richards & Rodgers, 2001, p. 6).

On the other hand, one can understand why Grammar Translation remains so popular. It requires few specialized skills on the part of teachers. Tests of grammar rules and of translations are easy to construct and can be objectively scored. Many standardized tests of foreign languages still do not attempt to tap into communicative abilities, so students have little motivation to go beyond grammar analogies, translations, and rote exercises. And it is sometimes successful in leading a student toward a reading knowledge of a second language. But, as Richards and Rodgers (2001, p. 7) pointed out, "it has no advocates. It is a method for which there is no theory. There is no literature that offers a rationale or justification for it or that attempts to relate it to issues in linguistics, psychology, or educational theory." As you continue to examine language-teaching methodology in this book, I think you will understand more fully the "theorylessness" of the Grammar Translation Method.

GOUIN AND THE SERIES METHOD

The history of "modern" foreign language teaching may be said to have begun in the late 1800s with François Gouin, a French teacher of Latin with remarkable insights. History doesn't normally credit Gouin as a founder of language-teaching methodology because, at the time, his influence was overshadowed by that of Maximillian Berlitz, the popular German founder of the Direct Method.

some attention to Gouin's unusually perceptive observations about language teaching helps us to set the stage for the development of language-teaching methods for the century following the publication of his book, *The Art of Learning and Studying Languages,* in 1880.

Gouin had to go through a painful set of experiences to derive his insights. Having decided in midlife to learn German, he took up residency in Hamburg for one year. But rather than attempting to converse with the natives, he engaged in a rather bizarre sequence of attempts to "master" the language. Upon arrival in Hamburg, he felt he should *memorize* a German grammar book and a table of the 248 irregular German verbs! He did this in a matter of only 10 days, and hurried to "the academy" (the university) to test his new knowledge. "But alas!" he wrote, "I could not understand a single word, not a single word!" (Gouin, 1880, p. 11). Gouin was undaunted. He returned to the isolation of his room, this time to memorize the German roots and to rememorize the grammar book and irregular verbs. Again he emerged with expectations of success. "But alas . . ." the result was the same as before. In the course of the year in Germany, Gouin memorized books, translated Goethe and Schiller, and even memorized 30,000 words in a German dictionary, all in the isolation of his room, only to be crushed by his failure to understand German afterward. Only once did he try to "make conversation" as a method, but this caused people to laugh at him, and he was too embarrassed to continue that method. At the end of the year Gouin, having reduced the Classical Method to absurdity, was forced to return home, a failure.

But there was a happy ending. After returning home, Gouin discovered that his three-year-old nephew had, during that year, gone through the wonderful stage of child language acquisition in which he went from saying virtually nothing at all to becoming a veritable chatterbox of French. How was it that this little child succeeded so easily, in a first language, in a task that Gouin, in a second language, had found impossible? The child must hold the secret to learning a language! So Gouin spent a great deal of time observing his nephew and other children and came to the following conclusions: Language learning is primarily a matter of transforming perceptions into conceptions. Children use language to represent their conceptions. Language is a means of thinking, of representing the world to oneself (see *PLLT,* Chapter 2). These insights, remember, were formed by a language teacher more than a century ago!

So Gouin set about devising a teaching method based on these insights. And thus the **Series Method** was created, a method that taught learners *directly* (without translation) and conceptually (without grammatical rules and explanations) a "series" of connected sentences that are easy to perceive. The first lesson of a foreign language would thus teach the following series of 15 sentences:

> I walk toward the door. I draw near to the door. I draw nearer to the door. I get to the door. I stop at the door.

(*continued*)

I stretch out my arm. I take hold of the handle. I turn the handle. I open the door. I pull the door.

The door moves. The door turns on its hinges. The door turns and turns. I open the door wide. I let go of the handle.

The 15 sentences have an unconventionally large number of grammatical properties, vocabulary items, word orders, and complexity. This is no simple *Voici la table* lesson! Yet Gouin was successful with such lessons because the language was so easily understood, stored, recalled, and related to reality. Yet he was a man unfortunately ahead of his time, and his insights were largely lost in the shuffle of Berlitz's popular Direct Method. But as we look back now over more than a century of language-teaching history, we can appreciate the insights of this most unusual language teacher.

THE DIRECT METHOD

The "naturalistic"—simulating the "natural" way in which children learn first languages—approaches of Gouin and a few of his contemporaries did not take hold immediately. A generation later, applied linguistics finally established the credibility of such approaches. Thus it was that at the turn of the century, the **Direct Method** became quite widely known and practiced.

The basic premise of the Direct Method was similar to that of Gouin's Series Method, namely, that second language learning should be more like first language learning—lots of oral interaction, spontaneous use of the language, no translation between first and second languages, and little or no analysis of grammatical rules. Richards and Rodgers (2001, p. 12) summarized the principles of the Direct Method:

1. Classroom instruction was conducted exclusively in the target language.
2. Only everyday vocabulary and sentences were taught.
3. Oral communication skills were built up in a carefully traded progression organized around question-and-answer exchanges between teachers and students in small, intensive classes.
4. Grammar was taught inductively.
5. New teaching points were taught through modeling and practice.
6. Concrete vocabulary was taught through demonstration, objects, and pictures; abstract vocabulary was taught by association of ideas.
7. Both speech and listening comprehension were taught.
8. Correct pronunciation and grammar were emphasized.

The Direct Method enjoyed considerable popularity at the beginning of the twentieth century. It was most widely accepted in private language schools where students were highly motivated and where native-speaking teachers could be employed. One of the best known of its popularizers was Charles Berlitz (who never used the term Direct Method and chose instead to call his method the Berlitz Method). To this day "Berlitz" is a household word; Berlitz language schools are thriving in every country of the world.

But almost any "method" can succeed when clients are willing to pay high prices for small classes, individual attention, and intensive study. The Direct Method did not take well in public education, where the constraints of budget, classroom size, time, and teacher background made such a method difficult to use. Moreover, the Direct Method was criticized for its weak theoretical foundations. Its success may have been more a factor of the skill and personality of the teacher than of the methodology itself.

By the end of the first quarter of the twentieth century, the use of the Direct Method had declined both in Europe and in the United States. Most language curricula returned to the Grammar Translation Method or to a "reading approach" that emphasized reading skills in foreign languages. But it is interesting that by the middle of the twentieth century, the Direct Method was revived and redirected into what was probably the most visible of all language-teaching "revolutions" in the modern era, the Audiolingual Method (see below). So even this somewhat short-lived movement in language teaching would reappear in the changing winds and shifting sands of history.

THE AUDIOLINGUAL METHOD

In the first half of the twentieth century, the Direct Method did not take hold in the United States the way it did in Europe. While one could easily find native-speaking teachers of modern foreign languages in Europe, such was not the case in the United States. Also, European high school and university students did not have to travel far to find opportunities to put the oral skills of another language to actual, practical use. Moreover, U.S. educational institutions had become firmly convinced that a reading approach to foreign languages was more useful than an oral approach, given the perceived linguistic isolation of the United States at the time. The highly influential Coleman Report (Coleman, 1929) had persuaded foreign language teachers that it was impractical to teach oral skills and that reading should become the focus. Thus schools returned in the 1930s and 1940s to Grammar Translation, "the handmaiden of reading" (Bowen, Madsen, & Hilferty, 1985).

Then World War II broke out, and suddenly the United States was thrust into a worldwide conflict, heightening the need for Americans to become orally proficient in the languages of both their allies and their enemies. The time was ripe for a language-teaching revolution. The U.S. military provided the impetus with funding for special, intensive language courses that focused on aural/oral skills; these courses came to be known as the Army Specialized Training Program (ASTP) or, more colloquially, the "Army Method." Characteristic of these courses was a great deal of oral activity—pronunciation and pattern drills and conversation practice—with virtually none of the grammar and translation found in traditional classes. It is ironic that numerous foundation stones of the discarded Direct Method were borrowed and injected into this new approach. Soon, the success of the Army Method and the revived national interest in foreign languages spurred educational institutions to adopt the new methodology. In all its variations and adaptations, the Army Method came to be known in the 1950s as the **Audiolingual Method**.

The Audiolingual Method (ALM) was firmly grounded in linguistic and psychological theory. Structural linguists of the 1940s and 1950s were engaged in what they claimed was a "scientific descriptive analysis" of various languages; teaching methodologists saw a direct application of such analysis to teaching linguistic patterns (Fries, 1945). At the same time, behavioristic psychologists (*PLLT,* Chapter 4) advocated conditioning and habit-formation models of learning that were perfectly married with the mimicry drills and pattern practices of audiolingual methodology.

The characteristics of the ALM may be summed up in the following list (adapted from Prator & Celce-Murcia, 1979):

1. New material is presented in dialogue form.
2. There is dependence on mimicry, memorization of set phrases, and overlearning.
3. Structures are sequenced by means of contrastive analysis and taught one at a time.
4. Structural patterns are taught using repetitive drills.
5. There is little or no grammatical explanation. Grammar is taught by inductive analogy rather than by deductive explanation.
6. Vocabulary is strictly limited and learned in context.
7. There is much use of tapes, language labs, and visual aids.
8. Great importance is attached to pronunciation.
9. Very little use of the mother tongue by teachers is permitted.
10. Successful responses are immediately reinforced.
11. There is a great effort to get students to produce error-free utterances.
12. There is a tendency to manipulate language and disregard content.

For a number of reasons, the ALM enjoyed many years of popularity, and even to this day, adaptations of the ALM are found in contemporary methodologies. The ALM was firmly rooted in respectable theoretical perspectives of the time. Materials were carefully prepared, tested, and disseminated to educational institutions. "Success" could be overtly experienced by students as they practiced their dialogues in off-hours. But the popularity was not to last forever. Challenged by Wilga Rivers's (1964) eloquent criticism of the misconceptions of the ALM and by its ultimate failure to teach long-term communicative proficiency, the ALM's popularity waned. We discovered that language was not really acquired through a process of habit formation and overlearning, that errors were not necessarily to be avoided at all costs, and that structural linguistics did not tell us everything about language that we needed to know. While the ALM was a valiant attempt to reap the fruits of language-teaching methodologies that had preceded it, in the end it still fell short, as all methods do. But we learned something from the very failure of the ALM to do everything it had promised, and we moved forward.

COGNITIVE CODE LEARNING

The age of audiolingualism, with its emphasis on surface forms and on the rote practice of scientifically produced patterns, began to wane when the Chomskyan revolution in linguistics turned linguists and language teachers toward the "deep structure" of language. Increasing interest in generative transformational grammar and focused attention on the rule-governed nature of language and language acquisition led some language-teaching programs to promote a deductive approach rather than the inductivity of the ALM. Arguing that children subconsciously acquire a system of rules, proponents of a **cognitive code learning** methodology (see Carroll, 1966) began to inject more deductive rule learning into language classes. In an amalgamation of Audiolingual and Grammar Translation techniques, classes retained the drilling typical of the ALM but added healthy doses of rule explanations and reliance on grammatical sequencing of material.

Cognitive code learning was not so much a method as it was an approach that emphasized a conscious awareness of rules and their applications to second language learning. It was a reaction to the strictly behavioristic practices of the ALM, and ironically, a return to some of the practices of Grammar Translation. As teachers and materials developers saw that incessant parroting of potentially rote material was not creating communicatively proficient learners, a new twist was needed, and cognitive code learning appeared to provide just such a twist. Unfortunately, the innovation was short-lived, for as surely as rote drilling bored students, overt cognitive attention to the rules, paradigms, intricacies, and exceptions of a language overtaxed the mental reserves of language students.

The profession needed some spice and verve, and innovative minds in the spirited 1970s were up to the challenge.

"DESIGNER" METHODS OF THE SPIRITED 1970S

The decade of the 1970s was historically significant on two counts. First, perhaps more than in any other decade in "modern" language-teaching history, research on second language learning and teaching grew from an offshoot of linguistics to a discipline in its own right. As more scholars specialized their efforts in second language acquisition studies, our knowledge of how people learn languages inside and outside the classroom mushroomed. Second, in this spirited atmosphere of pioneering research, a number of innovative if not revolutionary methods were conceived. These "designer" methods—to borrow a term from Nunan (1989a, p. 97)—were soon marketed by entrepreneurs as the latest and greatest applications of the multidisciplinary research findings of the day.

Today, as we look back at these methods, we can applaud them for their innovative flair, for their attempt to rouse the language-teaching world out of its audiolingual sleep, and for their stimulation of even more research as we sought to discover why they were *not* the godsend that their inventors and marketers hoped they would be. The scrutiny that the designer methods underwent has enabled us today to incorporate certain elements thereof in our current communicative approaches to language teaching. Let's look at five of these products of the spirited 1970s.

1. Community Language Learning

By the decade of the 1970s, as we increasingly recognized the importance of the affective domain, some innovative methods took on a distinctly affective nature. **Community Language Learning** is a classic example of an affectively based method.

In what he called the "Counseling–Learning" model of education, Charles Curran (1972) was inspired by Carl Rogers's view of education (*PLLT,* Chapter 4) in which learners in a classroom were regarded not as a "class" but as a "group"—a group in need of certain therapy and counseling. The social dynamics of such a group were of primary importance. In order for any learning to take place, group members first needed to interact in an interpersonal relationship in which students and teacher joined together to facilitate learning in a context of valuing each individual in the group. In such a surrounding, each person lowered the defenses that prevent open interpersonal communication. The anxiety caused by the educational context was lessened by means of the supportive community. The teacher's presence was not perceived as a threat, nor was it the teacher's purpose to impose limits and boundaries, but rather, as a true counselor, to center his or her attention on the clients (the students) and their needs. "Defensive" learning was made unnecessary by the empathetic relationship between teacher and students. Curran's Counseling-Learning model of education thus capitalized on the primacy of the needs of the learners—clients—who gathered together in the educational community to be counseled.

Curran's Counseling-Learning model of education was extended to language-learning contexts in the form of Community Language Learning (CLL). While particular adaptations of CLL were numerous, the basic methodology was explicit. The group of clients (for instance, beginning learners of English), having first established in their native language (say, Japanese) an interpersonal relationship and trust, were seated in a circle with the counselor (teacher) on the outside of the circle. When one of the clients wished to say something to the group or to an individual, he or she said it in the native language (Japanese) and the counselor translated the utterance back to the learner in the second language (English). The learner then repeated that English sentence as accurately as possible. Another client responded, in Japanese; the utterance was translated by the counselor into English; the client repeated it; and the conversation continued. If possible the conversation was taped for later listening, and at the end of each session, the learners inductively attempted together to glean information about the new language. If desirable, the counselor might take a more directive role and provide some explanation of certain linguistic rules or items.

The first stage of intense struggle and confusion might continue for many sessions, but always with the support of the counselor and of the fellow clients. Gradually the learner became able to speak a word or phrase directly in the foreign language, without translation. This was the first sign of the learner's moving away from complete dependence on the counselor. As the learners gained more and more familiarity with the foreign language, more and more direct communication could take place, with the counselor providing less and less direct translation and information. After many sessions, perhaps many months or years later, the learner achieved fluency in the spoken language. The learner had at that point become independent.

CLL reflected not only the principles of Carl Rogers's view of education, but also basic principles of the dynamics of counseling in which the counselor, through careful attention to the client's needs, aids the client in moving from dependence and helplessness to independence and self-assurance.

There were advantages and disadvantages to a method like CLL. The affective advantages were evident. CLL was an attempt to put Rogers's philosophy into action and to overcome some of the threatening affective factors in second language learning. The threat of the all-knowing teacher, of making blunders in the foreign language in front of classmates, of competing against peers—all threats that can lead to a feeling of alienation and inadequacy—were presumably removed. The counselor allowed the learner to determine the type of conversation and to analyze the foreign language inductively. In situations in which explanation or translation seemed to be impossible, it was often the client-learner who stepped in and became a counselor to aid the motivation and capitalize on intrinsic motivation.

There were some practical and theoretical problems with CLL. The counselor-teacher could become too nondirective. The student often needed direction, especially in the first stage, in which there was such seemingly endless struggle within the foreign language. Supportive but assertive direction from the counselor could strengthen the method. Another problem with CLL was its reliance on an inductive strategy of learning. It is well accepted that deductive learning is both a viable and efficient strategy of learning and that adults particularly can benefit from deduction as well as induction. While some intense inductive struggle is a necessary component of second language learning, the initial grueling days and weeks of floundering in ignorance in CLL could be alleviated by more directed, deductive learning, "by being told." Perhaps only in the second or third stage, when the learner has moved to more independence, is an inductive strategy really successful. Finally, the success of CLL depended largely on the translation expertise of the counselor. Translation is an intricate and complex process that is often "easier said than done"; if subtle aspects of language are mistranslated, there can be a less than effective understanding of the target language.

Today, virtually no one uses CLL exclusively in a curriculum. Like other methods in this chapter, it was far too restrictive for institutional language programs. However, the principles of discovery learning, student-centered participation, and development of student autonomy (independence) all remain viable in their application to language classrooms. As is the case with virtually any method, the theoretical underpinnings of CLL may be creatively adapted to your own situation.

2. Suggestopedia

Other new methods of the decade were not quite as strictly affective as CLL. **Suggestopedia,** for example, was a method that was derived from Bulgarian psychologist Georgi Lozanov's (1979) contention that the human brain could process great quantities of material if given the right conditions for learning, among which are a state of relaxation and giving over of control to the teacher. According to Lozanov, people are capable of learning much more than they give themselves credit for. In fact, as Larsen-Freeman (2000, p. 73) observed, it may be more appropriate to refer to "Desuggestopedia" to capture the importance placed on desuggesting *limitations* on learning. Learners all too often feel that learning a foreign language is so overwhelmingly difficult that they can never be successful.

Drawing on insights from Soviet psychological research on extrasensory perception and from yoga, Lozanov created a method for learning that capitalized on relaxed states of mind for maximum retention of material. Music was central to his method. Baroque music, with its 60 beats per minute and its specific rhythm, created the kind of "relaxed concentration" that led to "superlearning" (Ostrander & Schroeder, 1979, p. 65). According to Lozanov, during the soft playing of baroque music, one can take in tremendous quantities of material due to an increase in alpha brain waves and a decrease in blood pressure and pulse rate.

In applications of Suggestopedia to foreign language learning, Lozanov and his followers experimented with the presentation of vocabulary, readings, dialogues, role plays, drama, and a variety of other typical classroom activities. Some of the classroom methodology was not particularly unique. The primary difference lay in a significant proportion of activity carried out in soft, comfortable seats in relaxed states of consciousness. Students were encouraged to be as "childlike" as possible, yielding all authority to the teacher and sometimes assuming the roles (and names) of native speakers of the foreign language. Students thus became "suggestible." Lozanov (1979, p. 272) described the concert session portion of a Suggestopedia language class:

At the beginning of the session, all conversation stops for a minute or two, and the teacher listens to the music coming from a tape-recorder. He waits and listens to several passages in order to enter into the mood of the music and then begins to read or recite the new text, his voice modulated in harmony with the musical phrases. The students follow the text in their textbooks where each lesson is translated into the mother tongue. Between the first and second part of the concert, there are several minutes of solemn silence. In some cases, even longer pauses can be given to permit the students to stir a little. Before the beginning of the second part of the concert, there are again several minutes of silence and some phrases of the music are heard again before the teacher begins to read the text. Now the students close their textbooks and listen to the teacher's reading. At the end, the students silently leave the room. They are not told to do any homework on the lesson they have just had except for reading it cursorily once before going to bed and again before getting up in the morning.

Suggestopedia was criticized on a number of fronts. Scovel (1979) showed quite eloquently that Lozanov's experimental data, in which he reported astounding results with Suggestopedia, were highly questionable. Moreover, the practicality of using Suggestopedia is an issue when music and comfortable chairs are not available. More serious is the issue of the place of memorization in language learning. Scovel (1979, pp. 260–261) noted that Lozanov's "innumerable references to . . . memorization . . . to the total exclusion of references to 'understanding' and/or 'creative solutions of problems' convinces this reviewer at least that suggestopedy . . . is an attempt to teach memorization techniques and is not devoted to the far more comprehensive enterprise of language acquisition." On the other hand, other researchers, including Schiffler (1992, p. xv), have suggested a more moderate position on Suggestopedia, hoping "to prevent the exaggerated expectations of Suggestopedia that have been promoted in some publications."

Like some other designer methods (CLL and the Silent Way, for example), Suggestopedia became a business enterprise of its own, and it made promises in the advertising world that were not completely supported by research. Despite such dubious claims, Suggestopedia gave the language-teaching profession some insights. We learned to believe in the power of the human brain. We learned that deliberately induced states of relaxation may be beneficial in the classroom. And numerous teachers have at times experimented with various forms of music as a way to get students to sit back and relax.

3. The Silent Way

Like Suggestopedia, the **Silent Way** rested on more cognitive than affective arguments for its theoretical sustenance. While Caleb Gattegno, its founder, was said to be interested in a "humanistic" approach (Chamot & McKeon, 1984, p. 2) to education, much of the Silent Way was characterized by a problem-solving approach to learning. Richards and Rodgers (2001, p. 81) summarized the theory of learning behind the Silent Way:

1. Learning is facilitated if the learner discovers or creates rather than remembers and repeats what is to be learned.
2. Learning is facilitated by accompanying (mediating) physical objects.
3. Learning is facilitated by problem solving involving the material to be learned.

"Discovery learning," a popular educational trend of the 1960s, advocated less learning "by being told" and more learning by discovering for oneself various facts and principles. In this way, students constructed conceptual hierarchies of their own that were a product of the time they invested. Ausubel's "subsumption" (*PLLT,* Chapter 4) was enhanced by discovery learning since the cognitive categories were created meaningfully with less chance of rote learning taking place. Inductive processes were also encouraged more in discovery-learning methods.

The Silent Way capitalized on such discovery-learning procedures. Gattegno (1972) believed that learners should develop independence, autonomy, and responsibility. At the same time, learners in a Silent Way classroom had to cooperate with each other in the process of solving language problems. The teacher—a stimulator but not a hand-holder—was silent much of the time, thus the name of the method. Teachers had to resist their instinct to spell everything out in black and white, to come to the aid of students at the slightest downfall; they had to "get out of the way" while students worked out solutions.

In a language classroom, the Silent Way typically utilized as materials a set of Cuisenaire rods—small colored rods of varying lengths—and a series of colorful wall charts. The rods were used to introduce vocabulary (colors, numbers, adjectives [*long, short,* and so on]), verbs (*give, take, pick up, drop*), and syntax (tense, comparatives, pluralization, word order, and the like). The teacher provided single-word stimuli or short phrases and sentences once or twice, and then the students refined their understanding and pronunciation among themselves with minimal corrective feedback from the teacher. The charts introduced pronunciation models, grammatical paradigms, and the like.

Like Suggestopedia, the Silent Way has had its share of criticism. In one sense, the Silent Way was too harsh a method, and the teacher too distant, to encourage a communicative atmosphere. Students often need more guidance and overt correction than the Silent Way permitted. There are a number of aspects of language that can indeed be "told" to students to their benefit; they need not, as in CLL as well, struggle for hours or days with a concept that could be easily clarified by the teacher's direct guidance. The rods and charts wear thin after a few lessons, and other materials must be introduced, at which point the Silent Way classroom can look like any other language classroom.

And yet, the underlying principles of the Silent Way are valid. All too often we're tempted as teachers to provide everything for our students, neatly served up on a silver platter. We could benefit from injecting healthy doses of discovery learning into our classroom activities and from providing less teacher talk than we usually do to let the students work things out on their own.

4. Total Physical Response

James Asher (1977), the developer of **Total Physical Response** (TPR), actually began experimenting with TPR in the 1960s, but it was almost a decade before the method was widely discussed in professional circles. Today TPR, with simplicity as its most appealing facet, is a household word among language teachers.

You will recall from earlier in this chapter that more than a century ago, Gouin designed his Series Method on the premise that language associated with a series of simple actions will be easily retained by learners. Much later, psychologists developed the "trace theory" of learning in which it was claimed that memory is increased if it is stimulated, or "traced," through association with motor activity. Over the years, language teachers have intuitively recognized the value of associating language with physical activity. So while the idea of building a method of language teaching on the principle of psychomotor associations was not new, it was this very idea that Asher capitalized upon in developing TPR.

TPR combined a number of other insights in its rationale. Principles of child language acquisition were important. Asher (1977) noted that children, in learning their first language, appear to do a lot of listening before they speak, and that their listening is accompanied by physical responses (reaching, grabbing, moving, looking, and so forth). He also gave some attention to right-brain learning (*PLLT*, Chapter 5). According to Asher, motor activity is a right-brain function that should precede left-brain language processing. Asher was also convinced that language classes were often the locus of too much anxiety, so he wished to devise a method that was as stress-free as possible, where learners would not feel overly self-conscious and defensive. The TPR classroom, then, was one in which students did a great deal of listening and acting. The teacher was very directive in orchestrating a performance: "The instructor is the director of a stage play in which the students are the actors" (Asher, 1977, p. 43).

Typically, TPR heavily utilized the imperative mood, even into more advanced proficiency levels. Commands were an easy way to get learners to move about and to loosen up: *Open the window, Close the door, Stand up, Sit down, Pick up the book, Give it to John,* and so on. No verbal response was necessary. More complex syntax could be incorporated into the imperative: *Draw a rectangle on the chalkboard, Walk quickly to the door and hit it.* Humor is easy to introduce: *Walk slowly to the window and jump, Put your toothbrush in your book* (Asher, 1977, p. 55). Interrogatives were also easily dealt with: *Where is the book? Who is John?* (students pointed to the book or to John). Eventually students, one by one, would feel comfortable enough to venture verbal responses to questions, then to ask questions themselves, and to continue the process.

Like every other method we have encountered, TPR had its limitations. It seemed to be especially effective in the beginning levels of language proficiency, but it lost its distinctiveness as learners advanced in their competence. In a TPR classroom, after students overcame the fear of speaking out, classroom conversations and other activities proceeded as in almost any other communicative language classroom. In TPR reading and writing activities, students are limited to spinning off from the oral work in the classroom. Its appeal to the dramatic or theatrical nature of language learning was attractive. (See Smith, 1984, and Stern, 1983, for discussions of the use of drama in foreign language classrooms.) But soon learners' needs for spontaneity and unrehearsed language must be met.

5. The Natural Approach

Stephen Krashen's (1982, 1997) theories of second language acquisition have been widely discussed and hotly debated over the years (*PLLT,* Chapter 10). The major methodological offshoot of Krashen's views was manifested in the **Natural Approach**, developed by one of Krashen's colleagues, Tracy Terrell (Krashen & Terrell, 1983). Acting on many of the claims that Asher made for a **comprehension-based approach** such as TPR, Krashen and Terrell felt that learners would benefit from delaying production until speech "emerges," that learners should be as relaxed as possible in the classroom, and that a great deal of communication and "acquisition" should take place, as opposed to analysis. In fact, the Natural Approach advocated the use of TPR activities at the beginning level of language learning when "comprehensible input" is essential for triggering the acquisition of language.

There are a number of possible long-range goals of language instruction. In some cases second languages are learned for oral communication; in other cases for written communication; and in still others there may be an academic emphasis on, say, listening to lectures, speaking in a classroom context, or writing a research paper. The goal of the Natural Approach was to build the basic personal communication skills necessary for everyday language situations—daily conversations, shopping, listening to the radio, and the like. The initial task of the teacher was to provide comprehensible input, that is, spoken language that is understandable to the learner or just a little beyond the learner's level. Learners need not say anything during this "silent period" until they feel ready to do so. The teacher was the source of the learners' input and the creator of an interesting and stimulating variety of classroom activities—commands, games, skits, and small-group work.

In the Natural Approach, learners presumably move through what Krashen and Terrell defined as three stages:

a. The preproduction stage is the development of listening comprehension skills.
b. The early production stage is usually marked with errors as the student struggles with the language. The teacher focuses on meaning here, not on form, and therefore the teacher does not make a point of correcting errors

during this stage (unless they are gross errors that block or hinder meaning entirely).

c. The last stage is one of extending production into longer stretches of discourse involving more complex games, role plays, open-ended dialogues, discussions, and extended small-group work. Since the objective in this stage is to promote fluency, teachers are asked to be very sparse in their correction of errors.

The most controversial aspects of the Natural Approach were its advocacy of a "silent period"(delay of oral production) and its heavy emphasis on comprehensible input. The delay of oral production until speech "emerges" has shortcomings (see Gibbons, 1985). What about the student whose speech never emerges? And with all students on different timetables for this so-called emergence, how does the teacher manage a classroom efficiently? Furthermore, the concept of comprehensible input is difficult to pin down, as Langi (1984, p. 18) noted:

> How does one know which structures the learners are to be provided with? From the examples of "teacher talk" provided in the book (Krashen and Terrell, 1983), communication interactions seem to be guided by the topic of conversation rather than by the structures of the language. The decision of which structures to use appears to be left to some mysterious sort of intuition, which many teachers may not possess.

On a more positive note, most teachers and researchers agree that we are prone to insist that learners speak right away, and so we can take from the Natural Approach the good advice that for a period of time while students grow accustomed to the new language, their silence is beneficial. Through TPR and other forms of input, students' language egos are not as easily threatened, and they aren't forced into immediate risk-taking that could embarrass them. The resulting self-confidence eventually can spur a student to venture to speak out.

Innovative methods such as these five methods of the 1970s expose us to principles and practices that you can sift through, weigh, and adapt to multiple contexts. Your responsibility as a teacher is to choose the best of what others have experimented with and adapt those insights to your situation. Those insights and intuitions can become a part of your principled approach to language teaching.

FUNCTIONAL SYLLABUSES

As the innovative methods of the 1970s were being touted by some and criticized by many, some significant foundations for future growth were being laid in what soon came to be known as the **Notional-Functional Syllabus,** or more commonly the **Functional Syllabus.** Beginning with the work of the Council of Europe (Van Ek & Alexander, 1975) and later followed by numerous interpretations of "notional" syllabuses (Wilkins, 1976), Notional-Functional Syllabuses (NFS) began to be used in the United Kingdom in the 1970s.

The distinguishing characteristics of the NFS were its attention to functions (see *PLLT,* Chapter 8) as the organizing elements of English language curriculum, and its contrast with a structural syllabus in which sequenced grammatical structures served as the organizers. Reacting to methods that attended too strongly to grammatical form, the NFS focused strongly—and in some of its interpretations, exclusively—on the pragmatic purposes to which we put language. As such, it was not a method at all. It was close to what we can call an "approach" (see next chapter), but it was more specifically focused on curricular structure than a true approach would be.

"Notions," according to Van Ek and Alexander (1975), are both general and specific. General notions are abstract concepts such as existence, space, time, quantity, and quality. They are domains in which we use language to express thought and feeling. Within the general notion of space and time, for example, are the concepts of location, motion, dimension, speed, length of time, frequency, etc. "Specific notions" correspond more closely to what we have become accustomed to calling "contexts," or "situations." Personal identification, for example, is a specific notion under which name, address, phone number, and other personal information are subsumed. Other specific notions include travel, health and welfare, education, shopping, services, and free time.

The "functional" part of the NFS corresponded to language functions. Curricula were organized around such functions as identifying, reporting, denying, accepting, declining, asking permission, apologizing, etc. Van Ek and Alexander listed some 70 different language functions.

The NFS quickly provided popular underpinnings for the development of communicative textbooks and materials in English language courses. The functional basis of language programs has continued to the present day. In Brown (1999), for example, the following functions are covered in the first several lessons of an advanced beginner's textbook:

1. Introducing self and other people
2. Exchanging personal information
3. Asking how to spell someone's name
4. Giving commands
5. Apologizing and thanking
6. Identifying and describing people
7. Asking for information

A typical unit in this textbook includes an eclectic blend of conversation practice with a classmate, interactive group work, role plays, grammar and pronunciation focus exercises, information-gap techniques, Internet activities, and extra-class interactive practice.

It is important to emphasize, in this historical sketch of methodology, that the NFS did not necessarily develop communicative competence in learners. First, it was not a method, which would specify how you would teach something; it was a syllabus. And while it was clearly a precursor to what we now call Communicative Language Teaching (see Chapter 3), as a syllabus it still presented language as an inventory of units—functional rather than grammatical units—but units nonetheless. Communicative competence implies a set of strategies for getting messages sent and received and for negotiating meaning as an interactive participant in discourse, whether spoken or written. Therefore, the danger that the NFS could simply be "structural lamb served up as notional-functional mutton" (Campbell, 1978, p. 18) was ever-present. However, the NFS did indeed set the stage for bigger and better things. By attending to the functional purposes of language, and by providing contextual (notional) settings for the realization of those purposes, it provided a link between a dynasty of methods that were perishing and a new era of language teaching that is the subject of the next chapter.

As an aid to your recollection of the characteristics of some of the methods reviewed earlier, you may wish to refer to Table 2.1 (pages 36–37), in which the Audiolingual Method, the five "designer" methods, and the Communicative Language Teaching Approach are summarized according to eight different criteria.

✪   ✪   ✪   ✪   ✪

On looking back over this meandering history, you can no doubt see the cycles of changing winds and shifting sands alluded to earlier. In some ways the cycles were, as Marckwardt (1972) proposed, each about a quarter of a century in length, or roughly a generation. In this remarkable succession of changes, we learned something in each generation. We did not allow history simply to deposit new dunes exactly where the old ones lay. So our cumulative history has taught us to appreciate the value of "doing" language interactively, of the emotional (as well as cognitive) side of learning, of absorbing language automatically, of consciously analyzing it when appropriate, and of pointing learners toward the real world where they will use English communicatively.

In the next chapter we look at how we reaped those benefits to form a relatively well-integrated, unified, communicative approach to language teaching that is no longer characterized simply by a series of rising and falling methods.

TOPICS FOR DISCUSSION, ACTION, AND RESEARCH

[Note: (I) Individual work; (G) group or pair work; (C) whole-class discussion.]

1. (I) Since this chapter refers to some basic principles and issues that are normally covered in a course in second language acquisition (and in books like *PLLT* and Mitchell & Myles, 2004), it is quite important at this point for

you to review such material. For example, varied theories of learning are implied in all the methods just reviewed; the role of affective factors in second language acquisition is highlighted in some methods; conscious and subconscious (or focal and peripheral) processing assumes various roles, depending on the method in question. If you encountered concepts or issues that you needed to brush up on as you read this chapter, make some time for a thorough review.

2. (G) Given the choice of Richards and Rodgers's or Anthony's earlier model of looking at the concepts of approach, method, design, procedure, and technique, which do students prefer? Direct small groups to discuss preferences. If there is disagreement, groups should try to come to a consensus. Make sure groups deal with Richards and Rodgers's rationale for the change.

3. (G) Consider the Series Method, the Direct Method, and the Audiolingual Method. Assign a different method to each of several small groups. The task is to list the theoretical foundations on which the method rested and share findings with the whole class.

4. (C) Richards and Rodgers (2001, p. 7) said Grammar Translation "is a method for which there is no theory." Is this too harsh a judgment? Ask students if they agree with the theorylessness of Grammar Translation and why.

5. (G) If time permits, each of the methods described in this chapter could be assigned to a different small group of students. The group's task (which may require some extra-class research beyond what is provided in this chapter) is to specify, for the method assigned to them, the following descriptors (adapted from Larsen-Freeman, 2000) which differ from those in Table 2.1:

1. Characteristics of the teaching/learning process
2. The nature of teacher-student and student-student interaction
3. The ways in which students' feelings and emotions are handled
4. The role of the native language of students
5. The language skills that are emphasized
6. The way the teacher responds to student errors

Each group can then report their findings to the rest of the class. Students often find it useful to see the information formatted as a chart (on the chalkboard or computer generated) similar to Table 2.1.

6. (G/C) Review the five "designer" methods. If class size permits, assign a method to each of five different small groups, where each group will "defend" their method against the others. The group task is to prepare arguments in favor of their method, questions to ask of other methods, and counter-arguments against what other groups might ask them. After a modified debate, end with a whole-class discussion.

Table 2.1. An overview of methods (adapted from Nunan, 1989a)

	Theory of Language	Theory of Learning	Objectives	Syllabus
Audiolingual	Language is a system of rule-governed structures hierarchically arranged.	Habit formation; skills are learned more effectively if oral precedes written; analogy, not analysis.	Control of structures of sound, form, and order; mastery over symbols of the language; goal: native-speaker mastery.	Graded syllabus of phonology, morphology, and syntax. Contrastive analysis.
Total Physical Response	Basically a structuralist, grammar-based view of language.	L2 learning is the same as L1 learning; comprehension before production is "imprinted" through carrying out commands (right-brain functioning); reduction of stress.	Teach oral proficiency to produce learners who can communicate uninhibitedly and intelligibly with native speakers.	Sentence-based syllabus with grammatical and lexical criteria being primary, but focus on meaning, not form.
The Silent Way	Each language is composed of elements that give it a unique rhythm and spirit. Functional vocabulary and core structure are key to the spirit of the language.	Processes of learning a second language are fundamentally different from L1 learning. L2 learning is an intellectual, cognitive process. Surrender to the music of the language, silent awareness, then active trial.	Near-native fluency, correct pronunciation, basic practical knowledge of the grammar of the L2. Learner learns *how* to learn a language.	Basically structural lessons planned around grammatical items and related vocabulary. Items are introduced according to their grammatical complexity.
Community Language Learning	Language is more than a system for communication. It involves the whole person; culture; educational; developmental; and communicative processes.	Learning involves the whole person. It is a social process of growth from childlike dependence to self-direction and independence.	No specific objectives. Near-native mastery is the goal.	No set syllabus. Course progression is topic-based; learners provide the topics. Syllabus emerges from learners' intention and the teacher's reformulations.
The Natural Approach	The essence of language is meaning. Vocabulary, not grammar, is the heart of language.	There are two ways of L2 language development: "acquisition"—a natural subconscious process, and "learning"—a conscious process. Learning cannot lead to acquisition.	Designed to give beginners and intermediate learners basic communicative skills. Four broad areas: basic personal communicative skills (oral/written); academic learning skills (oral/written).	Based on selection of communicative activities and topics derived from learner needs.
Suggestopedia	Rather conventional, although memorization of whole meaningful texts is recommended.	Learning occurs through suggestion, when learners are in a deeply relaxed state. Baroque music is used to induce this state.	To deliver advanced conversational competence quickly. Learners are required to master prodigious lists of vocabulary pairs, although the goal is understanding, not memorization.	Ten unit courses consisting of 1,200-word dialogues graded by vocabulary and grammar.
Communicative Language Teaching	Language is a system for the expression of meaning; primary function—interaction and communication.	Doing activities that involve real communication, carrying out meaningful tasks, and using language which is meaningful to the learner promote learning.	Objectives will reflect the needs of the learner; they will include functional skills as well as linguistic objectives.	Will include some/all of the following: structures, functions, notions, themes, tasks. Ordering will be guided by learner needs.

Activity Types	Learner Roles	Teacher Roles	Roles of Materials
Dialogues and drills, repetition and memorization, pattern practice.	Organisms that can be directed by skilled training techniques to produce correct responses.	Central and active teacher-dominated method. Provides model, controls direction and pace.	Primarily teacher-oriented. Tapes and visuals, language lab often used.
Imperative drills to elicit physical actions.	Listener and performer, little influence over the content of learning.	Active and direct role; "the director of a stage play" with students as actors.	No basic text; materials and media have an important role later. Initially voice, action, and gestures are sufficient.
Learner responses to commands, questions, and visual cues. Activities encourage and shape oral responses without grammatical explanation or modeling by teacher.	Learning is a process of personal growth. Learners are responsible for their own learning and must develop independence, autonomy, and responsibility.	Teachers must (a) teach (b) test (c) get out of the way. Remain impassive. Resist temptation to model, remodel, assist, direct, exhort.	Unique materials: colored rods, color-coded pronunciation and vocabulary charts.
Combination of innovative and conventional. Translation, group work, recording, transcription, reflection and observation, listening, free conversation.	Learners are members of a community. Learning is not viewed as an individual accomplishment, but something that is achieved collaboratively.	Counseling/parental analogy. Teacher provides a safe environment in which students can learn and grow.	No textbook, which would inhibit growth. Materials are developed as course progresses.
Activities allowing comprehensible input, about things in the here-and-now. Focus on meaning, not form.	Should not try to learn language in the usual sense, but should try to lose themselves in activities involving meaningful communication.	The teacher is the primary source of comprehensible input. Must create positive low-anxiety climate. Must choose and orchestrate a rich mixture of classroom activities.	Materials come from realia rather than textbooks. Primary aim is to promote comprehension and communication.
Initiatives, question and answer, role play, listening exercises under deep relaxation.	Must maintain a passive state and allow the materials to work on them (rather than vice versa).	To create situations in which the learner is most suggestible and present material in a way most likely to encourage positive reception and retention. Must exude authority and confidence.	Consists of texts, tapes, classroom fixtures, and music. Texts should have force, literary quality, and interesting characters.
Engage learners in communication; involve processes such as information sharing, negotiation of meaning, and interaction.	Learner as negotiator, interactor, giving as well as taking.	Facilitator of the communication process, participants' tasks, and texts; needs analyst, counselor, process manager.	Primary role in promoting communicative language use; task-based materials; authentic.

7. (C) Three of the five "designer" methods (CLL, Silent Way, and Suggestopedia) were proprietary, with their own commercial publishing and educational company. Ask students to consider how that fact might have colored (a) the objectivity with which its backers promoted their method and (b) public reception to it.

8. (C) Chapter 1 described a classroom lesson in English as a second language. Ask students to look back through that lesson now and, in light of the various methodological positions that have occupied the last century or so of language teaching, to determine how the activities/techniques in the lesson reflect some of the theoretical foundations on which certain methods were constructed. For example, when the teacher did a quick choral drill (#10), how would one support that technique with principles that lay behind the ALM?

9. (G/C) Ask students in small groups to review the cycles of "shifting sands" since Gouin's time. How did each new method borrow from previous practices? What did each reject in previous practices? Each group will then share their conclusions with the rest of the class. On the board, you might reconstruct the historical progression in the form of a time line with characteristics listed for each "era." If time permits, try to determine what the prevailing intellectual or political mood was when certain methods were flowering. For example, the ALM was a product of a military training program and flourished during an era when scientific solutions to all problems were diligently sought. Are there some logical connections here?

FOR YOUR FURTHER READING

Kelly, L. (1969). *Twenty-five centuries of language teaching*. Rowley, MA: Newbury House Publishers.

For a fascinating look back into language teaching as long ago as 500 B.C., scan through this book (now out of print) that chronicles foreign language teaching practices. Examining a number of different skill areas, Kelly probes the origins of various methodological innovations through the centuries, ultimately showing that some of our "latest" methods may have roots that are hundreds of years old.

Anthony, E. (1963). Approach, method and technique. *English Language Teaching, 17*, 63–67.

In this seminal article, Anthony defines and gives examples of the three title terms. Methods are seen, perhaps for the first time, as guided by and built upon solid theoretical foundations. His definitions have prevailed to this day in informal pedagogical terminology.

Richards, J., & Rodgers, T. (2001). *Approaches and methods in language teaching* (2nd ed.). Cambridge, UK: Cambridge University Press.

Larsen-Freeman, D. (2000). *Techniques and principles in language teaching* (2nd ed.). Oxford, UK: Oxford University Press.

Both volumes offer excellent detailed summaries of the methods described in the present chapter. Richards and Rodgers redefine Anthony's original definitions and then present a useful overview of a number of different methods within the rubric of approaches that support them, course designs that utilize them, and classroom procedures (techniques) that manifest them. Larsen-Freeman analyzes each method from the perspectives of a standard set of questions, each of which helps to characterize the method. Questions focus on teacher goals, roles of the teacher, the nature of student-teacher interaction, undergirding theories of language and culture, assessment, and other topics.

CHAPTER 3

THE POSTMETHOD ERA:

TOWARD INFORMED APPROACHES

OBJECTIVES After reading this chapter, you will be able to:

- understand the concept of "postmethod" in a historical context

- apply principles of communicative language teaching to your understanding of an interactive language classroom

- distinguish among a variety of different approaches

- analyze the extent to which tenets of one or more approaches can enlighten your classroom methodology

The history of language teaching depicted in the previous chapter, characterized by a series of "methodical" milestones, had changed its course by the end of the 1980s. The profession had learned some profound lessons from our past wanderings. We had learned to be cautiously eclectic in making enlightened choices of teaching practices that were solidly grounded in the best of what we knew about second language learning and teaching. We had amassed enough research on learning and teaching that we could indeed formulate an integrated approach to language-teaching practices. And, perhaps ironically, the methods that were such strong signposts of our century-old journey were no longer of great consequence in marking our progress. How did that happen?

In the 1970s and early 1980s, there was a good deal of hoopla about the "designer" methods described in Chapter 2. Even though they weren't widely adopted as standard methods, they were nevertheless symbolic of a profession at least partially caught up in a mad scramble to invent a new method when the very concept of "method" was eroding under our feet. By the early 1990s it was readily apparent that we didn't need a new method. We needed, instead, to get on with the business of unifying our **approach** to language teaching and of designing effective tasks and techniques that were informed by that approach.

Perhaps the spirit of those times was best captured by the notion of a **postmethod** era of language teaching, a concept that continues to be used in pedagogical circles today (Kumaravadivelu, 2001, 2006b; Richards & Rodgers, 2001). Kumaravadivelu (1994), Clarke (1994), and Brown (1993), among others, expressed the need to put to rest the limited concept of method as it was used in the last century, and instead to focus on what Kumaravadivelu (2006b) calls a "pedagogy of particularity," by which he means being "sensitive to a particular group of teachers teaching a particular group of learners pursuing a particular set of goals within a particular institutional context embedded in a particular social milieu" (p. 538). A soundly conceived pedagogical approach underlies such attention to the particularities of contexts.

And so, today those clearly identifiable and enterprising methods are an interesting if not insightful contribution to our professional repertoire, but few practitioners look to any one of them, or their predecessors, for a final answer on how to teach a foreign language. Method, as a unified, finite set of design features, is now given only minor attention. Instead, as noted in the previous chapter, the notion of **methodology** nevertheless continues to be viable, as it is in any other behavioral science, as the systematic application of validated principles to practical contexts.

In all this discussion of method, you do well to keep in mind the comments of the previous chapter, namely, that some of the debate is simply a matter of semantics. Bell (2003) astutely observed that we have too many definitions attached to the same word. He suggested that methods with a lowercase *m* can mean any of a wide variety of classroom practices, while Methods with an uppercase *M* seem to connote a "fixed set of classroom practices that serve as a prescription" (p. 326). On the other hand, Richards and Rodgers (2001), as noted in the previous chapter, use the same term as an umbrella to comprise approach, design, and procedure. What are we to make of this confusion? Bell (2003) is joined by Larsen-Freeman (2000), among others, who remain comfortable with maintaining the notion of methods (with a small *m*) as long as we are clear about the referent. "Postmethod need not imply the end of methods but rather an understanding of the limitations of the notion of method and a desire to transcend those limitations" (Bell, 2003, p. 334).

So perhaps the profession has attained a modicum of maturity where we recognize that the diversity of language learners in multiple worldwide contexts demands an eclectic blend of tasks, each tailored for a specified group of learners studying for particular purposes in geographic, social, and political contexts. David Nunan (1991b, p. 228) summed it up nicely: "It has been realized that there never was and probably never will be a method for all, and the focus in recent years has been on the development of classroom tasks and activities which are consonant with what we know about second language acquisition, and which are also in keeping with the dynamics of the classroom itself."

THE DYSFUNCTION OF THE THEORY-PRACTICE DICHOTOMY

The now discarded concept of method (with a capital *M*) as a discrete set of unified techniques designed to meet a variety of contexts carried with it, in some opinions (Clarke, 1994; Kumaravadivelu, 2006b), an implicit assumption about the relationship between what we have customarily called "theory" and "practice." By **theory**, professional journals and books sometimes implied a creator, or theorist, who carried out research and proposed the rudiments of an organized set of hypotheses, and sometimes then further proposed a methodological "application" of the theory (hence the perhaps misguided term, "applied linguistics"). The **practice** part of the formula was thought to be the province of classroom teachers who all too gladly accepted the theorist's pronouncements, which came in the form of a method. The relationship between the theorist and practitioner was (and in some cases, still is) similar to that of a producer of goods and a consumer or customer.

Mark Clarke (1994) very eloquently argued against such a relationship in analyzing the "dysfunction" of the theory-practice relationship. He and others since then (Kumaravadivelu, 2006b; Larsen-Freeman, 2000; Nunan, 2003; Richards & Rodgers, 2001) offer strong arguments against perpetuating this "misleading dualism" (Hedgcock, 2002, p. 308). Not only does such an understanding promote the notion of "a privileged class of theorists and an underprivileged class of practitioners" (Kumaravadivelu, 2006, p. 166), but it also connotes a separation of researchers and teachers and, at worst, a one-way communication line from the former to the latter.

Recent work in the language-teaching profession shows a marked departure from the artificial dichotomy of theory and practice (Bailey, 2001; Johnson, 1999; McKay, 2006; Murphy & Byrd, 2001). In this newer mode of viewing the profession, teachers *are* researchers and are charged with the responsibility of reflecting on their own practice. Calls for "action research" and "classroom-based research" reflect a new and healthier attitude toward the relationship of research and practice. It has become increasingly inauthentic for university professors to generate ideas from the protective walls of an ivory tower without experiencing them in person in the classroom. Likewise, more and more teachers are engaging in the process of systematic observation, experimentation, analysis, and reporting of their own experiences in classrooms around the world. More detail on the language teacher as researcher is offered in Chapter 26 of this book.

As you continue to read on in this and following chapters, it is important to view yourself as a capable observer of your own—and others'—practice. You need not think of theorists as people that are removed from the arena of classroom reality, nor of teachers as anything less than essential participants in a dialogue. To assume a gap between theory and practice is dysfunctional indeed.

AN ENLIGHTENED, ECLECTIC APPROACH

It should be clear from the foregoing that as both an enlightened and eclectic teacher, you think in terms of a number of possible methodological options at your disposal for tailoring classes to particular contexts. Your **approach,** or rationale for language learning and teaching, therefore takes on great importance. Your approach includes a number of basic principles of learning and teaching (such as those that will be elaborated on in the next chapter) on which you can rely for designing and evaluating classroom lessons. Your approach to language-teaching methodology is a theoretically well-informed global understanding of the process of learning and teaching. It is inspired by the interconnection of all your reading and observing and discussing and teaching, and that interconnection underlies everything that you do in the classroom.

But your approach to language pedagogy is not just a set of static principles "set in stone." It is, in fact, a dynamic composite of energies within you that change, or should change, with your experiences in your learning and teaching. The way you understand the language-learning process—what makes for successful and unsuccessful learning—may be relatively stable across months or years, but don't ever feel too smug. There is far too much that we do not know collectively about this process, and there are far too many new research findings pouring in, to allow you to confidently assert that you know everything you already need to know about language and language learning.

The interaction between your approach and your classroom practice is the key to dynamic teaching. The best teachers always take a few calculated risks in the classroom, trying new activities here and there. The inspiration for such innovation comes from the approach level, but the feedback that these teachers gather from actual implementation then informs their overall understanding of the teaching-learning process. Which, in turn, may give rise to a new insight and more innovative possibilities, and the cycle continues.

If you have little or no experience in teaching and are perhaps now in a teacher education program, you may feel you cannot yet describe your own approach to language learning and teaching. On the other hand, you might just surprise yourself at the intuitions you already have about the foundations of teaching. Look at the list below of potential *choices* you have in designing a lesson. On the basis of what you know so far about second language acquisition and the pedagogical process, and for a particular context you're familiar with, think about:

a. which side of a continuum of possibilities you would generally lean toward,
b. why you would lean that way, and most importantly,
c. what contextual variables might influence a change away from your general inclination.

For example, the first item below offers a choice between "meaning" and "grammar" for a focus. While you might lean toward meaning because you know that too much focus on form could detract from communicative acquisition, certain classroom objectives and tasks might demand a focus on grammar. Here is the list:

For a particular course and context you are familiar with . . .

1. Should the course focus on *meaning* or *grammar?*
2. Will my students learn best by using plenty of *analysis* or *intuition?*
3. Would it be better for my students to *think directly* in the L2 or to *use translation* from the L1?
4. Will my students benefit more from *immediate* rewards or from *long-term* rewards?
5. As a teacher should I be *tough and demanding* or *gentle and empathetic?*
6. Should my feedback to students be given *frequently* or *infrequently*, so students will develop autonomy?
7. Should a communicative course give more attention to *accuracy* or *fluency?*

Were you able to respond to these items? If you could make a choice within each item, it indicates that you do indeed have some intuitions about teaching, and perhaps the beginnings of an approach. Your approach is guided by a number of factors: your own experience as a learner in classrooms, whatever teaching experience you may already have had, classroom observations you have made, books you have read, and previous courses in the field. But more importantly, if you found that in almost every choice you wanted to add something like "but it depends on . . ." then you are on the way toward developing an *enlightened* approach to language learning and teaching. Our approaches to language teaching must always be designed for specific contexts of teaching—what Kumaravadivelu (2006b) calls a pedagogy of "particularity," as mentioned earlier. Rarely can we say with absolute certainty that some methodological set of techniques applies to all learners in all contexts for all purposes.

Your approach also will differ on various issues from that of a colleague of yours, or even a supervising teacher, just as "experts" in the field differ in their interpretations of research on learning and teaching. There are three reasons for variation at the approach level:

a. an approach is by definition dynamic and therefore subject to alterations and modification as a result of one's observation and experience;
b. research in second language acquisition and pedagogy almost always yields findings that are not conclusive, but are subject to interpretation; and
c. we are constantly making new discoveries about language learning and teaching, as our professional stockpile of knowledge and experience builds.

COMMUNICATIVE LANGUAGE TEACHING

Is there a currently recognized approach that is a generally accepted norm in the field? The answer depends on whom you ask. For many (Savignon, 2005, among others), **Communicative Language Teaching** (CLT) is an accepted paradigm with many interpretations and manifestations. For others (Kumaravadivelu, 2006a, for example), CLT is laden with issues of "authenticity, acceptability, and adaptability" (p. 62), and instead we are exhorted to embrace **task-based language teaching** (TBLT) as a more appropriate model. (See below for a discussion of TBLT.)

The latter arguments represent what appears to be too strong a rejection of a tradition that has been viable in many language-teaching circles for several decades. In this chapter, in order to avoid a lot of nitpicking over the nuances of difference between the two approaches, we'll look at both CLT and TBLT, and then perhaps we can allow the progression of research in the next few years to sort out the pros and cons on each point of view. Suffice it to say that no model will be sufficient to satisfy *all* the criteria for a comprehensive theory of instructed second language acquisition. As long as the language-teaching community recognizes shortcomings and seeks to remedy them in local contexts, we can still use such models as foundation stones for our pedagogy.

In the previous chapter you were introduced to a progression of methods that defined a century or more of language-teaching history. Beneath those methods lay some important theoretical assumptions. In the 1940s and 1950s, the profession was to some extent convinced that teachers could behaviorally program a scientifically ordered set of linguistic structures into the minds of learners through conditioning. In the 1960s we were quite worried about how Chomsky's generative grammar was going to fit into our language classrooms and how to inject the **cognitive code** of a language into the process of absorption. The innovativeness of the 1970s brought affective factors to the forefront of some experimental language-teaching methods. This period saw a focus on emotional and sociocultural factors operating within learners. The late 1970s and early 1980s saw the beginnings of what we now recognize as a communicative approach as we better and better understood the functions that must be incorporated into a classroom. The late 1980s and 1990s saw the development of approaches that highlighted the fundamentally communicative properties of language, and classrooms were increasingly characterized by authenticity, real-world simulation, and meaningful tasks.

Today we continue our professional march through history. Beyond grammatical and discourse elements in communication, we continue to probe the nature of social, cultural, and pragmatic features of language. We are exploring pedagogical means for "real-life" communication in the classroom. We are trying to get our learners to develop linguistic fluency, and not just the accuracy that once consumed our predecessors. We are equipping our students with tools for generating unrehearsed language performance "out there" when they leave the womb of our classrooms. We are concerned with how to facilitate lifelong language learning among our students, and not just with the immediate classroom task. We are looking at learners as partners in a cooperative venture. And our classroom practices seek to draw on whatever intrinsically sparks learners to reach their fullest potential.

All of these theoretical interests underlie what we can best describe as CLT. It is difficult to offer a definition of CLT. It is a unified but broadly based, theoretically well-informed set of tenets about the nature of language and of language learning and teaching. From the earlier seminal works in CLT (Breen & Candlin, 1980; Savignon, 1983; Widdowson, 1978) up to more recent teacher education textbooks (Brown, 2007; Harmer, 2001; Jacobs & Farrell, 2003; Lee & VanPatten, 2003; Nunan, 2003; Richard-Amato, 2003; Savignon, 2005), we have definitions enough to send us reeling. For the sake of simplicity and directness, I offer the following seven interconnected characteristics as a description of CLT:

Characteristics of a CLT Approach

1. **Overall goals**. CLT suggests a focus on *all* of the components (grammatical, discourse, functional, sociolinguistic, and strategic) of communicative competence. Goals therefore must intertwine the organizational (grammatical, discourse) aspects of language with the pragmatic (functional, sociolinguistic, strategic) aspects.

2. **Relationship of form and function**. Language techniques are designed to engage learners in the pragmatic, authentic, functional use of language for meaningful purposes. Organizational language forms are not the central focus, but remain as important components of language that enable the learner to accomplish those purposes.

3. **Fluency and accuracy**. A focus on students' "flow" of comprehension and production and a focus on the formal accuracy of production are seen as complementary principles underlying communicative techniques. At times fluency may have to take on more importance than accuracy in order to keep learners meaningfully engaged in language use. At other times the students will be encouraged to attend to correctness. Part of the teacher's responsibility is to offer appropriate corrective feedback on learners' errors.

4. **Focus on real-world contexts**. Students in a communicative class ultimately have to use the language, productively and receptively, in unrehearsed contexts outside the classroom. Classroom tasks must therefore equip students with the skills necessary for communication in those contexts.

5. **Autonomy and strategic involvement**. Students are given opportunities to focus on their own learning process through raising their awareness of their own styles of learning (strengths, weaknesses, preferences) and through the development of appropriate strategies for production and comprehension. Such awareness and action will help to develop autonomous learners capable of continuing to learn the language beyond the classroom and the course.

6. **Teacher roles**. The role of the teacher is that of facilitator and guide, not an all-knowing font of knowledge. The teacher is an empathetic "coach" who values the students' linguistic development. Students are encouraged to construct meaning through genuine linguistic interaction with other students and with the teacher.

7. **Student roles**. Students in a CLT class are active participants in their own learning process. Learner-centered, cooperative, collaborative learning is emphasized, but not at the expense of appropriate teacher-centered activity.

These seven characteristics underscore some major departures from earlier methods and approaches. In some ways those departures were a gradual product of outgrowing the numerous methods that characterized a long stretch of history. In other ways those departures were radical. Structurally (grammatically) sequenced curricula were a mainstay of language teaching for centuries. CLT suggests that grammatical structure might better be subsumed under various pragmatic categories. In CLT we pay considerably less attention to the overt presentation and discussion of grammatical rules than we traditionally did. Using a great deal of authentic language is implied in CLT, as we attempt to build fluency. It is important to note, however, that fluency should never be encouraged at the expense of clear, unambiguous, direct communication. Much more spontaneity is present in communicative classrooms: Students are encouraged to deal with unrehearsed situations under the guidance, but not control, of the teacher. The importance of learners' developing a strategic approach to acquisition is a total turnabout from earlier methods that never broached the topic of strategies-based instruction. And finally, the teacher's facilitative role in CLT and students' collaborative role are the product of two decades or more of slowly recognizing the importance of learner initiative in the classroom.

Some of the characteristics of CLT make it difficult for a nonnative-speaking teacher who might not be very proficient in the second language to teach effectively. Dialogues, drills, rehearsed exercises, and discussions (in the first language) of grammatical rules are much simpler for some nonnative-speaking teachers to contend with. This drawback should not deter one, however, from pursuing communicative goals in the classroom. Technology (such as video, television, audio CDs, the Internet, the Web, and computer software) can aid such teachers. Moreover, in the last decade or so, we have seen a marked increase in English teachers' proficiency levels around the world. As educational and political institutions in various countries become more sensitive to the importance of teaching foreign languages for communicative purposes (not just for the purpose of fulfilling a requirement or of "passing a test"), we may be better able, worldwide, to accomplish the goals of communicative language teaching.

CLT is not by any means a brand-new approach. One of the most comprehensive lists of CLT features came a quarter of a century ago from Finocchiaro and Brumfit (1983, pp. 91–93) in a comparison of audiolingual methodology with what they then called the Communicative Approach. Because of its practicality, their list is reprinted in Table 3.1. In subsequent chapters, as you grapple with designing specific classroom techniques and planning lessons, you will be given chances to apply your understanding of CLT and, no doubt, to refine that understanding.

At the beginning of this section, it was noted that there are some who now argue that CLT may not be as sufficient a model as we once thought. Why the caution? Doesn't all the above make perfectly good sense? Haven't CLT principles been applied repeatedly, and successfully, in classrooms around the world? Indeed, you can with some assurance latch on to the CLT label and, like a member of a club, aver that you "believe in CLT," and be allowed to step inside the gates. But as with every issue in our field, there are caveats (see Kumaravadivelu, 2006, and Kramsch, 2006, for further discussion):

1. Beware of giving lip service to principles of CLT (and related principles like cooperative learning, interactive teaching, learner-centered classes, content-centered education, whole language, etc.—see the next sections in this chapter) but not truly grounding your teaching techniques in such principles (Kramsch, 2006). Few teachers would admit to a disbelief in principles of CLT; they would be marked as heretics. But if you believe the term characterizes your teaching, then make sure you do indeed understand and practice your convictions.
2. Avoid overdoing certain CLT features: engaging in real-life, authentic language in the classroom to the exclusion of any potentially helpful controlled exercises, grammatical pointers, and other analytical devices; or simulating the real world but refraining from "interfering" in the ongoing flow of language. Such an "indirect" approach* (Celce-Murcia, Dörnyei, & Thurrel, 1997) to CLT only offers the possibility of incidental learning without specific focus on forms, rules, and principles of language organization. A more effective application of CLT principles is manifested in a "direct" approach that carefully sequences and structures tasks for learners and offers optimal intervention to aid learners in developing strategies for acquisition.

---

*Howatt (1984), Littlewood (1981), and Nunan (1988) referred to this as the "strong" approach to CLT, noting that most practitioners would follow a "weak" version of CLT in which authenticity is coupled with structural and functional practice and other procedures of intervention.

Table 3.1. A comparison of the Audiolingual Method and Communicative Language
Teaching (Finocchiaro & Brumfit, 1983, pp. 91–93)

Audiolingual Method	Communicative Approach
1. Attends to structure and form more than meaning.	Meaning is paramount.
2. Demands more memorization of structure-based dialogues.	Dialogues, if used, center around communicative functions and are not normally memorized.
3. Language items are not necessarily contextualized.	Contextualization is a basic premise.
4. Language learning is learning structures, sounds, or words.	Language learning is learning to communicate.
5. Mastery or "overlearning" is sought.	Effective communication is sought.
6. Drilling is a central technique.	Drilling may occur, but peripherally.
7. Native-speaker-like pronunciation is sought.	Comprehensible pronunciation is sought.
8. Grammatical explanation is avoided.	Any device that helps the learners is accepted—varying according to their age, interest, etc.
9. Communicative activities come only after a long process of rigid drills and exercises.	Attempts to communicate are encouraged from the very beginning.
10. The use of the student's native language is forbidden.	Judicious use of native language is accepted where feasible.
11. Translation is forbidden at early levels.	Translation may be used where students need or benefit from it.
12. Reading and writing are deferred until speech is mastered.	Reading and writing can start from the first day, if desired.
13. The target linguistic system is learned through the overt teaching of the patterns of the system.	The target linguistic system is learned through the process of struggling to communicate.
14. Linguistic competence is the desired goal.	Communicative competence is the desired goal.
15. Varieties of language are recognized but not emphasized.	Linguistic variation is a central concept in materials and methods.
16. The sequence of units is determined solely by principles of linguistic complexity.	Sequencing is determined by any consideration of content function or meaning that maintains interest.
17. The teacher controls the learners and prevents them from doing anything that conflicts with the theory.	Teachers help learners in any way that motivates them to work with the language.
18. "Language is habit," so error must be prevented at all costs.	Language is often created by the individual through trial and error.
19. Accuracy, in terms of formal correctness, is a primary goal.	Fluency and acceptable language are the primary goals; accuracy is judged not in the abstract but in context.
20. Students are expected to interact with the language system, embodied in machines or controlled materials.	Students are expected to interact with other people, either in the flesh, through pair and group work, or in their writing.
21. The teacher is expected to specify the language that students are to use.	The teacher cannot know exactly what language the students will use.
22. Intrinsic motivation will spring from an interest in the structure of language.	Intrinsic motivation will spring from an interest in what is being communicated by the language.

3. Remember that there are numerous interpretations of CLT. Because it is a catchall term, it is tempting to figure that everyone agrees on its definition. As already noted above, they don't. In fact, some of those in the profession, with good reason, feel uncomfortable using the term, even to the point of wishing to exorcise it from our jargon. As long as you are aware of many possible versions of CLT, it remains a term that can continue to capture current language-teaching approaches.

Closely allied to CLT are a number of concepts that have, like CLT, become bandwagon terms: task-based language teaching (which is for some a candidate for replacing the notion of CLT), learner-centered, cooperative, interactive, whole language based, and content-based, to name a few. One way of looking at these terms is that they are simply expressions for the latest fads in language teaching and are therefore relatively meaningless. But another viewpoint would embrace them as legitimate attempts to label current concerns and recent developments within a CLT framework, as overlapping and confusing as those concerns sometimes are. I believe the latter is the more reasoned perspective. However, in order to take that perspective, some explanation is in order. Hence, in the sections that follow, a number of the current CLT-related approaches are summarized.

TASK-BASED LANGUAGE TEACHING

One of the most prominent perspectives within the CLT framework is **Task-based Language Teaching** (TBLT). While some researchers (Kumaravadivelu, 2006a) argue that TBLT is a significantly different approach, other proponents (Ellis, 2003) would claim that TBLT is at the very heart of CLT. This approach puts the use of tasks at the core of language teaching. While there is a good deal of variation among experts on how to describe or define **task,** Peter Skehan's (1998a, p. 95) concept of task still captures the essentials. He defines task as an activity in which

- meaning is primary;
- there is some communication problem to solve;
- there is some sort of relationship to comparable real-world activities;
- task completion has some priority; and
- the assessment of the task is in terms of outcome.

Perhaps more simply put, "a task is an activity which requires learners to use language, with emphasis on meaning, to attain an objective" (Bygate, Skehan, & Swain, 2001, p. 11). In some cases, task and technique may be synonymous (a problem-solving task/technique; a role-play task/technique, for example). But in other cases, a task may be comprised of several techniques (for example, a problem-solving task that includes, let's say, grammatical explanation, teacher-initiated questions, and a specific turn-taking procedure). Tasks are usually "bigger" in their ultimate ends than techniques. No small effort is demanded in designing effective tasks, as Johnson (2003) and Nunan (2004) ably demonstrate.

Task-based teaching makes an important distinction between **target tasks,** which students must accomplish beyond the classroom, and **pedagogical tasks,** which form the nucleus of the classroom activity. Target tasks are not unlike the **functions** of language that are listed in Notional-Functional Syllabuses (see Chapter 2, here, and Chapter 8 of *PLLT*); however, they are much more specific and more explicitly related to classroom instruction. If, for example, "giving personal information" is a communicative function for language, then an appropriately stated target task might be "giving personal information in a job interview." Notice that the task specifies a context. Pedagogical tasks include any of a series of techniques designed ultimately to teach students to perform the target task; the climactic pedagogical task actually involves students in some form of simulation of the target task itself (say, through a role-play simulation in which certain roles are assigned to pairs of learners).

Pedagogical tasks are distinguished by their specific goals that point beyond the language classroom to the target task. They may, however, include both formal and functional techniques. A pedagogical task designed to teach students to give personal information in a job interview might, for example, involve

1. doing exercises in comprehension of *wh-* questions with *do*-insertion ("When do you work at Macy's?")
2. doing drills in the use of frequency adverbs ("I usually work until five o'clock.")
3. listening to extracts of job interviews
4. analyzing the grammar and discourse of the interviews
5. modeling an interview: teacher and one student
6. role playing a simulated interview: students in pairs

While you might be tempted to think that only the climactic task (#6) fulfills the criterion of pointing beyond the classroom to the real world, all of the techniques build toward enabling the students to perform the final task.

A task-based curriculum, then, specifies what a learner needs to do with the English language in terms of target tasks and organizes a series of pedagogical tasks intended to reach those goals. Be careful that you do not look at task-based teaching as a hodgepodge of useful little things that the learner should be able to do, all thrown together haphazardly into the classroom. In fact, a distinguishing feature of task-based curricula is their insistence on pedagogical soundness in the development and sequencing of tasks. The teacher and curriculum planner are called upon to consider communicative dimensions such as goal, input from the teacher, interaction, teacher and learner roles, and assessment.

Task-based instruction is not a new method. Rather, it puts task at the center of one's methodological focus. It views the learning process as a set of communicative tasks that are directly linked to the curricular goals they serve, the purposes of which extend beyond the practice of language for its own sake. Research on task-based learning (Ellis, 2003; Kumaravadivelu, 2006; Nunan, 2004; Richards & Rodgers, 2001; Skehan, 2003) has attempted to identify types of tasks that enhance learning (such as open-ended, structured, teacher-fronted, small group, and pair work) to define task-specific learner factors (for example, roles, proficiency levels, and styles), and to examine teacher roles and other variables that contribute to successful achievement of objectives.

Task-based instruction is a perspective within a CLT framework that forces you to carefully consider all the techniques that you use in the classroom in terms of a number of important pedagogical purposes:

Characteristics of TBLT

- Tasks ultimately point learners beyond the forms of language alone to real-world contexts.
- Tasks specifically contribute to communicative goals.
- Their elements are carefully designed and not simply haphazardly or idiosyncratically thrown together.
- Their objectives are well specified so that you can at some later point accurately determine the success of one task over another.
- Tasks engage learners, at some level, in genuine problem-solving activity.

LEARNER-CENTERED INSTRUCTION

This term applies to curricula as well as to specific techniques. It can be contrasted with **teacher-centered instruction,** and has received various recent interpretations. **Learner-centered instruction** includes

- techniques that focus on or account for learners' needs, styles, and goals
- techniques that give some control to the student (group work or strategy training, for example)
- curricula that include the consultation and input of students and that do not presuppose objectives in advance
- techniques that allow for student creativity and innovation
- techniques that enhance a student's sense of competence and self-worth

Because language teaching is a domain that so often presupposes classrooms where students have very little language proficiency with which to negotiate with the teacher, some teachers shy away from the notion of giving learners the "power" associated with a learner-centered approach. Such restraint is not necessary because, even in beginning level classes, teachers can offer students certain choices.

All of these efforts help to give students a sense of "ownership" of their learning and thereby add to their intrinsic motivation (see Chapters 4 and 5 for discussions of intrinsic motivation).

COOPERATIVE LEARNING

A curriculum or classroom that is **cooperative**—and therefore not **competitive**—usually involves the above learner-centered characteristics. As students work together in pairs and groups, they share information and come to each other's aid. They are a "team" whose players must work together in order to achieve goals successfully. Research has shown an advantage for cooperative learning (as opposed to individual learning) on such factors as "promoting intrinsic motivation, . . . heightening self-esteem, . . . creating caring and altruistic relationships, and lowering anxiety and prejudice" (Oxford, 1997, p. 445). Some of the challenges of cooperative learning are accounting for varied cultural expectations, individual learning styles, and personality differences and an overreliance on the first language (Crandall, 1999). (The effective implementation of cooperative learning through group work in the language classroom is a topic that is covered in detail in Chapter 12 of this book.)

Cooperative learning is sometimes thought to be synonymous with **collaborative** learning. To be sure, in a cooperative classroom the students and teachers work together to pursue goals and objectives. But cooperative learning "is more structured, more prescriptive to teachers about classroom techniques, more directive to students about how to work together in groups [than collaborative learning]" (Oxford, 1997, p. 443). In cooperative learning models, a group learning activity is dependent on the socially structured exchange of information between learners. In collaborative learning, the learner engages "with more capable others (teachers, advanced peers, etc.), who provide assistance and guidance" (Oxford, 1997, p. 444). Collaborative learning models have been developed within social constructivist (see Chapter 1 of *PLLT*) schools of thought to promote communities of learners that cut across the usual hierarchies of students and teachers.

INTERACTIVE LEARNING

At the heart of current theories of communicative competence is the essentially **interactive** nature of communication. When you speak, for example, the extent to which your intended message is received is a factor of both your production and the listener's reception. Most meaning, in a semantic sense, is a product of negotiation, of give and take, as interlocutors attempt to communicate. Thus, the communicative purpose of language compels us to create opportunities for genuine interaction in the classroom. An interactive course or technique will provide for such negotiation. Interactive classes will most likely be found

- doing a significant amount of pair work and group work
- receiving authentic language input in real-world contexts
- producing language for genuine, meaningful communication
- performing classroom tasks that prepare them for actual language use "out there"
- practicing oral communication through the give and take and spontaneity of actual conversations
- writing to and for real audiences, not contrived ones

The theoretical foundations of interactive learning lie in what Michael Long (1985, 1996) described as the **interaction hypothesis** of second language acquisition (see *PLLT,* Chapter 10). Going beyond Stephen Krashen's (1985, 1997) concept of comprehensible input, Long and others have pointed out the importance of input and output in the development of language. As learners interact with each other through oral and written discourse, their communicative abilities are enhanced.

WHOLE LANGUAGE EDUCATION

A term that once swept through our profession and is still in common use is **whole language education.** Unfortunately, the term has been so widely and divergently interpreted that it unfortunately lost the impact that it once had (see Rigg, 1991, for an excellent review of whole language education). Initially the term came from reading research and was used to emphasize:

a. the "wholeness" of language as opposed to views that fragmented language into its bits and pieces of phonemes, graphemes, morphemes, and words;

b. the interaction and interconnections between oral language (listening and speaking) and written language (reading and writing); and

c. the importance, in literate societies, of the written code as natural and developmental, just as the oral code is.

Now the term has come to encompass a great deal more. Whole language is a label that has been used to describe:

- cooperative learning
- participatory learning
- student-centered learning
- focus on the community of learners
- focus on the social nature of language
- use of authentic, natural language
- meaning-centered language

- holistic assessment techniques in testing
- integration of the "four skills"

With all these interpretations, the concept of whole language has become considerably watered down. Edelsky (1993, pp. 550–551) noted that whole language is not a recipe, and it's not an activity that you schedule into your lesson; "it is an educational way of life. [It helps people to] build meaningful connections between everyday learning and school learning."

It is appropriate, then, that we use the term carefully so that it does not become just another buzzword for teachers and materials developers. Two interconnected concepts are brought together in whole language:

1. The wholeness of language implies that language is not the sum of its many dissectible and discrete parts. First language acquisition research shows us that children begin perceiving "wholes" (sentences, emotions, intonation patterns) well before "parts." Second language teachers therefore do well to help their students attend to such wholes and not to yield to the temptation to build language only from the bottom up. And since part of the wholeness of language includes the interrelationship of the four skills (listening, speaking, reading, and writing), we must conscientiously integrate two or more of these skills in our classrooms.

2. Whole language is a perspective "anchored in a vision of an equitable, democratic, diverse society" (Edelsky, 1993, p. 548). Because we use language to construct meaning and to construct reality, teaching a language enables learners to understand a system of social practices that both constrain and liberate. Part of our job as teachers is to empower our learners to liberate themselves from whatever social, political, or economic forces constrain them.

CONTENT-BASED INSTRUCTION

Content-based instruction (CBI), according to Brinton, Snow, and Wesche (1989, p. vii), is "the integration of content learning with language teaching aims. More specifically, it refers to the concurrent study of language and subject matter, with the form and sequence of language presentation dictated by content material." Such an approach contrasts sharply with many practices in which language skills are taught virtually in isolation from substantive content. Through CBI, language becomes the medium to convey informational content of interest and relevance to the learner. Language takes on its appropriate role as a vehicle for accomplishing a set of content goals.

A surge of interest in CBI in the 1990s resulted in widespread adoption of content-based curricula around the world, as chronicled by Brinton (2003), Stoller

(2004), Schleppegrell et al. (2004), and others, even to the point that Brinton et al.'s (1989) book was republished with an epilogue in 2003. Content-based classrooms have the potential of increasing intrinsic motivation and empowerment, since students are focused on subject matter that is important to their lives. Students are pointed beyond transient extrinsic factors, like grades and tests, to their own competence and autonomy as intelligent individuals capable of actually doing something with their new language.

The challenges of CBI range from a demand for a whole new genre of textbooks and other materials to the training of language teachers to teach the concepts and skills of various disciplines, professions, and occupations, and/or to teach in teams across disciplines. Allowing the subject matter to control the selection and sequencing of language items means that you have to view your teaching from an entirely different perspective. You are first and foremost teaching geography or math or culture; secondarily you are teaching language. So you may have to become a double expert! Some team-teaching models of content-based teaching alleviate this potential drawback. In some schools a subject-matter teacher and a language teacher link their courses and curricula so that each complements the other. Such an undertaking is not unlike what Brinton et al. (1989) describe as an "adjunct" model of content-based instruction.

Can content-based teaching take place at all levels of proficiency, even beginning levels? While it is possible to argue, for example, that certain basic survival skills are themselves content-based and that a beginning level class could therefore be content-based, such an argument extends the content-based notion beyond its normal bounds. Content-based instruction usually pertains to academic or occupational instruction over an extended period of time at intermediate-to-advanced proficiency levels. Talking about renting an apartment one day, shopping the next, getting a driver's license the next, and so on is certainly useful and meaningful for beginners, but would be more appropriately called task-based than content-based.

Several models of CBI have now emerged. **Theme-based** instruction may be the most common offshoot of CBI; in this model language remains the primary aim of a course, but special attention is given to meaningful, relevant themes as a point of departure for instruction in language. **Sheltered** content instruction is a form of CBI in which the teacher of a school subject (say, science or history) modifies the presentation of material to help L2 learners process the content. A little more recently, **sustained-content language teaching** involves a focus on a "single content area, or carrier topic . . . [along with] a complementary focus on L2 learning and teaching" (Murphy & Stoller, 2001, p. 3). Here, the L2 classroom simulates the structure and demands of mainstream courses but adds explicit instruction in language and academic skills. All three models are derived from the principle that students' meaningful involvement in relevant content will enhance acquisition.

OTHER CANDIDATES FOR CLT APPROACHES

The list of potential approaches, all related in some way to general principles of CLT, could become quite lengthy, depending on how you wish to narrow down your qualifications. Richards and Rodgers (2001) included Multiple Intelligences, Neurolinguistic Programming, the Lexical Approach, and Competency-based Teaching among their approaches and methods. Larsen-Freeman (2000) described the Participatory Approach, Learning Strategy Training, and Multiple Intelligences in her book on techniques and principles. Harmer (2001) adds Humanistic Teaching and the Lexical Approach to his list of approaches and methods. Just to be fair, we will take a brief look here at the Lexical Approach and Multiple Intelligences.

At the heart of the **Lexical Approach** is the hypothesis that the essential building blocks of language are words and word combinations, and that lexis therefore plays a central role in designing language courses and classroom methodology. Michael Lewis (1997) is perhaps the best-known advocate for a lexical approach to L2 teaching. His contention is not unlike that of Krashen (1997), who maintained that one can "do" almost anything in a language with vocabulary, and once those lexical units are internalized, other (grammatical and discourse) elements of language can be acquired, given a meaningful context. Lewis extends his approach to emphasize lexical phrases, or **collocations,** as central to a language course. Thus, phrases like *not so good, how's it going, easy does it, cover to cover,* and *I'll be in touch* are useful prefabricated patterns for a learner to internalize, along with certain predicable collocations like *do . . . my homework, . . . the laundry, . . . a good job, . . . lunch* and *make . . . some coffee, . . . my bed, . . . a promise, . . . a list.* The Lexical Approach has been considerably buoyed by the recent surge of corpus analysis, which now electronically provides literally millions of words and collocations within limited linguistic contexts.

A lexical emphasis has some obvious advantages. Sometimes in our penchant for communicative interaction, we overlook these basic foundation stones of language. And certainly a strategic language learner can accomplish a great deal with words alone. It remains somewhat unclear, however, how such an approach differs from other approaches (which certainly allow for a focus on lexical units). Nor is it clear how "an endless succession of phrase-book utterances, 'all chunks but no pineapple,' . . . can be incorporated into the understanding of a language system" (Harmer, 2001, p. 92).

Another possible qualifier as an approach lies in the current interest in the application of the concept of **Multiple Intelligences** (MI) to L2 teaching. As summarized in *PLLT,* Chapter 4 (pp. 107–109), Gardner's (1983, 1999, 2004) model of intelligence includes at least eight types of intelligence, which has led educators to view a number of forms of "smartness" that learners can manifest. A learner who is strong, for example, in interpersonal intelligence may thrive in the context of group work and interaction, while a student who has high spatial intelligence will perform well with plenty of charts, diagrams, and other visuals. Most educators who follow an MI approach advocate the use of a multiplicity of types of activities and techniques in order to appeal to as wide a swath of learners as possible (Armstrong, 1994). The foremost champion of MI in the language-teaching field is Mary Ann Christison (2005), author of numerous books and articles on the topic. Her most recent guidebook for teachers offers some 150 different activities for language learners, each emphasizing a specific intelligence, coded for age and proficiency level (Christison, 2005).

The efficacy of an MI approach to language learning may be obvious. Clearly, learners differ from each other in many ways, and MI is one way of categorizing those differences. If teachers can be guided to recognize students' unique strengths and weaknesses through attention to MI, and can follow with appropriately geared activities, they will certainly enrich their language courses and will possibly enable students to better accomplish their purposes. One might contend that the eight intelligences are culturally biased (though they were originally intended to be just the opposite), or in some cultures contrary to prevailing educational practices. Others could argue that MI hypotheses lack the empirical rigor necessary to qualify as a true theory. Whether or not history will recognize MI as a fully developed approach remains to be seen. Whatever we call it, it remains a perspective that prods teachers to look beyond traditional school smartness to find avenues of success for every student in our classrooms.

☆ ☆ ☆ ☆ ☆

Your approach to language teaching is obviously the keystone to all your teaching methodology in the classroom. By now, you may be able to "profess" at least some components of a personal approach to language learning and teaching and have a beginning of an understanding of how that approach enlightens—or will enlighten—your classroom practices. Many aspects of your approach will predictably mirror those that have been espoused here, especially since you are just beginning to learn your teaching craft. That's quite acceptable. But do keep in mind the importance of the dynamic nature of the theoretical stance of even the most experienced teachers. We have much to learn, collectively, in this profession. And we will best instruct ourselves, and the profession at large, when we maintain a disciplined inquisitiveness about our teaching practices. After all, that's how we got to this point after a century of questioning.

TOPICS FOR DISCUSSION, ACTION, AND RESEARCH

[Note: (I) Individual work; (G) group or pair work; (C) whole-class discussion.]

1. (I) Review the notion that your overall **approach** to language teaching can directly lead to curriculum design and lesson techniques, without subscribing

to a **method,** as the term was used in Chapter 2. Can you still comfortably use the term **methodology** to refer to pedagogical practice in general? As you read other research literature in the field of language teaching, pay special attention to how an author uses these terms. You will find some disparity in the various understandings of the terms.

2. (G) On page 44, a checklist of seven items was provided for readers to mentally respond to. Ask students to compare their responses with those of a partner. In pairs, they should talk about what contextual factors might cause one to change one's general inclination on any one or two of the items. Pairs will then present some of their discussion to the rest of the class.

3. (G/C) In anticipation of Chapter 4, in which readers will encounter 12 principles of language learning and teaching, ask students to brainstorm, in small groups, some assertions about language learning that one might include in a description of an approach to language teaching. For example, what would they say about the issue of age and acquisition; inhibitions; strategies for how to best store something in memory; and the relationship of intelligence to second language success? Direct the groups to come up with axioms or principles that would be relatively stable across many acquisition contexts. Then, as a whole class, list these on the board.

4. (G) Ask pairs to look at the seven features used as a general definition of CLT on pages 46–47 and to come up with some practical classroom examples of each of the seven factors. Should any characteristics be added to the list? or changed?

5. (G/C) Direct pairs to look again at the 22 characteristics of CLT (page 49) offered by Finocchiaro and Brumfit and to ask themselves if they are all in keeping with general CLT principles. Are they all sufficiently balanced in their viewpoint? Would students disagree with any of them? Pairs can share their ideas with the rest of the class.

6. (I/G) Have students observe an ESL class and use the characteristics as a gauge of how closely the lesson approximates CLT. Students should share their observations in small groups.

7. (I/G/C) Without looking back, students should write their own brief definitions of

   - task-based language teaching
   - learner-centered instruction
   - cooperative learning
   - interactive learning
   - whole language education
   - content-based instruction

Now, have them compare their definitions with those of a partner. If they are still confused by any terms, they should try to clear up the confusion through rereading and/or whole-class discussion.

8. (C) Ask members of the class to volunteer some examples from personal experience (learning or teaching) of the six types of teaching named above. How do your examples fit the types of teaching?
9. (C) Ask students to consider such approaches as the Lexical Approach and Multiple Intelligences. Do they qualify as legitimate, well-grounded approaches? What criteria are implied in deeming perspectives as approaches, as the term is used in this chapter?

FOR YOUR FURTHER READING

Kumaravadivelu, B. (2001). Toward a postmethod pedagogy. *TESOL Quarterly, 35,* 537–560.

Bell, D. (2003). Method and postmethod: Are they really so incompatible? *TESOL Quarterly, 37,* 325–336.

These two articles capsulize an interesting debate of a few years ago in which Kumaravadivelu asserted, as he had for a number of years, that language-teaching methodology was best characterized as a "postmethod" pedagogy. David Bell offered a thought-provoking response that put the discussion into a balanced perspective.

McKay, S. (2006). *Researching second language classrooms.* Mahwah, NJ: Lawrence Erlbaum Associates.

In keeping with the notion of narrowing the historical gap between "theory" and "practice," Sandra McKay offers a highly useful introduction to classroom-based research. She includes a survey of types of research, a description of various methods of research, and guidelines for writing research reports and theses.

Lee, J., & VanPatten, B. (2003). *Making communicative language teaching happen* (2nd ed.). New York: McGraw-Hill.

This professional reference book is a useful resource for teachers and teachers in training who would like a comprehensive view of classrooms operating under the principles of CLT. Sections of the book are devoted to teaching listening comprehension, grammar, spoken language, reading, and writing, all within a communicative framework. Connections between theory and practice are made.

Crandall, J. (1999). Cooperative language learning and affective factors. In J. Arnold (Ed.), *Affect in language learning* (pp. 226–245). Cambridge, UK: Cambridge University Press.

JoAnn Crandall's summary of cooperative learning describes the affective underpinnings of this approach, with plenty of practical examples of cooperative learning at work in the classroom.

Stoller, F. (2004). Content-based instruction: Perspectives on curriculum planning. *Annual Review of Applied Linguistics, 24,* 261–283.

The Annual Review series is always a fruitful source of summary articles on selected topics. Fredericka Stoller's overview offers descriptions of research and outlines current practice in content-based instruction.

Skehan, P. (2003). Task-based instruction. *Language Teaching, 36,* 1–14.

Peter Skehan provides an excellent overview of task-based language teaching in this review article. An extensive bibliography is included.

CHAPTER 4

TEACHING BY PRINCIPLES

OBJECTIVES After reading this chapter, you will be able to:

- develop a broadly based theoretical approach that incorporates a number of basic principles of language learning and teaching

- understand the unique nature of each principle and its specific contribution to the articulation of your approach to language pedagogy

- distinguish among 12 principles that form such a theoretical basis

- apply aspects of each principle to classroom methodological options

So far in this book you have observed a classroom in action, examined a century of language-teaching history, and taken a look at major constructs that define current practices in language teaching. In the foregoing chapters you may have already felt a little bewildered by the sheer number of methods and approaches that have characterized our profession. You may be asking questions like:

"Am I a learner-centered, interactive, or task-based teacher, or what?"

"The idea of CLT appeals to me, but out of a number of possible approaches within the tradition, how can I determine what my approach is?"

"Practicing a cautious, enlightened, eclectic approach is appealing, but isn't that way too broad a claim?"

"There are too many options here; how can I make informed choices about what to do in the particular context of my classroom?"

In order to sort through those questions and find some plausible answers, it is important for you to consider elements that are at the core of language pedagogy: foundational principles that can form the building blocks for your own theoretical rationale. For virtually all successful teachers, such principles comprise their **approach** to language teaching.

In *Principles of Language Learning and Teaching,* (Brown, 2007), which I refer to here as *PLLT,* I noted that the last few decades of research produced a complex storehouse of information on second language acquisition and teaching. We have discovered a great deal about how to best teach a second language in the classroom. And, while many mysteries still remain about why and how learners successfully acquire second languages, it is appropriate for you to focus on what we *do* know: what we have learned and what we can say with some certainty about second language acquisition. We can then clearly see that a great many of a teacher's choices are grounded in established principles of language learning and teaching. By perceiving and internalizing connections between practice (choices you make in the classroom) and theory (principles derived from research), you are more likely to engage in "enlightened" teaching. You will be better able to see why you have chosen to use a particular classroom technique (or set of techniques), to carry it out with confidence, and to evaluate its utility after the fact.

You may be thinking that such a principled approach to language teaching sounds only logical. How could one proceed otherwise? Well, I have seen many a novice language teacher gobble up teaching techniques without carefully considering the criteria that underlie their successful application in the classroom. "Just give me 101 recipes for Monday morning teaching," say some, "I just want to know what to do when I get into the classroom." Unfortunately, this sort of quick-fix approach to teacher education will not give you that all-important ability to comprehend when to use a technique, with whom it will work, how to adapt it for your audience, or how to judge its effectiveness.

We'll now take a broad, sweeping look at 12 overarching principles of second language learning that interact with sound practice and on which your teaching can be based. These principles form the core of an approach to language teaching, as discussed in the previous chapter. There is no magic about the number 12. If you read Tom Scovel (2001) you'll find 5 principles, but if you read Bernard Spolsky (1989) you'll discover 70! I have chosen 12 for the sake of simplicity and inclusiveness.

Before proceeding with a description of the 12 principles, a special note is in order to readers and instructors who have used the previous editions of *Teaching by Principles*. I continue to enumerate 12 principles in my list but have made two changes that reflect recent research and thinking. The revisions are as follows:

- Autonomy (#6) is a new principle.
- Willingness to Communicate (WTC) (#8) now replaces Self-confidence and Risk-taking since the latter are, in recent research, well accounted for in the concept of WTC.

One further note: As you are reading, it may be helpful to check referenced sections of *PLLT* to refresh your memory of certain terms and background information.

COGNITIVE PRINCIPLES

We will call the first set of principles "cognitive" because they relate mainly to mental and intellectual functions. It should be made clear, however, that all 12 of the principles outlined in this chapter spill across somewhat arbitrary cognitive, affective, and linguistic boundaries.

Principle 1: Automaticity

No one can dispute the success with which children learn foreign languages, especially when they are living in the cultural and linguistic milieu of the language (see *PLLT,* Chapter 3). We commonly attribute children's success to their widely observed tendency to acquire language subconsciously, that is, without overtly analyzing the forms of language themselves. Through an inductive process of exposure to language input and opportunity to experiment with output, they appear to learn languages without "thinking" about them.

This childlike, subconscious processing is similar to what Barry McLaughlin (1990; McLaughlin, Rossman, & McLeod, 1983) called automatic processing with peripheral attention to language forms (*PLLT,* Chapter 10). That is, in order to manage the incredible complexity and quantity of language—the vast numbers of bits of information—both adults and children must sooner or later move away from processing language unit by unit, piece by piece, focusing closely on each, and "graduate" to a form of high-speed, automatic processing in which language forms (words, affixes, word order, rules, etc.) are only on the periphery of attention. Children usually make this transition faster than adults, who tend to linger in analytical, controlled modes, focusing on the bits and pieces of language before putting those bits and pieces into the "hard drive" of their mind.

The Principle of Automaticity highlights the importance of

- subconscious absorption of language through meaningful use;
- efficient and rapid movement away from a focus on the forms of language to a focus on the purposes to which language is put;
- efficient and rapid movement away from a capacity-limited control of a few bits and pieces to a relatively unlimited automatic mode of processing language forms (often referred to as **fluency**); and
- resistance to the temptation to analyze language forms.

The Principle of Automaticity may be stated as follows:

> **Efficient second language learning involves a timely movement of the control of a few language forms into the automatic, fluent processing of a relatively unlimited number of language forms. Overanalyzing language, thinking too much about its forms, and consciously lingering on rules of language all tend to impede this graduation to automaticity.**

Notice that this principle does not say that focus on language forms is necessarily harmful. In fact adults, especially, can benefit greatly from certain focal processing of rules, definitions, and other formal aspects of language. What the principle does say is that adults can take a lesson from children by speedily overcoming our propensity to pay too much focal attention to the bits and pieces of language and to move language forms quickly to the periphery by using language in authentic contexts for meaningful purposes. In so doing, automaticity is built more efficiently.

What does this principle, which ordinarily applies to adult instruction, mean to you as a teacher? Here are some possibilities:

1. Because classroom learning normally begins with controlled, focal processing, there is no mandate to entirely avoid overt attention to language systems (grammar, phonology, discourse, etc.). That attention, however, should stop well short of blocking students from achieving a more automatic, fluent grasp of the language. Therefore, grammatical explanations or exercises dealing with what is sometimes called "usage" have a place in the adult classroom (see Principle 12), but you could overwhelm your students with grammar. If they become too heavily centered on the formal aspects of language, such processes can block pathways to fluency.
2. Make sure that a large proportion of your lessons are focused on the "use" of language for purposes that are as genuine as a classroom context will permit. Students will gain more language competence in the long run if the functional purposes of language are the focal point.
3. Automaticity isn't gained overnight; therefore, you need to exercise patience with students as you slowly help them to achieve fluency.

Principle 2: Meaningful Learning

Closely related to the Principle of Automaticity are cognitive theories of learning (*PLLT*, Chapter 4), which convincingly argue the strength of meaningful as opposed to rote learning (Ausubel, 1963). Meaningful learning "subsumes" new information into existing structures and memory systems, and the resulting associative links create stronger retention. Rote learning—taking in isolated bits and pieces of information that are not connected with one's existing cognitive structures—has little chance of creating long-term retention. Children are good meaningful acquirers of language (see Principle 1) because they associate sounds, words, structures, and discourse elements with that which is relevant and important in their daily quest for knowledge and survival.

The Principle of Meaningful Learning is quite simply stated:

> **The process of making meaningful associations between existing knowledge/experience and new material will lead toward better long-term retention than rote learning of material in isolated pieces.**

The language classroom has not always been the best place for meaningful learning. In the days when the Audiolingual Method (see *PLLT,* Chapter 4) was popular, rote learning occupied too much of the class hour as students were drilled and drilled in an attempt to "overlearn" language forms. The Principle of Meaningful Learning tells us that some aural-oral drilling is appropriate; selected phonological elements like phonemes, rhythm, stress, and intonation, for example, can indeed be taught effectively through pattern repetition. But drilling ad nauseam easily lends itself to rote learning.

Some classroom implications of the Principle of Meaningful Learning include the following:

1. Capitalize on the power of meaningful learning by appealing to students' interests, academic goals, and career goals.
2. Whenever a new topic or concept is introduced, attempt to anchor it in students' existing knowledge and background so that it becomes associated with something they already know.
3. Avoid the pitfalls of rote learning:
    a. too much grammar explanation
    b. too many abstract principles and theories
    c. too much drilling and/or memorization
    d. activities whose purposes are not clear
    e. activities that do not contribute to accomplishing the goals of the lesson, unit, or course
    f. techniques that are so mechanical or tricky that students focus on the mechanics instead of on the language or meanings

Principle 3: The Anticipation of Reward

B. F. Skinner and others have clearly demonstrated the strength of rewards in both animal and human behavior (see *PLLT,* Chapter 4). Virtually everything we do is inspired and driven by a sense of purpose or goal, and according to Skinner, the anticipation of reward is the most powerful factor in directing one's behavior. The principle behind Skinner's operant conditioning paradigm, which could be called the Reward Principle, can be stated as follows:

> **Human beings are universally driven to act, or "behave," by the anticipation of some sort of reward—tangible or intangible, short-term or long-term—that will ensue as a result of the behavior.**

The implications for the classroom are obvious. At one end of the spectrum, you can perceive the importance of the immediate administration of such rewards as praise for correct responses ("Very good, Maria!" "Nice job!"), appropriate grades or scores to indicate success, or other public recognition. At the other end, it behooves you to help students to see clearly why they are doing something and its relevance to their long-term goals in learning English. On the other hand, a reward-driven, conditioning theory of learning has some shortcomings that ultimately have a high impact on classroom instruction. These shortcomings are summarized under Principle 4, but for the moment, keep in mind that conditioning by rewards can (a) lead learners to become dependent on short-term rewards, (b) coax them into a habit of looking to teachers and others for their only rewards, and therefore (c) forestall the development of their own internally administered, intrinsic system of rewards.

Considering all sides of the Reward Principle, the following constructive classroom implications may be drawn:

1. Provide an optimal degree of immediate verbal praise and encouragement to students as a form of short-term reward (just enough to keep them confident in their ability but not so much that your praise simply becomes verbal gush).
2. Encourage students to reward each other with compliments and supportive action.
3. In classes with very low motivation, short-term reminders of progress may help students to perceive their development. Gold stars and stickers (especially for young learners), issuing certain "privileges" for good work, and progress charts and graphs may spark some interest.
4. Display enthusiasm and excitement yourself in the classroom. If you are dull, lifeless, bored, and have low energy, you can be almost sure that it will be contagious.
5. Try to get learners to see the long-term rewards in learning English by pointing out what they can do with English where they live and around the world, the prestige in being able to use English, the academic benefits of knowing English, jobs that require English, and so on.

Principle 4: Intrinsic Motivation

This principle is elaborated upon in detail in the next chapter as an example of how complex principles underlie a surprising number of our teaching practices. Simply stated, the Intrinsic Motivation Principle is:

> **The most powerful rewards are those that are intrinsically motivated within the learner. Because the behavior stems from needs, wants, or desires within oneself, the behavior itself is self-rewarding; therefore, no externally administered reward is necessary.**

If all learners were intrinsically motivated to perform all classroom tasks, we might not even need teachers! But you can perform a great service to learners and to the overall learning process by first considering carefully the intrinsic motives of your students and then by designing classroom tasks that feed into those intrinsic drives. Classroom techniques have a much greater chance for success if they are self-rewarding in the perception of the learner. The learners perform the task because it is fun, interesting, useful, or challenging, and not because they anticipate some cognitive or affective rewards from the teacher.

You may be wondering why such a principle is listed among "cognitive" principles. The development of intrinsic motivation does indeed involve affective processing, as most of these first five principles do, and so the argument is appropriate. But reward-directed behavior in all organisms is complex to the point that cognitive, physical, and affective processing are all involved. In the specific case of second language acquisition, mental functions may actually occupy a greater proportion of the whole than the other two domains, as we shall see in Chapter 5.

Principle 5: Strategic Investment

A few decades ago, the language-teaching profession largely concerned itself with the "delivery" of language to the student. Teaching methods, textbooks, or even grammatical paradigms were cited as the primary factors in successful learning. In more recent years, in the light of many studies of successful and unsuccessful learners, language teachers are focusing more intently on the role of the learner in the process. The "methods" that the learner employs to internalize and to perform in the language are as important as the teacher's methods—or more so. I call this the Principle of Strategic Investment:

> **Successful mastery of the second language will be due to a large extent to a learner's own personal "investment" of time, effort, and attention to the second language in the form of an individualized battery of strategies for comprehending and producing the language.**

This principle is laid out in full detail in Chapter 14, where practical classroom applications are made. For the time being, however, ponder two major pedagogical implications of the principle: (a) the importance of recognizing and dealing with the wide variety of styles and strategies that learners successfully bring to the learning process and, therefore, (b) the need for attention to each separate individual in the classroom.

As research on successful language learners has dramatically shown, the variation among learners poses a thorny pedagogical dilemma. Learning styles alone signal numerous learner preferences that a teacher needs to attend to (see *PLLT,* Chapter 5). For example, visual versus auditory preference and individual versus group work preference are highly significant factors in a classroom. In a related strain of research, we are finding that learners also employ a multiplicity of strategies for sending and receiving language and that one learner's strategies for success may differ markedly from another's.

A variety of techniques in your lessons will at least partially ensure that you will "reach" a maximum number of students. So you will choose a mixture of group work and individual work, of visual and auditory techniques, of easy and difficult exercises. Beware, however, of variety at the expense of techniques that you know are essential for the learner! If, for example, you know that three-quarters of your class prefers individual work, that should not dictate the proportion of time you devote to activities that involve silent work at their desks. They may need to be nudged, if not pushed, into more face-to-face communicative activities than their preferences would indicate.

A teacher's greatest dilemma is how to attend to each individual student in a class while still reaching the class as a whole group. In relatively large classes of 30 to 50 students, individual attention becomes increasingly difficult; in extra-large classes* it is virtually impossible. The Principle of Strategic Investment nevertheless is a reminder to provide as much attention as you can to each individual student.

---

* Around the world, far too many language class sizes are too large. Numbers in the range of 50–75 are not uncommon. For years I've tried to persuade administrators to lower those numbers and to understand that communicative acquisition of a language is very difficult to achieve under such circumstances. Nevertheless, the reality of school budgets sometimes provides few alternatives. See Chapter 15 for some practical suggestions for dealing with large classes.

Some aspects of the dilemma surrounding variation and the need for individualization can be solved through specific strategies-based instruction, the principal topic of Chapter 16. Meanwhile, simply as a "sneak preview" to that chapter, you might consider these questions as more grist for your teacher education mill:

1. Am I seizing whatever opportunity I can to let learners in on the "secrets" that will help them to develop and use strategies for learning and communication?
2. Am I helping students to become *aware* of their own preferences, styles, strengths, and weaknesses, so that they can then take appropriate *action* in the form of strategies for better learning?
3. Do my lessons and impromptu feedback adequately sensitize students to the wisdom of their taking responsibility for their own learning?
4. How can I ensure that my students will want to put forth the effort of trying out some strategies?

Principle 6: Autonomy

One way of looking at the history of language teaching, described in Chapter 2, is to consider the extent to which methodological trends have emphasized the respective roles of the teacher and the learner. Until some of the "designer" methods appeared in the 1970s, most of language-teaching methodology was teacher-centered. Students entered a classroom, sat down dutifully at their desks, and waited for the teacher to tell them what to do. Those directives might have been to translate a passage, to memorize a rule, or to repeat a dialogue. Then, the profession began to value the concept of learner **autonomy** (Benson, 2001, 2003; Schmenk, 2005; Wenden, 2002), which Benson (2001, p. 290) defined as "the capacity to control one's own learning." Autonomy is now almost universally manifested in the classroom in the form of allowing learners to do things like initiate oral production, solve problems in small groups, and practice language with peers.

Of utmost importance, language curricula recognized the crucial objective of helping learners to use the language *outside* of the classroom. We began to encourage learners to "take charge" of their own learning and to chart their own "pathways to success" (Brown, 1989, 2002b; Benson, 2003). With the principle of students' taking responsibility for their own learning, yet another important pedagogical foundation stone was set in place.

Briefly, the Principle of Autonomy states:

> **Successful mastery of a foreign language will depend to a great extent on learners' autonomous ability both to take initiative in the classroom and to continue their journey to success beyond the classroom and the teacher.**

Some have argued (Riley, 1988) that the Principle of Autonomy is a culturally loaded, ethnocentric construct—anything but universal in its conceptualization. Others suggest using some caution in making assumptions across cultural contexts and to account for "specific cultural backdrops and impacts" (Schmenk, 2005, p.115) in promoting autonomy in the language classroom. Once those accommodations have been appropriately addressed, you should by no means refrain from helping your students to participate actively in linguistic exchange and to continue their learning beyond the walls of your classroom. Consider a number of classroom implications of this principle:

1. Learners at the beginning stages of a language will of course be somewhat dependent on the teacher, which is natural and normal. But teachers can help even beginners to develop a sense of autonomy through guided practice and by allowing some creative innovation within limited forms.
2. As learners gain confidence and begin to be able to experiment with language, implement activities in the classroom that allow creativity but are not completely beyond the capacity of students.
3. Don't forget that pair and group work and other interactive activities in your classroom provide opportunities for students to "do" language on their own.
4. In oral and written production in the classroom, encourage creativity and praise students for trying language that's a little beyond their present capacity.
5. Remember, you're a facilitator and coach, so while your students are in your "care," provide feedback on their speech—just enough to be helpful, but not so much that you stifle their creativity.
6. Suggest opportunities for students to use their language (gauged for their proficiency level) outside of class. Examples include movies, TV, the Internet, books, magazines, practicing with each other, and—if feasible—using self-access centers available in some institutions.

SOCIOAFFECTIVE PRINCIPLES

The Principles of Intrinsic Motivation, Strategic Investment, and Autonomy are clearly not purely cognitive in nature. They share some attributes with socioaffective principles, the focus of this section of the chapter. But the next three principles are characterized by a more marked degree of emotional involvement, either within one's own self or as a learner relates socially to others. Here we look at feelings about self, about communicating with others in a community of learners, and about the ties between language and one's culture, worldview, and way of life.

Principle 7: Language Ego

The Language Ego Principle can be summarized in a well-recognized claim:

> **As human beings learn to use a second language, they also develop a new mode of thinking, feeling, and acting—a second identity. The new "language ego," intertwined with the second language, can easily create within the learner a sense of fragility, a defensiveness, and a raising of inhibitions.**

The Language Ego Principle might also be affectionately called the "warm and fuzzy" principle: All second language learners need to be treated with affective tender loving care. Remember when you were first learning a second language and how you sometimes felt silly, if not humiliated, when the lack of words or structure left you helpless in face-to-face communication? Otherwise highly intelligent adults can be reduced to babbling infants in a second language. Learners feel this fragility because the strategic arsenals of their native-language-based egos, which are normally well developed and resistant to attack, are suddenly—in the perception of the learner—obsolete. Now they must fend for their emotional selves with a paltry linguistic battery that leaves them with a feeling of total defenselessness.

How can you bring some relief to this situation and provide affective support? Here are some possibilities.

1. Overtly display a supportive attitude to your students. While some learners may feel quite stupid in this new language, remember that they are capable adults struggling with the acquisition of the most complex set of skills that any classroom has ever attempted to teach. Your "warm and fuzzy" patience and empathy need to be openly and clearly communicated, for fragile language egos have a way of misinterpreting intended input.
2. On a more mechanical, lesson-planning level, your choice of techniques and sequences of techniques needs to be cognitively challenging but not overwhelming at an affective level.
3. Considering learners' language ego states will probably help you to determine
    - who to call on
    - who to ask to volunteer information
    - when to correct a student's speech error
    - how much to explain something
    - how structured and planned an activity should be
    - who to place in which small groups or pairs
    - how "tough" you can be with a student

4. If your students are learning English as a second language (in the cultural milieu of an English-speaking country), they are likely to experience a moderate identity crisis as they develop a "second self." Help such students to understand that the confusion of developing that second self in the second culture is a normal and natural process (see *PLLT,* Chapter 7). Patience and understanding on your part will also ease the process.

Principle 8: Willingness to Communicate

Closely allied to the Language Ego Principle is a construct that is a relatively recent newcomer to second language acquisition research: Willingness to Communicate (WTC) (MacIntyre, Baker, Clément, & Conrod, 2001; MacIntyre, Clément, Dörnyei, & Noels, 1998; Yashima, 2002), simply defined as "the intention to initiate communication, given a choice" (MacIntyre et al., 2001, p. 369). Observations of language learners' *un*willingness to communicate, or what we commonly label as "shyness," have led us to emphasize classroom activity that encourages learners to "come out of their shells" and to engage communicatively in the classroom.

It has already been briefly noted that WTC combines concepts of **self-confidence** and **risk-taking**, as they are both interwoven in our human psyche. Of further importance are two other related constructs: **anxiety**, that is, the extent to which learners may "worry" about themselves; and **self-efficacy**, a person's belief in his or her ability to accomplish a task (See *PLLT,* Chapter 6, for further description). Linked to one's self-confidence (and allaying anxieties) is the ability to take calculated risks in attempting to use language—both productively and receptively. If learners recognize their own ego fragility and develop the firm belief that, yes, they can indeed do it (self-efficacy), then they are ready to take those necessary risks. They are ready to try out their newly acquired language, to use it for meaningful purposes, to ask questions, and to assert themselves.

This eighth principle may be summarized as follows:

> **Successful language learners generally believe in themselves and in their capacity to accomplish communicative tasks, and are therefore willing risk takers in their attempts to produce and to interpret language that is a bit beyond their absolute certainty. Their willingness to communicate results in the generation of both output (from the learner) and input (to the learner).**

The concept of WTC strikes at the heart of educational philosophy, and it appears to be applicable across many cultures (Yashima, 2002). Many instructional contexts do not encourage risk-taking; instead they encourage correctness, right answers, and withholding "guesses" until one is sure to be correct. Most educational research shows the opposite to be more conducive to long-term retention and intrinsic motivation. How can your classrooms reflect the Principle of WTC?

1. Give ample verbal and nonverbal assurances to students, affirming your belief in the student's ability. Energy that the learner would otherwise direct at avoidance or at erecting emotional walls of defense is thereby released to tackle the problem at hand.
2. Sequence techniques from easier to more difficult. As a teacher you are called on to sustain self-confidence where it already exists and to build it where it doesn't. Your activities in the classroom would therefore logically start with simpler techniques and simpler concepts. Students then can establish a sense of accomplishment that catapults them to the next, more difficult, step.
3. Create an atmosphere in the classroom that encourages students to try out language, to venture a response, and not to wait for someone else to volunteer language.
4. Provide reasonable challenges in your techniques—make them neither too easy nor too hard.
5. Help your students to understand what calculated risk-taking is, lest some feel that they must blurt out any old response.
6. Respond to students' attempts to communicate with positive affirmation, praising them for trying while at the same time warmly but firmly attending to their language.

Principle 9: The Language-Culture Connection

Language and culture are intricately intertwined. Any time you successfully learn a language, you will also learn something of the culture of the speakers of that language. This principle focuses on the complex interconnection of language and culture:

> **Whenever you teach a language, you also teach a complex system of cultural customs, values, and ways of thinking, feeling, and acting.**

Classroom applications include the following:

1. Discuss cross-cultural differences with your students, emphasizing that no culture is "better" than another, but that cross-cultural understanding is an important facet of learning a language.
2. Include among your techniques certain activities and materials that illustrate the connection between language and culture.

3. Teach your students the cultural connotations, especially the sociolinguistic aspects, of language.
4. Screen your techniques for material that may be culturally offensive.
5. Make explicit to your students what you may take for granted in your culture.

A second aspect of the language–culture connection is the extent to which your students will themselves be affected by the process of acculturation, which will vary with the context and the goals of learning. In many second-language-learning contexts, such as ESL in the United States, students are faced with the full-blown realities of adapting to life in a foreign country, complete with various emotions accompanying stages of acculturation (see Chapter 7 of *PLLT*). In such cases, acculturation, social distance, and psychological adjustment are factors to be dealt with. This aspect of the principle may be summed up in this way:

> **Especially in *second* (as opposed to *foreign*) language-learning contexts, the success with which learners adapt to a new cultural milieu will affect their language acquisition success, and vice versa, in some possibly significant ways.**

From the perspective of the classroom teacher, this principle is similar to the Principles of Language Ego and Willingness to Communicate, and all the concomitant classroom implications apply here as well. An added dimension, however, lies in the interaction between culture learning and language learning. An opportunity is given to teachers to enhance, if not speed up, both developmental processes. Once students become aware that some of their discouragement may stem from cultural sources, they can more squarely address their state of mind and emotion and do something about it.

In the classroom, you can do the following:

1. Help students to be aware of acculturation and its stages.
2. Stress the importance of the second language as a powerful tool for adjustment in the new culture.
3. Be especially sensitive to any students who appear to be discouraged, then do what you can to assist them.

LINGUISTIC PRINCIPLES

The last category of principles of language learning and teaching centers on language itself and on how learners deal with complex linguistic systems.

Principle 10: The Native Language Effect

It almost goes without saying that the native language of every learner is an extremely significant factor in the acquisition of a new language. Most of the time, we think of the native language as exercising an interfering effect on the target language, and indeed the most salient, observable effect does appear to be one of interference (see *PLLT,* Chapter 4). The majority of a learner's errors in producing the second language, especially in the beginning levels, stem from the learner's assumption that the target language operates like the native language.

But what we observe may, like the tip of an iceberg, be only part of the reality. The facilitating effects of the native language are surely as powerful in the process, or more so, even though they are less observable. When the native French speaker who is learning English says "I am here since January," there is one salient native language effect, a verb tense error stemming from French. But the learner's native French may also have facilitated the production of that sentence's subject-verb-complement word order, the placement of the locative (*here*), the one-to-one grammatical correspondence of the other words in the sentence, rules governing prepositional phrases, and the cognate word (*January*).

The Principle of the Native Language Effect stresses the importance of that native system in the linguistic attempts of the second language learner:

> **The native language of learners exerts a strong influence on the acquisition of the target language system. While that native system will exercise both facilitating and interfering effects on the production and comprehension of the new language, the interfering effects are likely to be the most salient.**

In your dealing with the Native Language Effect in the classroom, your feedback will most often focus on interference. That's perfectly sound pedagogy. Learners' errors stand out like the tips of icebergs, giving us salient signals of an underlying system at work. Errors are, in fact, windows to a learner's internalized understanding of the second language, and therefore they give teachers something observable to react to. Student non-errors—the facilitating effects—certainly do not need to be treated. Don't try to fix something that isn't broken.

Some classroom suggestions stemming from the Native Language Effect:

1. Regard learners' errors as important windows to their underlying system and provide appropriate feedback on them (see Principle 11 and Chapter 17 for more information on feedback). Errors of native language interference may be repaired by acquainting the learner with the native language cause of the error.

2. Ideally, every successful learner will hold on to the facilitating effects of the native language and discard the interference. Help your students to understand that not everything about their native language system will cause error.
3. Thinking directly in the target language usually helps to minimize interference errors. Try to coax students into thinking in the second language instead of resorting to translation as they comprehend and produce language. An occasional translation of a word or phrase can actually be helpful, especially for adults, but direct use of the second language will help to avoid the first language "crutch" syndrome.

Principle 11: Interlanguage

Just as children develop their native language in gradual, systematic stages, adults, too, manifest a systematic progression of acquisition of sounds and words and structures and discourse features (see *PLLT,* Chapter 8). The Interlanguage Principle tells us:

> **Second language learners tend to go through a systematic or quasi-systematic developmental process as they progress to full competence in the target language. Successful interlanguage development is partially a result of utilizing feedback from others.**

While the interlanguage of second language learners varies considerably (see *PLLT,* Chapter 9, on variability) between systematic and unsystematic linguistic forms and underlying rules, one important concept for the teacher to bear in mind is that at least some of a learner's language may indeed be systematic. In other words, in the mind's eye of learners, a good deal of what they say or comprehend may be logically "correct" even though, from the standpoint of a native speaker's competence, its use is incorrect. A learner who says "Does John can sing?" may believe it to be a correct grammatical utterance because of an internalized systematic rule that requires a pre-posed *do* auxiliary for English question formation.

Allowing learners to progress through such systematic stages of acquisition poses a delicate challenge to teachers. The collective experience of language teachers and a respectable stockpile of second language research (Doughty, 2003; Ellis, 2005) indicates that classroom instruction makes a significant difference in the speed and success with which learners proceed through interlanguage stages of development. This highlights the importance of the feedback that you give to learners in the classroom. In many settings (especially in EFL contexts where few opportunities arise outside the classroom to use the language communicatively), you are the only person the students have real-live contact with who speaks English. All eyes (and ears) are indeed upon you because you are the authority on the English language, whether you like it or not. Such responsibility means that virtually everything you say and do will be noticed (except when they're not paying attention)!

Much has been written about the role of feedback in second language acquisition. In Vigil and Oller's (1976) seminal study (see *PLLT*, Chapter 9), teachers were reminded of an important distinction between affective and cognitive feedback. The former is the extent to which we value or encourage a student's attempt to communicate; the latter is the extent to which we indicate an understanding of the "message" itself. Teachers are engaged in a never-ending process of making sure that we provide sufficient positive affective feedback to students and at the same time give appropriate feedback to students about whether or not their actual language is clear and unambiguous. (See Chapter 17 for more information on error feedback.)

How, then, do you know what kind of feedback to offer students? Are interlanguage errors simply to be tolerated as natural indications of systematic internalization of a language? These important questions are to some extent answered in Chapter 17. For the moment, however, a number of general classroom implications deserve your attention:

1. Try to distinguish between a student's systematic interlanguage errors (stemming from the native language or target language) and other errors; the former will probably have a logical source that the student can be made aware of.

2. Teachers need to exercise some tolerance for certain interlanguage forms that may arise out of a student's logical developmental process.

3. Don't make a student feel stupid because of an interlanguage error; quietly point out the logic of the erroneous form ("I can understand why you said 'I go to the doctor yesterday,' but try to remember that in English we have to say the verb in the past tense. Okay?").

4. Your classroom feedback to students should give them the message that mistakes are not "bad" but that most mistakes are good indicators that innate language acquisition abilities are alive and well. Mistakes are often indicators of aspects of the new language that are still developing.

5. Try to get students to self-correct selected errors; the ability to self-correct may indicate readiness to use that form correctly and regularly.

6. In your feedback on students' linguistic output, make sure that you provide ample affective feedback—verbal or nonverbal—to encourage them to speak.

7. As you make judicious selection of which errors to treat (see Chapter 17), do so with kindness and empathy so that the student will not feel thwarted in future attempts to speak.

Principle 12: Communicative Competence

While communicative competence (CC) has come to capture a multiplicity of meanings depending on who you ask, it is nevertheless a useful phrase. Look back at Chapter 3 here and recall the description of CLT, and you will see some combination of the following components of CC, which stem from Bachman (1990) and the seminal Canale and Swain (1980):

- organizational competence (grammatical and discourse)
- pragmatic competence (functional and sociolinguistic)
- strategic competence
- psychomotor skills

The array of studies on CC provides what is probably the most sweeping and comprehensive linguistic principle, if not the most important:

> **Given that communicative competence is the goal of a language classroom, instruction needs to point toward all its components: organizational, pragmatic, strategic, and psychomotor. Communicative goals are best achieved by giving due attention to language use and not just usage, to fluency and not just accuracy, to authentic language and contexts, and to students' eventual need to apply classroom learning to previously unrehearsed contexts in the real world.**

It is important to note that the CC principle still has a bit of a reactionist flavor: reacting to other paradigms that emphasized attention to grammatical forms; to "correct" language above all; to artificial, contrived language and techniques in the classroom; and to a finite repertoire of language forms and functions that might not have lent themselves to application in the world outside the classroom. But since most of our language-teaching generalizations are, after all, at least partially conceived against the backdrop of previous practices, such a statement can stand as a reasonably accurate description of our current understanding of CC.

To attempt to list all the applications of such a principle to the language classroom would be an exhaustive endeavor! Many such applications will become evident in later chapters of this book. But for the sake of closure and simplicity, consider the following six classroom teaching "rules" that might emerge:

1. Remember that grammatical explanations or drills or exercises are only part of a lesson or curriculum; give grammar some attention, but don't neglect the other important components (e.g., functional, sociolinguistic, psychomotor, and strategic) of CC.

2. Some of the pragmatic (functional and sociolinguistic) aspects of language are very subtle and therefore very difficult. Make sure your lessons aim to teach such subtlety.

3. In your enthusiasm for teaching functional and sociolinguistic aspects of language, don't forget that the psychomotor skills (pronunciation) are an important component of both. Intonation alone conveys a great deal of pragmatic information.

4. Make sure that your students have opportunities to gain some fluency in English without having to be constantly wary of little mistakes. They can work on errors some other time.

5. Try to keep every technique that you use as authentic as possible: Use language that students will actually encounter in the real world and provide genuine, not rote, techniques for the actual conveyance of information of interest.

6. Some day your students will no longer be in your classroom. Make sure you are preparing them to be independent learners and manipulators of language "out there."

☆   ☆   ☆   ☆   ☆

The 12 principles that have just been reviewed (listed for your convenience in Table 4.1) are some of the major foundation stones for teaching practice. While they are not by any means exhaustive, they can act for you as major theoretical insights on which your methodology can be based. With these 12 principles, you should be able to evaluate a course, a textbook, a group of students, and an educational context, and to determine courses of action in the classroom. You should be able to assess the strengths and weaknesses of lessons you've observed or lessons you plan to teach. In short, you should be able to frame your own *approach* by considering the extent to which the 12 principles inform your understanding of how languages are learned and taught.

I hope you have gained from this discussion a realization of the value of undergirding your teaching (and your teacher training process) with sound principles that help you to understand why you choose to do something in the classroom: what kinds of questions to ask yourself before the fact about what you are doing, how to monitor yourself while you are teaching, how to assess after the fact the effectiveness of what you did, and then how to modify what you will do the next time around.

Table 4.1. Principles of language learning and teaching

Cognitive Principles

1. Automaticity
2. Meaningful Learning
3. The Anticipation of Reward
4. Intrinsic Motivation
5. Strategic Investment
6. Autonomy

Socioaffective Principles

7. Language Ego
8. Willingness to Communicate
9. The Language-Culture Connection

Linguistic Principles

10. The Native Language Effect
11. Interlanguage
12. Communicative Competence

TOPICS FOR DISCUSSION, ACTION, AND RESEARCH

[Note: (I) Individual work; (G) group or pair work; (C) whole-class discussion.]

1. (G) The 12 principles summarized in this chapter are all important. Direct small groups to prioritize them, placing three principles at the top of the list. Then, have the groups compare their top three with others in the class. All may discover how difficult it is to choose only three to be at the top of the list.
2. (G) Have any principles been left out that should have been included? Ask small groups to pool their thoughts, describe any such principles, and justify their inclusion in such a list. Groups will then compare their own conclusions with those of others.
3. (G) Go back to Chapter 1. Notice that in the second part of the chapter, questions were raised regarding the lesson that was described. Assign one or more of those 30 comments to pairs. The task of each pair is (a) to determine which principles in this chapter justified the teacher's choice in each case, and (b) to decide whether any aspects of that lesson should have been altered and which principles support those alterations. Then, pairs can share their thoughts with the rest of the class.

4. (C) Look at Chapter 2, in which a number of methods were descriptive of a brief history of language teaching. A chalkboard list of methods should stimulate a class discussion of the extent to which each method can be justified by certain principles discussed in this chapter and criticized by other principles.

5. (I) As an exercise in articulating principles, write one or more sentences in your own words to describe each of the 12 principles cited here. Try doing this without looking back at the chapter, then compare your responses with what is written in the chapter.

6. (C) The 12 principles given here form elements of a theory of second language learning and teaching (see *PLLT,* Chapter 10). Using these 12 principles as a backdrop, ask the class to formulate a possible *theory* of second language learning and teaching. Chalkboard notes will remind students of various ideas and suggestions.

7. (I/C) The next time you observe a foreign language class (this could be one you are taking yourself), take a list of the 12 principles with you and determine the extent to which the principles are being applied. In some cases a principle may explain why students are successfully achieving lesson objectives; in other cases a principle might articulate why objectives were not reached. Your insights might be reported back to the class.

FOR YOUR FURTHER READING

Mitchell, R., & Myles, F. (2004). *Second language learning theories* (2nd ed.). London: Hodder Arnold.

This book provides an accessible alternative to PLLT in its survey of current theories and issues in the field of second language acquisition. It serves as a vantage point from which to view the backdrops to the 12 principles presented in this chapter.

Scovel, T. (2001). *Learning new languages: A guide to second language acquisition.* Boston: Heinle & Heinle.

Spolsky, B. (1989). *Conditions for second language learning.* Oxford, UK: Oxford University Press.

Tom Scovel's book offers a nice readable perspective on language learning (and teaching) by organizing principles around five domains: people, language, attention, cognition, and emotion, which spell out the acronym PLACE. Bernard Spolsky's book sets forth some 70 "principles," or conditions, for successful second language acquisition. They break down into quite specific conditions. The two lists are worth comparing to the list of 12 in this chapter.

Richards, J. (2002). Theories of teaching in language teaching. In J. Richards & W. Renandya (Eds.), *Methodology in language teaching: An anthology of current practice* (pp. 19–25). Cambridge, UK: Cambridge University Press.

Jack Richards offers yet another way of looking at language-teaching principles. He puts theories of teaching into a framework of four categories: science-research based, theory-philosophy, values-based, and art-craft conceptions. While you're reading this chapter, glance through other chapters in this useful anthology.

CHAPTER 5

INTRINSIC MOTIVATION IN

THE CLASSROOM

OBJECTIVES After reading this chapter, you will be able to:

- recognize differences among behavioral, cognitive, and constructivist perspectives on motivation

- identify the distinguishing characteristics of intrinsic motivation, especially in contrast to extrinsic motivation

- understand the role that motivation plays in all learning, not just in language learning

- apply principles of intrinsic motivation to the second language classroom

> For every complicated problem there is an answer
> that is short, simple, and wrong.
> — H. L. Mencken

One of the more complicated problems of second language learning and teaching has been to define and apply the construct of motivation in the classroom. On the one hand, it is an easy catchword that gives teachers a simple answer to the mysteries of language learning. "Motivation is the difference," I have heard people say, "between success and failure. If they're motivated, they'll learn, and if not, they won't." That simplification may hold some of the time. Why not all the time? Just what is motivation? Can it be acquired, or is it just "there"? Can it be taught? Where does it come from? Are there different kinds of motivation? If you don't address questions like these carefully, you run the risk of passing off motivation as one of H. L. Mencken's short, simple answers to learner success when it is neither short nor simple. Ironically, motivation is not the "wrong" answer to explaining learner success, but it is "right" only when its full complexity is recognized and applied appropriately in the language classroom.

In the previous chapter, 12 principles of language learning and teaching were examined. Underlying each of those 12 is a complex array of research and practice that should remind us that foundational principles are not simple constructs that can be adequately defined in a brief maxim. One of the 12 principles was intrinsic motivation. In this chapter we will take a long, careful look at the complexity and power of intrinsic motivation.

DEFINING MOTIVATION

How would you define motivation? Let me offer the following "dictionary definition" drawn from a number of different sources: Motivation is the extent to which you make choices about (a) goals to pursue and (b) the effort you will devote to that pursuit.

You can interpret this definition in varying ways, depending on the theory of human behavior you adopt. Let's look at theories of motivation in terms of three different viewpoints. One of these perspectives is a traditional view of motivation that accounts for human behavior through a behavioral paradigm that stresses the importance of rewards and reinforcement. Another cluster of perspectives contains a number of cognitive psychological theories that explain motivation through deeper, less observable phenomena. A third way of looking at motivation involves a constructivist view that emphasizes social context and personal choices. These three traditions are described below. (For further perspectives on defining motivation, especially constructivist views of motivation, see *PLLT*, Chapter 6.)

1. A behavioral definition

A behavioral psychologist like Skinner or Watson would stress the role of **rewards** (and perhaps punishments) in motivating behavior. In Skinner's operant conditioning model, for example, human beings, like other living organisms, will pursue a goal because they perceive a reward for doing so. This reward serves to **reinforce** behavior: to cause it to persist. This tradition gave us what I might facetiously refer to as the "M&M theory" of behavior, derived from the now seldom practiced administration of M&M candies to children for manifesting desired behavior.

A behaviorist would define motivation as "the anticipation of reinforcement." We do well to heed the credibility of such a definition. There is no question that a tremendous proportion of what we do is motivated by an anticipated reward. From eating to exercising to studying and even to altruistic acts of ministering to others, there is "something in it for me." The emotional overtones of the more intangible rewards must not be ignored. M&Ms, hugs, and laughter are all, at times, payoffs worth striving for.

Reinforcement theory is a powerful concept for the classroom. Learners, like the proverbial horse running after the carrot, pursue goals in order to receive externally administered rewards: praise, gold stars, grades, certificates, diplomas, scholarships, careers, financial independence, and ultimately, happiness.

2. Cognitive definitions

A number of cognitive psychological viewpoints offer quite a different perspective on motivation. While rewards are very much a part of the whole picture, the difference lies in the sources of motivation and in the power of self-reward. Three different theories illustrate this side of motivation.

A. Drive theory. Those who see human *drives* as fundamental to human behavior claim that motivation stems from basic innate drives. David Ausubel (1968) elaborated on six different drives:

- exploration
- manipulation
- activity
- stimulation
- knowledge
- ego enhancement

All of these drives act not so much as reinforcers, as in behavioristic theory, but as innate predispositions, compelling us, as it were, to probe the unknown; to control our environment; to be physically active; to be receptive to mental, emotional, or physical stimulation; to yearn for answers to questions; and to build our own self-esteem. It takes little imagination to see how motivation in the classroom is the fulfillment of these underlying drives.

B. Hierarchy of needs theory. One of the most widely cited theories of motivation comes from Abraham Maslow (1970), who, in the spirit of drive theory, elaborated further to describe a system of needs within each human being that propel us to higher and higher attainment. Maslow's hierarchy is best viewed metaphorically as a pyramid of needs (see Figure 5.1), progressing from the satisfaction of purely physical needs up through safety and communal needs, to needs of esteem, and finally to "self-actualization," a state of reaching your fullest potential.

Figure 5.1. Maslow's hierarchy of needs (Maslow 1970)

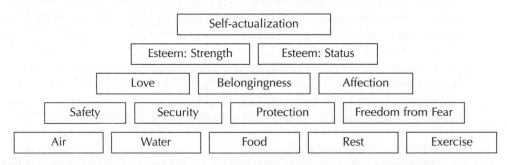

Of key importance here is that a person is not adequately energized to pursue some of the higher needs until the lower foundations of the pyramid have been satisfied. Therefore, a person who is hungry or cold, who has gotten little sleep, etc., has little motivation to see beyond those pressing physical discomforts to pursue anything higher. Likewise, needs for safety (comfort, routine, protection) and for a feeling of belonging (in a group of classmates or friends) must be met in order for a person to devote full energy to the higher needs of academic attainment, achievement of recognition for successes, and to the ultimate peak of "being all that you can be."

Maslow's theory tells us that what might be inappropriately viewed as rather ordinary classroom routines may in fact be important precursors to motivation for higher attainment. For an activity in the classroom to be considered motivating, then, it need not be outstandingly striking, innovative, or inspirational. Even familiar classroom procedures (taking roll, checking homework, small talk at the beginning of class, etc.), if they fulfill lower-order needs, can pave the way to meeting higher-order needs.

C. Self-control theory. Certain cognitive psychologists (for instance, Hunt, 1971) focus on the importance of people deciding for themselves what to think or feel or do. We define ourselves by making our own decisions, rather than by simply reacting to others. Motivation is highest when one can make one's own choices, whether they are in short-term or long-term contexts.

In the classroom, when learners have opportunities to make their own choices about what to pursue and what not to pursue, as in a cooperative learning context, they are fulfilling this need for autonomy. When learners get things shoved down their throats, motivation can wane, according to this branch of theory, because those learners have to yield to others' wishes and commands.

3. A constructivist definition

A constructivist view of motivation places even further emphasis on social context as well as individual personal choices (Williams & Burden, 1997, p. 120). Each person is motivated differently, and will therefore act on his or her environment in ways that are unique. But these unique acts are always carried out within a cultural and social milieu and cannot be completely separated from that context. In some ways Maslow's (1970) needs theory, summarized above, can be seen as constructivist in that ultimate attainment of goals is partly due to factors involving community, belonging, and social status. Motivation, in a constructivist view, is derived as much from our interactions with others as it is from one's self-determination.

Motivation is something that can, like self-esteem, be global, situational, or task oriented. Learning a foreign language requires some of all three levels of motivation. For example, a learner may possess high "global" motivation but low "task" motivation to perform well in, say, the written mode of the language. Motivation is also typically examined in terms of the intrinsic and extrinsic motives of the learner, which we will now consider.

INTRINSIC AND EXTRINSIC MOTIVATION

Before we look closely at intrinsic and extrinsic motivation, let me offer a disclaimer of sorts. For several decades, research on motivation in the field of second language acquisition research has been strongly influenced by the work of Robert Gardner and his associates (Gardner, 1985; Gardner & Lambert, 1972; Gardner & MacIntyre, 1991, 1993; Gardner & Tremblay, 1994). In this succession of research studies, a distinction has been made between **integrative** and **instrumental orientations** (see *PLLT,* Chapter 6). While the 1972 study claimed that an integrative orientation (desire to learn a language stemming from a positive affect toward a community of its speakers) was more strongly linked to success in learning a second language than an instrumental orientation (desire to learn a language in order to attain certain career, educational, or financial goals), later studies showed that both orientations could be associated with success.

Remember two important points. First, the research by Gardner and his colleagues centered on a dichotomy of *orientation,* not motivation. Orientation means a context or purpose for learning; motivation refers to the intensity of one's impetus to learn. An integrative orientation simply means the learner is pursuing a second language for a social or cultural purpose or both, and within that purpose, a learner could be driven by a high level of motivation or a low level. Likewise, in an instrumental orientation, learners are studying a language in order to further a career or academic goal. The intensity or motivation of a learner to attain that goal could be high or low.

Second, integrative and instrumental orientations are not to be confused with intrinsic and extrinsic motivation! They are separate issues. One (integrative/instrumental orientation) is a dichotomy and refers only to the context of learning. The other (intrinsic/extrinsic motivation) designates a continuum of possibilities of intensity of feeling or drive, ranging from deeply internal, self-generated rewards to strong, externally administered rewards from beyond oneself.

Now, let's move to specifying further what the intrinsic/integrative continuum implies. Edward Deci (1975, p. 23) defined intrinsic motivation this way:

> Intrinsically motivated activities are ones for which there is no apparent reward except the activity itself. People seem to engage in the activities for their own sake and not because they lead to an extrinsic reward. . . . Intrinsically motivated behaviors are aimed at bringing about certain internally rewarding consequences, namely, feelings of competence and self-determination.

Extrinsically motivated behaviors, on the other hand, are carried out in anticipation of a reward from outside and beyond the self. Typical extrinsic rewards are money, prizes, grades, and even certain types of positive feedback. Behaviors initiated solely to avoid punishment are also extrinsically motivated, even though numerous intrinsic benefits can ultimately accrue to those who, instead, view punishment avoidance as a challenge that can build their sense of competence and self-determination.

Which form of motivation is more powerful? A convincing stockpile of research on motivation strongly favors intrinsic drives, especially for long-term retention. Jean Piaget (1972) and others pointed out that human beings universally view incongruity, uncertainty, and "disequilibrium" as motivating. In other words, we seek out a reasonable challenge. Then we initiate behaviors intended to conquer the challenging situation. Incongruity is not itself motivating, but optimal incongruity—or what Krashen (1985) called "$i + 1$"—presents enough of a possibility of being resolved that we will go after that resolution.

Abraham Maslow (1970) claimed that intrinsic motivation is clearly superior to extrinsic. According to his hierarchy of needs, we are ultimately motivated to achieve "self-actualization" once the basic physical, safety, and community needs are met. No matter what extrinsic rewards are present or absent, we will strive for self-esteem and fulfillment.

Jerome Bruner (1962), praising the "autonomy of self-reward," claimed that one of the most effective ways to help both children and adults to think and learn is to free them from the control of rewards and punishments. One of the principal weaknesses of extrinsically driven behavior is its addictive nature. Once captivated, as it were, by the lure of an immediate prize or praise, we can become dependent on those tangible rewards, even to the point that their withdrawal can extinguish the desire to learn.

Now, you may be thinking, don't extrinsic rewards play a role in a learner's motivation? Wouldn't extrinsic rewards, coupled with intrinsic motivation, enhance the intrinsic? Not according to a surprising number of research studies. Two examples (Kohn, 1990) illustrate:

1. Subjects were asked to solve an intrinsically fascinating complex puzzle with no stated reward. Halfway through the process, the experimenter informed the subjects that there would be a monetary reward for solving the puzzle. From that point onward, intrinsic motivation (as measured by speed and correct steps toward a solution) waned.
2. Teenage girls were given the task of teaching some games to younger children. One group of "teachers" was simply given the teaching task; the others were told that they would receive a reward (a free ticket to the movies) for successfully completing the task. Results: The first group did their task faster, with more success, and reported greater pleasure in doing so than the second group!

It is interesting that the research shows that one type of extrinsic reward can indeed have an effect on intrinsic motivation: the positive feedback that learners perceive as a boost to their feelings of competence and self-determination. No other externally administered set of rewards has a lasting effect. So, for example, sincerely delivered positive feedback in a classroom, seen by students as a validation of their own personal autonomy, critical thinking ability, and self-fulfillment, can increase or maintain intrinsic motivation.

Intrinsic motivation is of course not the only determiner of success for a language learner. Sometimes, no matter how much you want to accomplish something or how hard you try, you may not succeed for a host of other reasons. But if the learners in your classroom are given an opportunity to "do" language for their own personal reasons of achieving competence and autonomy, those learners will have a better chance of success than if they become dependent on external rewards for their motivation.

INTRINSIC MOTIVATION IN EDUCATION

Educators like Maria Montessori, Rudolf Steiner, Paolo Freire, A. S. Neill, and Carl Rogers have all provided exemplary models of intrinsically motivated education. Traditionally, elementary and secondary schools are fraught with extrinsically motivated behavior. The school curriculum is dictated by institutions (sometimes politically influenced) and can be far removed from even the teacher's choice. Parents' and society's values and wishes are virtually forced onto pupils, whether they like it or not. Tests and exams, many of which are standardized and given high credence in the world "out there," are imposed on students with no consultation with the students themselves. The glorification of content, product, correctness, and competitiveness has failed to bring the learner into a collaborative process of competence building.

The consequence of such extrinsic motivators is that schools all too often teach students to play the "game" of pleasing teachers and authorities rather than developing an internalized thirst for knowledge and experience. The administration of grades and praises for being a "good child" builds a dependency on immediate M&M gratification. Competition *against* classmates (who might otherwise be allies or partners in learning) ensues. If a communal bond is created, it runs the risk of being motivated by the need to band together *against* teachers and authorities. Over the long haul, such dependency focuses students too exclusively on the material or monetary rewards of an education rather than instilling an appreciation for creativity and satisfying some of the more basic drives for knowledge and exploration. Ultimately, the product of this system is a student who has been taught to fear failure above all and therefore to refrain from potentially rewarding risk-taking or innovative behavior.

A bleak picture? Too harsh? Of course, there are many happy exceptions to such a depiction, but you don't have to look very far in any corner of the world to find major elements of the picture holding true. The question is: Can something be done to turn such a picture upside down? Or, more specifically to your quest, can your English classroom become a place where these extrinsic elements are diverted into a more positive direction? Or, better yet, can such elements be avoided entirely?

Table 5.1 depicts what can happen in an institution that takes eight extrinsic elements and, while accepting their reality in virtually any society or educational institution, turns those elements in an intrinsically oriented direction. The notion here is that an intrinsically oriented school can begin to transform itself into a more positive, affirming environment not so much by revolutionizing society (which takes decades if not centuries) but by shifting its view of the student.

Table 5.1. From extrinsic to intrinsic motivation in educational institutions

Extrinsic Pressures	Intrinsic Innovations	Motivational Results
SCHOOL CURRICULUM	learner-centered personal goal-setting individualization	self-esteem self-actualization decide for self
PARENTAL EXPECTATIONS	family solidarity negotiated agreements	love, intimacy acceptance, respect for wisdom
SOCIETY'S EXPECTATIONS (conformity)	security of comfortable routines task-based teaching	community, belonging identity, harmony security
TESTS & EXAMS	peer evaluation self-diagnosis level-check exercises	experience self-knowledge
IMMEDIATE GRATIFICATION ("M & Ms")	set long-term goals focus on big picture patience will reward	self-actualization
MAKE MONEY!	content-based teaching vocational education workplace ESL, ESP	cooperation harmony
COMPETITION	cooperative learning group work the class is a team	community strength, status security
NEVER FAIL!	risk-taking, innovation, creativity	learn from mistakes nobody's perfect "c'est la vie"

A curriculum that comes from "the administration" can be modified to some extent to include student-centered learning and teaching, to allow students to set some—not all, perhaps—of their own learning goals, and to individualize lessons and activities as much as possible. The result: higher student self-esteem, greater chances for self-actualization, more deciding for oneself.

Expectations of parents and other authority figures are a reality that we cannot simply dissolve by waving a magic wand. But teachers can help to convert the perception of those expectations into a sense of the positive effect of the immediate family on a student and of the importance of tradition not because it has been forced on them, but because its intrinsic worth is perceived. The result: an appreciation of love, intimacy, and respect for the wisdom of age. In turn, society's expectations may, through a process of education and counseling, be seen as a means for providing comfortable routines (time schedules, customs, mores). Class discussions can focus on a critical evaluation of society so that students aren't forced to accept some specific way of thinking or acting, but are coaxed into examining both sides of the issue. The result is a sense of belonging, of the value of the wider community, of harmony.

Tests and exams can incorporate some student consultation (see Chapter 24) and peer evaluation. Teachers can help students to view tests as feedback instruments for self-diagnosis, not as comparisons of one's performance against a norm. Students thus become motivated by the experience and by achieving self-knowledge.

The otherwise extrinsic values that are given in Table 5.1 (immediate gratification, material rewards, competition, and fear of failure) can also be redirected through

- emphasizing the "big" picture—larger perspectives
- letting students set long-term goals
- allowing sufficient time for learning
- cooperative learning activities
- group work
- viewing the class as a team
- content-centered teaching
- English for specific (vocational/professional) purposes
- English in the workplace
- allowing risk-taking behavior
- rewarding innovation and creativity

Such activities and attitudes on your part appeal to the deeper causes of motivation. They get at needs and drives, at self-control, at a balanced, realistic perception of self, and even at the simple joy of learning for its own sake!

INTRINSIC MOTIVATION IN THE SECOND LANGUAGE CLASSROOM

Turning to the role of intrinsic motivation in second language classrooms in particular, consider these activities that capitalize on the intrinsic by appealing to learners' self-determination and autonomy:

- teaching writing as a thinking process in which learners develop their own ideas freely and openly
- showing learners strategies of reading that enable them to bring their own information to the written word

- language experience approaches in which students create their own reading material for others in the class to read
- oral fluency exercises in which learners talk about what interests them and not about a teacher-assigned topic
- listening to an academic lecture in one's own field of study for specific information that will fill a gap for the learner
- communicative language teaching, in which language is taught to enable learners to accomplish certain specific functions
- grammatical explanations, if learners see in such explanations a potential for increasing their autonomy in a second language

Actually, every technique in your language classroom can be subjected to an intrinsic motivation "litmus test" to determine the extent to which they adhere to this powerful principle. Try using the checklist in Table 5.2 to help you determine whether something you're doing in the classroom is contributing to your students' intrinsic drives.

Table 5.2. A checklist of intrinsically motivating techniques

Yes	No	
❏	❏	1. Does the technique appeal to the genuine interests of your students? Is it relevant to their lives?
❏	❏	2. Do you present the technique in a positive, enthusiastic manner?
❏	❏	3. Are students clearly aware of the purpose of the technique?
❏	❏	4. Do students have some choice in a. choosing some aspect of the technique? b. determining how they go about fulfilling the goals of the technique?
❏	❏	5. Does the technique encourage students to discover for themselves certain principles or rules (rather than simply being "told")?
❏	❏	6. Does it encourage students in some way to develop or use effective strategies of learning and communication?
❏	❏	7. Does it contribute—at least to some extent—to students' ultimate autonomy and independence (from you)?
❏	❏	8. Does it foster cooperative negotiation with other students in the class? Is it truly interactive?
❏	❏	9. Does the technique present a "reasonable challenge"?
❏	❏	10. Do students receive sufficient feedback on their performance (from each other or from you)?

Throughout the rest of this book, you will be reminded of the importance of the Intrinsic Motivation Principle in achieving your goals as a teacher. Think of yourself not so much as a teacher who must constantly "deliver" information to your students, but more as a *facilitator* of learning whose job is to set the stage for learning, to start the wheels turning inside the heads of your students, to turn them on to their own abilities, and to help channel those abilities in fruitful directions.

Zoltàn Dörnyei (2001) offers an insightful set of strategies for creating what he calls "basic motivational conditions" (p. 31) in the classroom, based on a survey of Hungarian foreign language teachers (Dörnyei & Csizér, 1998). All eight strategies focus on what the teacher can do to start the process of creating intrinsic motivation.

1. Demonstrate and talk about your own enthusiasm for the course material, and how it affects you personally.
2. Take the students' learning very seriously.
3. Develop a personal relationship with your students.
4. Develop a collaborative relationship with the students' parents.
5. Create a pleasant and supportive atmosphere in the classroom.
6. Promote the development of group cohesiveness.
7. Formulate group norms explicitly, and have them discussed and accepted by the learners.
8. Have the group norms consistently observed.

These eight guidelines are followed, in Dörnyei's (2001) book, by 27 other strategies for generating initial motivation, maintaining and protecting motivation, and encouraging positive self-evaluation.

You might wish to compare Dörnyei's 35 strategies with my own six general guidelines for infusing your English language classroom with some intrinsically motivating dynamics:

1. Teachers are enablers, not rewarders. Therefore, when you teach, focus less on how to administer immediate or tangible rewards and more on how to get students to tune in to their potential and to be challenged by self-determined goals.
2. Learners need to develop autonomy, not dependence. Therefore, be careful not to let learners become dependent on your daily praise and other feedback. Rather, administer praise selectively and judiciously, helping students to recognize their own self-satisfaction in having done something well.
3. Help learners to take charge of their own learning through setting some personal goals and utilizing learning strategies.
4. Learner-centered, cooperative teaching is intrinsically motivating. Therefore, give students opportunities to make choices in activities, topics, discussions, etc.

Sometimes a simple either/or choice ("Okay, class, for the next 10 minutes we can either do this little cloze test or review for the test. Which do you want to do?") helps students to develop intrinsic motives. They feel less like puppets on a string if you can involve them in various aspects of looking at their needs and self-diagnosing, of planning lessons and objectives, of deciding in which direction a lesson might go, and of evaluating their learning.

5. Content-based activities and courses are intrinsically motivating. Therefore, you might strive to focus your students on interesting, relevant subject-matter content that gets them more linguistically involved with meanings and purposes and less with verbs and prepositions.

6. Tests, with some special attention from the teacher, can be intrinsically motivating. Allowing some student input to the test, giving well-thought-out classroom tests that are face-valid in the eyes of students, and giving narrative evaluations are just some of the topics covered in Chapter 25 on how your tests can contribute to intrinsic motivation.

☆   ☆   ☆   ☆   ☆

All of the above enthusiasm for intrinsic motivation shouldn't lure you into thinking that we now have a catchall concept that will explain everything about learning and teaching. Other factors affect learning outcomes: native ability, age, context of learning, style preferences, background experience and qualifications, availability of time to give the effort needed, and the quality of input that is beyond the immediate control of the learner. And clearly you will be able to use a combination of extrinsic (for more immediate concerns or for extremely low motivational contexts, for example) and intrinsic motives to your advantage in the classroom; there is indeed a place—and a very soundly supportable place—for extrinsic motives in the language classroom.

But when all these factors are duly considered, the students' long-term goals, their deepest level of feeling and thinking, and their global assessment of their potential to be self-actualized are much, much better served by promoting intrinsic motives. Your task is to maintain these intrinsically motivating factors on an underlying plane of awareness in your mind whenever and wherever learners are placed under your tutelage.

TOPICS FOR DISCUSSION, ACTION, AND RESEARCH

[Note: (I) Individual work; (G) group or pair work; (C) whole-class discussion.]

1. (I/G/C) This chapter has provided background information, research, and classroom applications of one of the 12 principles named in Chapter 4. Now, as a limited research project, pick one of the other 11 principles and (a) do some library research (you might begin by looking through *PLLT*) to find

sources on the topic and (b) draw some further practical implications for teaching. Write or orally present your report. This could be done as a collaborative project in pairs.

2. (G) Assign pairs to look once again at the ESL lesson described in Chapter 1, and make a list of aspects of that lesson that appeal to the Intrinsic Motivation Principle. Then, partners should scan through the list of methods described in Chapter 2 and consider the extent to which each method promoted intrinsic motivation among students.

3. (I) Review Gardner's concept of integrative and instrumental orientation (see *PLLT*, Chapter 6). Make sure you understand how both of his types of orientation could have either intrinsic or extrinsic motives.

4. (G) Ask pairs to look again at the six drives claimed by Ausubel to underlie human motivation, and describe classroom examples or illustrate how each of the six drives might be fulfilled.

5. (G) Maslow's pyramid of needs is a well-known model of motivation. Direct pairs to come up with some further examples—beyond those already cited— of how certain "ordinary classroom routines may in fact be important precursors to motivation for higher attainment" (page 87). At what point do these ordinary routines become dull, boring, or ineffective?

6. (I) What do the three cognitive definitions of motivation have in common?

7. (C) In some ways, traditional, largely extrinsically inspired educational systems are strongly criticized here. Ask the class to discuss whether that criticism is justified. Have the class share some examples of extrinsically oriented practices from their own experience in learning another language. What did they do to survive in that atmosphere? How can student survival techniques be turned around to inspire better teaching practices?

8. (G/C) Ask pairs to think of some counterexamples to the "bleak picture" of traditional education—that is, positive, intrinsically rewarding experiences in their own school experiences. Have pairs then share them with the rest of the class.

9. (G) If time and facilities permit, assign partners to design a simple classroom experiment in intrinsic motivation, perhaps following the model of the two little studies summarized on page 89. Since motivation can't be observed, it must be inferred. Therefore, students will need to be as specific as possible in determining how they will measure intrinsic motivation.

10. (C/G) As a whole class, brainstorm for just a minute to come up with half a dozen or so commonly used techniques in language classrooms that students have observed recently (e.g., pronunciation drill, fluency circle, information-gap activity, reading aloud, listening to a lecture, etc.). Then, assign one or two of those techniques to pairs or small groups for a rigorous examination of the 10 criteria for determining whether a technique is intrinsically motivating in Table 5.2. Groups should then share their "report card" for each technique. Did groups find that in most cases intrinsic motivation depended on how the teacher conducted the technique?

FOR YOUR FURTHER READING

Dörnyei, Z. (2005). Motivation and "self-motivation." In Z. Dörnyei, *The psychology of the language learner: Individual differences in second language acquisition* (pp. 65–119). Mahwah, NJ: Lawrence Erlbaum Associates.

Zoltan Dörnyei has published a number of books and articles on the subject of motivation in language learning. This chapter in his book on individual differences among language learners is an excellent summary of research on motivation worldwide.

Dörnyei, Z. (2001). *Motivational strategies in the language classroom.* Cambridge, UK: Cambridge University Press.

One of the most practical of his writings, this book is directed to teachers and offers 35 strategies for teachers to promote motivation. The strategies are classified into four categories: basic motivational conditions; generating initial motivation; maintaining and protecting motivation; and encouraging positive self-evaluation.

Deci, E. (1975). *Intrinsic motivation.* New York: Plenum Press.

Edward Deci is one of the principal players in a long list of those who have conducted research on intrinsic motivation. This book, though somewhat dated, is still applicable to current teaching practice. It explains the construct in full detail and describes supporting research.

Raffini, J. (1996). *150 ways to increase intrinsic motivation in the classroom.* Needham Heights, MA: Allyn & Bacon.

While not written for the foreign language teacher specifically, this very practically oriented book for teachers nevertheless gives a sense of many different approaches and classroom techniques that will instill a sense of intrinsic motivation in students.

PART II

CONTEXTS OF LEARNING

AND TEACHING

During the first six or seven decades of the twentieth century, language teaching as a disciplinary field seemed to operate on the assumption that there is—or should be—one standard, "orthodox" method for all contexts. Some claimed, for example, that the Audiolingual Method was "the" method for all language-teaching contexts.

One of the principal contributions of the last few decades of the twentieth century was an increasingly complex set of descriptions of the multiplicity of contexts in which foreign languages were learned and taught. As more and more research corroborated the concept that all learners and all contexts were *not* alike, teaching methodology followed with explorations of how to identify an array of needs and how to meet them.

The three chapters of Part II alert you to major variables in learning and teaching contexts. The most salient factor in a language classroom is age, treated in Chapter 6. Indeed, some classes may include a range of ages, from young adults to older adults. Chapter 7 treats the second most obvious contextual variable, proficiency level, with descriptions and applications for what are loosely labeled beginning, intermediate, and advanced levels of learning.

Chapter 8 examines a number of variables that were often swept under the rug in the last century: sociopolitical and institutional contexts. Issues of culture, identity, ethnicity, and the situational politics surrounding a language course are far-reaching and complex. Differences between teaching English in an English-speaking country and a non-English-speaking country, the controversy over nonnative English-speaking teachers (NNESTs), and the idiosyncracies of one's own institution can all affect the final outcome of learners in a language program.

CHAPTER 6

TEACHING ACROSS AGE LEVELS

OBJECTIVES After reading this chapter, you will be able to:

- appreciate the importance of age as a factor in designing lessons and courses

- understand the characteristics of children's learning that must be incorporated into lessons and courses

- distinguish differences between adults and children and how to accommodate such differences in your methodology

- recognize the characteristics of students "in between" childhood and adulthood, and provide tasks and activities that are appealing and challenging to teenagers

On occasion people who are quite unaware of the language-teaching field will walk into my office at the university looking for reassurance. They'll ask me, "Since English is my native language, I won't have any problem teaching it, will I?" Or they might ask, on the eve of their departure for Japan (without the slightest clue of who their future students will be), "Can you recommend a good textbook for my students?" Other naive inquirers who have had a little exposure to the vastness and complexity of the field still might assert, "I would like to learn how to teach ESL. Can you recommend a good workshop?" Such questions are prompted by advertisements in local newspapers that promise lifelong employment as an English teacher (in exotic places) if only you'll attend someone's weekend seminar (or two) and, of course, cough up a fairly hefty enrollment fee.

You are already aware of the array of questions, issues, approaches, and techniques that must be included in any training as a language teacher—a complexity that cannot be covered effectively in a weekend workshop. Part of this complexity is brought on by the multiplicity of contexts in which languages, and English more so than any other language, are learned and taught. Even if you could pack a suitcase full of the most current teaching resources, you would still have to face the question of *who* your learners are, *where* they are learning, and *why* they are learning.

This chapter begins to deal with contextual considerations in language teaching by addressing the learner variable of age. Chapter 7 then deals with the learner variable of language proficiency (beginning, intermediate, and advanced). And Chapter 8 grapples with several complex variables introduced by sociopolitical contexts of teaching (country, societal expectations, cultural factors, political constraints, the status of English); by the institution one is teaching in (school, university, language school, adult education, vocational/workplace courses); and by the implied purposes for learning English (academic, technical, social, cultural immersion, enrichment, survival). Your choices of techniques, lesson organization, and supporting materials must take all of these considerations into account.

TEACHING CHILDREN

Popular tradition would have you believe that children are effortless second language learners and far superior to adults in their eventual success. On both counts, some qualifications are in order.

First, children's widespread success in acquiring second languages belies a tremendous subconscious *effort* devoted to the task. As you have discovered in other reading (see *PLLT,* Chapters 2 and 3, for example), children exercise a good deal of both cognitive and affective effort in order to internalize both native and second languages. The difference between children and adults (that is, persons beyond the age of puberty) lies primarily in the contrast between the child's spontaneous, **peripheral** attention to language **forms** and the adult's overt, **focal** awareness of and attention to those forms. Therefore, the popular notion about children holds only if "effort" refers, rather narrowly, to focal attention (sometimes thought of as "conscious" attention—see *PLLT,* Chapter 10) to language forms.

Second, adults are not necessarily less successful in their efforts. Studies have shown that adults, in fact, can be superior in a number of aspects of acquisition (*PLLT,* Chapter 3). They can learn and retain a larger vocabulary. They can utilize various deductive and abstract processes to shortcut the learning of grammatical and other linguistic concepts. And, in classroom learning, their superior intellect usually helps them to learn faster than a child. So, while children's fluency and naturalness are often the envy of adults struggling with second languages, the context of classroom instruction may introduce some difficulties to children learning a second language.

Third, the popular claim fails to differentiate very young children (say, 4- to 6-year-olds) from pubescent children (12 to 13) and the whole range of ages in between. There are actually many instances of 6- to 12-year-old children manifesting significant difficulty in acquiring a second language for a multitude of reasons. Ranking high on that list of reasons are a number of complex personal, social, cultural, and political factors at play in elementary school education.

Teaching ESL to school-age children, therefore, is not merely a matter of setting them loose on a plethora of authentic language tasks in the classroom. In fact, for some TESOL professionals (Cameron, 2003), the challenge of teaching children warrants a separate acronym: TEYL (teaching English to young learners). Teacher reference books are devoted solely to the issues, principles, and methodology surrounding the teaching of children (Linse, 2005; Moon, 2000; Pinter, 2006; Reilly & Ward, 1997). To successfully teach children a second language requires specific skills and intuitions that differ from those appropriate for adult teaching. Five categories may help give some practical approaches to teaching children.

1. Intellectual development

An elementary school teacher asked her students to take a piece of paper and pencil and write something. A boy raised his hand and said, "Teacher, I ain't got no pencil." The teacher, somewhat perturbed by his grammar, embarked on a barrage of corrective patterns: "I *don't* have *a* pencil. You *don't* have *a* pencil. We *don't* have pencils." Confused and bewildered, the child responded, "Ain't nobody got no pencils?"

Since children (up to the age of about 11) are still in an intellectual stage of what Piaget (1972) called "concrete operations," we need to remember their limitations. Rules, explanations, and other even slightly abstract talk about language must be approached with extreme caution. Children are centered on the here and now, on the functional purposes of language. They have little appreciation for our adult notions of "correctness," and they certainly cannot grasp the metalanguage we use to describe and explain linguistic concepts. Here are some rules of thumb for the classroom:

- Don't explain *grammar* using terms like "present progressive" or "relative clause."
- *Rules* stated in abstract terms ("To make a statement into a question, you add a *do* or *does*") should be avoided.
- Some grammatical concepts, especially at the upper levels of childhood, can be called to learners' attention by showing them certain *patterns* ("Notice the *ing* at the end of the word") and *examples* ("This is the way we say it when it's happening right now: 'I'm walking to the door'").
- Certain more difficult concepts or patterns require more *repetition* than adults need. For example, repeating certain patterns (without boring students) may be necessary to get the brain and the ear to cooperate. Unlike the boy who had no pencil, children must understand the meaning and relevance of repetitions.

2. Attention span

One of the salient differences between adults and children is attention span. First, it is important to understand what attention span means. Put children in front of a TV showing a favorite cartoon and they will stay riveted for the duration. So, you cannot make a sweeping claim that children have short attention spans! But short attention spans do come into play when children have to deal with material that to them is boring, useless, or too difficult. Since language lessons can at times be difficult for children, your job is to make them interesting, lively, and fun. How do you do that?

- Because children are focused on the *here and now,* activities should be designed to capture their immediate interest.
- A lesson needs a *variety* of activities to keep interest and attention alive.
- A teacher needs to be *animated,* lively, and enthusiastic about the subject matter. Consider the classroom a stage on which you are the lead actor; your energy will be infectious. While you may think that you're overdoing it, children need this exaggeration to keep spirits buoyed and minds alert.
- A *sense of humor* will go a long way in keeping children laughing and learning. Since children's humor is quite different from adults', remember to put yourself in their shoes.
- Children have a lot of natural *curiosity.* Make sure you tap into that curiosity whenever possible, and you will thereby help to maintain attention and focus.

3. Sensory input

Children need to have all five senses stimulated. Your activities should strive to go well beyond the visual and auditory modes that we feel are usually sufficient for a classroom.

- Pepper your lessons with *physical* activity, such as having students act out things (role-play), play games, or do Total Physical Response activities.
- Projects and other *hands-on activities* go a long way toward helping children to internalize language. Small-group science projects, for example, are excellent ways to get them to learn words and structures and to practice meaningful language.
- *Sensory aids* help children to internalize concepts. The smell of flowers, the touch of plants and fruits, the taste of foods, liberal doses of audiovisual aids like videos, pictures, tapes, music—all are important elements in children's language teaching.
- Remember that your own *nonverbal language* is important because children will indeed attend very sensitively to your facial features, gestures, and body language.

4. Affective factors

A common myth is that children are relatively unaffected by the inhibitions that adults find to be a block to learning. Not so! Children are often innovative in language forms but still have a great many inhibitions. They are extremely sensitive, especially to peers: What do others think of me? What will so-and-so think when I speak in English? Children are in many ways much more fragile than adults. Their egos are still being shaped, and therefore the slightest nuances of communication can be negatively interpreted. Teachers need to help them to overcome such potential barriers to learning.

- Help your students to laugh *with* each other at various mistakes that they all make.
- Be patient and supportive to build self-esteem, yet at the same time be firm in your expectations of students.
- Elicit as much oral participation as possible from students, especially the quieter ones, to give them plenty of opportunities for trying things out.

5. Authentic, meaningful language

Children are focused on what this new language can actually be used for here and now. They are less willing to put up with language that doesn't hold immediate rewards for them. Your classes can ill afford to have an overload of language that is neither authentic nor meaningful.

- Children are good at sensing language that is not *authentic;* therefore, "canned" or stilted language will likely be rejected.
- Language needs to be firmly *context embedded.* Story lines, familiar situations and characters, real-life conversations, meaningful purposes in using language—these will establish a context within which language can be received and sent and thereby improve attention and retention. *Context-reduced* language in abstract, isolated, unconnected sentences will be much less readily tolerated by children's minds.
- A *whole language* approach is essential. If language is broken into too many bits and pieces, students won't see the relationship to the whole. And stress the interrelationships among the various skills (listening, speaking, reading, and writing), or they won't see important connections.

It takes a very special person to be able to teach children effectively. Along with all these guidelines, an elementary school teacher develops a certain intuition with increasing months and years of experience. If you don't yet have the experience, you will in due course of time. Meanwhile, you must begin somewhere, and these rules of thumb will help.

TEACHING ADULTS

Although many of the "rules" for teaching children can apply in some ways to teaching adults, the latter age group poses some different, special considerations for the classroom teacher. Adults have superior cognitive abilities that can render them more successful in certain classroom endeavors. Their need for sensory input can rely a little more on their imaginations (they can be told to "imagine" smelling a rose versus actually smelling one). Their level of shyness can be equal to or greater than that of children, but adults usually have acquired a self-confidence not found in children. And, because of adults' cognitive abilities, they can at least occasionally deal with language that isn't embedded in a "here and now" context.

So, as you consider the five variables that apply to children, keep in mind some specific suggestions and caveats.

1. Adults are more able to handle abstract rules and concepts. But beware! As you know, too much abstract generalization about usage and not enough real-life language use can be deadly for adults, too.
2. Adults have longer attention spans for material that may not be intrinsically interesting to them. But again, the rule of keeping your activities short and sweet applies also to adult-age teaching.
3. Sensory input need not always be as varied with adults, but one of the secrets of lively adult classes is their appeal to multiple senses.
4. Adults often bring a modicum of general self-confidence (global self-esteem) into a classroom. With children you must compensate for their fragile egos; such compensation may not be as critical with adults. Yet we should never underestimate the emotional factors that may be attendant to adult second language learning.
5. Adults, with their more developed abstract thinking ability, are better able to understand a context-reduced segment of language. Authenticity and mean-ingfulness are of course still highly important, but in adult language teaching, a teacher can take temporary digressions to dissect and examine isolated lin-guistic properties as long as students are returned to the original context.

Some implications for general classroom management (see Chapter 13 for a full treatment) can be drawn from what we know about differences between children and adults. Some management "do's" and "don'ts":

1. *Do* remember that even though adults cannot express complex thinking in the new language, they are nevertheless intelligent grown-ups with mature cognition and fully developed emotions. Show respect for the deeper thoughts and feelings that may be "trapped" for the moment by a low proficiency level.
2. *Don't* treat adults in your class like children by
    a. calling them "kids,"
    b. using "caretaker" talk (the way parents talk to children), or
    c. talking down to them.
3. *Do* give your students as many opportunities as possible to make *choices* (cooperative learning) about what they will do in and out of the classroom. That way, they can more effectively make an investment in their own learning process.
4. *Don't* discipline adults in the same way you would children. If discipline problems occur (showing disrespect, laughing, disrupting class, etc.), first assume that your students are adults who can be reasoned with like adults.

TEACHING TEENS

It is of course much too absolute to consider that a child ceases to be a child at the age of puberty and that all of the rules of adult teaching suddenly apply! It is therefore appropriate to consider briefly the sort of variables that apply in the teaching of "young adults," "teens," and high school–age children whose ages range between 12 and 18 or so.

The "terrible teens" are an age of transition, confusion, self-consciousness, growth, and changing bodies and minds. What a challenge for the teacher! Teens are in between childhood and adulthood, and therefore a very special set of considerations applies to teaching them. Perhaps because of the enigma of teaching teenagers, little is specifically said in the language-teaching field about teaching at this level. Nevertheless, some thoughts are worth verbalizing, even if in the form of simple reminders.

1. Intellectual capacity adds abstract operational thought around the age of 12. Therefore, some sophisticated intellectual processing is increasingly possible. Complex problems can be solved with logical thinking. This means that linguistic metalanguage can now, theoretically, have some impact. But the success of any intellectual endeavor will be a factor of the attention a learner places on the task; therefore, if a learner is attending to self, to appearance, to being accepted, to sexual thoughts, to a weekend party, to whatever, the intellectual task at hand may suffer.

2. Attention spans are lengthening as a result of intellectual maturation, but once again, with many diversions present in a teenager's life, those potential attention spans can easily be shortened.

3. Varieties of sensory input are still important, but again, increasing capacities for abstraction lessen the essential nature of appealing to all five senses.

4. Factors surrounding ego, self-image, and self-esteem are at their pinnacle. Teens are ultrasensitive to how others perceive their changing physical and emotional selves along with their mental capabilities. One of the most important concerns of the secondary school teacher is to keep self-esteem high by

   - avoiding embarrassment of students at all costs,
   - affirming each person's talents and strengths,
   - allowing mistakes and other errors to be accepted,
   - de-emphasizing competition between classmates, and
   - encouraging small-group work where risks can be taken more easily by a teen.

5. Secondary school students are of course becoming increasingly adultlike in their ability to make those occasional diversions from the "here and now" nature of immediate communicative contexts to dwell on a grammar point or

vocabulary item. But as in teaching adults, care must be taken not to insult them with stilted language or to bore them with overanalysis.

✯   ✯   ✯   ✯   ✯

This chapter is intended to offer a number of factors for you to consider as you attend to the age of your learners. These factors were noted as a series of pointers and reminders rather than as anecdotal or observational references to classrooms full of students. You can make those references yourself as you observe and as you begin to teach. The next time you're in an ESL classroom, notice how someone you're observing (or how you yourself) accounted for age variables in the overall lesson, in the type of techniques that were used, in the management of the classroom, in verbal registers as well as body language, in the teacher–student exchanges, and in the relationship that those exchanges conveyed. And remember that in some "adult" classes, students in their teens may be sitting next to classmates in their sixties, representing two or more generations! You may actually surprise yourself by how much of what we do and say as teachers is a factor of students' age.

TOPICS FOR DISCUSSION, ACTION, AND RESEARCH

[Note: (I) Individual work; (G) group or pair work; (C) whole-class discussion.]

1. (G) Direct small groups to think back to the ESL lesson that was described in Chapter 1. That was an adult class. Now, groups are to talk about how they would go about teaching virtually the same grammar and discourse to children of, say, ages seven and eight. Would the general topic fit? Would the same grammatical and communicative goals apply? What would you do differently? What would you delete, and what would you add? How would you alter the various techniques?

2. (G/C) Ask groups to brainstorm other considerations—beyond those mentioned in this chapter—that should be brought to bear on teaching ESL to (a) children, (b) adults, (c) teenagers. Groups should then share their thoughts with the rest of the class.

3. (G) Pair up students to look again at the five major categories of factors to consider in teaching children and to come up with some specific classroom examples that illustrate the factor under consideration. For example, it was suggested that teachers should have a sense of humor, use sensory aids, be patient and supportive, and use context-embedded language. Pairs should offer some examples of each of these and other suggestions in that section.

4. (C) Ask the class if they would like to take issue with any of the five factors regarding teaching ESL to children. For example, do children have inhibitions and fragile egos? How do adults' and children's inhibitions differ? See if there are other factors you might want to debate. Ask students to defend their assertions with examples.

5. (C) Engage the class in a discussion about whether one should teach language to children at all. Aren't their innate capacities sufficient without having to be instructed? What would happen if children (in a context you specify) were just "exposed" to English with no classroom instruction? What would they gain? What would they lose? You might want to debate this issue, with some class members arguing for the "no-classroom-instruction" position and others defending the contention that language classes for children can be beneficial.

6. (G/C) Assign groups of three to make three ESL observations: one person goes to an elementary school, one goes to a secondary school, and one goes to a class for adults. Each observer should take careful note of the following:

- topic or subject matter of the lesson
- teacher talk and student talk
- variety and type of techniques
- discipline or behavior problems
- physical activity and sensory input
- apparent motivation and interest

After their observations, group members should get together to share perceptions, compare differences, and see what insights were garnered about teaching at the different age levels. Each group's findings can then be shared with the rest of the class.

FOR YOUR FURTHER READING

Pinter, A. (2006). *Teaching young language learners.* Oxford, UK: Oxford University Press.

Linse, C. (2005). *Practical English language teaching: Young learners.* New York: McGraw-Hill.

Moon, J. (2000). *Children learning English.* Oxford, UK: Macmillan Education.

Reilly, V., & Ward, S. (1997). *Very young learners.* Oxford, UK: Oxford University Press.

All four of these very practically oriented books consist of different classroom activities suitable for young children, ranging in age from preschool to 10. Activities are thematically organized, either by skill area or by topic. In each, some general comments are made about the issues and principles of teaching children at various ages.

Schinke-Llano, L., & Rauff, R. (Eds.). (1996). *New ways in teaching young children.* Alexandria, VA: Teachers of English to Speakers of Other Languages.

Short, D. (Ed.). (1998). *New ways in teaching English at the secondary level.* Alexandria, VA: Teachers of English to Speakers of Other Languages.

Lewis, M. (Ed.). (1997). *New ways in teaching adults.* Alexandria, VA: Teachers of English to Speakers of Other Languages.

These three books are part of TESOL's New Ways series, designed as practical reference guides for teachers. Each book consists of many different activities suitable for the particular age level indicated. The books are subdivided by topics and skill areas. Also of interest is that each activity lists its appropriate proficiency level (e.g., beginning+, intermediate, etc.), exemplifying how activities vary by proficiency level as well as by age (see Chapter 7).

Cameron, L. (2003). Challenges for ELT from the expansion in teaching children. *ELT Journal, 57,* 105–112.

This article examines some of the challenges of teaching young children. Beginning with a summary of an approach to teaching children, the author then deals with such issues as meaningful learning, initial literacy, assessment, and teacher training needs.

TEACHING ACROSS

PROFICIENCY LEVELS

OBJECTIVES After reading this chapter, you will be able to:

- analyze the concept of language proficiency

- appreciate the difficulty of defining proficiency, especially in differentiating among what is commonly thought to be "beginning," "intermediate," and "advanced" levels

- recognize methodological differences among teaching classes of beginning, intermediate, and advanced students

- apply concepts of accuracy, fluency, comprehensibility, grammaticality, and sociolinguistic appropriateness to an understanding of proficiency

Hardly a teaching day goes by in this profession without someone referring to students' proficiency levels with the terms "beginning," "intermediate," or "advanced." And as long as Earth spins on its axis, I suppose, teachers will differ among themselves on just what those terms mean. At the American Language Institute of San Francisco State University, for example, what we call the "beginning" level consists of students who already may know a couple of hundred English words and are able to use a few common survival phrases. In some circles these students would be labeled "false beginners" as distinguished from "true beginners." The "advanced" level, on the other hand, is not as advanced as some of the ESL writing courses offered for credit in the same university's Department of English.

So, a certain sense of relativity must always be taken into account when these terms are used. What is beginning for some may not be for others. Certainly the language-teaching profession does not lay unique claim to such subjectivity. Consider, for example, how "Intermediate Algebra" might be variously interpreted according to the institution in which it is offered.

DEFINING PROFICIENCY LEVELS

Is there a standard set of guidelines by which these three mysterious terms may be uniformly understood? The answer is a qualified yes, in the form of the *ACTFL Proficiency Guidelines* (American Council on the Teaching of Foreign Languages, 1999). While textbooks and curricula do not by any means adhere to such guidelines universally, the guidelines nevertheless offer us a practical description of speaking, listening, reading, and writing proficiency at numerous gradations.

The *Guidelines,* produced by the American Council on the Teaching of Foreign Languages (ACTFL), are a recognized proficiency standard in many language-teaching circles. The current version of the *Guidelines* is historically related to what for many years was referred to as "FSI levels" of speaking proficiency. The FSI (Foreign Service Institute) levels, now referred to as "ILR" (Interagency Language Roundtable) levels in more formal research settings, represent points on an increasing scale of sophistication as determined by the FSI Oral Interview. The Oral Interview is a carefully designed set of structured tasks that elicit pronunciation; fluency and integrative ability; sociolinguistic and cultural knowledge; grammar; and vocabulary. The test-taker is judged to possess proficiency that falls into one of the following 11 different levels:

Level	Description
0	Unable to function in the spoken language.
0+	Able to satisfy immediate needs using rehearsed utterances.
1	Able to satisfy minimum courtesy requirements and maintain very simple face-to-face conversations on familiar topics.
1+	Able to initiate and maintain predictable face-to-face conversations and satisfy limited social demands.
2	Able to satisfy routine social demands and limited work requirements.
2+	Able to satisfy most work requirements with language usage that is often, but not always, acceptable and effective.
3	Able to speak the language with sufficient structural accuracy and vocabulary to participate effectively in most formal and informal conversations on practical, social, and professional topics.
3+	Often able to use the language to satisfy professional needs in a wide range of sophisticated and demanding tasks.
4	Able to use the language fluently and accurately on all levels normally pertinent to professional needs.
4+	Speaking proficiency is superior in all respects, usually equivalent to that of a well-educated, highly articulate native speaker.
5	Speaking proficiency is functionally equivalent to that of a highly articulate, well-educated native speaker and reflects the cultural standards of the country where the language is spoken.

The *ACTFL Proficiency Guidelines* were created to expand on the FSI/ILR levels so that listening, reading, and writing would also be included. The *Guidelines* have one other important difference: They are not connected with any one proficiency test, as the FSI/ILR levels are. Instead, they were created to guide any test-maker in the process of assessment. Today, numerous test designers utilize the *Guidelines* as a standard for assessment. While they were expressly not designed for assessing achievement in any one curriculum, the *Guidelines* can, when used with caution, provide a number of useful checkpoints for curriculum development and revision.

You will notice in the table of speaking guidelines (Table 7.1 on pages 114–118) that the term "novice" replaces the term "beginning" due to the difficulty of establishing a definitive beginning point in most language learners. For the distinction between what in ordinary conversation we might call "beginners" and "false beginners," the *Guidelines* offer the terms "novice-low" and "novice-mid." It is also important to note that the various levels of the speaking guidelines reprinted in Table 7.1 do *not* correspond to any one FSI level. In fact, in the introduction to the *Guidelines,* it is suggested that their "superior" level is "roughly equivalent to the ILR 3 range." Nevertheless, the *Guidelines* (presented here only for the one skill of speaking) can offer an informative overall picture of a range of proficiency in terms of assumed competencies at different levels. For other skills, you can visit the ACTFL Web site (http://www.actfl.org).

TEACHING BEGINNING LEVELS

Many teachers consider the beginning level of language instruction to be the most challenging. Since students at this level have little or no prior knowledge of the target language, the teacher (and accompanying techniques and materials) becomes a central determiner in whether students accomplish their goals. This can also be the most tangibly rewarding level for a teacher because the growth of students' proficiency is apparent in a matter of a few weeks.

At the beginning or even false-beginning level, your students have very little language "behind" them. You may therefore be tempted to go along with the popular misconception that the target language cannot be taught directly, that you will have to resort to a good deal of talking "about" the second language in the students' native language. Such is clearly not the case, as beginning language courses have demonstrated for many decades. But you do have to keep in mind that your students' capacity for taking in and retaining new words, structures, and concepts is limited. Foremost on your mind as a teacher should be the presentation of material in simple segments that don't overwhelm your students. Remember, they are just barely beginning!

The following 10 factors—and the words of advice accompanying each—will help you to formulate an approach to teaching beginners. As you adopt a theoretical stance on each factor, you will be able to design classroom techniques that are consistent with your approach.

1. Students' cognitive learning processes

In those first few days and even weeks of language learning, virtually all of the students' processing with respect to the second language itself is in a focal, controlled mode* (see *PLLT,* Chapter 10, for a review of McLaughlin's cognitive processes and some classroom applications). Therefore, you can expect to engage in plenty of repetition of a limited number of words, phrases, and sentences. Don't become frustrated if a considerable period of time goes by with little change in these learning modes.

Even in the first few days of class, however, you can coax your students into some peripheral processing by getting them to use practiced language for genuinely meaningful purposes. For example, getting information from a classmate whom a student does not know will require using newly learned language ("What's your name?" "Where do you live?"), but with a focus on the purposes to which the language is put, not on the forms of language. The forms themselves, although still controlled (limited in capacity), nevertheless move into a peripheral mode as students become immersed in the task of seeking genuine information.

2. The role of the teacher

Beginning students are highly dependent on the teacher for models of language, and so a teacher-centered or teacher-fronted classroom is appropriate for some of your classroom time. Students are able to initiate few questions and comments, so it is your responsibility to "keep the ball rolling." Still, your beginning level classes need not be devoid of a modicum of student-centered work. Pair work and group work (see Chapter 12) are effective techniques for taking students' focus off you as the center of attention and for getting them into an interactive frame of mind even at the most beginning level.

It follows that the degree of control of classroom time also leans strongly in the direction of the teacher at the beginning levels. In a second language context where instruction is carried out in the target language, virtually all of your class time will be teacher-controlled. Since students have no means, in the second language anyway, of controlling the class period, the onus is on you to plan topics, activity types, time-on-task, etc. As students gain in their proficiency, they will be able to initiate questions and comments of their own that may then occasionally shift the locus of control. In a foreign language situation, where your students speak the same native language (and you speak it as well), some negotiation might be possible in the native language, allowing for a small amount of student control (see #3 on page 118).

---

* A quick review of *PLLT* may remind you that controlled processing is common in any new skill where few bits of information can be managed at once. **Focal attention** is giving notice to something in particular: a language form, an attempted message, a person's physical appearance, a person's emotional state, etc. **Automatic processing** is the simultaneous management of a multitude of pieces of information. And **peripheral attention** refers to things that we give only incidental notice to.

Table 7.1. ACTFL Proficiency Guidelines–Speaking (ACTFL, 1999)

Superior Speakers at the Superior level are able to communicate in the language with accuracy and fluency in order to participate fully and effectively in conversations on a variety of topics in formal and informal settings from both concrete and abstract perspectives. They discuss their interests and special fields of competence, explain complex matters in detail, and provide lengthy and coherent narrations, all with ease, fluency, and accuracy. They explain their opinions on a number of topics of importance to them, such as social and political issues, and provide structured argument to support their opinions. They are able to construct and develop hypotheses to explore alternative possibilities. When appropriate, they use extended discourse without unnaturally lengthy hesitation to make their point, even when engaged in abstract elaborations. Such discourse, while coherent, may still be influenced by the Superior speakers' own language patterns, rather than those of the target language.

Superior speakers command a variety of interactive and discourse strategies, such as turn-taking and separating main ideas from supporting information through the use of syntactic and lexical devices, as well as intonational features such as pitch, stress and tone. They demonstrate virtually no pattern of error in the use of basic structures. However, they may make sporadic errors, particularly in low-frequency structures and in some complex high-frequency structures more common to formal speech and writing. Such errors, if they do occur, do not distract the native interlocutor or interfere with communication.

Advanced High Speakers at the Advanced-High level perform all Advanced-level tasks with linguistic ease, confidence and competence. They are able to consistently explain in detail and narrate fully and accurately in all time frames. In addition, Advanced-High speakers handle the tasks pertaining to the Superior level but cannot sustain performance at that level across a variety of topics. They can provide a structured argument to support their opinions, and they may construct hypotheses, but patterns of error appear. They can discuss some topics abstractly, especially those relating to their particular interests and special fields of expertise, but in general, they are more comfortable discussing a variety of topics concretely.

Advanced-High speakers may demonstrate a well-developed ability to compensate for an imperfect grasp of some forms or for limitations in vocabulary by the confident use of communicative strategies, such as paraphrasing, circumlocution, and illustration. They use precise vocabulary and intonation to express meaning and often show great fluency and ease of speech. However, when called on to perform the complex tasks associated with the Superior level over a variety of topics, their language will at times break down or prove inadequate, or they may avoid the task altogether, for example, by resorting to simplification through the use of description or narration in place of argument or hypothesis.

Advanced Mid Speakers at the Advanced-Mid level are able to handle with ease and confidence a large number of communicative tasks. They participate actively in most informal and some formal exchanges on a variety of concrete topics relating to work, school, home, and leisure activities, as well as to events of current, public, and personal interest or individual relevance.

Advanced-Mid speakers demonstrate the ability to narrate and describe in all major time frames (past, present, and future) by providing a full account, with good control of aspect, as they adapt flexibly to the demands of the conversation. Narration and description tend to be combined and interwoven to relate relevant and supporting facts in connected, paragraph-length discourse.

Advanced-Mid speakers can handle successfully and with relative ease the linguistic challenges presented by a complication or unexpected turn of events that occurs within the context of a routine situation or communicative task with which they are otherwise familiar. Communicative strategies such as circumlocution or rephrasing are often employed for this purpose. The speech of Advanced-Mid speakers performing Advanced-level tasks is marked by substantial flow. Their vocabulary is fairly extensive although primarily generic in nature, except in the case of a particular area of specialization or interest. Dominant language discourse structures tend to recede, although discourse may still reflect the oral paragraph structure of their own language rather than that of the target language.

Advanced-Mid speakers contribute to conversations on a variety of familiar topics, dealt with concretely, with much accuracy, clarity and precision, and they convey their intended message without misrepresentation or confusion. They are readily understood by native speakers unaccustomed to dealing with non-natives. When called on to perform functions or handle topics associated with the Superior level, the quality and/or quantity of their speech will generally decline. Advanced-Mid speakers are often able to state an opinion or cite conditions; however, they lack the ability to consistently provide a structured argument in extended discourse. Advanced-Mid speakers may use a number of delaying strategies, resort to narration, description, explanation or anecdote, or simply attempt to avoid the linguistic demands of Superior-level tasks.

Advanced Low

Speakers at the Advanced-Low level are able to handle a variety of communicative tasks, although somewhat haltingly at times. They participate actively in most informal and a limited number of formal conversations on activities related to school, home, and leisure activities and, to a lesser degree, those related to events of work, current, public, and personal interest or individual relevance.

Advanced-Low speakers demonstrate the ability to narrate and describe in all major time frames (past, present, and future) in paragraph length discourse, but control of aspect may be lacking at times. They can handle appropriately the linguistic challenges presented by a complication or unexpected turn of events that occurs within the context of a routine situation or communicative task with which they are otherwise familiar, though at times their discourse may be minimal for the level and strained. Communicative strategies such as rephrasing and circumlocution may be employed in such instances. In their narrations and descriptions, they combine and link sentences into connected discourse of paragraph length. When pressed for a fuller account, they tend to grope and rely on minimal discourse. Their utterances are typically not longer than a single paragraph. Structure of the dominant language is still evident in the use of false cognates, literal translations, or the oral paragraph structure of the speaker's own language rather than that of the target language.

While the language of Advanced-Low speakers may be marked by substantial, albeit irregular flow, it is typically somewhat strained and tentative, with noticeable self-correction and a certain grammatical roughness. The vocabulary of Advanced-Low speakers is primarily generic in nature.

Advanced-Low speakers contribute to the conversation with sufficient accuracy, clarity, and precision to convey their intended message without misrepresentation or confusion, and it can be understood by native speakers unaccustomed to dealing with non-natives, even though this may be achieved through repetition and restatement. When attempting to perform functions or handle topics associated with the Superior level, the linguistic quality and quantity of their speech will deteriorate significantly.

Intermediate High

Intermediate-High speakers are able to converse with ease and confidence when dealing with most routine tasks and social situations of the Intermediate level. They are able to handle successfully many uncomplicated tasks and social situations requiring an exchange of basic information related to work, school, recreation, particular interests and areas of competence, though hesitation and errors may be evident.

Intermediate-High speakers handle the tasks pertaining to the Advanced level, but they are unable to sustain performance at that level over a variety of topics. With some consistency, speakers at the Intermediate High level narrate and describe in major time frames using connected discourse of paragraph length. However, their performance of these Advanced-level tasks will exhibit one or more features of breakdown, such as the failure to maintain the narration or description semantically or syntactically in the appropriate major time frame, the disintegration of connected discourse, the misuse of cohesive devices, a reduction in breadth and appropriateness of vocabulary, the failure to successfully circumlocute, or a significant amount of hesitation.

Intermediate-High speakers can generally be understood by native speakers unaccustomed to dealing with non-natives, although the dominant language is still evident (e.g., use of code-switching, false cognates, literal translations, etc.), and gaps in communication may occur.

Intermediate Mid

Speakers at the Intermediate-Mid level are able to handle successfully a variety of uncomplicated communicative tasks in straightforward social situations. Conversation is generally limited to those predictable and concrete exchanges necessary for survival in the target culture; these include personal information covering self, family, home, daily activities, interests and personal preferences, as well as physical and social needs, such as food, shopping, travel and lodging.

Intermediate-Mid speakers tend to function reactively, for example, by responding to direct questions or requests for information. However, they are capable of asking a variety of questions when necessary to obtain simple information to satisfy basic needs, such as directions, prices and services. When called on to perform functions or handle topics at the Advanced level, they provide some information but have difficulty linking ideas, manipulating time and aspect, and using communicative strategies, such as circumlocution.

Intermediate-Mid speakers are able to express personal meaning by creating with the language, in part by combining and recombining known elements and conversational input to make utterances of sentence length and some strings of sentences. Their speech may contain pauses, reformulations and self-corrections as they search for adequate vocabulary and appropriate language forms to express themselves. Because of inaccuracies in their vocabulary and/or pronunciation and/or grammar and/or syntax, misunderstandings can occur, but Intermediate-Mid speakers are generally understood by sympathetic interlocutors accustomed to dealing with non-natives.

Intermediate Low

Speakers at the Intermediate-Low level are able to handle successfully a limited number of uncomplicated communicative tasks by creating with the language in straightforward social situations. Conversation is restricted to some of the concrete exchanges and predictable topics necessary for survival in the target language culture. These topics relate to basic personal information covering, for example, self and family, some daily activities and personal preferences, as well as to some immediate needs, such as ordering food and making simple purchases. At the Intermediate-Low level, speakers are primarily reactive and struggle to answer direct questions or requests for information, but they are also able to ask a few appropriate questions.

Intermediate-Low speakers express personal meaning by combining and recombining into short statements what they know and what they hear from their interlocutors. Their utterances are often filled with hesitancy and inaccuracies as they search for appropriate linguistic forms and vocabulary while attempting to give form to the message. Their speech is characterized by frequent pauses, ineffective reformulations and self-corrections. Their pronunciation, vocabulary and syntax are strongly influenced by their first language but, in spite of frequent misunderstandings that require repetition or rephrasing, Intermediate-Low speakers can generally be understood by sympathetic interlocutors, particularly by those accustomed to dealing with non-natives.

Novice High

Speakers at the Novice-High level are able to handle a variety of tasks pertaining to the Intermediate level, but are unable to sustain performance at that level. They are able to manage successfully a number of uncomplicated communicative tasks in straightforward social situations. Conversation is restricted to a few of the predictable topics necessary for survival in the target language culture, such as basic personal information, basic objects and a limited number of activities, preferences and immediate needs. Novice-High speakers respond to simple, direct questions or requests for information; they are able to ask only a very few formulaic questions when asked to do so.

Novice-High speakers are able to express personal meaning by relying heavily on learned phrases or recombinations of these and what they hear from their interlocutor. Their utterances, which consist mostly of short and sometimes incomplete sentences in the present, may be hesitant or inaccurate. On the other hand, since these utterances are frequently only expansions of learned material and stock phrases, they may sometimes appear surprisingly fluent and accurate. These speakers' first language may strongly influence their pronunciation, as well as their vocabulary and syntax when they attempt to personalize their utterances. Frequent misunderstandings may arise but, with repetition or rephrasing, Novice-High speakers can generally be understood by sympathetic interlocutors used to non-natives. When called on to handle simply a variety of topics and perform functions pertaining to the Intermediate level, a Novice-High speaker can sometimes respond in intelligible sentences, but will not be able to sustain sentence level discourse.

Novice Mid   Speakers at the Novice-Mid level communicate minimally and with difficulty by using a number of isolated words and memorized phrases limited by the particular context in which the language has been learned. When responding to direct questions, they may utter only two or three words at a time or an occasional stock answer. They pause frequently as they search for simple vocabulary or attempt to recycle their own and their interlocutor's words. Because of hesitations, lack of vocabulary, inaccuracy, or failure to respond appropriately, Novice-Mid speakers may be understood with great difficulty even by sympathetic interlocutors accustomed to dealing with non-natives. When called on to handle topics by performing functions associated with the Intermediate level, they frequently resort to repetition, words from their native language, or silence.

Novice Low   Speakers at the Novice-Low level have no real functional ability and, because of their pronunciation, they may be unintelligible. Given adequate time and familiar cues, they may be able to exchange greetings, give their identity, and name a number of familiar objects from their immediate environment. They are unable to perform functions or handle topics pertaining to the Intermediate level, and cannot therefore participate in a true conversational exchange.

3. Teacher talk

Your input in the class is crucial. All ears and eyes are indeed focused on you. Your own English needs to be clearly articulated. It is appropriate to slow your speech somewhat for easier student comprehension, but don't slow it so much that it loses its naturalness. And remember, you don't need to talk any louder to beginners than to advanced students if your articulation is clear. Use simple vocabulary and structures that are at or just slightly beyond their level.

Is it appropriate to use the students' native language? As noted above, in second language situations, especially multilingual classes, your use of a student's native language is seldom an issue. In foreign language situations, however, it becomes an option. It is important not to let your classes go to excess in the use of the students' native language. The rule of thumb here is usually to restrict classroom language to English unless some distinct advantage is gained by the use of their native language, and then only for very brief stretches of time. Examples of such advantages include

- negotiation of disciplinary and other management factors,
- brief descriptions of how to carry out a technique,
- brief explanations of grammar points,
- quick pointers on meanings of words that remain confusing after students have had a try at defining something themselves, and
- cultural notes and comments.

4. Authenticity of language

The language that you expose your students to should, according to principles of CLT discussed in Chapters 3 and 4, be authentic language; this is just as important at the beginning levels. Simple greetings and introductions, for example, are authentic and yet manageable. Make sure utterances are limited to short, simple phrases. At times such language may appear to be artificial because of all the repetition needed at this stage. Don't despair; your students will appreciate the opportunity to practice their new language.

5. Fluency and accuracy

Fluency is a goal at this level but only within limited utterance lengths. Fluency does not have to apply only to long utterances. The "flow" of language is important to establish, from the beginning, in reasonably short segments. Attention to accuracy should center on the particular grammatical, phonological, or discourse elements that are being practiced.

In teaching speaking skills, it is extremely important at this stage that you be very sensitive to students' need to practice freely and openly without fear of being corrected at every minor flaw. On the other hand, you need to correct some selected grammatical and phonological errors so that students don't fall into the trap of assuming that "no news is good news" (no correction implies perfection). Pronunciation work (on phonemes, phonemic patterns, intonation, rhythm, and stress) is very important at this stage. Neglecting phonological practice now may be at the expense of later fluency. Your job, of course, is to create the perfect balance. Chapter 17 will deal in more detail with this balance.

6. Student creativity

The ultimate goal of learning a language is to be able to comprehend and produce it in *unrehearsed* situations, which demand both receptive and productive creativity. But at the beginning level, students can be creative only within the confines of a highly controlled repertoire of language. Innovation will come later when students get more language under their control.

7. Techniques (activities, procedures, tasks)

Short, simple techniques must be used. Some mechanical techniques are appropriate—choral repetition and other drilling, for example. A good many teacher-initiated questions dominate at this level, followed only after some time by an increase in simple student-initiated questions. Group and pair activities are excellent techniques as long as they are structured and clearly defined with specific objectives. A variety of techniques is important because of limited language capacity.

8. Listening and speaking goals

Figure 7.1 on pages 120–123 is a reproduction of the Scope and Sequence chart for Level 1 of *New Vistas* (Brown, Aebarelli-Siegfried, Savage, & Shafiei, 2000). Notice that the listening and speaking functions for beginners are meaningful and authentic communication tasks. They are limited more by grammar, vocabulary, and length of utterance than by communicative function. It is surprising how many language functions can be achieved with very uncomplicated language.

Figure 7.1. Scope and Sequence chart

Scope and Sequence

UNIT	TOPICS	FUNCTIONS	GRAMMAR
1	**Meeting People** Introductions Greetings Leave-takings	• Introducing self and other people • Exchanging personal information • Asking for and giving a spelling	• Subject pronouns • Present tense: *Be* • Contractions • *Wh-* questions
2	**Personal Information** Numbers: Telephone Numbers & Addresses The Classroom	• Identifying objects in the classroom • Giving and performing commands • Confirming and correcting • Apologizing and thanking	• Indefinite articles *a, an* • Demonstratives: *this, that* • *Yes/No* questions; short answers
3	**The Family** Family Relationships Physical Characteristics	• Identifying and describing people • Exchanging information	• Adjectives used to describe people • Present tense: *has/have*
4	**The Home and the Neighborhood** The Classified Ads The Neighborhood	• Getting details from an ad • Ask for and give locations	• *yes/no* questions; short answers • *There isn't, There aren't* • Prepositions of location • Information questions
5	**Ongoing Concerns** The Time Clothes Colors Seasons/Weather	• Asking and telling time • Asking for and describing what people are doing and are wearing • Talking about the weather/seasons	• Present continuous: verb + *-ing* • Plural nouns: regular *vs.* irregular plural nouns • Adjectives: position

Scope and Sequence

PRONUNCIATION	COMMUNICATION SKILLS	
	Listening and Speaking	Reading and Writing
• Falling Intonation in greetings and leave-takings	• Introduce yourself and other people • Exchange information • Ask for and give a spelling • Listen for information	• Read for specific information • Make a class poster • Introduce oneself in writing
• Short /ɪ/ vs. long /i/	• Say and use numbers • Ask for the word in English of an object • Correct given information • Apologize	• Find information in phone and building directories • Make an address book
• Word stress	• Describe people • Listen for information • Get someone's attention • Ask someone to repeat	• Identify family members • Fill out a questionnaire • Write a paragraph
• Rising and falling intonation	• Ask about an apartment • Describe an apartment and the neighborhood • Describe locations	• Read real-estate ads • Write a simple ad • Write a description of one's neighborhood
• Word stress e.g., *thirteen* vs. *thirty*	• Ask and give the time • Talk about the weather and the seasons • Talk about on going actions • Talk about clothes and colors	• Read a weather map • Explain in writing one's opinion • Write a postcard

(Continued)

Scope and Sequence

UNIT	TOPICS	FUNCTIONS	GRAMMAR
6	**Daily Routines** Daily Routines The Calendar Ordinal Numbers	• Talking about routines • Negotiating schedules • Talking about holidays	• Simple present tense • Affirmative and negative statements with *do/does* • Adverbs of frequency
7	**Food and Food Shopping** Quantities The Supermarket Recipes	• Talking about availability of things • Asking for locations in a supermarket • Following a recipe	• Count and noncount nouns • *Some* and *any* • *How much* and *how many*
8	**Travel and Leisure** Transportation TV and Movies	• Asking for transportation information • Talking about likes and dislikes	• *Too* and *either* in compound structures • Adverbs of manner • Clauses: *before, after,* and *then*
9	**Skills and Abilities** The Interview The Application Form Skills and Abilities	• Responding to interview questions • Talking about ability • Asking for confirmation • Filling out an application form	• *Can* • Affirmative and negative statements • *How often;* frequency adverbs
10	**Past Activities and Future Plans** The Weekend The Immediate Future	• Talking about past activities • Ordering in a restaurant • Making a suggestion • Talking about future plans	• The simple past: *Yes/No* questions • *Wh-* questions • The future with *going to*

Scope and Sequence

PRONUNCIATION	COMMUNICATION SKILLS	
	Listening and Speaking	Reading and Writing
• Contrasting sounds: /t/ vs. /θ/	• Talk about daily routines • Talk about holidays	• Read for details • Write about daily routines • Write a short paragraph
• /a/ vs. /ə/, *e.g., cop* vs. *cup*	• Ask about availability • Ask for locations in a supermarket • Ask about prices • Discuss plans for a party	• Read advertisements • Follow directions in a recipe • Determine sequence in recipe instructions
• Questions with *or*	• Ask for information • Talk about likes/dislikes • Listen to recorded messages • Discuss use of leisure	• Read travel signs • Write a series of actions in proper sequence • Read entertainment schedules
• Rising intonation in *yes/no* questions	• Respond to interview questions • Talk about abilities • Discuss a person's suitability for a job	• Complete an application form • Create a Help Wanted ad • Read a performance review
• Final *-ed* sounds: /t/, /d/, /ɪd/	• Talk about past activities • Order in a restaurant • Make a suggestion, invite someone • Decline an invitation • Talk about future plans	• Read a menu • Create a personal time line

9. Reading and writing goals

A glance at the Scope and Sequence chart in Figure 7.1 demonstrates typical goals for a beginning level course: reading and writing topics are confined to brief but nevertheless real-life written material. Advertisements, forms, and recipes are grist for the beginner's reading mill, while written work may involve forms, lists, and simple notes and letters. The most important contextual factor that you should bear in mind in teaching reading and writing to beginners is their literacy level in their own native language, an issue that is covered in Chapter 18.

10. Grammar

Whether a curriculum or textbook is billed as functional, communicative, structural, or whatever, grammar and grammar sequencing is an issue. As the charts show, a typical beginning level will deal at the outset with very simple verb forms, personal pronouns, definite and indefinite articles, singular and plural nouns, and simple sentences, in a progression of grammatical topics from simple to complex. (See Chapter 22 for more information on grammar sequencing in textbooks and curricula.)

Whether or not you choose to overtly "explain" grammar in the classroom is another issue (also dealt with in Chapter 22). If you are teaching EFL (in a non-English-speaking country) and your students all speak the same native language, you may profit from occasionally using their native language to explain simple grammatical points. In ESL situations, where you usually rely only on English in the classroom, grammatical explanations of any complexity would at this level overwhelm the students. Therefore, an inductive approach to grammar with suitable examples and patterns will be more effective.

TEACHING INTERMEDIATE LEVELS

Now, turn your attention to that vague curricular territory that we call *intermediate,* where students have progressed beyond novice stages to an ability to sustain basic communicative tasks, to establish some minimal fluency, to deal with a few unrehearsed situations, to self-correct on occasion, to use a few compensatory strategies, and generally to "get along" in the language beyond mere survival. The picture changes somewhat. Your role and the students' capacities change. Consider the same 10 factors.

1. Students' cognitive learning processes

At the intermediate stage some automatic processing has taken hold. Phrases, sentences, structures, and conversational rules have been practiced and are increasing in number, forcing the mental processes to automatize. I like to think of automaticity as the placing of elements of language into the "hard drive" of our neurological computers. Our immediately controlled "desktops" (limited in capacity) are too small to contain all the information we need. One of your principal goals at this level is to get students to continue to automatize, to continue to allow the bits and pieces of language that might clutter the mind to be relegated to automaticity. There, in their linguistic hard drives, those bits and pieces are beneath the surface, as it were, yet readily available for immediate (automatic) use whenever needed.

2. The role of the teacher

You are no longer the only initiator of language. Students should be encouraged to ask questions, make comments, and negotiate certain options in learning where appropriate. More student–student interaction can now take place in pairs, small groups, and whole-class activity.

Learner-centered work is now possible for more sustained lengths of time as students are able to maintain topics of discussion and focus. By its very nature, the intermediate level is richly diverse; that diversity can work to your advantage with carefully designed cooperative activities that capitalize on differences among students. Don't set equal expectations for all students, however, since abilities, especially speaking abilities, can vary widely.

3. Teacher talk

Most of your oral production can be sustained at a natural pace, as long as your articulation is clear. Teacher talk should not occupy the major proportion of a class hour; otherwise, you are probably not giving students enough opportunity to talk. You should be using less of the native language of the learners at this level, but some situations may still demand it.

4. Authenticity of language

At this level students sometimes become overly concerned about grammatical correctness and may want to wander into esoteric discussions of grammatical details. This penchant for analysis might get them too far afield from authentic, real language. Make sure they stay on track.

5. Fluency and accuracy

The dichotomy between fluency and accuracy is a crucial concern here, more so than at either of the other ends of the proficiency spectrum. Some students are likely to become overly concerned about accuracy, possibly berating themselves for the mistakes they make and demanding constant corrections for every slip-up. Others may slide into a self-satisfied rut in which they actually become quite fluent, in the technical sense of the term, but in which they become very difficult to comprehend. Be on the lookout for both types of student and be prepared to offer individualized attention to each.

In general, fluency exercises (saying or writing a steady flow of language for a short period of time without any self- or other-correction at all) are a must at this level. They help to get students over the hump of always having to say or write everything absolutely correctly. You want them in due course of time to go through the "breakthrough" stage of language learning, often thought of as a stage after which a learner looks back and says, "Wow! I just carried on a whole conversation without thinking about my grammar!" A big part of your task with most students is to maintain their flow with just enough attention to error to keep them growing.

6. Student creativity

The fact that some of this new language is now under control gives rise to more opportunities for the student to be creative. Interlanguage errors such as

> Does John can sing?
>
> What means this?
>
> I must to make a lot of money.

are a good indication of the creative application of a system within the learner's mind. Try to recognize this form of creativity as a positive sign of language development and of the internalization of a coherent system. Students are also becoming more capable of applying their classroom language to unrehearsed situations. In EFL settings those situations may be more difficult to find, but through the various forms of media and the written word, applications to the real world, heretofore unrehearsed in the classroom, are available and should be encouraged.

7. Techniques

Because of the increasing language capacities of your students, techniques can increase in complexity. Common interactive techniques for intermediates include chain stories, surveys and polls, paired interviews, group problem solving, role plays, storytelling, and many others.

8. Listening and speaking goals

The linguistic complexity of communicative listening-speaking goals increases steadily. Along with the creation of novel utterances, students can participate in short conversations, ask and answer questions, find alternative ways to convey meaning, solicit information from others, and more. The functions themselves may not be intrinsically more complex, but the forms they use are. (For more information on teaching listening and speaking, see Chapters 18 and 19.)

9. Reading and writing goals

Increasing complexity in terms of length, grammar, and discourse now characterizes reading material as students read paragraphs and short, simple stories and begin to use skimming and scanning skills. Writing is similarly more sophisticated. (For more information on teaching reading and writing, see Chapters 20 and 21.)

10. Grammar

Grammar topics such as progressive verb tenses and clauses typify intermediate level teaching. Students can benefit from small doses of short, simple explanations of points in English. Whether through English or the native language medium, such overt attention to "sore spots" in grammar can, in fact, be exceedingly helpful at this stage. Students have been known to flounder in a sea of inductivity until one cogent tip from a teacher sets them back on a straight course. I once encountered a student who, for too many months (or years?), when referring to past events would say things like

> She can kept her child.

> He must paid the insurance [premium].

One day, a simple explanation from his teacher about modal auxiliaries in the past tense "cured" him when all the outright corrections in the world hadn't seemed to make an impact.

Keep grammatical metalanguage to an ideal minimum at this level; otherwise, your students will become English grammarians instead of English speakers. Remember, you are interested in grammar because that is where some of your training has been, but you don't need to make budding Ph.D.'s in linguistics out of your students! Overt grammatical explanation has its place, in the wings, if you will, as a prompter of sorts, but not as the dominant focus of student attention.

TEACHING ADVANCED LEVELS

As students move up the developmental ladder, getting closer and closer to their goals, developing fluency along with a greater degree of accuracy, able to handle virtually any situation in which target language use is demanded, they become "advanced" students. Toward the top of this ladder is what the ACTFL *Guidelines* describe as the "superior" level, which is not yet equivalent to an educated native-speaker level, but implies a high command of language for both social and professional purposes. Few if any ESL classes are designed for the superior level, so in order to be more in keeping with reality, we will simply focus on what the *Guidelines* describe as the "advanced" level.

1. Students' cognitive learning processes

As competence in language continues to build, students can realize the full spectrum of processing, assigning larger and larger chunks to automatic modes and gaining the confidence to put the formal structures of language on the periphery so that focal attention may be given to the interpretation and negotiation of meaning and to the conveying of thoughts and feelings in interactive communication. Some aspects of language, of course, need focal attention for minor corrections, refinement, and other "tinkering"; otherwise, teachers would almost be unnecessary. So your task at this level is to assist in the ongoing attempt to automatize language and in the delicate interplay between focal and peripheral attention to selected aspects of language.

2. The role of the teacher

On the surface, your job may appear easier with advanced students; you can sit back and let their questions and self-generated curiosity take over. In reality, the independence that students have acquired must be cleverly channeled into classroom routines that benefit most of the students most of the time. No mean task! The most common occurrence in advanced level teaching is that your class runs away with itself and you are left with only a quarter or half your plans fulfilled. So, while you want to take advantage of the self-starting personalities in your class, orderly plans are still important. A directive role on your part can create effective learning opportunities even within a predominantly learner-centered classroom.

3. Teacher talk

Natural language at natural speed is a must at this level. Make sure your students are challenged by your choice of vocabulary, structures, idioms, and other language features. But, after all, they are still learning the language, so remember that they have not yet turned into native speakers. The amount of teacher talk should be commensurate with the type of activity. Make sure your students have ample opportunities to produce language so that your role as a provider of feedback takes prominence. For some of your students, this is the last chance to benefit from informed, systematic feedback on their performance; from here on out, they will be "out there" where people, out of politeness or respect, rarely give corrections.

Very little, if any, reliance on the students' native language is now justified. Discipline, explanations, and other more complex language functions can be carried out in English. Occasionally, a teacher of an advanced class will resort to a word or two (a definition, for example) in the native language in order to help a student who is "stuck."

4. Authenticity of language

Everything from academic prose to literature to idiomatic conversation becomes a legitimate resource for the classroom. Virtually no authentic language material should be summarily disqualified at this stage. Certain restrictions may come to bear, depending on how advanced your class is, of course.

5. Fluency and accuracy

At this level most, if not all, of your students are "fluent" in that they have passed beyond the breakthrough stage and are no longer thinking about every word or structure they are producing or comprehending. A handful or two of problems still need attention. If errors are relatively rare, an occasional treatment from you or from peers may be quite helpful.

6. Student creativity

The joy of teaching at this level is in those moments of student performance when you know that they are now able to apply classroom material to real contexts beyond. Make sure that students keep their eyes fixed on those goals. Be ever wary of classroom activity that simply ends right there in the classroom.

7. Techniques

Techniques can now tap into a full range of sociolinguistic and pragmatic competencies. Typical activities include group debates and argumentation, and complex role plays. Students also benefit from scanning and skimming reading material, determining and questioning author's intent, and writing essays and critiques. Often at this level students have specific purposes for which they are planning to use English. Focus on those purposes as much as possible.

8. Listening and speaking goals

At this level students can focus more carefully on all the sociolinguistic and pragmatic nuances of language. The teacher needs to be on the lookout for common areas needing work and to guide students accordingly as they fine-tune their production and comprehension in terms of register, style, the status of the interlocutor, the specific context of a conversational exchange, turn-taking, topic nomination and termination, topic-changing, and culturally conditioned language constraints.

9. Reading and writing goals

Reading and writing skills similarly progress closer and closer to native-speaker competence as students learn more about such things as critical reading, the role of schemata in interpreting written texts, and how to write a document related to one's profession (laboratory reports, records of experimental research findings, etc.).

10. Grammar

The concern at the intermediate level for basic grammatical patterns now graduates beyond some of the elements of Level 4 in Figure 7.1 to functional forms, to sociolinguistic and pragmatic phenomena, and to strategic competence (see *PLLT,* Chapter 10). Linguistic metalanguage may now serve a more useful role as students perceive its relevance to refining their language. Your classes need not become saturated with language about language, but well-targeted deductive grammar has its place.

☆   ☆   ☆   ☆   ☆

You have now had a chance to contemplate quite a number of variables that change as you teach lower or higher levels of proficiency. The age and proficiency variables are two extremely important issues to incorporate into any attempt to plan and conduct language lessons. Chapter 8 will introduce more contextual variables that come to bear on decisions that you make when you teach in a classroom.

TOPICS FOR DISCUSSION, ACTION, AND RESEARCH

[Note: (I) Individual work; (G) group or pair work; (C) whole-class discussion.]

1. (I) Look again at the FSI levels (p. 111) and the *ACTFL Proficiency Guidelines* (Table 7.1 on pages 114–118). For a foreign language you know (or English, if it is a second language for you), try a quick self-assessment using the two scales. How confident do you feel about your self-rating? If someone else in your class knows your ability in this second language, ask them to place you on the scales, then see if you agree.

2. (G/C) Ask the class to imagine they have been asked to do an oral interview of a speaker of English as a second language. Direct small groups to collaborate to design a format and specific questions to include in such an interview so that one could determine an FSI and/or ACTFL level of the learner. After groups have compared formats, set up a role-played interview for selected students to perform for the rest of the class, perhaps in a language other than English.

3. (I) Think of several different foreign language classes that you're familiar with, preferably ranging from beginning to advanced levels. Use the ACTFL speaking guidelines to determine the level of each class. Are the *Guidelines* sufficient? What would you need to add?

4. (G) Ask groups to discuss how one would approach a class in which there are true beginners as well as "false" beginners. How would one keep the latter challenged without overwhelming the former? Have groups share their ideas with the rest of the class.

5. (C) Review the McLaughlin model in *PLLT*, Chapter 10, especially Table 10.2 in that chapter, listing on the board some classroom examples of each of the four cells in the model. Ask students to try to come up with some additional techniques that are controlled with respect to language forms. Then solicit some techniques in which students are automatically attending to language forms. Discuss where you would place each technique (both the ones given in the table and the added ones) on the scale ranging from beginning to advanced levels.

6. (G) It was noted on page 113 that in some EFL situations, teachers might "negotiate" certain elements of classroom practices with students. Ask pairs to identify some classroom contexts and to figure out some specific examples of negotiation. How do those differ, depending on proficiency level? For example, at the very beginning level, what form does negotiation take and how does that differ from negotiation at an advanced level?

7. (I) Can fluency be practiced at the very beginning level? Think about a foreign language class you have taken. Could you have produced anything you would call fluency? If not, or if only very little, at what stage would you say a fluency goal becomes feasible?

8. (G) Ten criteria were offered in this chapter for considering differences across proficiency levels. Divide the class into small groups and assign a different criterion to each group. Have them (a) note differences across proficiency levels and (b) illustrate each level with a specific classroom example. Groups will then share their thoughts with the rest of the class.

9. (G/C) Ask groups, in multiples of three, to design a mini-lesson of about 15 minutes (see Chapter 10 for some guidelines on lesson planning) that teaches students the function of requesting information in the context of transportation (tickets, timetables, departure times, etc.). Group A will design a mini-lesson for beginners; Group B, an intermediate lesson; Group C, an advanced lesson. Groups will then share their designs and discuss differences.

FOR YOUR FURTHER READING

American Council on the Teaching of Foreign Languages. (1999). *ACTFL proficiency guidelines—speaking.* Hastings-on-Hudson, NY. Author available online at http://www.actfl.org

These Guidelines *describe proficiency levels for all four skills: speaking, listening, writing, and reading. They are available at the above referenced Web site: Go to "publications" and click on "proficiency guidelines." The* Guidelines *for one of the four skills, speaking, are reprinted in Table 7.1, in this chapter.*

New ways in teaching series. Alexandria, VA: Teachers of English to Speakers of Other Languages.

TESOL's New Ways *series is a set of practical reference guides for teachers. A broad range of titles include teaching listening, speaking, reading, writing, grammar, and other topics. Each book consists of many different activities and each activity is indexed for age, skill area, and proficiency level (e.g., beginning+, intermediate, etc.).*

Christison, M. (2005). *Multiple intelligences and language learning.* San Francisco: Alta Book Center Publishers.

This book was referenced in Chapter 3, as it offers many activities in each of the multiple intelligences. I include it here as recommended reading because each of the activities is indexed for proficiency level, and a glance at those activities can give you a good idea of how methodology varies according to such levels.

CHAPTER 8

SOCIOCULTURAL, POLITICAL,

AND INSTITUTIONAL CONTEXTS

OBJECTIVES After reading this chapter, you will be able to:

- identify sociopolitical and institutional variables that affect how you would design and carry out a lesson or course

- appreciate the nuances of culture, identity, ethnicity, and situational politics that are deeply ingrained in students' minds and emotions

- evaluate the different factors involved in teaching in a "second" language situation and a "foreign" language situation

- develop a position on the advantages and disadvantages of native and nonnative English-speaking teachers

- understand how systems, regulations, and customs within an educational institution can affect your approach to teaching

Age and proficiency are two major contextual variables that will affect every aspect of your lesson or curriculum. They may, in fact, be the most important variables. But another cluster of factors also emerges for the language teacher: sociocultural, political, and institutional contexts, without consideration of which your classroom lessons may miss their mark. These domains intertwine in such a way that it is sometimes impossible to disentangle them and examine one without considering the other. Culture underlies every human being's emotion and cognition; governments, politics, and policies are equally powerful influences on our behavior; and finally, our educational institutions are products of culture and policy, and indeed are often microcosms of one's sociopolitical milieu.

While this chapter will not attempt to treat all such issues in detail, they are nevertheless important background variables to consider whenever you step into a language classroom.

CULTURAL CONTEXTS

Culture is a way of life. It is the context within which we exist, think, feel, and relate to others. It is the "glue" that binds a group of people together. It's our collective identity, our "blueprint" (Larson & Smalley, 1972, p. 39) that guides our behavior in a community. It makes us sensitive to matters of status, and helps us know what others expect of us and what will happen if we do not live up to their expectations. It's also dynamic, changing, situational, and at the same time, relatively stable (Matsumoto, 2000).

Culture also establishes for each person a context of cognitive and affective behavior, a template for personal and social existence. We tend to perceive reality within the context of our own culture, a reality that we have "created," and therefore not necessarily a reality that is empirically defined. Although the opportunities for world travel in the last several decades have increased markedly, there is still a tendency for us to believe that our own reality is the "correct" perception. Misunderstandings are therefore likely to occur between members of different cultures.

It should be obvious, then, that culture is highly important in the learning of a second language. A language is a part of a culture, and a culture is a part of a language. The two are intricately interwoven so that one cannot separate them without losing the significance of either language or culture. The acquisition of a second language, except for specialized, instrumental acquisition (as may be the case, say, in acquiring a reading knowledge of a language for examining scientific texts), is also the acquisition of a second culture. (For a more detailed treatment of culture, consult *PLLT,* Chapter 7.)

How does an understanding of the relationship of language to culture affect your own teaching? The possibilities are almost endless. Whether you're teaching ESL (in an "inner circle" country where English is the dominant language) or EFL (in an outer or expanding circle country), cultural factors affect you. In ESL contexts, your students are usually "guests" from other countries learning both a new language and a new culture simultaneously; in EFL contexts your students are in their home culture attempting to learn a language imbued with foreign cultural connotations. Those cultural connotations will be discussed in the next section.

For the moment, however, consider the following guidelines on accounting for cultural issues in your classroom:

1. A student's cultural identity is often a deeply seated bundle of emotions. Practice empathy as you relate to your students in cultural matters: behavior patterns and expectations; expected relationship to authority, family, and peers; ambiguity tolerance, and openness to new ideas and ways of thinking; students' attitudes toward their own and the L2 culture; their view of individualism versus collectivism; linguistic conventions of politeness, formality, and other sociopragmatic factors.
2. Recognize the cultural connotations and nuances of English and of the first language of your students. Capitalize on them in your teaching.
3. Use your classroom as an opportunity to educate your students about other cultures and help them to see that no one culture is "better" than another. Practice in words and deed your respect for your students' deeply ingrained emotions that stem from their cultural schemata.

4. As cultural differences emerge, help your students to appreciate and celebrate diversity. Especially in an ESL context where students in the same class may represent many different cultures, try to make your classroom a model of openness, tolerance, and respect.

SECOND AND FOREIGN LANGUAGE CONTEXTS

In some of our professional musing about teaching and learning, we interchange the terms **second** and **foreign** in referring to English language teaching. (See *PLLT*, Chapter 7, for a discussion of these two terms.) But some caution is warranted, particularly in relation to a curriculum or a lesson, because (a) the difference between the two is significant, and (b) this dichotomy has been overgeneralized in recent years.

To distinguish operationally between a second and a foreign language context, think of what is going on outside your classroom door. Once your students leave your class, which language will they hear in the hallways or, in case you are in the foreign language department hallway, out on the sidewalks and in the stores? **Second** language learning contexts are those in which the classroom target language is readily available out there. Teaching English in the United States or Australia clearly falls into this (ESL) category. **Foreign** language contexts are those in which students do not have ready-made contexts for communication beyond their classroom. They may be obtainable through language clubs, special media opportunities, books, or an occasional tourist, but efforts must be made to create such opportunities. Teaching English in Japan or Morocco or Thailand is almost always a context of English as a foreign language (EFL).

The seemingly clear dichotomy between ESL and EFL, however, has been considerably muddied in recent years with the increasing use of English worldwide for a variety of purposes (Nayar, 1997). First, ESL contexts vary from an American or British context, where monolingual native speakers abound, to countries such as India or Singapore, where English is a widely used second language for education, government, and commerce, to Scandinavian countries, where English has no official status but is commonly spoken by virtually every educated person. Likewise, in countries where a language might be quickly judged as foreign (for instance, Spanish or Chinese in the United States, English in Japan), learners may find readily available potential for authentic use of the language in such venues as indigenous language communities and the media (Internet, TV, film).

With that fair warning, it is still useful to consider the pedagogical implications for a *continuum* of contexts ranging from high-visibility, ready access to the target language outside the language classroom to no access beyond the classroom door. In a typical second language context, your students have a tremendous advantage. They have an instant "laboratory" available 24 hours a day. I often remind my students studying ESL at the American Language Institute that their classroom hours (about 25 hours a week) are only a fraction of their language-learning hours. After subtracting hours spent sleeping, they have more than 80 additional hours a week of opportunities to learn and practice English!

When you plan a lesson or curriculum in a context that falls into the **second** language category, students can capitalize on numerous opportunities. Here are some ways to seize this "ESL advantage":

- Give homework that involves a specific speaking task with a person outside the classroom, listening to a radio or TV program, reading a newspaper article, writing a letter to a store or a charity.
- Encourage students to seek out opportunities for practice.
- Encourage students to seek corrective feedback from others.
- Have students keep a log or diary of their extra-class learning.
- Plan and carry out field trips (to a museum, for example).
- Arrange a social "mixer" with native English speakers.
- Invite speakers into your classroom.

Communicative language teaching in what we might broadly categorize as an EFL context is clearly a greater challenge for students and teachers. Often, intrinsic motivation is a big issue, since students may have difficulty in seeing the relevance of learning English. Their immediate use of the language may seem far removed from their own circumstances, and classroom hours may be the only part of the day when they are exposed to English. Therefore, the language that you present, model, elicit, and treat takes on great importance. If your class meets for, say, only 90 minutes a week, which represents a little more than 1 percent of their waking hours, think of what students need to accomplish!

Can students learn English in an EFL setting? (or French in an "FFL" setting?) The answer is obviously yes because many people have done so. Here are some guidelines to help you compensate for the lack of ready communicative situations outside the classroom.

- Use class time for optimal authentic language input and interaction.
- Don't waste class time on work that can be done as homework.
- Provide regular motivation-stimulating activities.
- Help students to see genuine uses for English in their own lives.
- Play down the role of tests and emphasize more intrinsic factors.
- Provide plenty of extra-class learning opportunities, such as assigning an English-speaking movie, having them listen to an English-speaking TV or radio program, getting an English-speaking conversation partner, doing outside reading (news magazines, books), writing a journal or diary, in English, on their learning process.
- Encourage the use of learning strategies outside class.
- Form a language club and schedule regular activities.

ENGLISH AS AN INTERNATIONAL LANGUAGE

Closely related to the ESL/EFL distinction is the phenomenon of the role of internationalized varieties of English (see *PLLT,* Chapter 7). As English takes on more and more of a second language role in a country (such as in Singapore, for example), there is a greater likelihood of the growth of a nativized variety of English in that country. A good deal of research has been carried out on the "Indianization" of English (Kachru, 1992), with implications for notions of acceptability and standardization in other countries like the Philippines, Singapore, or Nigeria. Two basic issues for English teachers have emerged (Kachru, 2005; McKay, 2002):

1. English is increasingly being used as a tool for interaction among nonnative speakers. Well over one-half of the one billion English speakers of the world learned English as a second (or foreign) language. Most English language teachers across the globe are nonnative English speakers, which means that the norm is not monolingualism, but bilingualism.
2. English is not frequently learned as a tool for understanding and teaching U.S. or British cultural values. Instead, English has become a tool for international communication in transportation, commerce, banking, tourism, technology, diplomacy, and scientific research.

This multiplication of varieties of English poses some practical concerns for the teacher. One of those concerns is the issue of grammaticalness and correctness. What standard do you accept in your classroom? The practical issue boils down to the need for your open acceptance of the prevailing variety of English in use in the country where you're teaching, be it India, Nigeria, or the Philippines. It is certainly not necessary to think of English as a language whose cultural identity can lie only with countries like the United States, the United Kingdom, or New Zealand. Your students will no doubt be more interested in the practical, nonstigmatized uses of English in various occupational fields in their own country than in imitating American or British English.

If you're not teaching in a country whose people use a widely accepted variety of English, you will still, no doubt, find that your teaching must keep pace with the new pragmatism. Standards of grammaticalness and of pronunciation may well need to be viewed in terms of the practice of natives who are educated, proficient English speakers. In Japan, for example, "Japanized" forms of English are becoming more widely accepted by English specialists. Your own pronunciation, especially, may not be "perfectly nativelike" if you yourself are a nonnative English speaker (see the next section here for further comments). The goals that you set for your students may therefore more wisely be goals of clear, unambiguous pronunciation of English phonology.

Even if you are teaching English in what Kachru (1992) called **inner circle** countries (United States, United Kingdom, Canada, Australia, and New Zealand), you are well advised to base your judgments of the acceptability of students' production on the ultimate practical uses to which they will put the language: survival, social, occupational, academic, and technical uses. In a city like San Francisco, for example, we hear many varieties of English. On one occasion, as I interviewed a prospective ESL teacher, I concluded from her excellent but "Hong Kong-ized" variety of English that she was originally from Hong Kong. Upon asking her, I discovered she was a native San Franciscan!

NONNATIVE ENGLISH-SPEAKING TEACHERS

The foregoing discussion unavoidably leads into an issue that has been and continues to be debated in language-teaching circles: How important is it that a teacher of a language be a "native" speaker of that language? Take a look at the employment ads for language schools in newspapers in Taipei, Seoul, São Paulo, or any other city you choose, and you will find that at least 9 out of 10 ads ask for "native speakers only." The assumption, of course, is that a native speaker will provide a "correct" model of English. And as George Braine pointed out (1999), in such a job market, qualifications, ability, and experience are of little help for nonnative English-speakers. What's wrong with this picture?

For many decades the English language-teaching profession assumed that **native English-speaking teachers** (**NESTs**), by virtue of their superior model of oral production, comprised the ideal English language teacher. Then, Medgyes (1994), among others (Braine, 1999; Higgins, 2003; McArthur, 2001), showed in their research that **nonnative English-speaking teachers** (**NNESTs**) offer as many if not more inherent advantages. Not only are multiple varieties of English now considered legitimate and acceptable, but also teachers who have actually gone through the process of learning English possess distinct advantages over native speakers.

As we move into a new paradigm in which the concepts of native and nonnative *speaker* become less relevant, it is perhaps more appropriate to think in terms of the proficiency level of a *user* of a language. Speaking is one of four skills and may not deserve in all contexts to be elevated to the sole criterion for proficiency. So, with Murray (2006), Park (2006), Kachru (2005), Kamhi-Stein (2004), McKay (2002), and others, we see that the profession is better served by considering a person's communicative proficiency across the four skills. Teachers of English, regardless of their own variety of English, can then be judged accordingly, and in turn, their pedagogical training and experience can occupy focal attention.

What are the implications of the NEST versus NNEST issue for your teaching? Consider a few possibilities here:

1. NESTs are clearly and unequivocally *not* better teachers than NNESTs by virtue of their native language background. The most important qualification for a teaching position is *training* and *experience* in teaching English.
2. If you are a NNEST searching for a teaching position and you have training and experience, enter into interviews and application procedures with confidence, and capitalize on the *advantages* you bring to such a position over a NEST.
3. Try to dissuade any employers/administrators you know from insisting on native speakers as their primary criterion for employment. Try to show these managers that there are a number of legitimate varieties of world Englishes, and that the native-speaker model is outmoded in today's world.
4. If you are a NNEST and are now teaching English, and you feel you haven't quite yet reached a point of "satisfaction" in your own oral production ability, you can quite easily compensate for any slight disadvantage you might have in oral production through the following: using recorded media to provide models of speakers of English as a native language along with models of other English varieties; openly admitting to your students that your own pronunciation may not correspond to that of a NS (native speaker); consulting with other highly proficient users of English if you are not sure about a phonological or discourse matter; capitalizing on your ability in the skills of listening, reading, and writing.
5. If you are either a NEST or a NNEST and are now teaching English, consider doing the following: informing your students about varieties of English *among* native speakers themselves (regional and social dialects); informing your students about worldwide varieties of English and not insisting on the NS model as the only possibility; being patient with students whose fragile egos may be disturbed by criticism that is too harsh.

LANGUAGE POLICY ISSUES

A further contextual consideration at play in your English teaching is a set of sociocultural—or perhaps better termed **sociopolitical**—issues: What *status* does your country give to English? Does your country have an official language *policy* toward English? How does this policy or status affect the motivation and purpose of your students? Let me offer an example of such a debate from the United States.

The status of English in the United States is certainly not in question from a sociological or educational point of view. However, for a number of years the United States has experienced a language policy debate. At one end of the spectrum is the *English Only* movement, which advocates the exclusive use of the English language for all educational and political contexts and that carries an implicit assumption that the use of one's "home" language will impede success in learning English. In contrast, *English Plus* advocates respond with programs in which home languages and cultures are valued by schools and other institutions, but in which ESL instruction is promoted and given appropriate funding. The debate has polarized many Americans. On one side are those who raise fears of "wild and motley throngs" of people from faraway lands creating a linguistic muddle. On the other extreme, linguistic minorities lobby for recognition in what they see as a white supremacist governmental mentality. Yet enrollment in ESL classes across the United States is higher than ever, as recently and not-so-recently arrived immigrants appreciate the importance of English proficiency for survival and adaptation in the home, the workplace, and the community.

Current sociopolitical trends in the United States have created a unique challenge for some college-level ESL programs. As more and more families immigrate into the United States, children are placed into elementary and secondary schools according to their achievement in their home countries. Without adequate ESL or bilingual instruction (see below), they may get a "social pass" from one grade to the next without demonstrating mastery of the subject matter or the English proficiency necessary for that mastery. After a few years, they find themselves in the upper secondary school grades and in college courses, but with language skills inadequate for academic demands. They have typically gained **BICS** (basic interpersonal communication skills) (see *PLLT,* Chapter 8) that enable them to get along well socially, but not the cognitive academic language proficiency (**CALP**) needed to progress through a college program. They fall into neither ESL nor native language course categories in most colleges, and so specialized courses are sometimes developed to meet their special needs. Such courses stress study skills, reading strategies, academic listening skills, and techniques for successful academic writing.

Language policies and social climates may dictate the status accorded to native and second languages, which can, in turn, positively or negatively affect attitudes and eventual success in language learning. Two commonly used terms characterize the status of one's native language in a society where a second language is learned. A native language is referred to as **subtractive** if it is considered to be detrimental to the learning of a second language. In some regions of the United States, for example, Spanish may be thought to be sociopolitically less desirable than English. A native Spanish-speaking child, sensing these societal attitudes, may feel ashamed of Spanish (or in some cases the parents feel ashamed), and the child must conquer those feelings along with learning English. **Additive** bilingualism is found where the native language is held in prestige by the community or society. Children learning English in Quebec, for example, are proud of their native French language and traditions and can therefore approach the second language more positively.

Most EFL programs are additive since the native language is the accepted norm. Moreover, as the foremost international language, English is usually valued highly as a tool for upward mobility. But in many countries English is a required subject in secondary schools and higher education institutions, thereby diminishing possibilities of intrinsic motivation to learn. Teachers are in a constant state of war with institutional authorities (ministries of education) on curricular goals and on the means for testing the achievement of those goals. A student's proficiency is determined by a grueling computer-scorable standardized multiple-choice examination. That proficiency unfortunately often turns out to be related more to the ability to cram for a standardized test than to the ability to use English for communicative, meaningful purposes.

How can you teach a classroom of students under such circumstances? Can you focus their efforts and attention on language rather than on the exam at the end of the course? Can students develop an intrinsically oriented outlook on their motivation to succeed? As a start to answering such questions, go back to the principles of intrinsic motivation discussed in Chapter 5 and put them in practice, as suggested there. And always try to keep your students' vision fixed on useful, practical, reachable goals for the communicative use of English.

INSTITUTIONAL CONTEXTS

One of the most salient, if not relevant, contexts of language teaching is the institution in which you are teaching. ESL/EFL classes are found in such a wide variety of educational establishments that textbook publishers have a hard time tailoring material for the many contexts. Even within one "type" of institution, multiple goals are pursued. For example, language schools in many countries are now finely tuned to offer courses in conversation, academic skills, English for Specific Purposes (ESP), workplace English, vocational/technical English, test-taking strategies, and other specializations.

Institutional constraints are often allied to the sociopolitical considerations discussed above. Schools and universities cannot exist in a social (or political) vacuum. Public elementary and secondary schools are subject to official national language policy issues. In the United States and other countries, the type of second language program offered in schools is a product of legislation and governmental red tape. Students' purposes in taking English at the higher education level may be colored by institutional policies, certification and degree requirements, instructional staffing, and even immigration regulations.

Elementary and Secondary Schools

Language policies and programs in elementary and secondary schools differ greatly from country to country. Within some countries like the United States, **English Language Learner** (ELL) programs, designed for school-age children whose native language is not English, vary not only by state but also by school districts, which may number in the hundreds in larger states. In EFL countries, English is sometimes a required secondary school subject and almost always one of several foreign language options. In certain countries (Sweden and Norway, for example) English is even required in elementary schools.

A number of models are currently practiced in the United States for dealing with nonnative English-speaking students in elementary and secondary schools. Some of these models apply to other countries in varying adapted forms. A summary of these models follows (adapted from Richard-Amato, 2003, pp. 354–357).

1. **Submersion.** The first way of treating nonnative speakers in classrooms is really a lack of treatment: Pupils are simply "submerged" in regular content-area classes with no special foreign language instruction. The assumption is that they will "absorb" English as they focus on the subject matter. Research has shown that sometimes they don't succeed in either English or the content areas, especially in subtractive situations. So, a few schools may provide a **pull-out** program in which, for perhaps one period a day, students leave their regular classroom and attend special tutorials or an ESL class.
2. **Immersion.** Here, pupils attend specially designed content-area classes. All the students in a class speak the same native language and are at similar levels of proficiency in English. The teacher is not only certified in the regular content areas but also has some knowledge of the students' first language and culture. Immersion programs are found more commonly in EFL contexts than in ESL contexts. In most immersion programs, pupils are in an additive bilingual context and enjoy the support of parents and the community in this enriching experience.
3. **Sheltered English.** This is a specialized form of immersion program that has become popular in recent years. It differs from immersion in that students come from varying native language backgrounds and the teacher is trained in *both* subject-matter content *and* ESL methodology. Also, students often have a regular ESL class as part of the curriculum. At Newcomer High School in San Francisco, for example, newly arrived immigrants are given one year of sheltered instruction in which ESL-trained teachers combine content and ESL in every subject.
4. **Mainstreaming.** In some submersion programs, students first receive instruction in ESL before being placed into content areas. Once teachers and tests conclude that students are proficient enough to be placed into ongoing content classes, they are mainstreamed into the regular curriculum. We need to remember that this ESL instruction should be content-centered so that pupils will not be at a disadvantage once they are placed in an ongoing class.
5. **Transitional bilingual programs.** In the United States, three different forms of bilingual education—in which students receive instruction in some combination of their first and second languages—are in common use. Transitional programs teach subject-matter content in the native language, combined with an ESL component. When teachers and tests determine that they are ready, students are transitioned into regular all-English classes. This has the advantage of permitting students to build early cognitive concepts in their native language and then cross over later to the dominant language. The

major disadvantage is that students are too often mainstreamed before they are ready, before their academic and linguistic skills have been sufficiently built.

6. **Maintenance bilingual programs.** Here, students continue throughout their school years to learn at least a portion of their subject matter in the native language. This has the advantage of stimulating the continued development of pupils' native languages and of building confidence and expertise in the content areas. Disadvantages include discouraging the mastery of English and the high cost of staffing maintenance classes in budgetary hard times.

7. **Enrichment bilingual programs.** A third form of bilingual education has students taking selected subject-matter courses in a foreign language while the bulk of their education is carried on in their native language. Students in such programs in the United States are not doing so for survival purposes, but simply to "enrich" themselves by broadening their cultural and linguistic horizons.

Post-Secondary and Adult Education

At the next age level one finds a cluster of institutional English learning opportunities for adults who may or may not anticipate going on to college or university degree programs, but who nevertheless may need English for social or occupational purposes. Typical of these institutions are those classified as **language schools** (usually small proprietary schools exclusively focused on language instruction), **adult education** schools (in the United States, state- or city-sponsored centers for educational, vocational, and recreational classes), **community colleges** (two-year, non-baccalaureate-degree-granting institutions of higher education), and **extended learning** (also known as **continuing education**) programs affiliated with four-year colleges or universities. The following descriptions illustrate the variety of courses available in such institutions:

1. **Survival/social** curricula run the gamut from short courses that introduce adults to conversational necessities to full-blown curricula designed to teach adults a complete range of language skills for survival in the context of the second culture. By definition, such programs would not progress beyond intermediate skill levels. These courses are frequently offered in night-school adult education programs and private language schools such as Berlitz Schools.

2. **Literacy** programs are designed to teach students whose native language reading/writing skills are either nonexistent or very poor. Learning to be literate in English while learning aural-oral forms as well requires energy and motivation on the part of students. Teachers need special training to teach at this challenging level.

3. **VESL** (Vocational ESL) targets those who are learning trades (carpenters and electricians, for example), arts (such as photography), and other occupations not commonly included in university programs. VESL courses may be offered in **technical schools** or **trade schools** (institutions exclusively dedicated to teaching various arts and trades, ranging from art, fashion design, and architecture to carpentry, automotive mechanics, and masonry).

4. **Workplace ESL** programs may be housed in any one of the above-named types of institutions, or in the workplace itself. These are courses specifically devoted to teaching language needed for designated professional or occupational purposes. They differ from VESL programs in that a course will usually be narrowly focused on one context, and often offered in the workplace itself. For example, programs around the world are offered for hotel workers (or, even more specifically, housekeepers in hotels), grocery store workers, computer industry employees, and employees in multinational corporations that use English for international communication.

Institutions of Higher Education

English language teaching programs also exist, of course, in four-year colleges and universities and postgraduate universities. The types of programs listed below may also be found in two-year community colleges and language schools, referred to above. Following are descriptions of three broad types of curricula that are designed to fit varying student goals:

1. **IEPs** (Intensive English Programs) are pre-academic programs designed for students—usually from non-English-speaking countries—who anticipate entering a regular course of study in an English-speaking college or university. Some such programs are "full-time" and quite rigorous: Students attend classes for 20 to 25 hours per week, usually for a quarter or a semester. The focus varies in such programs from rather general language skills at the advanced-beginner level to advanced courses in reading, writing, study skills, and research.

2. **EAP** (English for Academic Purposes) is a term that is very broadly applied to any course, module, or workshop in which students are taught to deal with academically related language and subject matter. EAP is common at the advanced level of pre-academic programs as well as in colleges and universities, especially courses in writing at the academic level and in oral production (giving presentations, speeches, and participating in oral discourse in the classroom).

3. **ESP** (English for Specific Purposes) programs are specifically devoted to professional fields of study. A course in English for Agriculture or in Business Writing would fall under the general rubric of ESP. Usually ESP courses are differentiated from VESL English in that ESP refers to disciplines in which people can get university majors and degrees, while VESL refers to trades and other certificate programs.

All these institutional contexts, believe it or not, are somewhat oversimplified here! Not only are there other categories of institutions that one could consider, but a number of the types of courses named can easily "cross over" from membership in one list to another. So, beware of oversimplifying these lists and categories. In determining how to plan lessons and carry out your own methodology within each curriculum, a number of other institutional factors apply. Consider, for example:

- the extent to which institutional regulations demand a certain curriculum content;
- the extent to which budgetary and bureaucratic constraints dictate class size, number of hours, etc.;
- the extent to which an administrator or supervisor "forces" you to teach in a certain way;
- the textbook (which you may detest) assigned to your course;
- the support and feedback that you get from fellow teachers;
- how other teachers in your institution teach and the extent to which they may subtly coerce you into teaching "their" way;
- the number of hours you must teach in order to make a living and how that affects your energy level;
- the conditions of your classroom (room size, lighting, furniture, etc.); and
- whether or not your English course is required and the effect that has on the motivation of your students.

☆   ☆   ☆   ☆   ☆

Institutional constraints are sometimes the biggest hurdle you have to cross. Once you have found ways to compromise with the system and still feel professionally fulfilled, you can release more energy into creative teaching. Many of these issues will be dealt with in future chapters.

TOPICS FOR DISCUSSION, ACTION, AND RESEARCH

[Note: (I) Individual work; (G) group or pair work; (C) whole-class discussion.]

1. (C) Four implications of considering cultural issues are suggested on pages 133-134. The class might find it interesting to probe each possibility in a little more detail, specifically with personal viewpoints from students in the class, especially if some of those viewpoints vary to some extent.
2. (G) Ask pairs to think of some typical ESL and/or EFL contexts. Direct the pairs to think of other ways to (a) seize the "ESL advantage" and (b) compensate for the lack of ready communicative situations outside the EFL classroom door.

3. (I/C) Investigate the official policy on English (and, possibly, other second languages) in the government and educational system of your own country or a country of your choosing. Are there unofficial policies in business, educational, or social circles? Do they sustain or contradict the official stance? Share your findings with the class.

4. (C) The class may also find it enlightening to probe the NNEST versus NEST issue, especially if some students have personal experiences either with discrimination because of a NS bias in an institution, or with positive experiences of the NNEST advantages. If some "action" by students is warranted, the class could brainstorm some specific steps that could be taken to educate employees and advertisers on the issue.

5. (G) Ask pairs to describe other instances of subtractive (page 139) bilingualism. What could one do as a teacher to help students create a more positive outlook on their native and second languages?

6. (C) Solicit from students some specific steps that could be taken to lift the motivation level in countries where English is a compulsory subject in the schools and motivation to learn it is low. Would those steps lead to some intrinsic motivation? Are the steps practical?

7. (I/C) If possible, direct your students to observe different ESL classes that represent some of the models described on pages 141–142. Have them compare the differences and similarities in the programs and describe what seemed to be the most and the least effective elements in each program or class hour. Their findings might be shared with the rest of the class.

8. (G) Direct small groups to decide how they would deal with the following two scenarios. In each case, make sure each group specifies a targeted context (country, culture, language policy, institutional program):
   a. Your administrator insists that you teach a highly form-focused class, because your students will have to pass a multiple-choice grammar and vocabulary/reading test at the end of the term. You're convinced, however, that through a form of CLT your students would get excited and be motivated to learn, and you could *also* thoroughly cover the necessary grammar and vocabulary.
   b. You are a NNEST teaching in a non-English-speaking country, and your students have complained that your pronunciation is not nativelike (in spite of the fact that your English is "excellent," even if nonnative).

9. (G/C) The Brazilian educator Paolo Freire (1970) said that education empowers people: It enables them to become creative, productive people who will work toward political and social change. Ask small groups to discuss ways that English might empower learners. Groups should then share their ideas with the whole class.

FOR YOUR FURTHER READING

DeCapua, A., & Wintergerst, A. (2004). *Crossing cultures in the language classroom.* Ann Arbor: University of Michigan Press.

Fantini, A. (1997). *New ways in teaching culture.* Alexandria, VA: Teachers of English to Speakers of Other Languages.

These two very practically oriented books will give you an excellent survey of the possibilities of incorporating cultural issues into your classroom methodology. Even if you have to adapt some of the recommended activities for your own audience, there are plenty of ideas here.

Kachru, B. (1992). World Englishes: Approaches, issues, and resources. *Language Teaching, 25,* 1–14.

Kachru, Y. (2005). Teaching and learning of world Englishes. In E. Hinkel (Ed.), *Handbook of research in second language teaching and learning* (pp. 149–173). Mahwah, NJ: Lawrence Erlbaum Associates.

In one of the earlier surveys of world Englishes, Braj Kachru's 1992 article summarized a sweeping array of research at the time in what is now commonly referred to as "world Englishes." In the 2005 article, Yamuna Kachru brings us up to date on the state of the art in research and teaching of English as an international language (EIL).

Kamhi-Stein, L. (Ed.). (2004). *Learning and teaching from experience: Perspectives on nonnative English speaking professionals.* Ann Arbor: University of Michigan Press.

McKay, S. (2002). *Teaching English as an international language: Rethinking goals and approaches.* Oxford, UK: Oxford University Press.

Braine, G. (1999). *Nonnative educators in English language teaching.* Mahwah, NJ: Lawrence Erlbaum Associates.

Lia Kamhi-Stein's anthology presents a variety of perspectives on the issue of NNESTs in the classroom, from theoretical underpinnings to research, teacher preparation, and classroom practices. Sandra McKay views the topic from the perspective of a number of issues relevant to the growth of English as an international language, particularly from a pedagogical viewpoint. George Braine's book focuses on the various debates about NESTs and NNESTs in English language teaching, taking a balanced view, but with persuasive arguments for the advantages that NNESTs bring to the profession.

DESIGNING AND IMPLEMENTING CLASSROOM LESSONS

The previous two sections laid theoretical and contextual groundwork for Parts III and IV, which form the most practical core of *Teaching by Principles*. Part III presents a multiplicity of practical considerations involved in designing and implementing classroom lessons, while Part IV is a systematic compendium of teaching the four skills, along with form-focused instruction.

In Part III, the progression of logic begins with the "big" picture of curriculum design: Where do these daily lessons that we observe, plan, and carry out come from and how do they fit into a cohesive whole? Chapter 9 lays out the steps that are involved in such course development, not in so much detail that the reader becomes fully adept at curriculum design through this chapter, but with enough information to give you a good idea of the pedagogical context into which lessons are embedded. With that backdrop, Chapter 10 then offers specific guidelines on planning a lesson.

Chapters 11 and 12 turn your attention to the materials that we are constantly using in the process of carrying out those classroom lessons. The division between the two chapters lies in distinguishing traditional print media and realia (books, handouts, objects, etc., in Chapter 11) from technological material (audio, video, and computer technology, in Chapter 12). The latter offers a number of guidelines and information on using computer-based material in the language classroom.

The concept of interaction occupies the next two chapters. In Chapter 13, guidelines for initiating interaction are offered, while Chapter 14 is a primer on how to carry out successful interactive group work.

Part III concludes with a chapter on classroom management and a chapter on strategies-based instruction. Chapter 15 features, among other factors, problems of discipline; physical features in the classroom; the teacher's "presence," poise, roles, and styles; unplanned moments; and creating a positive climate. And then Chapter 16 offers some thoughts on how you can help students "learn how to learn" by using strategic competence techniques.

CHAPTER 9

CURRICULUM DESIGN

OBJECTIVES After reading this chapter, you will be able to:

- appreciate the complexity of curriculum design and the importance of a systematic process in such development

- evaluate the ways in which your own and others' lessons are embedded in the overall goals of a curriculum, and assess the effectiveness of lessons in that larger context

- identify a specific sequence of processes involved in course design: analyzing the situation and needs, specifying goals, developing a syllabus, choosing materials, creating assessments, and evaluating the course

- respond appropriately to demands placed on you, in the future, to undertake the process of course design or revision

In the previous eight chapters of this book, you have had a survey of language-teaching history and a description of how current views of methodology advocate principled, informed, eclectic approaches that consider all the varying nuances of age, proficiency, and sociocultural and institutional contexts. In this next section of eight chapters, we turn to the central focus of teaching: practical classroom methodological realities. We will consider the following: how a curriculum is designed; the fine art of planning a lesson; the multiplicity of choices you have among techniques, textbooks, other materials, and technological aids; guidelines for successful interactive classrooms; classroom management issues; how to incorporate an awareness and use of strategies by your students; and finally the concept of integrating skills.

The first step in this plethora of practicalities is to take a look at curriculum design: How is a curriculum "born"? How do courses evolve over years? What are some basic principles of effective curriculum design? How can you adapt a curriculum for your own context? How do you decide if a course has been successful?

These and many other questions will be addressed here, but an important warning is in order: This chapter is not intended to provide a comprehensive manual on course design; it serves merely as a *brief synopsis* of what would constitute at least one full teacher education course in curriculum design (which of course should eventually be taken in a teacher preparation program). This chapter is placed here because it's important—before you tackle the business of lesson planning—to possess at least a passing acquaintance with the place of a given lesson within the *larger framework* of a curriculum designed to meet particular goals for particular students in particular contexts. Here, Kumaravadivelu's (2001) "pedagogy of particularity" is highly relevant, for no one would dream of planning a lesson in a vacuum, or of assuming that lessons are *not* embedded in a much larger picture.

Before continuing, I would like to recommend five excellent sources of information on course design; these are books that I use in my own seminar on curriculum design. I have also referred to them frequently in the organizing and writing of this brief chapter. The five sources (Brown, 1995; Graves, 1996, 2000; Murphy & Byrd, 2001; Richards, 2001) are all listed and described at the end of this chapter under "For Your Further Reading."

CURRICULUM DEVELOPMENT: AN OVERVIEW

Here is one of several similar stories I have experienced. (Just for the sake of prudence, I will not name specific places or people.)

> A year or two ago I was approached by a university in Central America that wanted my university (San Francisco State University) to offer a four-week summer "short course" in English. My primary contact informed me that they would send 45 students between the ages of 18 and 24, that those students wanted a rigorous, serious course in academic English, and that they were at a high intermediate to advanced level of proficiency. We were told they wanted preparation in the TOEFL®, as many intended to apply to American universities for further study. They wanted to reside in our university dormitories and eat their meals there. They also wanted several weekday and weekend excursions to various sights in and around San Francisco, and asked for an activities leader to coordinate this part of the program. This, then, was in addition to the academic program, which was to be five days a week, for four to five hours a day.
>
> For reasons that are difficult to explain, we were not able to obtain any sort of verification of students' proficiency in advance. We had no test scores, grades, or writing samples. A very brief preliminary questionnaire, filled out by about 15 students, provided minimal demographic data and broadly verified their interest in academic English. It was now January and the program was proposed to start in mid-June, so we had to act quickly to prepare for this group; five months of lead time was minimal, but doable if communications could go back and forth efficiently. My contact asked for a proposed budget (which was a primary consideration in whether or not the program would happen) and a proposed curriculum for the 45 students.

I will now break at this point in this story, before continuing in installments throughout this chapter, and suggest that you are now a member of a committee of two or three charged with fulfilling the initial request of the Central American contact: a budget and a curriculum. What would you do? First, what further information would you need or desire from the contact? What further information would you like to get about the students and their purpose for traveling to San Francisco for a summer program in English? What problems would your committee anticipate not only in fulfilling the initial request but perhaps in ultimately seeing the program to fruition? Answering these questions would be the first steps in designing a curriculum, so let's turn to these questions, in succession.

In the flowchart shown in Figure 9.1, I offer my own "picture" of the process of designing a course, a sequence of steps that will be explained in the subsequent sections of this chapter. In the center of the chart are the basic steps normally followed in designing a curriculum. On each side are influential interacting factors. Toward the top, note that as goals are being defined and as a syllabus is being conceptualized, institutional constraints and available materials and resources must be simultaneously analyzed in order to maintain feasibility. In the lower part of the flowchart, the training, experience, and ability of the teacher will interact with the process of lesson design and teaching the course itself. Then, as instruction is ongoing, formative assessments will have the effect of monitoring students' progress. Finally, assessment of students, teacher, and program can fruitfully lead to appropriate revision of the course.

SITUATION ANALYSIS

The first—or perhaps among the first—steps in course design is an analysis of the setting, the audience, and needs of the students, otherwise known as a **situation analysis** (Richards, 2001). Every effective course is undergirded by a consideration of the following factors:

1. **Educational setting.** Within what societal and cultural norms is the course situated? What is the institutional framework into which the course must be integrated? What are the broad instructional goals of the program? In general what is the structure of the program? What are the physical conditions (e.g., classrooms) and resources (labs, computers, AV, materials)? Who are the learners, in very general terms? Basic questions here look at the larger educational context within which a course is placed.
2. **Class characteristics.** How would you describe the class in terms of the homogeneity of learners, the size of the class, and its relationship to others that learners are taking?

Figure 9.1 Second language curriculum development process

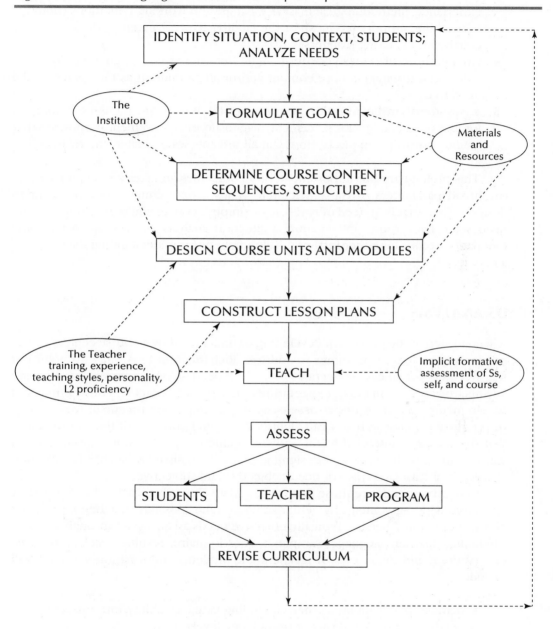

3. **Faculty characteristics.** What are the qualifications of teachers—training, experience, methodological biases? What are the working conditions (hours of teaching, support services) for the faculty? To what extent is there collaboration among teachers?
4. **Governance of course content.** Who determines course content? To what extent can teachers choose content and/or adapt content as they perceive the need to do so?
5. **Assessment and evaluation requirements.** What stipulations are in force for assessing students for placement, diagnostic, or achievement purposes? What grading norms are in place? How, if at all, are courses evaluated and revised?

This preliminary but important step in course design takes a sweeping look at the broad parameters of the curriculum. If it's a new course you are about to design, or one that is in need of revision, or simply a course you're teaching and you need some background information, a situation analysis allows you to lay some foundation stones for either further development or for understanding the nature of a course.

NEEDS ANALYSIS

A second step in the process of developing or understanding a course centers on the needs that the course presumes to address. Richards (2001) is quick to point out that **needs** is not an easy concept to define. Depending on whom you ask, they are "wants, desires, demands, expectations, motivations, lacks, constraints, and requirements" (p. 54). **A needs assessment** is an important precursor to designing the **goals** of a course in that it can identify the overall purposes of the course, "gaps" that the course is intended to fill, and the opinions of both course designers and learners about their reasons for designing/taking the course. As such, it is important to identify at least two types of needs: objective and subjective.

Objective needs are those that can be relatively easily measured, quantified, or specified with agreement by administrators (and possibly teachers) on what constitutes defined needs. Typically, objective needs are analyzed through test data (including learner language samples), questionnaire results, teacher reports, observations, and interviews of teachers and students. Information gathered will include:

- demographic data on learners, including language ability, interests, etc.
- needs expressed in terms of proficiency levels
- language skills to be addressed
- what learners need to *do* in English (target contexts for English use)

Subjective needs are often of equal or greater importance as they focus on needs as seen through the eyes of the learners themselves. Granted, sometimes learners' perceived needs do not match their actual needs. For example, students often feel that they should spend lots of time studying grammar in a class, when in reality they may actually need more time in communicative activities. But it still is wise for a curriculum developer to ascertain all subjectively perceived needs in order to address them in some way in the course itself. Subjective needs are more difficult to gather, but are typically sought through interviews, questionnaires, teachers' perceptions, observations, and the opinions of "experts." From these procedures, the following information may emerge:

- learners' attitudes toward the target language and culture
- expectations that students have of themselves and of the course
- purposes that students perceive for studying English
- specific language skills that students wish to focus on
- preferences (styles, strategies) that students have about their learning

PROBLEMATIZING

Graves (1996, p. 5) suggests that an important feature of course design is the careful consideration of the potentially large number of things that can go "wrong" with one's best-laid plans for a course. With all the societal, institutional, and pedagogical constraints already implied in simply *preparing* to design a curriculum, it may be obvious that problems are going to appear, and the better prepared you are to respond to such problems, the less likely it will be that insurmountable impediments will prevent the project from reaching its fruition. Problematizing a course, that is, anticipating impediments, issues, and other potential obstacles in advance, will save untold hours of effort that may otherwise be spent "patching up" the shortcomings later on.

Recently one of my graduate students proposed to design a workplace curriculum for grocery store workers for whom English was a second language, and who were having difficulties communicating with customers, colleagues, and bosses. A number of immediate problems came up: Did the learners perceive their own need to learn certain skills in English? Were managers supportive of the effort? Would workers receive paid time to take the course? Would prospective students have to pay to attend the course? Would the overall administrator of the grocery store pay the teacher for her services? Would there be money to pay for materials? Was there a convenient space available for the class? These and a host of other problems had to be addressed before the project could go forward, and many of them involved slowly turning wheels of bureaucracy.

Courses are usually successful because they have anticipated such problems in advance and have effectively determined realistic answers to them. Consider the following list as just scratching the surface of the process of addressing the challenges and conflicts of this particular task that faces you:

- What are institutional requirements and conditions that impact on the course?
- What administrative authorities must be brought into the process in order to obtain approval, budget, space, and staffing?
- What contradictions might exist between what learners want/need and institutional constraints?
- What budgetary constraints exist and how might a budget be effectively constructed for maximum efficiency and accomplishing of goals?
- Are there any problems surrounding faculty qualifications and availability that impact on the course?
- Are there conflicting expectations between administrator(s) and teachers on what the course can accomplish?
- What requirements for student assessment are in place and how can a teacher creatively work "within the system" to carry out appropriate assessments?

Before continuing with an enumeration of further steps in the process of curriculum design, let's go back to the story of the proposed Central American program.

> Our situation analysis proved to be the easiest part of the task. We had a readily available setting in the American Language Institute (ALI); we were familiar with academically bound international students and their needs; a course in academic English could easily be a spin-off of our existing courses; we had classrooms and resources. We knew the students would all be native Spanish speakers and a mix of men and women, and we were accustomed to classes of 15 students each, so the group would comprise three classes, each targeted at different proficiency levels (although here is where we eventually ran into some problems). Existing teachers at the ALI were happy at the prospect of summer employment and we easily arranged for them to teach about 10 hours a week. We planned a collaborative effort in which teachers and one coordinator would meet almost daily to deal with course content during the program. We easily put into place achievement tests and planned that the students would be given the TOEFL® at the end of the session.
>
> With our needs analysis we began to encounter serious problems. We wanted to get test scores ahead of time, to administer a self-check

questionnaire to determine interests, and to obtain writing samples of students (speech samples were not available). For reasons that I won't go into here, virtually none of the above were possible to obtain, except for the very brief aforementioned questionnaire returned by 15 of the prospective students. As time was rapidly marching on, we were forced to anticipate needs on the basis of past experience with similar groups.

An issue came up in our discussion of budgetary matters. We were informed that the initial figure that we proposed was too high and a request was made for a lower amount. We eventually agreed on a lower amount, but only by removing the activities leader and responsibility for the cultural aspects that were initially to be part of the whole package. We also had to dissociate what we had intended to be an interaction of language and culture in the course and plan a strictly academic program. Therein lay a further problem that arose later on!

We were now ready to tackle the next steps: stating goals, objectives, materials, and course content.

SPECIFYING GOALS

The terms **goal** and **objective** are often interchanged in pedagogical literature, and depending on whom you consult, you might find some confusion in defining the two terms. For the sake of clarity and brevity here, I will offer a distinction that seems to conform to the majority of uses of the two terms. It is really quite a simple distinction. **Goals** are rather broadly based aims and purposes in an educational context, and are therefore more appropriately associated with whole programs, courses, or perhaps sizable modules within a course. According to Brown (1995, p. 71), goals are "general statements concerning desirable and attainable program purposes and aims." **Objectives** are much more specific than goals, both in their conception and in their context. Objectives usually refer to aims and purposes within the narrow context of a lesson or an activity within a lesson. They are "specific statements that describe particular knowledge, behaviors, and/or skills" (Brown, 1995, p. 73). Obviously there can be some gray area in between the two concepts, but they are essentially distinguished by the size and scope of the context in question.

Most curriculum experts agree that once a situation analysis and needs analysis have confirmed some of the general parameters of a course, goals need to be carefully stated in order to be certain about what the course will accomplish and what it will not.

For the Central American program, to guide our thinking, we developed the following *speaking* goals for the lowest of the three levels we planned (we also had goals for listening, reading, and writing):

By the end of the course, students will be able to:

1. Participate in social conversations in English
2. Speak with few hesitations and with only minor (local) errors
3. Successfully apply some form-focused instruction to their speech
4. Self-monitor their speech for potential errors
5. Participate comfortably in pair, group, and whole-class discussions
6. Give a simple oral presentation on a familiar topic

These served as guidelines for determining course content and eventually lesson objectives.

CONCEPTUALIZING A COURSE SYLLABUS

The next *two* steps in many cases will be undertaken simultaneously or at least interactively: As you put together what most institutions call a **syllabus** (a sequential list of objectives, topics, situations, skills, and forms to be taught), it is often helpful to carry out a review of options in materials (textbooks and other resources) that are already available. It would be unrealistic to draw up a prototype of your course with no consultation of the potential materials that might support the course. You could end up having to redesign a great deal of your course if you find that the right materials don't exist!

So, how much time and effort should you spend on designing a syllabus before consulting the options for existing materials? This is a difficult question to answer because it depends on a number of factors, among which are time, expertise, money, and one's own need to offer the perfect course. Sometimes excellent courses are launched simply on the basis of an available textbook, and sometimes those curricula are unsuccessful. But it's also rare to design the perfect curriculum the first time around, and so perhaps through the revision process (the bottom box in Figure 9.1) a course can be redesigned quite successfully after a mediocre first run.

A communicative syllabus (function-focused as opposed to form-focused) should minimally consist of:

1. Goals for the course (and possibly goals for modules within the course).
2. Suggested objectives for units and possibly for lessons.
3. A sequential list of functions (purposes), following from the goals, that the curriculum will fulfill. Such a list is typically organized into weeks or days.

4. A sequential list of topics and situations matched to the functions in #3.
5. A sequential list of grammatical, lexical, and/or phonological forms to be taught, again matched to the sequence of functions.
6. A sequential list of skills (listening, speaking, reading, writing) that are also matched to the above sequences.
7. Matched references throughout to textbook units, lessons, and/or pages, and additional resources (audio, visual, workbooks, etc.) to be used.
8. Possible suggestions of assessment alternatives, including criteria to be tested and genres of assessment (traditional tests, journals, portfolios, etc.).

In addition, depending on how detailed the syllabus ultimately gets, it is not unusual to see syllabuses that include outlines of lesson plans (especially if a teacher's manual is included with a textbook) and/or suggested activities. In such lesson plans, one will often find suggestions for extra-class ("homework") activity to assign to students.

> In the case of the Central American program, with only about eight weeks remaining before their arrival, we began to get some mixed messages from our contact about the "real" purposes of the program—from less and less "academic" to more and more "cultural." We learned that the prospective students might only be at a low-intermediate level of English; and it looked like the initial 45 students would *not* materialize! We had neither time nor money available for course development, even though we clearly had the expertise. With a number of uncertainties entering into the planning of the program, we decided to conceptualize a course that was a hybrid of a published textbook series and our own ALI curriculum, with little further planning. This decision was expedient, and saved us from spending a lot of time in developing a course that might turn out to be the *wrong* course for a possible surprise audience!

SELECTING TEXTBOOKS, MATERIALS, AND RESOURCES

As noted above, the process of reviewing potential textbooks, materials, and resources, beyond those that you might design yourself, is one that ideally takes place in concert with conceptualizing the syllabus. Of great importance in this process is ascertaining that your goals—the outgrowth of a situation and needs analysis—are in central focus at all times. It is tempting to allow existing textbooks to drive your goals, but doing so can obviously lead you astray.

There are many different ways of approaching the process of reviewing textbooks and making a final decision. Richards (2001, p. 258), citing Cunningsworth (1995), suggests the following criteria as a set of guidelines:

1. They should correspond to learners' needs. They should match the aims and objectives of the language program.
2. They should reflect the uses (present or future) that learners will make of the language. Textbooks should be chosen that will help equip students to use language effectively for their own purposes.
3. They should take account of students' needs as learners and should facilitate their learning processes, without dogmatically imposing a rigid "method."
4. They should have a clear role as a support for learning. Like teachers, they should mediate between the target language and the learner.

J. Brown (1995, p. 161) lists five major categories to consider in choosing a textbook: (a) author's and publisher's reputation; (b) fit to the curriculum (meeting needs, goals, etc.); (c) physical characteristics (layout, organization, etc.); (d) logistical factors (price, auxiliary aids, workbooks); and (e) teachability (especially the usefulness of a teacher's edition).

A further consideration in reviewing and choosing materials is the extent to which a curriculum will involve teacher-made materials (additional activities and exercises, handouts, charts, review sheets, etc.). Such personalizing of a curriculum is of course highly recommended in that such material can be specifically gauged for the particular audience, and it is a motivating factor for teacher and students.

ASSESSMENT

Assessment of the students' attainment of objectives of lessons and units, and of the goals of the curriculum, may be offered in a wide array of possible formats. Traditional periodic tests such as quizzes, multiple-choice tests, fill-in-the-blank tests, and other somewhat mechanical test types offer the possibility of a practical, quick level check of students' attainment. Midterm and final examinations might include, along with some of the above techniques, short essays, oral production, and more open-ended responses. Alternatives in such assessment techniques are available in journals, portfolios, conferences, observations, interviews, and self- and peer-evaluation. Details on all these possibilities are described in Chapters 23, 24, and 25 of this book.

PROGRAM EVALUATION

No curriculum should be considered complete without some form of program evaluation—which you will see toward the bottom of the chart in Figure 9.1. Two manifestations of program evaluation are usually implied in a course: evaluation of the teacher and of the program itself. Of course, all three of these factors—students, teacher, and program—are interdependent. If *students* are successful, the cause could be either the teacher or the syllabus, and not just the performance of students. Likewise, the success of a *program* may be attributed to a great extent to a teacher's talent and ability to adapt a syllabus to an audience. And then again, a poorly motivated group of students and an inadequate program could make the world's best *teacher* look bad.

So, an effective program evaluation will consider all three factors in determining appropriate revisions. The most salient aspect of most program evaluations is the students' evaluation of both teacher and program elements, often in the form of a checklist or questionnaire. But hidden beneath the results of such questionnaires are several possible root causes of success or failure. Perhaps the teacher is so excellent or so poor that the program rises or falls on that alone. Perhaps the textbook and materials equally drove the success or failure of the course. It is also possible that students can give high ratings to teachers who are pedagogically mediocre but who are "nice" to their students; likewise, a stern, impassioned teacher might get some low student ratings but in the long run students will have learned a great deal from such a teacher.

How should one effectively account for all the possible variables contributing to the success of a program? First, all the "players" need to be consulted. This would include students, teachers, course developers, administrators, and if relevant, sponsors. Second, consider the audience of the evaluation. If the course is to be offered subsequently, then perhaps the primary audience is the administrator(s) and teachers. If it's money for further offerings that concerns you, the sponsors are your target. If you are concerned about which courses the students will move on into, then the students take central focus.

A third way to view program evaluation is to consider various aspects of the program, any or all of which might have contributed to the success or failure of a course:

- appropriateness of the course goals (in meeting needs and purposes)
- adequacy of the syllabus to meet those goals
- textbooks and materials used to support the curriculum
- classroom methodology, activities, procedures
- the teacher's training, background, and expertise
- appropriate orientation of teachers and students before the course
- the students' motivation and attitudes
- the students' perceptions of the course
- the students' actual performance as measured by assessments
- means for monitoring students' progress through assessment
- institutional support, including resources, classrooms, and environment
- staff collaboration and development before and during the course

It should be readily apparent that program evaluation extends well beyond the administration of a simple student evaluation form! If program evaluation is treated as a serious and comprehensive process, it will take time, effort, and focus to achieve its ends.

I can now relate the rest of the story of the Central American program, all in the light of the last few sections of this chapter.

As we approached the day of the students' arrival, we made sure all the physical arrangements were set: securing housing, confirming transportation, ordering textbooks and copies of the institutional TOEFL®, issuing contracts to teachers, reserving classroom space, and ascertaining that immigration regulations were being met. Difficulties with this last item almost forced us to cancel the program (another long story). At the last minute the crisis was averted, and the group was finally able to obtain visas from the U.S. immigration office in Central America.

About two weeks before the arrival date, we were informed that there would be only 25 students in the program. This had a significant impact on our plan to offer three sections, and the outcome of that was to offer only two sections, with another budgetary adjustment. The day after the students arrived, we had placement testing and discovered that they were clearly of lower proficiency than we had initially expected, but even more significant was their almost unanimous desire *not* to undertake a strictly academic course. Instead, their wishes indicated a course in conversation and culture, with only a light treatment of reading and writing skills, and with a liberal number of hours each day to enjoy the beautiful city of San Francisco!

What were we to do with our prepared syllabus? An "emergency" meeting among the teachers and coordinator resulted in an amazing collaborative effort to revise the curriculum on the spot and an agreement to meet together daily for the first two weeks and to share results of the previous day and to plan activities for the next. We were able to salvage some of the textbook lessons but the textbook proved to be marginally useful. Some of our own ALI curriculum was used to fill in certain gaps. Most of the four-week course was a daily process of creative design based on informal monitoring of student needs and their progress. We further arranged to have some cultural connections between class activity and afternoon and weekend tours. The TOEFL® prep part of the curriculum was reduced to two optional workshops.

At the end of the course, we found through various program evaluative measures that the students loved the course, the teachers, and the setting. They felt that their needs were more than fulfilled, as they showed excellent improvement in their English skills. They left San Francisco with cherished memories and experiences they might never again encounter.

This story could happen to you, but with a little bit of luck and better predictions of needs, it will not. What should have happened in order to prevent the numerous pitfalls encountered along the way? Here were our conclusions:

1. Carry out a more accurate needs analysis.
2. Begin the planning process much earlier in the academic year in order to better reach the desired numbers of participants, to establish a more realistic budget, and to plan the course accordingly.
3. With more accurate pinpointing of needs and purposes of the course, the syllabus, textbooks, and other resources would have been appropriate, and we would have avoided the "emergency" patching together of a course.

★   ★   ★   ★   ★

This survey of course design is intended to give you a picture of what lies behind the daily lessons and activities that you might observe or carry out in the classroom. It's important to place every class period against the backdrop of the course in which it is embedded and within the context of preceding and subsequent lessons. Without such a framework, from the point of view of the teacher, lessons might be inappropriately planned and executed, and from the point of view of an observer, inappropriately evaluated. We now turn to what many consider the "building blocks" of a course, the daily, time-framed sets of activities designed to meet specific objectives: the lesson.

TOPICS FOR DISCUSSION, ACTION, AND RESEARCH

[Note: (I) Individual work; (G) group or pair work; (C) whole-class discussion.]

1. (C) Brainstorm for one or two examples of courses that the class is familiar with. Then discuss what the situational context of the course is, and how such contextual variables are accounted for in the curriculum. Use the five points outlined in the section on Situation Analysis, on pages 150 and 152, as a guideline for the discussion.
2. (G) Have small groups look at the factors listed in the ovals at the sides of the chart in Figure 9.1 (page 151): institutional factors, materials, teacher variables, and formative ongoing assessment. Each group should pick one course that everyone in the group is familiar with and talk about how the four factors have influenced (or should influence) the course. Finally, have groups share results with the whole class.
3. (G) Have pairs quickly enumerate examples of objective needs and subjective needs in a course that both members of the pair are familiar with. Pairs can then write them on the board, followed by a whole-class reflection on the relative importance of selected items.

4. (C) Among the members of the class, solicit examples of "problems" that have arisen, or might arise, in a course familiar to everyone, in the process of developing a curriculum.

5. (I) Assign the task of finding an existing syllabus for a language course. Among possible sources are those found in Graves (1996) and in Murphy and Byrd (2001), where many different courses are described. The assignment is to describe, in abbreviated form, the eight elements of the syllabus (see pages 156–157 for the list).

6. (G/C) Among a number of coursebooks that have been brought to class, students will choose one, and in pairs, analyze it for a defined context using either Richards's (citing Cunningsworth) four criteria (pages 157–158) or J. Brown's five categories. Pairs can then make brief reports of findings.

7. (C) On page 159, 12 bulleted items are suggested as factors to consider in a program evaluation. Based on the Central America program that was synopsized in the chapter, ask students to briefly evaluate—on a scale of 5 (excellent) to 1 (poor)—the program's success. Note that in some cases there is incomplete information about the program.

8. (I/C) Have students interview a teacher or administrator who has developed and used a course (or textbook) in order to find out what steps were taken in the development process. The interview protocol should be designed to cover the major categories discussed in this chapter. A written and/or oral report should be submitted.

FOR YOUR FURTHER READING

Richards, J. (2001). *Curriculum development in language teaching.* Cambridge, UK: Cambridge University Press.

Graves, K. (2000). *Designing language courses: A guide for teachers.* Boston: Heinle & Heinle.

Brown, J.D. (1995). *The elements of language curriculum: A systematic approach to program development.* Boston: Heinle & Heinle.

Any one of these three books can be considered "standard" authoritative manuals for second language curriculum development. They are each comprehensive in scope and provide a wealth of information, ideas, guidelines, and practical examples.

Graves, K. (1996). *Teachers as course developers.* Cambridge, UK: Cambridge University Press.

Kathleen Graves has assembled a set of six different accounts of course design in several countries by individuals who have a remarkable ability to narrate their own journey through the stages of development. Each story includes both practical details as well as reflective thought on their processes. What is most refreshing about this book is that none of the accounts are examples of "perfect" curriculum design—they all exhibit certain shortcomings, but those instances are well analyzed.

Murphy, J., & Byrd, P. (Eds.). (2001). *Understanding the courses we teach: Local perspectives on English language teaching.* Ann Arbor: University of Michigan Press.

Not unlike the Graves (1996) book described above, John Murphy and Patricia Byrd's edited volume includes 18 real-world accounts of courses that teachers have taught (and in some cases developed themselves). The accounts are classified into workplace, adult education, EFL, university credit courses, and pre-university non-credit courses.

CHAPTER 10

LESSON PLANNING

OBJECTIVES After reading this chapter, you will be able to:

- understand the interdependent components of a successful lesson

- appreciate the paramount importance of establishing clear performance-based objectives for every lesson

- design your own lesson(s) using the guidelines that are suggested in this chapter

- evaluate the effectiveness of your own and observed lessons

Having taken a broad, sweeping look at the macro units of pedagogy, the curriculum or course, we now take the next logical step in a consideration of the process of teaching languages by zooming in on the organization of a course. Most courses are presented in a number of **units** of varying lengths (usually from one to three weeks in a normal 15-week term), whose focus is defined by goals that ultimately contribute to overall goals of the course. Such units are customarily characterized by a series of lessons: the building blocks of a unit and course, time-defined in-class sets of activities designed to accomplish one or more very specific objectives.

The term **lesson** is popularly considered to be a unified set of procedures that cover a period of classroom time, usually ranging from 45 to 120 minutes. These classroom time units are administratively significant for teachers because they represent steps in a curriculum before which and after which you have a hiatus (of a day or more) in which to evaluate and prepare for the next lesson. Sometimes your whole life seems to be caught up in a never-ending series of lesson plans. But those lessons, from the point of view of your own and students' time management, are practical, tangible units of effort that serve to provide a rhythm to a course of study.

How do you go about planning a lesson? This chapter should give you some guidelines.

FORMAT OF A LESSON PLAN

While variations abound, seasoned teachers generally agree on what the essential elements of a lesson plan should be. For examples of each element, turn to the sample lesson plan that begins on page 171 of this chapter.

1. Goal

As you discovered in the previous chapter, a well-designed course will specify a number of goals. Each lesson in the course will in some way address one or more of those "big" overall goals. A first step in a lesson, then, would be to acknowledge the way in which your lesson is designed to contribute to such goals. This goal may be generalized, but it provides a pedagogical context for you. Thus, in the sample lesson plan, "comprehending social conversations" generally identifies the curricular goal being addressed.

2. Objectives

It's very important to state explicitly what you want students to gain from the lesson. Explicit statements here help you to

a. be sure that you indeed know what it is you want to accomplish,
b. preserve the unity of your lesson,
c. predetermine whether or not you are trying to accomplish too much, and
d. evaluate students' success at the end of the lesson.

Objectives are most clearly captured in terms of stating what students will do— that is, what they will *perform*. Try to avoid vague, unverifiable statements like these:

- Students will learn about the passive voice.
- Students will practice some listening exercises.
- Students will do the reading selection.
- Students will discuss the homework assignment.

You would be unable to confirm the realization of any of these sorts of abstruse, loosely stated objectives. On the other hand, because they are stated in terms of expected student performance, the objectives in the sample lesson plan can more easily be verified. You can turn back to the objectives after a lesson and determine, to some extent anyway, how well students accomplished them.

Note, however, that some language objectives are not overtly observable, and therefore you may need to depart from strictly behavioral terms for such objectives. Notably, comprehension objectives (listening, reading) are tricky because you cannot actually *observe* either. You're forced to rely on performance that demonstrates or confirms correct comprehension; in other words, you have to *infer* the acquisition of those objectives.

In stating objectives, you should be able to identify an overall purpose that you will attempt to accomplish by the end of the class period. But there may be other supportive objectives that need to be stated as well, leading us to distinguish between two kinds of objectives: **Terminal objectives** are final learning outcomes that you will be responsible for assessing. **Enabling objectives** are interim steps within a lesson that build upon each other and ultimately lead to a terminal objective. Consider the following examples:

Terminal lesson objective:

- Students will successfully request information about airplane arrivals and departures.

Enabling objectives:

- Students will comprehend and produce the following 10 new vocabulary items. [vocabulary is listed]
- Students will read and understand an airline schedule.
- Students will produce questions with *when, where,* and *what time.*
- Students will produce appropriate polite forms of requesting.

You may be able to identify a number of other enabling objectives that will vary depending upon what students' proficiency level is and what they have already learned in the course. For another example, notice the difference between terminal and enabling objectives in the sample lesson plan.

3. Materials and equipment

It may seem a trivial matter to list materials needed, but good planning includes knowing what you need to take with you or to arrange to have in your classroom. It is easy, in the usually harried life of a teacher, to forget to bring to class a tape recorder, a poster, some handouts you left on your desk at home, or the workbooks that students gave you the night before.

4. Procedures

At this point, lessons clearly have tremendous variation. But, as a very general set of guidelines for planning, you might think in terms of making sure your plan includes

    a. an opening statement or activity as a warm-up
    b. a set of activities and techniques in which you have considered appropriate proportions of time for whole-class work, small-group and pair work, teacher talk, student talk,
    c. closure

5. Assessment

Next, how can you determine whether your objectives have been accomplished? If your lesson has no assessment component, you can easily find yourself simply making assumptions that are not informed by careful observation or measurement. Now, you must understand that every lesson does not need to end with a little quiz or a formal test, nor does evaluation need to be a separate element of your lesson. Informal assessment can take place in the course of "regular" classroom activity. Some forms of assessment may have to wait a day or two until certain abilities have had a chance to build. Whatever manifestation your assessment takes, make sure, after students have sufficient opportunities for learning, that you have appropriately considered how you will (a) assess the success of your students and possibly (b) make appropriate adjustments in your lesson plan for the next day.

6. Extra-class work

What we commonly call "homework" (but students don't necessarily do such work only at *home*), I like to call **extra-class work**. If it is warranted, extra-class work needs to be planned carefully and communicated clearly to the students. Whether you are teaching in an EFL or ESL situation, you can almost always find applications or extensions of classroom activity that will help students do some learning beyond the class hour.

GUIDELINES FOR LESSON PLANNING

1. How to begin planning

In most normal circumstances, especially for a teacher without much experience, the first step of lesson planning will already have been performed for you: choosing what to teach. No doubt you will be—or have already been— given a textbook and told to teach from it, with either a suggestion or a requirement of how many chapters or units you should cover. As you look over the chapter you are to cover for a class hour, you might go through the following sequence:

a. Assuming that you are already familiar with (i) the curriculum your students are following (see "Adapting to an Established Curriculum" on page 170 of this section) and (ii) the overall plan and "tone" of the textbook(s), look over the textbook chapter.
b. Based on (i) your view of the whole curriculum and (ii) your perception of the language needs of your students, determine what the topic and purpose of the lesson will be and write that down as the overall goal.
c. Again considering the curriculum and the students' needs, draft out perhaps one to three explicitly stated terminal objectives for the lesson.
d. For each exercise in the textbook, decide if you will use it as is, adapt it, or skip it entirely—all based on the objectives you have drafted.
e. Draft out a skeletal outline of what your lesson will look like.
f. Carefully plan step-by-step procedures for carrying out all techniques, especially those that involve changes and additions. State the purpose(s) of each technique and/or activity as enabling objectives.

For teachers who have never taught before, it is often very useful to write a script of your lesson plan in which your exact anticipated words are written down and followed by exactly what you would expect students to say in return. Scripting out a lesson plan helps you to be more specific in your planning and can often prevent classroom pitfalls where you get all tangled up in explaining something or students take you off on a tangent. Writing a complete script for a whole hour of teaching is probably too laborious and unreasonable, but more practical and instructive (for you) are *partial* scripts that cover

a. introductions to activities
b. directions for a task
c. statements of rules or generalizations
d. anticipated interchanges that could easily bog down or go astray
e. oral testing techniques
f. conclusions to activities and to the class hour

2. Variety, sequencing, pacing, and timing

As you are drafting step-by-step procedures, you need to look at how the lesson holds together as a whole. Four considerations come into play here:

a. Is there sufficient *variety* in techniques to keep the lesson lively and interesting? Most successful lessons give students a number of different activities during the class hour, keeping minds alert and enthusiasm high.
b. Are your techniques or activities *sequenced* logically? Ideally, elements of a lesson will build progressively toward accomplishing the ultimate goals. Easier aspects will usually be placed at the beginning of a lesson; tasks that require knowledge gained from previous exercises will be sequenced appropriately.
c. Is the lesson as a whole *paced* adequately? Pacing can mean a number of things. First, it means that activities are neither too long nor too short. You could, for example, have so many short activities that just as students are getting the "feel" for one activity, they get bounced to the next. Second, you need to anticipate how well your various techniques "flow" together. You would not, for example, find a smooth flow in a class that had five minutes each of whole-class work, pair work, whole-class work, group work, pair work, whole-class work, etc. Nor would you normally plan two silent reading activities in a row. Third, good pacing also is a factor of how well you provide a transition from one activity to the next. An example:

> **T:** Okay, you've just had a good chance to listen to the way a lecturer signals various segments of a class lecture. Now we're going to use this information to look at a reading passage about space exploration and figure out . . .

d. Is the lesson appropriately *timed,* considering the number of minutes in the class hour? This is one of the most difficult aspects of lesson planning to control. It's not unusual for new teachers to plan a lesson so tightly that they actually complete their lesson plan early, but after just a little experience it is more common that we don't complete our lessons within the planned time allotment. The latter is not a cardinal sin, for most likely it means you have given some time to students for genuine interaction and creative use of language. But timing is an element that you should build into a lesson plan: (i) If your planned lesson ends early, have some backup activity ready to insert; (ii) if your lesson isn't completed as planned, be ready to gracefully end a class on time and, on the next day, pick up where you left off.

3. Gauging difficulty

Figuring out in advance how easy or difficult certain techniques will be is usually learned by experience. It takes a good deal of cognitive empathy to put yourself in your students' shoes and anticipate their problem areas. Some difficulty is caused by tasks themselves; therefore, make your directions crystal clear by writing them out in advance (note the comments on "scripting" lessons, above). I have seen too many classes where teachers have not clearly planned exactly what task directions they will give. Writing them ahead of time allows you to be more objective in determining if everything is clear. And then, either give an example yourself or solicit an example of a subtask within a technique.

Another source of difficulty, of course, is linguistic. If you can follow the $i + 1$ principle of providing material that is just a little above, but not too far above, students' ability, the linguistic difficulty should be optimal. The main problem here lies in the heterogeneity of a classroom full of learners whose proficiency range is very broad. Individual attention, feedback, and small-group work can sometimes bring balance into the classroom.

4. Individual differences

For the most part, a lesson plan will aim at the majority of students in class who compose the "average" ability range. But your lesson plan should also take into account the variation of ability in your students, especially those who are well below or well above the classroom norm. You can take several steps to account for individual differences:

a. Design techniques that have easy and difficult aspects or items.
b. Solicit responses to easier items from students who are below the norm and to harder items from those above the norm.
c. Try to design techniques that will involve *all* students actively.
d. Use judicious selection to assign members of small groups so that each group has either (i) a heterogeneous range of ability or (ii) a homogeneous range (to encourage equal participation).
e. Use small-group and pair work time to circulate and give extra attention to those below or above the norm (see Chapter 14 on group work principles).

5. Student talk and teacher talk

Give careful consideration in your lesson plan to the balance between student talk and teacher talk. Our natural inclination as teachers is to talk too much! As you plan your lesson, and as you perhaps script out some aspects of it, see to it that students have a chance to talk, to produce language, and even to initiate their own topics and ideas.

6. Adapting to an established curriculum

In the previous chapter, you were introduced to the steps involved in designing a curriculum. The assumption then, and in this chapter, is that your primary task is *not* to write a new curriculum or to revise an existing one, but to follow an established curriculum and adapt to it in terms of your particular group of students, their needs, and their goals, as well as your own philosophy of teaching.

As you plan lessons, your first concern is that each class hour must contribute to the goals that a curriculum is designed to pursue. But perhaps your institution has no curriculum spelled out in a document; in other words, it is a "textbook-driven" curriculum that, in practice, simply tells you to teach everything in a textbook. Or you may find certain specifications for the course you are about to teach somewhere in the description of the institution. At best, you would be presented with a document that clearly delineates the goals of the curriculum and offers suggestions on how to meet those goals in terms of weekly or even daily lesson objectives.

If you don't have such overall course goals, it might be feasible to devise some for yourself so that you can keep your course focused on attainable, practical ends. To do so, consider the factors outlined in the previous chapter that contribute to curriculum planning:

- situation analysis (especially learner characteristics)
- needs analysis (especially learner factors and institutional factors)
- supporting materials and resources
- assessment requirements

By paying attention to the learner factors above, you will have a good chance of pointing your students toward pragmatic, communicative goals in which their real-life needs for English will be met. You will focus on the learners and their needs but temper those with the realities of your institution's needs. The latter will add some administrative practicality to your goals. After all, every educational institution is limited in some way in its capacity to deliver the very "best."

Your course goals might look like these goals of an advanced pre-university listening comprehension course:

a. Students will understand the teacher's instructions and demonstrate that understanding.
b. Students will understand the teacher's explanations and show that comprehension.

  c. Students will understand classroom peers in discussions, activities, and oral reports.
  d. Students will understand academic lectures given by different speakers.
  e. Students will identify topics and topic development.
  f. Students will infer relationships among topics.
  g. Students will recognize different points of view.
  h. Students will identify key information as signaled by vocabulary.
  i. Students will recognize key information as signaled by stress and intonation.
  j. Students will identify key information as signaled by grammatical structure.

7. Classroom lesson notes

A final consideration in your lesson planning process is a very practical one: What sort of lesson notes will you actually carry into the classroom with you? If you have pages and pages of notes and reminders and scripts, you will never free yourself for spontaneity. Most experienced teachers operate well with about *one page* of a lesson outline and notes. Some prefer to put lesson notes on a series of index cards for easy handling. By reducing your plans to such a physically manageable minimum, you will reduce the chances of getting bogged down in all the details that went into the planning phase, yet you will have enough in writing to provide order and clarity as you proceed.

SAMPLE LESSON PLAN

What follows here is a lesson plan* designed for an intermediate level pre-university class at the American Language Institute at San Francisco State University. The 16 students in the class range in age from 18 to 25. Their general goals are academically oriented. Their native languages are Japanese, Korean, Mandarin, Indonesian, Thai, and Arabic.

1. Goal

Students will comprehend social conversations. (Lesson focus: telephone conversations.)

2. Objectives

Terminal objectives:
  1. Students will develop inner "expectancy rules" that enable them to *predict* and anticipate what someone else will say on the telephone.
  2. Students will solicit and receive information by requesting it over the telephone.

---

*I am grateful to Karen Tenney, ALI Instructor, for permission to adapt one of her lesson plans here.

Enabling objectives:
1. Students will comprehend a simple phone conversation (played on a tape recorder).
2. In the conversation, students will identify who the participants are, what they are going to do, and when.
3. Students will comprehend and produce necessary vocabulary for this topic.
4. Students will comprehend cultural and linguistic background information regarding movies, theaters, and arranging to see a movie with someone.
5. Students will infer what a second speaker is saying on the phone by "eavesdropping" on one speaker only.
6. Each student will ask someone to go to a movie with him or her and respond appropriately to a reciprocal request.
7. Students will get "live" movie information over the phone.

3. Materials and equipment
- tape recorder with taped conversation
- a telephone (if possible) or a toy facsimile
- eight different movie advertisements
- movie guide page for extra-class work

4. Procedures

1. **PRELISTENING**
   (Place a phone on the front table. It will be used later.)
   To point the students' thinking in the right direction for this lesson, we will start off with the following "model" phone conversation on tape. It is very short and very easy, well below the students' level. There is no question that they will understand it fully; its purpose is to set up a framework for the lesson.

2. **LISTENING TO THE TAPE**
   Please listen

Phone:	Ring!
Tom:	Hullo?
Jack:	Tom, this is Jack. D'ya wanna go to th' movies?
Tom:	Mmm . . . When?
Jack:	Tonight. I have free passes.
Tom:	Uh, OK, sure. What time?
Jack:	Eight o'clock. I'll—I'll meet ya there, OK?
Tom:	Fine. See ya then.

   (This tape may be played twice.)

3. **WHOLE-CLASS DISCUSSION**
T:	Did Tom call Jack?
Ss:	No, Jack called Tom.

T:	Right. What are they going to do?
Ss:	Go to the movies.
T:	Good! When are they going?
Ss:	Tonight (and/or) Eight o'clock.
T:	Right! What are free passes?
S1:	Free tickets.
T:	Yes! Who has free passes?
S2:	Jack.
T:	Exactly. What movie are they going to?
Ss:	It doesn't say.
T:	Hmm . . . What could that mean?
S1:	There's only one theater in their town.
S2:	They always meet at the same place.
	etc.
T:	Good! Any of those things are possible. It sounds like they know each other very well. Maybe they go to the movies together often.

(A general discussion about movie-going [and phoning to arrange it] will involve students personally and will introduce one new term.)

4. **SCHEMATA-BUILDING DISCUSSION**

T:	Who's been to the movies lately?
S1:	(raises hand)
T:	S1, what did you see?
S1:	*Da Vinci Code.*
T:	*Da Vinci Code*—was it good?
S1:	Yes.
T:	Did you go with a friend?
S1:	Yes.
T:	Did you call him or her to arrange it?
S1:	She called me.

(This conversation will continue to include other Ss. The main subjects to come back to are what movies they saw, if they arranged it with a friend by phone, and whether they went to a bargain matinee.)

(During all interactions the teacher LISTENS with interest to student comments. The teacher gives feedback after each comment, making sure to let the students realize that they do already know a lot.)

5. **LISTENING ACTIVITY #1**

T:	(Indicates the phone on the front desk.) My friend Debbie is going to call me in a few minutes. Of course, you won't hear Debbie talking to me; you'll just hear me, right?
	I want you to listen carefully and try to figure out two things (write these on the board as you say them):
	One—What does Debbie want to do? (Repeat.)

Two—When? (Repeat.)
OK, listen for what Debbie wants to do and when. (Indicate questions on board.)

(Pause. The phone rings.)

T: Hullo?

Gap 1   _____

T: This is Karen.

Gap 2   _____

T: Oh, hi, Deb, how're you?

Gap 3   _____

T: The movies? (Look at watch.) When?

Gap 4   _____

T: Um, OK, this afternoon's fine. Whadda ya wanna see?

Gap 5: _____

T: Well, I'll only go to *Mission Impossible* if it's a bargain matinee.

Gap 6   _____

T: There is? One o'clock? Great! I'll meet you there. 'Bye.

T: What does Debbie want to do?

Ss: Go to the movies.

T: Right! When?

Ss: This afternoon (and/or) One o'clock.

T: Excellent! She wants to go to the movie this afternoon.
        Now you're going to hear the same phone call again. This time try to figure out three things:

1. What movie does Debbie suggest?
2. Am I willing to pay full price?
3. Does Debbie tell me I will have to pay full price?

(Erase the first two questions from the board and put the three new questions on the board.)

(Repeat the phone call.)

T: What movie does Debbie suggest?

S1:   *Mission Impossible.*

T: Right! Was I willing to pay full price?

S2:   No. You wanted to go to a bargain matinee.

T: Yes! And what does Debbie tell me? Will I have to pay full price?

S3:   No. She tells you that there is a bargain matinee.

T: At what time?

S3:   One o'clock.

T: OK, good! Now you're going to hear the phone call one last time. This time I'll stop every time Debbie should be speaking, and I want you to tell me what Debbie might have said. Many different answers may be correct.

T: (Go back to phone.) Hullo?

```
S1:   Hullo? . . .
S2:   Is Karen there?
S3:   Is Karen home?
T:    (Smile and nod to show answers are good.) This is Karen.
S4:   It's Debbie.
S5:   This is Debbie.
T:    Oh, hi, Deb, how're you?
S6:   Fine . . .
S7:   Do you want to go to the movies?
S8:   Do you have time to see a movie?
```
(Continue until all Ss have participated/taken a turn.)

6. **POST-LISTENING ACTIVITY**
   (Pass out eight different movie ads to eight students [see samples on ad page]. Put a second phone on the front table.)

   T: OK, everyone with an ad, please get a partner who does not have an ad. S1 and S2 (one pair-group), please come up to these phones. S1 has a newspaper ad for a movie. She will call S2 and ask him to go to that movie with her. Be sure to arrange the following things in your phone conversation (write these on the board):

   1. What movie?
   2. What time?
   3. Which theater?

   (The students come up in pairs and have very short phone conversations to arrange going to a movie together. If there is not time for each pair to come to the front and use the phones, pairs can work on their conversations at their desks.)

7. **EXTRA-CLASSWORK ASSIGNMENT**
   (Pass out DATEBOOK/MOVIE GUIDE page to each student.)

   T: Everyone please choose a theater from this page. (Make sure each student chooses a different theater.)
        Circle the theater and the phone number on your handout.
        Choose a movie at your theater.
        Circle the movie.
        Circle the times next to it.

   (Repeat these directions and demonstrate with your own movie list. Go around and make sure that everyone has circled:

   1. a theater.
   2. the right phone number,
   3. a movie at their theater,
   4. the times it's showing.)

   T: Tonight when you go home, please call the theater you've chosen. Listen to the recording. Find out two things:

> 1. Is "your" movie still playing?
> 2. Are the times the same?
> Please write these questions on the back of your handout (write them on the board):
> 1. Is the movie you've chosen still playing?
> 2. Are the times the same?
> Remember that you can call the theater as many times as you want. These are local calls.

5. Assessment

Terminal objective (1) and enabling objectives (1) through (5) are assessed as the activities unfold without a formal testing component. The culminating pair work activity is the assessment component for terminal objective (2) and enabling objective (6). As pairs work together, circulate to monitor students and to observe informally whether they have accomplished the terminal objective. The success of the extra-class assignment—enabling objective (7)—will be informally observed on the next day.

☆   ☆   ☆   ☆   ☆

This chapter has focused specifically on the planning stage of classroom teaching. When you walk into the classroom, all that planning (you hope!) will work to your advantage. We turn in the next two chapters to an overview of materials—textbooks, technology, and other resources—that support the delivery of successful lessons.

TOPICS FOR DISCUSSION, ACTION, AND RESEARCH

[Note: (I) Individual work; (G) group or pair work; (C) whole-class discussion.]

1. (I) Following are some curricular goals selected from various academic English language programs:

   - understand academic lectures
   - write a business letter
   - use greetings and "small talk"
   - request information in a restaurant
   - read informal essays

For each of the above, briefly describe a specific audience for which the goal might be appropriate, then (a) transform the goal into *terminal* objective(s) and (b) state a number of *enabling* objectives that would have to be reached in order to accomplish the terminal objective.

2. (G/C) Direct groups to practice stating other lesson objectives for a course everyone is familiar with, and to discuss the extent to which one could empirically evaluate students' achievement of the objectives. Groups can then share their conclusions with the rest of the class.

3. (I/C) Observe an ESL class in which you look for manifestations of variety, sequencing, pacing, and timing, or the lack thereof. Write down your observations and share them in the form of a brief report with the whole class.

4. (C) Accounting for individual differences is not as easy as it sounds. Ask members of the class to describe some dimensions of student differences they have experienced or observed. How would one ensure, in each case, that students on both ends of the continuum are "reached" in some way? Small groups sometimes provide a means for accounting for differences. What are some other ways (d on page 169) to divide the class into small groups? Justify each.

5. (G) Have groups look at the sample lesson plan (pages 171–176) and use the seven guidelines for lesson planning (pages 167–171) to evaluate the plan. Should any changes be made? Conclusions should be shared with the rest of the class.

6. (I/G) Transform the lesson plan (on pages 171–176) into some practical "lesson notes"—no more than one or two index cards perhaps—that you could carry into the classroom with you. What decisions did you have to make? On what basis did you decide to create your notes the way you did? Share your notes with others in a small group and discuss your reasons for doing what you did.

7. (G) A needs analysis normally considers such questions as who the learners are, why they are learning English, in what context(s) they use it, etc. Ask groups to identify learners they are familiar with, and devise a list of specific questions that one could use to analyze needs and, in turn, to determine how a curriculum or a set of lessons should be designed.

8. (I) Find a teacher's manual or instructor's edition of an ESL textbook. Look at a chapter or unit and read through the "plan" or "suggestions" for teaching. Using the principles cited in this and in previous chapters, evaluate it for an audience that you specify. How would the suggestions need to be changed or added to for your audience?

FOR YOUR FURTHER READING

Jensen, L. (2001). Planning lessons. In M. Celce-Murcia (Ed.), *Teaching English as a second or foreign language* (3rd ed.) (pp. 403–413). Boston: Heinle & Heinle.

Farrell, T. (2002). Lesson planning. In J. Richards & W. Renandya (Eds.), *Methodology in language teaching: An anthology of current practice* (pp. 30–39). Cambridge, UK: Cambridge University Press.

In both of these chapters within anthologies, the authors treat principles and practical guidelines for planning lessons. They will provide you with slightly different perspectives from what has been presented here. Sample lesson notes are included as appendices in both cases.

Brown, H. D. (1999). *New vistas: An interactive course in English.* Teacher's Editions. White Plains, NY: Pearson Education.

The teacher's editions of New Vistas *offer a number of ideas on how various techniques combine to form cohesive classroom lessons. Each unit has explicit directions for teachers that can be used as lesson plans or as general guidelines that can be adapted for various audiences.*

CHAPTER 11

TECHNIQUES AND MATERIALS

OBJECTIVES After reading this chapter, you will be able to:

- understand the historical progression of development that led to current communicative techniques and task-based instruction

- identify a wide variety of techniques that are viable for lessons, within certain parameters

- analyze a number of criteria that would lead to choosing or rejecting potential materials for a course or lesson

- use guidelines for textbook evaluation to revise, change, or adapt existing materials to better meet stated objectives

The previous two chapters have given you some important background for further considerations in language pedagogy: designing and implementing techniques in the classroom, and reviewing and choosing from a wide variety of materials. The progression here has been to first take a broad wide-angle view of a course, then to focus in on the lesson, that is, the basic units of a course, and now to zoom in further to the components of a lesson: the techniques and activities that comprise a lesson, and the materials that support those techniques.

It may be overstating the obvious, but you cannot even begin to design techniques in the classroom without considering the backdrops of curriculum and lesson, both of which set the stage for the minute-by-minute activity of a class hour. The choices that you make about what to do in the classroom are enlightened—and sometimes limited—by the factors enumerated in Chapter 9: learner characteristics, institution, faculty, needs, and more, as well as the all-important set of lesson objectives that have been established. With those elements in mind, let's look at techniques and materials.

TECHNIQUES REDEFINED

It is appropriate, before continuing, to make sure that certain terms are well defined. In Chapter 2, the term **technique** was introduced and defined, but it was noted in passing that some other commonly used terms are considered by some to be virtually synonymous. These other terms include *task, activity, procedure, practice, behavior, exercise,* and even *strategy.* Since the use of multiple terms may be confusing, you will no doubt find it helpful to do some clarifying. Bear in mind, however, that experts in the field may have slightly differing points of view about the working definitions here.

1. Task

We return to the term **task** again. You may recall from Chapter 3, in a discussion of task-based instruction, that task usually refers to a specialized form of technique or series of techniques closely allied with communicative curricula, and as such must minimally have communicative goals. The common thread running through half a dozen definitions of task is its focus on the authentic use of language for meaningful communicative purposes beyond the language classroom.

2. Activity

A very popular term in the literature, an **activity** may refer to virtually anything that learners *do* in the classroom. More specifically, when we refer to a classroom activity, we usually refer to a reasonably unified set of student behaviors, limited in time, preceded by some direction from the teacher, with a particular objective. Activities include role plays, drills, games, peer-editing, small-group information-gap exercises, and much more. Because an activity implies some sort of active performance on the part of learners, it is generally *not* used to refer to certain teacher behaviors like saying "good morning," maintaining eye contact with students, explaining a grammar point, or writing a list of words on the chalkboard. Such teacher behaviors, however, can indeed be referred to as techniques (see #5 below).

3. Procedure

Richards and Rodgers (2001) used the term **procedure** to encompass "the actual moment-to-moment techniques, practices, and behaviors that operate in teaching a language according to a particular method" (p. 26). Procedures, from this definition, include techniques, but the authors appear to have no compelling objection to viewing the terms synonymously. Thus, for Richards and Rodgers, this appears to be a catchall term.

4. Practice, behavior, exercise, strategy . . .

In the language-teaching literature, these terms, and perhaps some others, all appear to refer, in varying degrees of intensity, to what is defined below as technique.

5. Technique

Even before Anthony (1963) discussed and defined the term, the language-teaching literature generally accepted **technique** as a superordinate term to refer to various activities that either teachers or learners perform in the classroom. In other words, techniques include all tasks and activities. They are almost always planned and deliberate. They are the product of a choice made by the teacher. And they can, for your purposes as a language teacher, comfortably refer to the pedagogical units or components of a classroom session. You can think of a lesson as consisting of a number of techniques, some teacher-centered, some learner-centered, some production-oriented, some comprehension-oriented, some clustering together to form a task, and some as a task in and of themselves. We now turn to examine these classroom components of focus or activity.

CATEGORIZING TECHNIQUES: A BIT OF HISTORY

At last count there were 28,732 techniques for teaching language in the classroom. Okay, I'm joking. But a cursory glance at a few dozen textbooks and other teacher-activities books reveals many, many possible techniques! TESOL's *New Ways* series of teacher reference books is an excellent example of a plethora of techniques categorized into such areas as teaching speaking, listening, reading, and writing. Bailey (2005), for example, suggests at least 100 techniques for teaching speaking. Linse (2005), Nunan (2005), and Helgesen and Brown (2007) together offer hundreds of different techniques for teaching young children grammar and listening, respectively. Other teacher reference books from virtually every major publisher collectively describe thousands of techniques for different ages, skills, and proficiency levels (Claire, 1988; Klippel, 1984; Shoemaker & Shoemaker, 1991).

How can you best conceptualize this multitude of techniques? Over the years, several rubrics have been used to classify techniques.

1. From manipulation to communication

Techniques can be thought of as existing along a continuum of possibilities between highly manipulative and very communicative. At the extreme end of the **manipulative** side, a technique is totally controlled by the teacher and requires a predicted response from the student(s). Choral repetition and cued substitution drills are examples of oral techniques at this extreme. Other examples are dictation (listening/writing) and reading aloud.

At the **communicative** extreme, student responses are completely open-ended and therefore unpredictable. Examples include storytelling, brainstorming, role plays, certain games, etc. Teachers are usually put into a less controlled role here, as students become free to be creative with their responses and interactions with other students. However, keep in mind that a modicum of teacher control, whether overt or covert, should always be present in the classroom.

It is important to remember that the manipulation–communication scale does not correspond to the beginning-through-advanced proficiency continuum! For too many years the language-teaching profession labored under the incorrect assumption that beginners must have isolated, mechanical bits and pieces of language programmed into them (typically through a memorized audiolingual drill) and that only later could "real" communication take place. The whole CLT approach accentuates a diametrically opposed philosophy: that genuine communication can take place from the very first day of a language class.

The extent to which a communicative technique can sustain itself for long periods of time in the classroom will often be a factor of the overall proficiency level of your class. But even at the beginning level, students can engage in meaningful communication for significant stretches of time. Communicative techniques for beginners involve appropriately small chunks of language and build in some repetition of patterns for establishing fluency. On one of the very first days of class, for example, students can be taught to ask and respond to questions such as:

- How are you?
- What's your name?
- Where do you live?
- How old are you? (for children)
- What do you do? (for adults)

At an intermediate level, students can get involved in a "mixer" in which they go around the room, getting information from, say, four or five other students. At the more advanced levels, a simple question or problem posed by the teacher can lead to sustained, meaningful student communication between student and teacher, in pairs or in small groups.

2. Mechanical, meaningful, and communicative drills

In the decades of the 1940s through the 1960s, language pedagogy was obsessed with the drill. Great proportions of class time were often spent drilling: repeating, repeating, repeating. Today, thankfully, we have developed teaching practices that make only minimal—or optimal—use of such drilling.

A **drill** may be defined as a technique that focuses on a minimal number (usually one or two) of language forms (grammatical or phonological structures) through some type of repetition. Drills are commonly done chorally (the whole class repeating in unison) or individually. And they can take the form of simple repetition drills, substitution drills, and even the rather horrifying aberration known as the moving slot substitution drill. In a substitution drill, the teacher provides a sentence, students repeat; teacher cues students to change one word or structure in the sentence, students repeat. For example:

T: I went to the store yesterday.	**Ss:** I went to the store yesterday.
T: Bank.	**Ss:** I went to the bank yesterday.
T: Hospital.	**Ss:** I went to the hospital yesterday.

In a moving slot substitution drill, the slot moves, as in the following example:

T: I went to the store yesterday.	**Ss:** I went to the store yesterday.
T: Bank.	**Ss:** I went to the bank yesterday.
T: He.	**Ss:** He went to the bank yesterday.
T: In the morning.	**Ss:** He went to the bank in the morning.
T: Will go.	**Ss:** He will go to the bank in the morning.

By this time, if students haven't thrown up their arms in the frustration of having to retain each previous sentence alteration, they may have accomplished only the feat of overworking their short-term memories. They certainly have gained no communicative ability.

In referring to structural pattern drills, Paulston and Bruder (1976) used three categories: mechanical, meaningful, and communicative. **Mechanical drills** have only one correct response from a student, and have no implied connection with reality. Repetition drills require, for instance, that the student repeat a word or phrase whether the student understands it or not:

> **T:** The cat is in the hat.
> **Ss:** The cat is in the hat.
> **T:** The wug is on the gling.
> **Ss:** The wug is on the gling.

A **meaningful drill** may have a predicted response or a limited set of possible responses, but it is connected to some form of reality:

> **T:** The woman is outside. [*pointing out the window at a woman*]
>   Where is she, Hiro?
> **S1:** The woman is outside.
> **T:** Right, she's outside. Keiko, where is she?
> **S2:** She's outside.
> **T:** Good, Keiko, she's outside. Now, class, we are inside. Hiroko, where are we?
> **S3:** We are inside.

And the process may continue on as the teacher reinforces certain grammatical or phonological elements. To be frank, I see no reason to refer to such a technique as a drill; it is quite legitimately a form of meaningful practice, useful in many communicative classrooms.

Now, while Paulston and Bruder referred to "communicative" drills more than two decades ago, as we now understand and use the term, a **communicative drill** is an oxymoron. If the exercise is communicative, that is, if it offers the student the possibility of an open response and negotiation of meaning, then it is not a drill. Instead there is what we might call **form-focused** communicative practice that might go something like this, if you were trying to get students to practice the past tense:

> **T:** Good morning, class. Last weekend I went to a restaurant and I ate salmon. Juan, what did you do last weekend?
> **Juan:** I went to park and I play soccer.
> **T:** Juan, "I *play* soccer" or "I *played* soccer"?
> **Juan:** Oh . . . eh . . . I played soccer.
> **T:** Good! Ying, did you go to the park last weekend?
> **Ying:** No.
> **T:** What did you do?
> **Ying:** I went to a movie.
> **T:** Great, and what did you do, Fay?

This exercise is an attempt to force students to use the past tense, but allows them to choose meaningful replies. Juan chose the safety of the teacher's pattern, while Ying, perhaps because she was more focused on communicative reality than on past tense formation, initially broke out of the pattern before returning.

A final word about drills: A communicative approach to language teaching can make some use of drilling techniques, but only in moderation. A few short, snappy drills here and there, especially at the lower levels of proficiency, can be quite useful in helping students to establish structural patterns, rhythm, and certain pronunciation elements. But moderation is the key, especially if your drills are mechanical. There's nothing deadlier than a class hour filled with audiolingual parroting.

3. Controlled to free techniques

Perhaps the most useful classification of techniques for a teacher to use as a continuum not unlike the first one described on pages 181–182—a continuum of possibilities between highly manipulative and very communicative—but one that also specifically considers the extent to which the teacher maintains control over the learning activity. Accordingly, it is important to understand what is meant by *control*. In the lists below are a few generalizations.

Controlled	**Free**
Teacher-centered	Student-centered
Manipulative	Communicative
Structured	Open-ended
Predicted student responses	Unpredicted responses
Preplanned objectives	Negotiated objectives
Set curriculum	Cooperative curriculum

Clearly, the real picture is not as black-and-white as these generalizations seem to be. For example, many controlled techniques are manipulative, as described above. But controlled techniques sometimes have communicative elements. The form-focused communicative "drill" just described, for example, is highly controlled in that the teacher provides set questions and each student has a short time in which to respond. But there is an opportunity for students to venture out of the mold if they wish; that's communicative. So, if you are tempted to draw a clearly defined line between controlled and free, resist that temptation.

A TAXONOMY OF TECHNIQUES

A comprehensive taxonomy of common techniques for language teaching, adapted from Crookes and Chaudron (1991), is found in Table 11.1. Notice that three broad categories are used: controlled, semicontrolled, and free. Bearing in mind the somewhat slippery concept of control referred to above, you may be able to gain a broad picture from this taxonomy of a range of classroom language-teaching techniques. In the chapters that follow, many of these techniques will be discussed with examples and analysis.

Table 11.1. Taxonomy of language-teaching techniques (adapted from Crookes & Chaudron, 1991, pp. 52–54)

CONTROLLED TECHNIQUES

1. **Warm-up:** Mimes, dance, songs, jokes, play. This activity gets the students stimulated, relaxed, motivated, attentive, or otherwise engaged and ready for the lesson. It does not necessarily involve use of the target language.
2. **Setting:** Focusing in on lesson topic. Teacher directs attention to the topic by verbal or nonverbal evocation of the context relevant to the lesson by questioning or miming or picture presentation, possibly by tape recording of situations and people.
3. **Organizational:** Structuring of lesson or class activities includes disciplinary action, organization of class furniture and seating, general procedures for class interaction and performance, structure and purpose of lesson, etc.
4. **Content explanation:** Grammatical, phonological, lexical (vocabulary), sociolinguistic, pragmatic, or any other aspects of language.
5. **Role-play demonstration:** Selected students or teacher illustrate the procedure(s) to be applied in the lesson segment to follow. Includes brief illustration of language or other content to be incorporated.
6. **Dialogue/Narrative presentation:** Reading or listening passage presented for passive reception. No implication of student production or other identification of specific target forms or functions (students may be asked to "understand").
7. **Dialogue/Narrative recitation:** Reciting a previously known or prepared text, either in unison or individually.
8. **Reading aloud:** Reading directly from a given text.
9. **Checking:** Teacher either circulating or guiding the correction of students' work, providing feedback as an activity rather than within another activity.
10. **Question-answer, display:** Activity involving prompting of student responses by means of display questions (i.e., teacher or questioner already knows the response or has a very limited set of expectations for the appropriate response). Distinguished from referential questions by the likelihood of the questioner's knowledge of the response and the speaker's awareness of that fact.
11. **Drill:** Typical language activity involving fixed patterns of teacher prompting and student responding, usually with repetition, substitution, and other mechanical alterations. Typically with little meaning attached.
12. **Translation:** Student or teacher provision of L1 or L2 translations of given text.
13. **Dictation:** Student writing down orally presented text.
14. **Copying:** Student writing down text presented visually.
15. **Identification:** Student picking out and producing/labeling or otherwise identifying a specific target form, function, definition, or other lesson-related item.
16. **Recognition:** Student identifying forms, as in **Identification** (i.e., checking off items, drawing symbols, rearranging pictures), but without a verbal response.
17. **Review:** Teacher-led review of previous week/month/or other period as a formal summary and type of test of student recall performance.
18. **Testing:** Formal testing procedures to evaluate student progress.
19. **Meaningful drill:** Drill activity involving responses with meaningful choices, as in reference to different information. Distinguished from **Information exchange** by the regulated sequence and general form of responses. *(Continued)*

20. **Brainstorming:** A form of preparation for the lesson, like **Setting**, which involves free, undirected contributions by the students and teacher on a given topic, to generate multiple associations without linking them; no explicit analysis or interpretation by the teacher.

21. **Storytelling (especially when student-generated):** Not necessarily lesson-based, a lengthy presentation of story by teacher or student (may overlap with **Warm-up** or **Narrative recitation**). May be used to maintain attention, motivate, or as lengthy practice.

22. **Question-answer, referential:** Activity involving prompting of responses by means of referential questions (i.e., the questioner does not know beforehand the response information). Distinguished from **Question-answer, display**.

23. **Cued narrative/Dialogue:** Student production of narrative or dialogue following cues from miming, cue cards, pictures, or other stimuli related to narrative/dialogue (e.g., metalanguage requesting functional acts).

24. **Information transfer:** Application from one mode (e.g., visual) to another (e.g., writing), which involves some transformation of the information (e.g., student fills out diagram while listening to description). Distinguished from **Identification** in that the student is expected to transform and reinterpret the language or information.

25. **Information exchange:** Task involving two-way communication as in information-gap exercises, when one or both parties (or a larger group) must share information to achieve some goal. Distinguished from **Question-answer, referential** in that sharing of information is critical for the task.

26. **Wrap-up:** Brief teacher- or student-produced summary of point and/or items that have been practiced or learned.

27. **Narration/Exposition:** Presentation of a story or explanation derived from prior stimuli. Distinguished from **Cued narrative** because of lack of immediate stimulus.

28. **Preparation:** Student study, silent reading, pair planning and rehearsing, preparing for later activity. Usually a student-directed or -oriented project.

FREE TECHNIQUES

29. **Role play:** Relatively free acting out of specified roles and functions. Distinguished from **Cued dialogues** by the fact that cueing is provided only minimally at the beginning, and not during the activity.

30. **Games:** Various kinds of language game activity not like other previously defined activities (e.g., board and dice games making words).

31. **Report:** Report of student-prepared exposition on books, experiences, project work, without immediate stimulus, and elaborated on according to student interests. Akin to **Composition** in writing mode.

32. **Problem solving:** Activity involving specified problem and limitations of means to resolve it; requires cooperation on part of participants in small or large group.

33. **Drama:** Planned dramatic rendition of play, skit, story, etc.

34. **Simulation:** Activity involving complex interaction between groups and individuals based on simulation of real-life actions and experiences.

35. **Interview:** A student is directed to get information from another student or students.

36. **Discussion:** Debate or other form of grouped discussion of specified topic, with or without specified sides/positions prearranged.

37. **Composition:** As in **Report** (verbal), written development of ideas, story, or other exposition.

38. **A propos:** Conversation or other socially oriented interaction/speech by teacher, students, or even visitors, on general real-life topics. Typically authentic and genuine.

In a taxonomy such as this, not only will many techniques be somewhat difficult to categorize in terms of the control continuum, but some techniques will fit into more than one category. Consider the following "warm-up" activity suggested by Klippel (1984, pp. 13–14) for a beginning level class:

Step 1: Each student writes his/her full name on a piece of paper. All the papers are collected and redistributed so that everyone receives the name of a person he/she does not know.

Step 2: Everyone walks around the room and tries to find the person whose name he/she holds. Simple questions can be: "Is your name . . . ?" "Are you . . . ?"

Step 3: When everyone has found his/her partner, he/she introduces him/her to the group.

This exercise seems to fit into a number of possible categories: It involves *question-answer, referential* activity; there is some *information exchange* as well; and in some ways either *problem solving* or *games* may fit here. The purpose in referring to such a taxonomy, therefore, is not to be able to pinpoint every technique specifically. Rather, the taxonomy is more of a help to you as

- an aid to raising your awareness of the wide variety of available techniques
- an indicator of how techniques differ according to a continuum ranging from controlled to free
- a resource for your own personal brainstorming process as you consider types of techniques for your classroom

TEXTBOOKS

Techniques consist of the things you "do" in the classroom, but only a few techniques do not in some manner involve the use of materials to support and enhance them. What would language classes be without books, pictures, charts, realia, and technological aids (audiotapes, video, computers)? Yes, you could have conversations, role plays, discussions, and chalkboard work, but much of the richness of language instruction is derived from supporting materials. Today such materials abound for all levels and purposes.

What kinds of materials are available to you? How do you decide what will work and what won't? Is it worthwhile to create your own materials? If so, what sorts of things can be relatively easily made? We'll look at these and related questions here as we consider these all-important supporting elements in a lesson.

The most obvious and most common form of material support for language instruction comes through textbooks. Most likely, as a relatively new teacher, your first concern will not be to choose a textbook, but rather to find creative use for the textbook that has been handed to you by your supervisor. So, even though you may have idealistic thoughts about other (and better) textbooks, your challenge is to make the very best use of the textbook that you have. Sometimes new teachers, in their zeal for creating wonderful, marvelous written materials for their students, neglect the standard textbook prescribed by the school curriculum and fail to see that this resource may actually be quite useful. And you will no doubt find that, as a new teacher, you already have enough on your hands just preparing a lesson, carrying it out, monitoring its unfolding, and managing the dynamics of a classroom full of students. You don't need to add more stress to your life by trying to create brand-new materials.

Textbook Adaptation

So here you are, textbook in hand, preparing for tomorrow's lesson. If your textbook has a teacher's edition, by all means consult it and use as many of its suggestions as you feel are appropriate. If there is no teacher's edition, then your task becomes one of devising ways to present the content and the exercises of the book to your class.

On the next two pages is a lesson from Unit 13 in Book 1 of *Worldview* (Rost, 2002), pitched for a high-beginning level class. You will see that this lesson focuses on vocabulary related to food and, indirectly, on noun quantifiers. You note that you can classify possible techniques according to the taxonomy in Table 11.1:

> **Exercise 1:** (1) Warm-up; (2) Setting; (10) Question-answer, display;
> (16) Recognition; (9) Checking
> **Exercise 2:** (15) Identification; (11) Drill
> **Exercise 3:** (10) Question-answer, display; (24) Information transfer;
> (25) Information exchange; (14) Copying
> **Exercise 4:** (22) Question-answer, referential; (25) Information exchange
> **Exercise 5:** (15) Identification
> **Exercise 6:** (24) Information transfer
> **Exercise 7:** (6) Narrative presentation; (22) Question-answer, referential;
> (25) Information exchange; (9) Checking
> **Exercise 8:** (15) Identification; (10) Question-answer, display

Could you devise a plan (using the guidelines in the previous chapter) that would "teach" these eight exercises? Of course, each exercise has brief directions to students, but how would you contextualize the lesson for your audience and context? Let's say your objectives focus on (a) vocabulary for food, (b) talking about food you like, and (c) a message about unhealthy sweet food. Here are just a few of the questions you might ask yourself in the lesson planning stage:

UNIT
13

How sweet it is!

Vocabulary Food
Grammar Count and non-count nouns; *How much/How many*;
Quantifiers: *much, many, a lot of*
Speaking Talking about foods you like

Lesson A

Getting started

1 *PAIRS.* **Match the photos with the words in the box.**

bread ____	butter _A_	cake ____	candy ____	cheese ____
chocolate ____	coffee ____	cookies ____	crackers ____	fruit ____
ice cream ____	milk ____	nuts ____	potato chips ____	soda ____

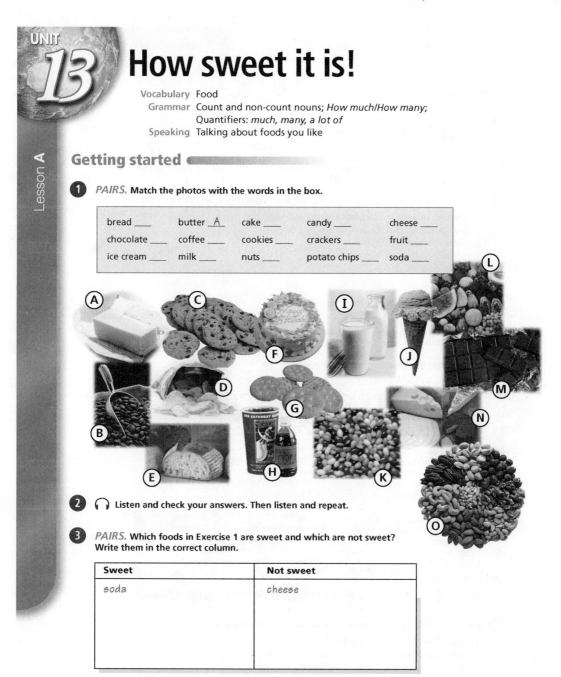

2 🎧 **Listen and check your answers. Then listen and repeat.**

3 *PAIRS.* **Which foods in Exercise 1 are sweet and which are not sweet?**
Write them in the correct column.

Sweet	Not sweet
soda	cheese

13

Listening

4 *PAIRS.* **Do you know what the following word and phrase mean:** *chocoholic* **and** *to have a sweet tooth*?

5 🎧 **Listen to the interview and check (✓) the words from Exercise 1 that you hear.**

6 🎧 **Listen again. Are the sentences true or false? Write *T* or *F* next to each one.**

1. Lorraine eats some chocolate almost every day. T
2. Tae-Soon eats a lot of sweet things.
3. Gustavo eats a lot of cookies.
4. Gustavo buys a lot of potato chips.
5. Janice prefers salty food.

Reading

7 *PAIRS.* **Do you think sweet foods are healthy or unhealthy for you? Read the article and compare your answers.**

Short and Sweet
The Truth about Sweets

Are you crazy about sweets? How many cookies do you eat in a day? How much chocolate? How much soda do you drink? A lot of people love sweets. In fact, a lot of people eat and drink too many sweet things. And that's not good. It can lead to health problems.

If you eat a lot of cookies, ice cream, or cake—be careful. Doctors say that too many sweets are bad for your health. They say to eat a variety of foods: lots of fruits and vegetables, and smaller portions of bread, meat, and dairy. Then have a cookie or two for dessert.

Are two cookies enough to satisfy your sweet tooth? If not, try these suggestions: eat some fruit instead of a lot of chocolate or ice cream, drink some juice instead of soda, or eat a few nuts instead of some candy.

8 **Read the article again. Underline the word that makes each sentence true.**

1. A lot of people love **sweets / butter**.
2. Too many **cookies / vegetables** are bad for your health.
3. It's OK to eat one or two **cookies / cakes** for dessert.
4. It's good to eat some **fruit / chocolate** instead of ice cream.

- Is Exercise 1 really the best way to begin this lesson? If they know these words, is this just a review?
- How will I direct students to perform Exercise 1? After the pairs have finished, what will the "reporting" process be?
- Is Exercise 2 too mechanical for my context?
- In Exercise 3, should I "teach" the word *sweet* first?
- Exercise 4 seems too complex for my high beginners. Should I just tell them about these two terms and then have a show of hands on those who feel they fall into one category or another? Or maybe at this point, they could take the lists of food in Exercise 3 and *talk about* what they like and don't like?
- I think I'll combine Exercises 5 and 6.
- Exercise 7 looks like it needs some background setting and some directions for what students should do *while* they read—what they should look for in the article as they are reading. Maybe I should follow this with some oral whole-class questions to serve as a comprehension check (rather than Exercise 8)?
- Instead of Exercise 8, I think I will consider a "mixer" in which I get students to line themselves up according to how much they like some of the foods listed in Exercise 1. That might wrap up this lesson with a focus on the message that sweet foods aren't all that healthy.

Textbook Evaluation

The above questions are issues of textbook adaptation that you face almost every time you sit down to plan a lesson. You see to it that the way you present the textbook lesson is appropriately geared for your particular students—their level, ability, and goals—and is just right for the number of minutes in your class.

If your teaching situation allows you to *choose* a textbook, you have an exciting but complex task ahead of you. In fact, the number of questions that need to be asked about a textbook can be overwhelming. (For the most comprehensive textbook evaluation checklist I have ever seen, see Skierso, 1991; this form occupies more than eight printed pages!) But once you have carried out a thorough investigation of textbooks using some kind of consistent evaluation procedure, you will be rewarded by having chosen a textbook that best fits all of your criteria.

Table 11.2 on page 192 provides an abridged evaluation form that can be a practical set of criteria for either (a) choosing a textbook for a course or (b) evaluating the textbook you are currently using. Even though this list was originally created several decades ago, it still stands as an excellent set of evaluative factors. As you read through this evaluation form, think of an ESL textbook that you are reasonably familiar with and ask yourself how well that book meets the criteria.

Table 11.2. Textbook evaluation criteria (adapted from Robinett, 1978, pp. 249–51)

1. **Goals of the course** (Will this textbook help to accomplish your course goals?)

2. **Background of the students** (Does the book fit the students' background?)
   - a. age
   - b. native language and culture
   - c. educational background
   - d. motivation or purpose for learning English

3. **Approach** (Does the theoretical approach reflected in the book reflect a philosophy that you and your institution and your students can easily identify with?)
   - a. theory of learning
   - b. theory of language

4. **Language skills** (Does the book integrate the "four skills"? Is there a balanced approach toward the skills? Does the textbook emphasize skills which the curriculum also emphasizes?)
   - a. listening
   - b. speaking
   - c. reading
   - d. writing

5. **General content** (Does the book reflect what is now known about language and language learning?)
   - a. validity—does the textbook accomplish what it purports to?
   - b. authenticity of language
   - c. appropriateness and currency of topics, situations, and contexts
   - d. proficiency level—is it pitched for the right level?

6. **Quality of practice material**
   - a. exercises—is there a variety from controlled to free?
   - b. clarity of directions—are they clear to both students and teacher?
   - c. active participation of students—is this encouraged effectively?
   - d. grammatical and other linguistic explanation—inductive or deductive?
   - e. review material—are there sufficient spiraling and review exercises?

7. **Sequencing** (How is the book sequenced?)
   - a. by grammatical structures
   - b. by skills
   - c. by situations
   - d. by some combination of the above

8. **Vocabulary** (Does the book pay sufficient attention to words and word study?)
   - a. relevance
   - b. frequency
   - c. strategies for word analysis

9. **General sociolinguistic factors**
   - a. variety of English—American, British, dialects, or international varieties
   - b. cultural content—is there a cultural bias?

10. **Format** (Is the book attractive, usable, and durable?)
    - a. clarity of typesetting
    - b. use of special notation (phonetic symbols, stress/intonation marking, etc.)
    - c. quality and clarity of illustrations
    - d. general layout—is it comfortable and not too "busy"?
    - e. size of the book and binding
    - f. quality of editing
    - g. index, table of contents, chapter headings

11. **Accompanying materials** (Are there useful supplementary materials?)
    - a. workbook
    - b. tapes—audio and/or video
    - c. posters, flash cards, etc.
    - d. a set of tests

12. **Teacher's guide** (Is it useful?)
    - a. methodological guidance
    - b. alternative and supplementary exercises
    - c. suitability for nonnative-speaking teacher
    - d. answer keys

OTHER TEXTS AND VISUAL AIDS

It needs to be made clear here how the word **text** is normally used in the profession and in this book, especially to distinguish *texts* from *textbooks.* Texts are any of a wide variety of types or genres of linguistic forms. Texts can be spoken or written. Among written texts, the range of possibilities extends from labels and forms and charts to essays and manuals and books. **Textbooks** are one type of text, a book for use in an educational curriculum.

Among other written texts available for your use in the classroom, an almost unlimited supply of real-world textual material is available. We daily encounter signs, schedules, calendars, advertisements, menus, memos, notes, etc. (see Chapter 20 for a long list of texts). Aside from written texts, other visual aids can support classroom lessons. Consider some possibilities of both texts and other supporting material:

a. **Teacher resource books.** Dozens of resource books are specifically designed to provide ideas for teachers. For example, books are available on speaking (e.g., Bailey, 2005), listening (Helgesen & Brown, 2007), reading (Anderson, 1999; Nuttall, 1996), grammar (Nunan, 2005), activities for children (Linse, 2005), and the list goes on.

b. **Other student textbooks.** Even a small library of student textbooks other than the one you are using will yield a book or two with some additional material that you can employ as supplementary material.

c. **Realia.** Realia are probably the oldest form of classroom aid. There is nothing like an "object" lesson. Objects—food items, cosmetics, household gadgets, tools, and other materials—always add some significant reality to the classroom. Their effectiveness in helping students to connect language to reality cannot be underestimated. Realia are especially useful and important for teaching children, who benefit from tangible objects that can stimulate kinesthetic connections.

d. **Self-made paper-based visual aids.** With the dominance of computer media in our world today, you may think it's odd to think about some of the more traditional forms of visual aids. Posters, charts, and magazine pictures represent "old-fashioned" but effective teaching aids. If you are artistically inclined, you should consider trying your hand at creating posters or charts for classroom use. Otherwise, a resource that many teachers find helpful is an assemblage of a couple of hundred magazine pictures that you can file and cross-index. Start with a pile of fairly recent magazines and pick out pictures (photos, diagrams, advertisements, etc.) that show people or objects large enough to be easily seen by all students in a classroom setting. Mounting them on cardboard or laminating them will protect your pictures from wrinkling.

e. **Commercially available visual aids.** Also, keep your eye open for commercially available slides, photographs, posters, and other illustrations. Some publishers still provide posters and charts with textbooks (even though most have now switched to DVDs that accompany textbooks). Media resource centers in many institutions offer a diversity of materials that should not be ignored.

✫   ✫   ✫   ✫   ✫

In the next chapter, you will find descriptions of what is commonly referred to as **technology** in the classroom, including the *audio* half of *audiovisual*. I have separated the technological elements into a separate chapter because of sweeping changes and the plethora of choices available due to advances in electronic media in a world that finds new words added to our vocabulary everyday!

TOPICS FOR DISCUSSION, ACTION, AND RESEARCH

[Note: (I) Individual work; (G) group or pair work; (C) whole-class discussion.]

1. (G) Ask pairs to review the differences among mechanical, meaningful, and quasi-communicative drills, and illustrate with more examples. What is the place of mechanical drills in an interactive CLT curriculum?
2. (I) Review the information on the continuum of techniques ranging from manipulation to communication, referring to both the manipulation-communication scale and the controlled-free scale. Look at the taxonomy of techniques in Table 11.1 (pages 185–186). For as many of the techniques as possible, decide if the arrangement in the table of controlled, semicontrolled, and free techniques matches the manipulation–communication scale.
3. (C/G) Refer students to the taxonomy of techniques referred to in Table 11.1, and try to clarify any questions they might have about what each technique is. If time permits, divide some or all of the techniques among pairs in the classroom, and have partners figure out how to demonstrate the technique to the rest of the class.
4. (G) On page 191 some questions were asked about the eight exercises reprinted from the *Worldview* series. Ask pairs to devise a plan that would "teach" selected exercises. For example, how would they introduce such a lesson? How would they direct Exercise 1? Or treat the reading passage in Exercise 7? Of the techniques listed earlier in this chapter, which might be appropriate additions to these exercises?
5. (I) Refer to the list of evaluative factors for a textbook in Table 11.2 (page 192) and convert them into questions that you could answer on a scale of 1 (poor) to 5 (excellent). Use your newly devised questionnaire to evaluate a textbook that is available to you. Write a brief review (or make an oral report) of the textbook based on your evaluation.

6. (G/C) Direct pairs to select approximately 10 magazine pictures for a lesson on foods and drugs and to brainstorm some ways that one might actually use them in a lesson. In the next class period, pairs will then share their ideas with the rest of the class.

FOR YOUR FURTHER READING

New Ways in TESOL series. (1993–1999). Alexandria, VA: Teachers of English to Speakers of Other Languages.

> *Any of the books in this series of 18 topically focused volumes will offer many different techniques which you can scan for an overview of things teachers have actually done in the classroom. Virtually all entries come from practicing teachers. Each entry is indexed by proficiency level, skill area, and sometimes age level.*

Bailey, K. (2005). *Practical English language teaching: Speaking.* New York: McGraw-Hill.

Helgesen, M., & Brown, S. (2007). *Practical English language teaching: Listening.* New York: McGraw-Hill.

Nunan, D. (2005). *Practical English language teaching: Grammar.* New York: McGraw-Hill.

Linse, C. (2005). *Practical English language teaching: Young learners.* New York: McGraw-Hill.

> *All four of these books are excellent examples of teacher reference books that offer a variety of different techniques for various contexts. Each book also includes principles, guidelines, and other commentary on teaching the designated skill area or age level.*

Graves, K. (2000). *Designing language courses: A guide for teachers.* Cambridge, UK: Cambridge University Press.

Brown, J.D. (1995). *The elements of language curriculum: A systematic approach to program development.* Boston: Heinle & Heinle.

> *Both of these books have separate chapters (for Graves, Chapter 9; for Brown, Chapter 5) that present useful comments and guidelines on choosing and adapting textbooks in the classroom. For an alternative to the textbook evaluation checklist that was offered in this chapter, see Brown, page 161.*

CHAPTER 12

TECHNOLOGY IN THE

CLASSROOM

OBJECTIVES After reading this chapter, you will be able to:

- identify numerous types of non-computer-based technology and their potential for contributing to a course or lesson

- understand the advantages as well as the disadvantages of using computer-based technology in your classroom

- examine the many possible forms of computer-based technology that are now available for classroom use, and their potential for contributing to linguistic interaction among students

- approach the use of technological innovations with caution but without the fear that could arise from your students being more cognizant of electronic hardware and software than you are

---

When someone mentions technology in the language classroom, your first impulse is to think computer technology, mostly because computers have so pervaded our daily home and workplace contexts. But technology covers everything from audiotapes to video to, yes, computers.

Some like to think that technology first entered the language classroom in the 1950s and 1960s in the form of the language laboratory. Institutions hastened to dedicate rooms to the installation of multiple tape-deck-equipped booths where students gathered to listen to native speakers modeling the drills of the current day's lesson. Often, users of language labs were able to record their own voices on one track of a tape in an attempt to match the native-speaker model; otherwise, they simply had the benefit of a listening lab. The advent of the language lab brought promises of great breakthroughs in language teaching: Technology would come to the rescue of less than totally effective methods. But when students were not being transformed into communicatively proficient speakers via the language lab, we discovered that there were some severe limitations to this new technological aid.

When the personal computer came on the scene in the 1980s, some practitioners in the language-teaching profession had similar hopes for salvation. Once again educational institutions had a promising new technology that could offer linguistic input and output, feedback, and a locus for student collaboration, interactivity, and fun. This time, however, the promises were more guarded as we were wary of the complexities involved in incorporating this powerful tool into our classrooms. The latter part of this chapter will specifically focus on **computer-assisted language learning** (CALL); but first, we take a look at *other* types of technological aids that are commonly available to a language teacher today.

NON-COMPUTER-BASED TECHNOLOGY

Believe it or not, there *is* technology available that is non-computer-based! If you went back a hundred years, you would find classrooms that had more than a piece of chalk and a chalkboard as teaching aids. In the previous chapter, photographs, posters, charts, and realia were mentioned—all time-tested, readily available, potentially interesting materials that are still viable in today's classrooms. But these don't fall into the category of technology—which I'm defining here as any equipment that requires electricity to operate. By the early part of the twentieth century, as electrical appliances became commonplace, motion pictures (movies), films and filmstrips, slides, and phonograph records joined the ranks of technology in the classroom. Then, in the middle part of the century, the tape recorder revolutionized foreign language learning in that, for the first time, ordinary people (and language students) could record their own and others' voices and play them back.

Some of that technology is still useful in today's ultra-fast-paced parade of ubiquitous gimmicks and devices and computer-based programs. Consider some of these perfectly useful, instructive, and convenient technologies:

1. Commercially produced audiotapes and CDs

It may be a surprise to some of the more youthful generation of tech-savvy language students that audiotapes *do* in fact exist and are still used in some circles today! True, cassette tapes have been replaced by CDs for virtually every textbook and program today. But in some cases, audiotapes are a financial necessity in an environment of budgetary cutbacks that prevent the purchase of the hardware and software necessary for CDs and CD players. Furthermore, "old" material may still be effective.

The more current and usually more readily available audio technology is of course the CD (compact disc), which accomplishes everything that a tape does, but with greater accuracy, durability, and storage capacity. Another feature is that the user can pinpoint a "spot" on a CD without the old fast-forward and rewind buttons. An advantage of both audiotapes and CDs is that they can be used for self-study beyond the language classroom. Many self-instructional language programs (Berlitz, Rosetta Stone, etc.) are available in this technology. (Note that CD-ROMs require a computer to operate them, while CDs can be accessed simply through a CD player.)

Whatever your own situation is, libraries and instructional resource centers may be able to provide a surprising variety of audiocassettes and a growing number of CDs with (a) listening exercises, (b) lectures, (c) stories, and (d) other authentic samples of native-speaker texts.

2. Commercially produced videotapes and DVDs

In the video category, tape-based technology is also waning with the advent of DVDs and the decreasing cost of digital video hardware. DVDs (digital video disc) offer the same convenience and accuracy that CDs give us, and so are of course the technology of choice. Many institutions still maintain videotape libraries, supplemented by an increasingly large collection of DVDs. Among some possible categories are (a) documentaries on special topics, (b) movies, films, and news media, and (c) programs designed specifically to instruct students on certain aspects of English. An option that some language teachers have found useful is closed-captioned video that offers students written-language input simultaneously with oral.

3. Self-made audiotapes and CDs

At the risk of sounding repetitious, I am listing audio*tapes* here for the same reasons specified above. However, since we are talking about *self*-made audio programs, we should note the ready availability and affordability today of digital recorders, usually no larger than a cell phone, with amazing memory on tiny mini-discs. This technology is quickly rendering the tape (cassette) recorder obsolete, and coupled with computer-based capacities to create your own recordings, offers a very convenient set of options. Teachers can now easily create their own supporting materials, with the possible drawback of amplifying devices suitable for classroom uses. Recordings of conversations, especially conversations of people known to one's own students, can be stimulating. Or just use your digital recorder for radio or TV excerpts of news, speeches, talk shows, etc., for listening techniques.

Included in the category of self-made audio segments is the possibility of students creating their own recordings. As long as playback hardware is available in your classroom, students' creations may be both instructive and fun.

4. Self-made videotapes and DVDs

Now that digital video cameras are also accessible, they too are making videotape recorders look like dinosaurs. Potentially interesting personalized video segments can be created in two ways. With a recordable DVD unit you can record television programs. They need not be long or complex. Sometimes a very simple advertisement or a segment of the news makes an excellent audiovisual stimulus for classroom work. With a camera, you can try your hand at creating your own "film" (a story, a "candid camera" episode, a skit, etc.), perhaps with some of your students as principal actors. Keep in mind, of course, the need for the hardware necessary to play back your creations to your students.

Students, too, can become the creators of video segments that are shown in the classroom (hardware permitting). I have seen some delightful little skits and interviews that students have created, and they act as intrinsic motivators as well as excellent practice in English.

5. Overhead projection

The advent of computerized visual presentations through such software as PowerPoint (see the next section) tends to dominate our profession. However, many classrooms around the world provide an overhead transparency projector as standard equipment (and, I must say, equipment that will probably have less chance of failing). Commercially available transparencies are available that can enhance a textbook lesson. Your own charts, lists, graphics, and other visually presented material can be easily reproduced (through most photocopying equipment or your computer printer) and offer stimulating visual input for students. Transparencies can save paper and can be reused in a subsequent term of teaching the same course.

COMPUTER-ASSISTED LANGUAGE LEARNING (CALL)

In the early 1980s the world was introduced to the personal computer, and it soon became a familiar household item. With its advent, dictionaries began to add new terms that are now commonplace: *keyboard, monitor, CPU, mouse, byte, joystick, modem,* and the list expanded daily. Now lexicographers can't even keep up as other words, phrases, and acronyms become components of people's everyday linguistic corpus: *iPods, MP3 players, flash drives, WiFi,* along with alphabet soup items like *CD-ROM, CD-RW, ISP, HTTP, JPEG, PDF, URL,* and *USB.* These terms run off the tips of our tongues and into usually understanding ears like pixels through FireWires. Undaunted, our silicon-driven culture clamors for more, better, and faster!

The recent advances in educational applications of computer hardware and software have provided a rapidly growing—and sometimes bewildering—set of resources for language classrooms. The practical applications of **computer-assisted language learning** (CALL) are growing at such a rapid pace that it is almost impossible for a classroom teacher to keep up with the field. But don't let the multitude of options discourage you from at least considering some CALL applications in your own teaching. At the same time, don't let the allure of computer-based technology fool you into thinking that computers will magically make your students happy and successful.

CALL, CMC, TMLL, or What?

First, a word or two about the popularly used acronym, CALL. Some practitioners are questioning whether the term is still viable (Bax, 2003; Kern, 2006; Warschauer, 1999). One issue is whether or not computers *assist* our instruction any more than books, pens, and libraries did in years past. Another question asks if the "computer" part of the acronym eliminates the use of other digital technologies, such as DVDs and CDs, which can be utilized without a computer. And finally, in an age in which computer science has pervaded all aspects of our lives, including our classrooms, why single out computers as some special case "when online communication has become a normal part of our daily life?" (Kern, 2006, p. 185). Instead, we should, according to Kern and others, "refer broadly to information and communication technologies rather than specifically to computers." This, then, could lead us better toward what Chapelle (2005) has suggested: integrating CALL into interactionist theories of second language learning and teaching. After all, technology is relatively useless if the science behind it is not fully amalgamated into language pedagogy.

So, is it still politically correct to refer to CALL? The alternatives are phrases like **computer-mediated communication** (CMC), which is becoming more widely accepted. Even better, perhaps, is the concept of **technology-mediated language learning** (TMLL). The latter captures the essence of current efforts to integrate technology into our pedagogical theories, and allows for technology beyond just computer science. Having said all that, I will side with Chapelle (2005), who wisely refrained from joining the alphabet soup argument, and simply accepted CALL as associated with "the broad range of activities associated with technology and language learning" (p. 743). For my part, because of the popularity and universal understanding of the term CALL, I too will use the latter acronym, begging the indulgence of any readers who yearn for a new term!

Principles and Benefits of CALL

There are some important principles to follow in using electronic technology to enhance your teaching. Following are some guidelines that capsulize those principles, adapted from Egbert (2005, pp. 11–14) and Beatty (2003):

- Use technology to *support* the pedagogical goals of the class and curriculum. That is, don't design instruction to fit the technology (what Egbert calls a **technocentric** approach); rather, focus on course goals and objectives and take advantage of whatever technology is available to enhance those purposes. Technology is a *tool* and we must remember that CALL includes the word *assisted,* implying that technology is not the "main event" in a classroom.
- Evaluate the *appropriateness* of software for your purpose and the availability of sufficient hardware. It is useful to look at such factors as expertise necessary for students to use a computer-based resource, their interest in the resource, the general cognitive difficulty of the task(s), the proficiency level required to do the task(s), and, of course, any budgetary costs involved in acquiring or using a resource.
- Create a classroom environment in which CALL is *affirmed* by the students. They need to "buy in" to the concept of computer-enhanced learning.

- Make the technology accessible to *all* learners. Varying styles and abilities among learners must be considered so that all learners can benefit and the risk of "losing" some learners is eliminated. We are well acquainted with "technophobic" learners and must not assume that everyone finds computers and computer programs easy to operate.
- Use technology *effectively.* Egbert (2005, p. 12) notes that "*effective* means that students learn language better or faster using the technology than they would have using the tools that would ordinarily be available." So, for example, the individualization and feedback possible with CALL may exceed the teacher's ability otherwise to reach all students.
- Use technology *efficiently.* Efficiency is related to *time.* When CALL enables a student (or teacher) to accomplish an objective in less time, then it is viable. For example, listening to a passage on a CD (as opposed to an audiotape) is more efficient when a student wishes to replay the passage a number of times. Dictionary searches can be faster, and with language corpus data available, a multiplicity of collocations can be instantly accessed. Speech analyzers can provide instant visual feedback to students wishing to improve pronunciation.
- Have a *backup plan* in case the technology fails. We've all witnessed at some time or another an electronically based presentation go awry due either to hardware or software problems. I have personally agonized over my own and my students' moments of frustration when something fails in the fragile links between preparation and delivery. You are wise to have something ready to substitute when these moments occur—and they will occur!

With those important guidelines as a backdrop, we can enumerate a number of benefits of CALL. Consider the following possible advantages of including a computer component in language instruction (adapted from Chapelle, 2005; Egbert, 2005; Miyagi, 2006; Nunan, 2006; Warschauer & Healy, 1998):

- opportunity for learners to *notice* language forms
- a means for providing optimal modified *input* to learners
- multimodal (visual, auditory, written) practice
- immediate, personalized feedback
- individualization in a large class
- self-pacing
- private space to make mistakes
- convenient mode for [distance] teacher feedback
- convenient venue for [written] practice of the L2
- collaborative projects
- variety in the resources available and learning styles used

- exploratory learning with large amounts of language (corpus) data
- real-life skill building in computer use
- the fun factor

Uses of CALL in the Language Classroom

The possible uses of computer technology in a language classroom are seemingly endless, as a glance through de Szendeffy's (2005) and Egbert's (2005) highly useful resources will reveal. Every time you turn around and read a new article or book or attend a conference presentation, a novel idea is presented. So, in some ways, because this book—and this chapter in particular—is designed as merely an *introduction* to technology, I will only scratch the surface here. In so doing, I hope your own explorations will go far beyond what is suggested here, and that in due course of time *you* will be the person presenting yet another effective way to use CALL in a language course.

Here are some thoughts to start the wheels of your mind turning. For further resources, consult the list of Web-based information as well as the list of printed books suggested at the end of this chapter.

1. Collaborative projects

With as many as two to four students to a terminal, research projects can be carried out utilizing data available on the Internet. Analysis of data can be done with data management or statistical processing software. Charts, graphics, and text can be generated for presentation of findings to the rest of the class. Miyagi (2006) reported a collaborative project on environmental awareness that involved students in Japan and in the United States working together.

2. Peer-editing of compositions

The exchange of information on discs, Web-based bulletin boards, or networked computers offers students an efficient means of peer-editing of drafts of compositions. Many instructors effectively use e-mail (see below) and bulletin boards (see below) to correspond with students, and vice versa. Instructors can easily manage comments on final drafts through this technology.

3. E-mail

The most obvious form of using e-mail for English teaching is giving students the possibility for actual communication with individuals around the world. Discussion lists provide opportunities for reading and writing on topics of interest. E-mail pen pals have become popular. Through the Web, chat programs offer students the novelty of asynchronous (delay in time between sending and responding) discussion. Teachers have used e-mail communication for such things as dialogue journals with students and collaboration with other teachers.

4. Blogs

The use of blogs (blogging) has become very popular, especially among young people. Blogs are easy-to-use simple Web sites where one can quickly write thoughts, interact with others, get feedback, post photos, and more. A number of blogs are free and can be easily set up in a minute or two. Blogs provide yet another venue for exchange of ideas in the L2.

5. Web-based bulletin board communication

With the increasing use of Web-based discussion venues, students are offered a means to accomplish objectives of a course (such as problem solving, resolving differences in data, drafting compositions, etc.). By setting up such bulletin board (BB) discussion sites, teachers also give students a means for using the L2 directly in writing.

6. Web page design

A rapidly growing number of educational institutions have offered courses to students in Web page design. Many computer users self-teach the art of Web-authoring, with the help of such books as Lynch and Horton's (2002) book and/or Web-based sites (listed at the end of this chapter). In the process, students not only become acquainted with computer technology in general but also utilize English in doing research on a topic, composing and designing, and collaborating with other students.

An interesting, motivating project for students in a class is to create their own class Web page, complete with stories, interviews, biographies, accounts of field trips, restaurant reviews, photos, video clips, sound bites, and graphics. Self-made or collaboratively designed videos also offer students a chance to "ham it up" and make their own video creations.

7. Videoconferencing

An increasingly popular technology is the carrying out of conferences over video. As long as the hardware (a digital video camera; wired or wireless access) is available, free software can be obtained from some Internet sites (Yahoo Messenger, Festoon with Skype). This adds the all-important nonverbal dimension of communication.

8. Reinforcement of classroom material

With ready availability of a wide array of software programs, course objectives can be reinforced, and added material can be made available. Many textbooks now come with an accompanying CD-ROM disc (accessible on a computer), if not a DVD (also accessible on many computers), filled with practice exercises, self-check tests, and extra reading and visual material. Some course programs include a dedicated Web site that is regularly updated and/or an online section in each unit, which encourages use of Internet-related activity. The process of learning to read a foreign language can be enhanced through computer-adaptive programs that offer lexical and grammatical information at predicted points of difficulty. And the list goes on!

9. Podcasting

Another relatively recent technology, podcasting is a method of distributing multimedia files—such as audio programs or music videos—over the Internet, for playback on mobile devices or personal computers. Podcasts can be a source of authentic listening for students of English, and, if students have a mobile device (an iPod, for example), they can access such material at their convenience outside of the classroom environment. Dervin (2006) offers a number of different sources and uses of podcasting (including what he calls "podwitnessing" in which learners can access material on various cultures), as well as a set of references.

10. Games and simulations

Not to be overlooked are the many engaging games and simulations, many of them involving verbal language, that present students with stimulating problem-solving tasks in which they must use functional language to pursue the goals of the games. Carefully planned uses of such games in the classroom (e.g., for practicing certain verbs, tenses, questions, locatives, etc.) add considerable interest to a classroom, especially if the curriculum or traditional textbook prescribes mechanical drills that are seen as boring to the learner.

11. Computer-adaptive testing

Many current standardized tests are now computer-adaptive. During the early items, right and wrong answers are electronically analyzed in order to present options for later items, from a bank of possible items, that will be neither too easy nor too difficult and therefore will present an optimal challenge. Test-takers need to be aware of the technology and to develop appropriate strategies for responding.

12. Speech recognition software

A remarkable degree of accuracy is now available and affordable in software designed to process human speech and analyze production. Speech recognition programs for the language classroom have a multitude of potential applications, including simple exercises in pronunciation and electronic visual feedback (EVF) that can show the accuracy of a learner's control of phonemic and prosodic elements (Igarashi, 2004).

13. Concordancing

With literally billions of linguistic corpus data now readily available, the process of concordancing (searching for words in context and collocations) has become relatively simple. Students wishing to research the possible contexts of words and teachers planning a grammar or vocabulary lesson are finding such sources enlightening.

14. Multimedia presentations

Finally, both students and language teachers have used PowerPoint and other media presentation software to enliven a presentation with graphics, charts, art, photos, lists, and audio "sound bites." Whether it's a student giving a presentation in class or a researcher presenting data at a professional conference, these computer-based technologies have proven to be universally popular.

☆   ☆   ☆   ☆   ☆

This chapter is intended to be simply a brief primer on technology in the language classroom. With so many books, Web sites, resources, software programs, and hardware options available, it is truly impossible to give adequate coverage to this burgeoning field. So consider this chapter as perhaps only an appetizer, promising a technological repast that will never be exhausted. At the end of the chapter, I have offered some ideas for you to begin that quest.

TOPICS FOR DISCUSSION, ACTION, AND RESEARCH

[Note: (I) Individual work; (G) group or pair work; (C) whole-class discussion.]

1. (I) How would you define *technology?* Are there other non-computer-based technological devices that you can think of?
2. (C) Is there anyone in the class who would describe him- or herself as a *technophobe?* If so, what are the root causes of this fear? Perhaps others can suggest ways to overcome or deal with such anxieties.
3. (C) Are there other principles and benefits of CALL that the class can think of and describe?
4. (G) In groups, brainstorm some of the *dis*advantages of CALL in the language classroom (which weren't specifically listed). How would one overcome or respond to such disadvantages?
5. (C) This chapter did not discuss the political and ethical consequences of the widespread use of Internet-based communication around the world. Issues of censorship, freedom of speech, junk e-mails, privacy, and appropriate Web-based verbal and nonverbal material are common. What thoughts might the class have to share on any of these or other similar issues?
6. (G/C) In small groups, class members can brainstorm other uses of CALL, beyond the 14 that were listed and described in this chapter. These could be from their own experience learning or teaching a foreign language, or from their reading and discussion in other courses such as this one. As a whole class, a composite list of suggestions might be put on the board and later distributed to the class via e-mail, bulletin board, or class Web site.

SOME USEFUL WEB RESOURCES

I gratefully acknowledge Tamotsu Miyagi (2006) for compiling this list. Please note, of course, that Web URLs often change, and that while this list is accurate on publication of this book, certain addresses may change or not be available.

General Resources Links

- Dave's ESL Café Web Links
  http://www.eslcafe.com/search/index.html
- ESL Lesson Plans and Resources
  http://www.csun.edu/~hcedu013/eslplans.html
- Ohio University English Student Resources
  http://www.ohiou.edu/esl/english/
- Using English for Academic Purposes
  http://www.uefap.com/index.htm
- TESOL Electronic Village
  http://webpages.csus.edu/%7Ehansonsm/announce.html
- TESL/TEFL/TESOL/ESL/EFL/ESOL Links
  http://iteslj.org/links/
- Interesting Things for ESL/EFL Students
  http://www.manythings.org/

Web Quiz Creation

- Hot Potato
  http://web.uvic.ca/hrd/hotpot/index.htm
- Hot Potatoes' Exercises
  http://perso.wanadoo.fr/michel.barbot/hotpot/exercises.htm
- Quia
  http://www.quia.com/web
- Discovery School
  http://school.discovery.com/quizcenter/quizcenter.html

Listening

- Randall's ESL Cyber Listening Lab
  http://esl-lab.com/index.htm
- BBC World Service Learning English
  http://www.bbc.co.uk/worldservice/learningenglish/index.shtml
- English Trailer
  http://www.english-trailers.com/index.php
- Apple Movie Trailers
  http://www.apple.com/trailers/

- Elllo
  http://www.elllo.org/index.htm
- World English
  http://www.wrn.org/listeners/stations/station.php?StationID=35
- Breaking News Easy/Hard
  http://www.breakingnewsenglish.com/
- Podcast Search
  http://www.podzinger.com/

Pronunciation
- Phonetics: The Sound of American English
  http://www.uiowa.edu/~acadtech/phonetics/english/frameset.html
- Sounds of English
  http://www.soundsofenglish.org/
- American English pronunciation practice
  http://www.manythings.org/pp/

Grammar and Vocabulary
- Activities for ESL Students
  http://a4esl.org/
- Grammar Station
  http://www.grammarstation.com/index.htm
- Englishpage
  http://www.englishpage.com/
- Phrasal Verb Demon
  http://www.phrasalverbdemon.com/
- Collocations
  http://www.eslflow.com/collocationsandphrasalvebs.html
- Vocabulary Power
  http://www.edumatic.qc.ca/English/activities/vocabularypower.htm
- Paul Nation
  http://www.vuw.ac.nz/lals/staff/paul-nation/nation.aspx
- AWL
  http://www.vuw.ac.nz/lals/research/awl/

Corpus
- Complete Lexical Tutor
  http://132.208.224.131/
- Online KWIC Concordancer
  http://ysomeya.hp.infoseek.co.jp/
- British National Corpus
  http://www.natcorp.ox.ac.uk/

Reading
- CNN Reading & Listening
  http://www.literacynet.org/cnnsf/home.html
- Reading Skills and Strategies
  http://www.eslgold.com/reading/skills.html
- Mystery.net
  http://www.mysterynet.com/
- English Independent Study Lab
  http://www.lclark.edu/~krauss/toppicks/reading.html
- Onlinenewspapers
  http://www.onlinenewspapers.com/

Writing
- Hostboard
  http://www.hostboard.com/cgi-bin/ultimatebb.cgi
- Advanced Composition for Non-Native English Speakers
  http://eslbee.com/
- Purdue University Online Writing
  http://owl.english.purdue.edu/
- Writing Center
  http://writing2.richmond.edu/writing/wweb.html
- Students' Web Publishing
  http://web.li.gatech.edu/~rdrury/500/writing/index.html
- Blogging
  http://www.blogger.com

Speaking
- Conversation Questions
  http://iteslj.org/questions/
- Speaks Itself
  http://www.speaksforitself.com/
- English Club
  http://www.englishclub.com/speaking/index.htm
- CILL
  http://elc.polyu.edu.hk/cill/default4.htm

Internet Activities
- WebQuests
  http://www.e4b.de/WebQuests/WebQuests.html
- WebQuest Portal
  http://webquest.org/
- ESL Cybersite
  http://station05.qc.ca/css/CyberSite/integrate/default.htm

CALL-Related Journals & Researchers

- CALL
  http://edvista.com/claire/call.html
- Language Learning & Technology
  http://llt.msu.edu/
- TESL-EJ
  http://www-writing.berkeley.edu/TESL-EJ/
- The Internet TESL Journal
  http://iteslj.org/
- Mark Warschauer
  http://www.gse.uci.edu/faculty/markw/
- Elizabeth Hanson-Smith
  http://www.geocities.com/ehansonsmi/
- Joy Egbert
  http://www.wsu.edu/~egbert/

FOR YOUR FURTHER READING

Chapelle, C. (2005). Computer-assisted language learning. In E. Hinkel (Ed.), *Handbook of research in second language teaching and learning* (pp. 743–755). Mahwah, NJ: Lawrence Erlbaum Associates.

Beatty, K. (2003). Computer-assisted language learning. In D. Nunan (Ed.), *Practical English language teaching* (pp. 247–266). New York: McGraw-Hill Contemporary.

Both of these summary articles—only accidentally with identical titles—give overviews of the state of the art in CALL. Carol Chapelle provides an excellent, authoritative overview of research in CALL, and effectively links second language acquisition issues to CALL pedagogy. Her extensive bibliography offers research references that are sometimes difficult to track down in the more practical manuals on CALL. Ken Beatty's chapter is more practical and classroom-based, with suggested approaches and activities.

de Szendeffy, J. (2005). *A practical guide to using computers in language teaching.* Ann Arbor: University of Michigan Press.

Egbert, J. (2005). *CALL essentials: Principles and practice in CALL classrooms.* Alexandria, VA: TESOL, Inc.

These two highly practical books offer a wealth of ideas and resources for using computer-based technology in language classrooms. Joy Egbert provides solid theoretical and research foundations along with practical methodological suggestions. John de Szendeffy's book is not only an excellent manual of practical CALL activities, but it also includes many simple explanations of technical concepts and terms. His glossary and other appendices are exceptionally useful for those who feel less than completely conversant in computer technology.

TESOL Quarterly, Autumn 2000 issue (volume 34, number 3).

The Autumn 2000 issue of the TESOL Quarterly *was a special issue devoted to the topic of "TESOL in the 21st Century." Especially useful are reviews of seven books that, at the time, described the state of the art in computer-based technology for language learning. A number of years have now passed since 2000, but this set of reviews is helpful, if for no other reason than to notice how many advances have been made since 2000!*

CHAPTER 13

INITIATING INTERACTION

IN THE CLASSROOM

OBJECTIVES After reading this chapter, you will be able to:

- apply principles of interaction to the design and observation of lessons

- embody in your own teaching (or future teaching) the roles necessary to be an interactive teacher

- approach interactive techniques and tasks with confidence, following guidelines that others before you have found to be successful

- understand various steps for initiating interaction in the classroom

- recognize a variety of questioning strategies that are likely to elicit responses from students

The quiet buzz of voices from the classroom echoes down the hallway. The 30-some-odd students in an intermediate English class in a Bangkok high school are telling stories, joking, gossiping, and talking about the latest popular songs. As the teacher walks in, the students fall silent, face forward, and open their textbooks in anticipation of another English lesson, another day of reciting, repeating, copying, reading aloud, translating sentences, and answering multiple-choice questions.

But today their usual teacher is absent, and a substitute teacher sits down at the front of the class and asks the students to rearrange their desks into concentric semicircles. Surprised, the students comply. Then the teacher speaks:

T: Kavin, what's your favorite movie?
S: [*after some silence*] I'm sorry. Please repeat.
T: What movie do you like best?
S: [*long silence, furtive glances to classmates*] Best?
T: Yeah, your favorite movie?
S: [*more silence*] I like best, uh, *United Nine-three* movie.
T: Ninety-three, uh-huh, okay. Arunee, what about you?
S: [*embarrassed, giggles*] About me?
T: Yeah, what do you think? What's your favorite movie?
S: Oh, uh, favorite movie is *Crash.*
T: Great. Now, Salinee, what's your favorite food?

This line of questioning continues for several minutes, with an increasing degree of ready participation by the students. Then the teacher changes the format a little:

T:	Now, Anchalee, ask Pravit what his favorite sport is.
Anchalee:	[*silence*] What your favorite sport?
Pravit:	Uh, soccer.
T:	Okay, Pravit, now ask Salinee a question.
Pravit:	[*long silence*] What sport you like?
T:	Okay, Pravit, good try. Now, say it this way: "What is your favorite sport?"
Pravit:	What is favorite sport?

Slowly, the students warm up to asking each other questions. The teacher then has students pair off and continue to ask about favorite movies, songs, sports, and food.

The teacher then asks the students to make four columns on a blank sheet of paper with the headings *Singer, TV program, Actress, Actor.* This time dividing the class into groups of four students each, the teacher directs each group to fill in their sheets with the favorites of the other members of the group—in English! Initial silence is gradually replaced by a buzz of voices in the groups as the teacher circulates and encourages the more reticent to participate. The exercise ends with "reports" of findings from appointed group leaders.

The last few minutes of the class hour are spent with the teacher pointing out certain grammatical reminders ("His favorite movie is _____," "I like _____ best").

WHAT IS INTERACTION?

You have been introduced to some basic issues in designing courses and lessons, and in using and adapting materials and resources, so your next move is to step into the classroom and begin the process of stimulating interaction. This chapter will offer some pointers on how to do that.

The class just described, whose students had been accustomed to recitation and mechanical output, just became—perhaps for the first time—interactive. Interaction is an important word for language teachers. In the era of communicative language teaching, interaction is, in fact, the heart of communication; it is what communication is all about. We send messages, we receive them, we interpret them in a context, we negotiate meanings, and we collaborate to accomplish certain purposes. And after several decades of research on teaching and learning languages, we have discovered that the best way to learn to interact is through interaction itself.

Interaction is the collaborative exchange of thoughts, feelings, or ideas between two or more people, resulting in a reciprocal effect on each other. Theories of communicative competence emphasize the importance of interaction as human beings use language in various contexts to "negotiate" meaning, or simply stated, to get an idea out of one person's head and into the head of another person and vice versa. From the very beginning of language study, classrooms should be interactive. Wilga Rivers (1987, pp. 4–5) puts it this way:

> Through interaction, students can increase their language store as they listen to or read authentic linguistic material, or even the output of their fellow students in discussions, skits, joint problem-solving tasks, or dialogue journals. In interaction, students can use all they possess of the language—all they have learned or casually absorbed—in real-life exchanges.... Even at an elementary stage, they learn in this way to exploit the elasticity of language.

INTERACTIVE PRINCIPLES

Most of the 12 principles listed and discussed in Chapter 4 form foundation stones for structuring a theory of interaction in the language classroom. Consider the following selected relationships:

Automaticity: True human interaction is best accomplished when focal attention is on meanings and messages and not on grammar and other linguistic forms. Learners are thus freed from keeping language in a controlled mode and can more easily proceed to automatic modes of processing.

Intrinsic motivation: As students become engaged with each other in speech acts of fulfillment and self-actualization, their deepest drives are satisfied. And as they more fully appreciate their own competence to use language, they can develop a system of self-reward.

Strategic investment: Interaction requires the use of strategic language competence both to make certain decisions on how to say or write or interpret language, and to make repairs when communication pathways are blocked. The spontaneity of interactive discourse requires judicious use of numerous strategies for production and comprehension.

Willingness to communicate: Interaction requires an attitude on the part of the learner that says, "I *want* to reach out to others and communicate." This willingness to communicate further implies the risk of failing to produce intended meaning, of failing to interpret intended meaning (on the part of someone else), of being laughed at, of being shunned or rejected. The rewards, of course, are great and worth the risks.

The language–culture connection: The cultural loading of interactive speech as well as writing requires that interlocutors be thoroughly versed in the cultural nuances of language.

Interlanguage: The complexity of interaction entails a long developmental process of acquisition. Numerous errors of production and comprehension will be a part of this development. And the role of teacher feedback is crucial to the developmental process.

Communicative competence: All of the elements of communicative competence (grammatical, discourse, sociolinguistic, pragmatic, and strategic) are involved in human interaction. All aspects must work together for successful communication to take place.

ROLES OF THE INTERACTIVE TEACHER

An interactive teacher is by definition one who is fully aware of the **group dynamics** of a classroom. As Dörnyei and Murphey (2003) explained, the success of classroom learning is very much dependent on how students relate to each other, what the classroom environment is, how effectively students cooperate and communicate with each other, and of course what roles the teacher and learners play. But it's important to remember that effective interaction within the dynamics of a classroom is a gradual incremental process. According to Vygotsky (1962, 1978), effective learning in students' "zones of proximal development" involves "[starting out with] firm leading and modeling on the part of the teacher and [shifting] as students internalize more and more of the processes and teachers learn how to let go" (Dörnyei & Murphey, 2003, p. 98).

Teachers can play many roles in the course of teaching. Just as parents are called upon to be many things to their children, teachers cannot be satisfied with only one role. Rebecca Oxford et al. (1998) pointed out that teacher roles are often best described in the form of metaphor: teacher as manufacturer, teacher as doctor, teacher as judge, teacher as gardener, and others. Following you will find another set of metaphors to describe a spectrum of possibilities of teacher roles, some of which are more conducive to creating an interactive classroom than others.

1. The teacher as controller

A role that is sometimes expected in traditional educational institutions is that of "master" controller, always in charge of every moment in the classroom. Master controllers determine what the students do, when they should speak, and what language forms they should use. They can often predict many student responses because everything is mapped out ahead of time, with no leeway for divergent paths. In some respects, such control may sound admirable. But for interaction to take place, the teacher must create a climate in which spontaneity can thrive, in which unrehearsed language can be performed, and in which the freedom of expression given over to students makes it impossible to predict everything that they will say and do.

Nevertheless, some control on your part is actually an important element of successfully carrying out interactive techniques. In the planning phase especially, a wise controller will carefully project how a technique will proceed, map out the initial input to students, specify directions to be given, and gauge the timing of a technique. So, granted that allowing for spontaneity of expression involves yielding certain elements of control to students, nevertheless, even in the most cooperative of interactive classrooms, the teacher must maintain some control simply to organize the class hour.

2. The teacher as director

Some interactive classroom time can legitimately be structured in such a way that the teacher is like a conductor of an orchestra or a director of a drama. As students engage in either rehearsed or spontaneous language performance, it is your job to keep the process flowing smoothly and efficiently. The ultimate motive of such direction, of course, must always be to enable students eventually to engage in the real-life drama of improvisation as each communicative event brings its own uniqueness.

3. The teacher as manager

This metaphor captures your role as one who plans lessons, modules, and courses, and who structures the larger, longer segments of classroom time, but who then allows each individual player to be creative within those parameters. Managers of successful corporations, for example, retain control of certain larger objectives of the company, keep employees pointed toward goals, engage in ongoing evaluation and feedback, but give freedom to each person to work in his or her own individual areas of expertise. A language class should not be markedly different.

4. The teacher as facilitator

A less directive role might be described as facilitating the process of learning, of making learning easier for students: helping them to clear away roadblocks, to find shortcuts, to negotiate rough terrain. The facilitating role requires that you step away from the managerial or directive role and allow students, with your guidance and gentle prodding, to find their own pathways to success. A facilitator capitalizes on the principle of intrinsic motivation by allowing students to discover language through using it pragmatically, rather than by telling them about language.

5. The teacher as resource

Here you take the least directive role. In fact, the implication of the resource role is that the student takes the initiative to come to you. You are available for advice and counsel when the student seeks it. It is of course not practical to push this metaphor to an extreme where you would simply walk into a classroom and say something like, "Well, what do you want to learn today?" Some degree of control, of planning, of managing the classroom is essential. But there are appropriate times when you can literally take a back seat and allow the students to proceed with their own linguistic development.

✦   ✦   ✦   ✦   ✦

In the lessons that you deliver, you should be able to assume all five of these roles on this continuum of **directive** to **nondirective** teaching, depending on the purpose and context of an activity. The key to interactive teaching is to strive toward the upper, nondirective end of the continuum, gradually enabling your students to move from their roles of total dependence (upon you, the class activities, the textbook, etc.) to relatively total independence. The proficiency level of your class will determine to some extent which roles will dominate. But even at the lowest levels, some genuine interaction can take place, and your role must be one that releases your students to try things for themselves.

We turn now to a more empirical and practical consideration of interaction in the communicative language classroom. In the remainder of this chapter you will get a sense of what you can do to initiate interaction in the classroom—that is, how your input can stimulate student interaction. (In Chapter 14, you will be given some guidance on maintaining interaction through effective group work techniques.)

FOREIGN LANGUAGE INTERACTION ANALYSIS

One way to begin to look at your role as an initiator of interaction in the classroom is to look at yourself (and other teachers) in terms of a well-known taxonomy for describing classroom interaction. Almost four decades ago, the work of Flanders (1970) and, more specific to foreign language teaching, of Gertrude Moskowitz (1971, 1976) gave us some categories for observation of classes known as the FLINT (Foreign Language Interaction Analysis) model (see Table 13.1).

How is a model like this helpful in developing interactive language teaching? There are several practical uses. First, it gives you a taxonomy for observing other teachers. Moskowitz recommends using a chart or grid to note instances of each category. You can also calculate how much classroom time is devoted to each. Then you can evaluate the wisdom of certain choices made by the teacher or look at the overall distribution of time and ask yourself (or your teacher trainer) about the appropriateness of such a distribution.

Second, it gives you a framework for evaluating and improving your own teaching. For example, how well do you balance teacher talk and student talk? While the FLINT model includes seven categories for teacher talk and only two for student talk, don't let that fool you into believing that your own talk should dominate. Depending on the objectives of the lesson, the level of the students, and other contextual factors, the proportions will vary, but most of the time we teachers tend to talk too much, without allowing enough time for students to respond to us or to initiate talk. A careful consideration of all seven of the teacher-talk categories

Table 13.1. Foreign Language Interaction Analysis (FLINT) system (adapted from Moskowitz, 1971)

TEACHER TALK	**Indirect Influence**	1. **Deals with feelings:** In a nonthreatening way, accepting, discussing, referring to, or communicating understanding of past, present, or future feelings of students.
		2. **Praises or encourages:** Praising, complimenting, telling students why what they have said or done is valued. Encouraging students to continue, trying to give them confidence, confirming that answers are correct.
		  2a. **Jokes:** Intentional joking, kidding, making puns, attempting to be humorous, providing the joking is not at anyone's expense. (Unintentional humor is not included in this category.)
		3. **Uses ideas of students:** Clarifying, using, interpreting, summarizing the ideas of students. The ideas must be rephrased by the teacher but still be recognized as being student contributions.
		  3a. **Repeats student response verbatim:** Repeating the exact words of students after they participate.
		4. **Asks questions:** Asking questions to which the answer is anticipated. (Rhetorical questions are NOT included in this category.)

	Direct Influence	5. **Gives information:** Giving information, facts, own opinion, or ideas: lecturing or asking rhetorical questions.
		  5a. **Corrects without rejection:** Telling students who have made a mistake the correct response without using words or intonations which communicate criticism.
		6. **Gives directions:** Giving directions, requests, or commands that students are expected to follow; directing various drills; facilitating whole-class and small-group activity.
		7. **Criticizes student behavior:** Rejecting the behavior of students; trying to change the nonacceptable behavior; communicating anger, displeasure, annoyance, dissatisfaction with what students are doing.
		  7a. **Criticizes student response:** Telling the student his or her response is not correct or acceptable and communicating criticism, displeasure, annoyance, rejection by words or intonation.

STUDENT TALK		8. **Student response, specific:** Responding to the teacher within a specific and limited range of available or previously practiced answers. Reading aloud, dictation, drills. 8a. **Student response, choral:** Choral response by total class or part of class. 9. **Student response, open-ended or student-initiated:** Responding to the teacher with students' own ideas, opinions, reactions, feelings. Giving one from among many possible answers that have been previously practiced but from which students must now make a selection. Initiating the participation.

OTHER		10. **Silence:** Pauses in the interaction. Periods of quiet during which there is no verbal interaction.
		  10a. **Silence—AV:** Silence in the interaction during which a piece of audiovisual equipment, e.g., a tape recorder, filmstrip projector, record player, etc., is being used to communicate.
		11. **Confusion, work-oriented:** More than one person at a time talking, so the interaction cannot be recorded. Students calling out excitedly, eager to participate or respond, concerned with the task at hand.
		  11a. **Confusion, non-work-oriented:** More than one person at a time talking so the interaction cannot be recorded. Students out of order, not behaving as the teacher wishes, not concerned with the task at hand.

		12. **Laughter:** Laughing and giggling by the class, individuals, and/or the teacher. 13. **Uses the native language:** Use of the native language by the teacher or the students. This category is always combined with one of the categories from 1 to 9. 14. **Nonverbal:** Gestures or facial expressions by the teacher or the student that communicate without the use of words. This category is always combined with one of the categories of teacher or student behavior.

217

can also serve as a blueprint for your teaching behavior in the classroom: Am I accepting a student's feelings in a nonthreatening way? Am I offering sufficient praise? Am I lecturing too much? Do I give my students opportunities to initiate language on their own?

Third, the FLINT model, especially the first seven categories, helps to set a learning climate for interactive teaching. In Chapter 5, under the rubric of intrinsically motivating classrooms, we discussed the importance of learners being brought into the decision-making process. You can establish a climate of cooperation by recognizing and openly accepting your students' emotional ups and downs, by recognizing each individual student in the class as special in his or her own way, by soliciting their ideas, and by careful framing of questions. We now turn to an extensive look at the latter.

QUESTIONING STRATEGIES FOR INTERACTIVE LEARNING

The most important key to creating an interactive language classroom is the initiation of interaction by the teacher. However nondirective your teaching style is, the onus is on you to provide the stimuli for continued interaction. These stimuli are important in the initial stage of a classroom lesson as well as throughout the lesson. Without such ongoing teacher guidance, classroom interaction may indeed be communicative, but it can easily fall prey to tangential chitchat and other behavior that is off-course from the class objectives.

One of the best ways to develop your role as an initiator and sustainer of interaction is to develop a repertoire of questioning strategies. In second language classrooms, where learners often do not have a great number of tools for initiating and maintaining language, your questions provide necessary stepping stones to communication. Appropriate questioning in an interactive classroom can fulfill a number of different functions (adapted from Christenbury & Kelly, 1983; Kinsella, 1991).

1. Teacher questions give students the impetus and opportunity to produce language comfortably without having to risk initiating language themselves. It's very scary for students to have to initiate conversation or topics for discussion. Appropriately pitched questions can give more reticent students an affective "green light" and a structured opportunity to communicate in their second language.
2. Teacher questions can serve to initiate a chain reaction of student interaction among themselves. One question may be all that is needed to start a discussion; without the initial question, however, students will be reluctant to initiate the process.
3. Teacher questions give the instructor immediate feedback about student com-prehension. After posing a question, a teacher can use the student response

to diagnose linguistic or content difficulties. Grammatical or phonological problem areas, for example, may be exposed through the student's response and give the teacher some specific information about what to treat.

4. Teacher questions provide students with opportunities to find out what they think by hearing what they say. As they are nudged into responding to questions about, say, a reading or a film, they can discover what their own opinions and reactions are. This self-discovery can be especially useful for a prewriting activity.

There are many ways to classify what kinds of questions are effective in the classroom. Perhaps the simplest way to conceptualize the possibilities is to think of a range of questions, beginning with **display** questions that attempt to elicit information already known by the teacher, all the way to highly **referential** questions that request information not known by the questioner; sometimes responses to the latter involve judgment about facts that are not clear or a statement of values. Table 13.2 on page 220 provides seven categories of questions, ranging from display to referential, with typical classroom question words associated with each category.

All of these types of questions have their place in the interactive classroom. Even those that are more on the display end of the continuum are very useful in eliciting both content and language from students. Usually, the higher the proficiency level you teach, the more you can venture into the upper, referential end of the continuum. One interesting study of high intermediate pre-university ESL students (Brock, 1986) found that teachers who incorporated more referential questions into their classes stimulated student responses that were longer and more grammatically complex. Make sure, then, that you challenge your students sufficiently but without overwhelming them.

Asking a lot of questions in your classroom will not by any means guarantee stimulation of interaction. Certain types of questions may actually discourage interactive learning. Beware of the following (adapted from Kinsella, 1991):

- Too much class time spent on display questions—students can easily grow weary of artificial contexts that don't involve genuine seeking of information.
- A question that insults students' intelligence by being so obvious that students will think it's too silly to bother answering.
- Vague questions that are worded in abstract or ambiguous language (for example, "Do you pretty much understand more or less what to do?").
- Questions stated in language that is too complex or too wordy for aural comprehension (e.g., "Given today's discussion, and also considering your previous experience in educational institutions, what would you say are the ramifications of, or the potential developmental impacts on, children functioning in an educational system in which assessment procedures largely consist of multiple-choice, paper-and-pencil instrumentation?").

Table 13.2. Categories of questions and typical classroom question words (adapted from Bloom, 1956; Kinsella, 1991)

1. **Knowledge questions:** Eliciting factual answers, testing recall and recognition of information.

   Common question words: *define, tell, list, identify, describe, select, name, point out, label, reproduce. Who? What? Where? When? Answer "yes" or "no."*

2. **Comprehension questions:** Interpreting, extrapolating.

   Common question words: *state in your own words, explain, define, locate, select, indicate, summarize, outline, match.*

3. **Application questions:** Applying information heard or read to new situations.

   Common question words: *demonstrate how, use the data to solve, illustrate how, show how, apply, construct, explain. What is _____ used for? What would result? What would happen?*

4. **Inference questions:** Forming conclusions that are not directly stated in instructional materials.

   Common question words: *How? Why? What did _____ mean by? What does _____ believe? What conclusions can you draw from . . . ?*

5. **Analysis questions:** Breaking down into parts, relating parts to the whole.

   Common question words: *distinguish, diagram, chart, plan, deduce, arrange, separate, outline, classify, contrast, compare, differentiate, categorize. What is the relationship between? What is the function of? What motive? What conclusions? What is the main idea?*

6. **Synthesis questions:** Combining elements into a new pattern.

   Common question words: *compose, combine, estimate, invent, choose, hypothesize, build, solve, design, develop. What if? How would you test? What would you have done in this situation? What would happen if . . . ? How can you improve . . . ? How else would you . . . ?*

7. **Evaluation questions:** Making a judgment of good or bad, right or wrong, according to some set of criteria, and stating why.

   Common question words: *evaluate, rate, defend, dispute, decide which, select, judge, grade, verify, choose why. Which is best? Which is more important? Which do you think is more appropriate?*

- Too many rhetorical questions (that you intend to answer yourself) that students think you want them to answer; they then get confused when you supply the answer.
- Random questions that don't fall into a logical, well-planned sequence, sending students' thought patterns into chaos.

There are, of course, other teacher strategies that promote interaction. Pair work and group work give rise to interaction. Giving directions ("Open your books," "Do the following exercise") can stimulate interaction. Organizational language ("Get into small groups") is important. Reacting to students (praise, recognition, or a simple "Uh-huh") cannot be dispensed with. Responding genuinely to student-initiated questions is essential. Encouraging students to develop their own strategies is an excellent means of stimulating the learner to develop tools of interaction. Even "lecturing" (and other forms of orally providing information) and having students read texts are part of the process of creating and maintaining an interactive classroom. Most of these strategies are dealt with in subsequent chapters; pair and group work is given extensive coverage in the next chapter. For the moment, however, as you build some tools for creating effective interactive classroom lessons, consider your questioning strategies as one of the most important teaching behaviors for you to master.

☆   ☆   ☆   ☆   ☆

This chapter focused on the first step in creating an interactive classroom: your role as an initiator of the interaction. What you do and say to get students started, to prime them, to stimulate them to further communication, is crucial to the success of interactive techniques. We now turn to the intricate process of managing what has come to be a hallmark of interactive language teaching: group work.

TOPICS FOR DISCUSSION, ACTION, AND RESEARCH

[Note: (I) Individual work; (G) group or pair work; (C) whole-class.]

1. (I/G) Define interaction in your own words (without looking back at the beginning of the chapter). How does an interactive classroom differ from a "traditional" classroom? List the factors and discuss them in a small group.
2. (G) Ask small groups each to consider one of the other interactive principles *not* mentioned on pages 213–214 (anticipation of reward, meaningful learning, language ego, self-confidence, the native language effect). Each group should discuss how its principle supports the notion of interactive learning. Do any of them speak to the importance of "individual study" as opposed to interaction with classmates?
3. (G/C) Direct pairs to answer the following: Of the five teacher roles described on pages 214–216, which one(s) do you think might come most naturally to you? Why? Which would come least naturally? Do your natural inclinations reflect the kind of balancing of roles that you think is appropriate for an interactive language classroom? How would those roles change depending on (a) the proficiency level, (b) the age, and (c) the culture of students? Conclusions should then be shared with the rest of the class.
4. (G/C) Have small groups brainstorm as many metaphors for *teachers* as possible (teacher as manufacturer, doctor, gardener, etc.), and then pick a few

to discuss in detail by extending the metaphor. For example, the teacher as gardener must offer a nurturing environment for students as plants/trees, considering the climate of context, etc. Groups can then present one such extended metaphor to the rest of the class.

5. (I/C) Using the FLINT taxonomy as a guide, in which you note teacher and student behavior, observe an ESL class. Did the taxonomy reveal anything new or interesting to you? Report briefly to the rest of the class on your observation.

6. (I) As you observe the same or another class, try to attend to the kinds of questions the teacher asks. Write them down. How many were **display** questions, and how many were **referential** questions? Do you think the teacher should have had a different proportion of display and referential questions? Justify your response.

7. (G/C) Direct pairs to list some specific examples of questions that *discourage* interaction and to discuss why they think those examples fail to promote interaction. Pairs will share their thoughts with other members of the class.

FOR YOUR FURTHER READING

Dörnyei, Z., & Murphey, T. (2003). *Group dynamics in the language classroom.* Cambridge, UK: Cambridge University Press.

Zoltán Dörnyei and Tim Murphey's book is an excellent survey of research on group dynamics from a psychological viewpoint. It is not a practical "how-to" book, but it offers a wealth of background on the psychodynamics of language classrooms in particular.

Oxford, R., et al. (1998). Clashing metaphors about classroom teachers: Toward a systematic typology for the language teaching field. *System, 26,* 3–50.

Rebecca Oxford joins seven other colleagues here in a discussion of the metaphorical roles of teachers in language classrooms. Many different metaphors are discussed in detail under the four general categories of social order, cultural transmission, learner-centered growth, and social reform.

Wright, T. (1987). *Roles of teachers and learners.* Oxford, UK: Oxford University Press.

A number of different teacher and learner roles are described with no less than 71 specific classroom techniques that illustrate those roles. This "teacher-friendly" book provides simple theoretical justification for the adoption of various roles.

CHAPTER 14

SUSTAINING INTERACTION

THROUGH GROUP WORK

OBJECTIVES After reading this chapter, you will be able to:

- identify the advantages of creating interactive group work tasks

- understand that excuses for avoiding group work are for the most part based on erroneous impressions, and that group work can be effectively implemented

- apply the steps leading to successful group work: designing the task, planning details, monitoring, and debriefing

- analyze successful and unsuccessful group work activity in lessons that you observe as well as your own

The teacher of the community college ESL class of 15 students has just played a DVD produced by the National Geographic Society on ocean ecology. The language of this 10-minute mini-lecture was comprehensible, but the subject matter itself offered a heavy cognitive load. Now, the teacher asks the class to get into groups of four students each to answer a set of comprehension questions. His directions are: "Get into groups now and answer the questions on the handout." He then gives each student a handout with 10 comprehension questions, such as, "What is the role of shrimp in ocean ecology?" and "According to the video, in what three ways are human beings dependent on the ocean for survival?"

The students comply with the first part of the directive by getting into previously arranged groups. Then, silence. Students spend a good three to four minutes silently reading the questions. Some students in some groups jot down answers to some of the questions. Others look up occasionally to see what other groups are doing or look at each other and then go back to studying the handout. Finally, in one group a student says to another:

> **S1:** You figure out number 3?
> **S2:** Um, no, and you?
> **S1:** No. How about number 6?
> **S2:** Well, answer is "plankton," I think.

Whereupon the group falls back into silence and more individual work.

In another group, one student has apparently finished jotting down answers to the questions, and a second student says:

S3: You got them all?
S4: Yes, I think so.
S3: So, what you write down?
S4: Number 1 is . . .

And S4 continues to read off his answers one by one as other students in the group fill in the answers in silence.

A third group seizes upon the latter group's method and queries one of their members who appears to have all the answers. And the fourth group works on in silence; students occasionally glance at each other's papers, mumble a comment or two, and make emendations. Meanwhile the teacher has circulated around once to watch the students, responding only if a student initiates a question directly. He then returns to his desk to record attendance and grade some papers.

After about 15 minutes, the teacher asks the class to report on their responses, question by question, students individually volunteering answers. For each question the teacher asks if anyone disagrees, then indicates whether the answer is right or wrong, then asks if everyone in the class understands.

There is something wrong with this picture! If the 15-minute time period in which students were in small groups is group work, then the language-teaching profession is in serious trouble. The description you have just read demonstrates just about everything that you should *not* do in conducting group work techniques in your classroom. Before reading on in this chapter, jot down (a) problems with the above lesson, and (b) what you think the teacher should have done to make a successful group activity following a 10-minute mini-lecture.

In this chapter, we will look at group work as central to maintaining linguistic interaction in the classroom. In so doing, you will get some answers to questions such as: What are the advantages of group work? What are some problems to overcome in successful group work? What different kinds of tasks are appropriate for group work? What are some steps for implementing group work? What are some rules for successful group work?

ADVANTAGES OF GROUP WORK

What is **group work**? It is a generic term covering a multiplicity of techniques in which two or more students are assigned a task that involves collaboration and self-initiated language. Note that what we commonly call pair work is simply group work in groups of two. It is also important to note that group work usually implies "small"-group work, that is, students in groups of perhaps six or fewer. Large groupings defeat one of the major purposes for doing group work: giving students more opportunities to speak.

Group work is solidly grounded in research principles (Dörnyei & Murphey, 2003; Long & Porter, 1985; McDonough, 2004). Consider the 12 principles cited in Chapter 4. You can think of other theoretical foundations of successful language teaching and learning already discussed in this and other books on second language learning and teaching. And consider the importance of interaction in the language classroom discussed in the previous chapter. An integration of these principles and issues yields a number of advantages of group work for your English language classroom.

1. Group work generates interactive language.

In so-called traditional language classes, teacher talk is dominant. Teachers lecture, explain grammar points, conduct drills, and at best lead whole-class discussions in which each student might get a few seconds of a class period to talk. Group work helps to solve the problem of classes that are too large to offer many opportunities to speak. By one estimate (Long & Porter, 1985), if just half of your class time were spent in group work, you could increase individual practice time five-fold over whole-class traditional methodology.

Closely related to the sheer *quantity* of output made possible through group work is the variety and *quality* of interactive language. With traditional methods, language tends to be restricted to initiation only by the teacher in an artificial setting where the whole class becomes a "group interlocutor." Small groups provide opportunities for student initiation, for face-to-face give and take, for practice in negotiation of meaning, for extended conversational exchanges, and for student adoption of roles that would otherwise be impossible.

2. Group work offers an embracing affective climate.

The second important advantage offered by group work is the security of a smaller group of students where each individual is not so starkly on public display, vulnerable to what the student may perceive as criticism and rejection. In countless observations of classes, I have seen the magic of small groups. Quite suddenly, reticent students become vocal participants in the process. The small group becomes a community of learners cooperating with each other in pursuit of common goals.

A further affective benefit of small-group work is an increase in student motivation. With Maslow's "security/safety" level satisfied through the cohesiveness of the small group, learners are thus freed to pursue higher objectives in their quest for success.

3. Group work promotes learner responsibility and autonomy.

Even in a relatively small class of 15 to 20 students, whole-class activity often gives students a screen to hide behind. I remember a college French class I took in which the teacher's single teaching technique was to call on students one by one to translate a sentence in our reading passage of the day. My way of playing that game was simply to keep one sentence ahead of the teacher so that when my name came up, I was ready. I paid no attention to what was currently being translated, to the meaning of the whole passage, to comments by the teacher, or to fellow classmates. An extreme case, to be sure! But even in less deadly classroom climates, students can "relax" too much in whole-class work. Group work places responsibility for action and progress upon each of the members of the group somewhat equally. It is difficult to "hide" in a small group.

4. Group work is a step toward individualizing instruction.

Each student in a classroom has needs and abilities that are unique. Usually the most salient individual difference that you observe is a range of proficiency levels across your class and, even more specifically, differences among students in their speaking, listening, writing, and reading abilities. Small groups can help students with varying abilities to accomplish separate goals. The teacher can recognize and capitalize upon other individual differences (age, cultural heritage, field of study, cognitive style, to name a few) by careful selection of small groups and by administering different tasks to different groups.

EXCUSES FOR AVOIDING GROUP WORK

Some teachers are afraid of group work. They feel they'll lose control or students will just use their native language, and so they shy away from it. Some of these apprehensions are understandable; group work does not mean simply putting students into groups and having them do what you would otherwise do as a whole class. But the limitations or drawbacks to group work are all surmountable obstacles when group work is used appropriately—that is, for objectives that clearly lend themselves to group work. Let's look at these limitations—or "myths," perhaps—and try to understand how to deal with them.

Excuse 1: The teacher is no longer in control of the class.

Now, you may be thinking, "Well, I don't mind giving control over to the students." But, depending on the context of your teaching, control could be a very important issue. If you are

- teaching in an institution where the administrator in charge requires that you teach through a traditional, whole-class methodology,
- teaching in a culture where "good teaching" is defined as students quietly working in orderly fashion, speaking only when spoken to by the teacher,
- teaching very large classes (of 75 or more) where a plethora of small groups becomes difficult to manage,
- teaching a group of unruly students—possibly of secondary school age—where discipline is a major issue,
- yourself a nonnative speaker of English without the confidence to "let your students go" in small groups,

then control may be an issue. There is no doubt that group work requires some yielding of control to the students. In numerous cultures, students are indeed primed to be under the complete control and authority of the teacher, and group work therefore is a very strange activity to engage in. In such contexts the teacher must be very clever to orchestrate successful small-group work.

But this is still a "drawback" rather than a reason to avoid group work. By quietly introducing small doses of group work into your otherwise traditional classroom, you may be able to convince administrators and students of the advantages. With careful attention to guidelines for implementation of group work, administrative or managerial dilemmas should be avoidable. And if you are unsure of your own English language ability, take heart in the fact that you are still quite a few steps ahead of your students.

As we noted earlier in Chapter 13, if control is thought of as *predicting* everything that is going to transpire in a class hour, then you do not want "control" because you will be thwarting virtually all possibility of an interactive language classroom. Group work still allows you to play the roles of director, manager, facilitator, and resource. In those roles, there is still an adequate degree of control; the class will not necessarily run away with you.

Excuse 2: Students will use their native language.

In ESL settings where a multiple number of languages are often represented in a single classroom, teachers can avoid the native language syndrome by placing students in heterogeneous language groups. But in EFL situations, where all of the students have a common native language, it is indeed possible, if not probable, that students in small groups will covertly use their native language. In fact, this is usually the primary reason teachers give me for shying away from group work. How can it be overcome?

Judicious following of guidelines for implementation (discussed in the following section) will help. If students feel that the task is too hard (or too easy), or that directions are not clear, or that the task is not interesting, or that they are not sure of the purpose of the task, then you may be inviting students to take shortcuts via their native language. The most important factor, however, is setting the climate for group work. Here are some suggestions:

- Impress upon your students the importance of *practice* in the second language for eventual success. Make sure—in whatever way you see fit— that they clearly understand that successful learners consistently practice using the target language in face-to-face contexts.
- Appeal to various *motivational* factors affecting them so that they can see some real uses for English in their own lives. Try to hone in on their *intrinsic* motivation to learn.
- Demonstrate how *enjoyable* the various small-group tasks and games and activities are. Careful selection and administration of group activities helps to ensure such pleasure. Your own overt display of enthusiasm will help to set a tone.
- Inform them of the *security* offered by the smaller groups. Get the groups to think of themselves as teams, the members of which are all working together. Remind them that, in the process, they can try out language

without feeling that the whole class (and the teacher!) is watching and criticizing.

- For students who argue that the only reason they are in your class is to pass an *examination,* remind them that research has shown that people do better on tests if they dive into the language itself rather than just study test items. If they can be convinced that small groups help to build their intuitions about language, they may also understand that those intuitions will be their ally in a test situation.

Excuse 3: Students' errors will be reinforced in small groups.

Teachers are usually concerned about the fact that, especially in large classes, students will simply reinforce each other's errors and the teacher won't get a chance to correct them. This concern can really be laid to rest. There is now enough research on errors and error correction (Long & Porter, 1985; McDonough, 2004) to tell us that (a) levels of accuracy maintained in unsupervised groups are as high as those in teacher-monitored whole-class work, and that (b) as much as you would like not to believe it, teachers' overt attempts to correct speech errors in the classroom have a negligible effect on students' subsequent performance. Errors are a "necessary" manifestation of inter-language development, and we do well not to become obsessed with their constant correction. Moreover, well-managed group work can encourage spontaneous peer feedback on errors within the small group itself.

Excuse 4: Teachers cannot monitor all groups at once.

Related to the issue of control is the sometimes misguided belief that a teacher should be "in on" everything a student says or does during the class hour. Interactive learning and teaching principles counter with the importance of meaningful, purposeful language and real communication, which in turn must allow the student to give vent to creative possibilities. Yes, the effective teacher will circulate among the groups, listen to students, and offer suggestions and criticisms. But it is simply not necessary—for reasons cited in #3 above—to be a party to all linguistic intercourse in the classroom.

Excuse 5: Some learners prefer to work alone.

It is true that many students, especially adult-age students, prefer to work alone because that is the way they have operated ever since they started going to school. As a successful manager of group work, you need to be sensitive to such preferences, acknowledging that some if not many of your students will find group work frustrating because they may simply want you just to give them the answers to some problem and then move on. Help your students to see that language learning is not a skill where you can simply bone up on rules and words in isolation. Language is for communicating with people (whether through oral or written modes), and the more they engage in such face-to-face communication, the more their overall communicative competence will improve.

Related to the work style issue are numerous other **learning style** variations among students that are magnified in small groups. Because the teacher isn't present within the group at all times, groups are often left to derive their own dynamic inductively. In the process, individual differences become more salient than they are in whole-class work. Below are several possible scenarios:

- A highly left-brain-oriented student is put off by the otherwise more right-brain members of the group.
- Quicker (impulsive) thinkers tend to blurt out their ideas, overwhelming the slower (reflective) thinkers.
- Impulsive learners get easily frustrated with the group process, which they perceive as circuitous.
- Competitive members of a group are reluctant to share information with others.
- "Talkative" students dominate the process.

While such problems can and do occur in group work, virtually every problem that is rooted in learning style differences can be solved by careful planning and management. In fact, when the group members know their task and know their roles in the group, learning style differences can be efficiently utilized and highly appreciated—much more so than in whole-class work.

IMPLEMENTING GROUP WORK IN YOUR CLASSROOM

As you saw in the scene that opens this chapter, group work can go wrong if it is not carefully planned, well executed, monitored throughout, and followed up on in some way. We'll now look at practical steps to take to carry out successful group work in your classroom.

Evaluating Classroom Language

One of the first considerations in implementing group work is to ascertain that your students have an appropriate command of **classroom language** with which to carry out the group task that you have in mind. Now, some group work is linguistically quite simple, and correctly so for lower proficiency levels. But at somewhat higher levels, we teachers love to direct our students to *discuss* some particular point or question, with no further explanation, assuming that our students know exactly what we mean by the word. When you say to your class, "Okay, everyone, get into pairs and discuss these ideas from the lecturette you just heard," what does that *mean* to students?

In order to make sure that a group task is accurately understood by students, not only are clear directions (see below) important, but students must be able to carry out the discourse necessary to accomplish the task. This means that prior (either in the same lesson or in previous lessons) to the task, students have performed the various bits and pieces of classroom language that the task presupposes. Consider the following excerpt from Sarosy and Sherak (2006, p. 54) that reviews expressions for agreeing and disagreeing:

To agree with others:
I agree with _____ , . . .
That's a good point, . . .
I agree with _____'s point, . . .
S/He's right, . . .
I think _____ has the right idea, . . .

To disagree with others:
I'm afraid I don't agree, . . .
I'm sorry, but I have to disagree, . . .
I disagree with _____ , . . .
No, I don't think that's true, . . .
I see your point, but . . .
Perhaps you're right about _____ , but I can't agree with you on . . .

There are other forms of classroom language that can make a difference in the success of a group task. Consider the following list (adapted from Sarosy & Sherak, 2006):

Agreeing and disagreeing ("I see your point, but . . .")
Interrupting another student (". . . Excuse me . . .")
Asking for clarification ("Sorry, what did you mean by _____?")
Asking for more information ("Could you elaborate, please?")
Supporting your opinion ("Let me tell you why . . .")
Coming to a consensus ("Would you all agree to . . . ?")
Going over exercises with a partner ("Oh, I wrote something different.")
Giving oral feedback to peers' written work ("Have you thought about . . . ?")

The important point here is *not* simply to assume your students have the necessary competence to perform the discourse required of a group task, without making sure those abilities are there. Once the necessary classroom language is in place, the task can proceed to its aims more efficiently.

Selecting Appropriate Group Techniques

So far in this chapter, as your attention has been focused on group work, differences between **pair work** and group work have not been emphasized. There are, in fact, some important distinctions. Pair work is more appropriate than group work for tasks that are (a) short, (b) linguistically simple, and (c) quite controlled in terms of the structure of the task. Appropriate pair activities (that are not recommended for groups of more than two) include:

1. practicing dialogues with a partner
2. simple question-and-answer exercises
3. performing certain meaningful substitution "drills"
4. quick (one minute or less) brainstorming activities
5. checking written work with each other
6. preparation for merging with a larger group
7. any brief activity for which the logistics of assigning groups, moving furniture, and getting students into the groups is too distracting

Pair work enables you to engage students in interactive (or quasi-interactive) communication for a short period of time with a minimum of logistical problems. But don't misunderstand the role of pair work. It is not to be used exclusively for the above types of activity; it is also appropriate for many group work tasks (listed below).

The first step in promoting successful group work, then, is to select an appropriate task. In other words, choose something that lends itself to the group process. Lectures, drills, dictations, certain listening tasks, silent reading, and a host of other activities are obviously not suitable for small-group work.

Typical group tasks are defined and briefly characterized below. For further examples and information, I highly recommend that you consult a few of a wide variety of teacher resource books that offer a multitude of tasks for you to consider. (Some are listed at the end of this chapter.)

1. Games

A game could be any activity that formalizes a technique into units that can be scored in some way. Several of the other group tasks outlined below could thus become "games." Guessing games are common language classroom activities. Twenty Questions, for example, is easily adapted to a small group. One member secretly decides that he or she is some famous person; the rest of the group has to find out who, within 20 yes/no questions, with each member of the group taking turns asking questions. The person who is "it" rotates around the group and points are scored.

2. Role plays and simulations

Role plays minimally involve (a) giving a role to one or more members of a group and (b) assigning an objective or purpose that participants must accomplish. In pairs, for example, student A is an employer; student B is a prospective employee; the objective is for A to interview B. In groups, similar dual roles could be assumed with assignments to others in the group to watch for certain grammatical or discourse elements as the roles are acted out. Or a group role play might involve a discussion of a political issue, with each person assigned to represent a particular political point of view.

Simulations usually involve a more complex structure and often larger groups (of 6 to 20) where the entire group is working through an imaginary situation as a social unit, the object of which is to solve some specific problem. A common genre of simulation games specifies that all members of the group are shipwrecked on a "desert island." Each person has been assigned an occupation (doctor, carpenter, garbage collector, etc.) and perhaps some other mitigating characteristics (has a physical disability, is an ex-convict, is a prostitute, etc.). Only a specified subset of the group can survive on the remaining food supply, so the group must decide who will live and who will die.

3. Drama

Drama is a more formalized form of role play or simulation, with a preplanned story line and script. Sometimes small groups may prepare their own short dramatization of some event, writing the script and rehearsing the scene as a group. This may be more commonly referred to as a "skit." Longer, more involved dramatic performances have been shown to have positive effects on language learning, but they are time consuming and rarely can form part of a typical school curriculum.

4. Projects

For learners of all ages, but perhaps especially for younger learners who can greatly benefit from hands-on approaches to language, certain projects can be rewarding indeed. If you were to adopt an environmental awareness theme in your class, for example, various small groups could each be doing different things: Group A creates an environmental bulletin board for the rest of the school; group B develops fact sheets; group C makes a three-dimensional display; group D puts out a newsletter for the rest of the school; group E develops a skit, and so on. As learners get absorbed in purposeful projects, both receptive and productive language is used meaningfully.

5. Interviews

A popular activity for pair work, but also appropriate for group work, interviews are useful at all levels of proficiency. At the lower levels, interviews can be very structured, both in terms of the information that is sought and the grammatical difficulty and variety. The goal of an interview could at this level be limited to using requesting functions, learning vocabulary for expressing personal data, producing questions, etc. Students might ask each other questions like

What's your name?

Where do you live?

What country (city) are you from?

and learn to give appropriate responses. At the higher levels, interviews can probe more complex facts, opinions, ideas, and feelings.

6. Brainstorming

Brainstorming is a technique whose purpose is to initiate some sort of thinking process. It gets students' "creative juices" flowing without necessarily focusing on specific problems or decisions or values. Brainstorming is often put to excellent use in preparing students to read a text, to discuss a complex issue, or to write on a topic. Brainstorming involves students in a rapid-fire, free-association listing of concepts or ideas or facts or feelings relevant to some topic or context.

Suppose you were about to read a passage on future means of transportation. You might ask small groups to brainstorm (a) different forms of transportation, past and present, and (b) current obstacles to more efficient means of transportation. The groups' task would be to make a composite list of everything they can think of within the category, without evaluating it. In brainstorming, no discussion of the relative merits of a thought takes place; everything and anything goes. This way, all ideas are legitimate, and students are released to soar the heights and plumb the depths, as it were, with no obligation to defend a concept. In whatever follow-up to brainstorming you plan, at that point evaluation and discussion can take place.

7. Information gap

These last four types of techniques are quite commonly used in adult classes around the world, up and down the proficiency continuum.

Information-gap activities include a tremendous variety of techniques in which the objective is to convey or to request information. The two focal characteristics of information-gap techniques are (a) their primary attention to information and not to language forms and (b) the necessity of communicative interaction in order to reach the objective. The information that students must seek can range from very simple to complex.

At the beginning level, for example, each member of a small group could be given the objective of finding out from the others their birthday, address, favorite food, etc., and filling in a little chart with the information. In intermediate classes you could ask groups to collectively pool information about different occupations: necessary qualifications, how long it takes to prepare for an occupation, how much the preparation costs, what typical job conditions are, what salary levels are, etc. In advanced classes, a small-group discussion on determining an author's message, among many other possibilities, would be an information-gap technique.

8. Jigsaw activities

Jigsaw techniques are a special form of information gap in which each member of a group is given some specific information and the goal is to pool all information to achieve some objective. Imagine four members of a group each with a [fictitious] application form, and on each form different information is provided. As students ask each other questions (without showing anyone their own application form), they eventually complete all the information on the form. Or you might provide maps to students in small groups, each student receiving different sets of information (where the bank is, where the park is, etc.). The goal for beginners might be simply to locate everything correctly, and for intermediate learners to give directions on how to get from one place on the map to another, requiring a collaborative exchange of information in order to provide complete directions.

One very popular jigsaw technique that can be used in larger groups is known as a "strip story." The teacher takes a moderately short written narrative or conversation and cuts each sentence of the text into a little strip, shuffles the strips, and gives each student a strip. The goal is for students to determine where each of their sentences belongs in the whole context of the story, to stand in their position once it is determined, and to read off the reconstructed story. Students enjoy this technique and almost always find it challenging.

9. Problem solving and decision making

Problem-solving group techniques focus on the group's solution of a specified problem. They might or might not involve jigsaw characteristics, and the problem itself might be relatively simple (such as giving directions on a map), moderately complex (such as working out an itinerary from train, plane, and bus schedules), or quite complex (such as solving a mystery in a "crime story" or dealing with a political or moral dilemma). Once again, problem-solving techniques center students' attention on meaningful cognitive challenges and not so much on grammatical or phonological forms.

Decision-making techniques are simply one kind of problem solving where the ultimate goal is for students to make a decision. Some of the problem-solving techniques alluded to above (say, giving directions to someone and solving a mystery) don't involve a decision about what to do. Other problem-solving techniques do involve such decisions. For example, students presented with several profiles of applicants for a job may be asked to decide who they would hire. The "desert island" simulation game referred to earlier involves a decision. Or a debate on environmental hazards might reveal several possible causes of air pollution, but if decision making is the goal, then the group would have to decide now what they would actually do to reduce toxins in our air.

10. Opinion exchange

An opinion is usually a belief or feeling that might not be founded on empirical data or what others could plausibly take issue with. Opinions are difficult for students to deal with at the beginning levels of proficiency, but by the intermediate level, certain techniques can effectively include the exchange of various opinions. Many of the above techniques can easily incorporate beliefs and feelings. Sometimes opinions are appropriate; sometimes they are not, especially when the objective of a task is to deal more with "facts."

Moral, ethical, religious, and political issues are usually "hot" items for classroom debates, arguments, and discussions. Students can get involved in the content-centered nature of such activity and thus pave the way for more automatic, peripheral processing of language itself. Issues for discussion include

- women's rights
- factors in choosing a marriage partner
- cultural taboos
- sexual orientation
- political candidates and their stands
- abortion
- euthanasia
- environmental crises (air, water, forests, atmosphere, oceans)
- war and peace

One warning: You play an important and sensitive role when you ask students to discuss their beliefs. Some beliefs are deeply ingrained from childhood rearing or from religious training, among other factors. So, it is easy for a student to be offended by what another student says. In such exchanges, do everything you can to assure everyone in your class that, while there may be disagreement on issues, all opinions are to be valued, not scorned, and respected, not ridiculed.

Planning Group Work

Possibly the most common reason for the breakdown of group work is an inadequate introduction and lead-in to the task itself. Too often, teachers assume that purposes are clear and directions are understood, and then have to spend an inordinate amount of time clarifying and redirecting groups. Once you have selected an appropriate type of activity, your planning phase should include the following seven "rules" for implementing a group technique.

1. **Introduce the technique.** The introduction may simply be a brief explanation. For example, "Now, in groups of four, you're each going to get different transportation schedules (airport limo, airplane, train, and bus), and your job is to figure out, as a group, which combination of transportation services will take the least amount of time." The introduction almost always should include a statement of the ultimate purpose so that students can apply all other directions to that objective.
2. **Justify the use of small groups for the technique.** You may not need to do this all the time with all your classes, but if you think your students have any doubts about the significance of the upcoming task, then tell them explicitly why the small group is important for accomplishing the task. Remind them that they will get an opportunity to practice certain language forms or functions, and that if they are reluctant to speak up in front of the whole class, now is their chance to do so in the security of a small group.
3. **Model the technique.** In simple techniques, especially those that your students have done before, modeling may not be necessary. But for a new and potentially complex task, it never hurts to be too explicit in making sure students know what they are supposed to do. After students get into their

groups, you might, for example, show them (possibly on an overhead projector) four transportation schedules (not the ones they will see in their groups). Then select four students to simulate a discussion of meshing arrival and departure times; your guidance of their discussion will help.

4. **Give explicit detailed instructions.** Now that students have seen the purpose of the task and have had a chance to witness how their discussion might proceed, give them specific instructions on what they are to do. Include

   - a restatement of the purpose,
   - rules they are to follow (e.g., Don't show your schedule to anyone else in your group. Use "if" clauses as in "If I leave at 6:45 A.M., I will arrive at the airport at 7:25."),
   - a time frame (e.g., You have 10 minutes to complete the task.),
   - assignment of roles (if any) to students (e.g., The airport limo person for each group is the "chair." The airplane person will present your findings to the rest of the class. The train person is the timekeeper, etc.).

5. **Divide the class into groups.** This element is not as easy as it sounds. In some cases you can simply number off (e.g., 1,2,3,4, . . .) and specify which area of the room to occupy. But to ensure participation or control you may want to preassign groups in order to account for one or two of the following:

   - native language (especially in ESL classes with varied native language backgrounds)
   - proficiency levels
   - age or gender differences
   - cultural or subcultural group
   - personality types
   - cognitive style preferences
   - cognitive/developmental stages (for children)
   - interests
   - prior learning experience
   - target language goals

   In classes of fewer than 30 people, preassigning groups is quite manageable if you come to class with the preassignments, having thought through the variables that you want to control. Just put the group names up on the chalkboard and tell people to get into their groups.

6. **Check for clarification.** Before students start moving into their groups, check to make sure they all understand their assignment. Do not do this by

asking, "Does everyone understand?"* Rather, test out certain elements of your lead-in by asking questions like, "Keiko, please restate the purpose of this activity."

7. **Set the task in motion.** This part should now be a simple matter of saying something like, "Okay, get into your groups and get started right away on your task." Some facilitation may be necessary to ensure smooth logistics.

Monitoring the Task

Your job now becomes one of facilitator and resource. To carry out your role, you need to tread the fine line between inhibiting the group process and being a helper or guide. The first few times you do group work, you may need to establish this sensitive role, letting students know you will be available for help and that you may make a suggestion or two here and there to keep them on task, but that they are to carry out the task on their own. There may actually be a few moments at the outset where you do not circulate among the groups so that they can establish a bit of momentum. The rest of the time it is very important to circulate so that, even if you have nothing to say to a group, you can listen to students and get a sense of the groups' progress and of individuals' language production.

A few *don'ts:*
- Don't sit at your desk and grade papers.
- Don't leave the room and take a break.
- Don't spend an undue amount of time with one group at the expense of others.
- Don't correct students' errors unless asked to do so.
- Don't assume a dominating or disruptive role while monitoring groups.

Debriefing

Almost all group work can be brought to a beneficial close by some sort of whole-class debriefing, once the group task is completed. This debriefing, or "processing," as some would refer to it, has two layers:

---

*Teachers are often tempted to assume that asking a blanket question like this provides an informal assessment of how well students comprehended something. Usually, whether students understood or not, a small minority of them will nod their heads affirmatively while the rest of the class shows no response. The few nodding heads must not be taken as a measure of comprehension by all. It is better, therefore, never (or rarely) to say such things as "Does everyone understand?" because it can lead to a false sense of satisfaction on the part of the teacher.

1. **Reporting on task objectives.** If groups were assigned a reporter to present something to the class, or if the task implicitly lends itself to some discussion of the "findings" of the groups, then make sure that you leave enough time for this to take place. As reporters or representatives of each group bring their findings, you may entertain some brief discussion, but be sure not to let that discussion steal time from other groups. This whole-class process gives each group a chance to perceive differences and similarities in their work. Some group work involves different assignments to different groups, and in these cases the reporting phase is interesting to all and provides motivation for further group work.

2. **Establishing affective support.** A debriefing phase also serves the purpose of exploring the group process itself and of bringing the class back together as a whole community of learners. If you or some students have questions about how smoothly the task proceeded, how comfortable people were with a topic or task, or problems they encountered in reaching their objective, now is an excellent time to encourage some whole-class feedback. This gives you feedback for your next group work assignment. Ultimately, even a very short period of whole-class discussion reminds students that everyone in the room is a member of a team of learners and that the groups, especially if any intergroup competition arose, are but temporary artifacts of classroom learning.

★ ★ ★ ★ ★

It's possible that this chapter on group work has been so explicit in its description that you feel overwhelmed or put off by the prospect of doing group work in your classroom. If so, that need not be the case! All of the guidelines and reminders and do's and don'ts included in this chapter will in due course of time become a part of your subconscious, intuitive teaching behavior. You won't have to process every minute of your class hour in terms of whether you've done all the "right" things. In the meantime, just remember that conscientious attention to what makes for successful group work will soon pay off.

TOPICS FOR DISCUSSION, ACTION, AND RESEARCH

[Note: (I) Individual work; (G) group or pair work; (C) whole-class discussion.]

1. **(G)** Direct pairs to do the following: Look again at the lesson described at the beginning of the chapter. Pick it apart: List the things about it that were problematic, and why they were problems. Can you put the lesson back together in a way that would promote successful group work? What would you do differently? Compare your findings with those of other pairs.

2. (I) What is "control"? Is control an issue for you? How might you do group work and still stay in control? Specifically, at what points should you relinquish control?

3. (G) What if, after all the precautions, students still use their native language in small groups? Ask pairs to brainstorm further solutions and then discuss their feasibility.

4. (G) Have pairs take one of the examples of the eight categories of classroom language listed on page 230 and brainstorm other phrases used in English to accomplish the discourse function. Each pair can write the list on the board for a composite list of samples from the eight categories.

5. (G) Have groups brainstorm other examples (besides those given in the book) of each of the 10 categories of small-group work starting on page 231, describe them carefully, and if possible, demonstrate selected techniques to their classmates.

6. (G/C) Direct pairs to think of other "hot topics" for opinion exchange (page 235). Which ones would be too "hot" to include in classroom discussion? Why? Pairs will then share their thoughts with the rest of the class.

7. (I/C) Try to observe an ESL class with several instances of group work. Use the criteria on pages 235–237 to evaluate the effectiveness of the group work that you observe. Report your findings back to your classmates.

8. (C) On page 236 some criteria were listed for preassigning group membership. Ask your students to justify the use of those criteria—that is, under what circumstances and for what reasons would one preassign small-group membership? Are there other criteria?

9. (G/C) Ask small groups, each assigned to a different one of the 10 categories of group work, to devise a role play in which they demonstrate how the technique would work with a defined group of students (age, proficiency level, context). They will then demonstrate it to their classmates. Ask the members of the class to criticize it with the criteria specified toward the end of the chapter. Groups should respond to the criticism as constructively as possible.

FOR YOUR FURTHER READING

Long, M., & Porter, P. (1985). Group work, interlanguage talk, and second language acquisition. *TESOL Quarterly, 19,* 207–228.

In this seminal, ground-breaking article on group work, Michael Long and Patricia Porter review the research relating to the effectiveness of group work in the second language classroom. They examine some "myths" about group work and encourage teachers to employ interactive small-group work in their classrooms. This article is a "must" for teachers wishing to understand the importance of group work in second language classrooms.

McDonough, K. (2004). Learner-learner interaction during pair and small group activities in a Thai EFL context. *System, 32,* 207–224.

Two decades after Long and Porter carried out their research, we still occasionally look for support for the concept of group work. In this article, Kim McDonough presents a brief survey of research on the effectiveness of pair and small-group activities in second language classrooms, then reports a study of English learners in Thailand who, after participation in pair and group work, manifested improved production of selected forms.

Sarosy, P., & Sherak, K. (2006). *Lecture ready: Strategies for academic listening, note-taking, and discussion.* New York, NY: Oxford University Press.

Peg Sarosy and Kathy Sherak provide a very practical, well-organized approach to academic listening in this textbook for ESL learners. In each unit are found examples of teaching classroom language.

Crandall, J. (1999). Cooperative language learning and affective factors. In J. Arnold (Ed.), *Affect in language learning* (pp. 226–245). Cambridge, UK: Cambridge University Press.

JoAnn Crandall provides an excellent chapter summarizing cooperative learning principles, virtually all of which apply to the successful implementation of group work tasks.

CHAPTER 15

CLASSROOM MANAGEMENT

> **OBJECTIVES** After reading this chapter, you will be able to:
>
> - recognize physical features in the classroom environment that affect the success of a lesson
>
> - monitor your voice and body language and make changes as necessary
>
> - apply guidelines for dealing with unexpected, unplanned moments, and turn them to your (and students') advantage
>
> - develop some strategies for teaching large classes
>
> - model roles and styles that are appropriate for a given lesson and audience
>
> - create a positive classroom climate

Is teaching an art or a science? Are teachers born or made? Is the learning-teaching connection poetic or predictable? These questions are commonly found swirling about in the minds of educators, not so much as "either-or" questions but rather as "both-and" questions. I think you can easily agree that teaching is both an art and a science, that some innate ability complements learned teaching skills, and that with all of our best-laid lesson plans there still remains an intangible aura surrounding acts of learning. But how do the two traditions coexist in practice? How do art and science mingle in the principles and approaches and techniques and plans of ESL teachers?

In the previous chapters in this section of *Teaching by Principles,* you have considered course and lesson design, materials and technological aids, and some guidelines for creating interaction in your methodology. The next step in a succession of practicalities for the language classroom is to grapple with what we call **classroom management**, which encompasses an abundance of factors ranging from how you physically arrange the classroom, to teaching "styles," to one of my favorite themes: classroom energy. By understanding what some of the variables are in classroom management, you can take some important steps to sharpening your skills as a language teacher. And then, as you improve some of those identifiable, overtly observable skills, you open the door to the intangible—to art, to poetics, to the invisible sparks of energy that kindle the flames of learning.

THE PHYSICAL ENVIRONMENT OF THE CLASSROOM

One of the simplest principles of classroom management centers on the physical environment for learning: the classroom itself. Consider four categories:

1. Sight, sound, and comfort

As trivial as it may first appear, in the face of your decisions to implement language-teaching principles in an array of clever techniques, students are indeed profoundly affected by what they see, hear, and feel when they enter the classroom. If you have any power to control the following, then it will be worth your time to do so:

- The classroom is neat, clean, and orderly in appearance.
- Chalkboards are erased.
- Chairs are appropriately arranged (see below).
- If the room has bulletin boards and you have the freedom to use them, can you occasionally take advantage of visuals?
- The classroom is as free from external noises as possible (machinery outside, street noise, hallway voices, etc.).
- Acoustics within your classroom are at least tolerable.
- Heating or cooling systems (if applicable) are operating.

Granted, you may be powerless to control some of the above. I have been in classrooms in tropical countries where there is no air conditioning, the concrete walls of the classroom echo so badly you can hardly hear anyone, and jackhammers are rapping away outside! But if these factors can be controlled, don't pass up the opportunity to make your classroom as physically comfortable as possible.

2. Seating arrangements

You may have had the experience of walking into a classroom and finding the movable desks all lined up in columns (not rows) that are perpendicular to the front wall of the room. Neat and orderly, right? Wrong. If you won't get fired from your teaching post by doing so, change the pattern immediately! Students are members of a team and should be able to see one another, to talk to one another (in English!), and not be made to feel like they just walked into a military formation.

If your classroom has movable desk-chairs, consider patterns of semicircles, U-shapes, concentric circles, or—if your class size is small enough—one circle so that students aren't all squarely facing the teacher. If the room has tables with two to four students at each, try to come up with configurations that make interaction among students most feasible. Give some thought to how students will do small-group and pair work with as little chaos as possible.

Should you determine who sits next to whom? Normally, students will soon fall into a comfortable pattern of self-selection in where they sit. You may not need to tamper with this arrangement unless you feel the need to force a different "mix" of students. In some ESL contexts, or where students come from varied native language backgrounds, English will be more readily practiced if students of the same native language are not sitting next to each other. And if some adjacent students are being disruptive, you may decide to selectively move a few people. When assigning small groups, as noted in Chapter 14, you may of course want to do so with a certain plan in mind.

3. Chalkboard use

The chalkboard is one of your greatest allies. It gives students added visual input along with auditory. It allows you to illustrate with words and pictures and graphs and charts. It is always there and it is recyclable! So, take advantage of this instant visual aid by profusely using the chalkboard. At the same time, try to be neat and orderly in your chalkboard use, erasing as often as appropriate; a messy, confusing chalkboard drives students crazy.

4. Equipment

Many courses now assume that equipment is either built into the classroom or readily available on portable carts. If you're using electrical equipment (say, a projector, or an audio or video player), make sure that

- the room's electrical outlets are within reach of the cord provided, and if not, that an extension cord is on your equipment list,
- the equipment fits comfortably in the room,
- everyone can see (and/or hear) the visual/auditory stimulus,
- you leave enough time before and after class to get the equipment and return it to its proper place,
- you try out the machine ahead of time to ascertain that it actually works,
- you know how to operate it,
- there is an extra lightbulb or battery or whatever else you'll need in case a routine replacement becomes necessary.

You would be surprised how many lesson plans go awry because of some very minor practicality surrounding the use of equipment.

YOUR VOICE AND BODY LANGUAGE

Another fundamental classroom management concern has to do with **you** and the messages you send through your voice and through your body language.

One of the first requirements of good teaching is good voice projection. You do not have to have a loud, booming voice, but you need to be heard by all the students in the room. When you talk, project your voice so that the person sitting farthest away from you can hear you clearly. If you are directing comments to a student in the first row sitting right in front of you, remember that in whole-class work, all the rest of the students need to be able to hear that comment. As you speak, articulate clearly; remember, these students are learning English, and they need every advantage they can get.

Should you slow down your normal rate of delivery? For beginning level classes, yes, but only slightly so, and not to the point that the rate of delivery is downright silly. Keep as natural a flow to your language as possible. Clear articulation is usually more of a key to comprehension than slowed speech.

Your voice isn't the only production mode available to you in the classroom. Nonverbal messages are very powerful. In language classes, especially, where students may not have all the skills they need to decipher verbal language, their attention is drawn to nonverbal communication. Here are some pointers:

- Let your body posture exhibit an air of confidence.
- Your face should reflect optimism, brightness, and warmth.
- Use facial and hand gestures to enhance meanings of words and sentences that might otherwise be unclear.
- Make frequent eye contact with all students in the class.
- Do not "bury yourself" in your notes and plans.
- Do not plant your feet firmly in one place for the whole hour.
- Move around the classroom, but not to distraction.
- Follow the conventional rules of proxemics (distance) and kinesthetics (touching) that apply for the culture(s) of your students.
- Dress appropriately, considering the expectations of your students and the culture in which you are teaching.

UNPLANNED TEACHING: MIDSTREAM LESSON CHANGES

Now that you have considered some of the factors in managing the physical space and your physical self, imagine that you have entered the classroom and begun your lesson. The warm-up has gone well. You have successfully (with clear, unambiguous directions) introduced the first major technique, which, let's say, has to do with different countries' forms of government. Students are clear about why they are doing this task and have launched themselves into it. Then one student asks about the political campaign happening right now. Another student responds, and then another, and before you know it, students are engaged in a very interesting, somewhat heated debate about current political issues. This theme is related to your lesson, but the discussion is not what you had in mind. Nevertheless, students are all alert, interested, participating, and using fairly complex English in the process. You realize that your lesson will have to change in some way.

This scene is commonplace. What would you do now? Should you have cut off the conversation early and nipped it in the bud? Or were you wise to let it continue and to discard some other activities you had in mind? Classroom management involves decisions about what to do when

- your students digress and throw off the plan for the day,
- *you* digress and throw off the plan for the day,

- an unexpected but pertinent question comes up,
- some technicality prevents you from doing an activity (e.g., a machine breaks down, or you suddenly realize you forgot to bring handouts that were necessary for the next activity),
- a student is disruptive in class,
- you are asked a question you don't know the answer to (e.g., a grammatical point),
- there isn't enough time at the end of a class period to finish an activity that has already started.

And the list could go on. In short, you are daily called upon to deal with the *unexpected.* You have to engage in what we'll call unplanned teaching that makes demands on you that were not anticipated in your lesson plan. One of the initiation rites that new teachers go through is experiencing these unexpected events and learning how to deal with them gracefully. And the key is *poise.* You will keep the respect of your students and your own self-confidence by staying calm, assessing the situation quickly, making a midstream change in your plan, and allowing the lesson to move on.

TEACHING UNDER ADVERSE CIRCUMSTANCES

Under the category of "adverse circumstances" are a number of management concerns of widely divergent nature. What is implied here is that no teaching-learning context is perfect. There are always imperfect institutions, imperfect people, and imperfect circumstances for you to deal with. How you deal with them is one of the most significant factors contributing to your professional success.

1. Teaching large classes

I was once asked by a student in a teacher education course about how to deal with large classes. I began to list the kinds of adjustments he could make with classes of 50 to 75 students, when he said that he meant really large classes: somewhere in the neighborhood of 600 students! As I caught my breath, my only response was to ask him how he would teach 600 people to swim in one swimming pool without displacing all the water in the pool!

Ideally, language classes should be comprised of no more than 12 to 15 students (LoCastro, 2001). They should be large enough to provide diversity and student interaction and small enough to give students plenty of opportunity to participate and to get individual attention. Unfortunately, with paltry educational budgets worldwide, too many language classes are significantly larger. Classes of 50 to 75 are not uncommon across the globe. While you need to keep reminding administrators (who too often believe that languages are learned by rote memorization) of the diminishing returns of classes in excess of 25 or 30, you nevertheless may have to cope with the reality of a large class for the time being. Large classes present some problems:

- Proficiency and ability vary widely among students.
- Individual teacher-student attention is minimized.
- Student opportunities to speak are lessened.
- Teacher's feedback on students' written work is limited.

Some solutions to these problems are available. Consider the following that apply to one or several of the above challenges:

a. Try to make each student feel important (and not just a "number") by learning names and using them. Name tags or desk "plates" serve as reminders in the early days of the course.

b. Assign students as much interactive work as possible, including plenty of "get-acquainted" activities at the beginning, so that they feel a part of a community and are not just lost in the crowd.

c. Optimize the use of pair work and small-group work to give students chances to perform in English. In grouping, consider the variation in proficiency levels (see next section, below).

d. Do more than the usual number of listening comprehension activities, using tapes, video, and yourself. Make sure students know what kind of response is expected from them. Through active listening comprehension, students can learn a good deal of language that transfers to reading, speaking, and writing.

e. Use peer-editing, feedback, and evaluation in written work whenever appropriate.

f. Give students a range of extra-class work, from a minimum that all students must do to challenging tasks for students with higher proficiency.

g. Don't collect written work from all of your students at the same time; spread it out in some systematic way both to lighten your load and to give students the benefit of a speedy return of their work.

h. Set up small "learning centers" in your class where students can do individualized work.

i. Organize informal conversation groups and study groups.

2. Teaching multiple proficiency levels in the same class

There is often a wide range of proficiency levels among students in the same class, especially in large classes, but even relatively small classes can be composed of students who in your estimation should not all be placed at the same level. In either case, you are faced with the problem of challenging the higher-level students and not overwhelming the lower-level students, and at the same time keeping the middle group well paced toward their goals. Most of the time, the phenomenon of widely ranging competencies in your class is a by-product of institutional placement procedures and budgetary limits, so there is little you can do to "kick out" the students at either extreme. So, how do you deal with this? Here are some suggestions to consider:

a. Do *not* overgeneralize your assessment of students' proficiency levels by blanket classifications into "the good students" and "the bad students." It is a common mistake among teachers (we all do it!) to talk about smart and dumb students in our classes. We must be very sensitive to the issue of *proficiency* versus *ability.* In a set of skills as complex as language, it is often difficult to determine whether a student's performance is a factor of aptitude, ability, a "knack," or a factor of time and effort.

b. For most students, competencies will vary among the four skills, within each skill (e.g., in reading, lexical knowledge, meaning-seeking strategies, speed, efficiency, etc.), and by context. As much as possible, identify the specific skills and abilities of each student in your class so that you can tailor your techniques to individualized needs. Through diagnostic tests and exercises and day-by-day monitoring of students, you may be able to pinpoint certain linguistic objectives and direct your students toward those.

c. Offer choices in individual (written and extra-class) techniques that vary according to needs and challenges. In doing so, sensitively convey to your students that they *all* have challenges and goals to pursue and that if some students seem to be "ahead" of others, it is no doubt due to previous instruction, exposure, and motivation (see item [a] above).

d. Take advantage of whatever learning centers or tutorial laboratories that may be available in your institution. All proficiency levels can benefit from laboratories that provide computer software for review and practice, or trained tutors that can diagnose needs and suggest avenues of further work. Students at higher levels and lower levels of proficiency can thereby be challenged to meet their needs.

e. Obviously, the tenor of your classroom teacher talk (instructions, explanations, lectures, etc.) will need to be gauged toward the middle of the levels of proficiency in your class. But group work tasks offer opportunities for you to solve multiple-proficiency issues. Sometimes you can place students of varying ranges in the same group, and at other times you can place students of the same range in a group together. Both scenarios offer advantages and disadvantages.

3. Using "English only" in the classroom?

In language-teaching circles across the globe, there is sometimes an undercurrent of opinion that claims that one should never use native languages in the classroom. Such convictions may stem from a bygone era when methods like the Direct Method endorsed "target language only" practices in the classroom, and from a reaction to Grammar Translation methodology that often saw little use at all of the target language. It is now clear from research and experience that "English only" prohibitions go too far (Atkinson, 1987; Harmer, 2001; Ur, 1996).

On the other hand, especially in EFL contexts, a common problem is too much use of the native language in the classroom. Teachers who may not feel supremely confident in their English proficiency are tempted to use more of the native language than may be pedagogically advisable. And students are naturally inclined to revert to various forms of code-switching (alternating between the native and target languages) in the classroom.

Is there a middle ground? Your cultural, institutional, and methodological contexts will usually lead to a reasonable solution. In EFL classes, where students all share the same native language, a good deal of time is saved by using the native language for certain definitions, grammatical explanations, directions for a task, or cultural comments. The most challenging context in EFL classes is in pair and group work: Students will by nature revert to their native language occasionally if they can "get away with it."

Some institutions pride themselves in advertising "direct" use of the target language in their classrooms, and you will have to discover for yourself how and when such proscriptions can be broken. In ESL contexts, with multiple languages often represented in a single classroom, the issue is not as acute, but even here clusters of students from the same country may engage in native language chatter, and it's up to you to determine how to deal with those possibilities.

Harmer (2001) and Gebhard (2006) offer some guidelines for dealing with issues of whether or not, and when, to use native languages in the classroom. The following is an amalgamation of the two sources:

a. Set clear guidelines. Students need to know when English use is essential, when it is more or less "okay" to use the native language, and when it is counterproductive to use the native language.

b. Negotiate with students on why it is important for them to use English in the classroom. If they understand the importance of practicing English, and the reasons for occasional uses of the native language, they will experience the "buy in" necessary for conforming to the negotiated standard.

c. Stimulate intrinsic motivation to use English in the classroom. If students use English because they themselves see the value in it, they will be less likely to use their native language. They will view the use of English in the classroom as an opportunity for practice and feedback from others.

d. Choose appropriate tasks for students, so that they are capable, at their level of English, of accomplishing the objectives of activities, and are therefore less tempted to "cheat" by using their native language.

e. Create in your classroom an English "atmosphere." Especially in EFL situations, if students are surrounded by posters, magazines, computer software, and other realia that stimulate the use of English, they will be more likely to be in the "mood" to speak English in the classroom.

4. Compromising with the "institution"

Another adverse circumstance is one that most teachers have to deal with at some time in their careers: teaching under institutional conditions that do not meet their ideal standards or philosophy of education. Sometimes such circumstances focus on an individual in charge, a director or principal. And sometimes they center on administrative constraints that are beyond the scope and power of one individual. Some examples:

- classes that are far too large to allow for the kind of results that the administration expects (see above),
- physical conditions in the classroom that are onerous,
- administratively imposed constraints on *what* you have to teach in your course (the curriculum, possibly in great detail),
- administratively imposed constraints on *how* you should teach (a specific methodology that you disagree with is required),
- courses that satisfy an institutional foreign language requirement, in which students simply want a passing grade,
- courses that are test-focused rather than language-focused.

5. Disciplining

Many volumes of research and practical advice have been written on the subject of classroom discipline. If all of your students were hard-working, intrinsically motivated, active, dedicated, intelligent learners—well, you would still have what we could label "discipline" problems! Without making this section a whole primer on discipline, I will simply offer some pointers here and let you make the applications to specific instances.

a. Learn to be comfortable with your position of authority.
b. Gain the respect of your students by treating them all with equal fairness.
c. Establish clearly and explicitly certain expectations regarding students' behavior in class, or what Harmer (2001, p. 127) calls a "code of conduct." Harmer suggested that if the code is established through negotiation with students, rather than as "rules" that you as the authority insist on, the democratically established code "has considerable power" (p. 128).
d. Include in the expectations such issues as: conventions for turn-taking, respect for others, the importance of listening to other students, attendance issues (tardiness and absence policy), and any extra-class ("homework") obligations.
e. Be firm but warm in dealing with variances to these expectations.
f. If a reminder, reprimand, or other form of verbal disciplinary action is warranted, do your best to preserve the dignity of the student (in spite of the fact that you could be frustrated enough to want to humiliate the student in front of classmates!) and the terms of any negotiated "rules."
g. Try, initially, to resolve disciplinary matters outside of class time (ask to see a student after class and quietly but firmly make your observation and let the student respond) so that valuable class minutes aren't spent focusing on one student.

  h. In resolving disciplinary problems, try to find the source of the problem rather than treating symptoms (for example, if a student isn't paying attention in class, it could be because of a lack of sleep caused by working a late night shift, in which case you could suggest a different shift or a different time bracket for the English class).
  i. If you cannot resolve a recurring disciplinary problem, then consult your institution's counselor or administrator.

6. Dealing with cheating

Cheating is a special disciplinary matter that warrants careful treatment. For the sake of definition, we will say *cheating* is a surreptitious violation of standards of individualized responses to tests or other exercises. The first step to solving a perceived problem of cheating is to ascertain a student's own perception: Did he or she honestly believe they were doing something wrong? There is a good deal of cultural variation in defining what is or isn't cheating, and for some, what you may think is cheating is merely an intelligent utilization of resources close at hand. In other words, if the answer that is written on the test is correct, then the means used to come up with the correct answer are justified. Once you have adequately ascertained a student's perception, then follow the disciplinary suggestions as a guide to a solution.

Minimizing opportunities to cheat—that is, prevention—may prove to be more fruitful than trying to tangle with the mixture of emotions that ensue from dealing with cheating after the fact. Why do students cheat? Usually because of pressure to "excel." So if you can lower that pressure (see Chapters 21 and 22), you may reduce the chance that someone will write notes on a fingernail or glance across the aisle. Remind students that you and the test are there to help them and to give them feedback, but if you don't see their "real" selves, you won't be able to help them. If the classroom size permits, get students spread out as much as possible (this "elbow room" also promotes some physical relaxation). Then, consider an "A" and "B" form of a test in which items are in a different order for every other person, thereby making it more difficult for someone to spot an answer.

All these and even further adverse circumstances are part of the reality of teaching and ultimately of classroom management because they all impinge in some way on what you can do in your lessons. Your handling of such situations will almost always demand some sort of compromise on your part. You must, as a professional "technician" in this field, be ready to bring professional diplomacy and efficiency to bear on the varying degrees of hardship.

TEACHERS' ROLES AND STYLES

In these final sections on classroom management, we turn a little more centrally to the affective or emotional side of being and becoming a good teacher.

1. Roles

A teacher has to play many **roles**, as was pointed out in Chapter 13. Think of the possibilities: authority figure, leader, knower, director, manager, counselor, guide, and even such roles as friend, confidante, and parent. Depending on the country you are in, on the institution in which you are teaching, on the type of course, and on the makeup of your students, some of these roles will be more prominent than others, especially in the eyes of your students.

For growing comfortable and confident in playing multiple roles, two rules of thumb are a willing acceptance of the many ways that students will perceive you, and a consistent fairness to all students equally. Know yourself, your limitations, your strengths, your likes and dislikes, and then accept the fact that you are called upon to be many things to many different people. Then, as you become more comfortable with, say, being an authority figure, be consistent in all your dealings with students. There is something quite unsettling about a teacher who is a sympathetic friend to some students and a dispassionate authority figure to others. Such waffling in playing out your roles can set students against each other, with many feeling shut out from an inner circle of "teacher's pets."

2. Teaching styles

Your **teaching style** is another affective consideration in the development of your professional expertise. Teaching style will almost always be consistent with your personality style, which can vary greatly from individual to individual. As you consider the teaching styles below, remember that each represents a continuum of possibilities:

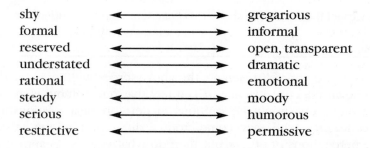

shy	⟷	gregarious
formal	⟷	informal
reserved	⟷	open, transparent
understated	⟷	dramatic
rational	⟷	emotional
steady	⟷	moody
serious	⟷	humorous
restrictive	⟷	permissive

Where do you place yourself on these continua? Do you feel it is necessary to lean toward one end in order to be an effective teacher? If you do, you may be succumbing to a stereotype that doesn't jibe with your most effective "self" in the classroom. I have seen excellent teachers on both ends of these style continua. As you grow more comfortable with your teaching roles in the classroom, make sure your style of teaching is also consistent with the rest of you and with the way you feel you can be most genuine in the classroom; then, learn how to capitalize on the strengths of your teaching style.

3. Cultural expectations

Western cultures emphasize the nondirective, nonauthoritarian roles and teaching styles listed in the right-hand column below. One major consideration, therefore, in the effectiveness of playing roles and developing styles is the culture in which you are teaching and the culture of your students.

The following are a number of cultural expectations of roles and styles as they relate to teachers and students and schools (adapted from Hofstede, 1986).

• Teachers are expected to have all the answers.	• Teachers are allowed to say "I don't know."
• Teachers are expected to suppress emotions (and so are students).	• Teachers are allowed to express emotions (and so are students).
• Teachers interpret intellectual disagreement as personal disloyalty.	• Teachers interpret intellectual disagreement as a stimulating exercise.
• Teachers reward students for accuracy in problem solving.	• Teachers reward students for innovative approaches to problem solving.
• Students admire brilliance in teachers.	• Students admire friendliness in teachers.
• Students should speak in class only when called on by the teacher.	• Students are encouraged to volunteer their thoughts.
• Teachers should never lose face; to do so loses the respect of students.	• Teachers can admit when they are wrong and still maintain students' respect.
• Students expect the teacher to show them "the way."	• Teachers expect students to find their own way.

Wherever you find yourself teaching, the above forces will come into play as you attempt to be an effective teacher. If you feel that one column is more "you" than the other, then you should be cautious in developing a relationship with students and colleagues who may come from a different tradition. Always be sensitive to the perceptions of others, but then do what you feel is appropriate to negotiate changes in attitude. Be ready to compromise your ideal self to some extent, especially when you begin a teaching assignment. There is little to be gained by coming into a teaching post like gangbusters, alienating all those around you, and than finding yourself unemployed a couple of months later. If you have convictions about what good teaching is, it pays to be patient in slowly reaching your goals. After all, you might learn something from your students and fellow teachers!

CREATING A POSITIVE CLASSROOM CLIMATE

The roles you play and the styles you develop will merge to give you some tools for creating a classroom climate that is positive, stimulating, and energizing.

1. Establishing rapport

Rapport is a somewhat slippery but important concept in creating positive energy in the classroom. Rapport is the relationship or connection you establish with your students, a relationship built on trust and respect that leads to students' feeling capable, competent, and creative. How do you set up such a connection? By

- showing interest in each student as a person,
- giving feedback on each person's progress,
- openly soliciting students' ideas and feelings,
- valuing and respecting what students think and say,
- laughing *with* them and not *at* them,
- working *with* them as a team, not *against* them, and
- developing a genuine sense of vicarious joy when they learn something or otherwise succeed.

2. Balancing praise and criticism

Part of the rapport you create is based on the delicate balance that you set between praise and criticism. Too much of either renders it less and less effective. Genuine praise, appropriately delivered, enables students to welcome criticism and to put it to use. Table 15.1 shows the contrast between effective praise and ineffective praise.

Table 15.1. Effective praise versus ineffective praise (adapted from Brophy, 1981)

Effective Praise	Ineffective Praise
• shows genuine pleasure and concern	• is impersonal, mechanical, and "robotic"
• shows verbal and nonverbal variety	• shows bland uniformity
• specifies the particulars of an accomplishment, so students know exactly what was performed well	• is restricted to global comments, so students are not sure what was performed well
• is offered in recognition of noteworthy effort on difficult tasks	• is offered equally strongly for easy and difficult tasks
• attributes success to effort, implying that similar success can be expected in the future	• attributes success to ability, luck, or other external factors
• fosters intrinsic motivation to continue to pursue goals	• fosters extrinsic motivation to perform only to receive more praise
• is delivered without disrupting the communicative flow of ongoing interaction	• disrupts the communicative flow of ongoing interaction

3. Generating energy

What is classroom "energy"? I like to use this term for a force that is unleashed in a classroom, perceivable only through a "sixth sense," if you will, that is acquired in the experience of teaching itself. Energy is what you react to when you walk out of a class period and say to yourself, "Wow! That was a great class!" or "What a great group of students!" Energy is the electricity of many minds caught up in a circuit of thinking and talking and writing. Energy is an aura of creativity sparked by the interaction of students. Energy drives students toward higher attainment. Students (and teachers) take energy with them when they leave the classroom and bring it back the next day.

How do you create this energy? Not necessarily by being dramatic or flamboyant, witty or wise. Sometimes energy is unleashed through a quiet, reserved, but focused teacher. Sometimes energy forces gather in the corporate intensity of students focused on rather mundane tasks. But you are the key. Because students initially look to you for leadership and guidance, you are the one to begin to get the creative sparks flying. And by whatever means you accomplish this, you do so through solid preparation, confidence in your ability to teach, a genuinely positive belief in your students' ability to learn, and a sense of joy in doing what you do. You also do so by overtly manifesting that preparation, confidence, positive belief, and joy when you walk into the classroom.

☆   ☆   ☆   ☆   ☆

Perhaps the art and the science of teaching converge on issues of classroom management. On the one hand, a good deal of the process of maintaining pace, rhythm, and energy in a class hour requires the artistic brush strokes of intuitive moment-by-moment decisions. When you have a classroom full of individuals with particular needs and moods and motivations, it's virtually impossible to predict everything that those individuals will do or say. But on the other hand, your intuitions are informed by the collective experience and best practices of those who have gone before you in the form of guidelines and parameters for successful management of a classroom full of students. By combining those well-tested principles with your personal intuition, you can enter the unpredictabilities of the classroom arena with confidence and creativity.

TOPICS FOR DISCUSSION, ACTION, AND RESEARCH

[Note: (I) Individual work; (G) group or pair work; (C) whole-class discussion.]

1. (C) Ask members of the class to volunteer stories about classes they have been in (or taught) where (a) something went wrong with the physical environment of the classroom, (b) some kind of unplanned or embarrassing moment occurred, or (c) some form of adverse circumstance took place. What did the teacher do? What *should* the teacher have done?

2. (G) Assign different groups to (a) large-class issues and (b) multiple-proficiency issues. Direct them to look at the lists of suggested solutions, and to discuss the extent to which the solutions are practical. Do they apply to actual classes that someone is familiar with? What further measures can be taken to maximize student learning in each of the two circumstances?

3. (G/C) Have groups brainstorm solutions to the following situations, then report back to the rest of the class: Suppose you have been assigned to teach in a language institute for adults in (you name the country). The director insists that students will learn best through the Grammar Translation Method, mainly because that's the way he learned three foreign languages. He has asked you to use this method, and the textbooks for the course are a grammar reference guide and a book of readings with vocabulary words listed at the end of each reading. Your class is a group of intermediate level young adults, all currently employed in various places around the city. They want to learn English in order to get into a university. What would you do? How would you resolve the difference between what you believe your students need and the dictates of your director? (You need the money, so don't get yourself fired!)

4. (C) Discuss the following questions with your class: What is cheating? How is it defined in your culture and how does that vary across cultures? Has a classmate ever tried to cheat in a class you have been a student in? What did the teacher do, if anything? What would you have done had you been the teacher?

5. (I/G) Rate yourself on the continua of teacher styles on page 251. Use four categories in between the extreme of each factor for your rating by designing a chart something like this:

shy   ❑   ❑   ❑   ❑   gregarious

Check just one box for each pair of adjectives. Check the left-most box if the left-hand adjective is *very* much like you, the second from the left if it *somewhat* describes you; check the right-most box if the right-hand adjective is *very* much like you, and the second from the right if it *somewhat* describes you. Do you feel that you need to change some of those natural styles when you enter a classroom? If not, why do you feel that your present styles are adequate? Are there any tendencies that might work against you? What should you do to prevent such a problem? Share your results with a partner.

6. (G) Arrange groups preferably with heterogeneous representations of people who are from or have knowledge of varied cultures. Consider the society your students know and ask them to address the following questions: Where does that society fall on the list of continua describing cultural expectations of students? Would you add any other expectations to the list? Consider each factor and discuss specific ways in which you would deal with a conflict of expectations between your students and yourself.

7. (I/G/C) In your own words, describe "energy." Share your description with a partner. Observe a class and see if you can identify things that the teacher or the students do that make you feel that the class is "energized." Share your observations with others in your class.

FOR YOUR FURTHER READING

Underwood, M. (1991). *Effective class management.* London: Longman.

Mary Underwood's timeless and very practical little book provides details of classroom management issues in a number of categories, ranging from the physical environment of the classroom to large classes to discipline. It applies as well today as it did when it was written, with the single exception of her chapter on audiovisual aids—a field that has changed markedly.

LoCastro, V. (2001). Large classes and student learning. *TESOL Quarterly, 35,* 493-496.

Sarwar, Z. (2001). Innovations in large classes in Pakistan. *TESOL Quarterly, 35,* 497-500.

These two articles provide some perspectives on issues and problems surrounding the teaching of large classes. Virginia LoCastro comments on how class size affects the purposes of a language class, and Zakia Sarwar reports on a classroom-based project in Pakistan in which teachers dealt with classes as large as 150 students.

Lewis, M. (2002). Classroom management. In J. Richards & W. Renandya (Eds.), *Methodology in language teaching: An anthology of current practice* (pp. 40-48). Cambridge, UK: Cambridge University Press.

Marilyn Lewis offers an interesting assortment of classroom management issues: student motivation, various behavior problems, group work issues, anxiety, and teachers' roles.

CHAPTER 16

STRATEGIES-BASED

INSTRUCTION

OBJECTIVES After reading this chapter, you will be able to:

- recognize the importance of students' understanding various tricks, gimmicks, and techniques for learning a language—embodying a "knack" for learning

- appreciate the value of fostering in students a sense of self-awareness of their styles and preferences

- understand the principle of strategic investment within practical classroom contexts

- identify a number of styles within students and their assets and liabilities in a given task or lesson

- apply the concept of leading students from awareness (of styles) to action (in the form of using strategies)

Did you ever see one of those enticing Web sites advertising a quick and easy foreign language course? It may have read something like this:

SPEAK JAPANESE LIKE A NATIVE!

Haven't you often wished you could speak a foreign language fluently and effortlessly? Well, now you can! With our online interactive technology, your computer becomes a convenient window to a Japanese classroom! Join the thousands who have mastered a foreign language from our scientifically proven method. All you have to do is . . .

The advertisement might have made additional guarantees and promises, and all this is yours for just $495 on your next credit card statement!

You know from your own experiences in learning and/or teaching a foreign language that there is no single magic formula for successful foreign language learning. One set of audio CDs or a software package may indeed be a good start or a great refresher. But with the vast complexity of second language learning, much more than this is necessary for ultimate mastery and the fluency that the advertisements promise.

What is required for such success is the persistent use of a whole battery of strategies for language learning, whether the learner is in a regular language classroom or working on a self-study program. Sometimes these strategies are subconsciously applied because certain learners seem to have a knack for language learning that they are not consciously aware of. But often, successful learners have achieved their goals only through conscious, systematic application of a battery of strategies.

STRATEGIC INVESTMENT

In recent years language-teaching methodology has seen a dramatic increase in attention to what I like to call the **strategic investment** that learners can make in their own learning process. The learning of any skill involves a certain degree of "investment" of one's time and effort. Every complex set of skills—like learning to play a musical instrument or tennis—is acquired through a combination of observing, focusing, practicing, monitoring, correcting, and redirecting. And so one develops strategies for perceiving others and for singling out relevant elements of language and all the other necessary behaviors essential for ultimate mastery. A language is probably the most complex set of skills one could ever seek to acquire; therefore, an investment is necessary in the form of developing multiple layers of strategies for getting that language into one's brain.

In Chapter 4 the Principle of Strategic Investment (Principle 5) was introduced. In this chapter we probe its implications for your teaching methodology in the classroom, specifically, how your language classroom techniques can encourage, build, and sustain effective language-learning strategies in your students. This facet of language teaching has come to be known as **strategies-based instruction** (SBI).

All 12 of the other principles outlined in Chapter 4 have a bearing on this issue. If one's language learning should sustain a modicum of automatic processing (Principle 1), what kind of strategies can students use to assist in converting controlled processes into automatic ones? If meaningful learning (Principle 2) is important, how can learners maximize meaning in their linguistic input and output? What kind of immediate, extrinsic rewards (Principle 3) and long-range, intrinsic motives (Principle 4) are necessary to keep learners pointed toward goals? As you run down the list of principles yourself, it becomes apparent how learning strategies are germane to the eventual success of learners. Strategies are, in essence, learners' techniques for capitalizing on the principles of successful learning.

In an era of communicative, interactive, learner-centered teaching, SBI simply cannot be overlooked. All too often, language teachers are so consumed with the "delivery" of language to their students that they neglect to spend some effort preparing learners to "receive" the language. And students, mostly unaware of the tricks of successful language learning, simply do whatever the teacher tells them to do, having no means to question the wisdom thereof. In an effort to fill class hours with fascinating material, teachers might overlook their mission of enabling learners to eventually become *independent* of classrooms—that is, to become autonomous learners.

One of your principal goals as an interactive language teacher is to equip your students with a sense of what successful language learners do to achieve success and to aid them in developing their own unique, individual pathways to success. Because by definition interaction is unrehearsed, mostly unplanned discourse, students need to have the necessary strategic competence to hold their own in the give and take of meaningful communication.

One could compare language learners to participants in an elaborate wine-tasting party. The color and sweetness of our linguistic corkage are enticing. But how are students to fully appreciate this event without some education on how to partake of the libations spread before them? Tips on what to look for and what goes with what and how to get the most out of something—these are necessary elements of our methodology. When students are taught how to look at themselves and how to capitalize on their talents and experiences, they learn lessons that carry them well beyond any language classroom. That's what SBI is all about.

GOOD LANGUAGE LEARNERS

SBI had its early roots in studies of "good" language learners. Research in this area tended first to identify certain successful language learners and then to extract— through tests of psycholinguistic factors, interviews, and other data analysis— relevant factors believed to contribute to their success. Some generalizations were drawn by Joan Rubin and Irene Thompson (1982) that will give you a sense of the flavor of this line of research. Good language learners

1. find their own way, taking charge of their learning
2. organize information about language
3. are creative, developing a "feel" for the language by experimenting with its grammar and words
4. make their own opportunities for practice in using the language inside and outside the classroom
5. learn to live with uncertainty by not getting flustered and by continuing to talk or listen without understanding every word
6. use mnemonics and other memory strategies to recall what has been learned
7. make errors work for them and not against them
8. use linguistic knowledge, including knowledge of their first language, in learning a second language
9. use contextual cues to help them in comprehension

10. learn to make intelligent guesses
11. learn chunks of language as wholes and formalized routines to help them perform "beyond their competence"
12. learn certain tricks that help to keep conversations going
13. learn certain production strategies to fill in gaps in their own competence
14. learn different styles of speech and writing and learn to vary their language according to the formality of the situation

It is important to remember that some of the above characteristics are not based on empirical findings, but rather on the collective observations of teachers and learners themselves. Therefore, do not assume that all successful learners exhibit all of these characteristics. Nor is this list of 14 an exhaustive one; in fact, later in this chapter, you will find a much more detailed taxonomy (Oxford, 1990) of successful learning strategies.

The good language learner studies are of obvious interest to teachers. The more your classroom activity can model the behavior exhibited by successful language learners, the better and more efficient your students will be, especially in developing their own autonomy as learners.

STYLES OF SUCCESSFUL LANGUAGE LEARNING

One step in understanding SBI is to make a distinction between styles and strategies (see *PLLT,* Chapter 5). **Styles**, whether related to personality (such as extroversion, self-esteem, anxiety) or to cognition (such as left/right-brain orientation, ambiguity tolerance, field sensitivity), characterize the consistent and enduring traits, tendencies, or preferences that may differentiate you from another person. They are ". . . an individual's natural, habitual, and preferred ways of absorbing, processing, and retaining new information and skills" (Kinsella, 1995, p. 171). You might, for example, tend to be extroverted or right-brain oriented, as opposed to being introverted or left-brain oriented. Or you could show a preference for solving problems in a linear, logical fashion versus an integrated, intuitive approach. These styles are an appropriate characterization of how you behave *in general,* even though you may for a multitude of conscious or subconscious reasons operate outside of those styles in a *specific* context.

Strategies, on the other hand, are specific methods of approaching a problem or task, modes of operation for achieving a particular end, or planned designs for controlling and manipulating certain information. Hsiao and Oxford (2002, p. 368) emphasize the role of strategies in *enhancing* students' learning. Strategies vary widely within an individual, while styles are more constant and predictable. You may almost simultaneously utilize a dozen strategies for figuring out what someone just said to you, for example. You may use strategies of "playback" (imagine an instant taped replay of the conversation), key word identification, attention to nonverbal cue(s), attention to context, dictionary look-up, grammatical analysis, numerous direct requests for repetition, rephrasing, word definition, or turning to someone else for interpretation. And the list could go on.

Successful second language learners are usually people who know how to manipulate style (as well as strategy) levels in their day-to-day encounters with the language. This means that they are first aware of general personality and cognitive characteristics or tendencies that usually lead to successful acquisition and strive to develop those characteristics. For example, a successful learner who is not a risk-taker (personality trait) and is left-brain dominant and somewhat intolerant of ambiguity (cognitive traits) recognizes her dominant traits and resolves to force herself to take more risks, to balance her brain, and to adopt a more tolerant attitude toward language she doesn't understand. Why? Because she has been informed of the importance of the latter styles for most language-learning contexts.

In other words, styles are not by any means immutable tendencies. Learners can, through a program of self-awareness, understand who they are and take steps to change what may be inhibiting traits within their general style. At this point in our collective knowledge about language acquisition, the number of personality and cognitive styles that lead toward successful learning is finite. In fact, the "10 commandments" listed in Table 16.1 in this chapter may sufficiently identify chief style factors that a language learner needs to be concerned with.

AWARENESS AND ACTION

Implied in the foregoing discussion is the all-important Principle of Autonomy (Principle 6, discussed in Chapter 4). In order for learners to become self-driven independent learners beyond the classroom, they must be fully aware of their own strengths, weaknesses, preferences, and styles, and be able to capitalize on that metacognition through the use of appropriate action in the form of strategic options. The importance of awareness-raising in language learning has caught the attention of researchers (Chamot, 2005; Nakatani, 2005; Parks & Raymond, 2004). Of course, the awareness-action relationship is fundamental to all human learning and especially to acquiring complex skills like foreign languages. When learners are aware of their own capacities and limitations, they can efficiently adopt pathways to success that capitalize on strengths and compensate for weaknesses.

Figure 16.1 on page 262 offers my visual picture of the awareness-action connection. A fully functioning learner is aware, on a number of levels, of styles, personality variables, the effect of early socialization, ego factors, self-efficacy, intellectual capabilities, cultural schemata, belief systems, and more. Such self-knowledge then leads to action in the form of strategies: direct, metacognitive, socioaffective, skill-specific (listening, speaking, reading, writing), and proficiency-based (varying from beginner to advanced) strategies, along with appropriate doses of compensating for weaknesses and capitalizing on style advantages.

Figure 16.1. Awareness and action in second language learning

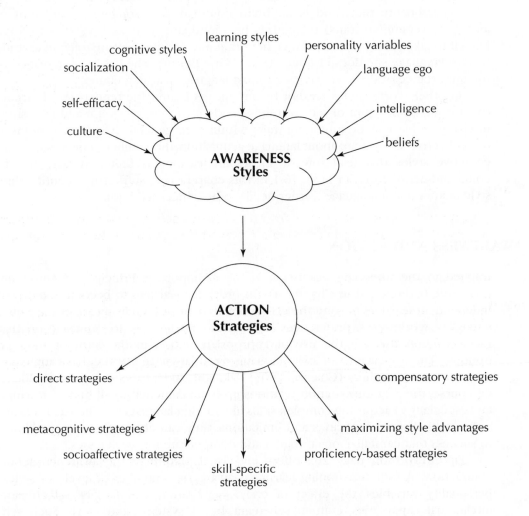

Successful language learners typically develop this self-awareness either subconsciously through experience and/or natural ability, or through conscious processes that may be stimulated by a teacher, a textbook, a guide to language learning, tips and hints from others, or a specific determination to assess one's various proclivities. The all-important follow-up, or "action" as I like to call it, comes in the form of a multitude of possible strategies. So, for example, a learner who is aware of his or her fondness for analysis, linear thinking, and clear structures will use that knowledge to tackle certain language-learning tasks at hand. Some tasks, such as generating input and using contextual cues to decipher information, will no doubt require strategic options that *compensate* for the tendency to overanalyze. Other tasks—for example, figuring out verb endings and determining L1/L2 contrasts—will offer this learner a chance to *capitalize* on preexisting strengths and preferences. The latter tasks will be fairly easy and automatic while the former tasks will probably take some special focus as the learner will need to move out of a strategic "comfort zone" and into territory that is a little less natural. This is where a teacher can be an excellent stimulator and facilitator.

DEVELOPING STUDENT SELF-AWARENESS OF STYLES

How do you help learners to develop the self-awareness necessary to work toward successful language-learning strategies? Several means are available to you as a teacher.

1. Informal self-checklists

One effective way to instill student awareness of successful styles is through an informal self-checklist (you might devise it yourself) that students fill out and then discuss. Such checklists are usually not formally scored or tallied; rather, they serve as focal points for discussion and enlightenment. Figure 16.2 on page 264 is an example of a checklist that has been used with ESL students. (For lower proficiency levels, the vocabulary can be simplified.)

You could adapt the following procedure for use in your classroom:

1. Hand out checklists to each student and tell them to fill them in on their own.
2. When they finish, put students into groups of four. Their objective is to compare answers, to justify individual responses, and to determine if anyone feels compelled to change his or her response category after discussion. The ultimate objective is to get students to talk openly about their own styles.
3. In whole-class activity, groups can be asked to share any major agreements and disagreements. Direct this discussion toward some conclusions about the best styles for successful language learning.
4. Summarize by explaining that no one side is necessarily good or bad, but that (a) if they are too dominant on one side, they may profit from allowing the

Figure 16.2. Learning styles checklist

Check one box in each item that best describes you. Boxes A and E indicate that the sentence is very much like you. Boxes B and D indicate that the sentence is somewhat descriptive of you. Box C indicates that you have no inclination one way or another.

A B C D E

1. I don't mind if people laugh at me when I speak. ❏ ❏ ❏ ❏ ❏ I get embarassed if people laugh at me when I speak.

2. I like to try out new words and structures that I'm not completely sure of. ❏ ❏ ❏ ❏ ❏ I like to use only the language that I am certain is correct.

3. I feel confident in my ability to succeed in learning this language. ❏ ❏ ❏ ❏ ❏ I feel quite uncertain about my ability to succeed in learning this language.

4. I want to learn this language because of what I can personally gain from it. ❏ ❏ ❏ ❏ ❏ I am learning this language only because someone else is requiring it.

5. I really enjoy working with other people in groups. ❏ ❏ ❏ ❏ ❏ I would much rather work alone than with others.

6. I like to "absorb" language and get the general gist of what is said or written. ❏ ❏ ❏ ❏ ❏ I like to analyze the many details of language and understand exactly what is said or written.

7. If there is an abundance of language to master, I try to take things one step at a time. ❏ ❏ ❏ ❏ ❏ I am very annoyed by an abundance of language material presented all at once.

8. I am not overly conscious of myself when I speak. ❏ ❏ ❏ ❏ ❏ I monitor myself closely and consciously when I speak.

9. When I make mistakes, I try to use them to learn something about the language. ❏ ❏ ❏ ❏ ❏ When I make a mistake, it annoys me because that's a symbol of how poor my performance is.

10. I find ways to continue learning the language outside the classroom. ❏ ❏ ❏ ❏ ❏ I look to the teacher and the classroom activities for everything I need for success.

other side of a continuum to operate, and (b) that most learners tend to lean too far to the right side of the chart, which is usually not the best learning style.

2. Formal personality and cognitive style tests

If formal personality or cognitive style tests are available to you, you might try using them in your class—but with caution! Often these tests are culturally biased, have difficult language, and need to be interpreted with a grain of salt. Many tests designed for North American English speakers are loaded with cultural references that learners from other countries may misinterpret. And if the language is too difficult, your attempts to paraphrase may destroy a test's validity. Always remember that any self-check test, however formal, is a product of a test-taker's own self-image; often they will simply want to see themselves in a good light, and therefore their responses may reflect a bit of self-flattery.

Nevertheless, a few simple scorable tests may be feasible for the second language classroom. Certain versions of the Myers-Briggs Type Inventory (MBTI) have been attempted with learners, especially the Keirsey Temperament Sorter (Keirsey & Bates, 1984), in order to give a measure of personality indices (see *PLLT*, Chapter 6). There is now enough research (Dörnyei, 2005; Ehrman & Dörnyei, 1998) to indicate that personality styles as measured by the MBTI (extroversion, intuition, logic, etc.) correspond to language-learning styles and that learners can benefit from knowing both the assets *and* liabilities of each style. For example, an extroverted style is beneficial for face-to-face conversation, but it can also entail dependency on outside stimulation and work against self-sufficiency.

More appropriate for the English classroom are two other examples of self-check inventories, provided in Figures 16.3 (page 266) and 16.4 (page 267), both taken from Brown (2002b), and constructed for intermediate students of English. The first is a left/right-brain dominance test; the second focuses on self-confidence and anxiety. Tests like these (or variations thereof) can be administered and treated in the same way as was suggested for the Learning Styles Checklist (Figure 16.2). In this way students can become aware of their possible style tendencies, consider the relationship between such styles and success in their language-learning goals, and take positive steps to capitalize on their assets and to overcome any liabilities.

3. Readings, lectures, and discussions

Yet another way of encouraging self-awareness of styles in your classroom is for you to assign occasional readings, or give mini-lectures or presentations followed by discussions about successful learning styles. In Brown's (2002b) *Strategies for Success,* a self-help guide for language learners, some chapters are devoted to raising style awareness, with simple, brief discussions that are comprehensible at a low intermediate level of English proficiency. Readings and questionnaires are followed by in-class exercises in which students further reinforce their knowledge of certain styles.

Figure 16.3. Left/right-brain dominance questionnaire

QUESTIONNAIRE: Left-Brain and Right-Brain Processing

Circle the number that best describes you. Circle only one number for each item. Use the following scale:

1   *The sentence on the left describes you well.*
2   *The sentence on the left somewhat describes you.*
3   *The sentence on the right somewhat describes you.*
4   *The sentence on the right describes you well.*

Example

   I prefer speaking to large groups.   1   2   ③   4   I prefer speaking to small groups.

Number 3 has been circled. This means that this person somewhat prefers speaking in small-group situations.

---

1. I try to make decisions based on facts.   **1   2   3   4**   I make decisions based on my feelings.

2. I like rules and exact information.   **1   2   3   4**   I like general guidelines and uncertain information.

3. I like to solve a problem by looking at all its parts.   **1   2   3   4**   I like to solve a problem by first looking at the whole problem.

4. I read slowly and try to analyze what I am reading.   **1   2   3   4**   I read fast and try to get the carefully general meaning of what I am reading.

5. I like teachers to tell me exactly what to do.   **1   2   3   4**   I like teachers to give me a lot of freedom to choose what I can do.

6. I like mathematics and science.   **1   2   3   4**   I like literature and art.

7. When I listen, I pay attention to people's exact words.   **1   2   3   4**   When I listen, I pay attention to the overall message.

8. I like multiple-choice tests.   **1   2   3   4**   I like open-ended essay tests.

Add up the numbers you circled. You should get a total score between 8 and 32.

Score: _____

Score	
28–32	High right-brain preference
23–27	Moderate right-brain preference
18–22	No particular preference for either side
13–17	Moderate left-brain preference
8–12	High left-brain preference

Figure 16.4. Self-confidence questionnaire

QUESTIONNAIRE: General Self-Confidence

Circle the number that best describes how you feel about yourself most of the time. Circle only one number for each item. Use the following scale:

4 *I strongly agree. This statement describes me very well.*
3 *I somewhat agree. This statement probably describes me.*
2 *I somewhat disagree. This statement probably does not describe me.*
1 *I strongly disagree. This statement definitely does not describe me.*

- -

Example

I am afraid a lot of the time.   4   3   2   ①

Number 1 has been circled. This means that this person strongly disagrees and thinks that this statement does not describe him or her well.

- -

1. I understand my own personality.   4   3   2   1
2. I make good judgments and choices in life.   4   3   2   1
3. I make good use of my time.   4   3   2   1
4. I enjoy other people.   4   3   2   1
5. I can succeed in goals that I really want to accomplish. 4   3   2   1
6. I am optimistic about the future.   4   3   2   1
7. I think for myself and defend my own beliefs and values. 4   3   2   1
8. I am a happy person most of the time.   4   3   2   1

Add up the numbers you circled. You should get a total score between 8 and 32.

Score: _____

Score
26–32   You have a very high level of general self-confidence.
20–25   Your general self-confidence is quite strong.
14–19   Your general self-confidence is satisfactory, but you might want to improve
            some aspects of your concept of yourself.
 8–13   Your general self-confidence is quite low; you should think seriously about
            how to improve your view of yourself.

Other sources of information on styles may be found in teacher reference books (Brown, 2007; Cohen, 1998; Dörnyei, 2005; Oxford, 1990; Weaver & Cohen, 1997), chapters or segments of which might be excerpted for students to read.

4. Encouraging "good language learner" behavior

Yet another form of instilling self-awareness in students is through frequent impromptu reminders of "rules" for good language learning and encouragement of discussion or clarification. Sometimes the little comments you make here and there have the effect of subtly urging students to take charge of their own destiny by understanding their own styles of learning and capitalizing on their abilities.

A set of successful styles for language learning might be appropriately capsulized in the form of 10 rules, or "commandments," as I have on occasion facetiously called them. In Table 16.1, they are given in a teacher's version and a learner's version. The former is stated in more technical terms; the latter uses words and clichés designed to catch the attention of learners. The learners' version, in the right-hand column with appropriate explanations, might be useful for a classroom bulletin board, for class discussions, or for student journal-writing topics.

It is extremely important to remember that these style continua do not always fit all learners. These rules encompass what most learners need to point to most of the time in most language-learning contexts. That is, most learners come to a language class with too many inhibitions, not enough willingness to take risks, relatively low self-confidence in their ability to learn a language, etc. Your mission to 90 percent of your students is to pull them away from this potentially interfering side of the continuum and to get them to grapple with these "problems" and overcome them. Ten percent (this is just a rough guess—it could be a higher or lower proportion depending on the makeup of your classroom and on the particular style tendency in question) of your students could lean the other way. For them your job is to put the brakes on things like high (and haphazard) risk taking, excessive impulsiveness, overinflated self-confidence, an approach that is too "laid back," and so forth. Further comments on this issue follow later in this chapter.

Table 16.1. "10 commandments" for good language learning

Teacher's Version	Learner's Version
1. Lower inhibitions.	Fear not!
2. Encourage risk taking.	Dive in.
3. Build self-confidence.	Believe in yourself.
4. Develop intrinsic motivation.	Seize the day.
5. Engage in cooperative learning.	Love thy neighbor.
6. Use right-brain processes.	Get the BIG picture.
7. Promote ambiguity tolerance.	Cope with the chaos.
8. Practice intuition.	Go with your hunches.
9. Process error feedback.	Make mistakes work FOR you.
10. Set personal goals.	Set your own goals.

HOW TO TEACH STRATEGIES IN THE CLASSROOM

Just what are all these tricks of the trade that we're calling "strategies"? Rebecca Oxford (1990) provides the most comprehensive taxonomy of learning strategies currently available. These strategies are divided into what have come to be known as direct or cognitive strategies, which learners apply directly to the language itself, and indirect or metacognitive strategies, in which learners manage or control their own learning process. Direct strategies include a number of different ways of

- remembering more effectively,
- using all your cognitive processes,
- compensating for missing knowledge.

Indirect strategies, according to Oxford's taxonomy, include

- organizing and evaluating your learning,
- managing your emotions,
- learning with others.

A list of 50 specific strategies falling into these six general categories is contained in Oxford's (1990) Strategy Inventory for Language Learning (SILL) in Figure 16.5 on pages 272–275. Turn to that inventory now, before reading on, in order to become familiar with some specific strategies for successful language learning.

Strategies, like styles, can be taught, and because of their specificity, even more easily than styles. There are at least four different approaches you can take to teaching strategies in the language classroom.

1. Teach strategies through interactive techniques.

Many strategies are related to, and actually become, the outward manifestation of styles. For example, a risk-taking style would result in seeking practice opportunities, making conversation even when it isn't "necessary," trying out language you're not sure of, asking for correction, making guesses about what someone said, etc.

One way to familiarize your students with this plethora of possible strategies is to promote the "10 commandments" above through your own classroom techniques. Some techniques will be the ones you would utilize anyway. Other techniques will perhaps be specifically geared toward building strategic competence. Table 16.2 on page 270 offers some suggestions for creating an atmosphere in your classroom in which students feel comfortable and are encouraged to develop their own strategies.

Rebecca Oxford (1990) offered one of the best teacher resource books to appear on the subject of SBI. She gave examples of many different classroom techniques and showed which strategies they encourage. For example, an information-gap listening technique was explained (pp. 109–110) in which students

Table 16.2. Building strategic techniques

1. **To lower inhibitions:** play guessing games and communication games; do role plays and skits; sing songs; use plenty of group work; laugh with your students; have them share their fears in small groups.
2. **To encourage risk-taking:** praise students for making sincere efforts to try out language; use fluency exercises where errors are not corrected at that time; give outside-of-class assignments to speak or write or otherwise try out the language.
3. **To build students' self-confidence:** tell students explicitly (verbally and nonverbally) that you do indeed believe in them; have them make lists of their strengths, of what they know or have accomplished so far in the course.
4. **To help them to develop intrinsic motivation:** remind them about the rewards for learning English; describe (or have students look up) jobs that require English; play down the final examination in favor of helping students to see rewards for themselves beyond the final exam.
5. **To promote cooperative learning:** direct students to share their knowledge; play down competition among students; get your class to think of themselves as a team; do a considerable amount of small-group work.
6. **To encourage them to use right-brain processing:** use movies and tapes in class; have them read passages rapidly; do skimming exercises; do rapid "free writes"; do oral fluency exercises where the object is to get students to talk (or write) a lot without being corrected.
7. **To promote ambiguity tolerance:** encourage students to ask you, and each other, questions when they don't understand something; keep your theoretical explanations very simple and brief; deal with just a few rules at a time; occasionally resort to translation into a native language to clarify a word or meaning.
8. **To help them use their intuition:** praise students for good guesses; do not always give explanations of errors—let a correction suffice; correct only selected errors, preferably just those that interfere with learning.
9. **To get students to make their mistakes work FOR them:** record students' oral production and get them to identify errors; let students catch and correct each other's errors; do not always give them the correct form; encourage students to make lists of their common errors and to work on them on their own.
10. **To get students to set their own goals:** explicitly encourage or direct students to go beyond the classroom goals; have them make lists of what they will accomplish on their own in a particular week; get students to make specific time commitments at home to study the language; give "extra credit" work.

listen to a conversation on a tape and then, in groups, fill in an information grid (with blank spaces for name, profession, address, age, and appearance) for each of four people mentioned in the conversation. Oxford explained that such a task involves direct strategies like practicing naturalistically, guessing, note taking, focusing attention, and cooperating with co-learners.

2. Use compensatory techniques.

A related avenue for SBI is in the specific identification of techniques that aim to compensate for certain style weaknesses. Some three decades ago, Alice Omaggio (1981) published a little book that applies as well today as it did when it was first published. Omaggio classified some 55 different techniques according to numerous cognitive style "problems" that might prevent students from reaching their highest potential. For example, "excessive reflectiveness/caution" is a problem that might apply to certain students in your class: They are unwilling to take risks; they pause too long before responding orally; they want to get everything right before they attempt to speak or write. Several dozen techniques are then "prescribed" to help such students overcome their problem. Here are some typical cognitive style "problems" and a few techniques you might prescribe to help overcome each problem.

1. *Low tolerance of ambiguity:* brainstorming, retelling stories, role playing, paraphrasing, finding synonyms, jigsaw techniques, skimming tasks
2. *Excessive impulsiveness:* making inferences, syntactic or semantic clue searches, scanning for specific information, inductive rule generalization
3. *Excessive reflectiveness/caution:* small-group techniques, role playing, brainstorming, fluency techniques
4. *Too much right-brain dominance:* syntactic or semantic clue searches, scanning for specific information, proofreading, categorizing and clustering activities, information-gap techniques
5. *Too much left-brain dominance:* integrative language techniques, fluency techniques, retelling stories, skimming tasks

3. Administer a strategy inventory.

Earlier in this chapter were some suggestions for using a self-checklist and formal style tests in the classroom. Following the same format, you could introduce a strategy inventory. The best and most comprehensive of such instruments is Rebecca Oxford's (1990) Strategy Inventory for Language Learning (SILL), mentioned in the introduction to this section of the chapter. The SILL has now been used with learners in a number of different countries including the United States, and has proven to be exceptionally enlightening to learners as they are exposed, perhaps for the first time, to so many different strategic options. The SILL is reprinted in Figure 16.5.

The SILL can be used in class for developing awareness of strategies in the same way suggested earlier for the self-checklist on styles. Or it could become an out-of-class assignment for later class discussion. Its scoring and interpretation can be tricky, however, so make sure that in either case students are fully aware of how to score it. AND the SILL can do double duty as an instrument that enlightens you about 50 different ways that your learners could become a little more successful in their language-learning endeavor.

Figure 16.5. Strategy Inventory for Language Learning (Oxford, 1990)

Strategy Inventory for Language Learning (SILL)
Version for Speakers of Other
Languages Learning English

Directions

This form of the STRATEGY INVENTORY FOR LANGUAGE LEARNING (SILL) is for students of English as a second or foreign language. You will find statements about learning English. Please read each statement. On the separate Worksheet, write the response (1, 2, 3, 4, or 5) that tells HOW TRUE OF YOU THE STATEMENT IS.

  1. **Never or almost never true of me**
  2. **Usually not true of me**
  3. **Somewhat true of me**
  4. **Usually true of me**
  5. **Always or almost always true of me**

Never or almost never true of me means that the statement is <u>very rarely</u> true of you.
Usually not true of me means that the statement is true <u>less than half the time.</u>
Somewhat true of me means that the statement is true of you <u>about half the time.</u>
Usually true of me means that the statement is true <u>more than half the time.</u>
Always or almost always true of me means that the statement is true of you <u>almost always.</u>

Answer in terms of <u>how well the statement describes you</u>. Do not answer how you think you <u>should</u> be, or what <u>other</u> people do. <u>There are no right or wrong answers to these statements.</u> Put your answers on the separate Worksheet. Please make no marks on the items. Work as quickly as you can without being careless. This usually takes about 20–30 minutes to complete. If you have any questions, let the teacher know immediately.

Part A
  1. I think of relationships between what I already know and new things I learn in English.
  2. I use new English words in a sentence so I can remember them.
  3. I connect the sound of a new English word and an image or picture of the word to help me remember the word.
  4. I remember a new English word by making a mental picture of a situation in which the word might be used.

5. I use rhymes to remember new English words.
6. I use flashcards to remember new English words.
7. I physically act out new English words.
8. I review English lessons often.
9. I remember new English words or phrases by remembering their location on the page, on the board, or on a street sign.

Part B

10. I say or write new English words several times.
11. I try to talk like native English speakers.
12. I practice the sounds of English.
13. I use the English words I know in different ways.
14. I start conversations in English.
15. I watch English language TV shows spoken in English or go to movies spoken in English.
16. I read for pleasure in English.
17. I write notes, messages, letters, or reports in English.
18. I first skim an English passage (read over the passage quickly), then go back and read carefully.
19. I look for words in my own language that are similar to new words in English.
20. I try to find patterns in English.
21. I find the meaning of an English word by dividing it into parts that I understand.
22. I try not to translate word-for-word.
23. I make summaries of information that I hear or read in English.

Part C

24. To understand unfamiliar English words, I make guesses.
25. When I can't think of a word during a conversation in English, I use gestures.
26. I make up new words if I do not know the right ones in English.
27. I read English without looking up every new word.
28. I try to guess what the other person will say next in English.
29. If I can't think of an English word, I use a word or phrase that means the same thing.

Part D

30. I try to find as many ways as I can to use my English.
31. I notice my English mistakes and use that information to help me do better.
32. I pay attention when someone is speaking English.
33. I try to find out how to be a better learner of English.
34. I plan my schedule so I will have enough time to study English.
35. I look for people I can talk to in English.
36. I look for opportunities to read as much as possible in English.
37. I have clear goals for improving my English skills.
38. I think about my progress in learning English.

(Continued)

Part E

39. I try to relax whenever I feel afraid of using English.
40. I encourage myself to speak English even when I am afraid of making a mistake.
41. I give myself a reward or treat when I do well in English.
42. I notice if I am tense or nervous when I am studying or using English.
43. I write down my feelings in a language learning diary.
44. I talk to someone else about how I feel when I am learning English.

Part F

45. If I do not understand something in English, I ask the other person to slow down or say it again.
46. I ask English speakers to correct me when I talk.
47. I practice English with other students.
48. I ask for help from English speakers.
49. I ask questions in English.
50. I try to learn about the culture of English speakers.

(Continued)

STRATEGY INVENTORY FOR LANGUAGE LEARNING

Your Name _____ Date _____

Worksheet for Answering and Scoring

1. Write your response to each item (that is, write 1, 2, 3, 4, or 5) in each of the blanks.
2. Add up each column. Put the result on the line marked SUM.
3. Divide by the number under SUM to get the average for each column. Round this average off to the nearest tenth, as in 3.4.
4. Figure out your overall average. To do this, add up all the SUMs for the different parts of the SILL. Then divide by 50.
5. When you have finished, your teacher will give you the Profile of Results. Copy your averages (for each part and for the whole SILL) from the Worksheet to the Profile.

Part A	Part B	Part C	Part D	Part E	Part F
1.____	10.____	24.____	30.____	39.____	45.____
2.____	11.____	25.____	31.____	40.____	46.____
3.____	12.____	26.____	32.____	41.____	47.____
4.____	13.____	27.____	33.____	42.____	48.____
5.____	14.____	28.____	34.____	43.____	49.____
6.____	15.____	29.____	35.____	44.____	50.____
7.____	16.____		36.____		
8.____	17.____		37.____		
9.____	18.____		38.____		
	19.____				
	20.____				
	21.____				
	22.____				
	23.____				

A	B	C	D	E	F	TOTAL
SUM ____	SUM ____	SUM ____	SUM ____	SUM ____	SUM ____	SUM _____
÷ 9= ____	÷14= ____	÷6= ____	÷9= ____	÷6= ____	÷6= ____	÷50=_____

(Overall average)

What These Averages Mean to You

The overall average tells how often you use strategies for learning English. Each part of the SILL represents a group of learning strategies. The averages for each part of the SILL show which groups of strategies you use the most for learning English.

The best use of strategies depends on your age, personality, and purpose for learning. If you have a very low average on one or more parts of the SILL, there may be some new strategies in these groups that you might want to use. Ask your teacher about these.

4. Make use of impromptu teacher-initiated advice.

Finally, as you may recall from the discussion of developing style awareness, learners can benefit greatly from your daily attention to the many little tricks of the trade that you can pass on to them. Think back to your own language-learning experiences and note what it was that you now attribute your success (or failure!) to, and pass these insights on. Did you use flash cards? Did you practice a lot? Did you see subtitled movies? Read books? Pin rules and words up on your wall? When the appropriate moments occur in your class, seize the opportunity to teach your students how to learn. By doing so you will increase their opportunities for strategic investment in their learning process.

"PACKAGED" MODELS OF SBI

Many of your opportunities for strategy training in the classroom will be "methodological." That is, you will opt for one of the four possible means suggested above. There remain three more formalized models of incorporating strategy awareness and practice in language classrooms. These are growing in popularity as more educational administrators appreciate the value of SBI for ultimate success in a foreign language.

1. Textbook-embedded instruction

An increasing number of ESL textbooks are offering guidelines and exercises for strategy awareness and practice within the stream of a chapter. Brown's (2000a) *New Vistas* series for ESL learners offers examples of embedding strategy work within the exercises of a textbook. Students are encouraged to continue their learning outside the classroom, sometimes individually, sometimes with a partner. One unit in the intermediate level suggests practicing communication strategies, identifying positive classroom learning strategies, and practicing conversation strategies in a discussion about cultural stereotypes. These "strategies for success" are reprinted in Figure 16.6 on page 277. The teacher's resource manual for this book gives detailed directions to teachers on how to facilitate these extra-class learning experiences.

Another series of ESL textbooks, *Lecture Ready* (Sarosy & Sherak, 2006), designed to teach academic listening, note taking, and discussion, also includes strategic suggestions for effectively comprehending academic lectures. Students' attention is explicitly drawn to cues for listening accurately to a lecture, for example, by attending to language that signals sequences of points, the "big picture," and signals for a new idea or topic. Similarly, Chamot, O'Malley, and Kupper (1992) include strategy training modules in each unit. One of their lessons recommends keeping a daily log for one week and checking how many times a student uses any of 14 different strategies. A grid is provided for easy checking (see Figure 16.7 on page 278).

Figure 16.6. Strategies for Success (from *New Vistas,* H.D. Brown, 2000a)

Strategies for Success

➤ **Practicing communication strategies**
➤ **Identifying behaviors for successful language learning**
➤ **Understanding cultural stereotypes**

1. With a Learning Partner, look at Lesson 1, Exercise 5 and add some more phrases for understanding someone in a conversation. You may think of expressions like: "uh-huh," "Sorry, what did you say?" or "You know what I mean?" Then, do some more practice using those phrases in the conversation below (#2).

2. With a partner, brainstorm some "classroom behaviors" that are especially helpful in learning English, specifically. You may want to list things like: listening to the teacher's directions carefully, raising your hand to volunteer answers or to ask questions, making sure you know the purpose of a task, etc. Write your list in your journal. Copy the list onto a bright-colored card or paper and put it on your bulletin board or some place where you will see it every day.

3. With your partner, brainstorm some stereotypes of several cultures or countries you are both familiar with (for example, "Americans are rich and friendly." "Japanese are smart and polite.") Decide whether the stereotypes are really true or not. Remember to practice the conversation strategies you discussed above.

2. Adjunct self-help guides

A second prepackaged way of enlightening students about strategies is through the assignment or recommendation of a self-help study guide (e.g., Brown, 2002b; Marshall, 1989; Rubin & Thompson, 1994). Such "how-to" guides tend to have short, easy-to-understand chapters with information, anecdotes, tips, and exercises that will help learners to use strategies successfully. They can be offered to students as recommended reading over and above their regular course assignments.

In my own (Brown, 2002b) *Strategies for Success,* students are systematically led through awareness + action sequences for 12 different topics, one topic for each chapter. Topics include self-confidence, anxiety, motivation, left- and right-brain processing, and risk taking, to name some. Each chapter opens with a self-check inventory in which students can raise awareness of their strengths, weaknesses, and

Figure 16.7. Self-help learning strategies (Chamot, O'Malley, & Kupper, 1992, p. 98)

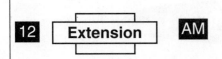

Keep a notebook about your learning

A. For the next week, keep a notebook about your learning. Pay attention to what you do in school. This includes: what you think, how you read, how you listen, when you take notes, when you listen hard, or when you don't listen. Use the chart below to help you.

WHAT I DO TO HELP MYSELF LEARN					
Strategies	**Day 1**	**Day 2**	**Day 3**	**Day 4**	**Day 5**
I paid attention to the teacher.					
I took notes when I listened.					
I took notes when I read.					
I read the questions before I listened.					
I read the questions before I read.					
I looked at my notes later.					
I repeated new words aloud.					
I used new words in a sentence.					
I looked for information in a reference book.					
I did all my homework.					
I helped a friend with homework.					
I asked the teacher questions.					
I asked a friend questions about schoolwork.					
I guessed at new words.					

preferences. (Figures 16.3 and 16.4 earlier in this chapter are examples of two such questionnaires.) This is followed by a brief discussion of the chapter's theme, including a list of suggested strategies, and each brief chapter concludes with four sets of exercises, each representing one of the four skills. By using such a book, students gain a heightened awareness of themselves, a battery of appropriate strategies they can use, and the opportunity to actually put the chapter's strategies into practice during class.

One drawback to books like these for English learners is that they are written in English, and one could argue that if students are proficient enough to read the book, they may not need all the strategies suggested therein! However, it has been found that intermediate level learners of English have profited from reading such books by simply skipping over some of the beginner level strategies. Brown's (2002b) guide, for example, compensates for potential learner obstacles by using very simple language and by embedding work on difficult vocabulary into the end-of-chapter exercises. Unlike the other two books, it also has detailed suggestions to the teacher in the preface, intended to enable teachers to integrate the material into virtually any curriculum.

Another type of book is a hybrid between textbook-embedded SBI and the adjunct guides described above: content-centered ESL textbooks in which the content itself is the study and utilization of learning strategies. For example, Gail Ellis and Barbara Sinclair (1989) get intermediate EFL learners to look systematically at successful learning strategies through readings, checklists, and various techniques in all four skills of listening, speaking, reading, and writing. Few institutional budgets can offer courses that focus only on SBI itself, but for those that can afford the time and cost of such a curriculum, students are well served.

3. Learning centers

Despite declining budgets in many schools and universities, a considerable number of learning centers around the world have an ESL-related component. Such centers typically make available to learners a number of possible types of extra-class assistance in writing, reading, academic study skills, pronunciation, and other oral production. Assistance can include diagnostic testing and interpretation, one-on-one tutorials, small-group tutorials, audio and video teaching programs, and computer programs ranging from grammatical brush-up to writing self-help. At San Francisco State University, for example, the Learning Assistance Center is an indispensable aid to students. It is well-known not just for its tutorials, but for the help it gives to students in developing study skills—which itself is a strategic factor.

A few progressive institutions view such learning centers not merely as a place to offer "remedial" help but as a resource for all learners for the improvement of their strategic competence in language learning. In one such center, at the Defense Language Institute of Monterey, California, students needing assistance get an initial interview to determine what kind of resources can benefit them the most. Then a number of diagnostic tests can be administered—tests of right/left-brain preference, ambiguity tolerance, self-esteem, extroversion, motivation, Oxford's SILL, and others. The test results identify areas needing attention, such as using both sides of style continua, motivation, strategy use, language-specific problems, and stress and time management. Numerous treatments are "prescribed": workshops, self-instructional programs, tutorials, clinics, and the like. Periodic evaluative instruments indicate progress.

☆ ☆ ☆ ☆ ☆

Interactive language teachers must not underestimate the importance of getting students strategically invested in their language-learning process. Perhaps the most powerful principles of learning that merge here are Intrinsic Motivation and Autonomy. One of the best ways of getting students intrinsically and autonomously involved in their language learning is to offer them the opportunity to develop their *own* strategies for success. Having thus invested their time and effort into the learning of English, they can take responsibility for much of their own learning. This, in turn, generates more motivation as they become autonomous learners.

TOPICS FOR DISCUSSION, ACTION, AND RESEARCH

[Note: (I) Individual work; (G) group or pair work; (C) whole-class discussion.]

1. (G/C) Direct groups to create a publicity flyer for an imaginary new program or school that they have started. One of the major selling points is an SBI component. What would the major features of the SBI program be? What kind of guarantees, if any, could one make? Groups will share flyers and comments with the rest of the class.
2. (C) What are some of the tricks of the trade that class members have used to try to be more successful language learners? List suggestions on the board.
3. (G) Groups will look at the list of characteristics of "good language learners" on pages 259–260 and the "10 commandments" in Table 16.1 (page 268). Among the items in those two lists, which three or four principles or characteristics should be placed at the top of the list as most important? Groups should be ready to explain their choices to the rest of the class. After the discussion, each group should decide whether they might qualify or change any of their choices.
4. (I/G) Fill out the checklist in Figure 16.2, based on a second language you have learned. How many D and E categories did you fall into? How many A and B? With a partner, see if you both agree that, in each case, A and B categories are more indicative of successful learning styles. If you fell into some D and E categories, talk about what steps you might take to change your learning style. How would you teach these changes in an ESL classroom?

5. (I) Take the two style tests on pages 266–267. Do the results seem to be indicative of the "real you"? What are some drawbacks to tests like these? Do you see any cross-cultural problems in their structure, conceptualization, or wording? How would you use such self-check inventories in an English classroom?

6. (C) Ask the class to cite examples or tell stories that recount any of their own experiences in the past with teachers that engaged in some form of SBI. Evaluate the effectiveness of each case, in retrospect.

7. (G) Direct small groups to look at Table 16.2 on page 270 and discuss the list. They should decide whether to add, subtract, or change some of the items to fit contexts that they are familiar with.

8. (I/C) Observe an ESL class and use the 10 items from Table 16.2 as a checklist to see how much the teacher instilled strategic competence in the learners. After observing, share your conclusions with other members of your class.

9. (I/C) Take the SILL, then, with the rest of the class, discuss how it could be used, in your context in an ESL classroom that you're familiar with. Could any of the 50 items be practiced in the classroom?

FOR YOUR FURTHER READING

Brown, H. D. (2002). *Strategies for success: A practical guide to learning English.* White Plains, NY: Pearson Education.

This is an adjunct strategies guide designed to accompany virtually any course in ESL. Students are led, through simply written, short chapters, to understand their own preferences and to develop strategies for successful acquisition of English. It is suitable for a low intermediate level of learners.

Anderson, N. (2003). L2 learning strategies. In E. Hinkel (Ed.), *Handbook of research in second language teaching and learning* (pp. 757–771). Mahwah, NJ: Lawrence Erlbaum Associates.

Chamot, A. (2005). Language learning strategy instruction: Current issues and research. *Annual Review of Applied Linguistics, 25,* 112–130.

These two articles summarize recent research and current issues in SBI, offering background research as well as pedagogical practices. Both give comprehensive bibliographies that include very recent as well as older references in the field.

Weaver, S., & Cohen, A. (1997). *Strategies-based instruction: A teacher-training manual.* Minneapolis: University of Minnesota, Center for Advanced Research on Language Acquisition.

A wealth of information is offered in this loose-leaf binder published by CARLA, well-known for its research on SBI. Susan Weaver and Andrew Cohen spell out in detail 20 lessons in learner strategy training, and include supporting materials for each lesson. An introduction to SBI, additional activities, and a bibliography are included.

Oxford, R. (1990). *Language learning strategies: What every teacher should know.* New York: Newbury House.

Rebecca Oxford's classic professional reference book still stands as an indispensable reference for teachers wishing to understand how they might incorporate strategy training in their language classrooms. Background theoretical information on learning strategies is provided along with carefully specified classroom techniques and materials.

Stevick, E. (1989). *Success with foreign languages: Seven who achieved it and what worked for them.* New York: Prentice-Hall.

Here, Earl Stevick chronicles the learning processes of seven foreign language learners who were interviewed in depth about the strategies they used—or failed to use—in their attempt to become successful in reaching their goals.

PART IV

TEACHING LANGUAGE SKILLS

This section of *Teaching by Principles* is focused on the details of teaching any one or a combination of the four skills of listening, speaking, reading, and writing. It is crucial to recognize that by attending to the four skills in four separate chapters I am not advocating the teaching of skills in separate classes or even lessons. In our language-teaching history we've "been there and done that" when classes were routinely divided skill by skill, with separate textbooks for each skill. We rather quickly discovered that in most contexts of human communication we do *not* separate those skills. We also discovered that the activation of one skill (listening, for example) can be readily reinforced by the use of another skill (speaking, reading, and/or writing).

So, Part IV begins with a chapter that emphasizes the importance of the integration of skills, lest you be misled into thinking that the subsequent four chapters are an argument for separation. I have chosen to illustrate the concept of integration by examining a number of approaches to language teaching that model integration. Chapter 17 describes some of those well-known approaches, all of which celebrate the integration of at least two, if not all four, skills.

Chapters 18, 19, 20, and 21 systematically analyze the unique factors and guidelines involved in teaching each of the four skills of listening, speaking, reading, and writing, respectively. A somewhat uniform outline is followed for each chapter so that you can easily compare characteristics of each skill.

Chapter 22 examines form-focused instruction, or what is commonly referred to as teaching grammar and vocabulary. Because all four skills inherently involve structure (grammar) and lexical items (vocabulary), this is a separate chapter devoted specifically to issues, problems, and guidelines for helping students to focus on form (the organizational components of language). Those issues and guidelines apply, of course, to whatever specific skill, or combination of skills, students are performing at a given time.

CHAPTER 17

INTEGRATING THE "FOUR SKILLS"

OBJECTIVES After reading this chapter, you will be able to:

- appreciate the importance of integrating skills for more authenticity and better reinforcement

- understand the characteristics of several different approaches that illustrate the integration of skills

- analyze a lesson from the point of view of its integration of skills

- apply concepts of skills integration to the next four chapters, which deal with the separate skills

For more than six decades now, research and practice in English language teaching has identified the "four skills"—listening, speaking, reading, and writing—as of paramount importance. ESL curricula and textbooks around the world tend to focus, all too often, on just one of the four skills, sometimes to the exclusion of the others. Books, articles, anthologies, research surveys, and conferences typically index or organize their contents according to each of the four skills.

It is perfectly appropriate to thus identify language performance. The human race has fashioned two forms of productive performance, oral and written, and two forms of receptive performance, aural (or auditory) and reading. There are, of course, offshoots of each mode. Lumped together under nonverbal communication are various visually perceived messages delivered through gestures, facial expressions, proximity, and so forth. Graphic art (drawings, paintings, and diagrams) is also a powerful form of communication. But attention to the four different skills does indeed pay off as learners of a second language discover the differences and interrelationships among these four primary modes of performance.

Despite our history of treating the four skills in separate segments of a curriculum, there is a recent trend toward skill **integration**. That is, rather than designing a curriculum to teach the many aspects of *one* skill, say, reading, curriculum designers are taking more of a **whole language** approach whereby reading is treated as one of two or more interrelated skills. A course that deals with reading skills, then, will more often than not also deal with related listening, speaking, and writing skills. A lesson in a so-called reading class, under this new paradigm, might include

- a prereading *discussion* of the topic to activate schemata;
- *listening* to a teacher's monologue or a series of informative statements about the topic of a passage to be read;

- a focus on a certain *reading* strategy, say, scanning;
- *writing* a response to or paraphrase of a reading passage.

This reading class, then, models for the students the real-life integration of language skills, gets them to perceive the relationship among several skills, and provides the teacher with a great deal of flexibility in creating interesting, motivating lessons.

WHY INTEGRATED SKILLS?

Some may argue that the integration of the four skills diminishes the importance of the rules of listening, speaking, reading, and writing that are unique to each separate skill. Such an argument rarely holds up under careful scrutiny of integrated-skills courses. If anything, the added richness of the latter gives students greater motivation that converts to better retention of principles of effective speaking, listening, reading, and writing. Rather than being forced to plod along through a course that limits itself to one mode of performance, students are given a chance to diversify their efforts in more meaningful tasks. Such integration can, of course, still utilize a strong, principled approach to the separate, unique characteristics of each skill.

So you may be wondering why courses weren't always integrated in the first place. There are several reasons:

1. In the pre–Communicative Language Teaching (CLT) days of language teaching, the focus on the **forms** of language almost predisposed curriculum designers to segment courses into the separate language skills. It seemed logical to fashion a syllabus that dealt with, say, pronunciation of the phonemes of English, stress and intonation, oral structural patterns (carefully sequenced according to presumed grammatical difficulty), and variations on those patterns. These language-based classes tended to be courses in "baby linguistics" where a preoccupation with rules and paradigms taught students a lot *about* language but sometimes at the expense of teaching language itself.
2. Administrative considerations still make it easier to program separate courses in reading and speaking, and so on, as a glance at current intensive and university English courses reveals. Such divisions can indeed be justified when one considers the practicalities of coordinating three-hour-per-week courses, hiring teachers for each, ordering textbooks, and placing students into the courses. It should be noted, however, that a proficient teacher who professes to follow principles of CLT would never conduct, say, a "reading" class without extensive use of speaking, listening, and writing in the class.
3. This leads to a third reason that not all classes are integrated. There are certain specific purposes for which students are studying English that may best be labeled by one of the four skills, especially at the high intermediate to advanced levels. In an academic setting such as a university, specialized

workshops, modules, tutorials, or courses may be constructed explicitly to improve certain specialized skills. Thus a module in listening comprehension might include instruction on listening effectively to academic lectures, to fellow students in the classroom, to audio programs where there are no visual cues, to the consultative register used in the professor's office, and even to fellow students in casual conversation. Such a course might encompass phonological, morphological, syntactic, lexical, semantic, and discourse elements.

Aside from these caveats, the integration of the four skills—or at least two or more skills—is the typical approach within a communicative, interactive framework. As Hinkel (2006, p. 113) noted, "In an age of globalization, pragmatic objectives of language learning place an increased value on *integrated and dynamic multiskill* [my italics] instructional models with a focus on meaningful communication and the development of learners' communicative competence." Most of the interactive techniques already described or referred to in this book involve the integration of skills. The following observations support such techniques.

1. Production and reception are quite simply two sides of the same coin; one cannot split the coin in two.
2. Interaction means sending *and* receiving messages.
3. Written and spoken language often (but not always!) bear a relationship to each other; to ignore that relationship is to ignore the richness of language.
4. For literate learners, the interrelationship of written and spoken language is an intrinsically motivating reflection of language and culture and society.
5. By attending primarily to what learners can *do* with language, and only secondarily to the forms of language, we invite any or all of the four skills that are relevant into the classroom arena.
6. Often one skill will reinforce another; we learn to speak, for example, in part by modeling what we hear, and we learn to write by examining what we can read.
7. Proponents of the **whole language** approach (see Chapter 3) have shown us that in the real world of language use, most of our natural performance involves not only the integration of one or more skills, but connections between language and the way we think and feel and act.

MODELS OF SKILLS INTEGRATION

How can you maintain an integrated-skills focus in your teaching? All of the models and approaches described in Chapter 3 are predicated on the use of at least two if not all four skills: learner-centered instruction; cooperative or collaborative learning, interactive learning, whole language education, content-based instruction, and task-based instruction. Even the added "candidates" for approaches, the Lexical Approach and Multiple Intelligences, imply several skills in developing communicative competence.

In order to illustrate a number of possible integrated approaches to language instruction, two of the previous models (content-based and task-based instruction) will be briefly analyzed here along with some further concepts that highlight the integration of listening, speaking, reading, and writing.

Content-Based Instruction

Content-based (sometimes referred to as "content-centered") instruction, described in Chapter 3, integrates the learning of some specific subject-matter content with the learning of a second language. The overall structure of a content-based curriculum, in contrast to many traditional language curricula, is dictated more by the nature of the subject matter than by language forms and sequences. The second language, then, is simply the medium to convey informational content of interest and relevance to the learner. Examples of content-based curricula include immersion programs for elementary school children, sheltered English programs (mostly found at elementary and secondary school levels), writing across the curriculum (where writing skills in secondary schools and universities are taught within subject-matter areas like biology, history, art, etc.), and English for Specific Purposes (ESP) (e.g., for engineering, agriculture, or medicine).

It is perhaps already clear that content-based teaching allows learners to acquire knowledge and skills that transcend all the bits and pieces of language that may occupy hours and days of analyzing in a traditional language classroom. Research on second language acquisition at various ages indicates the ultimate strength of learning that is pointed toward practical non-language goals. The meaningful learning principle applies well here. Learners are focused on useful, practical objectives as the subject matter is perceived to be relevant to long-term goals. This also increases the intrinsic motivation that is so important to learning of any kind.

Content-based instruction allows for the complete integration of language skills. As you plan a lesson around a particular subtopic of your subject-matter area, your task becomes how best to present that topic or concept or principle. In such lessons it would be difficult not to involve all four skills as your students read, discuss, solve problems, analyze data, and write opinions and reports.

Task-Based Language Teaching

Task-based language teaching (TBLT) was defined and discussed in Chapters 3 and 11. As you will recall, there are a number of different interpretations in the literature on what, exactly, a task is. What these various understandings all emphasize, however, is the centrality of the task itself in a language course and the importance of organizing a course around communicative tasks that learners need to engage in *outside* the classroom. At its heart, then, TBLT implies several integrated skills in its focus on language in the real world. Most real-world situations demand simultaneous use of two or more skills.

In task-based instruction, the priority is not the *forms* of language, but rather the functional *purposes* for which language must be used. While content-based instruction focuses on subject-matter content, task-based instruction focuses on a whole set of real-world tasks themselves. Input for tasks can come from a variety of authentic sources:

- speeches
- conversations
- narratives
- public announcements
- cartoon strips
- letters, e-mails
- poems
- directions
- invitations
- textbooks

- interviews
- oral descriptions
- media extracts
- games and puzzles
- photos
- diaries
- songs
- telephone directories
- menus
- labels

And the list could continue. Evident in this variety of source material is the necessity of attending to more than just one of the four skills. Course goals in TBLT are not linguistic in the traditional sense of just focusing on grammar or phonology; by maintaining the centrality of functions like exchanging opinions, reading newspapers and menus, writing letters and e-mails, etc., the course goals center on learners' **pragmatic** language competence.

So we have in task-based teaching a well-integrated approach to language teaching that asks you to organize your classroom around those practical tasks that language users engage in "out there" in the real world. These tasks virtually always imply several skill areas, not just one, and so by pointing toward tasks, we disengage ourselves from thinking only in terms of the separate four skills. Instead, principles of listening, speaking, reading, and writing become appropriately subsumed under the rubric of what it is our learners are going to *do* with this language.

Theme-Based Instruction

Another way of looking at the integration of skills is to consider the structure of many English language courses around the world. Courses tend to focus on topics, situations, or "themes" as one of their organizing parameters.

Theme-based instruction is not the same as content-based. In order to distinguish the two, let's think of the former as a "weak" version of the latter. In the strong version (content-based), the primary purpose of a course is to instruct students in a subject-matter area, and language is of secondary and subordinate interest. The examples of content-based instruction mentioned earlier in this chapter are good illustrations of the strong version. English for Specific Purposes

(ESP) at the university level, for example, gathers engineering majors together in a course designed to teach terminology, concepts, and current issues in engineering. Because students are ESL students, they must of course learn this material in English, which the teacher is prepared to help them with. Immersion and sheltered programs, along with programs in writing across the curriculum, are similarly focused.

A weak form of content-based teaching actually places an equal value on content and language objectives. While the curriculum, to be sure, is organized around subject-matter area, both students and teachers are fully aware that language skills don't occupy a subordinate role. Students have no doubt chosen to take a course or curriculum because their language skills need improvement, and they are now able to work toward that improvement without being battered with linguistically based topics. The ultimate payoff is that their language skills are indeed enhanced, but through focal attention to topic and peripheral attention to language.

This weak version is actually practical and effective in many instructional settings. It typically manifests itself in what has come to be called theme-based or **topic-based** teaching. Theme-based instruction provides an alternative to what would otherwise be traditional language classes by structuring a course around themes or topics. Theme-based curricula can serve the multiple interests of students in a classroom and can offer a focus on content while still adhering to institutional needs for offering a language course per se. So, for example, an intensive English course for intermediate pre-university students might deal with topics of current interest such as public health, environmental awareness, world economics, etc. In the classroom students read articles or chapters, view video programs, discuss issues, propose solutions, and carry out writing assignments on a given theme. English for Academic Purposes (EAP) in a university is an appropriate instance of theme-based instruction.

Granted, there is a fuzzy line of distinction between theme-based instruction and "traditional" language instruction. You could easily argue that many existing reading and writing courses, for example, are theme-based in that they offer students substantial opportunities to grapple with topics of relevance and interest. I don't think it is important, or necessary, to dichotomize here. What is important is to view theme-based instruction as a context for the integration of skills.

Numerous current ESL textbooks, especially at the intermediate to advanced levels, offer theme-based courses of study. Challenging topics in these textbooks engage the curiosity and increase motivation of students as they grapple with an array of real-life issues ranging from simple to complex and also improve their linguistic skills across all four domains of listening, speaking, reading, and writing.

Consider just one of an abundance of topics that have been used as themes through which language is taught: *environmental awareness and action.* With this topic, you are sure to find immediate intrinsic motivation—we all want to survive! Here are some possible theme-based activities:

1. **Use environmental statistics and facts for classroom reading, writing, discussion, and debate.** You don't have to look very far to find information about environmental crises, research on the issues, and pointers on what individuals can do to forestall a global disaster. Here are some modes of performance based on such material (coded for each of the skills):

[for intermediate to advanced students]
- (R) scan [reading selections] for particular information
- (W) do compare-and-contrast exercises
- (R) look for biases in statistics
- (L,S) use statistics in argument
- (W) use the discourse features of persuasive writing
- (W) write personal opinion essays
- (L,S) discuss issues
- (L,S) engage in formal debates

[for beginning students]
- (S,W) use imperatives ("Don't buy aerosol spray cans.")
- (S) practice verb tenses ("The ozone layer is vanishing.")
- (L,S,R,W) develop new vocabulary
- (S,W) use cardinal and ordinal numbers
- (L,S) practice simple conversations/dialogues like:

    A: Why do you smoke?
    B: Because I like it.
    A: You shouldn't smoke.
    B: Well, it makes me less nervous.
    A: But it's not good for your health.
    B: I don't care.
    A: Well, you will die young.

2. **Carry out research and writing projects.** When your ESL syllabus calls for a research project, an intrinsically motivating assignment is to research an environmental topic. Libraries, bookstores, newsstands, television and radio programs, and even political campaigns are fruitful sources of information. While individual projects are suitable, you can also encourage students to work in pairs or teams, each assigned to a different aspect of an issue. Data are sought, gathered, and synthesized; counter-arguments are explored; and results are presented orally and/or in writing to the rest of the class.

3. **Have students create their own environmental awareness material.** Whether you are teaching adults or children, beginning or advanced students, you can get a great deal of language and content material out of a **language experience approach** (see next section, below) in which students create

leaflets, posters, bulletin boards, newsletter articles, or even a booklet that outlines practical things they can do to "save the Earth." If time and equipment permit, some exciting projects can be done with a video camera, such as an information program, a drama, interviews, or news reports.

4. **Arrange field trips.** These could involve a pre-trip module (of perhaps several days) of reading, researching, and other fact-finding, and a post-trip module of summary and conclusions. Field trips can be made to recycling centers, factories that practice recycling, wildlife preserves, areas that need litter removed (abandoned lots, beaches, parks), etc.

5. **Conduct simulation games.** A number of simulation games are being created that use the environmental crisis as a theme around which to build various scenarios for the gaming process. Some games get quite elaborate, with countries of the world and their respective resources represented by objects like egg cartons, bottles, cans, newspapers, and the like, and players charged to resolve problems of unequal distribution of wealth as well as environmental controls.

It should be apparent from the foregoing that all four skills intertwine in these types of activities in the language classroom, and that it would be difficult *not* to involve several skill areas.

Experiential Learning

Yet another lens through which we could view the concept of integrated skills is the notion of **experiential** language learning. Experiential learning includes activities that engage both left- and right-brain processing, that contextualize language, that integrate skills, and that point toward authentic, real-world purposes. Experiential learning offers a dimension that may not necessarily be implied in the three concepts (content-based, task-based, theme-based) already discussed. What experiential learning highlights for us is giving students *concrete experiences* through which they "discover" language principles (even if subconsciously) by trial and error, by processing feedback, by building hypotheses about language, and by revising these assumptions in order to become fluent (Eyring, 1991, p. 347). That is, teachers do not simply tell students about how language works; instead, they give students opportunities to use language as they grapple with the problem-solving complexities of a variety of concrete experiences.

Experiential learning implies a direct encounter with the subject matter or topic being studied rather than simply reading or talking about it. Usually there is some physical involvement in the phenomenon as well. Experiential learning is not so much a novel concept as it is an emphasis on the marriage of two substantive principles of effective learning, principles espoused by the famous American educator John Dewey:

a. one learns best by "doing," by active experimentation, and
b. inductive learning by discovery activates strategies that enable students to "take charge" of their own learning progress.

As such it is an especially useful concept for teaching children, whose abstract intellectual processing abilities are not yet mature.

Experiential learning techniques tend to be learner-centered by nature. Examples of learner-centered experiential techniques include:

- hands-on projects (such as nature projects)
- computer activities (especially in small groups)
- research projects
- cross-cultural experiences (camps, dinner groups, etc.)
- field trips and other "on-site" visits (such as to a grocery store)
- role plays and simulations

But some teacher-controlled techniques may be considered experiential:

- using props, realia, visuals, show-and-tell sessions
- playing games (which often involve strategy) and singing
- utilizing media (television, radio, and movies)

Experiential learning tends to put an emphasis on the psychomotor aspects of language learning by involving learners in physical actions in which language is subsumed and reinforced. Through action, students are drawn into a utilization of multiple skills.

One specialized form of experiential learning that has been quite popular in elementary school teaching for several decades is the **Language Experience Approach** (LEA) (Van Allen & Allen, 1967), an integrated-skills approach initially used in teaching native language reading skills, but more recently adapted to second language learning contexts. With widely varying adaptations, students' personal experiences (a trip to the zoo, a television story, a picture, etc.) are used as the basis for discussion, and then the teacher writes down the "experience." Students can then recopy, edit, and/or illustrate the story, which is preserved in the form of a "book." A number of activities can then follow, including word study, spelling focus, semantic discussions, inference, prediction, etc. The benefit of the LEA is in the intrinsic involvement of students in creating their own stories rather than being given other people's stories. As in other experiential techniques, students are directly involved in the creative process of fashioning their own products, and all four skills are readily implied in carrying out a project.

The Episode Hypothesis

Well over a century ago, François Gouin, if you will recall from Chapter 2, designed a method of language teaching called the Series Method. One of the keys to the success of the method lay in the presentation of language in an easily followed storyline. You may remember the sequence of sentences about opening a door. In another lesson, Gouin teaches a number of verbs, verb forms, and other vocabulary in a little story about a girl chopping wood:

> The girl goes and seeks a piece of wood.
> She takes a hatchet.
> She draws near to the block.
> She places the wood on this block.
> She raises the hatchet.
> She brings down the hatchet.
> The blade strikes against the wood.
> etc.

In easily visualized steps, the students are led through the process of chopping and gathering wood, all at a very elementary level of the language.

In some ways, Gouin was utilizing a psychological device that, a hundred years later, John Oller called the **episode hypothesis**. According to Oller (1983b, p. 12), "text (i.e., discourse in any form) will be easier to reproduce, understand, and recall, to the extent that it is structured episodically." By this he meant that the presentation of language is enhanced if students receive interconnected sentences in an interest-provoking episode rather than in a disconnected series of sentences.

The episode hypothesis goes well beyond simple "meaningful" learning. Look at this dialogue:

> **Jack:** Hi, Tony. What do you usually do on weekends?
> **Tony:** Oh, I usually study, but sometimes I go to a movie.
> **Jack:** Uh-huh. Well, I often go to movies, but I seldom study.
> **Tony:** Well, I don't study as much as Greg. He always studies on the weekends. He never goes out.

You can see that this conversation, while easily understood, clearly presented, and perhaps quite relevant to students learning English, lacks a sense of drama—of "what's going to happen next?" Most of our communicative textbooks have many "Jack and Tony" types of presentation. They may illustrate certain grammatical or discourse features, but they don't grip the learner with suspense.

Now consider another conversation (Brinton & Neuman, 1982, p. 33) and notice how it differs from Jack and Tony's.

Darlene:	I think I'll call Bettina's mother. It's almost five and Chrissy isn't home yet.
Meg:	I thought Bettina had the chicken pox.
Darlene:	Oh, that's right. I forgot. Chrissy didn't go to Bettina's today. Where is she?
Meg:	She's probably with Gary. He has Little League practice until five.
Darlene:	I hear the front door. Maybe that's Gary and Chrissy.
Gary:	Hi.
Darlene:	Where's Chrissy? Isn't she with you?
Gary:	With me? Why with me? I saw her at two after school, but then I went to Little League practice. I think she left with her friend.
Darlene:	Which one?
Gary:	The one next door . . . the one she walks to school with every day.
Darlene:	Oh, you mean Timmy. She's probably with him.
Gary:	Yeah, she probably is.
Darlene:	I'm going next door to check.

This conversation uses a familiar setting and ordinary characters to whet the curiosity of the reader. Because the outcome is not clear, learners are motivated to continue reading and to become more involved in the content than in the language, therefore increasing its episodic flavor. Oller notes that the interaction of cognition and language enables learners to form "expectancies" as they encounter either logically or episodically linked sentences. Moreover, "stories" are universal, and therefore students from many different cultures can understand their organizational structure and identify with the characters.

You may be wondering how the episode hypothesis contributes or relates to integrated-skills teaching. Here are some possible ways:

- Stories or episodes challenge the teacher and textbook writer to present interesting, natural language, whether the language is viewed as written discourse or oral discourse.
- Episodes can be presented in either written or spoken form, thus requiring reading and/or writing skills on the students' part.
- Episodes can provide the stimulus for spoken or written questions that students respond to, in turn, by speaking or writing.
- Students can be encouraged to write their own episodes, or to complete an episode whose resolution or climax is not presented (such as the above conversation).
- Those written episodes might then be dramatized in the classroom by the students.

Now, it must be noted that the reality of the language classroom is such that not every aspect of language can be embedded in gripping dramatic episodes that have students yearning for the next day's events, as they might with a favorite soap opera! Linguistic samples like the conversation between Jack and Tony are quite respectable and pedagogically useful. Drills, writing practice, grammar explanations, essays on the world economy, and many other nonepisodic activities have a viable place in the classroom. But to the extent that a curriculum allows it, episodic teaching and testing may offer a rewarding alternative to sprinkle into your daily diet of teaching techniques.

AN INTEGRATED LESSON

We've considered five different ways to approach the integration of the four skills. The principal idea here is for you *not* to assume that all your techniques should be identified with just one of the four, but rather that most successful interactive techniques will include several skill areas. It may also be helpful to frame your lessons and lesson plans in terms of one or more of the five concepts discussed in this chapter. To illustrate just how such integration might work, consider the following lesson outline—with skills coded for each segment.

Context:	English Language School in Korea
Level:	High Intermediate
Course focus:	Multiple skills, emphasis on oral skills
Students:	Twelve young adults, wishing to improve English skills
Lesson:	Unit 7 (out of 10), Lesson 2 (out of 3)
	New Vistas, Book 3 (Brown, 2000a)
Class hour:	60 minutes
Focus:	[situational] Occupations, work, employment opportunities
	[functional] Expressing likes and dislikes
	[formal] *ing* gerunds; vocabulary for types of workers

Warm-up (5 min.) (L)

T asks Ss to name careers, jobs, and occupations and writes them on the board

T briefly tells about a job she had as a waitress in a restaurant—how she found the job, the interview, and what the job was like (5 min.)

A. Presentation (10 min.) (L, R, S)

T directs Ss to the opening page of Lesson 2, a full-page advertisement for summer employment at a "water park" in Clear Lake, Texas

T tells Ss to skim the page individually and decide if they would like to work at Clear Lake Water Park (3 min.)

T asks Ss to pair up and tell their partner what they like or don't like, and why they feel that way (4 min.)

T engages the whole class in a brief whole-class discussion of what Ss liked and didn't like, and puts a few key phrases on the board (good pay, benefits, discounts on rides in the park, flexible hours, etc.) (3 min.)

B. Listening focus (10 min.) (L, R, W, S)

T directs Ss to the second page, and plays a CD recording of a conversation in which a man named Jacques describes why he doesn't like his job. T plays the conversation once for general listening . . . (3 min.)

. . . and a second time for Ss to look at and complete the written exercise in the book that requires using the *ing* form of verbs like *work, write, apply,* etc. (4 min.)

T asks Ss to compare their responses with their partner and make any corrections (3 min.)

C. Grammar focus (15 min.) (L, R, W, S)

In the next exercise, Ss are asked to "make one list of job-related activities you like and another list of those you dislike" (5 min.)

T then calls attention to the expressions in the book: *I can't stand/I don't mind/I enjoy/I hate/I like/I prefer* + gerund [*ing* form of verb] (2 min.)

T puts Ss into groups of four and directs them to share their likes and dislikes, using the expressions + gerund. T offers some suggestions as prompts (8 min.)

D. Focus on types of workers (15 min.) (R, S, L, W)

On the next page, six types of workers are described and pictured: realistic, investigative, artistic, social, enterprising, and conventional

T directs Ss to the page and calls on six Ss to each read aloud one of the short descriptions; T makes a few pronunciation corrections (5 min.)

T then directs Ss to reread the descriptions and write a short paragraph describing themselves. Ss can use the gerunds used in the descriptions (10 min.)

Wind-down (5 min.) (L, S)

T asks Ss to look over their paragraph descriptions, and to revise them if they want to for homework

T calls on selected Ss and asks them about what type of worker they are, and if they like or dislike a job they have had

You can easily see in this typical lesson that all four skills are comfortably integrated into the sequence of activities. Some of the models of integration discussed in this chapter applied, but not all. Segments A, B, and C were examples of the *tasks* of expressing likes and dislikes. The whole lesson was on the *theme* of occupations and jobs. And there was to some extent a bit of an *episode* involved in the narrative that Jacques told. A follow-up to the next lesson in this same unit involved students in finding employment advertisements in an English newspaper and bringing them to class and reporting on the ones they liked or disliked, which incorporated an *experiential* flavor into the unit.

☆   ☆   ☆   ☆   ☆

In the next four chapters, we will look separately at the four skills, but *not* with a view to programming your language teaching into compartments. The four chapters are simply a convenient way to target the goals, problems, issues, and trends that relate to each of the four modes of communication. In so doing, we will not in any way neglect the paramount importance of the interconnection between and among the performance skills.

TOPICS FOR DISCUSSION, RESEARCH, AND ACTION

[Note: (I) Individual work; (G) group or pair work; (C) whole-class discussion.]

1. (I) Review the reasons (pages 285–286) for not integrating skills in ESL courses. Can you add others? If you know of certain courses that are not integrated, can these three—or any other—justifications be advanced for keeping them nonintegrated?

2. (G) Direct pairs to look at the seven observations (page 286) in support of integrated-skills classes. Pairs will discuss whether or not they apply to contexts they are familiar with. Would one be able to add anymore justification for integrating the skills?

3. (G/C) Ask pairs to collaborate in writing brief definitions of each of the five types of integrated-skills instruction discussed in this chapter: content-based, task-based, theme-based, experiential, and the episode hypothesis. Then, direct the whole class to make a list of various institutions that teach ESL and discuss the extent to which each model does or does not fit the institution.

4. (G) Ask pairs to consider the following: Suppose you are asked to employ a teacher for a content-centered curriculum. What qualifications would you draw up for such a teacher?

5. (G/C) Once again, the term "task-based" is presented in this chapter. Ask the class to define it again without referring to this chapter or to Chapter 3. Then have partners design a task that involves several techniques, share their task with the rest of the class, and give a rationale for the design.

6. (G) Direct groups each to consider a different audience and context, then to design a theme-based lesson or module on environmental action and awareness. As they plan the techniques, they should discuss any "political"

implications of what they might ask students to do. Groups will then share their lessons with the rest of the class.

7. (I/C) Look in a library or resource center for books that could be classified as theme-based. Select one to evaluate, perhaps with a partner. Are both language and content goals fulfilled? Are the four skills well integrated? Will students be intrinsically motivated to study the book? Share your thoughts with the rest of the class.

8. (G/C) Ask pairs to design an episodic activity and share the activity with the rest of the class.

9. (C) In the integrated lesson that was outlined at the end of the chapter, is there anything that could be altered to create better integration of skills?

FOR YOUR FURTHER READING

Hinkel, E. (2006). Current perspectives on teaching the four skills. *TESOL Quarterly, 40*, 109–131.

This article by Eli Hinkel appeared in the TESOL Quarterly's *40th anniversary issue, which was devoted to survey articles in a number of fields, as experts capsulized the state of the art in their specialties. The article is an excellent summary not only of why skills are integrated, but also of where we stand with respect to each of the four skills.*

Larsen-Freeman, D. (2000). *Techniques and principles in language teaching* (2nd ed.). Oxford, UK: Oxford University Press.

Richards, J., & Rodgers, T. (2001). *Approaches and methods in language teaching* (2nd ed.). Cambridge, UK: Cambridge University Press.

These two books were recommended earlier (Chapter 2) since they so aptly summarize a number of methods and approaches. It would be useful, in relation to the topic of this chapter, to look at their chapters on content-based, task-based, and participatory approaches, and on cooperative learning, as well as chapters on Multiple Intelligences, learner strategy training (Larsen-Freeman only), and the Lexical Approach (Richards & Rodgers only). View their descriptions with an eye for how each approach incorporates integration of skills.

Sarosy, P., & Sherak, K. (2006). *Lecture ready: Strategies for academic listening, note-taking, and discussion.* New York, NY: Oxford University Press.

Peg Sarosy and Kathy Sherak's textbook series is a superb example of skills integration. All four skills are interwoven in a book whose primary focus is on academic listening.

CHAPTER 18

TEACHING LISTENING

> **OBJECTIVES** After reading this chapter, you will be able to:
>
> - understand issues and concepts in pedagogical research that are related to teaching listening comprehension
>
> - appreciate factors that might make listening difficult for students
>
> - analyze types of spoken language, micro- and macroskills, and types of classroom listening performance
>
> - apply principles of designing listening techniques to your own lesson designs and to your observation of others' lessons
>
> - recognize some basic principles and formats for assessing listening comprehension

Three people were on a train in England. As they approached what appeared to be Wemberly Station, one of the travelers said, "Is this Wemberly?" "No," replied a second passenger, "it's Thursday." Whereupon the third person remarked, "Oh, I am too; let's have a drink!"

The importance of listening in language learning can hardly be overestimated. Through reception, we internalize linguistic information without which we could not produce language. In classrooms, students always do more listening than speaking. Listening competence is universally "larger" than speaking competence. Is it any wonder, then, that in recent years the language-teaching profession has placed a concerted emphasis on listening comprehension?

Listening comprehension has not always drawn the attention of educators to the extent that it now has. Perhaps human beings have a natural tendency to look at speaking as the major index of language proficiency. Consider, for example, our commonly used query, "Do you speak Japanese?" Of course we don't mean to exclude comprehension when we say that, but when we think of foreign language learning, we first think of speaking. In the decades of the 1950s and 1960s, language-teaching methodology was preoccupied with the spoken language, and classrooms full of students could be heard performing their oral drills. It was not uncommon for students to practice phrases orally they didn't even understand!

LISTENING COMPREHENSION IN PEDAGOGICAL RESEARCH

Listening as a major component in language learning and teaching first hit the spotlight in the late 1970s with James Asher's (1977) work on Total Physical Response (see Chapter 2). In TPR the role of comprehension was given prominence as learners were given great quantities of language to listen to before they were encouraged to respond orally. Similarly, the Natural Approach (again see Chapter 2) recommended a significant "silent period" during which learners were allowed the security of listening without being forced to go through the anxiety of speaking before they were "ready" to do so.

Such approaches were an outgrowth of a variety of research studies that showed evidence of the importance of **input** in second language acquisition (see *PLLT,* Chapter 10). Stephen Krashen (1985), for example, borrowing insights from first language acquisition, stressed the significance of **comprehensible input**, or the aural reception of language that is just a little beyond the learner's present ability. About the same time, researchers were also stressing the crucial importance of whatever mental processes were brought to bear on the learner's converting input into **intake**, or that which is actually stored in a learner's competence. In other words, you can be "exposed" to great quantities of input, but what counts is the linguistic information that you ultimately glean from that exposure through conscious and subconscious attention, through cognitive strategies of retention, through feedback, and through interaction. As we shall see, the conversion of input into intake is absolutely crucial in considering the role of listening in language learning. As you consider the role of listening techniques in your classes, you ultimately want to ask yourself what students have taken in from perhaps an array of comprehension activity.

Subsequent pedagogical research on listening comprehension made significant refinements in the process of listening. Studies looked at the effect of a number of different contextual characteristics and how they affect the speed and efficiency of processing aural language. Rubin (1994) identified five such factors: text, interlocutor, task, listener, and process characteristics. In each case, important elements of the listening process were identified. For example, the listener characteristics of proficiency, memory, attention, affect, age, gender, background schemata, and even learning disabilities in the L1 all affect the process of listening (pp. 206–10).

In more recent research, attention is being given to types of meaning involved in the act of comprehending language (Flowerdew & Miller, 2005). In this perspective, phonological, syntactic, semantic, and pragmatic knowledge are considered, along with nonverbal elements involved in most real-world (face-to-face) listening. Other studies have looked at the extent to which *first* language listening ability contributes to one's performance of second language listening, with the interesting suggestion by Vandergrift (2006) that if you're a good listener in your L1, you stand a good chance of doing well in L2 listening tasks. Further, the research has examined the role of strategic factors and of strategies-based instruction in listening comprehension (Flowerdew & Miller, 2005; Hinkel, 2006; Mendelsohn, 1998; Rost, 2005; Vandergrift, 2003, 2004). Studies tend to agree that listening, especially for academic and professional contexts, is a highly refined skill that requires a learner's attention to a battery of strategies for extracting meaning from texts (Flowerdew, 1994).

All of these issues prompt teachers to consider some specific questions about listening comprehension:

- What are listeners "doing" when they listen?
- What factors affect good listening?
- What are the characteristics of "real-life" listening?
- What are the many things listeners listen for?
- What are some principles for designing listening techniques?
- How can listening techniques be interactive?
- What are some common techniques for teaching listening?

These and other related questions will be addressed in this chapter.

AN INTERACTIVE MODEL OF LISTENING COMPREHENSION

Listening is not a one-way street. It is not merely the process of a unidirectional receiving of audible symbols. One facet—the first step—of listening comprehension is the psychomotor process of receiving sound waves through the ear and transmitting nerve impulses to the brain. But that is just the beginning of what is clearly an **interactive** process as the brain acts on the impulses, bringing to bear a number of different cognitive and affective mechanisms.

The following eight processes (adapted from Clark & Clark, 1977; Richards, 1983) are all involved in comprehension. With the exception of the initial and final processes below, no sequence is implied here; they all occur if not simultaneously, then in extremely rapid succession. Neurological time must be viewed in terms of microseconds.

1. The hearer processes what we'll call "raw speech" and holds an "image" of it in short-term memory. This image consists of the constituents (phrases, clauses, cohesive markers, intonation, and stress patterns) of a stream of speech.
2. The hearer determines the type of speech event being processed (for example, a conversation, a speech, a radio broadcast) and then appropriately "colors" the interpretation of the perceived message.
3. The hearer infers the objectives of the speaker through consideration of the type of speech event, the context, and the content. So, for example, one determines whether the speaker wishes to persuade, to request, to exchange pleasantries, to affirm, to deny, to inform, and so forth. Thus the function of the message is inferred.
4. The hearer recalls background information (or **schemata**; see Chapter 20 for more on this topic) relevant to the particular context and subject matter. A lifetime of experiences and knowledge is used to perform cognitive associations in order to bring a plausible interpretation to the message.

5. **The hearer assigns a literal meaning to the utterance.** This process involves a set of semantic interpretations of the surface strings that the ear has perceived. In many instances, literal and intended (see #6) meanings match. So, for example, if one of your students walks into your office while you are madly grading papers and says she has a question that she would appreciate your answer to, then says, "Do you have the time?," the literal meaning (Do you possess enough time now to answer me?) is appropriate. However, this process may take on a peripheral role in cases where literal meanings are irrelevant to the message, as in metaphorical or "idiomatic" language. If, for example, a stranger sitting beside you on a bus has been silent for a period of time and then says, "Do you have the time?," your appropriate response is not yes or no but rather, "It's a quarter to nine" or whatever. Second language learners must, in such cases, learn to go "beneath" the surface of such language in order to interpret correctly.

6. **The hearer assigns an intended meaning to the utterance.** The person on the bus intended to find out what time of day it was, even though the literal meaning didn't directly convey that message. How often do misunderstandings stem from false assumptions that are made on the hearer's part about the intended meaning of the speaker? A key to human communication is the ability to match **perceived** meaning with **intended** meaning. This matchmaking, of course, can extend well beyond simple metaphorical and idiomatic language. It can apply to short and long stretches of discourse, and its breakdown can be caused by careless speech, inattention of the hearer, conceptual complexity, contextual miscues, psychological barriers, and a host of other performance variables.

7. **The hearer determines whether information should be retained in short-term or long-term memory.** Short-term memory—a matter of a few seconds—is appropriate in contexts that call for a quick oral response from the hearer. Long-term memory is more common when, say, you are processing information in a lecture. There are, of course, many points in between.

8. **The hearer deletes the form in which the message was originally received.** The words, phrases, and sentences are quickly forgotten—"pruned"—in 99 percent of speech acts. You have no need to retain this sort of cognitive "clutter." Instead, the important information, if any (see #7 above), is retained conceptually. (See also *PLLT,* Chapter 4.)

It should be clear from the foregoing that listening comprehension is an interactive process. After the initial reception of sound, we human beings perform at least seven other major operations on that set of sound waves. In conversational settings, of course, further interaction takes place immediately after the listening stage as the hearer becomes speaker in a response of some kind. All of these processes are important for you to keep in mind as you teach. They are all relevant to a learner's purpose for listening, to performance factors that may cause difficulty in processing speech, to overall principles of effective listening techniques, and to the choices you make of what techniques to use and when to use them in your classroom.

TYPES OF SPOKEN LANGUAGE

Much of our language-teaching energy is devoted to instruction in mastering English conversation. However, numerous other forms of spoken language are also important to incorporate into a language course, especially in teaching listening comprehension. As you plan lessons or curricula, the classification of types of oral language shown in Figure 18.1 should enable you to see the big picture of what teaching aural comprehension entails.

In monologues, when one speaker uses spoken language for any length of time, as in speeches, lectures, readings, news broadcasts, and the like, the hearer must process long stretches of speech without interruption—the stream of speech will go on whether or not the hearer comprehends. Planned, as opposed to unplanned, monologues differ considerably in their discourse structures. Planned monologues (such as speeches and other prewritten material) usually manifest little redundancy and are therefore relatively difficult to comprehend. Unplanned monologues (impromptu lectures and long "stories" in conversations, for example) exhibit more redundancy, which makes for ease in comprehension, but the presence of more performance variables and other hesitations (see below) can either help or hinder comprehension.

Dialogues involve two or more speakers and can be subdivided into those exchanges that promote social relationships (**interpersonal**) and those for which the purpose is to convey propositional or factual information (**transactional**). In each case, participants may have a good deal of shared knowledge (background information, schemata); therefore, the familiarity of the interlocutors will produce conversations with more assumptions, implications, and other meanings hidden between the lines. In conversations between or among participants who are unfamiliar with each other, references and meanings have to be made more explicit to assure effective comprehension. When such references are not explicit, misunderstandings can easily follow.

Figure 18.1. Types of oral language (adapted from Nunan, 1991b, pp. 20–21)

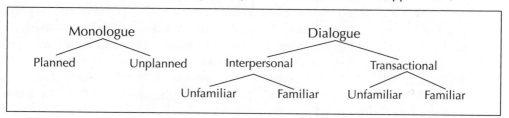

One could also have subdivided dialogues between those in which the hearer is a participant and those in which the hearer is an "eavesdropper." In both cases, the above conversational descriptions apply, but the major—and highly significant—difference is that in the latter the hearer is, as in monologues, unable to interrupt or otherwise participate vocally in the negotiation of meaning.

Remember that in all cases these categories are really not discrete, mutually exclusive domains; rather, each dichotomy, as usual, represents a continuum of possibilities. For example, everyday social conversations can easily contain elements of transactional dialogues, and vice versa. Similarly, "familiar" participants may share very little common knowledge on a particular topic. If each category, then, is viewed as an end point, you can aim your teaching at appropriate ranges in between.

WHAT MAKES LISTENING DIFFICULT?

As you contemplate designing lessons and techniques for teaching listening skills, or that have listening components in them, a number of special characteristics of spoken language need to be taken into consideration. Second language learners need to pay special attention to such factors because they strongly influence the processing of speech, and can even block comprehension if they are not attended to. In other words, they can make the listening process difficult. The following eight characteristics of spoken language are adapted from several sources (Dunkel, 1991; Flowerdew & Miller, 2005; Richards, 1983; Ur, 1984).

1. Clustering

In written language we are conditioned to attend to the sentence as the basic unit of organization. In spoken language, due to memory limitations and our predisposition for "chunking," or **clustering**, we break down speech into smaller groups of words. Clauses are common constituents, but phrases within clauses are even more easily retained for comprehension. In teaching listening comprehension, therefore, you need to help students to pick out manageable clusters of words; sometimes second language learners will try to retain overly long constituents (a whole sentence or even several sentences), or they will err in the other direction in trying to attend to every word in an utterance.

2. Redundancy

Spoken language, unlike most written language, has a good deal of redundancy. The next time you're in a conversation, notice the rephrasings, repetitions, elaborations, and little insertions of "I mean" and "you know." Such redundancy helps the hearer to process meaning by offering more time and extra information. Learners can train themselves to profit from such redundancy by first becoming aware that not every new sentence or phrase will necessarily contain new information and by looking for the signals of redundancy. Consider the following excerpt of a conversation.

Jeff:	Hey, Matt, how's it going?
Matt:	Pretty good, Jeff. How was your weekend?
Jeff:	Aw, it was terrible, I mean the worst you could imagine. You know what I mean?
Matt:	Yeah, I've had those days. Well, like what happened?
Jeff:	Well, you're not gonna believe this, but my girlfriend and I—you know Rachel? I think you met her at my party—anyway, she and I drove up to Point Reyes, you know, up in Marin County? So we were driving along minding our own business, you know, when this dude in one of those big ugly SUVs, you know, like a Hummer or something, comes up like three feet behind us and like tailgates us on these crazy mountain roads up there—you know what they're like. So, he's about to run me off the road, and it's all I can do to just concentrate. Then . . .

You can easily pick out quite a few redundancies in Jeff's recounting of his experience. Learners might initially get confused by this, but with some training, they can learn to take advantage of redundancies as well as other markers that provide more processing time.

3. Reduced forms

While spoken language does indeed contain a good deal of redundancy, it also has many reduced forms and sentence fragments. Reduction can be phonological ("Djeetyet?" for "Did you eat yet?"), morphological (contractions like "I'll"), syntactic (elliptical forms like "When will you be back?" "Tomorrow, maybe."), or pragmatic (phone rings in a house, child answers and yells to another room in the house, "Mom! Phone!"). These reductions pose significant difficulties, especially for classroom learners who may have initially been exposed to the full forms of the English language.

4. Performance variables

In spoken language, except for planned discourse (speeches, lectures, etc.), hesitations, false starts, pauses, and corrections are common. Native listeners are conditioned from very young ages to weed out such performance variables, whereas they can easily interfere with comprehension in second language learners. Imagine listening to the following verbatim excerpt of a sportsman talking about his game:

> But, uh—I also—to go with this of course if you're playing well—if you're playing well then you get uptight about your game. You get keyed up and it's easy to concentrate. You know you're playing well and you know . . . in with a chance then it's easier, much easier to—to you know get in there and—and start to . . . you don't have to think about it. I mean it's gotta be automatic.

In written form this looks like gibberish, but it's the kind of language we hear and process all the time. Learners have to train themselves to listen for meaning in the midst of distracting performance variables.

Everyday casual speech by native speakers also commonly contains ungrammatical forms. Some of these forms are simple performance slips. For example, "We arrived in a little town that there was no hotel anywhere" is something a native speaker could easily self-correct. Other ungrammaticality arises out of dialect differences ("I don't get no respect") that second language learners are likely to hear sooner or later.

5. Colloquial language

Learners who have been exposed to standard written English and/or "textbook" language sometimes find it surprising and difficult to deal with colloquial language. Idioms, slang, reduced forms, and shared cultural knowledge are all manifested at some point in conversations. Colloquialisms appear in both monologues and dialogues. Contractions and other assimilations often pose difficulty for the learner of English.

6. Rate of delivery

Virtually every language learner initially thinks that native speakers speak too fast! Actually, as Jack Richards (1983) points out, the number and length of pauses used by a speaker are more crucial to comprehension than sheer speed. Learners will nevertheless eventually need to be able to comprehend language delivered at varying rates of speed and, at times, delivered with few pauses. Unlike reading, where a person can stop and go back to reread, in listening the hearer may not always have the opportunity to stop the speaker. Instead, the stream of speech will continue to flow!

7. Stress, rhythm, and intonation

The prosodic features of the English language are very important for comprehension. Because English is a stress-timed language, English speech can be a terror for some learners as mouthfuls of syllables come spilling out between stress points. The sentence "The PRESident is INTerested in eLIMinating the emBARgo," with 4 stressed syllables out of 18, theoretically takes about the same amount of time to utter as "Dead men wear plaid." Also, intonation patterns are very significant (see Chapter 19) not just for interpreting straightforward elements such as questions, statements, and emphasis but for understanding more subtle messages like sarcasm, endearment, insult, solicitation, praise, etc.

8. Interaction

Unless a language learner's objective is exclusively to master some specialized skill like monitoring radio broadcasts or attending lectures, interaction will play a large role in listening comprehension. Conversation is especially subject to all the rules of interaction: negotiation, clarification; attending signals; turn-taking; and topic nomination, maintenance, and termination (see Chapter 8 of *PLLT*). So, to learn to listen is also to learn to respond and to continue a chain of listening and responding. Classroom techniques that include listening components must at some point include instruction in the two-way nature of listening. Students need to understand that good listeners (in conversation) are good responders. They know how to negotiate meaning (to give feedback, to ask for clarification, to maintain a topic) so that the process of comprehending can be complete rather than be aborted by insufficient interaction.

A fourth-century Chinese proverb says it more eloquently:

> *Not to let a word get in the way of its sentence,*
> *Nor to let a sentence get in the way of its intention,*
> *But to send your mind out to meet the intention as a guest;*
> *THAT is understanding.*

MICROSKILLS AND MACROSKILLS OF LISTENING

In his seminal article on teaching listening skills, Jack Richards (1983) provided a comprehensive taxonomy of aural skills, which he called **microskills**, involved in conversational discourse. I have adapted Richards's original microskills into a list of micro- and **macroskills**, the latter to designate skills that are technically at the *discourse* level. The former pertain to skills at the *sentence* level. Such lists are useful in helping you to break down just what it is that your learners need to actually *perform* as they acquire effective listening strategies. Through a checklist of micro- and macroskills, you can get a good idea of what your techniques need to cover in the domain of listening comprehension. As you plan a specific technique or listening module, such a list helps you to focus on clearly conceptualized objectives. And in your evaluation of listening, these micro- and macroskills can become testing criteria. Table 18.1 on page 308 is just such a checklist, adapted from Richards and other sources.

It is important to note that these 17 skills apply to conversational discourse. Less interactive forms of discourse, such as listening to monologues like academic lectures, include further, more specific micro- and macroskills (Blackwell & Naber, 2006; Flowerdew, 1994; Sarosy & Sherak, 2006). Students in an academic setting need to be able to perform such things as identifying the structure of a lecture, weeding out what may be irrelevant or tangential, detecting the possible biases of the speaker, critically evaluating the speaker's assertions, and developing means (through note taking, for example) of retaining the content of a lecture.

Table 18.1. Micro- and macroskills of listening comprehension (adapted from Richards, 1983)

Microskills

1. Retain chunks of language of different lengths in short-term memory.
2. Discriminate among the distinctive sounds of English.
3. Recognize English stress patterns, words in stressed and unstressed positions, rhythmic structure, intonational contours, and their role in signaling information.
4. Recognize reduced forms of words.
5. Distinguish word boundaries, recognize a core of words, and interpret word order patterns and their significance.
6. Process speech at different rates of delivery.
7. Process speech containing pauses, errors, corrections, and other performance variables.
8. Recognize grammatical word classes (nouns, verbs, etc.), systems (e.g., tense, agreement, pluralization), patterns, rules, and elliptical forms.
9. Detect sentence constituents and distinguish between major and minor constituents.
10. Recognize that a particular meaning may be expressed in different grammatical forms.

Macroskills

11. Recognize cohesive devices in spoken discourse.
12. Recognize the communicative functions of utterances, according to situations, participants, goals.
13. Infer situations, participants, goals using real-world knowledge.
14. From events, ideas, etc., described, predict outcomes, infer links and connections between events, deduce causes and effects, and detect such relations as main idea, supporting idea, new information, given information, generalization, and exemplification.
15. Distinguish between literal and implied meanings.
16. Use facial, kinesic, body language, and other nonverbal clues to decipher meanings.
17. Develop and use a battery of listening strategies, such as detecting key words, guessing the meaning of words from context, appealing for help, and signaling comprehension or lack thereof.

TYPES OF CLASSROOM LISTENING PERFORMANCE

With literally hundreds of possible techniques available for teaching listening skills, it will be helpful for you to think in terms of several kinds of listening performance—that is, what your students do in a listening technique. Sometimes these types of performance are embedded in a broader technique or task, and sometimes they are themselves the sum total of the activity of a technique.

1. Reactive

Sometimes you want a learner simply to listen to the surface structure of an utterance for the sole purpose of repeating it back to you. While this kind of listening performance requires little meaningful processing, it nevertheless may be a legitimate, even though a minor, aspect of an interactive, communicative classroom. This role of the listener as merely a "tape recorder" (Nunan, 1991b, p. 18) is very limited because the listener is not generating meaning. About the only role that reactive listening can play in an interactive classroom is in brief choral or individual drills that focus on pronunciation.

2. Intensive

Techniques whose only purpose is to focus on components (phonemes, words, intonation, discourse markers, etc.) of discourse may be considered to be intensive— as opposed to extensive—in their requirement that students single out certain elements of spoken language. They include the bottom-up skills (see page 312) that are important at all levels of proficiency. Examples of intensive listening performance include these:

- Students listen for cues in certain choral or individual drills.
- The teacher repeats a word or sentence several times to "imprint" it in the students' mind.
- The teacher asks students to listen to a sentence or a longer stretch of discourse and to notice a specified element, such as intonation, stress, a contraction, a grammatical structure, etc.

3. Responsive

A significant proportion of classroom listening activity consists of short stretches of teacher language designed to elicit immediate responses. The students' task in such listening is to process the teacher talk immediately and to fashion an appropriate reply. Examples include

- asking questions ("How are you today?" "What did you do last night?")
- giving commands ("Take a sheet of paper and a pencil.")
- seeking clarification ("What was that word you said?")
- checking comprehension ("So, how many people were in the elevator when the power went out?")

4. Selective

In longer stretches of discourse such as monologues of a couple of minutes or considerably longer, the task of the student is not to process everything that was said, but rather to *scan* the material selectively for certain information. The purpose of such performance is not to look for global or general meanings, necessarily, but to be able to find important information in a field of potentially distracting information. Such activity requires **field independence** (see *PLLT,* Chapter 5) on the part of the learner. Selective listening differs from intensive listening in that the discourse is in relatively long lengths. Examples of such discourse include

- speeches
- media broadcasts
- stories and anecdotes
- conversations in which learners are "eavesdroppers"

Techniques promoting selective listening skills could ask students to listen for

- people's names
- dates
- certain facts or events
- location, situation, context, etc.
- main ideas and/or conclusion

5. Extensive

This sort of performance, unlike the intensive processing (#2) described above, aims to develop a top-down, global understanding of spoken language. Extensive performance could range from listening to lengthy lectures, to listening to a conversation and deriving a comprehensive message or purpose. Extensive listening may require the student to invoke other interactive skills (e.g., note taking and/or discussion) for full comprehension.

6. Interactive

Finally, there is listening performance that can include all five of the above types as learners actively participate in discussions, debates, conversations, role plays, and other pair and group work. Their listening performance must be intricately integrated with speaking (and perhaps other) skills in the authentic give and take of communicative interchange.

PRINCIPLES FOR TEACHING LISTENING SKILLS

Several decades of research and practice in teaching listening comprehension have yielded some practical principles for designing classroom aural comprehension techniques. These principles should help you to create your own techniques and activities. Some of them, especially the second and third, actually apply to any technique; the others are more germane to listening.

1. Include a focus on listening in an integrated-skills course.

Assuming that your curriculum is dedicated to the integration of all four skills, remember that each of the separate skills deserves special focus in appropriate doses. It is easy to adopt a philosophy of just letting students "experience" language without careful attention to component skills. Because aural comprehension itself cannot be overtly "observed" (see #4 below), teachers sometimes incorrectly assume that the input provided in the classroom will always be converted into intake. The creation of effective listening techniques requires studied attention to all the principles of listening already summarized in this chapter.

2. Use techniques that are intrinsically motivating.

Appeal to listeners' personal interests and goals. Since background information (schemata) is an important factor in listening, take into full account the experiences, goals, and abilities of your students as you design lessons. Also, remember that the cultural background(s) of your students can be both facilitating and interfering in the process of listening. Then, once a technique is launched, try to construct it in such a way that students are caught up in the activity and feel self-propelled toward its final objective.

3. Utilize authentic language and contexts.

Authentic language and real-world tasks enable students to see the relevance of classroom activity to their long-term communicative goals. If you introduce natural texts (for a list of real-world texts, see page 288) rather than concocted, artificial material, students will more readily dive into the activity.

4. Carefully consider the form of listeners' responses.

Comprehension itself is not externally observable. We cannot peer into a learner's brain through a little window and empirically observe what is stored there after someone else has said something. We can only *infer* that certain things have been comprehended through students' overt (verbal or nonverbal) *responses* to speech. It is therefore important for teachers to design techniques in such a way that students' responses indicate whether or not their comprehension has been correct. Lund (1990) offered nine different ways that we can check listeners' comprehension:

- doing—the listener responds physically to a command
- choosing—the listener selects from alternatives such as pictures, objects, and texts
- transferring—the listener draws a picture of what is heard
- answering—the listener answers questions about the message
- condensing—the listener outlines or takes notes on a lecture
- extending—the listener provides an ending to a story heard
- duplicating—the listener translates the message into the native language or repeats it verbatim
- modeling—the listener orders a meal, for example, after listening to a model order
- conversing—the listener engages in a conversation that indicates appropriate processing of information

5. Encourage the development of listening strategies.

Most foreign language students are simply not aware of how to listen. One of your jobs is to equip them with listening strategies that extend beyond the classroom. Draw their attention to the value of such strategies as

- looking for key words
- looking for nonverbal cues to meaning
- predicting a speaker's purpose by the context of the spoken discourse
- associating information with one's existing cognitive structure (activating background information)
- guessing at meanings
- seeking clarification
- listening for the general gist
- various test-taking strategies for listening comprehension

As you "teach learners how to learn" by helping them to develop their overall strategic competence (see Chapter 16), strategies for effective listening can become a highly significant part of their chances for successful learning.

6. Include both bottom-up and top-down listening techniques.

Speech-processing theory distinguishes between two types of processing in both listening and reading comprehension. **Bottom-up** processing proceeds from sounds to words to grammatical relationships to lexical meanings, etc., to a final "message." **Top-down** processing is evoked from "a bank of prior knowledge and global expectations" (Morley, 1991a, p. 87) and other background information (schemata) that the listener brings to the text. Bottom-up techniques typically focus on sounds, words, intonation, grammatical structures, and other components of spoken language. Top-down techniques are more concerned with the activation of schemata, with deriving meaning, with global understanding, and with the interpretation of a text. It is important for learners to operate from both directions since both can offer keys to determining the meaning of spoken discourse. But in a communicative, interactive context, you don't want to dwell too heavily on the bottom-up, for to do so may hamper the development of a learner's all-important automaticity in processing speech.

LISTENING TECHNIQUES FROM BEGINNING TO ADVANCED

Techniques for teaching listening will vary considerably across the proficiency continuum. Chapter 7 has already dealt with general characteristics. Listening techniques are no exception to the general rule. Table 18.2 provides three lists of techniques for each of three proficiency levels. Each list is broken down into bottom-up, top-down, and interactive types of activity.

The importance of listening comprehension in language learning should by now be quite apparent. As we move on to look at speaking skills, always remember the ever-present relationship among all four skills and the necessity in authentic, interactive classes to integrate these skills even as you focus on the specifics of one skill area.

Table 18.2. Techniques for teaching listening comprehension (adapted from Peterson, 1991, pp. 114–121)

FOR BEGINNING LEVEL LISTENERS

Bottom-Up Exercises
1. Goal: *Discriminate Between Intonation Contours in Sentences*
    Listen to a sequence of sentence patterns with either rising or falling intonation. Place a check in column 1 (rising) or column 2 (falling), depending on the pattern you hear.
2. Goal: *Discriminate Between Phonemes*
    Listen to pairs of words. Some pairs differ in their final consonant, and some pairs are the same. Circle the word "same" or "different," depending on what you hear.
3. Goal: *Selective Listening for Morphological Endings*
    Listen to a series of sentences. Circle "yes" if the verb has an -*ed* ending, and circle "no" if it does not.
    Listen to a series of sentences. On your answer sheet, circle the one (of three) verb forms contained in the sentence that you hear.
4. Goal: *Select Details from the Text (Word Recognition)*
    Match a word that you hear with its picture.
    Listen to a weather report. Look at a list of words and circle the words that you hear.
    Listen to a sentence that contains clock time. Circle the clock time that you hear, among three choices (5:30, 5:45, 6:15).
    Listen to an advertisement, select the price of an item, and write the amount on a price tag.
    Listen to a series of recorded telephone messages from an answering machine. Fill in a chart with the following information from each caller: name, number, time, and message.
5. Goal: *Listen for Normal Sentence Word Order*
    Listen to a short dialogue and fill in the missing words that have been deleted in a partial transcript.

Top-Down Exercises
6. Goal: *Discriminate Between Emotional Reactions*
    Listen to a sequence of utterances. Place a check in the column that describes the emotional reaction that you hear: interested, happy, surprised, or unhappy.
7. Goal: *Get the Gist of a Sentence*
    Listen to a sentence describing a picture and select the correct picture.
8. Goal: *Recognize the Topic*
    Listen to a dialogue and decide where the conversation occurred. Circle the correct location among three multiple-choice items.
    Listen to a conversation and look at the pictured greeting cards. Decide which of the greeting cards was sent. Write the greeting under the appropriate card.
    Listen to a conversation and decide what the people are talking about. Choose the picture that shows the topic.

(Continued)

Interactive Exercises
9. Goal: *Build a Semantic Network of Word Associations*
    Listen to a word and associate all the related words that come to mind.
10. Goal: *Recognize a Familiar Word and Relate It to a Category*
    Listen to words from a shopping list and match each word to the store that sells it.
11. Goal: *Follow Directions*
    Listen to a description of a route and trace it on a map.

FOR INTERMEDIATE LEVEL LISTENERS

Bottom-Up Exercises
12. Goal: *Recognize Fast Speech Forms*
    Listen to a series of sentences that contain unstressed function words. Circle your choice among three words on the answer sheet—for example: "up," "a," "of."
13. Goal: *Find the Stressed Syllable*
    Listen to words of two (or three) syllables. Mark them for word stress and predict the pronunciation of the unstressed syllable.
14. Goal: *Recognize Words with Reduced Syllables*
    Read a list of polysyllabic words and predict which syllabic vowel will be dropped. Listen to the words read in fast speech and confirm your prediction.
15. Goal: *Recognize Words as They Are Linked in the Speech Stream*
    Listen to a series of short sentences with consonant/vowel linking between words. Mark the linkages on your answer sheet.
16. Goal: *Recognize Pertinent Details in the Speech Stream*
    Listen to a short dialogue between a boss and a secretary regarding changes in the daily schedule. Use an appointment calendar. Cross out appointments that are being changed and write in new ones.
    Listen to announcements of airline arrivals and departures. With a model of an airline information board in front of you, fill in the flight numbers, destinations, gate numbers, and departure times.
    Listen to a series of short dialogues after reading questions that apply to the dialogues. While listening, find the answers to questions about prices, places, names, and numbers. Example: "Where are the shoppers?" "How much is whole wheat bread?"
    Listen to a short telephone conversation between a customer and a service station manager. Fill in a chart which lists the car repairs that must be done. Check the part of the car that needs repair, the reason, and the approximate cost.

Top-Down Exercises
17. Goal: *Analyze Discourse Structure to Suggest Effective Listening Strategies*
    Listen to six radio commercials with attention to the use of music, repetition of key words, and number of speakers. Talk about the effect these techniques have on the listeners.
18. Goal: *Listen to Identify the Speaker or the Topic*
    Listen to a series of radio commercials. On your answer sheet, choose among four types of sponsors or products and identify the picture that goes with the commercial.
19. Goal: *Listen to Evaluate Themes and Motives*
    Listen to a series of radio commercials. On your answer sheet are four possible motives that the companies use to appeal to their customers. Circle all the motives that you feel each commercial promotes: escape from reality, family security, snob appeal, sex appeal.

20. Goal: *Find Main Ideas and Supporting Details*
    Listen to a short conversation between two friends. On your answer sheet are scenes from television programs. Find and write the name of the program and the channel. Decide which speaker watched which program.
21. Goal: *Make Inferences*
    Listen to a series of sentences, which may be either statements or questions. After each sentence, answer inferential questions such as "Where might the speaker be?" "How might the speaker be feeling?" "What might the speaker be referring to?"
    Listen to a series of sentences. After each sentence, suggest a possible context for the sentence (place, situation, time, participants).

Interactive Exercises
22. Goal: *Discriminate Between Registers of Speech and Tones of Voice*
    Listen to a series of sentences. On your answer sheet, mark whether the sentence is polite or impolite.
23. Goal: *Recognize Missing Grammar Markers in Colloquial Speech*
    Listen to a series of short questions in which the auxiliary verb and subject have been deleted. Use grammatical knowledge to fill in the missing words: ["Have you] got some extra?"
    Listen to a series of questions with reduced verb auxiliary and subject and identify the missing verb (*does it/is it*) by checking the form of the main verb. Examples: "'Zit come with anything else?", "'Zit arriving on time?"
24. Goal: *Use Knowledge of Reduced Forms to Clarify the Meaning of an Utterance*
    Listen to a short sentence containing a reduced form. Decide what the sentence means. On your answer sheet, choose the one (of three) alternatives that is the best paraphrase of the sentence you heard. Example: You hear "You can't be happy with that." You read: (a) "Why can't you be happy?" (b) "That will make you happy." (c) "I don't think you are happy."
25. Goal: *Use Context to Build Listening Expectations*
    Read a short want-ad describing job qualifications from the employment section of a newspaper. Brainstorm additional qualifications that would be important for that type of job.
26. Goal: *Listen to Confirm Your Expectations*
    Listen to short radio advertisements for jobs that are available. Check the job qualifications against your expectations.
27. Goal: *Use Context to Build Expectations. Use Bottom-Up Processing to Recognize Missing Words. Compare Your Predictions to What You Actually Heard*
    Read some telephone messages with missing words. Decide what kinds of information are missing so you know what to listen for. Listen to the information and fill in the blanks. Finally, discuss with the class what strategies you used for your predictions.
28. Goal: *Use Incomplete Sensory Data and Cultural Background Information to Construct a More Complete Understanding of a Text*
    Listen to one side of a telephone conversation. Decide what the topic of the conversation might be and create a title for it.
    Listen to the beginning of a conversation between two people and answer questions about the number of participants, their ages, gender, and social roles. Guess the time of day, location, temperature, season, and topic. Choose among some statements to guess what might come next.

(Continued)

FOR ADVANCED LEVEL LEARNERS

Bottom-Up Exercises

29. Goal: *Use Features of Sentence Stress and Volume to Identify Important Information for Note-Taking*

    Listen to a number of sentences and extract the content words, which are read with greater stress. Write the content words as notes.

30. Goal: *Become Aware of Sentence-Level Features in Lecture Text*

    Listen to a segment of a lecture while reading a transcript of the material. Notice the incomplete sentences, pauses, and verbal fillers.

31. Goal: *Become Aware of Organizational Cues in Lecture Text*

    Look at a lecture transcript and circle all the cue words used to enumerate the main points. Then listen to the lecture segment and note the organizational cues.

32. Goal: *Become Aware of Lexical and Suprasegmental Markers for Definitions*

    Read a list of lexical cues that signal a definition; listen to signals of the speaker's intent, such as rhetorical questions; listen to special intonation patterns and pause patterns used with appositives.

    Listen to short lecture segments that contain new terms and their definitions in context. Use knowledge of lexical and intonational cues to identify the definition of the word.

33. Goal: *Identify Specific Points of Information*

    Read a skeleton outline of a lecture in which the main categories are given but the specific examples are left blank. Listen to the lecture and find the information that belongs in the blanks.

Top-Down Exercises

34. Goal: *Use the Introduction to the Lecture to Predict Its Focus and Direction*

    Listen to the introductory section of a lecture. Then read a number of topics on your answer sheet and choose the topic that best expresses what the lecture will discuss.

35. Goal: *Use the Lecture Transcript to Predict the Content of the Next Section*

    Read a section of a lecture transcript. Stop reading at a juncture point and predict what will come next. Then read on to confirm your prediction.

36. Goal: *Find the Main Idea of a Lecture Segment*

    Listen to a section of a lecture that describes a statistical trend. While you listen, look at three graphs that show a change over time and select the graph that best illustrates the lecture.

Interactive Exercises

37. Goal: *Use Incoming Details to Determine the Accuracy of Predictions About Content*

    Listen to the introductory sentences to predict some of the main ideas you expect to hear in the lecture. Then listen to the lecture. Note whether or not the instructor talks about the points you predicted. If she/he does, note a detail about the point.

38. Goal: *Determine the Main Ideas of a Section of a Lecture by Analysis of the Details in That Section*

    Listen to a section of a lecture and take notes on the important details. Then relate the details to form an understanding of the main point of that section. Choose from a list of possible controlling ideas.

39. Goal: *Make Inferences by Identifying Ideas on the Sentence Level That Lead to Evaluative Statements*

    Listen to a statement and take notes on the important words. Indicate what further meaning can be inferred from the statement. Indicate the words in the original statement that serve to cue the inference.

40. Goal: *Use Knowledge of the Text and the Lecture Content to Fill In Missing Information*
    Listen to a lecture segment for its gist. Then listen to a statement from which words have been omitted. Using your knowledge of the text and of the general content, fill in the missing information. Check your understanding by listening to the entire segment.

41. Goal: *Use Knowledge of the Text and the Lecture Content to Discover the Lecturer's Misstatements and to Supply the Ideas That He or She Meant to Say*
    Listen to a lecture segment that contains an incorrect term. Write the incorrect term and the term that the lecturer should have used. Finally, indicate what clues helped you find the misstatement.

ASSESSING LISTENING IN THE CLASSROOM

Every classroom lesson involves some form of assessment, whether it's in the form of informal, unplanned, and intuitive teacher processing and feedback, or in formal, prepared, scored tests. In order to appropriately call some attention to this very important role that teachers must assume, I offer—in this and the next three chapters on the four skills—a few principles and practical guidelines for assessing those skills in the classroom. For a much more comprehensive treatment of the assessment of the four skills, as well as background research and theory, I refer you to my companion textbook, *Language Assessment: Principles and Classroom Practices* (Brown, 2004). For a detailed look at the assessment of listening, Buck's (2001) textbook is also very useful.

Understanding the Terms "Assessment" and "Test"

Before specifically considering the topic of assessing listening in particular, a word is in order about two commonly used terms. It's tempting at times to simply think that **assessment** and **test** are synonymous, appearing in free variation depending on the whim of the speaker or writer. A glance at some teacher reference books of 10 or more years ago could bear out such an assumption. However, in recent years, thankfully, the profession seems to have come to an appropriate consensus that the two terms are, in fact, *not* synonymous.

Tests are a subset of assessment. Assessment is an ongoing pedagogical process that includes a number of evaluative acts on the part of the teacher. When a student responds to a question, offers a comment, or tries out a new word or structure, the teacher subconsciously makes an evaluation of the student's performance. A student's written work, from notes or short answers to essays, is judged by the teacher. In reading and listening activities, students' responses are implicitly evaluated. All that is assessment. Technically it is referred to as **informal assessment**—because it is usually unplanned and spontaneous and without specific scoring or grading formats, as opposed to **formal assessment,** which is more deliberate and usually has conventionalized feedback. Tests fall into the latter category. They are planned sets of tasks or exercises, with designated time frames, often announced in advance, prepared for (and sometimes feared) by students, and characteristically offering specific scoring or grading formats.

In considering classroom assessment, then, be prepared to entertain a range of possible pedagogical procedures. In the comments that follow, for the most part more formal aspects of assessment are implied. The informal processes have already been subsumed into the various guidelines and examples of this chapter.

One of the first observations that needs to be made in considering assessment is that listening is unobservable. You cannot directly see or measure or otherwise observe either the process or the product of aural comprehension. Oh, yes, I can hear you saying that if you ask someone to close the window, and they close it, you have observed aural comprehension. Or that if someone nods and says, "uh-huh," while you're talking, you have evidence of comprehension. Well, what you have in these cases is indeed *evidence* of comprehension, but you have not actually observed receptors sending messages to the brain or the brain's processing of sound and converting it to meaning. So, when it comes to assessing listening, we're pretty well stuck with reliance on our best *inference* in determining comprehension. How you do that, and remain as accurate in your assessment as possible, is the challenge of assessing listening.

Assessing Types of Listening and Micro- and Macroskills

In this chapter, we have already looked at types of listening, from intensive listening on up to extensive and interactive. We have also considered the micro- and macroskills of listening, from processing tiny bits and pieces of language to strategic, interactive, and complex skills of extended discourse. These two related taxonomies are indispensable to valid, reliable assessment of students' listening comprehension ability. The more closely you can pinpoint exactly *what* you want to assess, the more reliably will you draw your conclusions.

What assessment methods (tasks, item formats) are commonly used at the various levels? Consider the following list of sample tasks (not an exhaustive list, by any means), and for further information consult Brown (2004).

1. Intensive listening tasks

   - distinguishing phonemic pairs (*grass-glass; leave-live*)
   - distinguishing morphological pairs (*miss-missed*)
   - distinguishing stress patterns (*I can go; I can't go.*)
   - paraphrase recognition (*I come from Taiwan; I'm Taiwanese.*)
   - repetition (S repeats a word)

2. Responsive listening tasks

- question (*What time is it?*—multiple choice [MC] response)
- question (*What time is it?*—open-ended response)
- simple discourse sequences (*Hello. Nice weather. Tough test.*)

3. Selective listening tasks

- listening cloze (Ss fill in blanks)
- verbal information transfer (Ss give MC verbal response)
- picture-cued information transfer (Ss choose a picture)
- chart completion (Ss fill in a grid)
- sentence repetition (Ss repeat stimulus sentence)

4. Extensive listening tasks

- dictation (Ss listen [usually 3 times] and write a paragraph)
- dialogue (Ss hear dialogue—MC comprehension questions)
- dialogue (Ss hear dialogue—open-ended response)
- lecture (Ss take notes, summarize, list main points, etc.)
- interpretive tasks (Ss hear a poem—interpret meaning)
- stories, narratives (Ss retell a story)

The fifth category of listening, interactive tasks, is deliberately omitted from this list since such interaction involves speaking and will be covered in the next chapter. With this brief outline, I hope you can gain a bit of a picture of some assessment possibilities in listening comprehension.

TOPICS FOR DISCUSSION, RESEARCH, AND ACTION

[Note: (I) Individual work; (G) group or pair work; (C) whole-class discussion.]

1. (G) Direct pairs to review the difference between input and intake (referring, if necessary, to *PLLT,* Chapter 10) and to illustrate with classroom examples how input gets converted into intake. What hints or ideas could one recommend for helping students to maximize the conversion of input to intake?

2. (C) Ask the class for specific language examples of each of the eight processes of listening referred to on pages 301–302. How are factors 2 through 8 interactive by definition?

3. (G) Ask pairs to look at the chart in Figure 18.1 and make sure they understand each type of oral language. Pairs will then devise an illustration of each and compare their illustrations with those of some other pairs.

4. (C) Pick an English language news program and audiotape a two- or three-minute segment. In class, have students listen to the tape and identify the "clusters" of words that form thought groups. Then direct them to brainstorm hints they could give to ESL students to help them to listen to such clusters rather than to each separate word.

5. (G) Instruct pairs to specifically identify the redundant words/phrases in the conversation between Matt and Jeff (page 305), and to brainstorm how they would teach students (a) to use such redundancies for comprehension and (b) to overlook them when comprehension is already sufficient.

6. (C) Tape-record a casual conversation between two native speakers of English. In class, play the tape and ask students to pick out as many "performance variables" as they can. How do these performance variables differ from those of a learner of English? Can students be taught to overlook or to compensate for such naturally occurring performance variables?

7. (G) Direct small groups to look again at the taxonomy of listening microskills (Table 18.1) and to make sure they understand each item by offering an example. Groups will then look at the six types of classroom listening performance (pages 309–310), share examples of each, and discuss their appropriateness in the classroom.

8. (G/C) Tell pairs to consider the listening strategies referred to on page 312 and to make sure they understand each strategy. Then, have them sketch out some techniques that they could use to teach such strategies to students. They can then share their techniques with the rest of the class.

9. (G) As a whole class, review the six principles for teaching effective listening techniques on pages 310–312. Then, assign to pairs one or two of the 41 techniques outlined in Table 18.2, and have them systematically evaluate the techniques they have been given. Their evaluation should be based on the six principles.

10. (I) One type of listening technique (combined with writing) not considered in this chapter is dictation (only mentioned in the final section). How useful is dictation? What are the pros and cons of using dictation in a classroom?

11. (G) In small groups, each assigned to one of the four categories listed in the section on assessment, brainstorm some other possible tasks (test methods) that could be employed in each category. Groups will report their findings on the chalkboard, and discuss any difficulties they had in categorizing their tasks.

FOR YOUR FURTHER READING

Rost, M. (2005). L2 listening. In E. Hinkel (Ed.), *Handbook of research in second language teaching and learning* (pp. 503–527). Mahwah, NJ: Lawrence Erlbaum Associates.

Vandergrift, L. (2004). Listening to learn or learning to listen? *Annual Review of Applied Linguistics, 24,* 3–25.

Both of these survey articles review research on listening comprehension. Between the two articles, there is almost no stone unturned as they cover a broad range of research. Both have extensive bibliographies that are useful for searching for references.

Flowerdew, J., & Miller, L. (2005). *Second language listening: Theory and practice.* Cambridge, UK: Cambridge University Press.

Rost, M. (2001). *Teaching and researching listening.* London: Longman.

These two books offer in-depth coverage of research on listening comprehension, as well as practical classroom implications. The authors are well-known experts in the field of L2 aural comprehension.

Helgesen, M., & Brown, S. (2007). *Practical English language teaching: Listening.* New York: McGraw-Hill.

Ur, P. (1984). *Teaching listening comprehension.* Cambridge, UK: Cambridge University Press.

You may think it's a bit unusual to recommend two books that were published 23 years apart! Both are highly practically oriented, with many suggested classroom tasks and activities. Mark Helgesen and Steven Brown give you a current view of listening pedagogy, while Penny Ur's book—a classic in the field—does the same for the early 1980s. A comparison of the two will reveal that there are some new trends, but that most of the "tried and true" tasks of two decades ago are still viable.

Brown, H. D. (2004). *Language assessment: Principles and classroom practices.* White Plains, NY: Pearson Education.

Buck, G. (2001). *Assessing listening.* Cambridge, UK: Cambridge University Press.

My own book gives a survey of language assessment in general, with separate chapters devoted to each of the four skills. The material is classroom-based, written for nonspecialist teachers, and does not require technical knowledge in the field of assessment to comprehend. Gary Buck gives you a detailed look at the assessment of listening; some of the material is a bit technical, but other parts of the book are practical and useful for classroom teachers.

CHAPTER **19**

TEACHING SPEAKING

OBJECTIVES After reading this chapter, you will be able to:

- understand issues and concepts in pedagogical research that are related to teaching speaking

- appreciate factors that might make speaking difficult for students

- analyze types of spoken language, micro- and macroskills, and types of classroom speaking performance

- apply principles of designing speaking techniques to your own lesson designs and to your observation of others' lessons

- evaluate when to treat and when not to treat spoken errors

- recognize some basic principles and formats for assessing speaking

From a communicative, pragmatic view of the language classroom, listening and speaking skills are closely intertwined. More often than not, ESL curricula that treat oral communication skills will simply be labeled as "Listening/Speaking" courses. The interaction between these two modes of performance applies especially strongly to conversation, the most popular discourse category in the profession. And, in the classroom, even relatively unidirectional types of spoken language input (speeches, lectures, etc.) are often followed or preceded by various forms of oral production on the part of students.

Some of the components of teaching spoken language were covered in the previous chapter as we looked closely at teaching listening comprehension: types of spoken language, idiosyncrasies of spoken language that make listening difficult, and listening microskills that are a factor of the oral code. This chapter will build on those considerations as we investigate the teaching of oral communication skills.

ORAL COMMUNICATION SKILLS IN PEDAGOGICAL RESEARCH

A review of some of the current issues in teaching oral communication will help to provide some perspective to the more practical considerations that follow in this chapter.

1. Conversational discourse

When someone asks you "Do you speak English?," they usually mean: Can you carry on a *conversation* reasonably competently? The benchmark of successful language acquisition is almost always the demonstration of an ability to accomplish pragmatic goals through interactive discourse with other speakers of the language. And yet, as Richards (1990, p. 67) noted, "the conversation class is something of an

322

enigma in language teaching." The goals and the techniques for teaching conversation are extremely diverse, depending on the student, teacher, and overall context of the class. Historically, "conversation" classes have ranged from quasi-communicative drilling to free, open, and sometimes agendaless discussions among students.

Recent pedagogical research on teaching conversation has provided some parameters for developing objectives and techniques (McCarthy & O'Keefe, 2004). We have learned to differentiate between transactional and interactional conversation (see Chapter 18). We have discovered techniques for teaching students conversation rules for topic nomination, maintaining a conversation, turn-taking, interruption, and termination. Our pedagogical storehouse has equipped us with ways to teach sociolinguistic appropriateness, styles of speech, nonverbal communication, and conversational routines (such as "Well, I've gotta go now." "Great weather today, huh?" "Haven't I met you somewhere before?"). Within all these foci, the phonological, lexical, and syntactic properties of language can be attended to either directly or indirectly.

2. Teaching pronunciation

There has been some controversy over the role of pronunciation work in a communicative, interactive course of study (Levis, 2005; Setter & Jenkins, 2005; Tarone, 2005). Because the overwhelming majority of adult learners will never acquire an accent-free command of a foreign language, should a language program that emphasizes whole language, meaningful contexts, and automaticity of production focus on these tiny phonological details of language? The answer is yes, but in a different way from what was perceived to be essential a couple of decades ago. This topic will be taken up later in the chapter.

3. Accuracy and fluency

An issue that pervades all of language performance is the distinction between **accuracy** and **fluency** (Bailey, 2003). In spoken language the question we face as teachers is: How shall we prioritize the two clearly important speaker goals of accurate (clear, articulate, grammatically and phonologically correct) language and fluent (flowing, natural) language?

In the mid to late 1970s, egged on by a somewhat short-lived antigrammar approach, some teachers turned away from accuracy issues in favor of providing a plethora of "natural" language activity in their classrooms. The argument was, of course, that adult second language acquisition should simulate the child's first language-learning processes. Our classrooms must not become linguistics courses but rather the locus of meaningful language involvement, or so the argument went. Unfortunately, such classrooms so strongly emphasized the importance of fluency— with a concomitant playing down of the bits and pieces of grammar and phonology—that many students managed to produce fairly fluent but barely comprehensible language. Something was lacking.

It's now very clear that fluency and accuracy are both important goals to pursue in CLT and/or TBLT. While fluency may in many communicative language courses be an *initial* goal in language teaching, accuracy is achieved to some extent by allowing students to focus on the elements of phonology, grammar, and discourse in their spoken output. If you were learning to play tennis instead of a second language, this same philosophy would initially get you out on the tennis court to feel what it's like to hold a racket, to hit the ball, to serve, etc., and then have you focus more cognitively on certain fundamentals. Fluency is probably best achieved by allowing the "stream" of speech to "flow"; then, as some of this speech spills over beyond comprehensibility, the "riverbanks" of instruction on some details of phonology, grammar, or discourse can channel the speech on a more purposeful course.

The fluency/accuracy issue often boils down to the extent to which our techniques should be **message oriented** (or, as some call it, teaching language use) as opposed to **language oriented** (also known as teaching language usage). Current approaches to language teaching lean strongly toward message orientation with language usage offering a supporting role.

4. Affective factors

One of the major obstacles learners have to overcome in learning to speak is the anxiety generated over the risks of blurting things out that are wrong, stupid, or incomprehensible. Because of the **language ego** (see *PLLT,* Chapters 3 and 6) that informs others that "you are what you speak," learners are reluctant to be judged by hearers. Language learners can put a new twist on Mark Twain's quip that "It's better to keep your mouth closed and have others think you are ignorant than to open it and remove all doubt." Our job as teachers is to provide the kind of warm, embracing climate that encourages students to speak, however halting or broken their attempts may be.

5. The interaction effect

The greatest difficulty that learners encounter in attempts to speak is not the multiplicity of sounds, words, phrases, and discourse forms that characterize any language, but rather the interactive nature of most communication. Conversations are collaborative as participants engage in a process of negotiation of meaning. So, for the learner, the matter of what to say—a tremendous task, to be sure—is often eclipsed by conventions of how to say things, when to speak, and other discourse constraints. For example, among the many possible grammatical sentences that a learner could produce in response to a comment, how does that learner make a choice?

Elaine Tarone (2005) reported on a number of studies that claim a crucial role for communication strategies in learning to participate in conversational discourse. A few such strategies are discussed later in this chapter. David Nunan (1991b, p. 47) noted yet another complication in interactive discourse: what he calls the **interlocutor effect**, or the difficulty of a speaking task as gauged by the skills of one's interlocutor.

In other words, one learner's performance is always colored by that of the person (interlocutor) he or she is talking with.

6. Questions about intelligibility

A now outdated model of English language teaching assumed that intelligibility should be gauged by whether nonnative speakers are intelligible to native speakers. This "rather arrogant" (Setter & Jenkins, 2005, p. 5) premise has now evolved into much more complex questions, especially since statistically, most interactions among English speakers are among *non*native speakers. So, materials, technology, and teacher education programs are being challenged to grapple with the issue of intelligibility, and to adopt new standards of "correctness" and new attitudes toward "accent" in order to meet current global realities (Derwing & Munro, 2005; Levis, 2005).

7. The growth of spoken corpora

The intelligibility issue is now being informed by what McCarthy and O'Keefe (2004) describe as a rapid growth of readily available **corpora** of spoken language—one of the key developments in research on teaching oral production. As the size and scope of corpora expand, so our understanding of what people *really* say is informed by empirical evidence. Of special interest to teachers of English worldwide is the wider range of language varieties that are now available through such projects as the International Corpus of English, which contains data from the spoken Englishes of Hong Kong, New Zealand, the United Kingdom, Ireland, Nigeria, the Caribbean, and others.

These data are spurring the language-teaching profession—especially textbook and course developers—to adopt new models that transcend the traditional native-speaker/nonnative-speaker dichotomy. Our notions of what is correct, acceptable, or appropriate, both phonologically and grammatically, are being forced to change.

8. Genres of spoken language

Finally, research on spoken language has recently attended to a specification of differences among various genres of oral interaction, and how to teach those variations (Hughes, 2002). What is judged to be acceptable and/or correct varies by contexts, or genres, such as small talk, discussion, and narrative, among others. As research more accurately describes the constraints of such genres on spoken language, we will be better able to pinpoint models of appropriateness for students' specific purposes in learning English.

TYPES OF SPOKEN LANGUAGE

In the previous chapter, several categories were defined for understanding types of spoken language (see especially Figure 18.1, page 303). In beginning through intermediate levels of proficiency, most of the efforts of students in oral production come in the form of conversation, or dialogue. As you plan and implement techniques in your interactive classroom, make sure your students can deal with both **interpersonal** (sometimes referred to as **interactional**) and **transactional** dialogue and that they are able to converse with a total stranger as well as someone with whom they are quite familiar.

WHAT MAKES SPEAKING DIFFICULT?

Again, Chapter 18 outlined some idiosyncrasies of spoken language that make listening skills somewhat difficult to acquire. These same characteristics must be taken into account in the productive generation of speech, but with a slight twist in that the learner is now the producer. Bear in mind that the following characteristics of spoken language can make oral performance easy as well as, in some cases, difficult.

1. Clustering
Fluent speech is phrasal, not word by word. Learners can organize their output both cognitively and physically (in breath groups) through such clustering.

2. Redundancy
The speaker has an opportunity to make meaning clearer through the redundancy of language. Learners can capitalize on this feature of spoken language.

3. Reduced forms
Contractions, elisions, reduced vowels, etc., all form special problems in teaching spoken English (see the section "Teaching Pronunciation" later in this chapter). Students who don't learn colloquial contractions can sometimes develop a stilted, bookish quality of speaking that in turn stigmatizes them.

4. Performance variables
One of the advantages of spoken language is that the process of thinking as you speak allows you to manifest a certain number of performance hesitations, pauses, backtracking, and corrections. Learners can actually be taught how to pause and hesitate. For example, in English our "thinking time" is not silent; we insert certain "fillers" such as *uh, um, well, you know, I mean, like,* etc. One of the most salient differences between native and nonnative speakers of a language is in their hesitation phenomena.

5. Colloquial language
Make sure your students are reasonably well acquainted with the words, idioms, and phrases of colloquial language and that they get practice in producing these forms.

6. Rate of delivery

Another salient characteristic of fluency is rate of delivery. One of your tasks in teaching spoken English is to help learners achieve an acceptable speed along with other attributes of fluency.

7. Stress, rhythm, and intonation

This is the most important characteristic of English pronunciation, as will be explained below. The stress-timed rhythm of spoken English and its intonation patterns convey important messages.

8. Interaction

As noted in the previous section, learning to produce waves of language in a vacuum—without interlocutors—would rob speaking skill of its richest component: the creativity of conversational negotiation.

MICRO- AND MACROSKILLS OF ORAL COMMUNICATION

In the previous chapter, 17 micro- and macroskills for listening comprehension (adapted from Richards, 1983) were presented. Here, many of the same skills apply, but because of major cognitive and physical differences between listening and speaking, some noticeable alterations have been made, as Table 19.1 on page 328 illustrates.

One implication of such a list is the importance of focusing on both the **forms** of language and the **functions** of language. In teaching oral communication, we don't limit students' attention to the whole picture, even though that whole picture is important. We also help students to see the pieces—right down to the small parts—of language that make up the whole. Just as you would instruct a novice artist in composition, the effect of color hues, shading, and brush stroke techniques, so language students need to be shown the details of how to convey and negotiate the ever-elusive meanings of language.

TYPES OF CLASSROOM SPEAKING PERFORMANCE

In Chapter 18, six types of listening performance were listed. With the obvious connection between listening and speaking, six similar categories apply to the kinds of oral production that students are expected to carry out in the classroom.

1. Imitative

A very limited portion of classroom speaking time may legitimately be spent generating "human tape recorder" speech, where, for example, learners practice an intonation contour or try to pinpoint a certain vowel sound. Imitation of this kind is carried out not for the purpose of meaningful interaction, but for focusing on some particular element of language form.

Table 19.1. Micro- and macroskills of oral communication

Microskills

1. Produce chunks of language of different lengths.
2. Orally produce differences among the English phonemes and allophonic variants.
3. Produce English stress patterns, words in stressed and unstressed positions, rhythmic structure, and intonational contours.
4. Produce reduced forms of words and phrases.
5. Use an adequate number of lexical units (words) in order to accomplish pragmatic purposes.
6. Produce fluent speech at different rates of delivery.
7. Monitor your own oral production and use various strategic devices—pauses, fillers, self-corrections, backtracking—to enhance the clarity of the message.
8. Use grammatical word classes (nouns, verbs, etc.), systems (e.g., tense, agreement, pluralization), word order, patterns, rules, and elliptical forms.
9. Produce speech in natural constituents—in appropriate phrases, pause groups, breath groups, and sentences.
10. Express a particular meaning in different grammatical forms.

Macroskills

11. Use cohesive devices in spoken discourse.
12. Accomplish appropriately communicative functions according to situations, participants, and goals.
13. Use appropriate registers, implicature, pragmatic conventions, and other sociolinguistic features in face-to-face conversations.
14. Convey links and connections between events and communicate such relations as main idea, supporting idea, new information, given information, generalization, and exemplification.
15. Use facial features, kinesics, body language, and other nonverbal cues along with verbal language to convey meanings.
16. Develop and use a battery of speaking strategies, such as emphasizing key words, rephrasing, providing a context for interpreting the meaning of words, appealing for help, and accurately assessing how well your interlocutor is understanding you.

New teachers in the field always want the answer to this question: Is *drilling* a legitimate part of the communicative language classroom? The answer is a qualified yes. Drills offer students an opportunity to listen and to orally repeat certain strings of language that may pose some linguistic difficulty—either phonological or grammatical. Drills are to language teaching what the pitching machine is to baseball. They offer limited practice through repetition. They allow one to focus on one element of language in a controlled activity. They can help to establish certain psychomotor patterns (to "loosen the tongue") and to associate selected grammatical forms with their appropriate context. Here are some useful guidelines for successful drills:

- Keep them short (a few minutes of a class hour only).
- Keep them simple (preferably just one point at a time).
- Keep them "snappy."
- Make sure students know why they are doing the drill.
- Limit them to phonology or grammar points.
- Make sure they ultimately lead to communicative goals.
- Don't overuse them.

2. Intensive

Intensive speaking goes one step beyond imitative to include any speaking performance that is designed to practice some phonological or grammatical aspect of language. Intensive speaking can be self-initiated, or it can even form part of some pair work activity, where learners are "going over" certain forms of language.

3. Responsive

A good deal of student speech in the classroom is responsive: short replies to teacher- or student-initiated questions or comments. These replies are usually sufficient and do not extend into dialogues (#4 and #5). Such speech can be meaningful and authentic:

T: How are you today?
S: Pretty good, thanks, and you?

T: What is the main idea in this essay?
S: The United Nations should have more authority.

S1: So, what did you write for question number one?
S2: Well, I wasn't sure, so I left it blank.

4. Transactional (dialogue)

Transactional language, carried out for the purpose of conveying or exchanging specific information, is an extended form of responsive language. Conversations, for example, may have more of a negotiative nature to them than does responsive speech:

T: What is the main idea in this essay?
S: The United Nations should have more authority.
T: More authority than what?
S: Than it does right now.
T: What do you mean?
S: Well, for example, the UN should have the power to force certain countries to destroy its nuclear weapons.

> **T:** You don't think the UN has that power now?
>
> **S:** Obviously not. Several countries are currently manufacturing nuclear bombs.

Such conversations could readily be part of group work activity as well.

5. Interpersonal (dialogue)

The other form of conversation mentioned in the previous chapter was interpersonal dialogue, carried out more for the purpose of maintaining social relationships than for the transmission of facts and information. These conversations are a little trickier for learners because they can involve some or all of the following factors:

- a casual register
- colloquial language
- emotionally charged language
- slang
- ellipsis
- sarcasm
- a covert "agenda"

For example:

> **Amy:** Hi, Bob, how's it going?
>
> **Bob:** Oh, so-so.
>
> **Amy:** Not a great weekend, huh?
>
> **Bob:** Well, far be it from me to criticize, but I'm pretty miffed about last week.
>
> **Amy:** What are you talking about?
>
> **Bob:** I think you know perfectly well what I'm talking about.
>
> **Amy:** Oh, that . . . How come you get so bent out of shape over something like that?
>
> **Bob:** Well, whose fault was it, huh?
>
> **Amy:** Oh, wow, this is great. Wonderful. Back to square one. For crying out loud, Bob, I thought we'd settled this before. Well, what more can I say?

Learners would need to learn how such features as the relationship between interlocutors, casual style, and sarcasm are coded linguistically in this conversation.

6. Extensive (monologue)

Finally, students at intermediate to advanced levels are called on to give extended monologues in the form of oral reports, summaries, or perhaps short speeches. Here the register is more formal and deliberative. These monologues can be planned or impromptu.

PRINCIPLES FOR TEACHING SPEAKING SKILLS

1. Focus on both fluency and accuracy, depending on your objective.

In our current zeal for interactive language teaching, we can easily slip into a pattern of providing zesty content-based, interactive activities that don't capitalize on grammatical pointers or pronunciation tips. We need to bear in mind a spectrum of learner needs, from language-based focus on accuracy to message-based focus on interaction, meaning, and fluency. When you do a jigsaw group technique, play a game, or discuss solutions to the environmental crisis, make sure that your tasks have a linguistic (language-based) objective, and seize the opportunity to help students to perceive and use the building blocks of language. At the same time, don't bore your students to death with lifeless, repetitious drills. As noted above, make any drilling you do as meaningful as possible.

2. Provide intrinsically motivating techniques.

Try at all times to appeal to students' ultimate goals and interests, to their need for knowledge, for status, for achieving competence and autonomy, and for "being all that they can be." Even in those techniques that don't send students into ecstasy, help them to see how the activity will benefit them. Often students don't know why we ask them to do certain things; it usually pays to tell them.

3. Encourage the use of authentic language in meaningful contexts.

This theme has been played time and again in this book, but one more reminder shouldn't hurt! It is not easy to keep coming up with meaningful interaction. We all succumb to the temptation to do, say, disconnected little grammar exercises where we go around the room calling on students one by one to pick the right answer. It takes energy and creativity to devise authentic contexts and meaningful interaction, but with the help of a storehouse of teacher resource material (see the recommended books and articles at the end of this chapter) it can be done. Even drills (see pages 342–344) can be structured to provide a sense of authenticity.

4. Provide appropriate feedback and correction.

In most EFL situations, students are totally dependent on the teacher for useful linguistic feedback. In ESL situations, they may get such feedback "out there" beyond the classroom, but even then you are in a position to be of great benefit. It is important that you take advantage of your knowledge of English to inject the kinds of corrective feedback that are appropriate for the moment.

5. Capitalize on the natural link between speaking and listening.

Many interactive techniques that involve speaking will also of course include listening. Don't lose out on opportunities to integrate these two skills. As you are perhaps focusing on speaking goals, listening goals may naturally coincide, and the two skills can reinforce each other. Skills in producing language are often initiated through comprehension.

6. Give students opportunities to initiate oral communication.

A good deal of typical classroom interaction is characterized by teacher initiation of language. We ask questions, give directions, and provide information, and students have been conditioned only to "speak when spoken to." Part of oral communication competence is the ability to initiate conversations, to nominate topics, to ask questions, to control conversations, and to change the subject. As you design and use speaking techniques, ask yourself if you have allowed students to initiate language.

7. Encourage the development of speaking strategies.

The concept of strategic competence (see Chapter 16; *PLLT,* Chapters 5 and 8) is one that few beginning language students are aware of. They simply have not thought about developing their own personal strategies for accomplishing oral communicative purposes. Your classroom can be one in which students become aware of, and have a chance to practice, such strategies as

- asking for clarification (*What?*)
- asking someone to repeat something (*Huh? Excuse me?*)
- using fillers (*Uh, I mean, Well*) in order to gain time to process
- using conversation maintenance cues (*Uh-huh, Right, Yeah, Okay, Hm*)
- getting someone's attention (*Hey, Say, So*)
- using paraphrases for structures one can't produce
- appealing for assistance from the interlocutor (to get a word or phrase, for example)
- using formulaic expressions (at the survival stage) (*How much does _____ cost? How do you get to the _____?*)
- using mime and nonverbal expressions to convey meaning

TEACHING CONVERSATION

Research on teaching conversational skills (McCarthy & O'Keefe, 2004; Tarone, 2005) historically describes two major approaches for teaching conversation. The first is an **indirect** approach in which learners are more or less set loose to engage in interaction. The second is a **direct** approach that "involves planning a conversation program around the specific microskills, strategies, and processes that are involved in fluent conversation" (Richards, 1990, pp. 76–77). The indirect approach implies that one does not actually *teach* conversation, but rather that students acquire conversational competence, peripherally, by engaging in meaningful tasks. A direct approach explicitly calls students' attention to conversational rules, conventions, and strategies.

While both approaches can be found in language-teaching institutions around the world, recent developments in such models as task-based language instruction have taken the learner well beyond simply using language. Nunan (2004), Ellis

(2003), and Willis (1996), in their descriptions of task-based instruction, for example, included focus on form, including analysis and practice, as an integral part of every task. Likewise, Skehan (1998a, p. 131) recommended that communicative tasks "maximize the chances of a focus on form through attentional manipulation." It is clear, upon scanning current English language textbooks, that the prevailing approach to teaching conversation includes the learner's inductive involvement in meaningful tasks as well as consciousness-raising elements of focus on form.

Richards (1990, pp. 79–80) offered the following list of features of conversation that can receive specific focus in classroom instruction:

- how to use conversation for both transactional and interactional purposes
- how to produce both short and long turns in conversation
- strategies for managing turn-taking in conversation, including taking a turn, holding a turn, and relinquishing a turn
- strategies for opening and closing conversations
- how to initiate and respond to talk on a broad range of topics, and how to develop and maintain talk on these topics
- how to use both a casual style of speaking and a neutral or more formal style
- how to use conversation in different social settings and for different kinds of social encounters, such as on the telephone and in informal and formal social gatherings
- strategies for repairing trouble spots in conversation, including communication breakdown and comprehension problems
- how to maintain fluency in conversation through avoiding excessive pausing, breakdowns, and errors of grammar or pronunciation
- how to produce talk in a conversational mode, using a conversational register and syntax
- how to use conversational fillers and small talk
- how to use conversational routines

It isn't possible in the context of one introductory chapter on teaching speaking to call attention to all the possible techniques and tasks available for teaching these features of conversation. I recommend that you turn to such books as Bailey (2005), Golebiowska (1990), and Klippel (1984) for an exploratory journey into some of the possibilities. What follows here (including Figures 19.1, 19.2, and 19.3) are some sample tasks that illustrate teaching various aspects of conversation, as well as an oral grammar practice technique (Figure 19.4). (Note: For more on oral grammar instruction, see Chapter 22.)

A. Conversation—Indirect (strategy consciousness-raising)

Figure 19.1. (adapted from Nolasco & Arthur, 1987, pp. 105–106)

<table>
<tr><td></td><td colspan="2">PLAN YOUR TIME</td></tr>
<tr><td>Level</td><td>Intermediate or above</td></tr>
<tr><td>Time</td><td>30–35 minutes</td></tr>
<tr><td>Aim</td><td>For students to consider ways in which they can learn English outside the classroom</td></tr>
<tr><td>Preparation</td><td>Make photocopies of the task sheet for your class.</td></tr>
<tr><td>Procedure</td><td>

1. Arouse student interest in the planning task.
2. Set up the initial pair work and give the students five to ten minutes to discuss, add to, or modify the list of suggestions.
3. When the initial discussion is over, you should facilitate the setting up of groups. Allow the groups a maximum of twenty minutes to complete the planning task.
4. Chair the report-back session in which each group presents its suggestions. Make OHTs or posters available to help the groups present their ideas.
</td></tr>
<tr><td>Task Sheet</td><td>

Here is a list of techniques that people use to help them learn English outside the classroom:
—memorizing a list of words
—reading a grammar book
—doing grammar exercises
—reading a book or magazine in English
—recopying things from their class notebook
—correcting mistakes made in written work
—preparing the next unit of the coursebook
Work with a partner and add any others of your own. Tell each other which ones in the list you find helpful, if any, then tell the class about the new ones you have added.

Arrange yourselves in groups and take a time period from this list:
—thirty minutes per day for six days a week
—one hour per day for five days a week
—two hours per day for four days a week
In your group, plan a program to show how you could make use of the time to do extra work on your English. Use the ideas from the earlier list, as well as any others you can think of. Choose one person to present your plan to the rest of the class.
</td></tr>
<tr><td>Remarks</td><td>If students agree to experiment with a study plan, some time should be allowed in class for them to discuss how they are getting on.</td></tr>
</table>

B. Conversation—Direct (gambits)

Figure 19.2. (adapted from Nolasco & Arthur, 1987, pp. 40–41)

IS THAT RIGHT?

Level	Elementary and above
Time	10–15 minutes
Aim	To help students recognize gambits
Preparation	Find a short cassette or video recording of two or three people chatting naturally. Identify examples of short responses being used and put them in random order on a task sheet, chalkboard, or OHT, along the following lines. You can add distractors if you wish. The task sheet might look like this:

Task Sheet

Read the following list of expressions, listen to the tape. Tick (✔) any of the expressions you hear. You may hear some expressions more than once:

Is that right?	_____	That's great!	_____
Really . . .?	_____	Oh, dear.	_____
How interesting!	_____	What a shame!	_____
Er . . . hum.	_____	Oh, no!	_____
Fine.	_____	You're joking!	_____
I see.	_____		

Procedure

1. Give a task sheet to each student and ask them to tick off the examples they hear on the tape.
2. When they have done this, choose two or three examples to focus on and see if the students can recall the utterances that precede or follow them on the tape.

C. Conversation—Transactional (ordering from a catalog)

Figure 19.3. (from H.D. Brown, *New Vistas 2*, 1999, pp. 131)

Information Gap Activity ✏️   Student A

You are a telephone salesperson for the Best Wear Company. Your partner is a customer. Your partner calls to order some items from your company's catalog. Take the order and fill out the order form. Make sure you have written the order correctly by asking your partner to confirm it. Don't look at your partner's page!

Ordered by:

Name _____

Address _____

City _____

State _____ Zip _____

Telephone _____

Ship to: (Use only if different from "ORDERED BY")

Name _____

Address _____

City _____

State _____ Zip _____

Item number	Quantity	Color	Size	Description	Unit price	Total

Check Method of Payment:

( ) check /   ( ) VISA

     money order   ( ) MASTERCARD

Card number: _____

Expiration date: _____

Merchandise Total	
Shipping and Handling	
Total	

Useful Language

Answering the telephone:	Hello, Best Wear Company.
Asking for information:	What's the item number (or price)?
	What color (or size) would you like?
Confirming the order:	Did you say the item number
	(or price or color or size) was . . .?
Ending the conversation:	Thank you for your order. Good-bye.

© 1999 Prentice Hall Regents. Duplication for classroom use is permitted.

Unit 7 Blackline Master 131

Figure 19.4. (from H.D. Brown, *New Vistas 2*, 1999, p. 132)

Information Gap Activity

Student B

You want to place a catalog order. Your partner is a telephone salesperson. Look at the catalog page below. Choose two items you want to buy. Call the Best Wear Company and give your order to your partner. Make sure that your partner takes the order correctly by confirming the information. Don't look at your partner's page!

40% OFF ALL SLEEPWEAR FOR BOYS

#1234X Boys' FLANNEL PAJAMAS
Sizes: S, M, L, XL.
Colors: Red, Blue, Green
Reg. $20, **Sale** $11.99

ALL WATCHES ARE ON SALE!
$29.99 *each*

WATER-RESISTANT SPORTS WATCHES
SHOWN:
A. # 7875P EXPLORER
B. # 7876Q GOLDMAN
C. # 7877F DECATHLON
Reg. $39.99, **Sale** $29.99

SAVE ON GIRLS' JEANS
$9.99

#0017G Girls' HIGH MOUNTAIN JEANS
Slim & Regular Sizes 7–16.
Colors: Blue, Brown, Black
Reg. $15, **Sale** $9.99

EVERY SWEATER FOR HER IS ON SALE!

$17.99

#2323W COTTON/ACRYLIC SWEATERS
Sizes: S, M, L.
Colors: Black, Red, Green, Blue
Reg. $28, **Sale** $17.99

SAVE ON GIFTS FOR MEN

$14.95

#1185D CLASSIC SUEDE SLIPPERS
Sizes: 7/8–12/13.
Reg. $20, **Sale** $14.95

25%–40% OFF ALL WOMENS' HANDBAGS!

A. #4440H VINYL TOTE
Black only. Reg. $14, **Sale** $10.99
B. #4445B PATCHED LEATHER BAG
Colors: Black, Brown.
Reg. $24.99, **Sale** $19.99
C. #4447B DENIM BACKPACK
Blue only. Reg. $20, **Sale** $14.99

Useful Language

Starting the conversation:	Hello. I'd like to place an order.
Placing an order:	I'd like ....
Confirming the order:	Yes, I said the item number (price or color or size) is ....

© 1999 Prentice Hall Regents. Duplication for classroom use is permitted.

D. Meaningful oral grammar practice (modal auxillary would)

Figure 19.5. (adapted from Nolasco & Arthur, 1987, pp. 45–46)

JE NE REGRETTE RIEN

Level	Intermediate and above
Time	15–20 minutes
Aim	To give students practice in hypothetical *would*
Preparation	None
Procedure	1. Put the following list on the board or on an OHT:

        —Your school
        —Your job or occupation
        —Your friends
        —Your habits, e.g., smoking, exercising, eating, etc.
        —Your hobbies, e.g., playing the piano, stamp collecting, etc.
        —Your skills, e.g., languages, carpentry, etc.

2. Ask the students to write a personal entry for each heading, i.e., the name of their school, job, etc. They should then decide which of these they would or would not change if they were to live their lives again.
3. Once they have done this, encourage them to share their thoughts in small groups of three or four.
4. Ask the students to take turns telling others in the group what they would change if they had their life again. The others can ask questions or comment.
5. Wind up the activity by seeing if there are any areas that most of the class would want to change.

Remarks The title of the activity comes from an Edith Piaf song. An English version is called "No Regrets." It would make a lively and stimulating start to this activity.

E. Individual practice: Oral dialogue journals

For extra-class practice, aside from recommending that your students seek out opportunities for authentic use of English, several teacher trainers (Celce-Murcia & Goodwin, 1991; McDonald, 1989) recommend using oral dialogue journals. Written dialogue journals (where the student records thoughts, ideas, and/or reactions, and the teacher reads and responds with written comments) have been in use for some time. Why not use the convenience of a voice (digital or tape) recorder for audio journals? With large classes, such a technique is too time-consuming for the teacher, but for individual students, tutees, or very small classes, it offers students a way to express themselves (without risking ridicule from peers) orally, to convey real concerns and thoughts, to practice speaking, and to get feedback from the teacher on both form and content.

F. Other interactive techniques

Of course, many other tasks and techniques can be applied to the teaching of conversation. They are almost impossible to categorize, but here are a few possible types, gleaned simply from the table of contents of Friederike Klippel's (1984) practical little resource book:

- interviews
- guessing games
- jigsaw tasks
- ranking exercises
- discussions

- values clarification
- problem-solving activities
- role plays
- simulations

TEACHING PRONUNCIATION

Views on teaching pronunciation changed dramatically over the last half of the twentieth century (see Tarone, 2005, for a synopsis). In the heyday of audiolingualism and its various behavioristic methodological variants, the pronunciation component of a course or program was a mainstay. In the 1970s, as the language-teaching profession began to experience a revolution of sorts (see Chapter 2), explicit pedagogical focus on anything that smacked of linguistic nuts and bolts was under siege by proponents of the various nondirective "let-it-just-happen" approaches to language teaching. Pronunciation instruction became somewhat incidental to a course of study. By the mid-1980s, with greater attention to grammatical structures as important elements in discourse, to a balance between fluency and accuracy, and to the explicit specification of pedagogical tasks that a learner should accomplish, it became clear that pronunciation was a key to gaining full communicative competence.

Current approaches to pronunciation contrast starkly with the early approaches. Rather than attempting only to build a learner's articulatory competence from the bottom up, and simply as the mastery of a list of phonemes and allophones, a top-down approach is now taken in which the most relevant features of pronunciation— stress, rhythm, and intonation—are given high priority. Instead of teaching only the role of articulation within words, or at best, phrases, we teach its role in a whole stream of discourse. Over two decades ago, Rita Wong (1987, p. 21) reminded us that "contemporary views [of language] hold that the sounds of language are less crucial for understanding than the way they are organized. The rhythm and intonation of English are two major organizing structures that native speakers rely on to process speech. . . . Because of their major roles in communication, rhythm and intonation merit greater priority in the teaching program than attention to individual sounds."

Wong's comments reflect an approach that puts all aspects of English pronunciation into the perspective of a communicative, interactive, whole language view of human speech. Once again, history taught us the lesson of maintaining balance.

Many learners of foreign languages feel that their ultimate goal in pronunciation should be accent-free speech that is indistinguishable from that of a native speaker. Such a goal is not only unattainable (see *PLLT*, Chapter 3) for virtually every adult learner, but in a multilingual, multicultural world, accents are quite acceptable. With the rapid spread of English as an international language, native accents have become almost irrelevant to cross-cultural communication. Moreover, as the world community comes to appreciate and value people's heritage, one's accent is just another symbol of that heritage.

Our goal as teachers of English pronunciation should therefore be more realistically focused on clear, comprehensible pronunciation. At the beginning levels, we want learners to surpass that threshold beneath which pronunciation detracts from their ability to communicate. At the advanced levels, pronunciation goals can focus on elements that enhance communication: intonation features that go beyond basic patterns, voice quality, phonetic distinctions between registers, and other refinements that are far more important in the overall stream of clear communication than rolling the English /r/ or getting a vowel to perfectly imitate a "native speaker."

What are the factors within learners that affect pronunciation, and how can you deal with each of them? Below is a list (adapted from Kenworthy, 1987, pp. 4–8) of variables that you should consider.

1. **Native language.** Clearly, the native language is the most influential factor affecting a learner's pronunciation (see *PLLT*, Chapter 9). If you are familiar with the sound system of a learner's native language, you will be better able to diagnose student difficulties. Many L1–L2 carryovers can be overcome through a focused awareness and effort on the learner's part.

2. **Age.** Generally speaking, children under the age of puberty stand an excellent chance of "sounding like a native" if they have continued exposure in authentic contexts. Beyond the age of puberty, while adults will almost surely maintain a "foreign accent," there is no particular advantage attributed to age (see *PLLT*, Chapter 3). A 50-year-old can be as successful as an 18-year-old if all other factors are equal. Remind your students, especially if your students are older, that "the younger, the better" is a myth.

3. **Exposure.** It is difficult to define exposure. One can actually live in a foreign country for some time but not take advantage of being "with the people." Research seems to support the notion that the quality and intensity of exposure are more important than mere length of time. If class time spent focusing on pronunciation demands the full attention and interest of your students, then they stand a good chance of reaching their goals.

4. **Innate phonetic ability.** Often referred to as having an "ear" for language, some people manifest a phonetic coding ability that others do not. In many cases, if a person has had exposure to a foreign language as a child, this "knack" is present whether the early language is remembered or not. Others are simply more attuned to phonetic discriminations. Some people would have you believe that you either have such a knack, or you don't. Strategies-based instruction (see Chapter 16), however, has proven that some elements of learning are a matter of an awareness of your own limitations combined with a conscious focus on doing something to compensate for those limitations. Therefore, if pronunciation seems to be naturally difficult for some students, they should not despair; with some effort and concentration, they can improve their competence.

5. **Identity and language ego.** Yet another influence is one's attitude toward speakers of the target language and the extent to which the language ego identifies with those speakers. Learners need to be reminded of the importance of positive attitudes toward the people who speak the language (if such a target is identifiable), but more important, students need to become aware of—and not afraid of—the second identity that may be emerging within them.

6. **Motivation and concern for good pronunciation.** Some learners are not particularly concerned about their pronunciation, while others are. The extent to which learners' intrinsic motivation propels them toward improvement will be perhaps the strongest influence of all six of the factors in this list. If that motivation and concern are high, then the necessary effort will be expended in pursuit of goals. You can help learners to perceive or develop that motivation by showing, among other things, how clarity of speech is significant in shaping their self-image and, ultimately, in reaching some of their higher goals.

All six of the above factors suggest that any learner who really wants to can learn to pronounce English clearly and comprehensibly. You can assist in the process by gearing your planned and unplanned instruction toward these six factors.

On the next few pages (including Figures 19.6 and 19.7), you will find three techniques for teaching different aspects of English pronunciation. Take note of how those techniques may capitalize on the positive benefits of the six factors above, and the extent to which they reflect a discourse-based view of pronunciation teaching. A significant factor for you in the success of such techniques lies in your ability to instill in your students the motivation to put forth the effort needed to develop clear, comprehensible pronunciation.

A. Intonation—Listening for pitch changes

Figure 19.6. (adapted from Wong, 1987, p. 61)

Record the following conversation and play it for the students. Establish the participants, the setting, and the event by asking the students to guess who and what they are.

He:	Ready? ↗
She:	No. ↘
He:	Why? ↘
She:	Problems. ↘
He:	Problems? ↗
She:	Yes. ↘
He:	What? ↘
She:	Babysitter. ↘

After the students have figured out what is going on, you can play the conversation again. This time put the transcription of the conversation on the board or on an overhead projector and ask the students to try to determine for each utterance whether the speaker's voice ends with a rising or falling pitch. Draw arrows next to each utterance and play the conversation once more. To isolate pitch from the words, you can use a kazoo, which can be purchased at a toy store (see Gilbert, 1978). By humming into it, you can demonstrate rising and falling pitch to the amusement and illumination of your students.

Ask the students to explain what each utterance means. Then point out that a change in pitch can indicate a change in meaning (e.g., "Ready?" with a rising pitch means "Are you ready?" but "Ready" with a falling pitch means "I am ready").

Additional practice dialogues are provided here. Make up more for your particular students. Follow the procedure described for the first conversation.

Conversation B	Conversation C	Conversation D
A: Single?	A: Good?	A: Locked?
B: Double.	B: Delicious.	B: Locked.
A: Double?	A: More?	A: Key?
B: Yes.	B: Please.	B: Key?
A: Cone?		A: Key.
B: Cup.		B: Oh-oh.

B. Stress—Contrasting nouns

Figure 19.7. (adapted from Nolasco & Arthur, 1987, pp. 67–68)

I WANT A BLUE ONE!

Level	Elementary to Intermediate
Time	10–15 minutes
Aim	To give students stress practice in the context of a drill
Preparation	Prepare 27 little cards with a picture on each to cover all the possible permutations of the following colors, fabrics, and items of clothing. The items can be increased and/or varied if required:

red	woolen	dress
blue	cotton	shirt
black	nylon	sweater

The cards should look like this:

woolen   cotton   nylon

Procedure

1. Set up a clothing store situation. Show students the cards to indicate what they can buy, and write a substitution table on the board like this:

I'd like a	red woolen dress,	please.
	blue cotton sweater,	
	black nylon shirt,	

2. Take the role of the salesclerk, and ask the students to take turns to ask for something in the shop. Whenever a student asks for something, you should hand over a picture, making an error in either the color, the fabric, or the item of clothing. The student then has to correct the error using appropriate stress and intonation. The dialogue should go like this:

> Student: I'd like a red cotton dress, please.
> Teacher: Here you are.
> Student: No. I asked for a *red* cotton dress, not a *blue* one.
> or
> Student: I'd like a black woolen shirt, please.
> Teacher: Here you are.
> Student: No. I said a black woolen *shirt*, not a black woolen *skirt*.

Remarks

3. When they have got the hang of the exercise, divide the cards out among pairs of students so that they can practice on their own.

This activity could be used with other objects and adjectives.

C. Meaningful minimal pairs

Traditional minimal-pair drills, used for decades in language teaching, go something like this:

> **T:** Okay, class, on the board, picture number 1 is a "pen," and picture number 2 is a "pin." Listen: Pen [*points to number 1*], pin [*points to number 2*] [*several repetitions*]. Now, I'm going to say either number 1 or number 2. You tell me which. Ready? [*pause*] Pin.
>
> **Ss:** Number 2.
>
> **T:** Good. Ready. Pin.
>
> **Ss:** Number 2.
>
> **T:** Okay. [*pause*] Pen.
>
> **Ss:** Number 1.

CLT and TBLT principles prod us to be a little more meaningful. In the following examples you can see that a little contextualization goes a long way:

> **1. T:** This pen leaks.
>   **S:** Then don't write with it.
>   **T:** This pan leaks.
>   **S:** Then don't cook with it.
>
> **2. T:** Where can I buy cold créam?
>   **S:** At the dairy.
>   **T:** Where can I buy cóld cream?
>   **S:** At the drugstore.
>
> **3. T:** The sun is hot on my head!
>   **S:** Then get a cap.
>   **T:** Oh, no, I missed the bus. I'm going to be late!
>   **S:** Then get a cab.

These are good examples of drilling techniques that have been modified to bring context, interest, and a modicum of authenticity to what would otherwise be a very mechanical task.

FOCUS ON FORM AND ERROR TREATMENT

One of the most frequently posed questions by teachers who are new to the trade is the following: When and how should I correct the speech errors of learners in my classroom? This happens also to be one of the most enigmatic questions in the language-teaching profession. I offer some guidelines here, but at the same time urge you to read the last part of Chapter 9 of *PLLT,* where issues surrounding form-focused instruction are described in more detail.

The Role of Feedback

One of the keys, but not the only key, to successful second language learning lies in the feedback that a learner receives from others. Chapter 9 of *PLLT* described Vigil and Oller's (1976) model of how affective and cognitive feedback affects the message-sending process. Figure 19.8 depicts, metaphorically at least, what happens in Vigil and Oller's model in the case of learners' orally produced utterances.

Figure 19.8. Affective and cognitive feedback

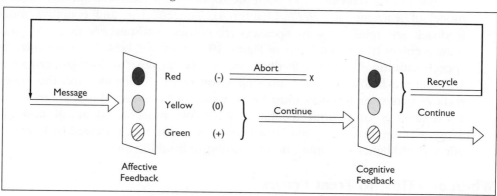

The "green light" of the affective feedback mode allows the sender to continue attempting to get a message across; a "red light" causes the sender to abort the attempt. (The metaphorical nature of such a chart is evident in the fact that affective feedback does not precede cognitive feedback, as this chart may lead you to believe; both modes can take place simultaneously.) The traffic signal of cognitive feedback is the point at which error treatment enters. A green light here symbolizes noncorrective feedback that says, "I understand your message." A red light symbolizes corrective feedback that takes on a myriad of possible forms (outlined below) and causes the learner to make some kind of alteration in production. To push the metaphor further, a yellow light could represent those various shades of color that are interpreted by the learner as falling somewhere in between a complete green light and a red light, causing the learner to adjust, to alter, to recycle back, to try again in some way. Note that fossilization may be the result of too many green lights when there should have been some yellow or red lights.

The most useful implication of Vigil and Oller's model for determining how you will administer error treatment is that cognitive feedback must be *optimal* in order to be effective. Too much negative cognitive feedback—a barrage of interruptions, corrections, and overt attention to malformations—often leads learners to shut off their attempts at communication. They perceive that so much is wrong with their production that there is little hope of getting anything right. On the other hand, too much positive cognitive feedback—willingness of the teacher-hearer to let errors go uncorrected, to indicate understanding when understanding may not have occurred—serves to reinforce the errors of the speaker-learner. The result is the persistence, and perhaps the eventual fossilization (or stabilization), of such errors. The task of the teacher is to discern the optimal tension between positive and negative cognitive feedback: providing enough green lights to encourage continued communication, but not so many that crucial errors go unnoticed; and providing enough red lights to call attention to those crucial errors, but not so many that the learner is discouraged from attempting to speak at all.

We do well to recall at this point the application of Skinner's operant conditioning model of learning (see *PLLT,* Chapter 4). The affective and cognitive modes of feedback are reinforcers to speakers' responses. As speakers perceive "positive" reinforcement (the green lights of Figure 19.8), they will be led to internalize certain speech patterns. Corrective feedback can still be "positive" in the Skinnerian sense, as we shall see below. Because ignoring erroneous behavior also has the effect of a positive reinforcer, teachers must be very careful to discern the possible reinforcing consequences of neutral feedback. What we must avoid at all costs is the administration of *punitive* reinforcement—correction that is viewed by learners as an affective red light—devaluing, dehumanizing, or insulting them.

When and How to Treat Errors

Against this theoretical backdrop we can evaluate some possibilities of when and how to treat errors in the language classroom. Michael Long (1977, p. 288) suggested that the question of *when* to treat an error (that is, which errors to provide some sort of feedback on) has no simple answer:

> Having noticed an error, the first (and, I would argue, crucial) decision the teacher makes is whether or not to treat it at all. In order to make the decision the teacher may have recourse to factors with immediate, temporary bearing, such as the importance of the error to the current pedagogical focus of the lesson, the teacher's perception of the chance of eliciting correct performance from the student if negative feedback is given, and so on. Consideration of these ephemeral factors may be preempted, however, by the teacher's beliefs (conscious or unconscious) as to what a language is and how a new one is learned. These beliefs may have been formed years before the lesson in question.

In a very practical article on error treatment, James Hendrickson (1980) advised teachers to try to discern the difference between global and local errors (to be described later in this chapter). Once a learner of English was describing a quaint old hotel in Europe and said, "There is a French widow in every bedroom." The local error is clearly—and humorously—recognized. Hendrickson recommended that local errors usually need not be corrected since the message is clear and correction might interrupt a learner in the flow of productive communication. Global errors need to be treated in some way since the message may otherwise remain garbled. "The different city is another one in the another two" is a sentence that would certainly need treatment because it is incomprehensible as is. Many utterances are not clearly global or local, and it is difficult to discern the necessity for corrective feedback. A learner once wrote, "The grammar is the basement of every language." While this witty little proclamation may indeed sound more like Chomsky than Chomsky does, it behooves the teacher to ascertain just what the learner meant here (no doubt "basis" rather than "basement"), and to provide some feedback to clarify the difference between the two. The bottom line is that we simply must not stifle our students' attempts at production by smothering them with corrective feedback.

The matter of *how* to treat errors is complex. Research on error correction methods is not at all conclusive on the most effective method or technique. It seems quite clear that students in the classroom generally want and expect errors to be corrected. However, some methods recommend no direct treatment of error at all (Krashen & Terrell, 1983). After all, in natural, untutored environments, nonnative speakers generally get corrected by native speakers on only a small percentage of errors that they make. Balancing these perspectives, I think we can safely conclude that a sensitive and perceptive language teacher should make the language classroom a happy optimum between some of the overpoliteness of the real world and the expectations that learners bring with them to the classroom.

Error treatment options can be classified in a number of possible ways, but one useful taxonomy was recommended by Kathleen Bailey (1985, p. 111). Seven "basic options" are complemented by eight "possible features" within each option.

Basic Options	**Possible Features**
1. To treat or to ignore	1. Fact of error indicated
2. To treat immediately or to delay	2. Location indicated
3. To transfer treatment (to, say, other learners) or not	3. Opportunity for new attempt given
4. To transfer to another individual, a subgroup, or the whole class	4. Model provided
5. To return, or not, to the original error maker after treatment	5. Error type indicated
6. To permit other learners to initiate treatment	6. Remedy indicated
7. To test for the efficacy of the treatment	7. Improvement indicated
	8. Praise indicated

All of the basic options and features within each option are viable modes of error treatment in the classroom. *It is important to understand that not all error treatment is error correction.* Among Bailey's eight features, it is possible to see *none* of them as a correction, in that none (with the possible exception of #6) specify the wrong form and supply the correct form. Error treatment encompasses a wide range of options, one of which—at the extreme end of a continuum—may be considered to be a correction. The research (Williams, 2005) shows that the best way to help a learner to repair malformed utterances is, first, to assist the learner in *noticing* an incorrect form (through recasts, prompts, and other attention-getting devices), and second, for the learner to initiate repair (with as little prompting as possible from the teacher).

The teacher needs to develop the intuition, through experience and established theoretical foundations, for ascertaining which option or combination of options is appropriate at given moments. Principles of optimal affective and cognitive feedback, of reinforcement theory, and of communicative language teaching all combine to form those intuitions.

One step toward developing such intuitions may be taken by considering the model in Figure 19.9, which illustrates what I would claim are the split-second series of decisions that a teacher makes when a student has uttered some deviant form of English in the classroom. In those few nanoseconds, information is accessed, processed, and evaluated, with a decision forthcoming on what the teacher is going to "do" about the deviant form. Imagine that you are the teacher and let me walk you through the flowchart.

Some sort of deviant utterance is made by a student. Instantly, you run this speech event through a number of nearly simultaneous screens:

1. You identify the type of deviation (lexical, phonological, etc.).
2. In addition, you often, but not always, identify its source, which will be useful in determining how you might treat the deviation.
3. Next, the complexity of the deviation may determine not only whether to treat or ignore but how to treat, if that is your decision. In some cases a deviation may require so much explanation, or so much interruption of the task at hand, that it isn't worth treating it.
4. Your most crucial and possibly the very first decision among these 10 factors is to quickly decide whether the utterance is interpretable (local) or not (global). Local errors can sometimes be ignored for the sake of maintaining a flow of communication. Global errors by definition often call for some sort of treatment, even if only in the form of a clarification request.
5. Then, from your knowledge of this student, you make a guess at whether it is a performance slip (mistake) or competence error (see *PLLT,* Chapter 2); this is not always easy to do, but you may be surprised to know that a teacher's intuition on this factor will often be correct. Mistakes rarely call for treatment, while errors more frequently demand some sort of teacher response.

Figure 19.9. A model for treatment of classroom speech errors

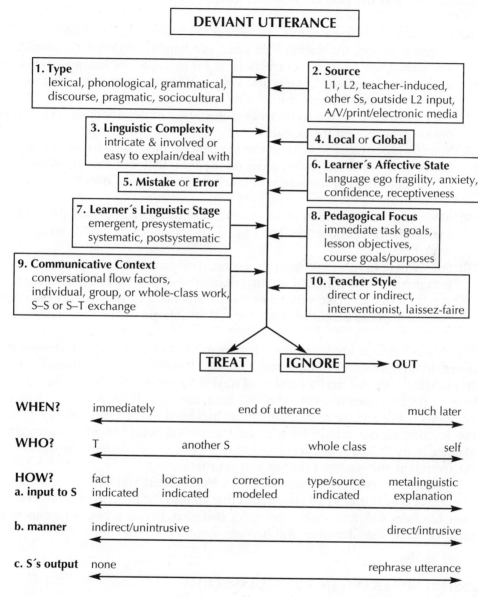

WHEN?	immediately		end of utterance		much later

WHO?	T	another S		whole class	self

HOW? a. input to S	fact indicated	location indicated	correction modeled	type/source indicated	metalinguistic explanation

b. manner	indirect/unintrusive				direct/intrusive

c. S's output	none				rephrase utterance

d. follow-up • affective	none		"okay"	"good"	[gush]
• cognitive	none	acknowledge		verbalize	further clarification

The above information is quickly stored as you perhaps simultaneously run through the next five possible considerations.

6. From your knowledge about this learner, you make a series of instant judgments about the learner's language ego fragility, anxiety level, confidence, and willingness to accept correction. If, for example, the learner rarely speaks in class or shows high anxiety and low confidence when attempting to speak, you may decide to ignore the deviant utterance.

7. Your knowledge of the learner's linguistic stage of development will help you decide how to treat the deviation.

8. Your own pedagogical focus at the moment (Is this a form-focused task to begin with? Does this lesson focus on the form that was deviant? What are the overall objectives of the lesson or task?) will help you to decide whether or not to treat.

9. Also consider the communicative context of the deviation (Was the student in the middle of a productive flow of language? How easily could you interrupt?).

10. Somewhere in this rapid-fire processing, your own style as a teacher comes into play: Are you generally an interventionist? laissez-faire? If, for example, you tend as a rule to make very few error treatments, a treatment now on a minor deviation would be out of character and misinterpreted by the student.

You are now ready to decide whether to *treat* or *ignore* the deviation! If you decide to do nothing, you simply move on. But if you decide to do something in the way of treatment, you have a number of treatment options, as discussed earlier. You have to decide when to treat, who will treat, and how to treat, and each of those decisions offers a range of possibilities, as indicated in the chart. Notice that you, the teacher, do not always have to be the person who provides the treatment. Manner of treatment varies according to the input to the student, the directness of the treatment, the student's output, and your follow-up.

After one very quick deviant utterance by a student, you have made an amazing number of observations and evaluations that go into the process of error treatment. New teachers will find such a prospect daunting, perhaps, but with experience, many of these considerations will become automatic.

ASSESSING SPEAKING IN THE CLASSROOM

Assessing speaking skills in the classroom has one clear advantage over assessing listening: Speech is observable, recordable, and measurable. However, once the criterion of your assessment moves beyond the phonological level, this advantage quickly disappears as *acceptable responses* are more difficult to specify reliably.

The prospect of designing classroom assessment procedures for oral production require the same preconsiderations that were outlined in the previous chapter: (1) Specify the category of speaking performance (from imitative to extensive) that is in question, and (2) describe the micro- and/or macroskills that are to be assessed. A further factor should also be taken into account: (3) the genre of spoken language that is being assessed. It's easier said than done, but the more specific you can be in pinpointing these three criteria, the greater the chances are that you will create a valid, reliable assessment procedure.

Item Types and Tasks for Assessing Speaking

So that you can gain an initial glimpse of options for assessing spoken language at the various levels of performance, I have listed some possibilities below. Again, for a further, more comprehensive survey, I refer you to my textbook on language assessment (Brown, 2004), in which I have provided a chapter on assessing speaking.

1. Imitative speaking tasks

   - minimal pair repetition
   - word/phrase repetition
   - sentence repetition

2. Intensive speaking tasks

   - directed response (*Tell me he went home. Tell him to come see me.*)
   - read-aloud (for either pronunciation or fluency)
   - oral sentence completion (*Yesterday, I _____.*)
   - oral cloze procedure (*Yesterday, I _____ to the grocery store.*)
   - dialogue completion (T: *May I help you?* S: _____.)
   - directed response (*What did you do last weekend?*)
   - picture-cued elicitation of a grammatical item (e.g., comparatives)
   - translation ([into the L2] of a word, phrase, or sentence or two)

3. Responsive speaking tasks

   - picture-cued elicitation of response or description
   - map-cued elicitation of directions (*How do I get to the post office?*)
   - question and answer—open-ended (*How do you like this weather?*)
   - question elicitation (*Ask me about my hobbies and interests.*)
   - elicitation of instructions (*What's the recipe for lasagna?*)
   - paraphrasing (of a short narrative or phone message)

4. Interactive speaking tasks

- oral interviews
- role plays
- discussions and conversations
- games

5. Extensive speaking tasks

- oral presentations (in academic or professional contexts)
- picture-cued (extensive) storytelling
- retelling a story or news event
- translation (into the L2) of an extended text (short story, news article)

Evaluating and Scoring Speaking Tasks

The evaluation of oral production performance can get quite complicated. First, you need to be clear in specifying the level of language you are targeting. One or more of at least six possible criteria may be your target:

- pronunciation
- fluency
- vocabulary
- grammar
- discourse features (cohesion, sociolinguistic appropriateness, etc.)
- task (accomplishing the objective of the task)

Some scales add "comprehension" to account for the extent to which a student has comprehended directions or elicitation. This category can be subsumed in the last two criteria above.

Within each of these categories you can judge a student's response(s) to be at one of several possible levels of performance. Typically, we think of beginning, intermediate, and advanced as potential levels. But as we saw in Chapter 7, those categories are quite slippery. Moreover, three levels may not be sufficient for your classroom purposes, and you may wish to score performance on five or six levels, ranging from "novice" or "true beginner" to "superior" or "completely acceptable." Whatever those categories are, it is important to describe them as clearly as possible in order to make reliable evaluations. For more on the issue of specifying scoring criteria, I suggest you consult my *Language Assessment* book (Brown, 2004) and/or Underhill's (1987) manual of oral testing techniques.

✯   ✯   ✯   ✯   ✯

Listening and speaking are the two skills that are most widely used for classroom interaction. By now, having covered the last two chapters, you have at least encountered many different parameters of these two skills, what they are, types of each, issues, some idea of the kinds of techniques that help to focus on either one or both of them; and you may have a few guidelines for assessment. We now move on to the next set of skills, reading and writing.

TOPICS FOR DISCUSSION, ACTION, AND RESEARCH

[Note: (I) Individual work; (G) group or pair work; (C) whole-class discussion.]

1. (C) Ask your students to think about the concept of fluency. Is it possible to devise an operational definition (in which measurable factors are specified) of fluency through such variables as rate, pronunciation accuracy, colloquial language, errors, clarity, and other factors? What does the operational definition say about what you should teach your students?

2. (G) Have pairs explain the difference between accuracy and fluency, and discuss which should come first in a curriculum and under what circumstances. Then tell them to think of some examples of how both fluency and accuracy might get attention within one task or technique.

3. (C) On pages 324–325 the interlocutor effect was described. Ask the class to think of some specific examples of this interlocutor effect and share them with the rest of the class. How might this effect help one to formulate certain plans for grouping or pairing students?

4. (C) With your students, review the eight factors (pages 326–327) that make spoken language difficult. Which is more difficult, speaking or listening (compare pages 304–307 and 326–327)? Ask for justifications of their responses.

5. (G/C) Richards (1990) listed many features of conversation that need to be attended to in an oral communication class. Divide up the features among pairs and ask each pair to (a) cite some examples of the feature and (b) speculate a little on how one would teach that aspect of conversation. Have pairs share their conclusions with the rest of the class.

6. (I) Observe a class in which there is a considerable amount of oral activity. Using the list of microskills (Table 19.1) as a checklist, take some notes that would enable you to report back to your class on how various microskills manifested themselves.

7. (G) Ask students to look again at the conversation between Bob and Amy (page 330) and, in pairs, to identify as many of the seven factors of interpersonal exchange (cited just prior to the conversation) as possible. Pairs should discuss how they would teach these factors, and then share their ideas with the rest of the class.

8. (G/C) Ask groups or pairs to demonstrate (peer-teach) the techniques described in the sections "Teaching Conversation" and "Teaching Pronunciation." Direct other members of the class to decide the extent to which the seven principles for designing speaking techniques were appropriately included.

9. (I/G) In the section "Focus on Form and Error Treatment," a number of principles of error correction are cited. In your own words, make up a short list (three or four) of "error correction maxims." Compare your maxims with those of others in the class, and make any changes you might want to. Then use those maxims as guidelines for observing a class in which you try to understand (a) why the teacher chose to correct something or not, and (b) how the correction was made.

10. (G) Have small groups, each assigned to one of the five levels of assessment described in the last section of this chapter, pick one of the suggested tasks and design a test for a classroom context that the group determines. Then the group should describe how one would score or evaluate student performance on such a test.

FOR YOUR FURTHER READING

McCarthy, M., & O'Keefe, A. (2004). Research in the teaching of speaking. *Annual Review of Applied Linguistics, 24,* 26–43.

Tarone, E. (2005). Speaking in a second language. In E. Hinkel (Ed.), *Handbook of research in second language teaching and learning* (pp. 485–502). Mahwah, NJ: Lawrence Erlbaum Associates.

These two survey articles summarize the state of the art in pedagogical research on the teaching of speaking. They both cover a range of topics and offer very useful extensive bibliographies.

Bailey, K. (2005). *Practical English language teaching: Speaking.* New York: McGraw-Hill.

Hughes, R. (2002). *Teaching and researching speaking.* London: Pearson Education.

If you wish to consult a volume completely devoted to the exploration of research and practice in teaching speaking, one or both of these two should be very useful. Bailey gives background research but is also very practically oriented, teacher-friendly, and organizes chapters by proficiency level. She includes comments on assessing speaking at each of the levels as well. Hughes offers historical and contextual background and suggestions for action research.

Celce-Murcia, M., Brinton, D., & Goodwin, J. (1996). *Teaching pronunciation: A reference for teachers of English to speakers of other languages.* Cambridge, UK: Cambridge University Press.

Still the best and most comprehensive teacher reference book on teaching pronunciation, this "classic" book combines the expertise and talent of all three authors. It is a comprehensive treatment of practice and research in pronunciation pedagogy. It includes techniques, diagnostic tools, assessment measures, and suggestions for syllabus design.

Setter, J., & Jenkins, J. (2005). Pronunciation. *Language Teaching, 38, 1-17.*

Levis, J. (2005). Changing contexts and shifting paradigms in pronunciation teaching. *TESOL Quarterly, 39,* 369-377.

For a good picture of research in the area of pronunciation teaching, these two articles summarize the state of the art. If you are able to secure a print copy of the issue of the TESOL Quarterly *(Number 3, September, 2005), you will see that the whole issue is devoted to issues of intelligibility, accent, world Englishes, and other related topics.*

Figure 19.10. (from Nilsen & Nilsen, 1971, p. ix)

CONSONANT/VOWEL CHARTS

English Consonants

								STOPS	
p			t			k			Voiceless
b			d			g			Voiced
								CONTINUANTS	
hw	f	θ	s		š		h		Voiceless
w	v	ð	z/y/l	r	ž				Voiced (Oral)
m			n			ŋ			Voiced (Nasal)
								AFFRICATES	
					č				Voiceless
					j				Voiced

(Place of articulation headings, left to right: two lips; top teeth/bottom lip; tongue tip/top teeth; tongue tip/tooth ridge; tongue tip/hard palate; tongue mid/hard palate; tongue back/soft palate; not localized)

English Vowels

		Front	Central	Back
High	Tense	iy		uw
	Lax	i		u
Mid	Tense	ey		ow
	Lax	e	ə	
Low	Tense	æ		
	Lax		a	ɔ

Diphthongs

ay
aw
oy

CHAPTER **20**

TEACHING READING

OBJECTIVES After reading this chapter, you will be able to:

- understand issues and concepts in pedagogical research that are related to teaching reading

- analyze types of written language, micro- and macroskills, and types of classroom reading performance

- apply principles of designing reading techniques to your own lesson designs and to your observation of others' lessons

- identify strategies for reading comprehension

- evaluate the effectiveness of reading lessons

- recognize some basic principles and formats for assessing reading

The written word surrounds us daily. It enlightens and confuses us, it amuses and depresses us, it heals and sickens us. At every turn, we who are members of a literate society are dependent on 20-some-odd letters and a handful of other written symbols for significant, even life-and-death, matters in our lives. How do we teach second language learners to master this written code? What do we teach them? What are the issues?

As you read this chapter, keep in mind that once again, interactive, integrated approaches to language teaching emphasize the interrelationship of skills. Reading ability will be developed best in association with writing, listening, and speaking activities. Even in those courses that may be labeled "reading," your goals will be best achieved by capitalizing on the connection between reading and other modes of performance, especially the reading-writing relationship. So, we focus here on reading as a component of general second language proficiency, but ultimately reading must be considered only in the perspective of the whole picture of interactive language teaching.

RESEARCH ON READING A SECOND LANGUAGE

By the 1970s, research on reading one's first language had been flourishing for a couple of decades as solutions were being sought to why some children couldn't read. But research on reading in a second language was almost nonexistent. Then, with Kenneth Goodman's (1970) seminal article, "Reading: A Psycholinguistic Guessing Game," and other subsequent work, second language specialists began to tackle the unique issues and questions facing second language reading pedagogy. A glance through what is now three decades of research reveals some significant

357

findings that will affect you and your approach to teaching reading skills. Some of the highlights are reviewed here.

1. Bottom-up and top-down processing

Led by Goodman's (1970) work, the distinction between bottom-up and top-down processing became a cornerstone of reading methodology for years to come. In **bottom-up processing**, readers must first recognize a multiplicity of linguistic signals (letters, morphemes, syllables, words, phrases, grammatical cues, discourse markers) and use their linguistic data-processing mechanisms to impose some sort of order on these signals. These data-driven operations obviously require a sophisticated knowledge of the language itself. From among all the perceived data, the reader selects the signals that make some sense, that cohere, that "mean."

Virtually all reading involves a risk—a guessing game, in Goodman's words—because readers must, through a puzzle-solving process, infer meanings, decide what to retain and not to retain, and move on. This is where a complementary method of processing written text is imperative: **top-down**, or **conceptually driven**, **processing** in which we draw on our own intelligence and experience to understand a text. Christine Nuttall (1996, pp. 16–17) compares bottom-up processes with the image of a scientist with a magnifying glass or microscope examining all the minute details of some phenomenon, while top-down processing is like taking an eagle's-eye view of a landscape below. Such a picture reminds us that field-independent and field-dependent cognitive styles (see *PLLT,* Chapter 5) are analogous to bottom-up and top-down processing, respectively.

A half-century ago, perhaps, reading specialists might have argued that the best way to teach reading is through bottom-up methodology: teach symbols, grapheme–phoneme correspondences, syllables, and lexical recognition first, then comprehension would be derived from the sum of the parts. More recent research on teaching reading has shown that a combination of top-down and bottom-up processing, or what has come to be called interactive reading, is almost always a primary ingredient in successful teaching methodology because both processes are important. "In practice, a reader continually shifts from one focus to another, now adopting a top-down approach to predict probable meaning, then moving to the bottom-up approach to check whether that is really what the writer says" (Nuttall, 1996, p. 17).

2. Schema theory and background knowledge

How do readers construct meaning? How do they decide what to hold on to, and having made that decision, how do they infer a writer's message? These are the sorts of questions addressed by what has come to be known as **schema theory,** the hallmark of which is that a text does not by itself carry meaning (Anderson, 2004; Eskey, 2005; Grabe, 2004). The reader brings information, knowledge, emotion, experience, and culture—that is, schemata (plural)—to the printed word. Schema theory is not a new construct. Three decades ago, Mark Clarke and Sandra Silberstein (1977, pp. 136–137) captured the essence of schema theory:

Research has shown that reading is only incidentally visual. More information is contributed by the reader than by the print on the page. That is, readers understand what they read because they are able to take the stimulus beyond its graphic representation and assign it membership to an appropriate group of concepts already stored in their memories. . . . Skill in reading depends on the efficient interaction between linguistic knowledge and knowledge of the world.

A good example of the role of schemata in reading is found in the following anecdote:

A 15-year-old boy got up the nerve one day to try out for the school chorus, despite the potential ridicule from his classmates. His audition time made him a good 15 minutes late to the next class. His hall permit clutched nervously in hand, he nevertheless tried surreptitiously to slip into his seat, but his entrance didn't go unnoticed.

"And where were you?" bellowed the teacher.

Caught off guard by the sudden attention, a red-faced Harold replied meekly, "Oh, uh, er, somewhere between tenor and bass, sir."

A full understanding of this story and its humorous punch line requires that the reader know two categories of schemata: **content** and **formal schemata.** Content schemata include what we know about people, the world, culture, and the universe, while formal schemata consist of our knowledge about language and discourse structure. For the above anecdote, these content schemata are a prerequisite to understanding its humor:

• Fifteen-year-old boys might be embarrassed about singing in a choir.
• Hall permits allow students to be outside a classroom during the class hour.
• Teenagers often find it embarrassing to be singled out in a class.
• Something about voice ranges.
• Fifteen-year-olds' voices are often "breaking."

Formal schemata also reveal some implied connections:

• The chorus tryout was the cause of potential ridicule.
• The audition occurred just before the class period.
• Continuing to "clutch" the permit means he did not give it to the teacher.
• The teacher did indeed notice his entry.
• The teacher's question referred to location, not a musical part.

The widespread acceptance of schema theory by reading researchers has not gone unchallenged. Nassaji (2002) provided an alternative view of the role of background knowledge, appealing to connectionist models of memory. In Nassaji's view, background knowledge is not "pre-stored," but "rather it emerges in the context of the task, and is relatively unstructured as opposed to the highly structured knowledge representations suggested by . . . schema theory" (p. 453). In this "construction-integration" model, the learner is seen to play a more active role in constructing meaning, while reading, than is proposed by schema theory.

3. Teaching strategic reading

One of the questions that has been asked about teaching reading has been the extent to which learners will learn to read better in a laissez-faire atmosphere of enriched surroundings than in an instructed sequence of direct attention to the strategies of efficient reading. Most experts in reading research side with the latter (Anderson, 1999, 2004; Eskey, 2005; Grabe, 2004), and cite research in support of their conclusion. A viable theory of instructed second language acquisition can hardly be sustainable without a solid component of strategic competence.

One of the ongoing themes among researchers and teachers of foreign languages is the tension between what in the last chapter we referred to as direct and indirect approaches to teaching language skills. This continuum of possibilities is highlighted in debates over conscious and subconscious acquisition, explicit and implicit learning, focal and peripheral processing, and Krashen's (1985) learning versus acquisition. Instruction should of course provide an optimal mix of each, but Neil Anderson (1999, 2004) advocated a healthy dose of strategy-based instruction, including metacognitive strategies of self-planning, monitoring, and evaluating one's own reading processes. William Grabe (2004) stressed the coordinated use of multiple strategies *while* students are reading. David Eskey (2005) reminds us of research on prereading, while reading, postreading, and follow-up strategies for reading, will be discussed later in this chapter.

4. Extensive reading

On the other hand, there is a place for extensive reading of longer texts with little or no conscious strategic intervention. Elley (2001), Day and Bamford (1998), and Krashen (1993) all made the case that extensive reading (free voluntary reading [FVR], as Krashen called it) is a key to student gains in reading ability, linguistic competence, vocabulary, spelling, and writing. Green and Oxford (1995) found that reading for pleasure and reading without looking up all the unknown words were both highly correlated with overall language proficiency.

This research suggests that instructional programs in reading should give consideration to the teaching of extensive reading. It does not suggest, of course, that focused approaches to specific strategies for intensive reading ought to be abandoned, but strengthens the notion that an extensive reading component in conjunction with other focused reading instruction is highly warranted.

5. Fluency and reading rate

Paralleling the research on other language skills, fluency, or reading rate, has drawn the attention of some research. In L1 reading, fluency and reading rate have long been a concern (Grabe, 2004; Kuhn & Stahl, 2003), but surprisingly few studies have been carried out in L2 reading. Anderson's (1999) teacher reference book is a notable exception, in which a chapter is devoted to increasing reading rate, with suggestions for using skimming, scanning, predicting, and identifying main ideas as approaches to increasing fluency.

6. Focus on vocabulary

In recent years there has been a resurgence of interest in the role of vocabulary knowledge on the acquisition of reading skills (Nation, 2003, 2005; Read, 2004), with findings that support a strong relationship between vocabulary knowledge and later reading ability. This topic will be taken up in further detail in Chapter 22 of this book.

7. The role of affect and culture

It's readily apparent from just a cursory survey of research on second language acquisition that affective factors play major roles in ultimate success. Just as language ego, self-esteem, empathy, and motivation undergird the acquisition of spoken discourse, reading is subject to variability within the affective domain. The "love" of reading has propelled many a learner to successful acquisition of reading skills. Instruction has been found to be effective when students' self-esteem is high (Dole, Brown, & Trathen, 1996). The autonomy gained through the learning of reading strategies has been shown to be a powerful motivator (Bamford & Day, 1998), not to mention the affective power of reading itself. Similarly, culture plays an active role in motivating and rewarding people for literacy. We cannot simply assume that cognitive factors alone will account for the eventual success of second language readers (Fitzgerald, 1994).

8. Adult literacy training

As ESL materials and methods continue to apply both bottom-up and top-down models of reading to programs and curricula, one particularly challenging focus of effort for researchers and teachers has been literacy-level teaching of adults (August, et al., 2002; Devine & Eskey, 2004; Elley, 2001; Schleppegrell & Colombi, 2002; Verhoeven & Snow, 2001). A significant number of immigrants arriving in various nonnative countries and cultures are nonliterate in their native languages, posing special issues in the teaching of English. What are sometimes referred to as "skills-based" (bottom-up) and "strategies-based" (top-down) approaches are both used in adult literacy training. For more information on this specialized field, a particularly good reference is August et al.'s (2006) Center for Applied Linguistics anthology.

Aside from the eight major issues touched on above, a multitude of other topics are grist for current researchers' mills:

- the role of cognition in reading
- the role of automaticity in word recognition
- reading as sociocultural practice
- effective techniques for activating schemata
- relationships of reading to writing

And the list goes on. At this stage in your professional career when you are learning to teach, rather than immersing you in oceans of research data, it is perhaps more important to lay some basic foundations for the development of an effective teaching approach, which we now turn to.

GENRES OF WRITTEN LANGUAGE

In the previous two chapters we looked at types of spoken language so that you could identify the kinds of language your listening and speaking techniques should include. Here, we do the same for types, or **genres**, of reading and writing.

In our highly literate society, there are literally hundreds of different types of written texts, a much larger variety than found in spoken texts. Each of the types listed below represents, or is an example of, a *genre* of written language. Each has certain rules or conventions for its manifestation, and we are thus able immediately to identify a genre and to know what to look for within the text. Consider the following nonexhaustive list:

- nonfiction: reports, editorials, essays, articles, reference (dictionaries, etc.)
- fiction: novels, short stories, jokes, drama, poetry
- letters: personal, business
- greeting cards
- diaries, journals
- memos (e.g., interoffice memos)
- messages (e.g., phone messages)
- announcements
- newspaper "journalese"
- academic writing: short-answer test responses, reports, papers, theses, books
- forms, applications
- questionnaires
- directions
- labels
- signs
- recipes
- bills (and other financial statements)

- maps
- manuals
- menus
- schedules (e.g., transportation tables)
- advertisements: commercial, personal
- invitations
- directories (e.g., telephone, yellow pages)
- comic strips, cartoons

And I'm sure you could name a few more! It's interesting that every literate adult knows the distinctive features of each of these genres. You can immediately distinguish a menu from a map, an interoffice memo from a telephone message, and a bill from an invitation—well, okay, some bills are invitations to pay! When you encounter one of the above, you usually know what your purpose is in reading it, and therefore you know what to select and what not to select for short- and long-term memory—in other words, you bring various schemata to bear on the message that you have chosen to retain. What would happen if you didn't know some of these differences? That is what your students may encounter when they read English, so part of your job as a teacher is to enlighten your students on features of these genres and to help them to develop strategies for extracting necessary meaning from each.

CHARACTERISTICS OF WRITTEN LANGUAGE

There are quite a number of salient and relevant differences between spoken and written language. Students already literate in their native languages will of course be familiar with the broad, basic characteristics of written language; however, some characteristics of English writing, especially certain rhetorical conventions, may be so different from their native language that reading efforts are blocked. The characteristics listed below will also be of some help for you in

a. diagnosing certain reading difficulties arising from the idiosyncrasies of written language,
b. pointing your techniques toward specific objectives, and
c. reminding students of some of the advantages of written language over spoken.

1. Permanence
Spoken language is fleeting. Once you speak a sentence, it vanishes (unless there is a tape recorder around). The hearer, therefore, is called upon to make immediate perceptions and immediate storage. Written language is permanent (or as permanent as paper and computer disks are!), and therefore the reader has an opportunity to return again and again, if necessary, to a word or phrase or sentence, or even a whole text.

2. Processing time

A corollary to the above is the processing time that the reader gains. Most reading contexts allow readers to read at their own rate. They aren't forced into following the rate of delivery, as in spoken language. A good deal of emphasis is placed on reading speed in our fast-paced, time-conscious society, which is good news and bad news. The good news is that readers can indeed capitalize on the nature of the printed word and develop very rapid reading rates. The bad news is that many people who are "slow" readers are made to feel inferior. In practice, except for the time factor itself, fast readers do not necessarily have an advantage over slow readers.

3. Distance

The written word allows messages to be sent across two dimensions: physical distance and temporal distance. The pedagogical significance of this centers on interpretation. The task of the reader is to interpret language that was written in some other place at some other time with only the written words themselves as contextual clues. Readers can't confront an author and say, "Now, what exactly did you mean by that?" Nor can they transport themselves back through a time machine and "see" the surrounding context, as we can in face-to-face conversations. This sometimes decontextualized nature of writing is one of the things that makes reading difficult.

4. Orthography

In spoken language, we have phonemes that correspond to writing's graphemes. But we also have stress, rhythm, juncture, intonation, pauses, volume, voice quality settings, and nonverbal cues, all of which enhance the message. In writing we have graphemes—that's it! Yes, sometimes punctuation, pictures, or charts lend a helping hand. And, yes, a writer can describe the aforementioned phonological cues, as in, "With loud, rasping grunts, punctuated by roars of pain, he slowly dragged himself out of the line of enemy fire." But these written symbols stand alone as the one set of signals that the reader must perceive. Because of the frequent ambiguity that is present in a good deal of writing, readers must do their best to infer, to interpret, and to "read between the lines."

English orthography itself, in spite of its reputation for being "irregular," is highly predictable from its spoken counterpart, especially when one considers morphological information as well. For literate learners of English, our spelling system presents only minor difficulties, even for those whose native languages have quite different systems. Actually, most of the irregularity in English manifests itself in high-frequency words (*of, to, have, do, done, was,* etc.), and once those words are in place, the rest of the system can usually be mastered without special instruction.

5. Complexity

You might be tempted to say that writing is more complex than speech, but in reality, that would be difficult to demonstrate. Writing and speech represent different modes of complexity, and the most salient difference is in the nature of clauses. Spoken language tends to have shorter clauses connected by more coordinate conjunctions, while writing has longer clauses and more subordination. The shorter clauses are often a factor of the redundancy we build into speech (repeating subjects and verbs for clarity). Look at the following pair:

1. Because of the frequent ambiguity that therefore is present in a good deal of writing, readers must do their best to infer, to interpret, and to "read between the lines."
2. There's frequent ambiguity in a lot of writing. And so, readers have to infer a lot. They also have to interpret what they read. And sometimes they have to "read between the lines."

The cognitive complexity of version 1, the written version, is no greater than version 2, the spoken version. But structurally, four clauses were used in version 2 to replace the one long clause in version 1.

Readers—especially second language readers who may be quite adept in the spoken language—have to retool their cognitive perceptors in order to extract meaning from the written code. The linguistic differences between speech and writing are another major contributing cause to difficulty.

6. Vocabulary

It is true that written English typically utilizes a greater variety of lexical items than spoken conversational English. In our everyday give and take with family, friends, and colleagues, vocabulary is limited. Because writing allows the writer more processing time, because of a desire to be precise in writing, and simply because of the formal conventions of writing (see #7 below), lower-frequency words often appear. Such words can present stumbling blocks to learners. However, because the meaning of a good many unknown words can be predicted from their context, and because sometimes the overall meaning of a sentence or paragraph is nevertheless still clear, learners should refrain from the frequent use of a bilingual dictionary.

7. Formality

Writing is quite frequently more formal than speech. What do we mean by that? Formality refers to prescribed **forms** that certain written messages must adhere to. The reason that you can both recognize a menu and decide what to eat fairly quickly is that menus conform to certain conventions. Things are categorized (appetizers, salads, entrees, desserts, etc.) in logical order and subcategorized (all seafood dishes are listed together); exotic or creative names for dishes are usually defined; prices are given for each item; and the menu isn't so long that it overwhelms you. We have **rhetorical,** or organizational, formality in essay writing that demands a writer's conformity to conventions like paragraph topics; we have logical order for, say, comparing and contrasting something; we have openings and closings, and a preference for nonredundancy and subordination of clauses, etc. Until a reader is familiar with the formal features of a written text, some difficulty in interpretation may ensue.

MICRO- AND MACROSKILLS FOR READING COMPREHENSION

Table 20.1 on page 367, an adaptation of the models of micro- and macroskills offered in the previous two chapters, is a breakdown of what students of ESL need to do to become efficient readers.

STRATEGIES FOR READING COMPREHENSION

For most second language learners who are already literate in a previous language, reading comprehension is primarily a matter of developing appropriate, efficient comprehension strategies. Some strategies are related to bottom-up procedures, and others enhance the top-down processes. Following are 10 such strategies, each of which can be practically applied to your classroom techniques.

1. Identify the purpose in reading.

How many times have you been told to read something without knowing why you've been asked to read it? You do only a mediocre job of retaining what you "read" and perhaps are rather slow in the process. Efficient reading consists of clearly identifying the purpose in reading something. By doing so, you know what you're looking for and can weed out potential distracting information. Whenever you are teaching a reading technique, make sure students know their purpose in reading something.

2. Use graphemic rules and patterns to aid in bottom-up decoding.

At the beginning levels of learning English, one of the difficulties students encounter in learning to read is making the correspondences between spoken and written English. In many cases, learners have become acquainted with oral language and have some difficulty learning English spelling conventions. They may need hints and explanations about certain English orthographic rules and peculiarities. While you can often assume that one-to-one grapheme–phoneme correspondences will be acquired with ease, other relationships might prove difficult. Consider how you might provide hints and pointers on such patterns as these:

- "short" vowel sound in VC patterns (*bat, him, leg, wish,* etc.)
- "long" vowel sound in VCe (final silent *e*) patterns (*late, time, bite,* etc.)
- "long" vowel sound in VV patterns (*seat, coat,* etc.)
- distinguishing "hard" *c* and *g* from "soft" *c* and *g* (*cat* vs. *city, game* vs. *gem,* etc.)

Table 20.1. Micro- and macroskills for listening comprehension

---

Microskills

1. Discriminate among the distinctive graphemes and orthographic patterns of English.
2. Retain chunks of language of different lengths in short-term memory.
3. Process writing at an efficient rate of speed to suit the purpose.
4. Recognize a core of words, and interpret word order patterns and their significance.
5. Recognize grammatical word classes (nouns, verbs, etc.), systems (e.g., tense, agreement, pluralization), patterns, rules, and elliptical forms.
6. Recognize that a particular meaning may be expressed in different grammatical forms.

Macroskills

7. Recognize cohesive devices in written discourse and their role in signaling the relationship between and among clauses.
8. Recognize the rhetorical forms of written discourse and their significance for interpretation.
9. Recognize the communicative functions of written texts, according to form and purpose.
10. Infer context that is not explicit by using background knowledge.
11. Infer links and connections between events, ideas, etc.; deduce causes and effects; and detect such relations as main idea, supporting idea, new information, given information, generalization, and exemplification.
12. Distinguish between literal and implied meanings.
13. Detect culturally specific references and interpret them in a context of the appropriate cultural schemata.
14. Develop and use a battery of reading strategies such as scanning and skimming, detecting discourse markers, guessing the meaning of words from context, and activating schemata for the interpretation of texts.

These and a multitude of other *phonics* approaches to reading can prove useful for learners at the beginning level and especially useful for teaching children and nonliterate adults.

3. Use efficient silent reading techniques for improving fluency.

If you are teaching beginning level students, this particular strategy will not apply because they are still struggling with the control of a limited vocabulary and grammatical patterns. Your intermediate-to-advanced level students need not be speed readers, but you can help them increase reading rate and comprehension efficiency by teaching a few silent reading rules:

- You don't need to "pronounce" each word to yourself.
- Try to visually perceive more than one word at a time, preferably phrases.
- Unless a word is absolutely crucial to global understanding, skip over it and try to infer its meaning from its context.

Aside from these fundamental guidelines, which if followed can help learners to be efficient readers, reading speed is usually not much of an issue for all but the most advanced learners. Academic reading, for example, is something most learners manage to accomplish by allocating whatever time they personally need in order to complete the material. If your students can read 250 to 300 words per minute, further concern over speed may not be necessary.

4. Skim the text for main ideas.

Perhaps the two most valuable reading strategies for learners (as well as native speakers) are skimming and scanning. **Skimming** consists of quickly running one's eyes across a whole text (such as an essay, article, or chapter) for its gist. Skimming gives readers the advantage of being able to predict the purpose of the passage, the main topic, or message, and possibly some of the developing or supporting ideas. This gives them a head start as they embark on more focused reading. You can train students to skim passages by giving them, say, 30 seconds to look through a few pages of material, close their books, and then tell you what they learned.

5. Scan the text for specific information.

The second in the most valuable category is **scanning**, or quickly searching for some particular piece or pieces of information in a text. Scanning exercises may ask students to look for names or dates, to find a definition of a key concept, or to list a certain number of supporting details. The purpose of scanning is to extract specific information without reading through the whole text. For academic English, scanning is absolutely essential. In vocational or general English, scanning is important in dealing with genres like schedules, manuals, forms, etc.

6. Use semantic mapping or clustering.

Readers can easily be overwhelmed by a long string of ideas or events. The strategy of **semantic mapping**, or grouping ideas into meaningful clusters, helps the reader to provide some order to the chaos. Making such semantic maps can be done individually, but they make for a productive group work technique as students collectively induce order and hierarchy to a passage. Early drafts of these maps can be quite messy—which is perfectly acceptable. Figure 20.1, for example, shows a first attempt by a small group of students to draw a semantic map of an article by Rick Gore called "Between Fire and Ice: The Planets," an article about a total solar eclipse as seen through the eyes of villagers in Patuk, Java.

Figure 20.1. Semantic map

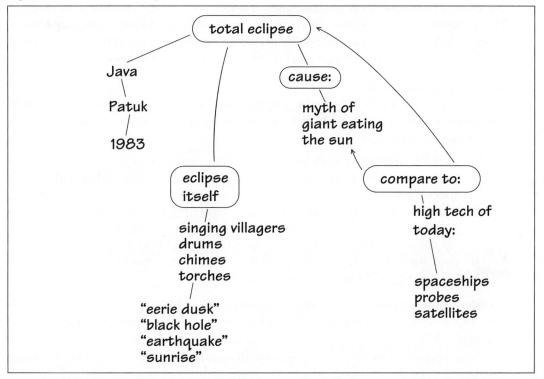

7. Guess when you aren't certain.

This is an extremely broad category. Learners can use guessing to their advantage to do the following

- guess the meaning of a word
- guess a grammatical relationship (e.g., a pronoun reference)
- guess a discourse relationship
- infer implied meaning ("between the lines")
- guess about a cultural reference
- guess content messages

Now, you of course don't want to encourage your learners to become haphazard readers! They should utilize all their skills and put forth as much effort as possible to be on target with their hypotheses. But the point here is that reading is, after all, a guessing game of sorts, and the sooner learners understand this game, the better off they are. The key to successful guessing is to make it reasonably *accurate*.

You can help learners to become accurate guessers by encouraging them to use effective **compensation strategies** in which they fill gaps in their competence by intelligent attempts to use whatever clues are available to them. Language-based clues include word analysis (see #8 below), word associations, and textual structure. Nonlinguistic clues come from context, situation, and other schemata.

8. Analyze vocabulary.

One way for learners to make guessing pay off when they don't immediately recognize a word is to analyze it in terms of what they know about it. Several techniques are useful here:

  a. Look for prefixes (*co-, inter-, un-,* etc.) that may give clues.
  b. Look for suffixes (*-tion, -tive, -ally,* etc.) that may indicate what part of speech it is.
  c. Look for roots that are familiar (e.g., *intervening* may be a word a student doesn't know, but recognizing that the root *ven* comes from Latin "to come" would yield the meaning "to come in between").
  d. Look for grammatical contexts that may signal information.
  e. Look at the semantic context (topic) for clues.

9. Distinguish between literal and implied meanings.

This requires the application of sophisticated top-down processing skills. The fact that not all language can be interpreted appropriately by attending to its literal, syntactic surface structure makes special demands on readers. Implied meaning usually has to be derived from processing *pragmatic* information, as in the following examples:

  a. Bill walked into the frigid classroom and immediately noticed Bob, sitting by the open window, with a heavy sweatshirt on.
     "Brrr!" he exclaimed, simultaneously eyeing Bob and the open windows, "It's sure cold in here, Bob."
     Bob glanced up from his book and growled, "Oh, all right, I'll close the window."
  b. The policeman held up his hand and stopped the car.
  c. Mary heard the ice cream man coming down the street. She remembered her birthday money and rushed into the house . . . (Rummelhart, 1977, p. 265).

Each of these excerpts has implied information. The request in (a) is obvious only if the reader recognizes the nature of many indirect requests in which we ask people to do things without ever forming a question. We can't be sure in (b) if the policeman literally (physically) stopped the car with his hand, but the assumption is that this is a traffic policeman whose hand signal was obeyed by a driver. Rummelhart's classic example in (c) leads the reader, without any other context, to believe Mary is going into the house to get money to buy ice cream until the last few words are supplied: ". . . and locked the door!"

10. Capitalize on discourse markers to process relationships.

Many discourse markers in English signal relationships among ideas as expressed through phrases, clauses, and sentences. A clear comprehension of such markers can greatly enhance learners' reading efficiency. Table 20.2 enumerates almost 100 of these markers with which learners of intermediate proficiency levels ought to be thoroughly familiar.

TYPES OF CLASSROOM READING PERFORMANCE

Variety of reading performance in the language classroom is derived more from the variety of texts (refer to the list earlier in this chapter) to which you can expose students than from the variety of overt types of performance. Consider Figure 20.2.

Figure 20.2. Types of classroom reading performance

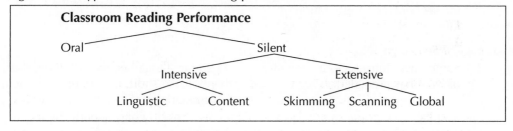

1. Oral and silent reading

Occasionally, you will have reason to ask a student to read orally. At the beginning and intermediate levels, oral reading can

   a. serve as an evaluative check on bottom-up processing skills,
   b. double as a pronunciation check, and
   c. serve to add some extra student participation if you want to highlight a certain short segment of a reading passage.

For advanced levels, usually only advantage (c) can be gained by reading orally. As a rule of thumb, you want to use oral reading to serve these three purposes because the *disadvantages* of too much oral reading can easily come into play:

   a. Oral reading is not a very authentic language activity.
   b. While one student is reading, others can easily lose attention (or be silently rehearsing the next paragraph!).
   c. It may have the outward appearance of student participation when in reality it is mere recitation.

2. Intensive and extensive reading

Silent reading may be subcategorized into intensive and extensive reading. **Intensive reading**, analogous to intensive listening (described in Chapter 18), is

Table 20.2. Types of discourse markers (Mackay, 1987, p. 254)

Notional category/Meaning	Marker
1. *Enumerative.* Introduce in order in which points are to be made or the time sequence in which actions or processes took place.	first(ly), second(ly), third(ly), one, two, three / a, b, c, next, then, finally, last(ly), in the first / second place, for one thing / for another thing, to begin with, subsequently, eventually, finally, in the end, to conclude
2. *Additive*	
2.1 Reinforcing. Introduces a reinforcement or confirmation of what has preceded.	again, then again, also, moreover, furthermore, in addition, above all, what is more
2.2 Similarity. Introduces a statement of similarity with what has preceded.	equally, likewise, similarly, correspondingly, in the same way
2.3 Transition. Introduces a new stage in the sequence of presentation of information.	now, well, incidentally, by the way, O.K., fine
3. *Logical Sequence*	
3.1 Summative. Introduces a summary of what has preceded.	so, so far, altogether, overall, then, thus, therefore, in short, to sum up, to conclude, to summarize
3.2 Resultative. Introduces an expression of the result or consequence of what preceded (and includes inductive and deductive acts).	so, as a result, consequently, hence, now, therefore, thus, as a consequence, in consequence
4. *Explicative.* Introduces an explanation or reformulation of what preceded.	namely, in other words, that is to say, better, rather, by (this) we mean
5. *Illustrative.* Introduces an illustration or example of what preceded.	for example, for instance
6. *Contrastive*	
6.1 Replacive. Introduces an alternative to what preceded.	alternatively, (or) again, (or) rather, (but) then, on the other hand
6.2 Antithetic. Introduces information in opposition to what preceded.	conversely, instead, then, on the contrary, by contrast, on the other hand
6.3 Concessive. Introduces information which is unexpected in view of what preceded.	anyway, anyhow, however, nevertheless, nonetheless, notwithstanding, still, though, yet, for all that, in spite of (that), at the same time, all the same

usually a classroom-oriented activity in which students focus on the linguistic or semantic details of a passage. Intensive reading calls students' attention to grammatical forms, discourse markers, and other surface structure details for the purpose of understanding literal meaning, implications, rhetorical relationships, and the like.

As a "zoom lens" strategy for taking a closer look at a text, intensive reading also may be a totally content-related reading initiated because of subject-matter difficulty. A complex cognitive concept may be "trapped" inside the words of a sentence or paragraph, and a good reader will then very slowly and methodically extract meaning therefrom.

Extensive reading is carried out to achieve a general understanding of a usually somewhat longer text (book, long article, essay, etc.). Most extensive reading is performed outside of class time. Pleasure reading is often extensive. Technical, scientific, and professional reading can, under certain special circumstances, be extensive when one is simply striving for global or general meaning from longer passages.

The advantages of extensive reading were discussed in the first section of the chapter. By stimulating reading for enjoyment or reading where all concepts, names, dates, and other details need not be retained, students gain an appreciation for the affective and cognitive window of reading: an entrée into new worlds. Extensive reading can sometimes help learners get away from their tendency to overanalyze or look up words they don't know, and read for understanding.

PRINCIPLES FOR TEACHING READING SKILLS

1. In an integrated course, don't overlook a specific focus on reading skills.

ESL students who are literate in their own language sometimes are left to their own devices when it comes to learning reading skills. We often assume that they will learn good reading simply by absorption through generous offerings of extensive reading opportunities. In reality, there is much to be gained by your focusing on reading skills. This chapter has provided some guidelines on how to direct that focus. On the other hand, it should be clear from previous comments in this chapter that it is important to make sure that your students have ample time for extensive reading. Sustained silent reading allows them to develop a sense of fluency. Also, silent reading then becomes an excellent method for self-instruction on the part of the learner.

2. Use techniques that are intrinsically motivating.

What do you think makes for interesting and relevant reading for your students? Of the long list of genres at the beginning of this chapter, how many will your students encounter in "real life"? Use those texts. What are your students' goals in learning to read English? Focus on those goals. Choose material that is *relevant* to those goals.

One popular and intrinsically motivating approach to reading instruction is the **Language Experience Approach** (LEA), referred to in Chapter 17, where students create their own material for reading. Other approaches in which learners are given choices in selecting reading material offer a degree of intrinsic motivation. Carefully sequenced readings and instructional strategies that are *success-oriented* give further intrinsic involvement in the process. Another way to enhance intrinsic motives is to offer opportunities for learners to gauge their progress through periodic instructor-initiated assessments and self-assessments.

3. Balance authenticity and readability in choosing texts.

By now, the importance of authentic language should be more than clear. But in teaching reading, one issue that has invited some controversy is the advisability of what are called "simplified texts," in which an otherwise authentic text is edited to keep language within the proficiency level of a set of students. In order for you to make a decision on this issue, it is important to distinguish between (a) simple texts and (b) simplified texts and to understand sources of complexity in reading material.

Authentic simple texts can either be devised or located in the real world. From ads to labels to reports to essays, texts are available that are grammatically and lexically simple. Simplifying an existing potential reading selection may not be necessary. Yet if simplification must be done, it is important to preserve the natural redundancy, humor, wit, and other captivating features of the original material.

Second, you might ask yourself what "simplicity" is and then determine if a so-called simplified text is really simpler than its original. Sometimes simplified texts remove so much natural redundancy that they actually become difficult. And what you perceive as textual complexity may be more a product of background schemata than of linguistic complexity. Take another look at the list of characteristics of written language earlier in this chapter and you will no doubt see what it is that makes a text difficult. In light of those criteria, is a simplified text really simpler? The answer may be no. Richard Day and Julian Bamford (1998, p. 53), in warning against "the cult of authenticity and the myth of simplification," contended that our CLT approach has overemphasized the need for so-called authenticity, and that there is indeed a place for simplified texts in reading instruction.

Christine Nuttall (1996) offered three criteria for choosing reading texts for students: (1) *suitability* of content: material that students will find interesting, enjoyable, challenging, and appropriate for their goals in learning English; (2) *exploitability:* a text that facilitates the achievement of certain language and content goals, that is exploitable for instructional tasks and techniques, and that is integratable with other skills (listening, speaking, writing); (3) *readability:* a text with lexical and structural difficulty that will challenge students without overwhelming them.

4. Encourage the development of reading strategies.

Already in this chapter, 10 different reading strategies have been discussed. To what extent are you getting your students to use all these strategies?

5. Include both bottom-up and top-down techniques.

In our craze for communicative, authentic language activity in the classroom, we sometimes forget that learners can indeed benefit from studying the fundamentals. Make sure that you give enough classroom time to focusing on the building blocks of written language, geared appropriately for each level.

6. Follow the SQ3R sequence.

One effective series of procedures for approaching a reading text has come to be labeled the **SQ3R** technique, a process consisting of the following five steps:

1. *Survey*: Skim the text for an overview of main ideas.
2. *Question:* The reader asks questions about what he or she wishes to get out of the text.
3. *Read*: Read the text while looking for answers to the previously formulated questions.
4. *Recite*: Reprocess the salient points of the text through oral or written language.
5. *Review*: Assess the importance of what one has just read and incorporate it into long-term associations.

This series of techniques of course may not fit all classes and contexts, but it serves as a general guide for a reading class.

7. Plan on prereading, during-reading, and after-reading phases.

It's tempting, especially at intermediate and advanced levels, to tell students, "Okay now, class, read the next two pages silently." No introduction, no hints on anything special to do while reading, and nary a thought about something to follow the silent reading period. A good rubric to keep in mind for teaching reading is the following three-part framework:

1. *Before you read:* Spend some time introducing a topic, encouraging skimming, scanning, predicting, and activating schemata. Students can bring the best of their knowledge and skills to a text when they have been given a chance to "ease into" the passage.
2. *While you read:* Not all reading is simply extensive or global reading. There may be certain facts or rhetorical devices that students should take note of while they read. Give students a sense of purpose for reading rather than just reading because you ordered it.
3. *After you read:* Comprehension questions are just one form of activity appropriate for postreading. Also consider vocabulary study, identifying the author's purpose, discussing the author's line of reasoning, examining grammatical structures, or steering students toward a follow-up writing exercise.

8. Build an assessment aspect into your techniques.

Because reading, like listening comprehension, is totally unobservable (we have to infer comprehension from other behavior), it is as important in reading as it is in listening to be able to accurately assess students' comprehension and development of skills. Consider some of the following overt responses (modeled after the list in Chapter 18 for listening) that indicate comprehension:

1. Doing—the reader responds physically to a command.
2. Choosing—the reader selects from alternatives posed orally or in writing.
3. Transferring—the reader summarizes orally what is read.
4. Answering—the reader answers questions about the passage.
5. Condensing—the reader outlines or takes notes on a passage.
6. Extending—the reader provides an ending to a story.
7. Duplicating—the reader translates the message into the native language or copies it (beginning level, for very short passages only).
8. Modeling—the reader puts together a toy, for example, after reading directions for assembly.
9. Conversing—the reader engages in a conversation that indicates appropriate processing of information.

TWO READING LESSONS

Following are excerpts from two different ESL textbooks designed to teach reading skills. In both cases, of course, the other three skills are implied in the unfolding of the lesson.

The first excerpt (Figure 20.3), on rain forests, is designed for beginners (Boone, Bennett, & Motai, 1988). It illustrates the use of natural, authentic language and tasks at the beginning level. Some attention is given to bottom-up skills, but not at the expense of top-down processing, even at this level.

The second excerpt (Figure 20.4 on pages 379–385), on genetic engineering and DNA, is for advanced students (Silberstein, Dobson, & Clarke, 2002). It illustrates the use of an article from a newspaper as the main focal point for reading. Notice that the lesson begins with top-down processing, on the assumption that at this level, the greater need is for activating schemata (note the "Before You Begin" and "Skimming and Scanning" sections) and understanding the organization and purpose of the article. Another genre is also presented: a chart of the human genome. Students are then led to take a more detailed look at their level of comprehension of each genre, followed by "Critical Reading," which calls for students to articulate their beliefs. Open discussion or writing is then encouraged, and followed by an exercise in strategic study of "Vocabulary from Context."

Figure 20.3. Rain forests (from Boone, Bennett, & Motai, 1988, pp. 14–15)

RAIN FORESTS
by Scott Adelson

Have you ever seen a rain forest? Where do rain forests grow? What is unusual or unique about rain forests? Are they important to the world?

This text is about special forests in tropical areas of the world that are being cut down, and about a special group that is trying to save them.

Vocabulary to Watch for

debt	—money you owe to another person
organization	—group
conservation	—saving the land and the animals
reserve	—a safe place for animals and nature
basin	—valley where there is a river
region	—area; large place
savannah	—dry, flat land; plain

READ

In many tropical countries, people are cutting down rain forests to make room for farms. They hope that the farms will make money for them so that they can pay their **debts**. But a new **organization** is trying to help these countries save their forests. The name of this organization is **Conservation International**. Conservation International pays countries not to cut down their rain forests.

Their first agreement was with Bolivia, for a 4,000,000 acre **reserve** in the Amazon River **basin** in northeast Bolivia. The **region** has **savannahs**, deep woods, and rain forests. It is famous for the different plants and unusual wildlife that live there. Bolivia and Conservation International will take care of the reserve together.

This idea of helping countries make rain forest reserves is so unusual that Brazil and Ecuador, which are both interested in this program, are already having talks with Conservation International.

(Continued)

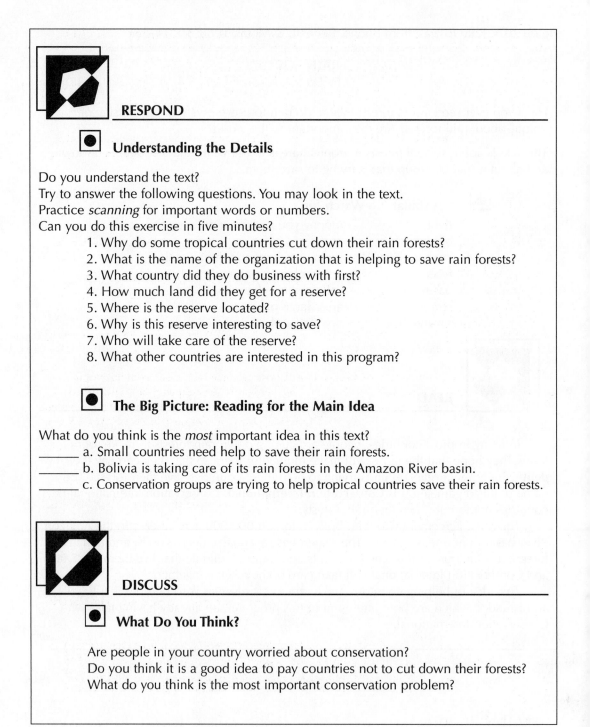

RESPOND

⬤ Understanding the Details

Do you understand the text?
Try to answer the following questions. You may look in the text.
Practice *scanning* for important words or numbers.
Can you do this exercise in five minutes?

1. Why do some tropical countries cut down their rain forests?
2. What is the name of the organization that is helping to save rain forests?
3. What country did they do business with first?
4. How much land did they get for a reserve?
5. Where is the reserve located?
6. Why is this reserve interesting to save?
7. Who will take care of the reserve?
8. What other countries are interested in this program?

⬤ The Big Picture: Reading for the Main Idea

What do you think is the *most* important idea in this text?

_____ a. Small countries need help to save their rain forests.
_____ b. Bolivia is taking care of its rain forests in the Amazon River basin.
_____ c. Conservation groups are trying to help tropical countries save their rain forests.

DISCUSS

⬤ What Do You Think?

Are people in your country worried about conservation?
Do you think it is a good idea to pay countries not to cut down their forests?
What do you think is the most important conservation problem?

Figure 20.4. Science reporting (from Silberstein, Dobson, & Clark, 2002, pp. 163–169)

Reading Selection 3
Science Reporting

Before You Begin   1. Here are some common English sayings. What do they mean? Do they contain some elements of truth? Are there similar sayings in the languages you speak?

     a. Like father, like son.
     b. He's a chip off the old block.
     c. The apple never falls far from the tree.

2. How might recent discoveries in genetics contribute to an understanding of the assumptions that underlie these sayings?

3. In discussions of personality, most explanations can be described as emphasizing "nature" or "nurture." Where do you stand with regard to these explanations?

4. Would you care if others had a copy of your medical records and learned about your genetic makeup?

Recent discoveries by scientists working on the Human Genome Project have been reported in scholarly publications and the popular press. They report success in mapping the human genome. Gene mapping is the process of identifying which genes lie where on the DNA strands that make up biological inheritance. The following article, which appeared in newspapers across the United States, examines potential dangers of the research.

Skimming and Scanning

Skim the article quickly to discover the author's main ideas, and study the accompanying illustration. Then scan to answer the following questions.*

1. Look at the illustration on page 165. What is the human genome?

2. What sort of discrimination could gene mapping encourage?

Now read the article more carefully. Your teacher may want you to do the Vocabulary from Context exercise on pages 168–69 before you begin reading.

☞ | For further discussion of issues surrounding genetic research, see "Grains of Hope," pages 258–60.

(Continued)

Gene mapping may foster discrimination

■ Employers could reject new hires predisposed to disease.

by PAUL RECER

WASHINGTON — Mapping the human genome opens a new era for medical science— and a new frontier for potential discrimination.

New genetic research may make it possible to identify an individual's lifetime risk of cancer, heart attack and other diseases. Experts worry that this information could be used to discriminate in hiring, promotions, or insurance.

Employers and insurers could save millions of dollars if they could use predictive genetics to identify in advance, and then reject, workers or policy applicants who are predisposed to develop chronic disease.

Thus, genetic discrimination could join the list of other forms of discrimination: racial, ethnic, age and sexual.

Genetic discrimination is drawing attention this week because of the first publication of the complete human genome map and sequence. Two versions, virtually identical, were compiled separately by an international public consortium and by a private company.

The journal *Nature* is publishing the work of the public consortium and the journal *Science* is publishing the sequence by Celera Genomics, a Rockville, Md., company.

Fear of such discrimination already is affecting how people view the medical revolution promised by mapping the human genome. A Time/CNN poll last summer found that 75 percent of 1,218 Americans surveyed did not want insurance companies to know their genetic code, and 84 percent wanted that information withheld from the government.

"There has been widespread fear that an individual's genetic information will be used against them," said Sen. Bill Frist, R-Tenn. "If we truly wish to improve quality of health care, we must begin taking steps to eliminate patients' fears."

The Equal Employment Opportunity Commission filed its first lawsuit challenging genetic testing last week in U.S. District Court in the Northern District of Iowa.

'Without adequate safeguards, the genetic revolution could mean one step forward for science and two steps backward for civil rights.'

—Sens. James Jeffords, R-Vt., and Tom Daschle, D-S.D.

Burlington Northern Santa Fe Railroad was charged in the suit with conducting genetic testing on employees without their permission. At least one worker was threatened with dismissal unless he agreed to the test, the agency charges.

The EEOC said the genetic tests were being run on employees who filed for worker's compensation as the result of carpal tunnel syndrome, a type of repetitive motion injury common to keyboard operators. Some studies have suggested that a mutation on chromosome 17 predisposes to the injury.

A survey of 2,133 employers this year by the American Management Association found that seven are using genetic testing for either job applicants or employees, according to the journal *Science.*

Many experts believe the only solution to potential genetic discrimination is a new federal law that specifically prohibits it.

"Genetic testing has enormous potential for improving health care in America, but to fully utilize this new science, we must eliminate patients' fears and the potential for insurance discrimination," said Frist, the only physician in the Senate.

Frist and Sen. Olympia Snowe, R-Maine, are introducing legislation that would prevent insurance companies from requiring genetic testing and ban the use of genetic information to deny coverage or to set rates.

Writing this week in the journal *Science,* Senators James M. Jeffords, R-Vt., and Tom Daschle, D-S.D., say they both favor legislation prohibiting genetic discrimination. "Without adequate safeguards, the genetic revolution could mean one step forward for science and two steps backward for civil rights," they write. "Misuse of genetic information could create a new underclass: the genetically less fortunate."

From the *Ann Arbor News,* February 12, 2001.

The human genome

The human genome is the genetic code contained in the tightly coiled strands of 23 pairs of chromosomes in each cell's nucleus.

The Human Genome Project and Celera Genomics have been racing to be the first to decode the three billion base pairs that make up the human genome and to identify genes revealed in the process.

HUMAN CELL

NUCLEUS

CHROMOSOMES

Chromosomes

Mostly made of long chains of a chemical called DNA, chromosomes carry thousands of genes, the specific portions of DNA that contain hereditary instructions.

DNA

The hereditary instructions of genes are written in a four-letter code. Each letter corresponds to one of the chemical components of DNA: A, G, C, T.

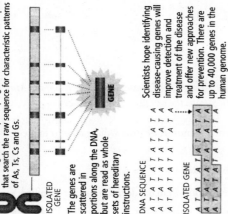

A
ADENINE

T
THYMINE

G
GUANINE

C
CYTOSINE

DNA

The bases are linked so that A always links to T, and C always links to G.

Gene discovery

To find genes, computer programs have been developed that search the raw sequence for characteristic patterns of As, Ts, Cs and Gs.

ISOLATED GENE

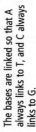

GENE

The genes are scattered in portions along the DNA, but are read as whole sets of hereditary instructions.

DNA SEQUENCE

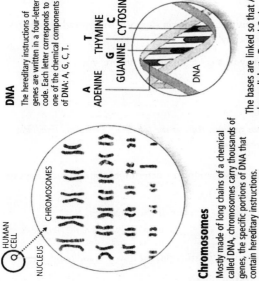

A T A T A T A T A T A
A T A T A T A T A T A
A T A T A T A T A T A

ISOLATED GENE

A T A T A T A T A
A T A T A T A T A
A T A T A T A T A

Scientists hope identifying disease-causing genes will improve detection and treatment of the disease and offer new approaches for prevention. There are up to 40,000 genes in the human genome.

Complete reports online

The world's two leading scientific journals are publishing reports by the competing teams online today. Science magazine is publishing the work by the private company Celera. Nature is publishing the work of an international public consortium.

Science magazine
● Web site:
www.sciencemag.org

Nature Science
● Web site:
www.nature.com

From the *Seattle Post-Intelligencer*/*New York Times*, February 12, 2001.

(Continued)

(Figure 20.4, continued)

Comprehension

Exercise 1

Indicate if each of the statements below is true (T) or false (F) based on "Gene Mapping May Foster Discrimination" or inferences that can be drawn from the article.

1. T / F As a result of research on the human genome, doctors will be able to make better decisions about their patients.

2. T / F Genome mapping could help you make lifestyle decisions.

3. T / F Businesses could use genetic information to make decisions about employees.

4. T / F According to a Time/CNN poll conducted around the time of the publication of the article, the majority of Americans do not want insurance companies or the government to know their genetic code.

5. T / F The Equal Employment Opportunity Commission supports widespread genetic testing as a way to improve the nation's economy.

6. T / F A mutation on a chromosome may be a cause of injured or sore wrists.

Exercise 2

Examine the illustration describing the human genome. Answer the following questions. True/False questions are indicated by a T / F preceding the item.

1. T / F The human genome contains the information that determines your physical appearance and other characteristics.

2. T / F Each human cell contains a nucleus with 23 pairs of chromosomes.

3. T / F Each chromosome contains thousands of genes.

4. T / F Genes are sections of DNA that contain instructions for how you look and act.

5. T / F There are four chemical components of DNA.

6. How many genes are contained in the human genome?

7. Where might you go for more information about the Human Genome Project?

Critical Reading

1. Following is a list of potential consequences of the genome project. Put a plus sign (+) next to those that you believe are positive and a minus sign (−) next to those that you believe are negative.

   a. _____ You will know your genetic history.

   b. _____ Genetic counselors will be able to give advice to couples who are considering having children.

   c. _____ Employers will be able to hire people with healthy family histories.

   d. _____ Doctors will be able to make more precise prescriptions.

   e. _____ Researchers will be able to suggest ways of improving babies.

   f. _____ Surgeons will be able to modify your genetic structure so that you can live longer.

   g. _____ Insurance companies will be able to save money by insuring only healthy individuals.

   h. _____ It will be possible for the government to issue ID cards with individuals' genetic profiles on them.

   i. _____ The armed forces will be able to recruit individuals whose genetic history indicates that they will be good soldiers.

   j. _____ Universities will be able to recruit students with strong academic potential.

   k. _____ Selective decisions before marriage could result in children whose genetic profiles promise genius in the arts, sports, or other areas.

   l. _____ Countries could improve their chances of healthy citizens by issuing guidelines for marriage and childbearing.

   m. _____ Parents could make medical decisions about their children long before a potential disease appeared.

   n. _____ Young people could learn about their health risks in time to alter their lifestyle choices and improve their chances for a healthy future.

2. Who are the following individuals, and what are their scientific qualifications? What role do they play in the debate over genetics and discrimination?

   a. Paul Recer   c. Olympia Snowe

   b. Bill Frist   d. Tom Daschle

Discussion/Composition

1. Which potential consequence of genetic mapping most excites or most worries you? Why?

2. Should an employer be required to hire a worker who is otherwise qualified for a job but whose family history indicates a risk of a serious illness? Consider the issue from the perspective of both employer and employee. Present your perspective either orally or in writing. Include reasons and examples.

(Continued)

(Figure 20.4, continued)

Vocabulary from Context

Both the ideas and the vocabulary in the following passage are taken from "Gene Mapping May Foster Discrimination." Use the context provided to determine the meanings of the italicized words. Write a definition, synonym, or description of each of the italicized vocabulary items in the space provided.

1. _____

2. _____

3. _____

4. _____

5. _____

6. _____

7. _____

8. _____

9. _____

The gene is often called the building block of life because it is the smallest unit to carry information from one generation to another. Scientists working in the field of *genetics* are able to understand how one generation inherits important characteristics from the previous generation. But we are able to understand much more than merely why a particular family has a large number of red-haired children. We are also able to discover whether an individual is likely to live a long life or suffer from particular diseases. This is called *predictive genetics,* and the benefits of such research are many.

This description of the genetic code of the human being has long been the goal of scientists. Doctors are interested in this research because of the possibilities it would provide for treating long-term illnesses. The treatment of *chronic* diseases such as asthma and diabetes, for example, could be greatly improved by early diagnosis. There is also the possibility that an understanding of *mutations* in genetic sequences could be used to cure disease. Some researchers believe, for example, that genetic changes are responsible for many common diseases. Predictive genetics can also help in situations where there is a *predisposition* for illness. In some cases, a family history indicates a high probability of developing a disease. Genetic mapping could indicate if that will happen, thereby increasing the chances of early diagnosis and treatment.

While no one doubts the benefits of gene mapping, it is also true that there is a dark side to all this knowledge. As with all scientific advances, the possibility exists that knowledge would be used to violate basic human rights. For example, you might be denied a job or a chance to move up in the company because your genetic map indicates that you have a high probability of contracting a certain disease. The possibility that this would be used as a reason not to hire an employee or *promote* within the company is what worries people.

The *insurance* industry is another area where these concerns arise. Insurance companies provide financial security for people by promising that they will continue to be paid in the event that they are unable to work. There is widespread fear that employees needing *workers' compensation* would be denied because of their genetic history. This type of *discrimination* is illegal, just as it is illegal to reject you because of your gender or race. However, the dangers increased recently because of research reports published in

10. _____

11. _____

12. _____

13. _____

two respected journals, *Nature* and *Science,* which describe the work of scientists to map the human *genome.*

Many experts believe that the only way to address this risk is to pass national laws that *prohibit* discrimination. Such laws would forbid employers from failing to promote an employee or from *dismissing* an employee from the company merely because of genetic makeup. It is clear that such laws would not *eliminate* genetic discrimination entirely, but they would greatly reduce such practices.

ASSESSING READING

The classic principles of classroom assessment apply to your attempts to assess reading comprehension: Be specific about which micro- or macroskill(s) you are assessing; identify the genre of written communication that is being evaluated; and choose carefully among the range of possibilities from simply perceiving letters or words all the way to extensive reading. In addition, for assessing reading, some attention should be given to the highly strategic nature of reading comprehension by accounting for which of the many strategies for reading are being examined. Finally, reading assessment implies differentiating bottom-up from top-down tasks, as well as focus on form versus focus on meaning.

In your efforts to design tests at any one or a combination of these levels and categories, consider the following taxonomy of tasks. These are not meant to be exhaustive, but rather to provide an overview of some possibilities.

1. Perceptive reading (recognition of symbols, letters, words)

   - reading aloud
   - copying (reproduce in writing)
   - multiple-choice recognition (including true-false and fill-in-the-blank)
   - picture-cued identification

2. Selective reading (focus on morphology, grammar, lexicon)

   - multiple choice grammar/vocabulary tasks
   - contextualized multiple choice (within a short paragraph)
   - sentence-level cloze tasks
   - matching tasks
   - grammar/vocabulary editing tasks (multiple choice)
   - picture-cued tasks (Ss choose among graphic representations)
   - gap-filling tasks (e.g., sentence completion)

3. Interactive reading

- discourse-level cloze tasks (requiring knowledge of discourse)
- reading + comprehension questions
- short-answer responses to reading
- discourse editing tasks (multiple choice)
- scanning
- re-ordering sequences of sentences
- responding to charts, maps, graphs, diagrams

4. Extensive reading

- skimming
- summarizing
- responding to reading through short essays
- note taking, marginal notes, highlighting
- outlining

☆   ☆   ☆   ☆   ☆

This chapter has only begun to scratch the surface of information on the teaching of reading, but you should now have a grasp of some issues surrounding this challenging task, and a sense of how to go about designing effective tasks and activities. Of further importance is the reading-writing connection, the second half of which we turn to in the next chapter.

TOPICS FOR DISCUSSION, ACTION, AND RESEARCH

[Note: (I) Individual work; (G) group or pair work; (C) whole-class discussion.]

1. (G/C) Bring to class a number of different samples of types (genres) of written language (see pages 362–363), such as a memo, a newspaper article, a questionnaire, a telephone directory, and give one each to small groups. The group's task is to review the meaning of bottom-up and top-down processing of written material, then offer examples of each for its assigned genre. Ask groups to then report back to the whole class.

2. (G/C) Tell small groups to think of an anecdote or joke that one could tell classmates. Then, after reviewing the meaning of content and formal schemata, identify examples of each type of schemata in the anecdote. They will then report back to the class.

3. (G/C) Ask small groups to choose a pair of contrasting genres of written language and list their distinctive features, that is, what readers need to know about each with a specific focus on formal characteristics. Next, tell them to devise a technique that would teach the genres and demonstrate them to the rest of the class.

4. (C) Review the meaning of skimming and scanning. What are the differences between them? What purposes does each serve? Ask your students to suggest hints they would give to a student who just doesn't seem to be able to skim a passage.

5. (G) Ten reading strategies are discussed on pages 366–371. Direct pairs to look at the textbook lesson reprinted in Figure 20.4 beginning on page 379, and (a) note which strategies are being encouraged in each activity, and (b) think of other activities that would fill any gaps.

6. (C/G) Review with the class the discussion of semantic mapping on page 368. Ask pairs to skim the reading selection "Gene Mapping May Foster Discrimination" in Figure 20.4 and to draw a semantic map of it. Then have pairs compare their maps with others in the class and talk about why they drew theirs the way they did.

7. (I) On page 370, compensation strategies were mentioned. What are these? Give some concrete examples. How might they be taught?

8. (G) Tell pairs to look at the textbook lesson on rain forests (Figure 20.3) and to critique it in terms of its adherence to principles of teaching interactive reading. What changes might they recommend and why? Have them share their conclusions with the rest of the class. If time permits, they could talk about how they would teach this lesson to a specified group of beginning students, and to share those ideas with the rest of the class.

9. (I) Skim the textbook lesson reprinted in Figure 20.4 at the end of the chapter. Evaluate this lesson on the basis of (a) opportunities for students to learn strategies of reading and (b) the eight principles for designing interactive techniques (especially #3 on choosing texts).

10. (G/C) Divide that lesson (Figure 20.4) into segments and give a segment to each of a number of small groups. The group task is to decide how they would teach that segment to a specified group of learners, then demonstrate those techniques to the rest of the class.

FOR YOUR FURTHER READING

Anderson, N. (1999). *Exploring second language reading: Issues and strategies.* Boston: Heinle & Heinle.

Nuttall, C. (1996). *Teaching reading skills in a foreign language.* (2nd ed.). Oxford, UK: Heinemann.

Neil Anderson's and Christine Nuttall's teacher reference books offer comprehensive treatments of research issues and classroom practice in teaching reading skills. The material is useful for teachers in training, but they give excellent reviews of issues and techniques for experienced teachers as well.

Eskey, D. (2005). Reading in a second language. In E. Hinkel (Ed.), *Handbook of research in second language teaching and learning* (pp. 563–579). Mahwah, NJ: Lawrence Erlbaum Associates.

Grabe, W. (2004). Research on teaching reading. *Annual Review of Applied Linguistics, 24,* 44–69.

Anderson, N. (2003). Reading. In D. Nunan (Ed.), *Practical English language teaching* (pp. 67–86). New York: McGraw-Hill Contemporary.

David Eskey, William Grabe, and Neil Anderson are recognized experts in the field of second language reading. These three survey articles provide synopses of research and practice in the teaching of reading to second language learners. The first two articles have extensive bibliographies which can serve as a set of references for further research and exploration. Anderson's article is more practically oriented.

Nation, I. S. P. (2003). Vocabulary. In D. Nunan (Ed.), *Practical English language teaching* (pp. 129–152). New York: McGraw-Hill Contemporary.

Nation, I. S. P. (2005). Teaching and learning vocabulary. In E. Hinkel (Ed.), *Handbook of research in second language teaching and learning* (pp. 581–595). Mahwah, NJ: Lawrence Erlbaum Associates.

Read, J. (2004). Research in teaching vocabulary. *Annual Review of Applied Linguistics, 24,* 146–161.

These three articles, also by leading experts in the field, Paul Nation and John Read, like Eskey's, Grabe's, and Anderson's above, survey issues in vocabulary acquisition and teaching. They, too, provide useful bibliographic references.

Nassaji, H. (2002). Schema theory and knowledge-based processes in second language reading comprehension: A need for alternative perspectives. *Language Learning, 52,* 439–481.

For a real professional challenge, try reading Nassaji's article about an alternative approach to schema theory. It's highly technical material, so be forewarned, this is not for the faint-hearted!

Silberstein, S., Dobson, B., & Clarke, M. (2002). *Reader's choice* (4th ed.). Ann Arbor: University of Michigan Press.

Here's a highly recommended example of a textbook that has almost every imaginable genre of reading! Now in its fourth edition, a sign of its success since its first edition in 1977, it is a superior example of a very student-friendly textbook that focuses on reading while involving students in other integrated skills.

Alderson, J. (2000). *Assessing reading.* Cambridge, UK: Cambridge University Press.

Read, Alderson, J. (2000). *Assessing vocabulary.* Cambridge, UK: Cambridge University Press.

These two volumes are part of a series on language assessment. They both contain research background, issues, theoretical foundations, and practical applications in their respective areas.

CHAPTER 21

TEACHING WRITING

> **OBJECTIVES** After reading this chapter, you will be able to:
>
> - understand issues and concepts in pedagogical research that are related to teaching writing
>
> - appreciate some of the unique difficulties involved in learning to write effectively
>
> - analyze types of written language, micro- and macroskills, and types of classroom writing performance
>
> - apply principles of designing writing techniques to your own lesson designs and to your observation of others
>
> - recognize some basic principles and formats for evaluating and assessing writing

The psycholinguist Eric Lenneberg (1967) once noted, in a discussion of "species-specific" human behavior, that human beings universally learn to walk and to talk, but that swimming and writing are culturally specific, learned behaviors. We learn to swim if there is a body of water available and usually only if someone teaches us. We learn to write if we are members of a literate society, and usually only if someone teaches us.

Just as there are nonswimmers, poor swimmers, and excellent swimmers, so it is for writers. Why isn't everyone an excellent writer? What is it about writing that blocks so many people, even in their own native language? Why don't people learn to write "naturally," as they learn to talk? How can we best teach second language learners of English how to write? What should we be trying to teach? Let's look at these and many other related questions as we tackle the last of the "four skills."

RESEARCH ON SECOND LANGUAGE WRITING

Trends in the teaching of writing in ESL and other foreign languages have, not surprisingly, coincided with those of the teaching of other skills, especially listening and speaking. You will recall from earlier chapters that as communicative language teaching gathered momentum in the 1980s, teachers learned more and more about how to teach fluency, not just accuracy, how to use authentic texts and contexts in the classroom, how to focus on the purposes of linguistic communication, and how to capitalize on learners' intrinsic motives to learn. Those same trends and the principles that undergirded them also applied to advances in the teaching of writing in second language contexts.

Over the past few decades of research on teaching writing to second language learners, a number of issues have appeared, some of which remain controversial in spite of reams of data on second language writing. Here is a brief look at some of those issues.

1. Composing versus writing

A simplistic view of writing would assume that written language is simply the graphic representation of spoken language, and that written performance is much like oral performance, the only difference lying in graphic instead of auditory signals. Fortunately, no one holds this view today. The process of writing requires an entirely different set of competencies and is fundamentally different from speaking in ways that have already been reviewed in the last chapter. The permanence and distance of writing, coupled with its unique rhetorical conventions, indeed make writing as different from speaking as swimming is from walking.

One major theme in pedagogical research on writing is the nature of the **composing** process of writing (O'Brien, 2004; Silva & Brice, 2004). Written products are often the result of thinking, drafting, and revising procedures that require specialized skills, skills that not every speaker develops naturally. Further, students exhibit a number of different styles and preferences in their composing processes (Chen, 2005). The upshot of the compositional nature of writing has produced writing pedagogy that focuses students on how to generate ideas, how to organize them coherently, how to use discourse markers and rhetorical conventions to put them cohesively into a written text, how to revise text for clearer meaning, how to edit text for appropriate grammar, and how to produce a final product.

2. Process versus product

Recognition of the compositional nature of writing has changed the face of writing classes. A half a century ago, writing teachers were mostly concerned with the final **product** of writing: the essay, the report, the story, and what that product should "look" like. Compositions were supposed to (a) meet certain standards of prescribed English rhetorical style, (b) reflect accurate grammar, and (c) be organized in conformity with what the audience would consider to be conventional. A good deal of attention was placed on "model" compositions that students would emulate and on how well a student's final product measured up against a list of criteria that included content, organization, vocabulary use, grammatical use, and mechanical considerations such as spelling and punctuation.

There is nothing inherently wrong with attention to any of the above criteria. They are still the concern of writing teachers. But in due course of time, we became better attuned to the advantage given to learners when they were seen as creators of language, when they were allowed to focus on content and message, and when their own individual intrinsic motives were put at the center of learning. We began to develop what is now termed the **process** approach to writing instruction. Process approaches do most of the following (adapted from Shih, 1986):

- focus on the process of writing that leads to the final written product;
- help student writers to understand their own composing process;
- help them to build repertoires of strategies for prewriting, drafting, and rewriting;
- give students time to write and rewrite;
- place central importance on the process of revision;
- let students discover what they want to say as they write;
- give students feedback throughout the composing process (not just on the final product) as they attempt to bring their expression closer and closer to intention;
- encourage feedback from both the instructor and peers;
- include individual conferences between teacher and student during the process of composition.

Perhaps you can personally appreciate what it means to be asked to write something—say, a letter to an editor, an article for a newsletter, a paper for a course you're taking—and to allow the very process of putting ideas down on paper to transform thoughts into words, to sharpen your main ideas, to give them structure and coherent organization. As your first draft goes through perhaps several steps of revision, your thesis and developing ideas more and more resemble something that you would consider a final product. If you have done this, you have used your own process approach to writing.

You may also know firsthand what it is like to try to come up with a "perfect" final product without the above process. You may have experienced "writer's cramp" (mental blocks) that severely hampered any progress. You may have felt a certain level of anxiety building within you as you felt the pressure to write an in-class essay that would be judged by the teacher, graded, and returned with no chance for your future revision. The process approach is an attempt to take advantage of the nature of the written code (unlike conversation, it can be planned and given an unlimited number of revisions before its "release") to give students a chance to think as they write. Another way of putting it is that writing is indeed a *thinking process*.

Over three decades ago, Peter Elbow (1973) expressed the concept of process writing in urging teachers to discard the notion that "first you figure out what you want to say... don't start writing till you do" (p. 14). Elbow and many experts since then have noted that "this idea of writing is backwards" (Elbow, 1973, p. 15). Instead, process approaches feature the following practices (adapted from Hedgcock, 2005, pp. 604–605):

- allowing students to discover their own voice (see #7 below)
- freewriting, journaling, and fluency activities
- tasks that engage learners in meaningful writing
- giving writers a sense of audience and authentic tasks

- encouraging invention, prewriting, and revision strategies
- providing formative feedback through conferencing

The current emphasis on process writing must of course be seen in the perspective of history and future developments (Casanave, 2004; Hedgcock, 2005; O'Brien, 2004; Silva & Leki, 2004). Some research (Atkinson, 2003) has already claimed that we are now in a "post-process" era, while others (Matsuda, 2003) are more circumspect by noting that the concept of post-process, in fact, only rejects "the dominance of process at the expense of other aspects of writing and writing instruction" (Matsuda, 2003, pp. 78–79). As in most language-teaching approaches, it is quite possible for you to go to an extreme in emphasizing process to the extent that the final product diminishes in importance. Try not to let this happen! The product is, after all, the ultimate goal; it is the reason that we go through the process of prewriting, drafting, revising, and editing. Without that final product firmly in view, we could quite simply drown ourselves in a sea of revisions. Process is not the end; it is the means to the end.

3. Contrastive rhetoric

Robert Kaplan's (1966) article on contrastive rhetoric has been the subject of much discussion and debate ever since. Kaplan's thesis was that different languages (and their cultures) have different patterns of written discourse. English discourse, according to Kaplan (p. 14), was schematically described as proceeding in a straight line, Semitic writing in a zigzag formation, Oriental [*sic*] written discourse in a spiraling line, and so forth (see Figure 21.1).

The point of Kaplan's conclusions about how we write was, of course, that learners of English bring with them certain predispositions, which come from their native languages, about how to organize their writing. If English writers get "straight" to the point, and Chinese writers "spiral" around the point, then a Chinese speaker who is learning English will encounter some difficulty in learning to write English discourse.

Figure 21.1. Patterns of written discourse (Kaplan, 1966, p. 14)

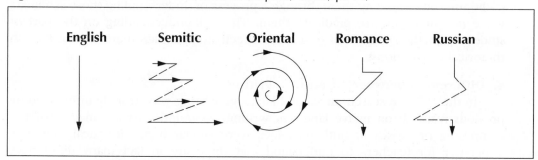

There were problems with Kaplan's study (Casanave, 2004; Connor, 2002), some of which Kaplan has recently responded to (Kaplan, 2005). His diagrams and conclusions were simplistic and overgeneralized. Simplistic, because he based his conclusions about English discourse on style manuals rather than using data from actual writing in English. Overgeneralized, because one cannot conclude that English writers consistently use a "straight-line" attack on a thesis and certainly cannot make any generalization that applies, for example, to all Oriental languages. Furthermore, without a native-speaking English control group, one cannot determine if the "difficulty" of his sample data is simply the difficulty any inexperienced writer might encounter in learning to write.

Nevertheless, there was and still is a ring of truth to Kaplan's claims, as both Kaplan (2005) himself and Connor (2002) have noted. In fact, Connor has done much "to move contrastive rhetoric out of the quagmire in which it had been lodged for so long" (Casanave, 2004, p. 41). No one can deny the effect of one's native culture, or one's predispositions that are the product of perhaps years of schooling, reading, writing, thinking, asserting, arguing, and defending. In our current paradigm of attending carefully to schemata and scripts, native language patterns of thinking and writing simply cannot be ruled out. A balanced position on this issue, then, would uphold the importance of your carefully attending to the rhetorical first language interference that may be at play in your students' writing. But rather than holding a dogmatic or predictive view (that certain writers *will* experience difficulty because of their native language), you would be more prudent to adopt a "weak" position (see *PLLT,* Chapter 9) in which you would consider a student's cultural/literary schemata as only one possible source of difficulty.

In recent years new research studies have appeared that tackle the issue of contrastive rhetoric (Casanave, 2004; Connor, 2002). According to Connor, a theory of contrastive rhetoric is influenced by more than first language patterns; factors such as linguistic relativity, theory of rhetoric, text linguistics, discourse types and genres, literacy, and translation all contribute toward a comprehensive theory of contrastive rhetoric. One important conclusion from this renewed wave of research is the significance of valuing students' native-language-related rhetorical traditions, and of guiding them through a process of understanding those schemata while *not* attempting to eradicate them. That self-understanding on the part of students may then lend itself to a more effective appreciation and use of English rhetorical conventions.

4. Differences between L1 and L2 writing

In the 1970s, research on second language writing was strongly influenced by previous research on native language writing. Assumptions were made that the composing processes in both instances were similar if not identical. But it is imperative for teachers to understand that there are in fact many differences between the two, as Tony Silva (1993) so clearly demonstrated in a comprehensive survey of L2 writing. Silva found that L2 writers did less planning, and that they were less fluent (used fewer words), less accurate (made more errors), and less effective in stating goals and organizing material. Differences in using appropriate grammatical and rhetorical conventions and lexical variety were also found, among other features.

The questions that are currently being addressed in this area (Hedgcock, 2005) center on differences between L1 and L2 writing and sorting out appropriate approaches to L2 writing. Some pedagogical implications of these questions are that (a) it is important to determine appropriate approaches to writing instruction for L2 writers in different contexts, (b) writing teachers need to be equipped to deal effectively with the sociocultural and linguistic differences of L2 students, and (c) the assessment of L2 writing may need to take into account the fundamental differences between most L1 and L2 writing.

5. Authenticity

Another issue in the teaching of writing surrounds the question of how much of our classroom writing is "real" writing (Casanave, 2004; Hedgcock, 2005; Silva & Brice, 2004). That is, how authentic are the classroom writing exercises that we ask students to perform? One could address this question by asking how much writing the average college-educated person in Western society actually does, and what kind of writing. I would venture to say very little, and that little amounts to filling out forms, writing telephone messages, e-mailing, and occasionally dashing off a letter or postcard. In the era of electronic communication (video, phone, computer, etc.) we are less and less called upon to *compose*. I was recently consulted by a friend who is studying to be certified as a realtor. Part of his certification examination involved a simple one- or two-page written essay. The prospect frightened him!

So, why do we want students to write? In school, writing is a way of life. Without some ability to express yourself in writing, you don't pass the course. Across the age levels from elementary school through university graduate courses, we write in order to succeed in mastering the subject matter. In **English for Academic Purposes** (EAP), writing ranges from short phrases (as in fill-in-the-blank tests), to brief paragraphs (as in essay question exercises and tests), to brief reports of many different kinds, to a full-length research paper. In vocational-technical English (where students are studying English in connection with a trade or occupation), students need to fill out forms, write simple messages, write certain conventional reports (for example, a bid on a contract, an inspection report), and at the most "creative" end of the continuum, write a brief business letter. In adult education and survival English classes, filling out simple forms and questionnaires may be as sophisticated as students' needs get. This leaves EAP as the major consumer of writing techniques, especially writing techniques that concern themselves with the composing process: development of ideas, argument, logic, cause and effect, etc., as Paltridge (2004) aptly describes in a survey of teaching EAP.

Another way to look at the authenticity issue in classroom writing is to distinguish between **real writing** and **display writing**. Real writing, as explained by Ann Raimes (1991), is writing when the reader doesn't know the answer and genuinely wants information. In many academic/school contexts, however, if the instructor is the sole reader, writing is primarily for the display of a student's knowledge. Written exercises, short-answer essays, and other writing in test situations are instances of display writing.

Should we as teachers incorporate more real writing in our classrooms? In some ways, yes. If ESL courses strive to be more content-based, theme-based, or task-based, students are more likely to be given the opportunity to convey genuine information on topics of intrinsic interest. But display writing is not totally unjustified. Writing to display one's knowledge is a fact of life in the classroom, and by getting your students to perform well in display writing exercises, they can learn skills that will help them to succeed in further academic pursuits.

6. Responding to student writing

The gradual recognition of writing as a process of thinking and composing was a natural by-product of CLT. With its emphasis on learner-centered instruction, student-student negotiation, and strategies-based instruction that values the variability of learners' pathways to success, CLT is an appropriate locus for process writing. As students are encouraged (in reading) to bring their own schemata to bear on understanding texts, and in writing to develop their own ideas, offer their own critical analysis, and find their own voice (see #7 below), the role of teacher must be one of facilitator and coach, not an authoritative director and arbiter.

This facilitative role of the writing teacher has inspired research on the role of the teacher as a responder to students' writing (Casanave, 2004; Ferris & Hedgcock, 2005; Hedgcock, 2005; Silva & Brice, 2004). As a facilitator, the teacher offers guidance in helping students to engage in the thinking process of composing but, in a spirit of respect for student opinion, must not impose his or her own thoughts on student writing. However, as Joy Reid (1994, p. 273) pointed out, our penchant for laissez-faire approaches to commenting on student writing may have gone too far. "Instead of entering the conversation of composing and drafting, instead of helping students negotiate between their interests and purposes and the experiences and intentions of their academic readers, many teachers have retreated into a hands-off approach to student writing." Short of "appropriating" student text, we can offer useful feedback that respects students' values and beliefs. Dana Ferris (1997) offered useful guidelines for making teacher commentary more effective. For example, Ferris found that when teachers (a) requested specific information and (b) made summary comments on grammar, more substantive student revisions ensued than when teachers (a) posed questions and (b) made positive comments. We are still exploring ways to offer optimal feedback to student writing.

7. Voice and identity

Weaving in and out of several of the above topics, especially the last one, is the issue of how to preserve the cultural and social identities of students but at the same time to teach English language writing conventions. This issue is especially acute in the case of EAP writing programs where a major goal is for students to write acceptable academic prose in their respective subject-matter fields (Paltridge, 2004). In other writing courses, however, the problem is also significant as course designers and instructors must attend to "the socially and politically situated contexts of writing and how these contexts influence both how writing gets done and the end products of writing" (Casanave, 2004, p. 84). In some ways the issue is one of authenticity, mentioned above, and in other ways it has overtones of critical pedagogy (see Chapter 26). Recent research indicates that some progress is being made toward focusing students on writing for meaningful purposes within their own sociopolitical contexts (Atkinson, 2003; Casanave, 2003), and not just creating writing assignments that will force certain rhetorical competencies.

These seven categories comprise just a few of the many intriguing current questions in teaching writing. By acquainting yourself with these issues, you will begin to gain an appreciation of some of the challenges of becoming an effective writing teacher.

TYPES OF WRITTEN LANGUAGE

In Chapter 20, on pages 362–363, were some 30-odd types of written language "forms." As you consider an ESL class that you might be teaching, how many of these types of writing will your students be likely to produce themselves? Those types that they will indeed need, either for further study of English or for their ultimate academic/vocational goals, should then become the prime focus of "real" writing in your classroom.

CHARACTERISTICS OF WRITTEN LANGUAGE: A WRITER'S VIEW

In Chapter 20, some characteristics of written language from the perspective of a reader were set forth. Let's revisit those from a writer's viewpoint.

1. Permanence
Once something is written down and delivered in its final form to its intended audience, the writer abdicates a certain power: the power to emend, to clarify, to withdraw. That prospect is the single most significant contributor to making writing a scary operation! Student writers often feel that the act of releasing a written work to an instructor is not unlike putting themselves in front of a firing squad. Therefore, whatever you can do as a teacher, guide, and facilitator to help your students to revise and refine their work before final submission will help give them confidence in their work.

2. Production time
The good news is that, given appropriate stretches of time, a writer can indeed become a "good" writer by developing efficient processes for achieving the final product. The bad news is that many educational contexts demand student writing within time limits, or "writing for display" as noted in the previous section (examination

writing, for example). So, one of your goals, especially if you are teaching in an EAP context, would be to train your students to make the best possible use of such time limitations. This may mean sacrificing some process time, but with sufficient training in process writing, combined with practice in display writing, you can help your students deal with time limitations.

3. Distance

One of the thorniest problems writers face is anticipating their audience. That anticipation ranges from general audience characteristics to how specific words, phrases, sentences, and paragraphs will be interpreted. The distance factor requires what might be termed "cognitive" empathy, in that good writers can "read" their own writing from the perspective of the mind of the targeted audience. Writers need to be able to predict the audience's general knowledge, cultural and literary schemata, specific subject-matter knowledge, and very important, how their choice of language will be interpreted.

4. Orthography

Everything from simple greetings to extremely complex ideas is captured through the manipulation of a few dozen letters and other written symbols. Sometimes we take for granted the mastering of the mechanics of English writing by our students. If students are nonliterate in the native language, you must begin at the very beginning with fundamentals of reading and writing. For literate students, if their native language system is not alphabetic, new symbols have to be produced by hands that may have become accustomed to another system. If the native language has a different phoneme–grapheme system (most do!), then some attention is due here.

5. Complexity

In the previous chapter, the complexity of written—as opposed to spoken—language was illustrated. Writers must learn how to remove redundancy (which may not jibe with their first language rhetorical tradition), how to combine sentences, how to make references to other elements in a text, how to create syntactic and lexical variety, and much more.

6. Vocabulary

As was noted in Chapter 20, written language places a heavier demand on vocabulary use than does speaking. Good writers will learn to take advantage of the richness of English vocabulary.

7. Formality

Whether a student is filling out a questionnaire or writing a full-blown essay, the conventions of each form must be followed. For ESL students, the most difficult and complex conventions occur in academic writing where students have to learn how to describe, explain, compare, contrast, illustrate, defend, criticize, and argue.

MICRO- AND MACROSKILLS FOR WRITING

Following the format from the previous three chapters, micro- and macroskills for writing production are enumerated in Table 21.1.

Table 21.1. Micro- and macroskills for writing

Microskills

1. Produce graphemes and orthographic patterns of English.
2. Produce writing at an efficient rate of speed to suit the purpose.
3. Produce an acceptable core of words and use appropriate word order patterns.
4. Use acceptable grammatical systems (e.g., tense, agreement, pluralization), patterns, and rules.
5. Express a particular meaning in different grammatical forms.

Macroskills

6. Use cohesive devices in written discourse.
7. Use the rhetorical forms and conventions of written discourse.
8. Appropriately accomplish the communicative functions of written texts according to form and purpose.
9. Convey links and connections between events and communicate such relations as main idea, supporting idea, new information, given information, generalization, and exemplification.
10. Distinguish between literal and implied meanings when writing.
11. Correctly convey culturally specific references in the context of the written text.
12. Develop and use a battery of writing strategies, such as accurately assessing the audience's interpretation, using prewriting devices, writing with fluency in the first drafts, using paraphrases and synonyms, soliciting peer and instructor feedback, and using feedback for revising and editing.

TYPES OF CLASSROOM WRITING PERFORMANCE

While various genres of written texts abound, classroom writing performance is, by comparison, limited. Consider the following five major categories of classroom writing performance:

1. Imitative, or writing down

At the beginning level of learning to write, students will simply "write down" English letters, words, and possibly sentences in order to learn the conventions of the orthographic code. Some forms of **dictation** fall into this category, although dictations can serve to teach and test higher-order processing as well. Dictations typically involve the following steps:

a. Teacher reads a short paragraph once or twice at normal speed.
b. Teacher reads the paragraph in short phrase units of three or four words each, and each unit is followed by a pause.
c. During the pause, students write exactly what they hear.
d. Teacher then reads the whole paragraph once more at normal speed so students can check their writing.
e. Scoring of students' written work can utilize a number of rubrics for assigning points. Usually spelling and punctuation errors are not considered as severe as grammatical errors.

2. Intensive, or controlled

Writing is sometimes used as a production mode for learning, reinforcing, or testing grammatical concepts. This intensive writing typically appears in controlled, written grammar exercises. This type of writing does not allow much, if any, creativity on the part of the writer.

A common form of **controlled** writing is to present a paragraph to students in which they have to alter a given structure throughout. So, for example, they may be asked to change all present tense verbs to past tense; in such a case, students may need to alter other time references in the paragraph.

Guided writing loosens the teacher's control but still offers a series of stimulators. For example, the teacher might get students to tell a story just viewed on a videotape by asking them a series of questions: Where does the story take place? Describe the principal character. What does he say to the woman in the car?

Yet another form of controlled writing is a **dicto-comp**. Here, a paragraph is read at normal speed, usually two or three times; then the teacher asks students to rewrite the paragraph to the best of their recollection of the reading. In one of several variations of the dicto-comp technique, the teacher, after reading the passage, puts key words from the paragraph, in sequence, on the chalkboard as cues for the students.

3. Self-writing

A significant proportion of classroom writing may be devoted to self-writing, or writing with only the self in mind as an audience. The most salient instance of this category in classrooms is note taking, where students take notes during a lecture for the purpose of later recall. Other note taking may be done in the margins of books and on odd scraps of paper.

Diary or **journal** writing also falls into this category. However, in many circumstances a **dialogue journal,** in which a student records thoughts, feelings, and reactions and which an instructor reads and responds to, while ostensibly written for oneself, has two audiences.

Figure 21.2 is an entry from a journal written by an advanced ESL student from China, followed by the teacher's response (contributed by Lauren Vanett and Donna Jurich).

Figure 21.2. Journal entry—advanced student from China

Journal Entry:

Yesterday at about eight o'clock I was sitting in front of my table holding a fork and eating tasteless noodles which I usually really like to eat but I lost my taste yesterday because I didn't feel well. I had a headache and a fever. My head seemed to be broken. I sometimes felt cold, sometimes hot. I didn't feel comfortable standing up and I didn't feel comfortable sitting down. I hated eveything around me. It seemed to me that I got a great pressure from the atmosphere and I could not breath. I was so sleepy since I had taken some medicine which functioned as an antibiotic.

The room was so quiet. I was there by myself and felt very solitary. This dinner reminded me of my mother. Whenever I was sick in China, my mother always took care of me and cooked rice gruel, which has to cook more than three hours and is very delicious, I think. I would be better very soon under the care of my mother. But yesterday, I had to cook by myself even though I was sick, The more I thought, the less I wanted to eat, Half an hour passed. The noodles were cold, but I was still sitting there and thinking about my mother, Finally I threw out the noodles and went to bed.

Ming Ling, PRC

Teacher's Response:

This is a powerful piece of writing because you really communicate what you were feeling. You used vivid details, like ". . . eating tasteless noodles . . .", "my head seemed to be broken . . ." and ". . . rice gruel, which has to cook more than three hours and is very delicious." These make it easy for the reader to picture exactly what you were going through. The other strong point about this piece is that you bring the reader full circle by beginning and ending with "the noodles."

Being alone when you are sick is difficult. Now, I know why you were so quiet in class.

If you want to do another entry related to this one, you could have a dialogue with your "sick" self. What would your "healthy" self say to the "sick" self? Is there some advice that could be exchanged about how to prevent illness or how to take care of yourself better when you do get sick? Start the dialogue with your "sick" self speaking first.

4. Display writing

It was noted earlier that writing within the school curricular context is a way of life. For all language students, short-answer exercises, essay examinations, and even research reports will involve an element of display. For academically bound ESL students, one of the academic skills that they need to master is a whole array of display writing techniques.

5. Real writing

While virtually every classroom writing task will have an element of display writing in it, some classroom writing aims at the genuine communication of messages to an audience in need of those messages. The two categories of real and display writing are actually two ends of a continuum, and in between the two extremes lies some combination of display and real writing. Three subcategories illustrate how reality can be injected:

a. **Academic.** The Language Experience Approach gives groups of students opportunities to convey genuine information to each other. Content-based instruction encourages the exchange of useful information, and some of this learning uses the written word. Group problem-solving tasks, especially those that relate to current issues and other personally relevant topics, may have a writing component in which information is genuinely sought and conveyed. Peer-editing work adds to what would otherwise be an audience of one (the instructor) and provides real writing opportunity. In certain ESP and EAP courses, students may exchange new information with each other and with the instructor.

b. **Vocational/technical.** Quite a variety of real writing can take place in classes of students studying English for advancement in their occupation. Real letters can be written; genuine directions for some operation or assembly might be given; and actual forms can be filled out. These possibilities are even greater in what has come to be called "English in the Workplace," where ESL is offered within companies and corporations.

c. **Personal.** In virtually any ESL class, diaries, letters, postcards, notes, personal messages, and other informal writing can take place, especially within the context of an interactive classroom. While certain tasks may be somewhat contrived, nevertheless the genuine exchange of information can happen.

PRINCIPLES FOR TEACHING WRITING SKILLS

Out of all of these characteristics of the written word, along with micro- and macroskills and research issues, a number of specific principles for teaching writing skills emerge.

1. Incorporate practices of "good" writers.

This first guideline is sweeping. But as you contemplate devising a technique that has a writing goal in it, consider the various things that efficient writers do, and see if your technique includes some of these practices. For example, good writers

- focus on a goal or main idea in writing,
- perceptively gauge their audience,
- spend some time (but not too much!) planning to write,
- easily let their first ideas flow onto the paper,
- follow a general organizational plan as they write,
- solicit and utilize feedback on their writing,
- are not wedded to certain surface structures,
- revise their work willingly and efficiently,
- patiently make as many revisions as needed.

2. Balance process and product.

Because writing is a composing process and usually requires multiple drafts before an effective product is created, make sure that students are carefully led through appropriate stages in the process of composing. This includes careful attention to your own role as a guide and as a responder (see #8). At the same time, don't get so caught up in the stages leading up to the final product that you lose sight of the ultimate attainment: a clear, articulate, well-organized, effective piece of writing. Make sure students see that everything leading up to this final creation was worth the effort.

3. Account for cultural/literary backgrounds.

Make sure that your techniques do not assume that your students know English rhetorical conventions. If there are some apparent contrasts between students' native traditions and those that you are trying to teach, try to help students to understand what it is, exactly, that they are accustomed to and then, by degrees, bring them to the use of acceptable English rhetoric.

4. Connect reading and writing.

Clearly, students learn to write in part by carefully observing what is already written. That is, they learn by observing, or reading, the written word. By reading and studying a variety of relevant types of text, students can gain important insights both about how they should write and about subject matter that may become the topic of their writing.

5. Provide as much authentic writing as possible.

Whether writing is real writing or for display, it can still be authentic in that the purposes for writing are clear to the students, the audience is specified overtly, and there is at least some intent to convey meaning. Sharing writing with other students in the class is one way to add authenticity. Publishing a class newsletter, writing letters to people outside of class, writing a script for a skit or dramatic presentation, writing a résumé, writing advertisements—all these can be seen as authentic writing.

6. Frame your techniques in terms of prewriting, drafting, and revising stages.

Process writing approaches tend to be framed in three stages of writing. The **prewriting** stage encourages the generation of ideas, which can happen in numerous ways:

- reading (extensively) a passage
- skimming and/or scanning a passage
- conducting some outside research
- brainstorming (see below)
- listing (in writing—individually)
- clustering (begin with a key word, then add other words, using free association)
- discussing a topic or question
- instructor-initiated questions and probes
- freewriting (see below)

Examples of **brainstorming** and **freewriting**, from *Challenges* (Brown, Cohen, & O'Day, 1991), are shown in Figure 21.3.

The **drafting** and **revising** stages are the core of process writing. In traditional approaches to writing instruction, students either are given timed in-class compositions to write from start to finish within a class hour, or they are given a homework writing assignment. The first option gives no opportunity for systematic drafting, and the second assumes that if students did any drafting at all, they would simply have to learn the tricks of the trade on their own. In a process approach, drafting is viewed as an important and complex set of strategies, the mastery of which takes time, patience, and trained instruction.

Several strategies and skills apply to the drafting/revising process in writing:

- getting started (adapting the freewriting technique)
- "optimal" monitoring of one's writing (without premature editing and diverted attention to wording, grammar, etc.)
- peer-reviewing for content (accepting/using classmates' comments)
- using the instructor's feedback
- editing for grammatical errors
- "read-aloud" technique (in small groups or pairs, students read their almost-final drafts to each other for a final check on errors, flow of ideas, etc.)
- proofreading

Figure 21.3. Brainstorming and freewriting (from Brown, Cohen, & O'Day, 1991, pp. 4–5)

GENERATING IDEAS

• Brainstorming

Let's think about the future for a moment. Let's focus our attention on how it might affect your present or future job. Have you thought about the changes that might occur in your field? To help you think about this question, you are going to make two lists of ideas concerning changes in your field or in the field you plan to enter.

DIRECTIONS: Use your knowledge and imagination to follow these steps.

1. Prepare two sheets of paper with the following:
   a. What changes have occurred in my field in the last twenty years?
      Your field—today's date
   b. What changes do I expect to occur in my field in the next twenty years?
      Your field—the date twenty years from now
2. As quickly as possible, think of as many ideas as you can to answer the question on sheet a.
   a. Take between five and ten minutes to list every idea that comes to your mind.
   b. Do not evaluate your ideas. That will come later.
3. When you have written down everything you can think of, go over the list to evaluate what you have written. Cross out the ideas that don't fit.
4. Repeat this process (steps 2 and 3) for sheet b.

This process, called **brainstorming**, is a useful technique in writing because it permits you to approach a topic with an open mind. Because you do not judge your ideas as they emerge, you free yourself to come up with ideas that you might not even know you had. Brainstorming is one of several different ways to begin writing. In the following pages, we will introduce some other methods that will help you to explore ideas that you might want to write about.

• Working in a Group

In the preceding exercise you worked individually, using brainstorming to establish your own ideas, to follow your own train of thought. Another effective way to generate ideas is to work in a small group where you share your brainstormed ideas with the rest of the group members. By doing this, each of you will have an opportunity to further expand your own ideas.

DIRECTIONS: Form a small group (three to five people). Use the following guidelines for your group discussion.

1. Take turns reading your lists of changes in your field to each other.
2. Compare your classmates' lists to yours, looking for similarities and differences.
   a. Mark the changes on your list that are similar.
   b. Add to your list new ideas of changes that apply to your field.
3. As a group, select three changes that applied to the fields of each group member. If you have time, you can discuss these three ideas.

(Continued)

4. Choose a reporter from your group to share your three changes with the rest of the class.

Here is an example of what the compared lists of a group of three students might look like. (Notice that each list has some ideas that have been crossed out. These ideas had already been eliminated by the student in the last step of the brainstorming exercise because they did not fit.) The changes that were similar in each list have been labeled.

Teaching—Today	Sales—Today	Health Care—Today
attitudes toward teachers Ⓐ information explosion Ⓑ union activity more job security better benefits Ⓒ ~~use of textbooks~~ larger class size computers as teaching tools computers for record keeping Ⓓ competition for jobs greater student maturity higher diplomas	computerized inventory Ⓓ customers' bad attitudes Ⓐ distance from owners pressure ~~meeting people~~ incentive pay consumer action need to know more about products Ⓑ more responsibility more advancement changes fewer personnel time clocks students' increased knowledge better benefits Ⓒ	malpractice suits less respect Ⓐ ~~hours~~ pay educational demands pressure information increase Ⓑ consulting with others competition for clients advertising computerized business Ⓓ computerized diagnosis less pay, greater benefits Ⓒ

• Freewriting

You have just begun to explore the question of changes in your field. Some of your ideas will interest you more than others. Now you will have an opportunity to develop your thinking about one of these ideas.

DIRECTIONS: Follow these steps to generate further ideas on this topic.

1. From your lists of changes, choose one idea that interested you.
2. Write that idea at the top of a clean sheet of paper.
3. For ten minutes, write about this topic without stopping. This means that you should be writing something constantly.
    a. Write down everything that comes to your mind.
    b. Do not judge your ideas.
    c. Do not worry about your spelling and grammar.
    d. If you run out of things to say, continue writing whatever comes to your mind.

This process is called **freewriting**. It is designed to help you free ideas that you might not realize that you have. An important aspect of freewriting is that you write without being concerned about spelling, punctuation, or grammar. Of course, these elements of writing are important, but students' concern about them can sometimes inhibit the free flow of their ideas. Freewriting is a technique to generate ideas; it should be used as a beginning, as an initial exploration of the ideas that you have about a topic.

You can use your freewriting to help you get started with related tasks. In fact, you might want to refer to this freewriting when you are doing other writing tasks later in this unit. Therefore, you should put this and all other freewriting that you do into a notebook that you can refer to when you are generating ideas for future assignments.

Figure 21.4 is another sample from the student book of *Challenges*, illustrating some of the above strategies, especially **peer-editing**, from the drafting and revising stages.

Figure 21.4. Additional writing strategies (from H.D. Brown, Cohen, & O'Day, 1991, pp. 42–45)

LESSON 3

COMPOSING
ON YOUR OWN

In this unit you have read about the issues surrounding the predicted population explosion. You have also worked with important writing techniques such as showing and using facts and statistics. Let's now try to apply what you have learned to the writing process.

THE FIRST DRAFT

Choosing a Topic

DIRECTIONS: Choose one of the following topics to write about in a paragraph.

A. Explain the information introduced in the following bar graph.

B. In the final paragraphs of the article "The World's Urban Explosion," the author raises the question of what the effects of the population explosion might be in the future. Imagine your city, town, or village in the year 2025. Imagine that the population predictions did, in fact, come true. Place yourself in the scene, and describe what you see.

Note: Notice how different these topics are from one another. The first topic asks you to write an explanation which analyzes a graph. The second topic asks for a description. Think about the possible purposes of each topic. How do you think these purposes will affect the tone of each piece?

(Continued)

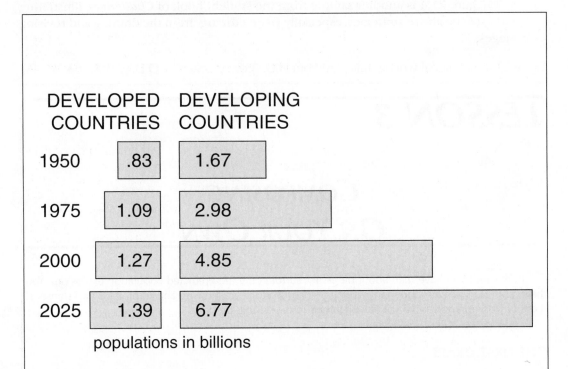

DEVELOPED   DEVELOPING
COUNTRIES   COUNTRIES

1950   .83   1.67

1975   1.09   2.98

2000   1.27   4.85

2025   1.39   6.77

populations in billions

Generating Ideas

First, we need to find ways to unlock the hidden ideas we have in our minds. In this unit you have learned to use brainstorming, freewriting, and looping. Try these techniques in any combination that works for you. Reading also helps to generate ideas. As you write, keep in mind the information you learned about this topic in the readings.

Writing the First Draft

After exploring your ideas, put them into paragraph form, keeping in mind how showing and using facts and statistics makes writing powerful and convincing. Our task here is to discover how we can best express our ideas in the clearest manner possible so that our readers will receive the same message, with the same impact, that we intended.

Peer-editing

What follows is an element of the writing process that is especially important: sharing what we have written with others, our readers, to see if we have been successful in conveying our intended meaning. This step can be a fascinating adventure. We step out of our own selves, to see what we have created through the eyes of others, to discover the impact of our words on the thoughts of our readers, so that we can then use the information to improve what we have written. We call this peer-editing. Peer-editing is a true sharing process. Not only do you get feedback from your classmates, but you also give feedback to them. It is a two-way street. You learn to be a better writer and a better reader. In the following exercise you will work with several classmates, taking the roles of both reader and writer.

DIRECTIONS: Work with four other classmates who chose to write on the same topic as you did.

1. Discuss the idea-generating techniques that you each used to write this composition.
2. Read each other's papers silently, and answer the following questions for each paper:
   a. What do you like the most about the writing?
   b. What is the main idea?
   c. Who is the audience, and what is the purpose?
   d. What convincing details does the writer use?
   e. Where could the writer add details to make the piece more convincing?
   f. What areas in the writing seem unclear?
   g. How could the writer make the piece clearer?
3. Now, for each paper, compare your notes on the questions to help the writer think of ways to improve the piece.

Revising

You have gotten feedback about your composition from several classmates. Now you can use what you learned about your writing to improve it, to make it clearer and more convincing. Writers call this step of the process revising. All good writers go through several steps of revision because they want to make their writing the best it can be. At this point they reconsider what they have written, get feedback from others, and then make changes.

(Continued)

Review your notes from your peer-editing session. Think about the comments made by your peer readers; in particular, comments they agreed on. If you agree with them, you can revise the piece. Remember, however, that you are the final judge as to what you want to include or eliminate in your writing.

Make corrections directly on your first draft. Do not be afraid to mark up this paper. You can scratch out unnecessary or irrelevant information, squeeze ideas that you want to add into the margin, and even cut up and repaste your paper to change the order or make additions. You might be surprised to see the revising process of professional writers. Their drafts will often be illegible to anyone but themselves!

THE SECOND DRAFT

Writing the Second Draft and Proofreading

Once you have made the necessary changes in your paper, you can rewrite it legibly. As you are rewriting, you may think of more changes that you would like to make. Do not hesitate to continue revising during this step. Writing takes time and a lot of thought, so take advantage of this stage to keep improving what you have already done. After you have rewritten your paper, go over it carefully to see if the language sounds correct and if your message seems complete and understandable. Finally, submit your paper to your teacher.

Using Your Teacher's Feedback

When your paper is returned to you, spend time examining the comments your teacher made. This is a good time to compare your classmates' responses to your teacher's, taking into account the changes you made between the original draft and the revised paper. Did you improve on the parts of your original paper that your classmates encouraged you to work on? Did your teacher comment on aspects of your paper that your classmates did not comment on? Share this information with the classmates you did peer-editing with. For each paper you looked at, compare the comments you made to the teacher's comments. Keep in mind the ideas you and your teacher had in common about each paper. Also, notice comments that your teacher made that you missed. This is valuable information. You'll use it the next time you write and the next time you do peer-editing.

Keeping a Journal

In this unit we read about population growth, about changes that we expect to take place in the future that will affect our lives. For a moment, reflect back in time. Try to visualize a place from your distant past, any place that sticks out in your mind. Now roll the clock back up to the present. If the place looks very different in the present, you've found your journal topic. If not, start again until you come up with a scene that has changed over a period of time. When you've found this place that has changed, write about it. You can choose to describe it as it was in the past, in the present, or you can do both. You might want to write about how the changes in the place have affected you. Whatever aspect of the place you choose to write about, make sure that you have a single purpose, a central focus, and try to include detail that helps to develop that main point only. Remember that when you choose to write about something that is familiar and important to you, the task of writing is easier and more pleasurable.

7. Strive to offer techniques that are as interactive as possible.

It is no doubt already apparent that a process-oriented approach to writing instruction is, by definition, interactive (as students work in pairs and groups to generate ideas and to peer-edit), as well as learner-centered (with ample opportunities for students to initiate activity and exchange ideas). Writing techniques that focus on purposes other than compositions (such as letters, forms, memos, directions, short reports) are also subject to the principles of interactive classrooms. Group collaboration, brainstorming, and critiquing are as easily and successfully a part of many writing-focused techniques. Don't buy into the myth that writing is a solitary activity! Some of it is, to be sure, but a good deal of what makes a good writer can be most effectively learned within a community of learners.

8. Sensitively apply methods of responding to and correcting your students' writing.

In Chapter 19, some principles of error correction were suggested for dealing with learners' speech errors. Error correction in writing must be approached in a different manner. Because writing, unlike speaking, often includes an extensive planning stage, error treatment can begin in the drafting and revising stages, during which time it is more appropriate to consider errors among several features of the whole process of responding to student writing. As a student receives responses to written work, errors—just one of several possible things to respond to—are rarely changed outright by the instructor; rather, they are treated through self-correction, peer-correction, and instructor-initiated comments.

As you respond to your students' writing, remember that you are there as an ally, as a guide, as a facilitator. After the final work is turned in, you may indeed have to assume the position of judge and evaluator (see below for some comments on evaluation), but until then, the role of consultant will be the most productive way to respond. Ideally, your responses—or at least some of them—will be written and oral as you hold a conference, however short, with a student. Under less than ideal conditions, written comments may have to suffice.

Here are some guidelines for responding to the *first draft*.

  a. Resist the temptation to treat minor (local) grammatical errors; major (global) errors within relevant paragraphs—see (e) below—can at this stage be indicated either directly (say, by underlining) or indirectly (for example, by a check next to the line in which an error occurs).
  b. Generally resist the temptation to rewrite a student's sentences.
  c. Comment holistically, in terms of the clarity of the overall thesis and the general structural organization.
  d. Comment on the introductory paragraph.
  e. Comment on features that appear to be irrelevant to the topic.
  f. Question clearly inadequate word choices and awkward expression within those paragraphs/sentences that are relevant to the topic.

For the *subsequent drafts,* your responses can include all of the above except that (a) now may change its character slightly:

g. Minor ("local") grammatical and mechanical (spelling, punctuation) errors should be indicated, but not corrected for the student.
h. Comment on the specific clarity and strength of all main ideas, supporting ideas, and on argument and logic.
i. Comment on any further word choices and expressions that may not be "awkward" but are not as clear or direct as they could be.
j. Check cohesive devices within and across paragraphs.
k. In academic papers, comment on documentation, citing sources, evidence, and other support.
l. Comment on the adequacy and strength of the conclusion.

9. Clearly instruct students on the rhetorical, formal conventions of writing.

Each type of writing has its formal properties. Don't just assume that students will pick these up by absorption. Make them explicit. A reading approach to writing is very helpful here. For academic writing, for example, some of the features of English rhetorical discourse that writers use to explain, propose solutions, debate, and argue are as follows:

- a clear statement of the thesis or topic or purpose
- use of main ideas to develop or clarify the thesis
- use of supporting ideas
- supporting by "telling": describing
- supporting by "showing": giving evidence, facts, statistics, etc.
- supporting by linking cause and effect
- supporting by using comparison and/or contrast

ASSESSING WRITING

The assessment of writing, especially in a process-oriented classroom, is a thorny issue (see Ferris & Hedgcock, 2005, for an overview). If you are a guide and facilitator of students' performance in the ongoing process of developing a piece of written work, how can you also be the judge? What do you judge? The answer to the first question—how can you be a judge and a guide at the same time—is one of the primary dilemmas of all teachers. Juggling this dual role requires wisdom and sensitivity. The key to being a judge is fairness and explicitness (reliability) in what you take into account in your evaluation.

Evaluation Checklists

One way to view writing assessment is through various rating checklists or grids that can indicate to students their areas of strength and weakness, and in many cases such taxonomies are scoring rubrics. Table 21.2 is a typical list of general categories that are often the basis for the evaluation of student writing.

Table 21.2. Categories for evaluating writing (adapted from J. D. Brown, 1991, pp. 42–46)

Content
- thesis statement
- related ideas
- development of ideas through personal experience, illustration, facts, opinions
- use of description, cause/effect, comparison/contrast
- consistent focus

Organization
- effectiveness of introduction
- logical sequence of ideas
- conclusion
- appropriate length

Discourse
- topic sentences
- paragraph unity
- transitions
- discourse markers
- cohesion
- rhetorical conventions
- reference
- fluency
- economy
- variation

Syntax

Vocabulary

Mechanics
- spelling
- punctuation
- citation of references (if applicable)
- neatness and appearance

Writing specialists disagree somewhat on the system of weighting each of the above categories, that is, which of the six is most important, next, and so on. Nevertheless, the order in which the six are listed here at the very least emphasizes the importance of content over syntax and vocabulary, which traditionally might have had high priority.

In your evaluation of student writing, the most instructive evaluative feedback you can give is your comments, both specific and summative, regarding the student's work. The six-category list in Table 21.2 can serve as the basis for such evaluations. If numerical scores are either pedagogically or administratively important to you, then you can establish a point scale (say, 0 to 5) for each of the categories and return papers with six different scores on them. By avoiding a single overall score, you can help students to focus on aspects of writing to which they need to give special attention. If you still need to assign a single "grade" or score to each paper, then consider weighting the first few categories more heavily. You can thereby emphasize the content-based flavor of your evaluation. Such a weighting scale might look like this:

Content:	0 – 24
Organization:	0 – 20
Discourse:	0 – 20
Syntax:	0 – 12
Vocabulary:	0 – 12
Mechanics:	0 – 12
TOTAL	100

A key, of course, to successful evaluation is to get your students to understand that your grades, scores, and other comments are varied forms of feedback from which they can benefit. The final evaluation on one composition simply creates input to the learner for the next composition.

Writing Assessment Tasks

Writing an essay in successive drafts, with checklists to guide evaluation, is one general category of writing assessment. There are many more. Hedge (2005) describes over 50 different writing techniques, all of which can have an assessment component. In my *Language Assessment* textbook (Brown, 2004), in the chapter on assessing writing, I have described a number of possible writing tasks according to their level of linguistic complexity, and list them here just to stimulate your own creativity.

1. Imitative writing

- exercises in handwriting letters, words, and punctuation
- keyboarding (typing) exercises

- copying
- listening cloze selection tasks (listen and write)
- picture-cued writing exercises
- completing forms and questionnaires
- converting numbers and abbreviations to words and phrases
- spelling tasks
- one-word dictation tasks

2. Intensive (controlled) writing

- dictation of phrases and simple sentences
- dicto-comp (rewrite a story just heard)
- grammatical transformation exercises
- picture description tasks
- use vocabulary in a sentence
- ordering tasks (re-order a list of words in random order)
- short-answer tasks
- sentence completion tasks

3. Responsive writing

- paraphrasing
- guided writing, e.g., question and answer
- paragraph construction tasks (topic sentence, main idea, etc.)
- responding to a reading or lecture

4. Extensive writing

- essay writing tasks
- tasks in types of writing (narrative, description, argument, etc.)
- tasks in genres of writing (lab report, opinion essay, research paper)

It is of course of paramount importance to be absolutely clear, in your designing of assessment tasks in writing, about *what* you are trying to test and *why* you are testing written performance. The concept of **formative** assessment is prominent in a course that uses a process approach to writing: Our assessments should serve the purpose of facilitating improvement in a student's written work, and judgment of the final product should occur only when such **summative** evaluation is warranted. Ferris and Hedgcock (2005), Sokolik (2003), and Weigle (2002) all stress the need for teachers to act responsibly in evaluating writing: Respect the time-tested principles of validity, reliability, and washback in writing assessment.

☆   ☆   ☆   ☆   ☆

Writing instruction in a communicative, interactive language course should be deeply rooted in the 12 principles of language learning and teaching that have formed a train of thought throughout this book. As you think about each principle, you can make the connections. Automaticity, for example, is gained as students develop fluency in writing, which can best be promoted through the multiple stages of a process writing approach. Meaningful learning and intrinsic motivation are paramount as you try to get your students involved in topics of interest and significance to them and in authentic writing tasks. Strategic investment is clearly at the center of the composing process. Perhaps you can continue down the list yourself.

TOPICS FOR DISCUSSION, ACTION, AND RESEARCH

[Note: (I) Individual work; (G) group or pair work; (C) whole-class discussion.]

1. (C) Review with your students what is meant by a **process** approach to teaching writing. Ask if they discern any cross-cultural issues involved in teaching writing as a process. Are these viable alternatives to teaching through a process approach?

2. (G/C) Direct groups to review the comments on cross-cultural differences and contrastive rhetoric (pages 393–394), and then to discuss the validity of Kaplan's diagrams. How do writing conventions differ between or among cultures that they are familiar with? Ask the groups to pick one other culture to contrast English writing to, and to sketch out salient differences between the two sets of rhetorical conventions. What does this indicate about what to teach in an ESL writing class? Have groups report back to the whole class.

3. (G) Direct pairs to pick an ESL audience, brainstorm reasons or purposes for that audience to write, and talk about how one would teach toward those purposes by getting students to do as much **real writing** as possible.

4. (C) Engage the class in a discussion of what it means to recognize and respect a student's voice and sociocultural identity. Have any students experienced, in their prior language-learning classes, writing assignments or evaluation systems that violate their sense of cultural or personal identity? If so, what might the teacher have done to change these situations into more authentic, respectful experiences?

5. (G) Ask pairs to turn back to pages 362–363 in Chapter 20 and review the types of written language listed there. Then have them pick several familiar audiences or contexts and decide which of the genres their students might actually need to produce. Finally, tell them to prioritize them and share their conclusions with the rest of the class.

6. (C) On page 403, things that "good" writers do are listed. Ask your students the following: Do you agree with the list? Can you add to the list? In what way do the other suggestions that follow implement these behaviors?

7. (I) On page 404, some specific steps for guiding students through stages of drafting and revising a composition are listed. Review those steps again. If possible, sit in on a teacher–student conference in which the student's essay is being discussed. Notice the interaction between student and teacher. Was the session effective? Why?

8. (C) Ask your class to carefully look through the guidelines on methods of responding to written work (pages 411–412). Supply them with a sample first draft and ask them to try to provide some written responses that would stimulate the writer to make some appropriate revisions. In a whole-class discussion, solicit some responses and evaluate their effectiveness.

9. (I/G) If possible, observe an ESL writing class. Use the list of nine principles (pages 403–404, 411–412) for teaching writing skills to evaluate what you see. Discuss your observations in a small group.

10. (I/G) There are numerous scales and inventories for rating and scoring written work. The one presented here (Table 21.2 on page 413) is not exhaustive by any means. Can students think of things they would add to the inventory? Distribute to pairs an actual student's composition and ask them to rate the student's performance on the basis of the taxonomy. To do so, pairs might want to experiment with assigning a numerical weighting scale (page 414). Facilitate the comparison of the various "diagnoses," and discuss how well the scale served its purpose.

FOR YOUR FURTHER READING

Ferris, D., & Hedgcock, J. (2005). *Teaching ESL composition: Purpose, process, and practice* (2nd ed.). Mahwah, NJ: Lawrence Erlbaum Associates.

In this excellent teacher reference book, now in its second edition, Dana Ferris and John Hedgcock have provided many references to research and a practical orientation to second language writing courses.

Casanave, C. (2004). *Controversies in second language writing.* Ann Arbor: University of Michigan Press.

Christine Casanave offers a unique perspective in this survey of writing pedagogy by describing a number of issues and controversies over the last few decades. She provides a balanced perspective to each.

Hedgcock, J. (2005). Taking stock of research and pedagogy in L2 writing. In E. Hinkel (Ed.), *Handbook of research in second language teaching and learning* (pp. 597–613). Mahwah, NJ: Lawrence Erlbaum Associates.

O'Brien, T. (2004). Writing in a foreign language: Teaching and learning. *Language Teaching, 37,* 1–28.

Silva, T., & Brice, C. (2004). Research in teaching writing. *Annual Review of Applied Linguistics, 24,* 70-106.

These three survey articles offer overviews of the state of the art in second language writing pedagogy. Extensive lists of references are included in each article.

Hedge, T. (2005). *Writing.* Oxford, UK: Oxford University Press.

Tricia Hedge describes over 50 different writing activities, categorized into sections on communication, composing, crafting, and improving. It is highly practical and teacher friendly. A bibliography is included.

CHAPTER 22

FORM-FOCUSED INSTRUCTION

OBJECTIVES After reading this chapter, you will be able to:

- appreciate the value of focus on form in a communicative language curriculum

- understand issues surrounding form-focused instruction, in terms of both grammar focus and vocabulary focus

- identify techniques for teaching both grammar and vocabulary

- examine guidelines for grammar sequencing in textbooks and curricula

A glance through the last century of language-teaching practices reveals mixed opinions about the place of teaching language **forms**, depending on the method or era. In the Grammar Translation Method and in cognitive code learning (see Chapter 2), formal aspects of language received central attention. In the Direct Method and the Natural Approach, overt focus on form was almost forbidden. Some manifestations of CLT, especially **indirect** approaches, advocated only a passing attention to form, while other proponents of CLT injected healthy doses of form-focused techniques into a communicative curriculum. A decade ago, perhaps, our profession was inundated with a swarm of mixed messages about the place of grammar and vocabulary in the communicative language classroom, with strong advocates on both sides.

Today, only a handful of language-teaching experts advocate *no* focus on form ("zero option") at all, a prime proponent of which is Krashen (1997) with his input hypothesis (see *PLLT,* Chapter 10). Current views of second language classroom methodology are almost universally in agreement on the importance of some **form-focused instruction** within the communicative framework, ranging from explicit treatment of rules to **noticing** and **consciousness-raising** (Ellis, 2001, 2006; Williams, 2005) techniques for structuring input to learners. This of course still leaves open a wide range of options from which you must choose, depending on your students, their purposes, and the context.

The **forms** of language include the organizational components of language and the systematic rules that govern their structure. Phonological, grammatical, and lexical forms occupy the three principal formal categories that typically appear in a language curriculum. Since phonology was discussed in Chapter 19 in the form of pronunciation teaching, our focus here will be on the place of grammar and vocabulary in language teaching. First, grammar.

THE PLACE OF GRAMMAR

Grammar is the system of rules governing the conventional arrangement and relationship of words in a sentence. In place of "words," I could, for more specificity, have said "morphemes," but for the moment just remember that the components of words (prefixes, suffixes, roots, verb and noun endings, etc.) are indeed a part of grammar. Technically, grammar refers to sentence-level rules only, and not to rules governing the relationship among sentences, which we commonly refer to as **discourse** rules. But for the sake of simplicity, I will include discourse considerations in this discussion of grammar-focused instruction.

In the widely accepted definition of communicative competence that was reviewed in Chapters 3 and 4 (see also *PLLT,* Chapter 8), grammatical competence occupies a prominent position as a major component of communicative competence. **Organizational competence** is an intricate, complex array of rules, some of which govern the sentence (grammar), while others govern how we string sentences together (discourse). Without the structure that organizational constraints impose on our communicative attempts, our language would simply be chaotic.

Organizational competence is *necessary* for communication to take place, but not *sufficient* to account for all production and reception in language. As Diane Larsen-Freeman (2003) pointed out, grammar is one of three dimensions of language that are interconnected. Grammar gives us the form or the structures of language, but those forms are literally meaningless without a second dimension, that of **semantics** (meaning), and a third dimension, **pragmatics**. In other words, grammar tells us how to construct a sentence (word order, verb and noun systems, modifiers, phrases, clauses, etc.), and discourse rules tell us how to string those sentences together. Semantics tells us something about the meaning(s) of words and strings of words. Then pragmatics tells us about which of several meanings to assign given the context of an utterance or written text. Context takes into account such things as

- who the speaker/writer is,
- who the audience is,
- where the communication takes place,
- what communication takes place before and after a sentence in question,
- implied versus literal meanings,
- styles and registers,
- the alternative forms among which a producer can choose.

It's important to grasp the significance of the interconnectedness of all three dimensions: No one dimension is sufficient. In such a view, grammar, according to Larsen-Freeman (2003), is a dynamic process and learners are called on to engage in what she called "grammaring." The latter departs from the usual traditions of teaching grammar as a body of *knowledge,* and instead treats grammar as a skill.

So, no one can tell you that grammar is irrelevant, or that grammar is no longer needed in a CLT framework. No one seriously questions the prominence of grammar as an organizational framework within which communication operates.

TO TEACH OR NOT TO TEACH GRAMMAR

The next question, then, is whether to teach grammar in language classes, and if so, how to teach it. As noted above, varied opinions on the question can be found in the literature on language teaching. Reason, balance, and the experience of teachers in recent communicative methodology tell us that judicious attention to grammatical form in the adult classroom is not only helpful, if appropriate techniques are used, but essential to a speedy learning process (see Ellis, 2006; Nassaji & Fotos, 2004; Nunan, 2005). Appropriate grammar-focusing techniques

- are embedded in meaningful, communicative contexts,
- contribute positively to communicative goals,
- promote accuracy within fluent, communicative language,
- do not overwhelm students with linguistic terminology,
- are as lively and intrinsically motivating as possible.

For adults, the question is not so much whether to teach grammar, but rather, what the optimal conditions for the teaching of grammar are, and what degree of overt attention should be included in such form-focused instruction. Rod Ellis (2006, pp. 102–103) offered some of his own answers to questions about when and how to teach grammar, which are capsulized here:

- Both form and meaning should be emphasized; learners need to have the opportunity to practice forms in communicative tasks.
- Focus more strongly on forms that are problematic for learners.
- Explicit grammar teaching is more effective at the intermediate to advanced levels than beginning levels.
- Attend to both input-based (comprehension) and output-based (production) grammar.
- Both deductive and inductive approaches can be useful, depending on the context and purpose of instruction.
- *Incidental* focus on form is valuable in that it treats errors that occur while learners are engaged in meaningful communication.
- Corrective feedback can facilitate acquisition if it involves a mixture of implicit and explicit feedback.
- Separate grammar lessons ("focus on forms") and grammar integrated into communicative activities ("focus on form") are both viable, depending on the context.

Another way of viewing the role of grammar in language teaching is to look at variables that Celce-Murcia (1991a) first proposed, but that have been addressed repeatedly, in one form or another, since then (Larsen-Freeman, 2003; Nassaji & Fotos, 2004; Nunan, 2005; Williams, 2005). We'll look at six variables.

1. Age

It is clear that due to normal intellectual developmental variables, young children can profit from a focus on form if attention to form is offered through structured input and incidental, indirect error treatment. Somewhat older children may benefit as well from very simple generalizations (such as "This is the way we say it when we're talking about yesterday") and concrete illustrations. Adults, with their abstract intellectual capabilities, can use grammatical pointers to advance their communicative abilities.

2. Proficiency level

If we force too much grammar focus on beginning level learners, we run the risk of blocking their acquisition of fluency skills. At this level, grammatical focus is helpful as an occasional "zoom lens" with which we zero in on some aspect of language but not helpful if it becomes the major focus of class work. Most research agrees that at the intermediate to advanced levels, a more explicit focus on form is less likely to disturb communicative fluency, and can assist learners in developing accuracy (Celce-Murcia, 1991a; Ellis, 2006).

3. Educational background

Students who are nonliterate or who have no formal educational background may find it difficult to grasp the complexity of grammatical terms and explanations. Highly educated students, on the other hand, are cognitively more receptive to grammar focus and may insist on error correction to help refine their already fluent skills.

4. Language skills

Because of the permanence of writing and the demand for perfection in grammatical form in written English, grammar focus is absolutely necessary in improving written English. In speaking skills, focus on form, especially through incidental feedback, has been shown in some studies to be effective (Williams, 2005). For input-based skills (listening and reading), there is some evidence that treatment of perceived sources of error can aid learners (Larsen-Freeman, 2003).

5. Style (register)

Informal contexts often make fewer demands on a learner's grammatical accuracy. In casual conversation among peers, for example, minor errors are acceptable, while more formal contexts (say, a student consulting with a teacher) usually require greater grammatical accuracy. Similarly, in writing, tolerance for error is higher in, say, a quick e-mailed message than in a formal essay.

6. Needs and goals

If learners are headed toward professional goals, they may need to stress formal accuracy more than learners at the survival level. In either case, message clarity is a prime criterion.

These six categories should be looked on as general guidelines for judging the need for conscious grammatical focus in the classroom, but none of these suggestions is absolute! For example, you can probably think of numerous situations where it is important to focus on form with beginners, or to get learners away from too intense a grammatical focus in the context of a formal register.

ISSUES ABOUT HOW TO TEACH GRAMMAR

While the professional community in general agrees on the importance of form-focused instruction (Nassaji & Fotos, 2004; Williams, 2005), there are still degrees of opinion on what kind of instruction should be offered to learners. Four primary issues characterize this ongoing professional discussion.

1. Should grammar be presented inductively or deductively?

Do learners benefit from an inductive approach in which various language forms are practiced but in which the learners are left to discover or induce rules and generalizations on their own? Or would they be better off being given a rule/generalization by the teacher or textbook and then allowed to practice various instances of language to which the rule applies? These two approaches are often contrasted with each other when questions about grammar teaching arise.

In most contexts, an inductive approach is more appropriate because of the following:

- It is more in keeping with natural language acquisition (where rules are absorbed subconsciously with little or no conscious focus).
- It conforms more easily to the concept of interlanguage development in which learners progress, on variable timetables, through stages of rule acquisition.
- It allows students to get a communicative "feel" for some aspect of language before possibly being overwhelmed by grammatical explanations.
- It builds more intrinsic motivation by allowing students to discover rules rather than being told them.

There may be occasional moments, of course, when a deductive approach—or a blend between the two—is indeed warranted. In practice, the distinction is not always apparent. Consider the following excerpt from a low intermediate classroom (the T has asked Ss to tell the rest of the class about a recent journey):

> **S1:** And so, you see, I tell the, eh, uh, stewardess, to bring me hot tea! Well, she doesn't!
>
> **T:** Uh-huh, okay. [*pause; Kamal raises his hand*] Kamal?
>
> **S2:** Yes, eh, well, I am also very, eh, frustrated last week. When I, eh, travel in the airplane, I get no sleep . . .
>
> **T:** Okay, Kamal, before you go on, since we need to review the past tense anyway, let me remind you that you should be using the past tense here, okay? So, you want to say "I *was* frustrated," "I *got* no sleep," "I *told* the stewardess." Okay, Kamal, go ahead and continue your story.

After Kamal finished his story, this time with a more accurate use of the past tense, the teacher put the verbs they used on the board, listed their past tense forms, and had students practice them. While you might question the appropriateness of the interruption here, the point is that the lesson's objective was to use the past tense, and the teacher's focus on the past tense in this particular instance was deductive for the rest of the students in the class who were listening. But it was inductive in that the focus on the past actually was triggered by students' meaningful performance.

2. Should we use grammatical explanations and technical terminology in a CLT classroom?

Our historical roots (in Grammar Translation methodology) placed a strong emphasis on grammatical explanations (in the mother tongue) and on the terminology necessary to carry out those explanations. Many foreign language learners in the United States have remarked that their first and only encounter with grammatical concepts was not in English (language arts classes) but in a foreign language class, where that they learned about subjects, predicates, direct objects, and intransitive verbs.

In CLT classes, the use of grammatical explanation and terminology must be approached with care. We teachers are sometimes so eager to display our hard-earned metalinguistic knowledge that we forget that our students are so busy just learning the language itself that the added load of complex rules and terms is too much to bear. But clearly, adults can benefit from occasional explanations. Following a few simple (but not always easily interpreted) rules of thumb will enhance any grammatical explanations you undertake.

- Keep your explanations brief and simple. Use the mother tongue if students cannot follow an explanation in English.
- Use charts and other visuals whenever possible to graphically depict grammatical relationships.
- Illustrate with clear, unambiguous examples.
- Try to account for varying cognitive styles among your students (for example, analytical learners will have an easier time picking up on grammatical explanations than will holistic learners).

- Do not get yourself (and students!) tied up in knots over so-called exceptions to rules.
- If you don't know how to explain something (for instance, if a student asks you about a point of grammar and you are not sure of the rule), do not risk giving false information (that you may have to retract later, which will cause even more embarrassment). Rather, tell students you will research that point and bring an answer back the next day.

3. Should grammar be taught in separate "grammar only" classes?

The collective experience of the last two decades or so of CLT practice, combined with the research on the effectiveness of grammatical instruction (Nassaji & Fotos, 2004; Nunan, 2005), indicates the advisability of embedding grammatical techniques into general language courses, rather than singling grammar out as a discrete "skill" and treating it in a separate course. Grammatical information, whether consciously or subconsciously learned, is an enabling system, a component of communicative competence like phonology, discourse, the lexicon, etc. Therefore, as courses help students to pursue relevant language goals, grammar is best brought into the picture as a contributor toward those goals.

In some curricula, however, certain class hours, workshops, or courses are set aside for grammar instruction. In a language-teaching paradigm that stresses communicative, interactive, meaningful learning, such courses may appear to be anachronisms. Under certain conditions, however, they can provide a useful function, especially for high intermediate to advanced learners, where a modicum of fluency is already in place (Ellis, 2006). Those conditions are as follows:

- The grammar course is explicitly integrated into the total curriculum so that students can readily relate grammatical pointers to their other work in English.
- The rest of the curriculum (or the bulk of students' use of language outside of the grammar class) controls the content of the grammar course, and not vice versa. That is, the grammar course "serves" (enhances) the curriculum. For example, a significant portion of the agenda for the grammar class should come from students' work in other courses.
- Grammar is contextualized in meaningful language use.
- The course is tailored as much as possible for specific problems students are experiencing. For example, in grammar "workshops" for intermediate and advanced students, grammatical topics come from the students' own performance in other classes, rather than being preset by a curriculum or textbook.
- Sometimes grammar modules in a standardized test preparation course serve as helpful reviews of grammatical principles that may be incorporated into the test.
- The ultimate test of the success of such courses is in the improvement of students' performance outside of the grammar class, not in their score on discrete-point grammar tests.

Under these conditions, then, grammar assumes its logical role as one of several supporting foundation stones for communication.

4. Should teachers correct grammatical errors?

Many student errors in speech and writing performance are grammatical. It is interesting that research evidence shows that rarely is overt grammatical correction by teachers in the classroom of any consequence in improving learners' language. But we do have evidence that various other forms of attention to and treatment of grammatical errors have an impact on learners. (See *PLLT,* Chapter 9, for an overview of error treatment in SLA and Chapter 19 of this book for a discussion of the treatment of spoken errors.) Therefore, it is prudent for you to engage in such treatment, as long as you adhere to principles of maintaining communicative flow, of maximizing student self-correction, and of sensitively considering the affective and linguistic place the learner is in.

The treatment of grammatical (and discourse) errors in writing is a different matter. In process writing approaches, overt attention to **local** grammatical and rhetorical (discourse) errors is normally delayed until learners have completed one or two drafts of a paper. **Global** errors that impede meaning must of course be attended to earlier in the process. Studies have shown (Ferris & Hedgcock, 2005) that certain attention to errors does indeed make a difference in final written products.

GRAMMAR TECHNIQUES

Following are some sample techniques for teaching grammar, using Sandra McKay's (1985) classifications that have withstood the test of time.

1. Charts

Charts and graphs are useful devices for practicing patterns, clarifying grammatical relationships, and even for understanding sociolinguistic and discourse constraints. The exercise in Figure 22.1 stimulates students to practice frequency adverbs.

Another grammatical system that lends itself well to charts is the verb system. Figure 22.2 on pages 428–429 illustrates a commonly used system of depicting some verb tenses.

2. Objects

Objects brought into the classroom not only liven up the context but provide a kinesthetic, hands-on dimension to your teaching. By engaging students in communication with each other, you also stimulate them to practice conversation rules and other discourse constraints. To teach the possessive to beginning level students, for example, bring in a few small items such as a necklace, a purse, and some glasses. Then ask students to put two or three of their own things on their desks. Then do something like the three exercises in Figure 22.3 on page 430.

Figure 22.1. Frequency adverbs (from H. D. Brown, 1992, p. 99)

EXERCISE 1

Read the paragraphs on page 98 again. Then choose the appropriate adverb of frequency.

	never	seldom	sometimes	often	usually	always
1. Keiko works hard.						✔
2. She is on time for work.						
3. She is late or sick.						
4. She is early for work.						
5. She types letters.						
6. She files.						
7. She makes copies.						
8. She makes mistakes when she types.						
9. She answers the phone politely.						
10. She is angry.						

Now say the complete sentences.

> 1. Keiko always works hard.
> 2. She is always on time for work.

3. _____   7. _____
4. _____   8. _____
5. _____   9. _____
6. _____   10. _____

Notice that embedded in grammatical attention to possessives are politeness forms ("Excuse me") and discoursal ellipsis rules that allow a person to say "No, it's Lucy's," rather than "No, it's Lucy's handbag."

3. Maps and drawings

Maps, also mentioned in Chapter 14 in the discussion about group work, are practical and simple visual aids in a classroom. Useful for jigsaw, information-gap, and other interactive techniques, they can also serve to illustrate certain grammatical structures. For example, maps can stimulate learners' use of

- prepositional phrases (*up the street, on the left, over the hill,* etc.),
- question forms (*where, how do I get to, can you tell me, is this,* etc.),
- imperatives (*go, walk, look out for,* etc.),
- appropriate discourse for getting someone's attention, asking for directions, receiving and clarifying given information, and terminating the conversation.

Sandra McKay suggested using drawings of circles, squares, and other familiar shapes to teach locative words (see Figure 22.4 on page 431).

Figure 22.2. Tense diagrams (from Cross, 1991, pp. 29–30)

Introducing Tenses

A visual representation can often be clearer than a verbal one to introduce a tense. This is especially true where students do not have similar tense systems in their mother tongue. Time can be shown by a line across the board. An arrow pointing down indicates this moment now. To the left of the arrow is past time, to the right is the future. A cross indicates a single event, a row of dots denotes an action that lasted or will last for a period of time. The uses of most tenses can be shown and contrasted pictorially on such a time line, as shown in the following examples.

1. *He used to smoke* (in the past, not anymore).

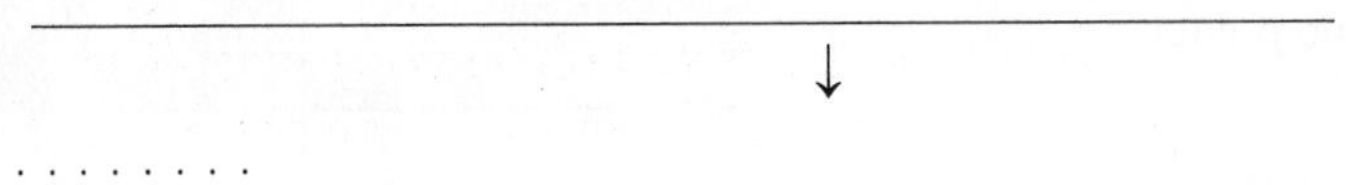

$$\downarrow$$

. . . .

2. *She works in the market* (did in the past and will continue in the future).

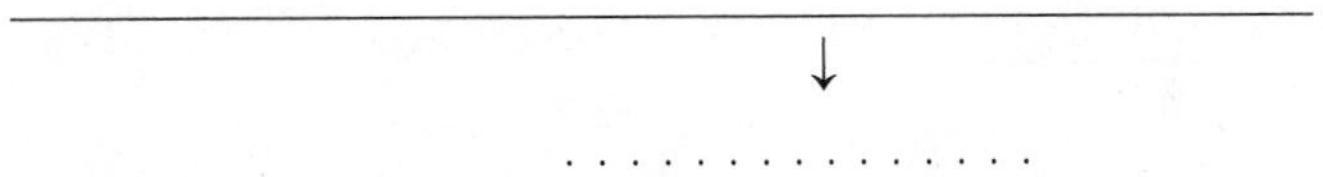

$$\downarrow$$

. . . .

3. *He is having his supper* (eating now, having started a short while ago in the past, but this will not continue for any appreciable length of time).

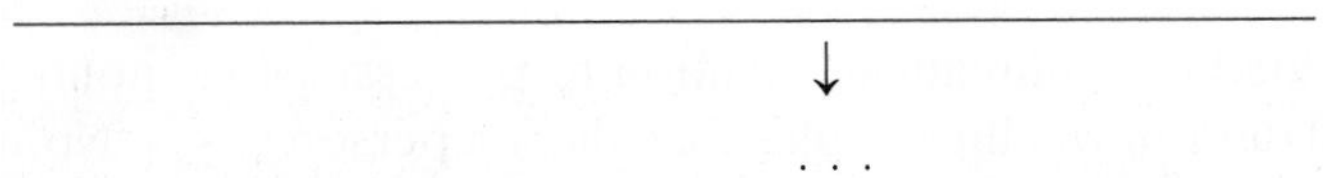

$$\downarrow$$

. . .

4. *He got up at six o'clock* (in the past, a single event).

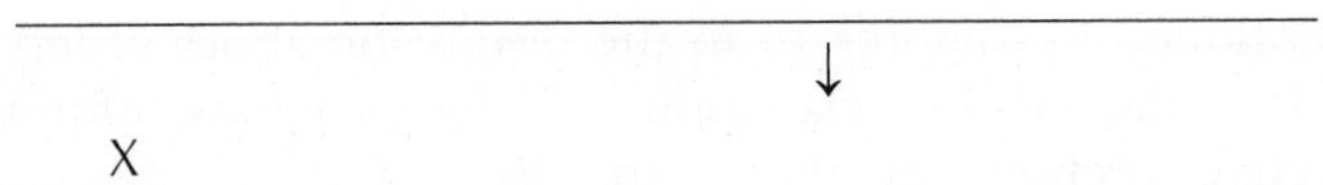

$$\downarrow$$

X

5. *I've been teaching for a long time* (started in the past, still doing it today).

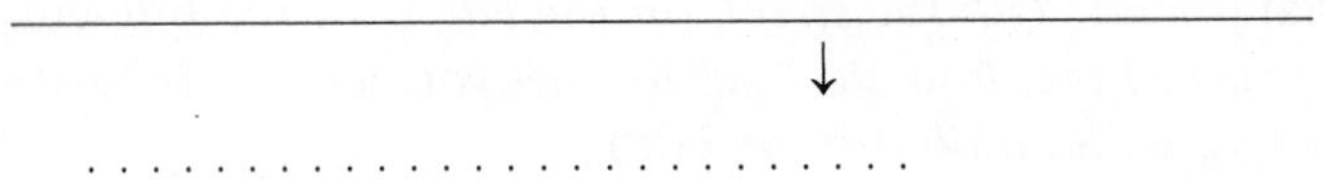

$$\downarrow$$

. . . .

6. *We'll travel by plane* (in the future).

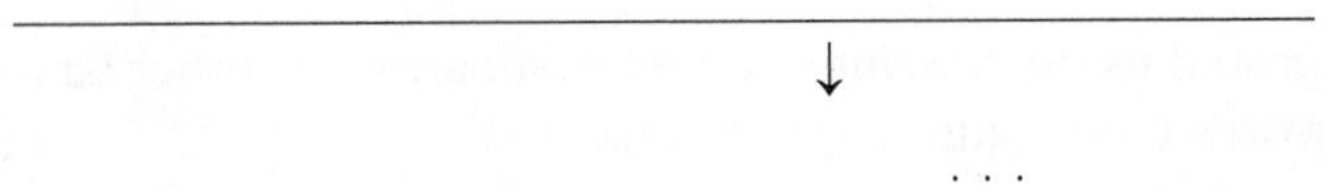

$$\downarrow$$

. . .

7. *We were out walking when it started to rain* (a continuous past action interrupted by a single event).

$$\downarrow$$

. . . . . . X. . . .

8. *It's 6 o'clock now, I shall have finished by 8 o'clock* (a task started earlier and which will continue for 2 more hours).

4 5 6 7 8 9 10 11

$$\downarrow$$

. X

This is by no means the full range of tenses, but once you have grasped the idea you will be able to use the technique to introduce others the same way. You can also use a time scale to show concepts like *for 2 months, since April* and *from April to mid June.* This is done in the following example.

Jan.   Feb.   March   April   May   June   July   Aug.   Sept.   Oct.   Nov.   Dec.

. . . .

4. Dialogues

Dialogues are an age-old technique for introducing and practicing grammatical points. Consider the dialogue in Figure 22.5 on page 432, with the suggestions for teachers in Figure 22.6 on page 433.

5. Other written texts

At the very simple, mechanical level, a short paragraph can become an exercise in processing selected verb tenses, such as in the passage in Figure 22.7. In such texts, discourse rules for paragraphing and sequencing ideas can also be attended to. Notice, however, that in the text in Figure 22.7 (page 434) the grammatical category is then applied meaningfully to students' own lives in the form of questions like "What do you usually do every day?"

Figure 22.3. Picture-cued vocabulary exercises (from H. D. Brown, 1992, p. 43)

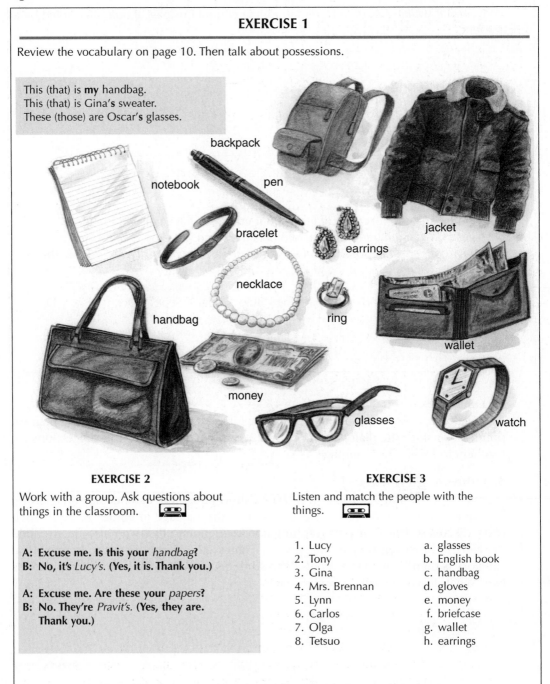

EXERCISE 1

Review the vocabulary on page 10. Then talk about possessions.

This (that) is **my** handbag.
This (that) is Gina**'s** sweater.
These (those) are Oscar**'s** glasses.

backpack

notebook pen

bracelet jacket

earrings

necklace

handbag ring

wallet

money

glasses watch

EXERCISE 2

Work with a group. Ask questions about things in the classroom.

A: **Excuse me. Is this your** *handbag***?**
B: **No, it's** *Lucy's*. **(Yes, it is. Thank you.)**

A: **Excuse me. Are these your** *papers***?**
B: **No. They're** *Pravit's*. **(Yes, they are. Thank you.)**

EXERCISE 3

Listen and match the people with the things.

1. Lucy   a. glasses
2. Tony   b. English book
3. Gina   c. handbag
4. Mrs. Brennan   d. gloves
5. Lynn   e. money
6. Carlos   f. briefcase
7. Olga   g. wallet
8. Tetsuo   h. earrings

Figure 22.4. Locatives (from McKay, 1985, p. 61)

SIMPLE DRAWINGS

With Prepositional Phrases **To Describe Locations**
of Location **To Give Directions**

Drawings of simple shapes can be used to provide practice in stating locations and giving directions. In order to do this, you might begin by using the following drawing, modeling the expressions which follow.

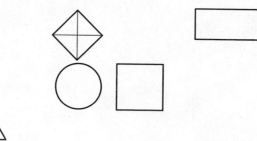

The circle is *in the center of* the paper.
The diamond is *directly above* the circle.
The square is *to the right of* the circle.
The rectangle is *in the upper right-hand corner.*
The triangle is *in the lower left-hand corner.*

    After you have introduced these terms tell the students to take out a piece of paper. Give them a series of commands and have them draw these on this paper. (E.g., Draw a square in the upper left-hand corner. Draw a circle inside the square.)

    Later you might use this same technique to introduce more technical vocabulary of shapes along with the relative proportion (E.g., Draw a triangle in the center of the paper. Draw a circle above the triangle. The diameter of the circle should be the same length as the base of the triangle.)

GRAMMAR SEQUENCING IN TEXTBOOKS AND CURRICULA

Grammatical sequencing received a great deal of attention in the 1950s and 1960s when curricula and textbooks were organized around grammatical categories. Some language professionals were of the opinion that difficulty could be predicted (especially if the native language were taken into consideration) and that therefore grammar in a curriculum should be sequenced in a progression of easier to more difficult items. Yet no one had been able to verify empirically such hierarchies of difficulty by the time the debate over grammatical sequencing whimpered to a halt and situational and notional-functional curricula assumed popularity. At that point the question shifted more to whether or not there was an optimal **functional** sequence.

Figure 22.5. Opening dialogue (from H. D. Brown, 1992, p. 360)

Lesson 2

What are you doing next week?

Look at the picture. Then listen as you read the conversation.

Carlos: What are you doing during the school break?

Tetsuo: I'm going to New York. What about you? Are you staying in Dallas, or are you going away?

Carlos: I'm going to Los Angeles for a week. I want to go to the beach.

Tetsuo: When are you leaving?

Carlos: Tomorrow.

Tetsuo: I'm really happy we have a vacation. I need a rest.

Carlos: I know. I need a rest, too. Say, I'm thirsty. Let's get something to drink.

Tetsuo: Good idea. How much is a soda?

Carlos: Fifty cents. Do you have change for a dollar?

Tetsuo: Yes, I think so.

Figure 22.6. Suggestions for the teacher (from H. D. Brown, 1992, p. 361)

Lesson 2

What are you doing next week?

Preparing the Students

A. Introduce future time expressions and the future with the present continuous tense. On the board, write the following sentence. Underline *is* and *-ing:*

Mark <u>is</u> driv<u>ing</u> to Colorado tomorrow.

Tell the students that you want them to help you continue to write a story about Mark. Write another sentence on the board:

He's leaving early in the morning, and he's taking a friend with him.

Now have the class suggest other lines for the story. Write them on the board. Finally, call on students to underline all the examples of the present continuous tense.

B. Review the word *let's* used in making suggestions or invitations. Have the students perform actions which you suggest. For example, with appropriate gestures, say "Let's stand up and stretch." (The students stand up and stretch.) Make several other suggestions and have the class carry out the actions. Be sure that you participate.

Presentation: Conversation

A. Have the students look at the picture. Establish the context—Carlos and Tetsuo are talking about a school break. Read the conversation or play the cassette. Have the students listen as they read along silently in their books.

B. Answer any questions students have about vocabulary or structures. Introduce or review the words *during, break, stay, go away, beach, vacation,* and *rest.* Then have the students close their books. Ask them questions about the conversation. For example:

Do Carlos and Tetsuo have a break soon?
Are they both staying in Dallas?
Where are they going?
Why's Carlos going to Los Angeles?
When's he leaving?
Do they think they need a rest?
Are they both going to drink a soda?
How much does a soda cost?

C. In pairs, have the students practice the conversation. Encourage them to use their own ideas by changing the names of places, times, and activities. Call on several pairs to present their conversations to the class.

In recent years, we have witnessed a return to a more balanced viewpoint in which grammar is seen as one of several organizational aspects of communicative competence, all of which should be considered in programming a textbook or a curriculum. In this perspective, the question of an optimal sequence of grammatical structures is not irrelevant, but with our current disciplinary maturity, we seem to agree that

- grammatical categories are one of several considerations in curricular sequencing

Figure 22.7. Exercise in choice of tense (from H. D. Brown, 1992, p. 362)

EXERCISE 6

What does Lucy do every day? What is she doing now? Choose the correct form of the verb.

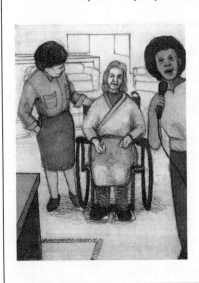

"Lucy Mendoza is a nurse. She is never bored because she is always busy. She usually (**1.** works/is working) in a hospital, but sometimes she (**2.** works/is working) in a special home for old people. Lucy (**3.** enjoys/is enjoying) her work every day, and she never (takes/is taking) a day off. She is always happy. She is never sad. Today she (**4.** doesn't work/isn't working) in the hospital. She (**5.** works/is working) in the home for old people. Right now she (**6.** talks/is talking) to a woman. The woman is very lonely because her children never (**7.** visit/are visiting)."

> **What about you?**
> What do you usually do every day?
> What are you doing right now?

- a curriculum usually manifests a logical sequence of basic grammatical structures (such as introducing the past perfect tense after the past tense, relative clauses after question formation), but such a sequence may be more a factor of frequency and usefulness than of clearly identified degrees of linguistic difficulty
- beyond those basic structures, a few permutations here and there will make little difference in the eventual success of students, as long as language is being learned in the context of a communicative curriculum

"Scope and sequence" charts found in most textbooks are good examples of how a course sequences grammatical, functional, and situational elements of the course. The chart shown in Chapter 7 (pages 120–123) is illustrative of a typical sequence of grammatical structures in a basal ESL series. In arranging the order of structures, the principles of simplicity and frequency were followed. Therefore, the more "complex" tenses and clause formations come later in the series. While one could quibble with certain elements and suggest alternative permutations, nevertheless learners' success in a course like this seems to be more a factor of (a) clear, unambiguous presentation of material and (b) opportunity for meaningful, interactive practice, rather than a factor of a grammar point presented a week earlier or later.

CURRENT ISSUES IN VOCABULARY TEACHING

The other "half" of form-focused instruction is vocabulary—the thousands of lexical building blocks that are available to the average user of a language. As we consider vocabulary teaching, be reminded again that lexical items are basic to all of the four skills, and so vocabulary is not a "skill" as we normally use the term. The skill comes in the efficient storage (competence) and adept retrieval (performance) of those units. How vocabulary should be taught has stimulated some controversies over time, which we'll first take a brief look at here.

One of the casualties of the early approaches to CLT was a loss of a concerted focus on the lexical forms of language. While traditional language-teaching methods highlighted vocabulary study with lists, definitions, written and oral drills, and flash cards, there was a period of time when "the teaching and learning of vocabulary [were] undervalued" (Zimmerman, 1997, p. 5). In the zeal for natural, authentic classroom tasks and activities, vocabulary focus was swept under the rug. Further, as teachers more and more perceived their role as facilitators and guides, they became more reluctant to take the directive and sometimes intrusive steps to turn students' focus to lexical form.

Toward the end of the twentieth century, we saw a revival of systematic attention to vocabulary learning across a number of proficiency levels and contexts. Ranging from very explicit focus, such as that found in Michael Lewis's (1993, 1997, 2000) Lexical Approach, to more indirect approaches in which vocabulary is incorporated into communicative tasks, attention to lexical forms is now more central to the development of language curricula (Nation, 2001, 2003, 2005; Read, 2004).

One of the "hot topics" of the last decade in vocabulary teaching is whether learners are better served in the long run with **incidental** exposure to lexical items (that is, as a by-product of communicative activities), or with **intentional**, explicit focus on vocabulary. In the earlier years of CLT approaches, "the concept of incidental learning offered the seductive prospect that, provided the learners had access to sufficient comprehensible input, L2 vocabulary acquisition would largely take care of itself" (Read, 2004, p. 147). However, as Read (2004), Hulstijn (2001), and others have shown, intentional vocabulary focus accounts for significant gains in acquisition, and it may therefore be "necessary to re-visit such unfashionable procedures as regular rehearsal of words, rote learning, and training in automatic word recognition . . . particularly for beginning and intermediate level learners" (Hulstijn, 2001, p. 275).

A further development in vocabulary teaching is the rapid growth of **corpus linguistics** and the volumes of raw data that are now available in corpora that encompass spoken and written language, genres of each, as well as data from a number of varieties of world Englishes. Conrad (2005) and others have described numerous ways in which corpus linguistics has improved our collective capacity to expose learners to real-world language. We have ready access not just to statistics such as word frequency counts, but more important, **collocations** (words that tend to appear in the company of other words). **Concordancing** enables learners (and textbook writers) to see words in context (McCarthy, 2004). And these voluminous copora provide data banks through which we can more closely examine and appreciate associations between grammatical and lexical units (Hunston & Francis, 2000).

Current practices in teaching vocabulary, especially in view of the technology of corpus linguistics, are clearly not simply a rebirth of the same methods of half a century ago. Rather than viewing vocabulary items as a long and boring list of words to be defined and memorized, lexical forms now play a central role in contextualized, meaningful language. Learners can be guided in specific ways to internalize these important building blocks of language.

PRINCIPLES FOR TEACHING VOCABULARY

Below are some guidelines for the communicative treatment of vocabulary instruction.

1. Allocate specific class time to vocabulary learning.

In the hustle and bustle of our interactive classrooms, sometimes we get so caught up in lively group work and meaningful communication that we don't pause to devote some attention to words. After all, words are basic building blocks of language; in fact, survival-level communication can take place quite intelligibly when people simply string words together—without applying any grammatical rules at all! So, if we're interested in being communicative, words are among the first priorities.

2. Help students to learn vocabulary in context.

The best internalization of vocabulary comes from encounters (comprehension or production) with words within the context of surrounding discourse. Data from linguistic corpora can provide real-world actual language that has been printed or spoken. Rather than isolating words and/or focusing on dictionary definitions, learners can benefit from attending to vocabulary within a communicative framework in which items appear. Students will then associate new words with a meaningful context to which they apply.

3. Play down the role of bilingual dictionaries.

A corollary to the above is to help students to resist the temptation to overuse their bilingual dictionaries. In recent years, with the common availability of electronic pocket dictionaries, students are even more easily tempted to punch in a word they don't know and get an instant response. It is unfortunate that such practices rarely help students to internalize the word for later recall and use.

However, recent years have seen an increasing popularity of learners' dictionaries—which are English-English dictionaries modified for more learner-friendly definitions, metaphors, idioms, and contrasts. When a dictionary is warranted, such publications can be very useful.

4. Encourage students to develop strategies for determining the meaning of words.

Included in the discussion of learning strategies in Chapter 16 are references to learning words. Also, Chapter 20 referred to such strategies as guessing vocabulary in context. A number of "clues" are available to learners to develop "word attack" strategies. Figure 22.8 on pages 438–439 provides a detailed taxonomy of such strategies with examples.

5. Engage in "unplanned" vocabulary teaching.

In all likelihood, most of the attention you give to vocabulary learning will be unplanned: those moments when a student asks about a word or when a word has appeared that you feel deserves some attention. These impromptu moments are very important. Sometimes, they are simply brief little pointers; for example, the word "clumsy" once appeared in a paragraph students were reading and the teacher volunteered:

> **T:**   Okay, "clumsy." Does anyone know what that means? [*writes the word on the board*]
>
> **Ss:** [*silence*]
>
> **T:**   No one? Okay, well, take a look at the sentence it's in. "His clumsy efforts to imitate a dancer were almost amusing." Now, was Bernard a good dancer? [*S1 raises her hand.*] Okay, Mona?
>
> **S1:** Well, no. He was a very bad dancer, as we see in the next sentence.
>
> **T:**   Excellent! So, what do you think "clumsy" might mean?
>
> **S2:** Not graceful?
>
> **T:**   Good, what else? Anyone?
>
> **S3:** Not smooth, eh, . . . uncoordinated?
>
> **T:**   Great! Okay, so "clumsy" means awkward, ungraceful, uncoordinated. [*writes synonyms on the board*] Is that clear now?
>
> **Ss:** [*most Ss nod in agreement*]

Sometimes, such impromptu moments may be extended: The teacher gives several examples and/or encourages students to use the word in other sentences. Make sure that such unplanned teaching, however, does not detract from the central focus of the activity by drifting into a long and possibly irrelevant tangent.

☆   ☆   ☆   ☆   ☆

Figure 22.8. Vocabulary development strategies (from Kruse, 1987, p. 315–316)

A PROGRAM FOR TEACHING VOCABULARY DEVELOPMENT SKILLS

1. Goals

a. To improve the reading vocabulary skills of ESL students.

b. To teach ESL students word-building skills.

c. To teach ESL students to guess word meanings from context clues.

2. Word Building

a. *Suffixes:* It may be a good idea simply to give a list of these to the student for memorization. Roots used for this section should be familiar.

   (1) Practice in suffix recognition, i.e., simple exercises in isolation of suffixes:

   good*ness*   famili (ar) (ly)

   (2) Lesson and practice in noting grammatical changes effected by suffixes. Word tables might be very useful here.
   Adj. (good)+ness=N (goodness)
   Adj. (gloomy)+ly=Adv. (gloomily)

   (3) Practice in word *formation* through exercises in which the student adds and subtracts suffixes. Again the word table is useful. The student fills in the appropriate forms of a word by manipulating suffixes. It is of great importance to group words by the way they form variations so that all words being studied at one time add the same suffixes in the same manner and regularity of change can be emphasized.

b. *Prefixes:* These are more varied and less regular and therefore should not be presented until after suffixes have been mastered. A list of these can also be memorized.

   (1) Practice in prefix recognition.

   (2) Lesson and practice in meaning changes resulting from the use of prefixes, e.g., *in + formal =* not formal=casual. This is fairly difficult. The examples used should be straightforward in the early stages. Here again, the groupings must be of words that add the same prefixes in the same manner to achieve the same type of meaning. Groupings like *un* in *untie* and *un* in *unfair* must be avoided. As these are mastered, more difficult items requiring progressively higher degrees of interpretation may be introduced.

   (3) Practice in word formation:

   (a) Addition of prefixes. These exercises should progress in difficulty. E.g., Make a word meaning "not natural" (*unnatural*).

   (b) Addition of prefixes and suffixes.

c. *Roots:* These are quite difficult and should not be taught at all unless the student is fairly advanced and flexible in his approach to word forms. For a good list of Latin and Greek roots, refer to Dechant (1970, Ch. 12).

   (1) Recognizing roots. Isolation of root forms.

   (2) Effect of prefixes and suffixes on root forms.

3. Definition Clues

a. *Parentheses and footnotes* X (Y); X*

   (1) A lesson would first be given on these two types of clues, stressing their physical structure and how to read them correctly.

   (2) Practice in recognizing these clues. E.g., Draw a line under the words in parentheses: *The panther (<u>a large black animal related to a cat</u>) is very dangerous and deadly.*

   (3) Practice in using the clue. Here exercises of the following sort are useful: *The principal (main) reason for wearing clothes is to keep warm.* What is the meaning of *principal* in the sentence?

b. *Synonyms and antonyms:* Most students have studied and enjoy learning words with similar and opposite meanings. The task is to get them to recognize the definitional role these often play.

(1) X *is* Y; X, *that is,* Y. Students can be taught that an unfamiliar word is often defined in a sentence using the copula *be* and a synonym.

(a) Clue recognitions, both of signal words and synonyms. E.g., Underline the signal word <u>is</u> or <u>that is</u>: *A birthday party is an observance, <u>that is</u>, a remembrance of someone's day of birth.*

(b) Practice in using the clue. Again exercises in producing or recognizing a synonym are useful.

(2) X—Y—; X, *which* is Y; X. *or* Y; X, Y. Appositival constructions. This can be approached in essentially the same manner as the *is* and *that is* clues were.

4. Inference Clues

These types of clues require a higher level of analytical skill and practice than previous types dealt with. They should be approached slowly, moving from obvious answers to increasingly vague exercises. The ESL student should never be expected to do the same kind of inferring that a native speaker could do, but should be encouraged to go as far as possible as long as the guessing is not allowed to become wild. For all three types of clues (example, summary, and experience) the same method of practice in (i) recognition of clue elements and (ii) obtaining meaning from the elements can be followed.

a. *Example:*

(1) Specific clues: X, *e.g.,* Y; X, *i.e.,* Y; X, *for example,* Y.
E.g., *Iran is trying to <u>restore</u> many of its ancient monuments. Persepolis, for example, is being partly rebuilt by a group of Italian experts.*

(2) No physical clue.
E.g., *Roberta Flack, Aretha Franklin, and Olivia Newton-John are popular female <u>vocalists</u>.*

b. *Summary:*

(1) Restatement

(a) With a physical clue: . . . X. This Y . . . ; . . . X. X is Y.
E.g., *Many products are sold to stop <u>perspiration</u>. This wetness that comes from your body whenever you are too warm, work very hard, or are afraid, usually doesn't smell very good.*

(b) Without physical clue.
Either: The same meaning. X, Y.
E.g., *He's a really good <u>athlete</u>. He plays sports well.*
Or: Opposite meaning. X. (neg) Y.
E.g., *He's <u>bound</u> to win. He can't lose.*

(2) Information. E.g., *The <u>forsythia</u> was covered with the golden flowers that bloom early in the spring.*

c. *Experience:* The reader must decide from his own experiences what is probably meant by a word. E.g., *The old dog <u>snuffled</u> and <u>moped</u> as he slowly walked from the room.*

Unfortunately, professional pendulums have a disturbing way of swinging too far one way or the other, and sometimes the only way we can get enough perspective to see these overly long arcs is through hindsight. Hindsight has now taught us that there was some overreaction to the almost exclusive attention that grammar and vocabulary received in the first two-thirds of the twentieth century. So-called "natural" approaches in which grammar was considered damaging were equally overreactive. Advocating the "absorption" of grammar and vocabulary with no overt attention whatsoever to language forms went too far. We now seem to have a healthy respect for the place of form-focused instruction—attention to those basic "bits and pieces" of a language—in an interactive curriculum. And now we can pursue the business of finding better and better techniques for getting these bits and pieces into the communicative repertoires of our learners.

TOPICS FOR DISCUSSION, ACTION, AND RESEARCH

[Note: (I) Individual work; (G) group or pair work; (C) whole-class discussion.]

1. (I) It might be useful to review the section on form-focused instruction and error treatment in *PLLT,* Chapter 9, where background research and terminology are explained.
2. (G) Sometimes grammatical knowledge isn't sufficient to understand "hidden" or implied meanings of what people say or write. Tell pairs to look at the following:
    a. "Oh! That's just great!" [falling intonation]
    b. "Good to see you again, Helen. You've lost some weight, haven't you?"
    c. "Brrrr! It's sure cold in this house!"
    The "surface" grammatical meaning differs from potential "deep" structure meanings. Ask the pairs to identify those meanings, and, if possible, to think of other examples. Then have them devise a few techniques that could be used to teach such pragmatic aspects of English, and share their ideas with the rest of the class.
3. (I/C) Observe a class in which the teacher uses some form-focused instruction. Evaluate the effectiveness of the class using the five grammar focusing techniques on page 421. Share your observations with the whole class.
4. (G) Assign a separate, different grammar "point" to every *two* pairs and have them do the following: One pair figures out how to teach that point with a deductive approach and describes students for which such an approach is justified; the other pair is directed to do the same with an inductive approach. Pairs then present their suggestions to the whole class for comparison.
5. (C) On page 424, an example of a teacher's intervention is given. Discuss the following as a whole class: Was the teacher's interruption warranted? What are

some rules for interruption? (See the section on error treatment in Chapter 19.)

6. (C) On page 425 some justifications are offered for separate grammar classes. Ask the class if they agree with all the reasons. Do they know of any institutions that offer such courses? Do they follow all the criteria listed here?

7. (I) Review the section on error treatment in Chapter 19 (pages 344–350). Observe a class and try to determine if all the principles of error correction were followed. How, specifically, did the teacher treat grammatical (as opposed to vocabulary, pronunciation, etc.) errors?

8. (G/C) A number of grammar-focusing techniques are illustrated in this chapter (pages 426–431). Tell groups or pairs, each assigned to one technique, to demonstrate (peer-teach) that technique to the rest of the class. Ask the class to offer collective critiques of what worked well, what didn't, and why.

9. (G/C) Ask pairs to look back at the scope and sequence chart in Chapter 7 (pages 120–123) and decide if all the grammatical items are in an appropriate sequence. Which items could be placed significantly earlier or later in the course without posing undue difficulty for the students? Pairs will then share their thoughts with the rest of the class.

10. (I/G) As an extra-class project, pairs or individuals could be directed to consult one of the many available online linguistic corpora. Some corpora contain hundreds of millions of words in their data banks. So that I don't provide web URLs that may not exist as you read this, try searching for "Corpus Linguistics" in your favorite search engine (Google, Yahoo, etc.), and you will find many possible corpora, as well as further corpus searches in many different languages. Reports back to the class could include what was found, with some evaluative comments on pedagogical usefulness.

11. (G) Direct pairs to review the sections of Chapters 16 and 20 that deal with strategies for vocabulary acquisition. Then, referring to Kruse's taxonomy (Figure 22.8), pairs should figure out what word-attack skills are appropriate for a context with which they are familiar.

FOR YOUR FURTHER READING

Ellis, R. (2006). Current issues in the teaching of grammar: An SLA perspective. *TESOL Quarterly, 40,* 83–107.

Williams, J. (2005). Form-focused instruction. In E. Hinkel (Ed.), *Handbook of research in second language teaching and learning* (pp. 671–691). Mahwah, NJ: Lawrence Erlbaum Associates.

Nassaji, H., & Fotos, S. (2004). Current developments in research on the teaching of grammar. *Annual Review of Applied Linguistics, 24,* 126–145.

These three articles offer comprehensive surveys of research on form-focused instruction, with an emphasis on the teaching of grammar. Extensive bibliographies are included.

Nunan, D. (2005). *Practical English language teaching: Grammar.* New York: McGraw-Hill.

Larsen-Freeman, D. (2003). *Teaching language: From grammar to grammaring.* Boston: Heinle & Heinle.

David Nunan and Diane Larsen-Freeman both offer book-length perspectives on teaching grammar in current communicative frameworks. Nunan's treatment has practical exercises and materials, graded into beginning, intermediate, and advanced levels, along with a survey of issues and approaches. Larsen-Freeman's book is more like a series of essays, each offering interesting perspectives on approaches to grammar, all in support of what she calls "grammaring," or learners' processes of using grammatical knowledge in their performance of language.

Nation, I. S. P. (2005). Teaching and learning vocabulary. In E. Hinkel (Ed.), *Handbook of research in second language teaching and learning* (pp. 581–595). Mahwah, NJ: Lawrence Erlbaum Associates.

Read, J. (2004). Research in teaching vocabulary. *Annual Review of Applied Linguistics, 24,* 146–161.

Paul Nation and John Read each describe current research on teaching vocabulary in these review articles, with useful bibliographic references.

PART V

ASSESSING LANGUAGE SKILLS

Assessment is an integral aspect of the pedagogical process of designing lessons, implementing them, and evaluating their success. Without an assessment component in every lesson, every unit, and every course, we couldn't determine the attainment of objectives and goals.

This section of *Teaching by Principles* addresses concepts, issues, and practicalities of assessment in the classroom. It is intended to serve simply as an introduction to classroom-based assessment—enough to supply you with some useful tools for creating or adapting your own assessment procedures. For a comprehensive treatment of language assessment, I recommend reading my companion textbook, *Language Assessment: Principles and Classroom Practices* (Brown, 2004).

Chapter 23 offers a survey of principles and basic concepts in language assessment, beginning with the articulation of five basic principles that underlie virtually every assessment procedure, from formal *tests* to informal, incidental *assessments* that are part of virtually every moment of teaching. These principles are followed by a look at historical developments in the field, a look at large-scale and standards-based testing, and an analysis of the critical ethical issues involved in assessment.

Chapter 24 is focused directly on the classroom, and on what you as a teacher can do to develop principled, effective, informative assessments in your teaching process. After a primer on writing formal tests and test items, you're led through a succession of alternatives in assessment: the feasibility of using portfolios, journals, conferences, observations, and self- and peer-assessment. The chapter concludes with a closer look at the dilemmas presented by balancing principles of practicality/reliability with principles of authenticity and washback in the classroom.

CHAPTER **23**

LANGUAGE ASSESSMENT:

PRINCIPLES AND ISSUES

OBJECTIVES After reading this chapter, you will be able to:

- distinguish between the terms *assessment* and *testing*
- define five basic principles of language assessment and apply them to practical, classroom-based tests and other assessment procedures
- identify a number of different genres of tests
- examine historical developments as well as current issues in language testing
- analyze large-scale standardized tests and apply standards to those tests
- appreciate the critical nature of testing, especially the moral and ethical issues involved in large-scale commercial testing

So far, if you have been reading this book chapter by chapter from the beginning, you have gathered a great deal of information about the process of the classroom teaching of second language learners: principles underlying a sound approach, contextual considerations, lesson design and classroom management, and language skills instruction. In all these discussions, the notion of language assessment has emerged implicitly on a number of occasions, and explicitly at the end of each of the chapters on the four skills, but not to the point of taking a broad look at the field of language assessment and the principles and issues involved in the discipline.

This and the subsequent chapter offer a survey of principles and issues in language assessment, a look at designing language tests, and a primer on classroom alternatives in assessment. These three chapters are intended to be a rather sweeping survey of this important aspect of your pedagogy—enough to acquaint you with some basic tools for considering the role of assessment in your classroom. Obviously, in a field so complex and diverse, a complete, comprehensive understanding of language assessment will require more reading. For the latter, in a book-length treatment of language assessment, I refer you to my companion text, *Language Assessment: Principles and Classroom Practices* (Brown, 2004).

TESTING, ASSESSING, AND TEACHING

Before diving into a description of the language assessment field, it's important to define some frequently misunderstood terms. The word *assessment* has, in recent years, become a popular word for educators—in much the same way that

444

communicative or *interactive* have gained widespread acceptance in language-teaching circles. You are said to be on the cutting edge if you *assess* your students in lieu of *testing* them. This is a misunderstanding.

On the one hand, sometimes you find writers using *test* and *assessment* synonymously, which is not the case. A **test** is a method of measuring a person's ability or knowledge in a given domain, with an emphasis on the concepts of *method* and *measuring*. Tests are instruments that are (usually) carefully designed and that have identifiable scoring rubrics. Tests are prepared administrative procedures that occupy identifiable time periods in a curriculum when learners muster all their faculties to offer peak performance, knowing that their responses are being measured and evaluated.

Assessment, on the other hand, is an ongoing process that encompasses a much wider domain. Whenever a student responds to a question, offers a comment, or tries out a new word or structure, the teacher subconsciously makes an assessment of the student's performance. Written work—from a jotted-down phrase to a formal essay—is performance that ultimately gets assessed by self, teacher, and possibly other students. Reading and listening activities usually require some sort of productive performance that the teacher implicitly judges, however peripheral that judgment may be. A good teacher never ceases to assess students, whether those assessments are incidental or intentional.

In this view of these two concepts, tests are subsets of assessment; they are certainly not the only form of assessment that a teacher can make. Tests can be useful devices, but they are only one among many procedures and tasks that teachers can ultimately use to assess students.

But now, you might be thinking, if you make assessments every time you teach something in the classroom, does all *teaching* involve assessment? Are teachers constantly assessing students with no room for interaction that is assessment-free? The answer depends on your perspective. For optimal learning to take place, students must have the freedom in the classroom to experiment, to try out their own hypotheses about language without feeling that their overall competence is being "judged" in terms of those trials and errors. In the same way that, say, tournament tennis players must, before a tournament itself begins, have the freedom to practice their skills with no implications for their final placement on that day of days, so also must your learners have ample opportunities to "play" with language in your classroom without being formally graded. Teaching, in part, sets up the practice games of language learning, the opportunities for learners to listen, think, take risks, set goals, and process feedback from the "coach" and then recycle through whatever it is that they are trying to set in place.

At the same time, during these practice activities, teachers (and tennis coaches) are indeed observing students' performance and making various evaluations of the learner: How did the performance compare to previous performance? Which aspects of the performance were better than others? Is the learner performing up to an expected potential? How does the performance compare to that of others in the same learning community? And, in the ideal classroom, all these observations then feed into the way the teacher provides instruction to each student.

What you're doing when you're "coaching" your students and giving them feedback is essentially **informal** assessment: incidental, unplanned comments and responses like "Nice job!" "Did you say *can* or *can't?*" "You *go* to the movies yesterday?" or a marginal comment on a paper. A good deal of a teacher's informal assessment is embedded in classroom tasks designed to elicit performance but *not* with the intent of recording results and making fixed judgments about a student's competence.

On the other hand, **formal** assessment includes exercises or procedures specifically designed to tap into a storehouse of skills and knowledge. They are systematic, planned sampling techniques constructed to give teacher and student an appraisal of student achievement. To extend the tennis analogy, formal assessments are the tournament games that periodically occur in the course of a daily or weekly regimen of practice.

Is formal assessment the same as a test? We can say that all tests are formal assessments, but not all formal assessment is testing. For example, you might use a student's journal or portfolio of materials as a formal assessment of the attainment of certain course objectives, but it is problematic to call those two procedures "tests." A systematic set of observations of a student's frequency of oral participation in class is certainly a formal assessment, but it too is hardly what anyone would call a test. Tests are usually relatively time-constrained (usually spanning a class period or at most several hours) and draw on a limited sample of behavior.

PRINCIPLES OF LANGUAGE ASSESSMENT

Whether you are focusing on testing or assessing, a finite number of principles can be named that serve as guidelines for the design of a new test or assessment and for evaluating the efficacy of an existing procedure. I offer five such principles here. They represent a synthesis of what various assessment specialists cite as priorities for the design of language assessments. As I explain each principle, I will use the term *test* here as a generic term for both *test* and *formal assessment,* since all the principles apply to both.

Practicality

A good test is **practical.** It is within the means of financial limitations, time constraints, ease of administration, and scoring and interpretation. A test that is prohibitively expensive is impractical. A test of language proficiency that takes a student 10 hours to complete is impractical. A test that requires individual one-to-one proctoring is impractical for a group of 500 people and only a handful of examiners. A test that takes a few minutes for a student to take and several hours for an examiner to evaluate is impractical for most classroom situations. A test that can be scored only by computer is impractical if the test takes place a thousand miles away from the nearest computer. The value and quality of a test are dependent upon such nitty-gritty, practical considerations.

The extent to which a test is practical sometimes hinges on whether a test is designed to be **norm-referenced** or **criterion-referenced.** In norm-referenced tests, each test-taker's score is interpreted in relation to a mean, median, standard deviation, and/or percentile rank. The purpose in such tests is to place test-takers along a mathematical continuum in rank order. Typical of norm-referenced tests are standardized tests intended to be administered to large audiences, with results quickly disseminated to test-takers. Such tests must have fixed, predetermined responses in a format that can be electronically scanned. Practicality is a primary issue.

Criterion-referenced tests, on the other hand, are designed to give test-takers feedback on specific course or lesson objectives, that is, the "criteria." Classroom tests involving smaller numbers, and connected to a curriculum, are typical of criterion-referenced testing. Here, more time and effort on the part of the teacher (test administrator) are usually required in order to deliver the feedback. One could say that criterion-referenced tests may, in the opinion of some, consider practicality as a secondary issue in the design of the test; teachers may sacrifice time and effort in order to offer students appropriate and useful feedback—the instructional value of a test. Testing (assessing) and teaching are interrelated, as noted already in this chapter.

Reliability

A **reliable** test is consistent and dependable. A number of sources of unreliability may be identified:

- the test itself (its construction), known as test reliability
- the administration of a test
- the test-taker, known as student-related reliability
- the scoring of the test, known as rater (or scorer) reliability

I once participated in the administration of a test of aural comprehension in which a tape recorder played items for comprehension, but because of street noise outside the testing room, students in the room who were sitting next to windows were impaired from hearing the tape accurately. That was a clear case of test administration unreliability. Sometimes a test yields unreliable results because of factors beyond the control of the test writer, but within the test-taker, such as illness, a "bad day," or no sleep the night before (student-related reliability).

Scorer reliability sometimes refers to the consistency of scoring by two or more scorers, but for classroom teachers and your own classroom-based assessment, it's rare that you will have the luxury of a second scorer or grader. So, how does scorer reliability enter into the picture when you are the only scorer? Interestingly enough, reliability is an extremely important issue that every teacher has to contend with.

Because we are all human, we can be unreliable in the consistency we apply to test evaluation. Unclear scoring criteria, fatigue, carelessness, or a bias toward "good" and "bad" students can all play a part in our own unreliability. If subjective techniques are employed in the scoring or grading of a test, reliability can suffer. A test of pronunciation in which the scorer is to assign a number between one and five might be unreliable if the scoring specifications are not clear. Or let's say you have 40 tests to evaluate and it's late the night before you must return the tests: You can be tempted toward inconsistent application of your criteria for judgment. If scoring directions are clear and specific as to the exact details that you should attend to, then such scoring can become reasonably consistent and dependable.

Validity

By far the most complex criterion of a good test is **validity,** the degree to which the test actually measures what it is intended to measure. A valid test of reading ability is one that actually measures reading ability and not, say, 20/20 vision, previous knowledge of a subject, or some other variable of questionable relevance. To measure writing ability, one might conceivably ask students to write as many words as they can in 15 minutes, then simply count the words for the final score. Such a test would be easy to administer (practical) and the scoring quite dependable (reliable). But it would hardly constitute a valid test of writing ability unless some consideration were given to the communication and organization of ideas, among other factors. Some have felt that standard language proficiency tests, with their context-reduced, CALP (cognitive academic language proficiency)-oriented language and limited stretches of discourse, are not valid measures of language "proficiency" since they do not appear to tap into the communicative competence of the learner. There is good reasoning behind such criticism; nevertheless, what such proficiency tests lack in validity, they gain in practicality and reliability. We will return to the question of large-scale proficiency later in this chapter.

How does one establish the validity of a test? Statistical correlation with other related measures is a standard method. But ultimately, validity can be established only by observation and theoretical justification. There is no final, absolute, and objective measure of validity. We have to ask questions that give us convincing evidence that a test accurately and sufficiently measures the test-taker for the particular objective, or criterion, of the test. If that evidence is there, then the test may be said to have criterion validity.

In tests of language, validity is supported most convincingly by subsequent personal observation by teachers and peers. The validity of a high score on the final exam of a foreign language course will be substantiated by "actual" proficiency in the language. A classroom test designed to assess mastery of a point of grammar in communicative use will have validity if test scores correlate either with observed subsequent behavior or with other communicative measures of the grammar point in question.

How can teachers be somewhat assured that a test, whether it is a standardized test or one constructed for classroom use, is indeed valid? Three types of validation are important in your role as a classroom teacher: content validity, face validity, and construct validity.

Content validity

If a test actually samples the subject matter about which conclusions are to be drawn, if it requires the test-taker to perform the behavior that is being measured, it can claim **content validity**. You can usually determine content validity, observationally, if you can clearly define the achievement that you are measuring. A test of tennis competency that asks someone to run a 100-yard dash lacks content validity. If you are trying to assess a person's ability to speak a second language in a conversational setting, a test that asks the learner to answer paper-and-pencil multiple-choice questions requiring grammatical judgments does not achieve content validity. A test that requires the learner actually to speak within some sort of authentic context does.

In most human situations, we are best tested in something when we are required to perform a sampling of the criterion behavior. But there are a few highly specialized and sophisticated testing instruments that do not have high content validity yet are nevertheless valid. Projective personality tests are a prime example. The Thematic Apperception Test and the Rorschach "inkblot" tests have little content validity, yet they have been shown to be accurate in assessing certain types of deviant personality behavior. A test of field independence as a prediction of language success in the classroom may have potentially good criterion validity but poor content validity in that the ability to detect an embedded geometric figure bears little direct resemblance to the ability to speak and hear a language. As already noted, standard proficiency tests often don't get high scores on content validity.

Face validity

A concept that is very closely related to content validity is **face validity**, which asks the question "Does the test, on the 'face' of it, appear from the learner's perspective to test what it is designed to test?" To achieve "peak" performance on a test, a learner needs to be convinced that the test is indeed testing what it claims to test. Once I administered a dictation test and a cloze test (see below for a discussion of cloze tests) as a placement test for an experimental group of learners of English as a second language. Some learners were upset because such tests, on the face of it, did not appear to them to test their true abilities in English. Face validity is almost always perceived in terms of content: If the test samples the actual content of what the learner has achieved or expects to achieve, then face validity will be perceived.

Construct validity

A third category of validity that teachers must be aware of in considering language tests is construct validity. One way to look at construct validity is to ask the question "Does this test actually tap into the theoretical construct as it has been defined?" "Proficiency" is a construct. "Communicative competence" is a construct. "Self-esteem" is a construct. Virtually every issue in language learning and teaching involves theoretical constructs. Tests are, in a manner of speaking, operational definitions of such constructs in that they operationalize the entity that is being measured (see Davidson, Hudson, & Lynch 1985).

A teacher needs to be satisfied that a particular test is an adequate definition of a construct. Let's say you have been given a procedure for conducting an oral interview. The scoring analysis for the interview weighs several factors into a final score: pronunciation, fluency, grammatical accuracy, vocabulary use, and sociolinguistic appropriateness. The justification for these five factors lies in a theoretical construct that claims those factors as major components of oral proficiency. So, on the other hand, if you were asked to conduct an oral proficiency interview that accounted only for pronunciation and grammar, you could be justifiably suspicious about the construct validity of such a test.

Most of the tests that you will encounter as a classroom teacher can be validated adequately through content; if the test samples the outcome behavior, then validity will have been achieved. But when there is low, or questionable, content validity in a test, it becomes very important for a teacher to be assured of its construct validity. Standardized tests designed to be given to large numbers of students typically suffer from poor content validity but are redeemed through their construct validation. The TOEFL® (Test of English as a Foreign Language), for example, does not sample oral production, yet oral production is obviously an important part of succeeding academically in a university course of study. The TOEFL's absence of oral production content is justified by research that has shown positive correlations between oral production and the behaviors (listening, reading, grammaticality detection, and writing) actually sampled on the TOEFL. Because of the crucial need to offer a financially affordable proficiency test and the high cost of administering and scoring oral production tests, the omission of oral content from the TOEFL has been accepted as a necessity in the professional community.

There are other forms of validity that you might want to consider (see Brown, 2004, pp. 22–27), but these three are the most relevant to classroom-based assessment, and are at the same time indispensable to your understanding of what makes a "good" test.

Authenticity

A fourth major principle of language testing is **authenticity**, a concept that is a little slippery to define, especially within the art and science of evaluating and designing tests. Bachman & Palmer (1996, p. 23) define authenticity as "the degree of correspondence of the characteristics of a given language test task to the features of a target language task," and then suggest an agenda for identifying those target language tasks and for transforming them into valid test items.

Essentially, when you make a claim for authenticity in a test task, you are saying this is a task that is likely to be enacted in the "real world." Many test item types fail to simulate real-world tasks. They may be contrived or artificial in their attempt to target a grammatical form or a lexical item. The sequencing of items that bear no relationship to one another lacks authenticity. One does not have to look very long to find reading comprehension passages in proficiency tests that hardly reflect a real-world passage.

In a test, authenticity may be present in the following ways:

- The language in the test is as natural as possible.
- Items are contextualized rather than isolated.
- Topics and situations are interesting, enjoyable, and humorous.
- Some thematic organization to items is provided, such as through a story line or episode.
- Tasks represent, or closely approximate, real-world tasks.

The authenticity of test tasks in recent years has increased noticeably. Two or three decades ago unconnected, boring, contrived items were accepted as a necessary by-product of testing. Things have changed. It was once assumed that large-scale testing could not stay within budgetary constraints and include performance of the productive skills, but now many such tests offer speaking and writing components. Reading passages are selected from real-world sources that test-takers are likely to have encountered or will encounter some day. Listening comprehension sections feature natural language with hesitations, white noise, and interruptions. More and more tests offer items that are "episodic," in that they are sequenced to form meaningful units, paragraphs, or stories.

Washback

When students take a test, ideally they will receive information (feedback) about their competence, based on their performance. That feedback should "wash back" to them in the form of useful diagnoses of strengths and weaknesses. **Washback** also includes the effects of an assessment on teaching and learning prior to the assessment itself, that is, on preparation for the assessment. Informal assessment is by nature more likely to have built-in washback effects, because the teacher is usually providing interactive feedback. Formal tests can also have positive washback, but they are also subject to an inadvertent absence of washback if students simply receive a letter grade or a single overall numerical score.

The challenge to teachers is to create classroom tests that serve as learning devices through which washback is achieved. Students' incorrect responses can become windows of insight into further work. Their correct responses may need to be praised, especially when they represent accomplishments in a student's interlanguage. Teachers can suggest strategies for success as part of their "coaching" role. Washback enhances a number of basic principles of language acquisition: intrinsic motivation, autonomy, self-confidence, language ego, interlanguage, and strategic investment, among others.

One way to enhance washback is to comment generously and specifically on test performance. Many teachers, in our overworked (and underpaid!) lives, return tests to students with a single letter grade or numerical score on them, and consider their job done. In reality, letter grades and a score showing the number of right or wrong give absolutely no information of intrinsic interest to the student. Grades and scores reduce a mountain of linguistic and cognitive performance data to an absurd molehill. At best, they give a relative indication of a formulaic judgment of performance as compared to others in the class—which fosters competitive, not cooperative, learning.

With this in mind, when you return a written test or a data sheet from an oral production test, consider giving more than a number, grade, or phrase as your feedback. Even if your evaluation is not a neat little paragraph appended to the test, at least you can respond to as many details throughout the test as time will permit. Give praise for strengths—the "good stuff"—as well as constructive criticism of weaknesses. Give strategic hints on how a student might improve certain elements of performance. In other words, take some time to make the test performance an intrinsically motivating experience through which a student will feel a sense of accomplishment and challenge.

A little bit of washback may also accrue to students through a specification to the student of the numerical scores on the various subsections of the test. A section on verb tenses, for example, that yields a relatively low score may serve the diagnostic purpose of showing the student an area of challenge.

Washback also implies that students have ready access to you to discuss the feedback and evaluation you have given. I'm sure you have known teachers in your life with whom you wouldn't dare "argue" about a grade. In an interactive, cooperative, collaborative classroom, one could hardly promote such an atmosphere. For learning to continue, students need to have a chance to "feed back" on your feedback, to seek clarification of any issues that are fuzzy, and to appropriately set new goals for themselves for the days and weeks ahead.

Washback may also imply the benefit learners experience in their preparation for a test, before the fact. (I like to facetiously call this "wash forward.") By using appropriate strategies for reviewing, synthesizing, and consolidating of material before taking a test, students may find that the preparation time is as beneficial as the feedback received after the fact. Sometimes, preparation and reviewing before a test is even *more* instructive than the test itself! You can be a facilitator in this process by helping to direct your students toward productive and relevant reviewing techniques.

You now have five basic principles for designing effective tests and assessments in your classroom:

1. Practicality
2. Reliability
3. Validity (content, face, and construct)

4. Authenticity
5. Washback

If in your language teaching you can attend to these principles in evaluating or adapting existing procedures, or in designing new ones on your own, then you are well on the way to making accurate judgments about the competence of the learners with whom you are working.

KINDS OF TESTS

There are many kinds of tests, each with a specific purpose and a particular criterion to be measured. Below you will find descriptions of five test types that are in common use in language curricula. Explanations here are only for the purpose of helping you to identify and differentiate among types, not to serve as a manual for designing such tests.

Proficiency Tests

If your aim in a test is to tap global competence in a language, then you are, in conventional terminology, testing proficiency. A **proficiency test** is not intended to be limited to any one course, curriculum, or single skill in the language. Proficiency tests have traditionally consisted of standardized multiple-choice items on grammar, vocabulary, reading comprehension, aural comprehension, and sometimes a sample of writing. Such tests often have content validity weaknesses, as already noted above, but after several decades of construct validation research, some great strides have been made toward constructing communicative proficiency tests.

Typical examples of standardized proficiency tests are the *Test of English as a Foreign Language* (TOEFL®) and the *International English Language Testing System* (IELTS). Together, they are used by thousands of educational institutions as an indicator of a prospective student's ability to undertake academic or professional work in an English medium. Both TOEFL and IELTS consist of performance on all four skills and both are now computer-based. The comprehension sections (listening and reading) of virtually all large-scale proficiency tests are computer-scorable for rapid turnaround and cost effectiveness. Production performance (speaking and writing) usually demand human scorers.

Diagnostic Tests

A **diagnostic test** is designed to diagnose a particular aspect of a language. A diagnostic test in pronunciation might have the purpose of determining which phonological features of English are difficult for a learner and should therefore become a part of a curriculum. Usually, such tests offer a checklist of features for the administrator (often the teacher) to use in pinpointing difficulties. A writing diagnostic would first elicit a writing sample from students. Then the teacher would identify, from a list of rhetorical features that are already present in a writing course, those on which a student needs to have special focus. It is not advisable to use a general achievement test (see below) as a diagnostic, since diagnostic tests need to be specifically tailored to offer information on student need that will be worked on imminently. Achievement tests are useful for analyzing the extent to which students have acquired language features that have already been taught.

Placement Tests

Certain proficiency tests and diagnostic tests can act in the role of **placement tests,** whose purpose is to place a student into an appropriate level or section of a language curriculum or school. A placement test typically includes a sampling of material to be covered in the curriculum (that is, it has content validity), and it thereby provides an indication of the point at which the student will find a level or class to be neither too easy nor too difficult, but appropriately challenging.

Achievement Tests

An **achievement test** is related directly to classroom lessons, units, or even a total curriculum. Achievement tests are limited to particular material covered in a curriculum within a particular time frame, and are offered after a course has covered the objectives in question. Achievement tests can serve as indicators of features that a student needs to work on in the future, but the primary role of an achievement test is to determine acquisition of course objectives at the end of a period of instruction.

Aptitude Tests

Finally, we need to consider the type of test that is given to a person *prior* to any exposure to the second language, a test that predicts a person's future success. A language **aptitude test** is designed to measure a person's capacity or general ability to learn a foreign language and to be successful in that undertaking. Aptitude tests are considered to be independent of a particular language. Two standardized aptitude tests were once in popular use—the *Modern Language Aptitude Test* (MLAT) (Carroll & Sapon, 1958) and the *Pimsleur Language Aptitude Battery* (PLAB) (Pimsleur, 1966). Both are English language tests and require students to perform such tasks as memorizing numbers and vocabulary, listening to foreign words, and detecting spelling clues and grammatical patterns. The validity of both tests rested on correlations between such tasks and subsequent performance in foreign language courses.

This genre of aptitude test is seldom used today. Instead, the measurement of language aptitude has taken the direction of examining the relationship between more pragmatic and strategic abilities of would-be language learners and their eventual success in natural, real-world input generation, interaction, and output performance (Dörnyei & Skehan, 2003; Robinson, 2005; Skehan, 1998a). Any test that claims to *predict* success in learning a language is undoubtedly flawed, because we now know that with appropriate self-knowledge, active strategic involvement in learning, and/or strategies-based instruction, virtually everyone can succeed eventually. (A full discussion of language aptitude and aptitude tests can be found in *PLLT,* Chapter 4.)

Within each of the five categories of tests above, there are a variety of different possible techniques and procedures. These range from

- objective to subjective scoring procedures,
- open-ended to structured response options,
- multiple-choice to fill-in-the-blank item design formats,
- written to oral performance modes.

Tests of each of the modes of performance can be focused on a continuum of linguistic units, from smaller to larger: phonology and orthography, words, sentences, and discourse. In interpreting a test it is important to note which linguistic units are being tested. Oral production tests can be tests of overall conversational fluency or pronunciation of a particular subset of phonology, and can take the form of imitation, structured responses, or free responses. Similarly, listening comprehension tests can concentrate on a particular feature of language or on overall listening for general meaning. Tests of reading can cover the range of language units and can aim to test comprehension of long or short passages, single sentences, or even phrases and words. Writing tests can take on an open-ended form with free composition, or be structured to elicit anything from correct spelling to discourse-level competence.

HISTORICAL DEVELOPMENTS IN LANGUAGE ASSESSMENT

Historically, language testing trends and practices have followed the changing winds and shifting sands of methodology described earlier in this book (Chapter 2). For example, in the 1950s, an era of behaviorism and special attention to contrastive analysis, testing focused on specific language elements such as the phonological, grammatical, and lexical contrasts between two languages. In the 1970s and 1980s, communicative theories of language brought on more of an integrative view of testing in which testing specialists claimed that "the whole of the communicative event was considerably greater than the sum of its linguistic elements" (Clark, 1983, p. 432). Today, test designers are still challenged in their quest for more authentic, content-valid instruments that simulate real-world interaction while still meeting reliability and practicality criteria (Leung & Lewkowicz, 2006).

This historical perspective underscores two major approaches to language testing that still prevail, even if in mutated form, today: the choice between discrete-point and integrative testing methods. Discrete-point tests were constructed on the assumption that language can be broken down into its component parts and those parts adequately tested. Those components are basically the skills of listening, speaking, reading, writing, the various hierarchical units of language (phonology/graphology, morphology, lexicon, syntax, discourse) within each skill, and subcategories within those units. So, for example, it was claimed that a typical proficiency test with its sets of multiple-choice questions divided into grammar, vocabulary, reading, and the like, with some items attending to smaller units and others to larger units, can measure these discrete points of language and, by adequate sampling of these units, can achieve validity. Such a rationale is not unreasonable if one considers types of testing theory in which certain constructs are measured by breaking down their component parts.

The discrete-point approach met with some criticism as we emerged into an era of emphasizing communication, authenticity, and context. The earliest criticism (Oller, 1979) argued that language competence is a unified set of interacting abilities that cannot be tested separately. The claim was, in short, that communicative competence is so global and requires such integration (hence the term "integrative" testing) that it cannot be captured in additive tests of grammar and reading and vocabulary and other discrete points of language. Others (Cziko, 1982; Savignon, 1982) soon followed in their support for integrative testing.

Just what does an integrative test look like? Two types of test have been held up as examples of integrative tests: cloze tests and dictations. A cloze test is a reading passage (of, say, 150 to 300 words) that has been "mutilated" by the deletion of roughly every sixth or seventh word; the test-taker is required to supply words that fit into those blanks. John Oller (1979) claimed that cloze test results are good measures of overall proficiency. According to theoretical constructs underlying this claim, the ability to supply appropriate words in blanks requires a number of abilities that lie at the very heart of competence in a language: knowledge of vocabulary, grammatical structure, discourse structure, reading skills and strategies, and an internalized "expectancy" grammar (that enables one to predict an item that will come next in a sequence). It is argued that successful completion of cloze items taps into all of those abilities, which are the essence of global language proficiency.

The dictation is familiar to virtually all classroom language learners. (The steps for administering a dictation are outlined in Chapter 21.) The argument for claiming dictation as an integrative test is that it taps into grammatical and discourse competencies required for other modes of performance in a language. Further, dictation test results tend to correlate strongly with other tests of proficiency. Success on a dictation requires careful listening, reproduction in writing of what is heard, efficient short-term memory, and, to an extent, some expectancy rules to aid the short-term memory. Dictation testing remains more classroom-centered because large-scale administration of dictations is quite impractical from a scoring standpoint. Reliability of scoring criteria is also a problem that is not present in multiple-choice, exact-word cloze test scoring.

Proponents of integrative test methods (Lowe & Stansfield, 1988; Oller, 1979) soon centered their argument on what became known as the unitary trait hypothesis, which suggested an "indivisible" view of language proficiency, namely, that vocabulary, grammar, phonology, the "four skills," and other discrete points of language cannot, in fact, be distinguished from each other. The unitary trait hypothesis contended that there is a general factor of language proficiency such that all the discrete points do not add up to that whole.

Others argued strongly against the unitary trait position. For example, Hossein Farhady (1982) found significant and widely varying differences in performance on six different components of an ESL proficiency test, depending on subjects' native country, major field of study, and graduate versus undergraduate status. So, for example, Brazilians scored very low in listening comprehension and relatively high in reading comprehension. Filipinos, whose scores on five of the six components of the test were considerably higher than Brazilians' scores, were actually lower than Brazilians in reading comprehension scores. Farhady's contentions were supported in other research that seriously questioned the unitary trait hypothesis. Finally, in the face of the evidence, Oller (1983b, p. 352) backed down and admitted that "the unitary trait hypothesis was wrong."

CURRENT ISSUES IN LANGUAGE ASSESSMENT

In some ways, recent work in language assessment makes the above account seem like ancient history. So many steps have been taken to improve the construction, delivery, and scoring of assessments that it's difficult to capsulize them here. From an era not too many decades ago when virtually all tests were thought to necessitate decontextualized linguistic stimuli of dubious authenticity, we have emerged into a new world of more communicative, learner-centered, performance-based assessment. Nevertheless, many challenges remain—in the world of commercial production of language tests and in the language classroom. Let's look at a few of those highlights.

Large-Scale Language Proficiency Testing

The first issue that springs into the mind of most of us when "language testing" is mentioned is our global obsession over standardized tests, mass produced by corporations and government agencies, hailed as empirically validated, and thought to provide accurate measures of ability. Are such tests valid? Are they authentic? What are the consequences for test-takers of such testing? To what use are they put?

The accumulated research on language testing in the last half of the twentieth century produced some bad news and some good news for the daunting task of large-scale, standardized proficiency assessment.

In order to test hundreds, if not tens of thousands, in the case of tests like the TOEFL®, TOEIC, and IELTS, the principle of practicality is always foremost. In a world of commercial competition, costs must be within reach of customers. Assessing multitudes of test-takers (either manually, in paper-and-pencil formats, or in computer-delivered technology) requires intricate procedures to protect the security of items and forms. Tasks need to be designed to mirror language tasks of the real world, yet allow for rapid scoring at a marketable cost. To be sure, virtually no one is looking for the magic of a unitary trait in order to accomplish this end. Furthermore, language-testing specialists are not banking entirely on a discrete-point approach for solutions, either. The crux of the issue lies in finding ways to tap into the *communicative* abilities of language users.

The good news is that researchers continue to focus on the components of communicative competence in their efforts to specify the multiple language traits that must be measured in a valid test. Listening, speaking, reading, and writing are but one dimension of a multi-trait approach to testing. Bachman's (1990) model of communicative language proficiency is still a viable template for designing large-scale tests. Along with the components of organizational (phonology, grammar, discourse) competence, language tests of the new millennium are focusing on the pragmatic (sociolinguistic, functional), strategic, and interpersonal/affective components of language ability (Kunnan, 2005; Leung & Lewkowicz, 2006).

According to criteria set forth by Bachman (1991), a communicative test needed to meet some rather stringent criteria. It had to test for grammatical, discourse, sociolinguistic, and illocutionary competence as well as strategic competence. It had to be pragmatic in that it requires the learner to use language naturally for genuine communication and to relate to thoughts and feelings, in short, to put authentic language to use within a context. It needed to be direct (as opposed to indirect tests that may lose content validity). And it should test the learner in a variety of language functions. These criteria represented a departure from earlier language proficiency tests by requiring multiple sources of input (skills), task dependency (tasks building on previous tasks in the test), and more emphasis on pragmatic and sociolinguistic factors than was found in previous tests.

At the present time, designers of large-scale language tests are still struggling with some of Bachman's criteria, but some progress has been made. Tests such as the TOEFL®, in a new incarnation in 2005, include performance on all four skills, interactive response techniques, and improved tasks requiring pragmatic, discourse, and sociolinguistic competence in order to accurately respond. Computer delivery, scoring, and reporting technology has helped test designers to venture into more complex tasks without incurring undue costs (Jamieson, 2005). Further, corpus linguistics has contributed to designers' ability to create authentic tasks (Conrad, 2005).

Further challenges of course remain. A perplexing and extremely complex issue in language assessment globally is the increasing recognition of varieties of international English. A few years ago one could be smugly content to include among test stimuli a variety of "accents" and consider the matter of world Englishes to be covered. Today, we are confronted with the challenge of assessing multi-modal skills across grammatical, lexical, discourse, pragmatic, and sociolinguistic planes—far beyond the simple question of accent (Leung & Lewkowicz, 2006). Yet another challenge in large-scale proficiency testing is the assessment of language within the **specific purposes** to which language will be put. Douglas (2005) raises interesting questions about how to conceive of "overall" language ability if there are multiple contexts in which a second language is used. Is a "general purpose" proficiency test really of much use to anyone? Douglas argues for greater attention to specific purposes tests.

Authenticity

A second and certainly not unrelated current issue in language assessment is authenticity. Earlier in this chapter you were introduced to authenticity as one of five major underlying principles of language assessment. The focus in language pedagogy on communication in real-world contexts has spurred many attempts to create more communicative assessment procedures. Lyle Bachman's (1990) seminal book was a call for communicative testing to include *all* the components of communicative competence (including pragmatic and interpersonal competence). Current approaches, as described by Leung (2005) and Alderson and Banerjee (2001, 2002), reveal that assessment specialists *and* classroom teachers are answering the call. Important strides have been made to enable both technicians and teachers to design authentic tests, yet even further steps are being made as we speak.

One of the keystones of communicative competence theories is the interactive nature of language. Users of a language creatively interact with other people as well as with texts (including test items). Simply put, this means that tests have to involve people in actually performing the behavior that we want to measure. Paper-and-pencil or computer-delivered multiple-choice tests certainly do not involve test-takers in speaking, requesting, responding, interacting, or in combining listening and speaking, or reading and writing. Interactive testing involves them in all of the above rather than relying on the assumption that a good paper-and-pencil test-taker is a good overall language performer.

More than two decades ago, Mueller (1987, p. 124) noted that what we are being asked to do is to "take the audacious step of making testing truly interactive: . . . a lively exchange of stimulating ideas, opinions, impressions, reactions, positions or attitudes. Students can be actively involved and interested participants when their task is not restricted to providing the one and only correct answer."

Creating authentic tasks within formal assessment procedures presents some dilemmas. Authentic tasks are often complex and lack practicality (Alderson &

Banerjee, 2002). They are difficult to create and even more difficult to evaluate because they often involve reliability issues. An oral interview can go a long way toward authenticity, but the possibility of unpredictable responses from test-takers sometimes means we have to make a "judgment call" that could be inconsistent. Another problem raised by authentic assessment tasks is how to judge the difficulty of a task, an important factor in standardized testing (Leung & Lewkowicz, 2006). Authentic tasks are rarely confined to one simple level of difficulty across phonological, syntactic, discourse, and pragmatic planes. Finally, authenticity almost always means the integration of two or more skills, and so how is an evaluator to judge, say, both the listening competence and the speaking competence of a learner on an interview task? They are interdependent skills, and so a speaking error may actually stem from a listening error, or vice versa.

Performance-Based Assessment

Closely related to the issue of authenticity is what has come to be called **performance-based assessment**. An authentic task in any assessment implies that the test-taker (or classroom student) must engage in actual performance of the specified linguistic objective. In educational settings around the world, test designers and classroom teachers are now tackling this new agenda (Leung, 2005). Instead of just offering paper-and-pencil single-answer tests of possibly hundreds of discrete items, performance-based testing of typical school subjects involves

- open-ended problem solving tasks
- hands-on projects
- student portfolios
- experiments
- tasks in various genres of writing
- group projects

To be sure, such testing is time-consuming and therefore expensive, but the losses in practicality are made up for in higher validity. Students are tested as they actually perform the behavior itself. In technical terms, higher content validity is achieved as learners are measured in the process of performing the objectives of a lesson or course.

In the ESL context, performance-based testing means that you may have a difficult time distinguishing between formal and informal testing. If you do a little less setting aside of formally structured techniques labeled as "tests" and a little more formative evaluation during students' performance of various tasks, you will be taking some steps toward meeting some of the goals of performance-based testing.

Challenges from Innovative Theories of Intelligence

Intelligence was once viewed strictly as the ability to perform (a) linguistic and (b) logical-mathematical problem solving. This "IQ" concept of intelligence permeated the Western world and its way of testing for almost a century. Since "smartness" in general is measured by timed, discrete-point tests consisting of many little items, then why shouldn't every field of study be so measured? Today we still live in a world of standardized, norm-referenced tests that are timed, multiple-choice, tricky, long, and artificial.

Research on intelligence by psychologists like Gardner (1983, 1999), Sternberg (1988, 1997), and Goleman (1995) challenged the traditional psychometric orthodoxy. Standard theories of intelligence, on which standardized IQ (and other) tests are based, were expanded to include inter- and intrapersonal, spatial, kinesthetic, contextual, and emotional intelligences, among others. (For a summary of these theories of intelligence, see *PLLT,* Chapter 4.)

These new conceptualizations of intelligence infused the decade of the 1990s with a sense of both freedom and responsibility in our testing agenda. We were freed from exclusive reliance on timed, discrete-point, analytical tests in measuring language. We were liberated from the tyranny of "objectivity" and its accompanying impersonalness. But we also assumed the responsibility for tapping into whole language skills, learning processes, and the ability to negotiate meaning. Our challenge was to test interpersonal, creative, communicative, interactive skills, and in doing so, to place some trust in our subjectivity, our intuition.

Expanding "Alternatives" in Classroom-Based Assessment

Implied in some of the above discussion are two interconnected current challenges. Performance-based assessment that embodies a learner-centered, authentic approach to designing assessment tasks goes hand in hand with an increasing recognition (and celebration) of classroom teachers as wholly capable professionals who can design their own classroom-based procedures with confidence. In the "old" days teachers labored under the impression that test design must be left to the experts and it was the teacher's job to simply trust those experts and administer their tests. There was something wrong with this picture!

Current practice sees a great deal of action by teachers more and more involved in the creation of their own instruments and/or the willing adaptation of published tests for their own classroom context. In what has been termed "classroom-based teacher assessment" (Leung, 2005), or more commonly simply **classroom-based assessment**, a number of current challenges and issues merge: authentic assessment, performance-based assessment, formative assessment (designed to facilitate a student's continued *formation* of language competence), informal assessment, and alternatives in assessment.

Some references to alternatives in assessment refer to "alternative assessment," a term that conveys the wrong message, as Brown and Hudson (1998) note. To speak of *alternative* assessment implies something that is outside of or "exempt from the requirements of responsible test construction" (Brown & Hudson, 1998, p. 657). Instead, *alternatives* in assessment recognize that tests are one of many possible alternatives within the superordinate concept of assessment. Table 23.1 (adapted from Armstrong, 1994; Bailey, 1998, p. 207) highlights how such alternatives differ from traditional tests.

It should be noted here that traditional testing offers significantly higher levels of practicality. Considerably more time and higher institutional budgets are required to administer and evaluate assessments that presuppose more subjective evaluation, more individualization, and more interaction in the process of offering feedback. The payoff for the latter, however, comes with more useful washback to students, better possibilities for intrinsic motivation, and ultimately greater validity. We'll return to the topic of alternatives in assessment in Chapter 24.

Ethical Issues: Critical Language Assessment

The first issue described in this section, large-scale proficiency testing, brings with it more than simply linguistic and psychometric challenges. One of the by-products of a rapidly growing testing industry is the danger of an abuse of power. "Tests represent a social technology deeply embedded in education, government, and business; as such they provide the mechanism for enforcing power and control. Tests are most powerful as they are often the single indicators for determining the future of individuals" (Shohamy, 1997, p. 2). Test designers, and the corporate sociopolitical infrastructure that they represent, have an obligation to maintain certain standards as specified by their client educational institutions. These standards bring with them certain ethical issues surrounding the "gatekeeping" nature of "high-stakes" standardized tests.

Table 23.1. Traditional and alternative assessment

Traditional Tests	Alternatives in Assessment
One-shot, standardized exams	Continuous long-term assessment
Timed, multiple-choice format	Untimed, free-response format
Decontextualized test items	Contextualized communicative tasks
Scores suffice for feedback	Formative, interactive feedback
Norm-referenced scores	Criterion-referenced scores
Focus on the "right" answer	Open-ended, creative answers
Summative	Formative
Oriented to product	Oriented to process
Noninteractive performance	Interactive performance
Fosters extrinsic motivation	Fosters intrinsic motivation

Elana Shohamy (2001) and others (Bachman, 2005) see the ethics of testing as a case of critical language testing (see Chapter 26 for a discussion of critical pedagogy in general). Critical-language-testing research asks incisive questions about possible bias in large-scale testing, and claims in some cases that such tests are the "agent of cultural, social, political, educational, and ideological agendas that shape the lives of individual participants, teachers, and learners"(Shohamy, 1997, p. 3). The issues of critical language testing are numerous:

- Psychometric traditions are challenged by interpretive, individualized procedures for predicting success and evaluating ability.
- Test designers have a responsibility to offer multiple modes of performance to account for varying styles and abilities among test-takers.
- Tests are deeply embedded in culture and ideology.
- Test-takers are political subjects in a political context.

These issues are not new. More than a century ago, British educator F. Y. Edgeworth (1888) challenged the potential inaccuracy of contemporary qualifying examinations for university entrance. But in recent years, the debate has heated up. In 1997, an entire issue of the journal *Language Testing* was devoted to questions about ethics in language testing. And Shohamy's (2001) book, *The Power of Tests*, takes a long critical look at current issues worldwide.

One of the problems of critical language testing surrounds the widespread belief that standardized tests designed by reputable test manufacturers are infallible in their predictive validity. Universities, for example, will deny admission to a student whose TOEFL® score falls one point below the requisite score, even though that student, if offered other measures of language ability, might demonstrate abilities necessary for success in a university program. One standardized test is deemed to be sufficient; follow-up measures are considered to be too costly.

A further problem with our test-oriented culture lies in the agendas of those who design and those who utilize the tests. Tests are used in some countries to deny citizenship (Shohamy, 2001). Tests are by nature culture-biased and therefore may disenfranchise members of a nonmainstream value system. Test producers are always in a position of power over test-takers and therefore can impose social and political ideologies on test-takers through standards of acceptable and unacceptable items. Tests promote the notion that answers to real-world problems have unambiguous right and wrong answers with no shades of gray. A corollary to the latter is that tests presume to reflect an appropriate core of common knowledge and acceptable behavior; therefore the test-taker must buy into such a system of beliefs in order to make the cut.

As a language teacher, you might be able to exercise some influence in the ways tests are used and interpreted in your own context. Perhaps, if you are offered a variety of choices in standardized tests, you could choose a test that offers the least degree of culture bias. Better yet, can you encourage the use of multiple measures of performance (varying item types, oral and written production, for example) even though this may cost more money? Furthermore, you might be instrumental in establishing an institutional system of evaluation that places less emphasis on standardized tests and more emphasis on the ongoing process of formative evaluation you and your co-teachers can offer. In so doing, you might offer educational opportunity to a few more people who would otherwise be eliminated from contention.

TOPICS FOR DISCUSSION, ACTION, AND RESEARCH

[Note: (I) Individual work; (G) group or pair work; (C) whole-class discussion.]

1. (G) In groups each assigned to one of the four skills, have students brainstorm some techniques, activities, or tasks in about two minutes or less. Then groups can discuss the extent to which selected techniques have an *assessment* component to them, either explicit or implicit.

2. (C) Find a published classroom test (many textbook series include ready-made tests), photocopy it (be sure to check for copyright limitations), and distribute it. With the class, analyze it according to each of the five principles described in this chapter. Is it a "good" test?

3. (I) Distinguish between content and construct validity. If content validity is absent, why does construct validity assume greater importance? Explain the fact that there is no final, absolute, and objective measure of validity. Why does validity ultimately go back to the rather subjective opinion of testers and theorists?

4. (G/C) Ask pairs to share experiences from their past about tests that they thought had high and low face validity. Why is face validity important? Have pairs share their examples with the rest of the class.

5. (C) Language aptitude tests were discussed briefly here, and in more detail in *PLLT,* Chapter 4. In light of the discussion at the end of this chapter about ethical issues in language testing, ask your students if aptitude testing is ethical.

6. (C) Solicit comments from students in the class on any experiences they have had taking large-scale standardized language tests (TOEFL®, IELTS, TOEIC, etc.). To what extent can they be argued to be "communicative" in Bachman's terms? What were the scores used for? Were specific purposes represented in the test?

7. (G) One of the current issues discussed here is authenticity. Have pairs brainstorm tests (or other more informal assessments) that fit into the category of either authentic or *in*authentic. Pairs can then share findings with the rest of the class.

8. (C) Review the description of alternative views of intelligence described in *PLLT,* Chapter 4. Ask the class to describe some assessment tasks that would tap into such intelligences as interpersonal, intrapersonal, spatial, contextual, and emotional.

9. (C) How confident do students feel about their ability to design a classroom test? What are advantages and disadvantages of teachers designing their own classroom tests?

10. (C) Review with the class the notion that tests serve as "gatekeepers" in society. Among familiar standardized tests, what ethical issues might emerge? Does the testing industry promote a widening of gaps between educated and uneducated, rich and poor, "haves" and "have-nots"?

FOR YOUR FURTHER READING

Leung, C., & Lewkowicz, J. (2006). Expanding horizons and unresolved conundrums: Language testing and assessment. *TESOL Quarterly, 40,* 211-234.

Kunnan, A. (2005). Language assessment from a wider context. In E. Hinkel (Ed.), *Handbook of research in second language teaching and learning* (pp. 779-794). Mahwah, NJ: Lawrence Erlbaum Associates.

Leung, C. (2005). Classroom teacher assessment of second language development: Construct as practice. In E. Hinkel (Ed.), *Handbook of research in second language teaching and learning* (pp. 869-888). Mahwah, NJ: Lawrence Erlbaum Associates.

Alderson, J. C., & Banerjee, J. (2001). Language testing and assessment (Part 1). *Language Teaching, 34,* 213-236.

Alderson, J. C., & Banerjee, J. (2002). Language testing and assessment (Part 2). *Language Teaching, 35,* 79-113.

All five of these articles offer surveys of the field of language assessment and deal comprehensively with current issues, dilemmas, and problems on a wide range of subtopics. The extensive bibliographies in each article are very useful.

Robinson, P. (2005). Aptitude and second language acquisition. *Annual Review of Applied Linguistics, 25,* 46-73.

Peter Robinson traces historical developments in language aptitude research and describes current research that has brought a bit of a resurgence of interest in the construct. A substantial portion of the article is devoted to assessment issues.

Shohamy, E. (2001). *The power of tests: A critical perspective on the use of language tests.* Harlow, UK: Pearson Education.

Elana Shohamy has for years been a strong advocate for the rights of test-takers and for watch-dogging political and governmental agencies that are in positions to usurp their power through large-scale mandatory language testing. This book is an excellent exposé.

CHAPTER 24

CLASSROOM-BASED

ASSESSMENT

OBJECTIVES After reading this chapter, you will be able to:

- distinguish between norm-referenced and criterion-referenced testing

- apply principles for designing tests to the creation of your own classroom-based tests and other assessment procedures

- create revised, modified versions of existing tests that adhere more closely to principles of authenticity and washback

- explore alternatives in assessment: portfolios, journals, conferences, observations, and self- and peer-assessment

- appreciate the difficulty of balancing principles of practicality and validity with principles of authenticity and washback, especially in the alternatives in assessment

- develop an attitude toward assessment that views assessment and teaching as partners in the learning process

Tests have become a way of life in the educational world. In every learning experience there comes a time to pause and take stock, to put our focal processes to their best use, and to demonstrate accumulated skills or knowledge. From pop quizzes to final exams to standardized entrance exams, tests are crucial milestones in the journey to success. It is unfortunate that learners all too often view tests as dark clouds hanging over their heads, upsetting them with lightning bolts of anxiety as they anticipate a hail of questions they can't answer and, worst of all, a flood of disappointment if they don't make the grade. Students tend to feel "prodded, jostled, or dragged by an establishment bent on spoiling what might otherwise be a pleasant student life" (Mueller, 1987, p. 124).

Within this atmosphere of gloom and doom, can tests be positive experiences? Can they build a person's confidence? Can they be part of an ongoing interaction between teacher and learners? Can they bring out the best in students? The answer, surprisingly, is an encouraging yes when teachers and other educators understand the benefits of tests and their place within the larger domain of assessment.

In this chapter, we turn from the macro-issues and challenges of language assessment as a discipline to the day-to-day micro-issues that you face as a classroom teacher. The discussion in this chapter is designed to briefly acquaint you with some principles for designing your own tests, some steps to take in that process, and some of the alternatives in assessment that were mentioned in the previous chapter. The underlying theme of this exploration is an emphasis on assessment as a positive, motivating, feedback-giving element of second language learning in the classroom.

NORM-REFERENCED AND CRITERION-REFERENCED TESTS

Before proceeding directly to the process of designing and implementing tests in your classroom, a few words are necessary in order to make one more distinction. The dichotomy between norm- and criterion-referenced testing is not just another technical construct that you can soon forget once you've read this chapter. Rather, the two concepts help to resolve many a misunderstanding that teachers have had. Sometimes teachers think that every classroom test, quiz, or exercise should be mathematically scored, charted, and assigned percentiles or quartiles. Not so! Nor should a large-scale proficiency test be expected to be responsive to some of the criteria demanded of classroom tests.

In **norm-referenced** tests, each test-taker's score is interpreted in relation to a mean (average score), median (middle score), standard deviation (extent of variance in scores), and/or percentile rank. The purpose in such tests is to place test-takers along a mathematical continuum in rank order, and little else. If test-takers are *differentiated* through their performance on the instrument, the mission of a norm-referenced test has virtually been accomplished. Scores are usually reported back to the test-taker in the form of a numerical score (e.g., 230 out of 300) and/or a *percentile* rank (e.g., 84 percent, which means that the test-taker's score was better than 84 percent of the total number of test-takers, but below 16 percent of the test-takers in that administration). Typical of norm-referenced tests are standardized tests like the Scholastic Aptitude Test (SAT) or the Test of English as a Foreign Language (TOEFL®), intended to be administered to large audiences, with results efficiently disseminated to test-takers. Such tests usually have fixed, predetermined responses in a format that can be quickly scored at minimum expense. Money and efficiency are important concerns in these tests. Therefore, the principles of practicality, reliability, and validity are primary.

Criterion-referenced tests, on the other hand, are designed to give test-takers feedback on specific course or lesson objectives, or the "criteria" of the course. Classroom achievement tests involving just the students in one class, and connected to a curriculum, are typical of criterion-referenced testing. Here, there is a significant responsibility on the part of the teacher (as the test administrator) to deliver useful, appropriate feedback to students, or what Oller (1979, p. 52) called "instructional value." In a criterion-referenced test, the distribution of students' scores across a continuum may be of little concern, as long as the instrument assesses appropriate objectives. In the following sections of this chapter, with its emphasis on classroom-based assessment (as opposed to standardized, large-scale testing), criterion-referenced testing emerges as a more significant focus. The principle of practicality still remains important to you, but authenticity and especially washback are of primary concern.

So, the next time you're perplexed about why a large-scale test doesn't provide washback, or why students' scores on your bi-weekly quizzes don't adhere to a normal curve, or why it takes such a long time to evaluate your students' essays, or why a multiple-choice test may not elicit actual language performance from students in your classroom, you might find answers in the nature of criterion-referenced versus norm-referenced testing. For the remainder of this chapter, we'll be looking strictly at the former: tests and assessments in your classroom designed to elicit performance on the specific criteria, or objectives, of your course.

SOME PRACTICAL STEPS TO TEST CONSTRUCTION

If you haven't already had an occasion to create and administer a classroom test, your time is coming soon! Now that you have read about testing issues in this and the previous chapter, you may be thinking that you must now go out there and create a wonderfully innovative instrument that will garner the accolades of your colleagues and the admiration of your students. Well, don't be too hard on yourself! Traditional testing techniques can be applied in an interactive, communicative language curriculum. Your best tack as a new teacher is to work within the guidelines of accepted, known testing techniques, yet you can still give an authentic, interesting flavor to your tests. Slowly, with experience, you can get bolder in your attempts—which we'll talk about in the next section of the chapter. In that spirit, here are some practical steps to take in constructing classroom tests.

1. Test toward clear, unambiguous objectives.

In Chapters 9 and 10, you were strongly advised to state clear, specific objectives for courses and lessons. Doing so enables you to focus clearly on such objectives when it comes to either informal or formal assessment. Likewise, for a test that you design, make sure that students actually perform the criterion objectives that your test was designed to assess. You *don't* want your students to say, after a test, "I don't see a connection between your test and what we studied."

You need to know as specifically as possible what it is you want to test. Sometimes teachers give tests simply because it's Friday or it's the third week of the course; after hasty glances at the chapter(s) covered during the period, they dash off some test items so the students will have something to do during the class period. This is no way to approach a test! Instead, carefully list everything that you think your students should "know" or be able to "do," based on the material the students are responsible for.

Your "objectives" can, for testing purposes, be as simple as the following list of grammatical structures and communicative skills in a unit that, let's say, you have recently taught:

Grammar:

Tag questions
Simple past tense in negative statements and information questions
Irregular past tense verbs
Who as subject
Anyone, someone, and *no one*
Conjunctions *so* and *because*

Communication skills:

Guessing what happened
Finding out who did something
Talking about family and friends
Talking about famous people and events
Giving reasons
Asking for confirmation

2. From your objectives, draw up test specifications.

Now, this sounds like you're supposed to have a Ph.D. in psychometrics! Wrong. Test specifications for classroom use can be a simple and practical outline of your test.* Let's say you are testing the above unit. Your specifications will indicate how you will divide up the 40-minute test period, what skills you will test, and what the items will look like. Your "specs" may look something like this:

Listening (15 minutes)

Part 1: Minimal sentence pairs (choose the sentence that you think you
hear) [10 pairs, 2 themes]

Cover: tag questions

negative statements

guessing what happened

finding out who did something

Part 2: Conversation (choose the correct answer) [5 items]

Cover: information questions

talking about family and friends

Multiple choice (10 minutes) [15 items in a story line (cloze) format]

Cover: simple past tense

past irregular verbs

anyone, someone, and *no one*

---

*Note that for standardized, large-scale tests that are intended to be widely distributed and therefore are widely generalized, test specifications are much more formal and detailed.

Writing production (15 minutes) [topic: Why I liked/didn't like a recent movie]

> Cover: affirmative and negative statements
>
> conjunctions *so* and *because*
>
> giving reasons

These informal classroom-oriented specifications give you an indication of (a) which of the topics (objectives) you will cover, (b) what the item types will be, (c) how many items will be in each section, and (d) how much time is allocated for each. Notice that a couple of communication skills and one grammatical structure are not tested—this may be a decision based on the time you devoted to these objectives, or only on the finite number of minutes available to administer the test. Notice, too, that this course quite likely has a good deal of oral production in it, but for reasons of practicality (perhaps oral testing was done separately?), oral production is also not included on this test.

3. Draft your test.

A first draft will give you a good idea of what the test will look like, how students will perceive it (face validity), the extent to which authentic language and contexts are present, the length of the listening stimuli, how well a storyline comes across, how things like the cloze testing format will work, and other practicalities. Your items may look like these:

Listening, Part 1 (theme: last night's party)

1. Teacher says:	We sure made a mess last night, didn't we?
Student reads:	(a) We sure made no mess last night, did we?
	(b) We sure made a mess last night, didn't we?

Listening, Part 2 (theme: still at the party)

2. Teacher says:*	A. Mary, who was that gorgeous man I saw you with at the party?
	B. Oh, Nancy, that was my brother!
Student reads:	(a) Mary's brother is George.
	(b) Nancy saw Mary's brother at the party.
	(c) Nancy's brother is gorgeous.

Multiple choice (theme: still at the party)

Student reads:	Then we _____ the loudest thunder you have
	$\overset{3}{}$
	ever heard! And of course right away lightning

---

*Ideally, for the sake of authenticity, you should enlist the aid of a colleague and make a tape in which each of you reads a different part so that students will readily perceive that two people are speaking. If time, equipment, and colleagues don't permit this, make sure that when you read the two parts, you differentiate clearly (with voice and also by bodily facing in two different directions) between the two characters.

_____ right outside the house!
₄

3. (a) heared   (b) did hear   (c) heard
4. (a) struck   (b) stricken   (c) strack

As you can see, these items are quite traditional. In fact, you could justifiably object to them on the grounds that they ask students to rely on short-term memory and on spelling conventions. But the thematic format of the sections, the authentic language, and the contextualization add face validity, interest, and intrinsic motivation to what might otherwise be a mundane test. And the essay section adds some creative production to help compensate for the lack of an oral production component.

4. Revise your test.

At this stage, you will work through all the items you have devised and ask a number of important questions:

- Are the directions to each section absolutely clear?
- Is there an example item for each section?
- Does each item measure a specified objective?
- Is each item stated in clear, simple language?
- Does each multiple-choice item have appropriate distractors, that is, are the wrong items clearly wrong and yet sufficiently "alluring" that they aren't ridiculously easy?
- Does the difficulty of each item seem to be appropriate for your students?
- Do the sum of the items and test as a whole adequately reflect the learning objectives?

5. Final-edit, word-process, and print the test.

In an ideal situation, you would try out all your tests on some students before actually administering them. In our daily classroom teaching, the tryout phase is virtually impossible, and so you must do what you can to bring to your students an instrument that is, to the best of your ability, practical, reliable, and valid. So, after careful completion of the drafting phase, a final edit is in order.

In your final editing of the test before typing it for presentation to your class, imagine that you are one of your students. Go through each set of directions and all items slowly and deliberately, timing yourself as you do so. Often we underestimate the time students will need to complete a test. If the test needs to be shortened or lengthened, make the necessary adjustments. Then make sure your test is neat and uncluttered on the page, reflecting all the care and precision you have put into its construction. If your test has a listening component, make sure your script is clear and that the audio equipment you will use is in working order.

6. Utilize your feedback after administering the test.

After you give the test, you will have some information about how easy or difficult it was, about the time limits, and about your students' affective reaction to it and their general performance. Take note of these forms of feedback and use them for making your next test.

7. Provide ample washback.

As you evaluate the test and return it to your students, your feedback should reflect the principles of washback discussed earlier. Use the information from the test performance as a springboard for review and/or for moving on to the next unit.

TURNING EXISTING TESTS INTO MORE EFFECTIVE PROCEDURES

For many language learners, the mention of the word *test* evokes images of walking into a classroom after a sleepless night, of anxiously sitting hunched over a test page while a clock ticks ominously, and of a mind suddenly gone empty as they vainly attempt to "multiple guess" their way through the ordeal. How can you, as a classroom teacher and designer of your own tests, change this image?

Now that you have considered standard steps for creating a somewhat traditional classroom test, let's go a little further. Consider the following four guidelines for converting what might be ordinary, traditional tests into authentic, interesting, appropriately challenging, washback-giving learning opportunities designed for learners' best performance and for optimal feedback.

1. Facilitate strategic options for test-takers.

The first principle is to offer your learners appropriate, useful strategies for taking the test. With some preparation in test-taking strategies, learners can allay some of their fears and put their best foot forward during a test. Through strategies-based test-taking, they can avoid miscues due to the format of the test alone. They should also be able to demonstrate their competence through an optimal level of performance. Years ago, Merrill Swain (1984) referred to the principle of "bias for best" as an important goal for teachers in designing tests. In other words, design, prepare, administer, and evaluate tests in such a way that the *best* performance of your students will be elicited! One of the ways to bias your test for best performance is by encouraging before-, during-, and after-test options, as listed in Table 24.1.

2. Establish face validity.

Sometimes students don't know what is being tested when they tackle a test. Sometimes they feel, for a variety of possible reasons, that a test isn't testing what they feel it was intended to test. Face validity, as we saw in the previous chapter, means that in the students' perception, the test is valid. You can help to foster that perception with

- a carefully constructed, well-thought-out format,
- a test that is clearly doable within the allotted time limit,

Table 24.1. Before-, during-, and after-test strategies

Before the Test

1. Give students all the information you can about the test. Exactly what will the test cover? Which topics will be the most important? What kind of items will be included? How long will it be?

2. Encourage students to do a systematic review of material. For example, skim the textbook and other material, outline major points, write down examples, etc.

3. Give them practice tests or exercises, if available.

4. Facilitate formation of a study group, if possible.

5. Caution students to get a good night's rest before the test.

6. Remind students to get to the classroom early.

During the Test

1. As soon as the test is distributed, tell students to quickly look over the whole test in order to get a good grasp of its different parts.

2. Remind them to mentally figure out how much time they will need for each part.

3. Advise them to concentrate as carefully as possible.

4. Alert students a few minutes before the end of the class period so that they can proofread their answers, catch careless errors, and still finish on time.

After the Test

1. When you return the test, include feedback on specific things the student did well, what he or she did not do well, and if possible, the reasons for such a judgment on your part.

2. Advise the student to pay careful attention in class to whatever you say about the test results.

3. Encourage questions from students.

4. Advise students to make a plan to pay special attention in the future to points that they are weak on.

- items that are clear and uncomplicated,
- directions that are crystal clear,
- tasks that are familiar and relate to their course work, and
- a difficulty level that is appropriate for your students.

3. Design authentic tasks.

Make sure that the language in your test is as natural and authentic as possible. Also, try to give language some context so that items aren't just a string of unrelated language samples. Thematic organization of items may help in this regard. Or consider a storyline that may run through your items.

Also, the tasks themselves need to be tasks in a form that students have practiced and feel comfortable with. A classroom test is not the time to introduce brand-new tasks because you won't know if student difficulty is a factor of the task itself or of the language you are testing.

4. Work for washback.

Washback, described in the previous chapter, is the benefit that tests offer to learning. When students take a test, they should be able, within a reasonably short period of time, to utilize the information about their competence that test feedback offers. Formal tests must therefore be learning devices through which students can receive a diagnosis of areas of strength and weakness. Their incorrect responses can become windows of insight about further work. Your prompt return of written tests with your feedback is therefore very important to intrinsic motivation.

One way to enhance washback is to provide a generous number of specific comments on test performance. Many teachers, in our overworked (and underpaid!) lives, are in the habit of returning tests to students with a letter grade or number score on them, and considering their job done. In reality, letter grades and a score showing the number right or wrong give absolutely no information of intrinsic interest to the student. Grades and scores reduce a mountain of linguistic and cognitive performance data to an absurd minimum. At best they give a relative indication of a formulaic judgment of performance as compared to others in the class—which fosters competitive, not cooperative, learning.

So, when you return a written test, or even a data sheet from an oral production test, consider giving more than a number or grade or phrase as your feedback. Even if your evaluation is not a neat little paragraph, at least you can respond to as many details in the test as time permits. Give praise for strengths—the "good stuff"—as well as constructive criticism of weaknesses. Give strategic hints on how a student might improve certain elements of performance. In other words, take some time to make the test performance an intrinsically motivating experience through which a student will feel a sense of accomplishment and challenge.

Another way to increase intrinsic motivation among students is to involve them in the design and review process (what I called the "wash forward" effect in the previous chapter), and in the evaluation of responses afterward. Depending on a number of contextual variables in your plan to assess students, peer feedback can be an excellent way for learners to gain washback from the test.

Finally, washback also implies that students have ready access to *you* to discuss the feedback and evaluation you have given. I'm sure you have known teachers with whom you wouldn't dare argue about a grade. Such a tyrannical atmosphere is out of place in an interactive, cooperative, intrinsically motivating classroom. For learning to continue, learners need to have a chance to feed back on your feedback, to seek clarification of any fuzzy issues, and to set new appropriate goals for themselves for the days and weeks ahead.

ALTERNATIVES IN ASSESSMENT

So far in this chapter, the focus has been on the administration of formal tests in the classroom. It was noted earlier that assessment is a broad term covering any conscious effort on the part of a teacher or student to draw some conclusions on the basis of performance. Tests are a special subset of the range of possibilities within assessment; of course they constitute a very salient subset, but not all assessment consists of tests.

In recent years language teachers have stepped up efforts to develop non-test assessment options that are nevertheless carefully designed and that adhere to the criteria for adequate assessment. Sometimes such innovations are referred to as alternative assessment, if only to distinguish them from *traditional* formal tests. However, as you saw in the previous chapter, I prefer Brown and Hudson's (1998) phrase, **alternatives in assessment,** which emphasizes the responsibility to apply all assessment principles to such options, and *not* to treat them as strange aberrations of normal assessment practices.

Several alternatives in assessment will be briefly discussed here. For a more detailed description and analysis of these options, I recommend that you take a look at my companion text, *Language Assessment* (Brown, 2004), Chapter 10.

Portfolios

One of the most popular forms of alternative assessment now within a communicative framework is the construction of portfolios. A portfolio is "a purposeful collection of students' work that demonstrates to students and others their efforts, progress, and achievements in given areas" (Genesee & Upshur, 1996, p. 99). Portfolios include essays, compositions, poetry, book reports, artwork, video- or audiotape recordings of a student's oral production, journals, and virtually anything else one wishes to specify. In earlier decades of our history, portfolios were thought to be applicable only to younger children, who assembled a portfolio of art and written work for presentation to a teacher and/or a parent. But now, learners of all ages and in all fields of study are benefiting from the tangible, hands-on nature of portfolio development.

Following are some guidelines for using portfolios in a classroom:

- Specify to students what the purpose of the portfolio is (to emphasize accomplishments, to offer tangible material for feedback from the teacher, etc.).
- Give clear directions to students on how to get started (many students will never have compiled a portfolio before and may be mystified about what to do). Showing a sample portfolio from a previous student might help to stimulate thoughts on what to include.
- Give guidelines on acceptable material to include.
- Collect portfolios on pre-announced dates and return them promptly.
- Be clear yourself on the principal purpose of the portfolio and make sure your feedback speaks to that purpose.
- Help students to process your feedback and show them how to respond to your responses. This processing might take place in a conference or simply through written feedback.

Journals

Usually one thinks of journals simply as opportunities for learners to write relatively freely without undue concern for grammaticality. Journals can have a number of purposes: language-learning logs; grammar discussions; responses to readings; self-assessment; and reflections on attitudes and feelings about oneself. Recently, the assessment qualities of journal writing have assumed an important role in the teaching–learning process. Because journal writing is a dialogue between student and teacher, journals afford a unique opportunity for a teacher to offer various kinds of feedback to learners.

Using journals as assessment instruments requires a carefully specified, systematic approach, using guidelines similar to those recommended for portfolios:

- Specify to students what the purpose of the journal is (response to reading, learning log, grammar commentary, etc.).
- Give clear directions to students on how to get started (many students will never have written a journal before and may be mystified about what to do). Sometimes an abbreviated model journal entry helps.
- Give guidelines on length of each entry and any other format expectations.
- Collect journals on pre-announced dates and return them promptly.
- Be clear yourself on the principal purpose of the journal and make sure your feedback speaks to that purpose.
- Help students to process your feedback, and show them how to respond to your responses.

Conferences

For a number of years, conferences have been a routine part of language classrooms, especially courses in writing. Conferencing can serve a number of possible functions; among them are the following:

- commenting on drafts of essays and reports
- reviewing portfolios
- responding to journals
- advising on a student's plan for a paper or presentation
- exploring compensatory strategies to overcome weaknesses
- giving feedback on the results of performance on a test
- setting learning goals for the near future

Conferencing has become a standard part of the process approach to teaching writing, as the teacher, in a conversation about a draft, facilitates the improvement of the written work. Such interaction has the advantage of allowing one-on-one interaction between teacher and student such that the specific needs of a student can receive direct feedback. Through conferences, a teacher can assume the role of a facilitator and guide, rather than a master controller and deliverer of final grades. In this intrinsically motivating atmosphere, students can feel that the teacher is an ally who is encouraging self-reflection. It is important to consider a conference as a dialogue that is *not* to be graded. Conferences are by nature formative, not summative; formative assessment points students toward further development, rather than offering a final summation of performance.

Observations

One of the characteristics of an effective teacher is the ability to *observe* students as they perform. Teachers are constantly engaged in a process of taking students' performance and intuitively assessing it and using those evaluations to offer feedback. Without ever administering a test or a quiz, teachers know a lot about their students. In fact, experienced teachers are so good at this almost subliminal process of assessment that their estimates of a student's competence are often highly correlated with actual independently administered test scores.

On the other hand, teachers' intuitions about students' performance are not infallible, and certainly both the reliability and face validity of their feedback to students can be increased with the help of empirical means of observing their language performance. Observations can become systematic, planned procedures for real-time, almost surreptitious recording of student verbal and nonverbal behavior. One of the objectives of such observation is to assess students as much as possible without their awareness (and possible consequent anxiety) of the observation, so that the naturalness of their linguistic performance will be maximized. Checklists, charts, rating scales, systematic note taking, and teachers' journals can all help to support our intuitive observations and to provide a source of identifiable feedback to students.

What kinds of student performance can be the subject of such observations? Consider a few possibilities:

- sentence-level oral production
- interaction with classmates (cooperation, frequency of oral production)
- frequency of student-initiated responses (whole class, group work)
- quality of teacher-elicited responses
- evidence of listening comprehension (questions, clarifications, attention-giving verbal and nonverbal behavior)
- evidence of attention span issues, learning style preferences, etc.
- use of strategic options in comprehension or production (use of communication strategies, avoidance, etc.)
- culturally specific linguistic and nonverbal factors (kinesics, proxemics, use of humor, slang, metaphor, etc.)

In order to carry out classroom observation, it is of course important to be clear about why you are observing, what you are observing, how you will observe (what system you will use), and how you will convey your perceptions to your students. Checklists and grids are a common form of recording observed behavior. In Spada and Fröhlich's (1995) system, grids capture such variables as whole-class, group, and individual performance; formal versus functional errors; and which one of the four skills is involved. The observer identifies performance and checks appropriate boxes in the grid. Checklists need not be that elaborate. Simpler options—noting occurrences of student errors in certain grammatical categories, or "action zones" in the classroom, for example—may be more realistic.

Rating scales have also been suggested for recording observations. One type of rating scale asks teachers to indicate the frequency of occurrence of target performance either on a separate frequency scale (always = 5; never = 1). Rating scales may be appropriate for recording observations after the fact—on the same day but after a class period, for example. Specific quantities of occurrences may be difficult to record while teaching a lesson and managing a classroom, but immediate subsequent evaluations might offer some data on observations that will certainly fade from memory by the next day or so.

You will probably find moderate practicality and reliability in observations, especially if the objectives are kept simple. Face validity and content validity are likely to get high marks since observations are likely to be integrated into the ongoing process of a course. Authenticity is high because, if an observation goes relatively unnoticed by the student, then there is little likelihood of contrived situations. Washback can be high if you take the time and effort to help students to become aware of your data on their performance.

Self- and Peer-Assessments

A conventional view of language pedagogy might consider self- and peer-assessment to be an absurd reversal of the teaching–learning process. After all, how could learners who are still in the process of acquisition, especially the early processes, be capable of rendering an accurate assessment of their own performance? But a closer look at the acquisition of any skill reveals the importance, if not the necessity, of self-assessment and the benefit of peer-assessment. What successful learner has not developed the ability to monitor his or her own performance and to use the data gathered for adjustments and corrections? Successful learners extend the learning process well beyond the classroom and the presence of a teacher or tutor, autonomously mastering the art of self-assessment. And where peers are available to render assessments, why not take advantage of such additional input?

Research has shown (Alderson & Banerjee, 2001; Brown & Hudson, 1998; O'Malley & Pierce, 1996) a number of advantages of self- and peer-assessment: speed, direct involvement of students, the encouragement of autonomy, and increased motivation because of self-involvement in the process of learning. Of course, the disadvantage of subjectivity looms large, and must be considered whenever you propose to involve students in self- and peer-assessment.

Following are some ways in which self- and peer-assessment can be implemented in language classrooms.

- Oral production: completing student self-checklists and/or peer checklists; offering and receiving a holistic rating of an oral presentation; listening to tape-recorded oral production to detect pronunciation or grammar errors; in natural conversation, asking others for confirmation checks; setting goals for creating opportunities to speak
- Listening comprehension: listening to TV or radio broadcasts and checking comprehension with a partner; in pair or group work, asking when you don't understand something; listening to an academic lecture and checking yourself on a "quiz" of the content; setting goals for increasing opportunities for listening
- Writing: revising written work on your own; revising written work with a peer (peer-editing); proofreading; setting goals for increasing opportunities to write
- Reading: reading textbook passages followed by self-check comprehension questions; reading and checking comprehension with a partner; taking vocabulary quizzes; self-assessing reading habits; setting goals

SCRUTINIZING THE ALTERNATIVES

As you consider using some of the alternatives that have just been described, two factors deserve your attention and application: maximizing practicality and reliability in your procedures, and focusing on your students' actual language performance.

Maximizing Practicality and Reliability

The classroom-based tests described in the first part of this chapter, as well as the alternatives in assessment, are contextualized to a specific curriculum, are referenced to criteria (objectives) of a course or module, offer greater potential for both authenticity and washback, and in the case of the "alternatives," are open-ended in their response format and time orientation. This is a very different picture from large-scale standardized tests structured for computer delivery and rapid machine scoring.

One way of looking at this contrast poses a rather tantalizing challenge to you as a teacher and test designer. Formal standardized tests are almost by definition highly practical, reliable instruments. They are designed to minimize time and money on the part of test designer and test-taker, and to be painstakingly accurate in their scoring. Alternatives such as portfolios, or conferencing with students on drafts of written work, or observations of learners over time all require considerable time and effort on the part of the teacher and the student. Even more time must be spent if the teacher hopes to offer an evaluation that is reliable—within students across time, as well as across students (taking care not to favor one student or group of students). But the latter techniques also offer markedly greater washback, are superior formative measures, and, because of their authenticity, usually carry greater face validity.

Does this mean that multiple-choice formats are inevitably devoid of authenticity and washback? And that the more open-ended, long-term alternatives are by nature unreliable and will forever cost teachers sleepless nights? I hope not. The challenge that faces us all as conscientious teachers and assessors in our profession is to change this perception. With some creativity and effort, we can transform otherwise inauthentic and negative-washback-producing tests into more pedagogically fulfilling learning experiences by doing the following:

- building as much authenticity as possible into multiple-choice task types and items
- designing classroom tests that have both objective-scoring sections and open-ended response sections: varying the performance tasks
- turning multiple-choice test results into diagnostic feedback on areas of needed improvement
- maximizing the preparation period before a test to elicit performance relevant to the ultimate criteria of the test
- teaching test-taking strategies

- helping students to see beyond the test: don't "teach to the test"
- triangulating information on a student before making a final assessment of competence

The flip side of this challenge is to understand that the alternatives in assessment are not by nature destined to flounder in a quagmire of impracticality and unreliability. As we look at alternatives in assessment in this chapter, we must be mindful of Brown and Hudson's (1998) admonition to scrutinize the practicality, reliability, and validity of those alternatives at the same time that we celebrate their face validity, washback potential, and authenticity. It is easy to fly out of the cage of traditional testing rubrics, but it is tempting in doing so to flap our wings aimlessly in accepting virtually any classroom activity as a viable alternative. Assessments that are proposed to serve as triangulating measures of competence imply a responsibility to be rigorous in determining objectives, response modes, and criteria for evaluation and interpretation.

Performance-Based Assessment

A second interesting factor at play in the alternatives in assessment is a recognition of the importance of **performance-based assessment**, sometimes merely called performance assessment (Leung & Lewkowicz, 2006). The push toward more performance-based assessment is part of the same general educational reform movement that has raised strong objections to using standardized test scores as the only measures of student competencies (Kohn, 2000). The argument, as you can guess, is that standardized tests, to a large extent, do not elicit actual performance on the part of test-takers.

Performance-based assessment implies productive, observable skills, such as speaking and writing, of content-valid tasks. Such performance usually, but not always, brings with it an air of authenticity—real-world tasks that students have had time to develop. They often imply an integration of language skills, perhaps all four skills in the case of portfolios and conferencing. Because the tasks that students perform are consistent with course goals and curriculum, students and teachers are likely to be more motivated to perform them, as opposed to a set of multiple-choice questions about grammaticality or reading comprehension.

O'Malley and Valdez-Pierce (1996, p. 5) considered performance-based assessment to be a subset of authentic assessment, with the following characteristics:

1. Students make a *constructed response*.
2. They engage in *higher-order thinking*, with *open-ended* tasks.
3. Tasks are *meaningful, engaging, and authentic*.
4. Tasks call for the *integration of language skills*.
5. Both *process and product* are assessed.
6. The *depth* of a student's mastery is emphasized over breadth.

Performance-based assessment needs to be approached with care. It is tempting for teachers to assume that if a student is *doing* something, then the process has fulfilled its own goal, and the evaluator needs only to make a checkmark in the grade book next to a particular competency. In reality, performances as assessment procedures need to be treated with the same rigor as traditional tests. This implies that teachers should:

- state the overall goal of the performance
- specify the objectives (criteria) of the performance in detail
- prepare students for performance in stepwise progressions
- use a reliable evaluation form, checklist, or rating sheet
- treat performances as opportunities for giving feedback and provide that feedback systematically
- if possible, utilize self- and peer-assessments judiciously

To sum up, performance assessment is not completely synonymous with the concept of alternative assessment. Rather, it is best understood as one of the primary traits of the many alternatives in assessment that are available to us.

☆   ☆   ☆   ☆   ☆

It's quite obvious by now, I hope, that assessment is an integral part of the teaching-learning cycle. In an interactive, communicative curriculum, assessment is almost constant. Tests, as a subset of all assessment processes, do not necessarily need to violate principles of authenticity, intrinsic motivation, and student-centeredness. Along with some newer alternatives in assessment, tests become indispensable components of a curriculum.

As a reminder of the value of assessment in the classroom, remember that assessment and teaching are partners in the learning process:

- Periodic assessments, both formal and informal, can increase motivation as they serve as milestones of student progress.
- Assessments encourage retention of information through the feedback they give on learners' competence.
- Assessments can provide a sense of periodic closure to various units and modules of a curriculum.
- Assessments can encourage students' self-evaluation of their progress, and spur them to set goals for themselves.
- Assessments can promote student autonomy as they confirm areas of strength and areas needing further work.
- Assessments can aid in evaluating teaching effectiveness.

TOPICS FOR DISCUSSION, ACTION, AND RESEARCH

[Note: (I) Individual work; (G) group or pair work; (C) whole-class discussion.]

1. (G/C) Teachers are called upon to play dual roles in the classroom. One is the role of a coach or guide, and the other is the role of a judge who administers tests and assigns grades. Ask pairs to discuss whether these two roles are conflicting. Then ask them to brainstorm some ways that a teacher can lessen the potential conflict such that one can play both roles. Then have them share their ideas with the rest of the class.

2. (I) Review the distinction between norm- and criterion-referenced testing. In your own words explain the difference.

3. (G/C) This one might take up a full class hour to complete. Direct small groups to devise a relatively simple, brief classroom test for a specified purpose and an audience that they are familiar with, following the practical steps for test design in this chapter.

4. (G) Four guidelines were offered in this chapter (pages 472–475) for turning traditional tests into more authentic, washback-giving, intrinsically motivating experiences. Photocopy some existing published classroom tests, distribute them to groups, and ask the groups to redesign aspects of the test to fit some or all of the principles. They can then share the result with the rest of the class.

5. (C) Ask your class to look again at the lists of strategies for test-takers and ask them what strategies they could add to this list.

6. (C) The alternatives in assessment described here all fall into the category of *formal* (as opposed to informal) assessment. How do the alternatives in assessment differ from what you would describe as a *test*, in technical terms?

7. (G/C) Ask groups to consider the five different alternatives in assessment and to describe to each other any examples of any of the five that they have experienced in a previous class. Groups will then share those findings with the rest of the class.

8. (C) Ask the class to brainstorm (a) specific ways, with examples from tests that they know, in which large-scale standardized tests can be made to be more authentic and washback-giving, and (b) ways that the alternatives could become more practical (less time-consuming to evaluate) and reliable (consistent evaluation criteria).

FOR YOUR FURTHER READING

Genesee, F., & Upshur, J. (1996). *Classroom-based evaluation in second language education.* Cambridge, UK: Cambridge University Press.

The authors offer a comprehensive treatment of language assessment by first connecting assessment with instructional objectives and evaluation, then focusing, in some detail, on alternative testing (observation, portfolios, conferences, journals, questionnaires, interviews), and finally, discussing testing as it is traditionally understood.

Brown, H. D. (2004). *Language assessment: Principles and classroom practices.* White Plains, NY: Pearson Education.

Brown, J. D. (2005). *Testing in language programs: A comprehensive guide to English language assessment.* New York: McGraw-Hill.

Hughes, A. (2003). *Testing for language teachers* (2nd ed.). Cambridge, UK: Cambridge University Press.

All three of these books are practical in their attention to classroom testing techniques. Teachers are given numerous examples of tests covering varying skills and proficiency levels. In all three, general guidelines and principles are also offered so that the teacher isn't simply an item-writing machine.

Brown, J. D., & Hudson, T. (1998). The alternatives in language assessment. *TESOL Quarterly, 32,* 653–675.

This article summarizes testing methods and formats in use today, starting with traditional methods (true-false, matching, multiple choice, fill-in, short answer), and in the last half of the article describing alternatives (performance, conferences, portfolios, self- and peer-assessment) that depart from traditional testing methods.

O'Malley, J. M., & Pierce, L. (1996). *Authentic assessment for English language learners: Practical approaches for teachers.* White Plains, NY: Addison-Wesley.

A practical guide for teachers in elementary and secondary schools in the United States, this book provides a comprehensive selection of strategies for assessing oral language, reading, writing, and the content areas. Many of their suggestions fall into the category of alternatives in assessment. The authors and publisher give blanket permission to photocopy most of their sample assessments.

PART VI

LIFELONG LEARNING

Your course in teacher education is not the end of the road for you! Every successful teacher knows that the pursuit of excellence is a lifelong journey. From the first days of apprenticeship and training to the final stretches of experience perhaps decades later, we're in a constant state of change. Every day I learn something from my students, and every time I attend a conference or read an article or book, I try to internalize some little nugget that will help me to be a better teacher.

This final section addresses the need for us as teachers to engage in the kind of reflection and learning that will continue to sharpen our senses and to improve our craft. In the last decade or two a great deal of research has been done to help us in this journey toward excellence. Articles, books, conference presentations, and Internet sources abound on the topic of professional development. These last two chapters synthesize some of those resources and offer some suggestions and guidelines for your reflective practice.

Chapter 25 begins by giving you some general suggestions for peak performance and optimal development of your talents and skills, followed by comments on two forms of professional development: classroom observations and action research in the classroom. Then a number of suggestions are made for creative ways you can engage in collaborative teacher development through such means as peer coaching, team teaching, support groups, and other activities. Finally, several means for individual development are offered: journals, teaching portfolios, reading and study, and writing, among others.

Chapter 26 strikes at the "heart" of teaching: What beliefs, convictions, and personal ambitions drive you and challenge you every day in this profession of service to others? One way of looking at this personal side of teaching is to examine the concept of social responsibility in our professional pursuits. How can I be an effective agent of change in a world that cries out for communication, understanding, healing, and peace? Another way of framing this issue is to examine the "critical" nature of our pedagogy, our responsibility as teachers to help students to be open-minded, empowered, critical thinkers. Ghandi said, "You must *be* the change you want to see in the world." This final chapter challenges you to carry out that mission.

CHAPTER 25

TEACHER DEVELOPMENT

OBJECTIVES After reading this chapter, you will be able to:

- challenge yourself to set personal goals for optimal performance as a teacher

- identify elements in a lesson that you wish to observe and to evaluate them in terms of their effectiveness

- design your own classroom-based research projects in pursuit of answers to systematically framed questions

- engage in various forms of collaboration with your colleagues in an effort to improve your professional skills

- carry out several forms of individualized professional development

---

One of the most invigorating things about teaching is that you never stop learning. The complexity of the dynamic triangular interplay among teachers and learners and subject matter continually gives birth to an endless number of questions to answer, problems to solve, issues to ponder. Every time you walk into a classroom to teach, you face some of those issues, and if you're a growing teacher, you learn something new yourself. You find out how well a technique works, how a student processes language, how classroom interaction can be improved, how to assess a student's competence, how emotions enter into learning, or how your teaching style affects learners. The discoveries go on and on—for a lifetime.

As you embark on this journey into the teaching profession, how can you best continue to grow professionally? How can you most fruitfully meet the challenges that lie ahead? Are there some practical goals that you can pursue? So far, as you have worked through the material of this book, you have already begun your own teacher development. Richards and Farrell (2005, pp. 6-7) frame this developmental process in terms of four conceptualizations of teacher learning:

1. **Skill learning.** Teachers develop a range of the basic skills (such as those addressed in this book) of designing lessons, managing classrooms, assessing performance, etc.

2. **Cognitive process.** Teachers' background, experience, knowledge, and beliefs all contribute to an underlying set of cognitive assumptions about language learning and teaching.

3. **Personal construction.** Teachers' knowledge is actively constructed (not passively received) in an ongoing process of reorganization and reconstruction as new learning and experiences form a personal framework.

4. **Reflective practice.** Teachers can benefit greatly from focused reflection and critical examination of their own teaching experiences, which then lead to improvement and further development.

One of the major themes that continues to be expressed in current research on teacher development is a constructivist approach to development that highlights the active and responsible role of teachers to forge their own personal frameworks within their respective situated contexts (Bailey, Curtis, & Nunan, 2001; Borg, 2003b; Freeman, 2002; Hedgcock, 2002; Johnson, 2006; Mann, 2005; Mullock, 2006; Richards & Farrell, 2005). Teachers are trained and continue their training in what Hedgcock (2002, p. 301) described as "communities of practice" in which teachers of varying degrees of experience carry out their roles as practicing technicians who learn from each other. We best fulfill the goal of professional development not through a "transmission" model of education in which knowledge is simply deposited into the brains of teachers, but through a process model in which teachers learn and continue to develop their skill in dialogue with a professional community (Johnson, 2006). If you are a novice teacher reading and studying this book, your dialogue is just beginning. You have perhaps begun to move through the first two (skill learning, cognitive process) of the four elements of teacher development cited by Richards and Farrell (2005). Continuing to strengthen those two factors and moving into stages of personal construction and reflective practice is a process that will demand your patience and perseverance. Don't expect to become a "master" teacher overnight!

Right now, as you begin your teaching career, you can set some realistic, practical goals that you can focus on without being overwhelmed by everything you have to attend to when you teach. Just as beginning language learners are in a **controlled** mode of operation, able to manage only a few bits of information at a time with capacity-limited systems, so it is with your teaching. If you try to focus on everything in the classroom (the management issues, techniques, delivery, body language, feedback, individual attention, lesson goals, mid-lesson alterations, etc.) all at once, you may end up doing nothing well. In due course of time, however, dealing with the abundance of cognitive/emotional phenomena in the classroom will be sufficiently **automatic** that you will indeed manage to operate on many planes simultaneously.

As you read on here, you will find some ideas that you can immediately put to work and others that may apply to you after you have gained some experience.

PEAK PERFORMERS

Are you doing the best you can do? Are you "being all that you can be," in a process of self-actualization, in Maslow's terms? Or are you satisfied with getting by? In the stressful (but rewarding) world of teaching, it's easier than you might imagine to slip into a pattern of just keeping a step ahead of your students as you struggle through long working hours and cope with large classes. This pattern is the beginning of a downward spiral that you should avoid at all costs. How do you do that? In part by practicing the behaviors of peak performers, people who are reaching their fullest potential and therefore who, in turn, reap success. Consider the following five maxims (among many) of peak performers (adapted from Covey, 1990, and others) that you might apply to yourself, even at this early stage in your career:

1. Believe in yourself.

Teaching is no easy profession. It requires deep dedication, a willingness to work long hours, a genuine desire to help other people, a commitment sometimes to "walk the second mile" in facilitating students' best performance, cognizance of a professional core of knowledge, an ability to be "on tap" in front of students many hours in a day, and more. Are you up to the (possibly) daunting prospect of being a teacher? Almost every "formula" for success begins with the importance of believing that you are fully capable of undertaking the task(s) at hand. So, at the outset, you need to be convinced that you can indeed be a teacher and be an excellent one!

2. Set realistic goals.

Peak performers know their limitations and strengths and their feelings and needs, and then set goals that will be realistic within this framework. They set their own goals and don't let the world around them (colleagues, supervisors, or friends) dictate goals to them. If you have a sense of overall purpose in your career as a mission, then this mission will unfold in the form of daily, weekly, monthly, or annual goals.

It's always a good idea to write down some short-term and long-term goals. Be realistic in terms of what you can accomplish. Be specific in your statements. Here are some examples to get the wheels turning.

- Read x number of teacher resource books this year.
- Design my next test to be more authentic, biased for best, with maximum washback.
- Observe five other teachers this semester.
- Monitor my error treatments in the classroom.
- Attend two professional conferences/workshops this year.

3. Set priorities.

It's crucial that you have a sense of what is most important, what is least important, and everything in between in your professional goals and tasks. If you don't, you can end up spending too much time on low-priority tasks that rob you of the time you should be spending on higher priorities. Priority-setting requires a sense of your whole professional and personal life, and how you are going to use your waking hours.

4. Take risks.

Peak performers don't play it safe all the time. They are not afraid to try new things. Nor are they put off by limiting circumstances: what cannot be done, or "the way" things are done. They don't linger in the safety of a "comfort zone"; instead, they reach out for new challenges.

The key to risk taking as a peak performance strategy, however, is not simply in taking the risks. It is in learning from your "failures." When you risk a new technique in the classroom, try a new approach to a difficult student, or make a frank comment to a supervisor, you must be willing to accept possible "failure" in your attempt. Then you assess all the facets of that failure and turn it into an experience that teaches you something about how to calculate the next risk.

5. Reduce and manage stress factors.

Contrary to some perceptions from outside our profession, teaching is a career with all the makings for high-stress conditions. Think of some of the sources of stress in this business: long hours, large classes, low pay, pressure to "perform" in the classroom, high student expectations, professional demands outside the classroom, emotional connections with students' lives, bureaucracies, pressure to keep up with a rapidly changing field, information overload. Managing those potential stress factors is an important key to keeping yourself fresh, creative, bright, and happy.

One of the cardinal rules of stress management is setting priorities, which has already been dealt with above. Another rule was also touched on: Know your limitations. Other rules follow—don't take on too many extra duties; take time for yourself; and balance your personal and professional time. Peak performers don't spend 18 hours a day working. They don't get so consumed with their profession that the rest of their life is a shambles. They work hard but stop to play. They know how to relax, and do so regularly. And they develop fulfilling personal relationships with family and friends that provide enrichment and renewal.

As you begin a teaching career, you may feel the weight of heavy demands. And teaching is not one of those careers where you can necessarily leave all the cognitive and emotional load in the office. So, you can expect to be the proverbial overworked and underpaid laborer. But in the midst of those demands, try to balance your life, and take everything in perspective.

THE "GOOD" LANGUAGE TEACHER

One way to begin setting goals and priorities is to consider the qualities of successful language teachers. Numerous "master" teachers have come up with their lists of attributes, and they all differ in a variety of ways. Three decades ago, Harold B. Allen (1980) suggested the following down-to-earth list of characteristics of good English language teachers:

- competent preparation leading to a degree in English language teaching
- a love of the English language
- critical thinking

- the persistent urge to upgrade oneself
- self-subordination
- readiness to go the extra mile
- cultural adaptability
- professional citizenship
- a feeling of excitement about one's work

A decade later, Martha Pennington (1990) enumerated what she saw as key attributes of a successful language teacher:

- knowledge of the theoretical foundations of language learning and language teaching
- analytical skills necessary for assessing different teaching contexts and classroom conditions
- awareness of alternative teaching techniques and the ability to put these into practice
- confidence and skill to alter your teaching techniques as needed
- practical experience with different teaching techniques
- informed knowledge of yourself and your students
- interpersonal communication skills
- attitudes of flexibility and openness to change

I have my own list of good language-teaching characteristics (see Table 25.1), a synthesis of several unpublished sources. You may wish to use this list as a self-check to earmark some areas for continued professional growth, to prioritize those areas, and to articulate some specific goals to pursue.

The items on all three lists together make a substantive list of challenges for your professional growth. However, I must make a very important caveat here: *Simply aspiring to fulfill items on a list of "good teacher" attributes does NOT constitute the totality of teacher development!* It's tempting to pin lists like these up on your bulletin board, and perhaps measure yourself against items, as if they were *prescribed* attributes. They are not prescriptions! The key to healthy teacher development is to take a reflective approach which "requires that teachers have the opportunities to observe, evaluate, and reflect systematically on their classroom practices in order to promote understanding and self-awareness and to make changes when necessary" (McDonough, 2006, p. 33). So, if you use such lists, treat them as suggestions, possibilities, and perhaps mental prods to stimulate some further growth.

CLASSROOM OBSERVATION

One of the most neglected areas of professional growth among teachers is the mutual exchange of classroom observations. Once you get into a teaching routine,

Table 25.1. Characteristics of a good language teacher

GOOD LANGUAGE-TEACHING CHARACTERISTICS

Technical Knowledge
1. Understands the linguistic systems of English phonology, grammar, and discourse.
2. Comprehensively grasps basic principles of language learning and teaching.
3. Has fluent competence in speaking, writing, listening to, and reading English.
4. Knows through experience what it is like to learn a foreign language.
5. Understands the close connection between language and culture.
6. Keeps up with the field through regular reading and conference/workshop attendance.

Pedagogical Skills
7. Has a well-thought-out, informed approach to language teaching.
8. Efficiently designs and executes lesson plans.
9. Understands and appropriately uses a variety of techniques.
10. Monitors lessons as they unfold and makes effective mid-lesson alterations.
11. Effectively perceives students' linguistic and personal needs, along with their various styles, preferences, strengths, and weaknesses.
12. Gives optimal feedback to students.
13. Stimulates interaction, cooperation, and teamwork in the classroom.
14. Uses appropriate principles of classroom management.
15. Uses effective, clear presentation skills.
16. Creatively adapts textbook material and other audio, visual, and mechanical aids.
17. Innovatively creates brand-new materials when needed.
18. Uses interactive, intrinsically motivating techniques to create effective tests.

Interpersonal Skills
19. Is aware of cross-cultural differences and is sensitive to students' cultural traditions.
20. Enjoys people; shows enthusiasm, warmth, rapport, and appropriate humor.
21. Values the opinions and abilities of students.
22. Is patient in working with students of lesser ability.
23. Offers challenges to students of exceptionally high ability.
24. Cooperates harmoniously and candidly with colleagues, including seeking opportunities to share thoughts, ideas, and techniques.

Personal Qualities
25. Is well-organized, conscientious in meeting commitments, and dependable.
26. Is flexible when things go awry.
27. Engages in regular reflection on one's own teaching practice and strives to learn from those reflective practices.
28. Maintains an inquisitive mind in trying out new ways of teaching.
29. Sets short-term and long-term goals for continued professional growth.
30. Maintains and exemplifies high ethical and moral standards.

it is very difficult to make time to go and see other teachers and to invite the same in return. Too often, teachers tend to view observations as necessary while "in training" but unnecessary thereafter unless a supervisor is forced by regulations to visit their class in order to write up a recommendation for rehiring. If one of your colleagues comes up to you and says, "Hey, guess what? I was observed today," your answer might be something like "Oh, no! How bad was it?"

Fortunately, in an era of classroom-based research (see the next section in this chapter), the prevailing attitude toward observations is changing. Teachers are coming to understand that seeing one's actions through another's eyes is an indispensable tool for classroom research as well as a potentially enlightening experience for both observer and the one being observed. Before you get into the nasty habit of filling your time with everything else, why not carve out some time in your work schedule to visit other teachers and to invite reciprocity? As long as such visits pose no undue complication in schedules and other institutional constraints, you will reap rewarding benefits as you gain new ideas, keep fresh, and sharpen your own skills.

A second form of observation, which can be very effective in different ways, is self-observation. Actually, self-observation is no more than a systematic process of monitoring yourself, but it's the *systematic* part that is crucial. It requires discipline and perseverance, but the results are worth it. How do you go about observing yourself?

1. Select an element of your teaching to "keep an eye out for" as you teach. Make sure it's one finite element, like teacher talk, eye contact, teaching predominantly to one side of the classroom, or chalkboard work. If you try to take in too many things, you could end up becoming too self-conscious to the detriment of the rest of the lesson.
2. Monitor that particular element during the class period. If you can, video-record yourself (it's always less stressful for you if you can designate a colleague to come in and operate the camera—you can then do the same for your colleague).
3. After class, set aside a few moments to give these elements careful assessment through reflection, perhaps in a personal journal, on an audio-recorder, or in a discussion with a colleague.
4. Synthesize your reflections into a specific set of personal objectives for the very near future.

The most common and instructive means to go about observing oneself or others is to use an observation checklist. Dozens of such instruments are in active use by teacher trainers, supervisors, and teachers across the profession. Two such checklists follow. Figure 25.1 is a checklist for observing other teachers; Figure 25.2 is designed for self-observation.

Figure 25.1. Teacher observation form: observing other teachers

Circle or check each item in the column that most clearly represents your evaluation: 4 = excellent, 3 = above average, 2 = average, 1 = unsatisfactory, N/A = not applicable. You may also write comments in addition to or in lieu of checking a column.

I.   Preparation

1. The teacher was well-prepared and well-organized in class.   4 3 2 1 N/A
   Comment:

2. The lesson reviewed material and looked ahead to new material.   4 3 2 1 N/A
   Comment:

3. The prepared goals/objectives were apparent.   4 3 2 1 N/A
   Comment:

II.   Presentation

4. The class material was explained in an understandable way.   4 3 2 1 N/A
   Comment:

5. The lesson was smooth, sequenced, and logical.   4 3 2 1 N/A
   Comment:

6. The lesson was well-paced.   4 3 2 1 N/A
   Comment:

7. Directions were clear and concise and students were able to   4 3 2 1 N/A
   carry them out.
   Comment:

8. Material was presented at the students' level of comprehension.   4 3 2 1 N/A
   Comment:

9. An appropriate percentage of the class was student production   4 3 2 1 N/A
   of the language.
   Comment:

10. The teacher answered questions carefully and satisfactorily.   4 3 2 1 N/A
    Comment:

11. The method(s) was(were) appropriate to the age and ability   4 3 2 1 N/A
    of students.
    Comment:

12. The teacher knew when the students were having trouble understanding.   4 3 2 1 N/A
    Comment:

(Continued)

13. The teacher showed an interest in, and enthusiasm for,   4 3 2 1 N/A
    the subject taught.
    Comment:

III. Execution/Methods

14. There were balance and variety in activities during the lesson.   4 3 2 1 N/A
    Comment:

15. The teacher was able to adapt to unanticipated situations.   4 3 2 1 N/A
    Comment:

16. The material was reinforced.   4 3 2 1 N/A
    Comment:

17. The teacher moved around the class and made eye contact   4 3 2 1 N/A
    with students.
    Comment:

18. The teacher knew students' names.   4 3 2 1 N/A
    Comment:

19. The teacher positively reinforced the students.   4 3 2 1 N/A
    Comment:

20. Student responses were effectively elicited (i.e., the order in   4 3 2 1 N/A
    which the students were called on).
    Comment:

21. Examples and illustrations were used effectively.   4 3 2 1 N/A
    Comment:

22. Instructional aids or resource material was used effectively.   4 3 2 1 N/A
    Comment:

23. Drills were used and presented effectively.   4 3 2 1 N/A
    Comment:

24. Structures were taken out of artificial drill contexts and applied to   4 3 2 1 N/A
    the real contexts of the students' culture and personal experiences.
    Comment:

25. Error perception.   4 3 2 1 N/A
    Comment:

26. Appropriate error correction.   4 3 2 1 N/A
    Comment:

IV. Personal Characteristics

27. Patience in eliciting responses.   4 3 2 1 N/A
    Comment:

28. Clarity, tone, and audibility of voice.   4 3 2 1 N/A
    Comment:

29. Personal appearance.   4 3 2 1 N/A
    Comment:

30. Initiative, resourcefulness, and creativity.   4 3 2 1 N/A
    Comment:

31. Pronunciation, intonation, fluency, and appropriate and acceptable   4 3 2 1 N/A
    use of language.
    Comment:

V. Teacher/Student Interaction

32. Teacher encouraged and assured full student participation in class.   4 3 2 1 N/A
    Comment:

33. The class felt free to ask questions, to disagree, or to express their   4 3 2 1 N/A
    own ideas.
    Comment:

34. The teacher was able to control and direct the class.   4 3 2 1 N/A
    Comment:

35. The students were attentive and involved.   4 3 2 1 N/A
    Comment:

36. The students were comfortable and relaxed, even during intense   4 3 2 1 N/A
    intellectual activity.
    Comment:

37. The students were treated fairly, impartially, and with respect.   4 3 2 1 N/A
    Comment:

38. The students were encouraged to do their best.   4 3 2 1 N/A
    Comment:

39. The teacher was relaxed and matter-of-fact in voice and manner.   4 3 2 1 N/A
    Comment:

40. The teacher was aware of individual and group needs.   4 3 2 1 N/A
    Comment:

41. Digressions were used positively and not overused.   4 3 2 1 N/A
    Comment:

Figure 25.2. Teacher self-observation form (adapted from Christison & Bassano, 1984)

Thoughtfully consider each statement. Rate yourself in the following way:

3 = Excellent   2 = Good   1 = Needs Improvement   0 = Not Applicable

Write your ratings in the blanks. When you've finished, give overall consideration to the various areas.

I. Learning Environment

A. Relationship to Students

_____ 1. I establish good eye contact with my class. I do not talk over their heads, to the chalkboard, or to just one person.

_____ 2. If I tend to teach predominantly to one area of the classroom, I am aware of this. I make a conscious effort at all times to pay attention to all students equally.

_____ 3. I divide my students into small groups in an organized and principled manner. I recognize that these groups should differ in size and composition, varying with the objective of the group activity.

B. The Classroom

_____ 1. If possible, I arrange the seating in my class to suit the class activity for the day.

_____ 2. I consider the physical comfort of the room, such as heat and light.

_____ 3. When I need special materials or equipment, I have them set up before the class begins.

C. Presentation

_____ 1. My handwriting on the chalkboard and charts is legible from all locations in the classroom. It is large enough to accommodate students with vision impairments.

_____ 2. I speak loudly enough to be heard in all parts of the classroom, and I enunciate clearly.

_____ 3. I vary the exercises in class, alternating rapid and slow-paced activities to keep up the maximum interest in the class.

_____ 4. I am prepared to give a variety of explanations, models, or descriptions for all students.

_____ 5. I help the students form working principles and generalizations.

_____ 6. Students use new skills or concepts long enough so that they are retained and thus future application is possible.

_____ 7. I plan for "thinking time" for my students so they can organize their thoughts and plan what they are going to say or do.

D. Culture and Adjustment

_____ 1. I am aware that cultural differences affect the learning situation.

_____ 2. I keep the cultural background(s) of my students in mind when planning daily activities and am aware of cultural misunderstandings that might arise from the activities I choose.

_____ 3. I promote an atmosphere of understanding and mutual respect.

II. The Individuals

A. Physical Health

_____ 1. I know which students have visual or aural impairments and seat them as close to my usual teaching positions as possible.

_____ 2. I am aware that a student's attention span varies from day to day, depending on mental and physical health and outside distractions. I pace my class activities to accommodate the strengths. I don't continue with an activity that may exhaust or bore them.

_____ 3. I begin my class with a simple activity to wake students up and get them working together.

_____ 4. I am sensitive to individual students who have bad days. I don't press a student who is incapable of performing at the usual level.

_____ 5. I try to challenge students who are at their best.

_____ 6. If I am having a bad day and feel it might affect my normal teaching style, I let my students know it so there is no misunderstanding about my feelings for them.

B. Self-Concepts

_____ 1. I treat my students with the same respect that I expect them to show me.

_____ 2. I plan "one-centered" activities that give all students an opportunity at some point to feel important and accepted.

_____ 3. I like to teach and have a good time teaching—on most days.

C. Aptitude and Perception

_____ 1. I am aware that my students learn differently. Some students are visual-receptive, some are motor-receptive, and others are audio-receptive.

_____ 2. My exercises are varied; some are visual, aural, oral, and kinesthetic. I provide models, examples, and experiences to maximize learning in each of these areas.

_____ 3. I know basic concepts in the memory process. When applicable, I use association to aid students in rapid skills acquisition.

D. Reinforcement

_____ 1. I tell students when they have done well, but I don't let praise become mechanical.

_____ 2. I finish my class period in a way that will review the new concepts presented during the class period. My students can immediately evaluate their understanding of those concepts.

_____ 3. My tests are well-planned and -produced.

_____ 4. I make my system of grading clear to my students so that there are no misunderstandings of expectations.

E. Development

_____ 1. I keep up to date on new techniques in the ESL profession by attending conferences and workshops and by reading pertinent professional articles and books.

_____ 2. I realize that there is no one right way to present a lesson. I try new ideas where and when they seem appropriate.

_____ 3. I observe other ESL teachers so that I can get other ideas and compare them to my own teaching style. I want to have several ideas for teaching one concept.

(Continued)

III. The Activity

A. Interaction
_____ 1. I minimize my role in conducting the activities.
_____ 2. I organize the activities so they are suitable for real interactions among students.
_____ 3. The activities maximize student involvement.
_____ 4. The activities promote spontaneity or experimentation on the part of the learner.
_____ 5. The activities generally transfer attention away from "self" and outward toward a "task."
_____ 6. The activities are organized to ensure a high success rate, leaving enough room for error to make the activity challenging.
_____ 7. I am not always overly concerned with error correction. I choose the appropriate amount of correction for the activity.

B. Language
_____ 1. The activity is focused.
_____ 2. The content of the skill presented will be easily transferrable for use outside the class.
_____ 3. The activity is geared to the proficiency level of my class or slightly beyond.
_____ 4. The content of the activity is not too sophisticated for my students.
_____ 5. I make the content of the activity relevant and meaningful to my students' world.

CLASSROOM-BASED "ACTION" RESEARCH

Research is a scary word for many of us. We are happy to leave it in someone else's hands because it involves statistics (which we hate), experimental design (which we don't know), and the interpretation of ambiguous results (which we think is best left to the "experts"). Even so, leaving all the research in the hands of researchers is an upside-down policy, as Anne Meek (1991, p. 34) noted: "The main thing wrong with the world of education is that there's this one group of people who do it—the teachers—and then there's another group who think they know about it—the researchers. The group who think they know about teaching try to find out more about it in order to tell the teachers about teaching—and that is total reversal." She goes on to stress the importance of teachers doing their own research in their classrooms.

Actually, research doesn't have to be a scary prospect at all. You're researching ideas all the time, whether you know it or not. If, as a growing teacher, you have as a goal to improve the quality of your teaching, then you'll ask some relevant questions, hypothesize some possible answers or solutions, put the solutions to a practical tryout in the classroom, look for certain results, and weigh those results in some manner to determine whether your hypothesized answer held up. Such a process is quite formal in following classic steps for experimental research. It may not be a habitual practice for you.

A good deal of classroom research is an informal, everyday occurrence. You divide up small groups in a different way to stimulate a better exchange of ideas; you modify your usual nondirective approach to getting students to study harder and take a bold, direct, no-nonsense approach; you try a videotape as a conversation stimulus; you try a deductive approach to presenting a grammar point instead of your usual inductive approach. Other classroom research may be more of a long-term process that covers a term or more. In this mode, still in an informal manner, you may try out some learner strategy training techniques to see if students do better at conversation skills; you may do a daily three-minute pronunciation drill to see if students' pronunciation improves; you may assign specific extra-class reading to see if reading comprehension improves.

This kind of classroom-based research has commonly been called **action research,** in which "participants in a given social situation [a language class] are themselves centrally involved in a systematic process of inquiry arising from their own practical concerns" (Burns, 2005, p. 241). Action research is carried out not so much to fulfill a thesis requirement or to publish a journal article as to improve your own understanding of the teaching–learning process in the classroom. The payoff for treating your teaching–learning questions seriously is, ultimately, your becoming a better teacher. And, yes, you might also find that what you have learned is worth sharing with other teachers, either through informal conversations in the teacher's lunchroom or through a conference presentation.

David Nunan (1989b, p. 36) suggested the following possible questions, divided into four categories, that might form the central focus of some action research:

Linguistic features of learners' language

1. In my teaching, I generally provide an application task to follow up a formal presentation. What kind of language items do learners actually use in the application task?
2. Do learners more easily learn closed class items (e.g., pronouns/demonstratives) when these are presented as paradigms, or when they are taught separately over a period of time?

Interactive features of classroom language

3. In what ways do turn-taking and topic management vary with variations in the size and composition of learner groups?
4. Are learners more effective at conversational management when techniques such as holding the floor, bringing in another speaker, etc., are consciously taught?

Tasks

5. Which tasks stimulate more interaction?
6. Which tasks work best with mixed-ability groups?

Strategies

7. Is there a conflict between the classroom activities I favor and those my learners prefer?
8. Do my best learners share certain strategy preferences that distinguish them from less efficient learners?

One of the possible benefits of action research is its stimulus for collaboration among teachers. A few years ago I instigated a collaborative effort at the American Language Institute at San Francisco State University to study the effect of error treatment on the performance of our ESL students. Two matched sections of the same low-intermediate intensive English course were selected for investigation over a seven-week period. An oral pre-test was designed by the research group and administered to each student. In one section, teachers deliberately withheld any treatment of present tense, present progressive, and third person singular speech errors committed by the students. In the other section, teachers attempted to treat overtly all such errors that they noticed. During the seven-week study time, teachers observed each other, and other members of the research group not teaching those sections also came in to observe, mostly to check up on the extent to which teachers were carrying out their respective charge. At the end of the seven-week period, the pre-test was readministered as a post-test, and gain scores were calculated.

The statistical findings of this little study were disappointing: no significant difference between the two sections! But the pedagogical gains accrued by the collaboration among eight teachers were more than worth the effort. In the process of investigating a potentially interesting instructional variable, teachers did the following, all collaboratively: They formulated research hypotheses; they designed the study; they designed a test; they observed and gave feedback to each other; they were sensitized to the complexities of error treatment; and they lowered their fear of performing research!

You still may be feeling a little queasy about labeling some of your teacher inquisitiveness as *research*. Can I really ask the "right" questions? How do I know if my research methodology is sound? How will I deal with numerical results (statistics)? Will my conclusions be valid? Good questions. First of all, I recommend that you consult a teacher resource book on classroom research (Burns, 1999; Edge, 2001; Freeman, 1998; Wallace, 1998).

Second, consider the following pointers to get yourself started on some simple but potentially effective action research.

1. Convert your "ideas" into specific questions.

You may have quite a few "ideas" about things that you could investigate in the classroom. That's good; keep those creative juices flowing. But in order to be able to draw conclusions, your ideas have to be converted into questions that you can answer. Sometimes those questions are too broad: Is communicative language teaching effective? How useful is reading aloud in class? Does process writing work?

So, make sure that your questions are specific enough that you can look back after your investigation and really come up with an answer. The questions do not have to be long and drawn out, just specific, like the eight questions listed earlier. As an example here, let's consider the following question:

*Given a selection of six commonly used techniques, how do they
compare with each other in terms of stimulating interaction?*

2. Operationally define the elements of your question.

Next, take your question and operationally define all the elements in it.
"Operational" means that you have a measurable means for determining something.
So, in the example question above, let's say that for the purpose of your research
you have selected six small-group techniques (jigsaw, role play, etc.). You will limit
your investigation to those six. Interaction then has to be defined. Suppose you
define interaction as the total number of turns taken in each group. And, for a
possible additional interesting statistic, total up the number of minutes of student
talk as well.

3. Determine how you will answer your question.

Now you are ready to launch the investigation. How will you answer the
question? Your research methodology may call for several weeks of data collecting
and, in this particular case, some tape recorders, since you will not be able to record
data for several small groups at once and attend to the techniques as well. For each
of the six designated techniques, you will have a tape recorder placed in each small
group and running during the entire technique. (Yes, the tape recorders may inhibit
some students, but that's the risk you have to take.) You will (perhaps with the help
of a colleague?) then listen to each tape and tally the number of turns for each and
add up minutes of talk as well. Assuming that you have allowed all the groups an
equal number of total minutes within each technique, you can come up with a
grand total of turns and minutes for each technique. The number of turns for each
technique will determine its rank order among the six.

4. Interpret your results appropriately.

According to your findings (see below), technique A stimulates the most
interaction, B is next, and so on. But your conclusion may not be so simple. Every
research study has its necessary caveats, so before you make a sweeping
generalization about your findings, it will help to state, even if only for yourself, some
of the limitations of your results. Here are the results you found:

Technique	Turns	Minutes Student talk/Total time
A	137	73/90
B	133	85/90
C	116	79/90
D	114	69/90
E	102	71/90
F	91	79/90

First, can you be sure that technique A stimulated significantly more turns than technique B? And B more than C, etc.? Ask a statistician to help you to determine how probable it is that your results stemmed from the technique rather than from just random possibilities. This way you will be able to determine the statistical significance of your findings.

Second, notice that the number of minutes of student talk didn't correspond, meaning that in some techniques (A, for example) there was some relatively rapid turn-taking interspersed with student silence, and in other techniques (F, for example) certain students talked for longer stretches of time. This may give you cause to redefine interaction or at least to interpret your results accordingly.

Finally, results need to be seen in terms of other limitations in the study itself: the choice and number of tasks, the number of students, the operational definitions chosen, and your particular group of students. You may, for example, be tempted to generalize results of classroom research to the world at large. Beware. Your safest conclusion is one that reports what you found for your class, and to invite others to replicate your study if they wish to see if similar results are obtained.

Classroom-based research is ideally suited to current practice in language teaching where we are not in the business of buying into one of the "designer" methods with their prescriptions of what teachers should do in the classroom. Instead, our communicative, interactive language-teaching approach asks every teacher to assess his or her own classroom of students and to design instructional techniques that work under those particular conditions, for those particular learners, who are pursuing particular purposes in learning the English language.

Further, action research is an excellent way to promote teacher development within a framework that values the personal construction of teacher knowledge as opposed to a transmission model. It fosters a spirit of understanding of one's own beliefs, knowledge, and experience. It forces teachers to look at their own situated context. And, almost inevitably, action research encourages collaborative relationships among teachers (Burns, 2005; Freeman, 2002; Mann, 2005).

TEACHER COLLABORATION: LEARNING FROM EACH OTHER

The process of continuing to develop your professional expertise as a teacher is sometimes difficult to manage alone. The challenges of teaching in a rapidly changing profession almost necessitate collaboration with other teachers in order to stay on the cutting edge (Murphey & Sato, 2005). Can you successfully collaborate with other teachers to fulfill your expectations? Let me suggest six forms of collaboration—of teachers learning from each other—that have worked for others and that may work for you.

1. Peer coaching

Already in this chapter you have been given some guidelines for observation of both yourself and other teachers. *Peer coaching* is a systematic process of collaboration in which one teacher observes and gives feedback to another teacher, usually with some form of reciprocity. Kate Kinsella (1994, p. 35) defines and elaborates as follows:

> Peer coaching is a structured process by which trained faculty members voluntarily assist each other in enhancing their teaching within an atmosphere of collegial trust and candor, through: (1) development of individual instructional improvement goals and clear observation criteria; (2) reciprocal, focused, nonevaluative classroom observations; and (3) prompt constructive feedback on those observations.

Observers need not technically be "peers" in every sense of the word, but as colleagues, observer and teacher engage in a cooperative process of mutual communication about the actual teaching–learning process as directly observed in the classroom. Feedback is classified as **formative** rather than **summative**. It is offered and received as information for the enhancement of one's future teaching, not as data for summing up one's competencies as a teacher.

Peer coaching can be especially helpful if you focus on certain aspects of your teaching. If you've been concerned, say, about the quantity of teacher talk versus student talk in your teaching, a peer observer may be able to give you some feedback that could lead you to make some adjustments. Among topics that peer-coaching programs have centered on are distribution of student participation across the classroom; teacher speech mannerisms, patterns, eye contact, and nonverbal distractors; group and pair work management; and transitions from one activity to the next, to the next.

Peer coaching is able to offer a personalized opportunity for growth. Both sides of the team benefit: The observer is called upon to carefully analyze another's teaching and thereby sharpen his or her own metacognitive ability to reflect on the teaching process; the teacher being observed is nudged out of what might otherwise be some complacency into a heightened awareness of his or her own areas of strength and weakness.

2. Team teaching

To the extent that the structure and budget of your program permit, team teaching can be an extraordinarily rewarding experience. Several models of team teaching are common: (1) Two teachers are overtly present throughout a class period, but divide responsibility between them; (2) two teachers take different halves of a class period, with one teacher stepping aside while the other performs; and (3) two or more teachers teach different consecutive periods of one group of learners, and must collaborate closely in carrying out and modifying curricular plans.

The first two models are less frequently found among English language programs not because of absence of reward for student and teacher, but because of budgetary limitations. The third model is extremely common in the English language–teaching world, especially whenever a group of learners compose an intact set of students across two or more class periods. Within this model, the importance of collaboration is sometimes underestimated. Teachers may be too ready to assume that a curriculum spanning a whole term of, say, 10 to 15 weeks will simply proceed as planned, only to discover that another teacher has not been able to follow the time-plan, throwing off the expected sequencing of material.

The advantages of team teaching, especially in the first two models, parallel those of peer coaching. Teachers are encouraged to collaborate, to consider respective strengths, and to engage in reflective practice. In the third model, teachers must develop a pattern of frequent communication and exchange, the fruits of which often are greater professional growth.

3. Action research

Classroom-based, or "action," research has already been described in a previous section of this chapter. Research in the language classroom offers another opportunity for you to collaborate with other teachers in creative and ultimately rewarding ways.

4. Collaborative curriculum development and revision

The process of curriculum development and revision warrants a similar collaborative effort. In the same way that teachers are sometimes all too happy to turn over research to the experts, so we are tempted to get curriculum specialists to do course and program development. Growing, dynamic language programs are a product of an ongoing creative dialogue between teachers and among teachers and those that are assigned to compile curricula. Not to involve teachers in the process is to run the risk of programs that are generated in a vacuum of sorts, devoid of a dynamic interaction among student, teacher, and administrator.

At the American Language Institute, our curriculum supervisors are in daily communication with teachers. As teachers consult with them on lesson design, textbook adaptation, and pedagogical innovations, new curricula are born every day. This kind of collaboration results in solicited teacher contributions to course syllabuses, which are then adapted and incorporated into established, revised curricula. Thus the curricula for courses are in a slow but constant state of creative change.

5. Presenting at a professional conference

At San Francisco State University, the graduating class in the M.A. program in TESOL plans and administers a semi-annual professional conference at which each graduate makes a professional presentation. Graduates find that this is not just an excellent training ground for conference planning, but that it forces them to prepare and deliver a high-quality presentation on a topic of professional interest. A number of those presentations are co-presented, giving the presenters an opportunity to collaborate and pool their efforts.

I include the suggestion of conference presentations here because it's difficult *not* to collaborate in some way on such events. Even if you do a solo presentation, some collaboration is often involved in preparing, in critiquing, and, of course, in interacting with one's audience. A conference presentation is a superb opportunity to develop some of your own ideas and to share them with a professional community. It gives you an impetus to focus on some background reading, to systematically pull together an idea or topic, to present it clearly and enthusiastically, and ultimately to establish new professional connections beyond your own institution. It's also an excellent addition to your résumé! Some ideas for presentations:

- a task or activity that demonstrates a principle or theme (e.g., environmental action)
- a set of tasks or activities (e.g., a project involving all four skills) focused on a theme
- a study of students' language development in a specific area (e.g., relative clauses, verb tenses)
- a curriculum or module that you created for a course
- a focus on a learning principle (e.g., anxiety) with background research and practical examples for facilitating learning
- a report on some teacher development projects (e.g., formation of a support group, peer coaching)
- a focus on an age group (e.g., very young learners) with examples of classroom tasks and activities
- a cross-cultural analysis of a subtopic within education with practical classroom examples

This list could continue for pages, as a glance at any conference handbook will reveal. By organizing your thoughts clearly and carefully following directions for submitting a proposal for a presentation, you have an excellent chance of having your proposal accepted. I can guarantee you that it will be a very rewarding experience!

6. Teacher support groups

Finally, collaboration can take the form of gatherings of teachers at a number of different levels (Murphey & Sato, 2005). At the local level of the day-to-day routine that we all find ourselves in, the importance of purposeful gatherings of teachers cannot be too strongly stressed. Even if agendas are rather informal—empathetic support will readily be found even within informal agendas—it is important to have times when a staff of teachers gets together to cover a number of possible issues: student behavior problems, teaching tips, curricular issues, and even difficulties with administrative bureaucracy. When teachers talk together, there is almost always a sense of solidarity and purpose, and ultimately a morale boost.

JOURNALS, TEACHING PORTFOLIOS, READING, AND WRITING

So far in this chapter, we've looked at teacher development in the form of observations and action research, and in the section above, at several methods of collaborative development. The latter endeavors, but to some extent the former two as well, involve *collaboration* with fellow teachers, which in many circumstances may be difficult to arrange vis-à-vis a language teacher's hectic schedule and pace. Other effective ways to continue your professional growth include efforts that you can *individually* make according to your own timetable and pace (Bailey et al., 2001). We'll conclude this chapter with some thoughts about these rewarding possibilities.

1. Teaching journals

The use of student-generated journals in our classrooms has already been discussed in previous chapters. Journal-writing has in recent years evolved from simply a matter of keeping a diary into a potentially integral aspect of a learner's process of acquisition. Now, in the burgeoning field of teacher development, teacher journal-writing has been prominently featured (Mann, 2005; Richards & Farrell, 2005; Bailey, 1990).

Journals enable a teacher to record events, observations, questions, and feelings more or less immediately, before recollections fade in the memories of our busy minds. Teacher journals serve much the same purpose that student journals serve in enabling the writer to focus more clearly on relevant phenomena, to reflect on them, and to resolve to take action on goals that are derived from the insights that accrue. Richards and Farrell (2005) suggest that the primary audience for such journals is the writer, but that at times journals can be fruitfully shared with other teachers or a supervisor.

A key to successful journal writing lies in commitment: Set goals; address specific questions; set aside a regular time for writing; and review and evaluate your entries in order to learn something from them (Bailey, 1990).

2. Teaching portfolios

The creation of a professional portfolio is a second method of individual development that one can accomplish without the difficulty imposed by collaborative efforts. Although you are ultimately likely to want to share your portfolio with someone else, much of it can be assembled on your own time. A portfolio is an assembly of your professional handiwork, thoughts and reflections, beliefs and principles, and personal data (Tanner, 2003; Constantino & De Lorenzo, 2002). A portfolio might take on a summative nature by serving as a demonstration of your professional qualifications for, say, a job that you're interviewing for, or it can play a more formative role in putting together a personally oriented set of documents that show your progress in selected areas of concern. Like a journal, a portfolio can be an instrument for reflection and goal-setting.

At San Francisco State University, graduates of the M.A. program in TESOL all create a professional portfolio as part of their culminating experience in the program. Their portfolios consist of an introduction, a résumé, a statement of one's philosophy of education (beliefs about teaching and learning), annotated bibliographies on selected topics, one or two sample (revised) academic papers from their program, and two lesson plans with reflections on each. These portfolios are then used for imminent job applications and interviews, but their greatest value is in the process of synthesizing two or more years of graduate study.

3. Professional reading on your own

In a teacher's busy existence, it's all too often the case that you simply "run out of time" for things like reading professional journals and books. At the end of the day—literally—you end up being mentally spent and your body craves some physical exercise, a good meal, a friendly conversation, or anything but more reading! By then it's late at night, you need some sleep, and the cycle starts over. There's no question that selective reading to "keep up with the field," and simply to discover what other people are thinking and doing, is essential to the growing, dynamic teacher (Borg, 2003a). So what's the solution?

I find it difficult to maintain a discipline of *regular* reading and study. I tend to put these sorts of professional activities off until summertime, a January break, or some other "block" of time. I don't recommend this practice! I have to force the issue by trying to do some of the following:

- Designate times during the day for catching up on professional reading. Build these times into your calendar and don't let other things interfere.
- Make use of "empty" periods of time during the day (waiting for a bus; riding a commuter train; sitting in the doctor's waiting room).
- When a journal comes in the mail, scan it quickly for the articles you really want (or need) to read, flag them with a colored tag, and put the journal on an actual (or mental) list of "things to do."
- Practice the art of skimming and scanning—since there are so many possible things to read and there's *no way* you can read them all from cover to cover. Reading the abstract of a journal article is usually an excellent way to determine its utility for your professional purposes, and to help you decide whether to later read the article in detail.
- Devise a system of note taking for future retrieval, such as index cards, file folders, electronic notes, etc.
- Focus on some *production* goals for directing your reading (see #4 on p. 508). With an overwhelming number of possible books, journals, articles, and electronic information to cover, if you can set the goal of writing (for a journal, newsletter, or Web-based source) or presenting (at a conference), it will channel your reading and help to prevent haphazard reading here and there with no direct, tangible end.

4. Writing for publication

One of the most rewarding endeavors in a teacher's life is professional writing for publication. My first journal article was an outgrowth of a little classroom-based experiment that I did on the English spelling system (Brown, 1970). I did background reading, devised a hypothesis, set up the research methodology, gathered data, and came up with some interesting results. I never dreamed that my "little" study was worthy of publication in a "big" journal, but at the encouragement of others, I edited the piece, submitted it, and much to my surprise at the time, it was accepted!

Your reading, action research, journal-writing, or curriculum development projects, among many other possibilities, can become a potentially useful, interesting, and innovative addition to professional literature in the field of language teaching. With a huge variety of journals in our field, in addition to newsletters, local professional booklets, and a growing number of Web-based opportunities for writing (Murphey et al., 2005), you should by all means consider this creative outlet for your energies.

Consider these possible genres of writing that you can do:

- writing a professional journal article on some action research you have done
- responding to a recent journal article that particularly interested you
- reviewing a book (Kupetz, 2003) that you recently read
- writing up a "teaching tip" on a task you developed in your class
- writing a curriculum for your institution (Seymour, 2003)
- publishing a student textbook
- compiling a teacher's manual for a student textbook
- editing a textbook for a publisher
- reviewing a manuscript for a publisher
- creating Web-based blogs or other electronic resources
- compiling an annotated bibliography of references on a specific topic

It's tempting for teachers to assume that professional writing must be undertaken by "experts" (Ph.D.'s and professors and the like), and certainly not by "ordinary" teachers. Nonsense! In the same way that research is not the exclusive province of fancy psychometricians, as we noted above, professional writing is (or should be) equally shared by classroom teachers. Many teachers find that professional writing is not only an excellent motivating experience, but also a rewarding one that opens up new personal and professional vistas.

✬   ✬   ✬   ✬   ✬

I think you can now see that teacher development is indeed a lifelong process. If you're just "starting out" in the profession, you have many adventures ahead of you, and the best way to fully appreciate those adventures is to keep growing. As you do so, remember that there's no ideal "model" teacher that you need to aspire to. Every teacher is unique, with individual experiences, knowledge, and beliefs, and you are now forming your own construction of yourself as a teacher. Proceed with pride in who you are already and with dedication to who you will become.

TOPICS FOR DISCUSSION, ACTION, AND RESEARCH

[Note: (I) Individual work; (G) group or pair work; (C) whole-class discussion.]

1. (G) If students have been systematically reading and studying the chapters of this book, they have by now picked up a reasonably comprehensive picture of principles and issues in language teaching and how they apply to the classroom. With that background information, ask pairs to go back now to Chapter 1 and look through the lesson that was described there. Then, have them look at the 30 questions posed in the subsequent section ("Analyzing the Lesson," pp. 8–10). Dividing the questions among pairs or small groups, direct them to propose answers to those questions. What aspects of this class hour should one change, and why? Groups will present their responses and rationale for changes to the whole class.

2. (I) Look again at the 12 principles of language learning and teaching outlined in Chapter 4. Restate them in your own words. Would you now like to add any further principles or refine any of the 12? Which principles are most applicable to your own context(s) of teaching English?

3. (I) Over the next several months, see what you can do to be more of a "peak performer" as a teacher. Set some goals for yourself, and list them in order of priority or in chronological order. Resolve to take some risks, and if you think you need to do so, take specific steps to lower stress in your life. Consider writing a journal to keep track of your progress.

4. (I/C) Using the information provided in the section on "The 'Good' Language Teacher" (pp. 489–490), write your own description of the top four or five characteristics that you think apply to excellence in language teaching. Share your essay, or a summary of it, with the rest of the class.

5. (I/C) (For class members who are *not* currently teaching) Use the observation form in Figure 25.1 to observe a language class. Report back to the class on the usefulness of the form for identifying significant elements of the class and the teacher's methodology.

6. (I/G) (For class members who *are* currently teaching) Use the self-observation form (Figure 25.2.) the next time you teach. What did you learn? Use Figure 25.1 to arrange a peer-coaching exchange of observations of each other. Make sure you give verbal feedback to each other as well.

7. (G) (For class members who are *not* currently teaching) In assigned groups, using the list of research questions on page 499 as a starting point, have students brainstorm some other researchable ideas using a chalkboard or poster paper to write the ideas down. They will pick several ideas to carry out individually or as a small team, making plans (using steps 1 through 4 in this chapter) for some action research to carry out someday. Ask groups to share their ideas with the rest of the class.

8. (G) (For class members who *are* currently teaching) Form groups of three or four people each who are currently teaching. Have them brainstorm some forms of collaboration that would work in their institution and write down the ideas that are generated. Ask them to share their thoughts with the rest of the class, and to make a resolution to make this plan actually happen in the near future.

9. (C) Engage the class in a discussion of the feasibility of the collaborative methods of teacher development and the individual means that were suggested in the last section. If members of the class have tried any of these, they could share their experiences with the class and offer comments on what worked and what did not work.

10. (G) In small groups, have students brainstorm ideas for either (a) a conference presentation or (b) professional writing. First, they should generate some ideas or topics to present/write about. Then, they need to establish the type of presentation or genre of writing for the idea, and talk about how to go about seeking acceptance or publication. Finally, they can develop the idea in a brief outline, and report back to the class.

FOR YOUR FURTHER READING

Richards, J., & Farrell, T. (2005). *Professional development for language teachers: Strategies for teacher learning.* Cambridge, UK: Cambridge University Press.

Bailey, K., Curtis, A., & Nunan, D. (2001). *Pursuing professional development: The self as source.* Boston: Heinle & Heinle.

Jack Richards and Thomas Farrell's book is comprehensive in its presentation of a number of professional development options for teachers. The 12 chapters include such topics as teacher support groups, teaching journals, peer observation, portfolios, and action research. Bibliographies at the end of each chapter are useful. Kathleen Bailey, Andy Curtis, and David Nunan also offer a wealth of information and practical ideas for professional development in their book.

Mann, S. (2005). The language teacher's development. *Language Teaching, 38,* 103–118.

Borg, S. (2003). Teacher cognition in language teaching: A review of research on what language teachers think, know, believe, and do. *Language Teaching, 36,* 81–109.

Freeman, D. (2002). The hidden side of the work: Teacher knowledge and learning to teach. *Language Teaching, 35,* 1–13.

These three survey articles together provide a comprehensive overview of recent work in teacher development. Each article includes an extensive bibliography.

Burns, A. (2005). Action research. In E. Hinkel (Ed.), *Handbook of research in second language teaching and learning* (pp. 241–256). Mahwah, NJ: Lawrence Erlbaum Associates.

Edge, J. (Ed.). (2001). *Action research.* Alexandria, VA: Teachers of English to Speakers of Other Languages.

Wallace, M. (1998). *Action research for language teachers.* Cambridge, UK: Cambridge University Press.

Anne Burns offers a succinct survey of current developments in action research in her article. Julian Edge's edited volume contains examples of classroom-based research from contributing writers. Michael Wallace's manual provides some detailed suggestions on how to go about conducting research in your language classroom.

Professional Development in Language Education Series:

Egbert, J. (Ed.). (2003). *Becoming contributing professionals.* Alexandria, VA: Teachers of English to Speakers of Other Languages.

Murphey, T. (Ed.). (2003). *Extending professional contributions.* Alexandria, VA: Teachers of English to Speakers of Other Languages.

Byrd, P., & Nelson, G. (2003). *Sustaining professionalism.* Alexandria, VA: Teachers of English to Speakers of Other Languages.

Murphey, T., & Sato, K. (2005). *Communities of supportive professionals.* Alexandria, VA: Teachers of English to Speakers of Other Languages.

This series of short books (125–150 pages each) is an excellent resource on many different ideas for professional development. Each edited book has 12 or more chapters written by practicing classroom teachers around the world.

CHAPTER 26

TEACHERS FOR SOCIAL

RESPONSIBILITY

OBJECTIVES After reading this chapter, you will be able to:

- take up the challenge to be a socially responsible teacher

- understand and put into practice various interpretations of what it means to engage in critical pedagogy

- identify a number of controversial issues and topics and treat them sensitively in the classroom

- recognize moral dilemmas in taking up the challenge to be an agent for change

- develop a personal set of ethics for language teaching that is consonant with your beliefs and that at the same time respects students' cultural values

You must be the change you want to see in the world.
—Gandhi

In this final chapter I want to address another aspect of language teaching, beyond that of teacher development, that penetrates well below the surface of the cognitive and technical skills implied in effective teaching. The *critical* nature of language learning and teaching can in many ways be pervasive in your professional life. Ask yourself what, in the deepest part of your soul, drives you in your chosen profession. What convictions and beliefs directed you into the profession? What sense of purpose continues to propel you through hours and days and weeks of teaching (possibly at a fairly low wage)? What is it that somehow prods you to wake up every Monday morning, a bit blurry-eyed perhaps, but ready to face new challenges and opportunities?

Somewhere in those deep recesses of your mind and emotion you are guided by a sense of mission, of purpose, and of dedication to a profession in which you believe you can make a difference. Your sense of social responsibility directs you to be an agent for change. You're driven by convictions about what this world should look like, how its people should behave, how its governments should control that behavior, and how its inhabitants should be partners in the stewardship of the planet. In the words of Giroux and McLaren (1989, p. xiii), you strive to "embody in [your] teaching a vision of a better and more humane life."

CRITICAL PEDAGOGY

These fundamental moral principles within us have been examined in recent years in what educational professionals have called **critical pedagogy**. Suresh Canagarajah (2005) shied away from a direct, empirical definition of critical pedagogy, but noted that it implies a way of "doing" learning and teaching, motivated by our beliefs about education and its place in society: "Critical students and teachers are prepared to situate learning in the relevant social contexts, unravel the implications of power in pedagogical activity, and commit themselves to transforming the means and ends of learning, in order to construct more egalitarian, equitable, and ethical educational and social environments" (p. 932).

Critical pedagogy has been a focus of interest in the language-teaching profession for some time. In 1999, the *TESOL Quarterly* devoted its entire (Autumn) issue to critical pedagogy, with contributions from a number of authors representing various perspectives and subfields (Pennycook, 1999). Now, it would be remiss of any language teacher to skirt around issues of power and politics and religion in the classroom, simply because they evoke strong emotions.

Teaching As A Subversive Activity

The call for teachers to act critically, as agents for change, is not a new one. Four decades ago, Postman and Weingartner (1969) shook some educational foundations with their best seller, *Teaching as a Subversive Activity*. In their stinging critique of the American educational establishment, they challenged teachers to enable their students to become "crap" detectors: (a) crap detectors in creating major *changes* in our social, economic, and political systems; (b) crap detectors who can cut through burgeoning *bureaucracies* (which, they note, are repositories of conventional assumptions and standard practices); and (c) crap detectors who can release us from the stranglehold of the *media,* which creates its own version of censorship.

The call for subversive teaching is not unlike the challenge to English language teachers today to engage in critical pedagogy. Those of us who teach languages may indeed have a special responsibility to "subvert" attitudes and beliefs and assumptions that ultimately impede the attainment of such goals as equality, justice, freedom, and opportunity.

In recent years some educators, notably Henry Giroux (2006) and Peter McLaren (2005), along with Julian Edge (2003) in our own profession of language educators, have taken a strong interpretation of the implications of critical pedagogy. The title alone of McLaren's (2005) book, *Capitalists and Conquerors: A Critical Pedagogy Against the Empire,* provides a clear picture of its contents: a call to teachers for classroom practices that assertively direct students toward becoming critical thinkers (and doers) in the face of war, violence, corruption, imperialism, greed, and waste of natural resources.

Some Cautionary Observations

Debates over the means and ends of carrying out critical pedagogies bring with them some warnings. We are reminded that our learners must be free to be themselves, to think for themselves, to behave intellectually without coercion from a powerful elite (Clarke, 1990, 2003), to cherish their beliefs and traditions and cultures without the threat of forced change (Benesch, 2001; Edge, 1996; Norton & Toohey, 2004). In our classrooms, where "the dynamics of power and domination permeate the fabric of classroom life" (Auerbach, 1995, p. 9), we are alerted to a possible "covert political agenda [beneath our] overt technical agenda" (Phillipson, 1992, p. 27). Julian Edge (2003, p. 705) cautions against those who might teach English out of a religious "conversion-motivated" zeal, lest the very act of teaching English create its own hegemony, a theme echoed by Scollon (2004).

What has come to be known as **liberation education,** among other terms (see Clarke, 1990, 2003; Freire, 1970), must no doubt be tempered with some cautionary observations. Some have recently argued that our ostensibly benign assumptions about teaching methodology (see Canagarajah, 2005; Holliday, 1994; Pennycook, 2001) have an element of controversy in them. Why, there's hardly a person in this profession who would not stand up with your hand over your heart to salute "communicative language teaching" or "cooperative learning"! But are all these warm and fuzzy, soft and tender approaches to the classroom universally accepted by all cultures and all educational traditions? Probably not. In an article titled "Towards Less Humanistic English Teaching," Gadd (1998) cautioned against viewing ourselves as a "nurturer of souls . . ." because this "inappropriate and oppressive role . . . does not encourage or permit the students' intellectual and cognitive development." (Arnold's reply to Gadd in the same issue is worth careful reading.)

The counterpoint to this rallying of teachers to change a world mired in bureaucracies is epitomized, as I see it, in what Skutnabb-Kangas and Phillipson (1994) called *linguicism.* Phillipson (1992) argued that, historically at least, worldwide English language teaching has served to "legitimate . . . an unequal division of power and resources," as "the dominant language [English] is glorified, [and] dominated languages are stigmatized" (p. 27). Now, while Holliday (1994) rightfully argues, I think, that Phillipson's stance ". . . implies a conspiracy view of English language teaching which is over-simplistic and naive" (p. 99), nevertheless I think all of us, if we haven't done so already, need to take heed lest we become the inadvertent perpetuators of a widening of the gap between haves and have-nots. Language is power, and the unequal distribution of language programs across the world surely could contribute to the ultimate unequal distribution of power (Macedo, Dendrinos, & Gounari, 2003; Norton & Toohey, 2004).

Is there a middle ground? A number of recent articles and books suggest that there is (Canagarajah, 2005; Clarke, 2003; Edge, 2003; Johnston, 2003; Snow, 2001). In the face of current mounting threats from terrorist organizations, warring nations, and religious crusades, especially since the September 11, 2001 incidents, we are in a period of dire need of information, understanding, and communication.

Such educative processes must be undertaken with the utmost care (Dewaele, 2004).

Your own language classroom is an excellent place to begin the quest for a more humane world. Our classrooms can themselves become models of mutual respect across cultural, political, and religious boundaries. As we take up Julian Edge's (2006) challenge to engage in nonjudgmental discourse in our classrooms, we begin the journey. Can English language teachers facilitate the formation of classroom communities of learners who critically examine moral, ethical, and political issues surrounding them, and do so sensitively, without pushing a personal subversive agenda? In the next section, I offer some guidelines for teaching, along with some examples of engaging in critical pedagogy while respecting the values and beliefs of our students.

HOT TOPICS IN THE LANGUAGE CLASSROOM

A number of the so-called "hot topics" that we sometimes address in our classrooms, such as nonviolence, human rights, gender equality, racial/ethnic discrimination, health issues, environmental action, and political activism, are controversial. They demand critical thinking and the need to be sensitive to students' value systems. They cannot, in any context, be simply thrown into a classroom routine without risking alienation, anger, or resentment on the part of students.

Guidelines for Dealing with Controversial Issues in the Classroom

I would like to suggest three guiding principles for engaging in teaching with **social responsibility**, that is, critical pedagogy that fully respects the values and beliefs of your students.

1. **Teachers are responsible for giving students opportunities to learn about important social / moral / ethical issues and to analyze all sides of an issue.** A language class is an ideal locus for offering information on topics of significance to students. The objectives of a curriculum are not limited to linguistic factors alone, but also include developing the art of critical thinking. Complex issues (say, religious fundamentalism or homosexuality, for example) can become the focus of intrinsically motivating content-based language learning.

2. **Teachers are responsible for creating an atmosphere of respect for each other's opinions, beliefs, and ethnic/cultural diversity.** The classroom becomes a model of the world as a context for tolerance and for the appreciation of diversity. Discourse structures such as "I see your point, but ..." are explicitly taught and used in classroom discussions and debates. Students learn how to disagree without imposing their own belief or opinions

on others. In all this, it is important that the teacher's personal opinions or beliefs remain sensitively covert, lest a student feel coerced into thinking something because the teacher thinks that way.

3. **Teachers are responsible for maintaining a threshold of morality and ethics in the classroom climate.** Occasionally a teacher needs to exercise some discipline when students show disrespect or hatred based on, say, race, religion, ethnicity, or gender. Teachers should ensure that "universal" moral principles (love, equality, tolerance, freedom) are manifested in the classroom. This guideline is, in effect, a paradox because it presupposes certain values to be beyond reproach. Such a presupposition violates the very principle of respect captured in the guideline #2 above. Nevertheless, this is where one's pedagogy becomes "critical" in that the teacher's vision of "a better and more humane life" is usually predicated on such basic values.

Examples of Socially Responsible Teaching from Around the World

Consider the following examples of classroom activities from around the world. Do they abide by the above guidelines? Can your classroom re-create any of them?

In Brazil, a curriculum for children takes them on an adventure trip searching for "magic glasses" which, they discover, will enable them to see the world as it could be if everyone respected it. The program teaches appreciation for Native Indians of Brazil, their culture, stories, and music; it teaches gender-role equity, animal rights, and environmental stewardship. (Maria Rita Vieira)

In Japan, a classroom research project called "Dreams and Dream Makers" had students choose a person who "worked to make the world a more peaceful place." (Donna McInnis)

In Singapore, an activity called "stamping out insults" focused on why people insult others and helped students to learn and use kind, affirming words as they disagreed with one another. (George Jacobs)

In China, a teacher had students study oppression and suppression of free speech in the former Soviet Union, calling for critical analysis of the roots and remedies of such denial of freedom. Without espousing any particular point of view himself, and under the guise of offering criticism of another country's practices, students were led to comprehend alternative points of view. (Anonymous by request)

In Armenia, a teacher had students share their grandparents' experiences during the 1915 Armenian genocide when more than 1.5 million Armenians were killed in Turkey. Nearly every student had family members who had been killed. Discussions focused on how ethnic groups could overcome such catastrophes and learn to live together as cooperative, peaceful neighbors. (Nick Dimmitt)

A teacher in Israel told of a unit in which students had to create an ethical marketing and advertising campaign for a product. Cases of Colgate's widening the mouth of toothpaste tubes and of Revlon's making the glass on nail polish bottles a little thicker led students to debate ethical business issues. (Stuart Carroll)

In Egypt, a culture where equal opportunities and rights of women are abridged, a teacher used an activity in a class with both men and women in it that culminated in the students' collaboratively writing up a "bill of rights" for women in Egypt. (Mona Grant Nashed)

In the United States, following the September 11, 2001 terrorist attacks, a student asked the teacher what "Middle East" meant; when the teacher defined the term, the student responded with, "Oh, you mean 'terrorists'." The teacher used the next 10 minutes to sensitively guide students through a discussion of stereotypes and the misinformation that they often convey. (Anonymous)

A number of recent presentations and publications reveal that teachers are increasingly taking bold steps to incorporate global concerns and social responsibility in their classrooms (Garfield, 2003; Givner, 2004; Graybill & Shehane, 2006; Sampedro & Hillyard, 2004). At TESOL conferences one can always find a substantial number of presentations on controversial issues. In the TESOL organization, one of the strongest caucuses is Teachers for Social Responsibility. Similar interest groups in other organizations are strengthening teachers' abilities to engage in critical pedagogy. In Japan, a quarterly publication, *Global Issues in Language Education Newsletter,* has a national readership.

Can you, in turn, engage in sensitive critical pedagogy in your classroom? What are some activities you can do that would respect students' points of view yet stir them to a higher consciousness of their own role as agents of change? The little differences here and there that you make can add up to fulfilling visions of a better and more humane world.

MORAL DILEMMAS AND MORAL IMPERATIVES

The process of engaging in a socially responsible approach in which we teachers take up the challenge of being agents for change brings with it some moral dilemmas. How far should we push our own personal beliefs and agendas in our zeal for realizing visions of a better world and for creating critically thinking future leaders among our students? Do you have the right to subversively push your vision of the ideal world out there? At least five moral dilemmas present themselves, but each dilemma carries with it what I claim is a moral imperative. Consider the following dilemmas, and their corollaries in the form of imperatives, that call us to action as socially responsible teachers:

1. Risking the cultural biases of communicative approaches

Our widely accepted communicative approach to language teaching (CLT), which aims to empower and value students, may itself reflect a cultural bias that is not universally embraced. Not all educational traditions value the learner-centered, interactive approaches that could—in the mind of a teacher—usurp the teacher's authority (and power) in the classroom. I believe such a dilemma can be resolved in the following moral imperative:

> Respect the diversity of cultural patterns and expectations among our students, while utilizing the best methodological approaches available to accomplish course goals and objectives.

2. Avoiding contributing to *dis*empowerment

Our altruistic "agendas" for bringing English to the world at large have the potential of legitimizing an unequal division of power and resources. As noted above, the very act of teaching English may have the residual effect of widening the gap between "haves" and "have-nots" by enabling an elite class to distinguish itself from a less powerful group by the ability to use English. Here's a possible moral imperative that may resolve this:

> Help students to claim their own power and resources and to bridge the gaps that separate countries, political structures, religions, and values through a unifying language, but do all we can to celebrate indigenous heritage languages and cultures.

3. Creating inoffensive yet interesting materials

In our curricular materials, our choices of topics and issues present us with opportunities to stimulate critical thinking but also to offend and polarize students. But those materials risk being very bland and uninteresting if everything that has a remote potential of being offensive is deleted. Perhaps some middle ground can be achieved in this moral imperative:

> Sensitively, with due attention to the potential for students to be offended and polarized, approach critical, relevant, and informative issues in appropriate pedagogical contexts with as balanced a perspective as possible, and with the particular cultural sensitivities of your students well in mind.

4. Remaining as neutral as possible

Our discussions, debates, group work activities, essays, and other classroom tasks offer opportunities for us to be agents for change, but does our zeal for realizing our own vision of a better world stand in the way of *genuinely* equal, balanced treatment of all sides of controversial issues? Is it realistic to think that a teacher can completely hide his or her own beliefs on such fundamental issues as racial hatred, nonviolence, gender equality, treatment of those with homosexual orientations, environmental stewardship, or freedom of expression, to name a few? Students have an uncanny ability to "psych out" their teachers, and it's difficult for you to remain staunchly neutral on issues about which you feel very passionately. Perhaps this dilemma can be at least partially resolved in the following imperative:

> Guided by a clear vision of your own mission as a teacher, promote critical thinking on complex issues, remain as neutral as possible in the process, but be fully aware that you are almost certainly promoting a set of values in your classroom, even if somewhat covertly or "subversively."

5. Dealing with assessment standards

Large-scale standardized tests are widely embraced by a budget-conscious establishment, but are they all free of cultural and socioeconomic bias? It was noted in Chapter 24 that critical language testing is another prominent issue in our classrooms today. Perhaps a route to some solutions can be found in the following moral imperative:

> Carry out research to improve the authenticity and predictive validity of standardized testing, lobby for funding for more performance-based assessment, and in our classroom assessments, model principles of authenticity, biased-for-best performance, and beneficial washback to students.

AGENTS FOR CHANGE

I'm sure that all five of the above dilemmas are commonly experienced among teachers around the world. However, if we're too daunted by the dilemmas, we risk becoming passive supporters of a status quo that may be in dire need of change. If we shrink from our responsibility as change agents, surely we will have lost the opportunity to act on the imperatives that can drive us as teachers. We will have lost the chance, in Gandhi's words at the beginning of this chapter, to *be* the change we want to see in the world!

Can you take a bold step forward and at the same time respect the beliefs and attitudes of your students? What are some activities you can do that would respect students' points of view yet stir them to a higher consciousness of their own role as agents of change? How would you respond to statements from students that seem to support hate, violence, or intolerance? The little differences here and there that you make can add up to fulfilling visions of a better and more humane world.

Your role as a socially responsible teacher serves to highlight the fact that you're not merely a *language* teacher. You're much more than that. You're an agent for change in a world in desperate need of change: change from competition to cooperation, from war to peace, from powerlessness to empowerment, from conflict to resolution, from prejudice to understanding.

☆   ☆   ☆   ☆   ☆

What could be more intrinsic to the spirit of all language teachers around the world than to finely tune our ability to become agents for change? Our professional commitment drives us to help the inhabitants of this planet to communicate with each other, to negotiate the meaning of peace, of goodwill, and of survival on this tender, fragile globe. Surely it is our moral imperative, therefore, with all the professional tools available to us, to passionately pursue these ultimate goals!

TOPICS FOR DISCUSSION, ACTION, AND RESEARCH

[Note: (I) Individual work; (G) group or pair work; (C) whole-class discussion]

1. **(I/C)** Have each student write a definition of what he or she now understands to be *critical pedagogy*, in his or her own words, and provide one or two illustrative examples. Students can then share these examples with the class, either in a class hour or on a class Web site.

2. **(C)** Ask students their opinion of Phillipson's claim that English language teaching can lead to what he called *linguicism*. What examples or counterexamples might students have? What are some suggestions for

circumventing the possible outcome that knowledge of English could create a further gap between socioeconomic classes?

3. (G) As a whole class, brainstorm a list of "hot topics" that includes, but goes beyond, the topics mentioned in this chapter. Then, in groups, with one or two topics for each group, students will (a) rate the topic from 1 to 5 on its "heat" for a specified audience in a specified culture, and (b) suggest some tasks or activities that would treat the topic in some way while respecting students' opinions, beliefs, and values.

4. (C) Some have claimed that teachers have no business "meddling" with students' belief systems and traditions by exposing them to controversial moral, ethical, and political topics. Ask your class to explore this side of the critical pedagogy issue and compare it with the position espoused here at the end of the chapter.

5. (C) Three guidelines were offered here for treating controversial issues in the classroom (pages 515-516). To what extent do students in the class agree that these guidelines are useful? Would they add or change any of them?

6. (C) Some have suggested that teachers should never express their personal opinion on a controversial topic, and that they should therefore remain neutral and balanced in equally treating both (or all) sides of a touchy issue. Do you agree with this rule of thumb? If a student in class says something like, "I admire Hitler because he killed many Jews in the Holocaust," would you remain *completely* neutral in your various responses to such a comment? Or might your response(s) ultimately convey your conviction that hateful remarks will not be tolerated in your classroom?

7. (C) Ask students to share some of their own experiences in classroom tasks or activities that treated controversial issues—either in classes where they were learning a language or where they were teaching.

8. (G/C) Ask pairs to do some research to find information on organizations, Internet sources, or print media that promote social responsibility and the treatment of global and/or controversial issues, and then to bring the information back to class or to post their findings on a class Web site.

9. (G) Five "moral dilemmas" were proposed in this chapter. Assign one dilemma to each group and have them discuss (a) the extent of their agreement or disagreement with the dilemma as stated, (b) any additional information they would add to the statement of the dilemma, (c) personal experiences either learning or teaching a language that any have had that illustrate the dilemma, and (d) any cautionary statements they would add to the "moral imperative" that was stated here.

10. (I/C) What is your "vision of a better and more humane life"? Write down your thoughts about teaching for a better world. Share some of those thoughts with the rest of the class.

FOR YOUR FURTHER READING

Canagarajah, A. S. (2005).   Critical pedagogy in L2 learning and teaching.   In E. Hinkel (Ed.), *Handbook of research in second language teaching and learning* (pp. 931–949).   Mahwah, NJ: Lawrence Erlbaum Associates.

Suresh Canagarajah surveys developments, research, and controversies in critical pedagogy in this state-of-the-art article.   An extensive bibliography is included.

Giroux, H. (2006). *America on the edge: Henry Giroux on politics, culture, and education.* New York: Palgrave Macmillan.

McLaren, P. (2005). *Capitalists and conquerors: A critical pedagogy against the empire.* Lanham, MD: Rowman & Littlefield.

Henry Giroux and Peter McLaren are well-known figures in educational fields outside of language teaching, but their commentaries on critical pedagogy are incisive and always challenging.

Norton, B., & Toohey, K. (Eds.).   (2004).   *Critical pedagogies and language learning.* Cambridge, UK: Cambridge University Press.

In this collection of papers, put together by Bonnie Norton and Kelleen Toohey, the editors provide a number of different international perspectives on critical pedagogy in English-language-teaching contexts.

Johnston, B.   (2003).   *Values in English language teaching.*   Mahwah, NJ: Lawrence Erlbaum Associates.

Bill Johnston writes in lucid, readable fashion about a variety of personal and moral issues that arise in the process of language teaching. He shows excellent balance in treating the controversies, and offers suggestions and ideas that classroom teachers can appreciate.

Tollefson, J. (Ed.).   (1995).   *Power and inequality in language education.*   Cambridge, UK: Cambridge University Press.

Among the possible resources on critical pedagogy, this anthology offers quite a number of different perspectives on the sensitive role of education in societies, with a special focus in each chapter on the mingling of power and politics and education. In spite of its date of publication, its contents remain relevant to many of today's current contexts.

Sampedro, R., & Hillyard, S.   (2004).   *Global issues.*   Oxford, UK: Oxford University Press.

This very practically oriented book describes several dozen classroom activities that focus on global issues. Sections of the book are divided into awareness raising, personal experience, major global issues, music and global issues, and drama.

<u>Some useful Web sites for your reference:</u>
- Educators for Social Responsibility:
  http://www.esrnational.org
- Global Issues Newsletter:
  http://www.jalt.org/global/
- Peace Education Foundation:
  http://www.peace-ed.org
- TESOLers for Social Responsibility:
  http://www.tesol.org/mbr/caucuses/tsr.html

BIBLIOGRAPHY

Aebersold, J. A., & Field, M. (1997). *From reader for reading teacher: Issues and strategies for second language classrooms.* Cambridge, UK: Cambridge University Press.

Alatis, J. (Ed.). (1990). *Georgetown University round table on languages and linguistics.* Washington, DC: Georgetown University Press.

Alderson, J. C. (2000). *Assessing reading.* Cambridge, UK: Cambridge University Press.

Alderson, J. C., & Banerjee, J. (2001). Language testing and assessment (Part 1). *Language Teaching, 34,* 213-236.

Alderson, J. C., & Banerjee, J. (2002). Language testing and assessment (Part 2). *Language Teaching, 35,* 79-113.

Allen, H. (1980, April). What it means to be a professional in TESOL. Lecture presented at the conference of TEXTESOL.

Allen, V. (1983). *Techniques in teaching vocabulary.* Oxford, UK: Oxford University Press.

Allwright, R., & Bailey, K. (1991). *Focus on the language classroom: An introduction to classroom research for language teachers.* Cambridge, UK: Cambridge University Press.

American Council on the Teaching of Foreign Languages. (1986). *ACTFL proficiency guidelines.* Hastings-on-Hudson, NY: ACTFL.

American Council on the Teaching of Foreign Languages. (1999). *ACTFL proficiency guidelines—speaking.* Hastings-on-Hudson, NY. Author available online at: www.actfl.org.

Anderson, N. (1999). *Exploring second language reading: Issues and strategies.* Boston: Heinle & Heinle.

Anderson, N. (2003a). L2 learning strategies. In E. Hinkel (Ed.), *Handbook of research in second language teaching and learning* (pp. 757-771). Mahwah, NJ: Lawrence Erlbaum Associates.

Anderson, N. (2003b). Reading. In D. Nunan (Ed.), *Practical English language teaching* (pp. 67-86). New York: McGraw-Hill Contemporary.

Anderson, N. (2004). Metacognitive reading strategy awareness. *CATESL Journal, 16,* 11-27.

Anthony, E. (1963). Approach, method, and technique. *English Language Teaching 17,* 63-67.

Armstrong, T. (1994). *Multiple intelligences in the classroom.* Philadelphia: Association for Curriculum Development.

Arnold, J. (Ed.). (1999). *Affect in language learning.* Cambridge, UK: Cambridge University Press.

Asher, J. (1977). *Learning another language through actions: The complete teacher's guidebook.* Los Gatos, CA: Sky Oaks Productions.

Atkinson, D. (1987). The mother tongue in the classroom: A neglected resource? *ELT Journal, 41,* 292-298.

Atkinson, D. (2003). L2 writing in the post-process era: Introduction. *Journal of Second Language Writing, 12,* 3-15.

Au, S. (1988). A critical appraisal of Gardner's social-psychological theory of second language learning. *Language Learning, 38,* 75-100.

Auerbach, E. (1995). The politics of the ESL classroom: Issues of power in pedagogical choice. In J. Tollefson (Ed.), *Power and inequality in language education* (pp. 9-33). Cambridge, UK: Cambridge University Press.

August, D., Shanahan, T., Christian, D., & Beck, I. (2002). *Developing literacy in second-language learners: A report of the national literacy panel on language minority children and youth.* Washington, DC: Center for Applied Linguistics.

Ausubel, D. (1963). Cognitive structure and the facilitation of meaningful verbal learning. *Journal of Teacher Education, 14,* 217-221.

Ausubel, D. (1968). *Educational psychology: A cognitive view.* New York: Holt, Rinehart & Winston.

Bachman, L. (1988). Problems in examining the validity of the ACTFL oral proficiency interview. *Studies in Second Language Acquisition, 10,* 149-164.

Bachman, L. (1990). *Fundamental considerations in language testing.* New York: Oxford University Press.

Bachman, L. (1991). What does language testing have to offer? *TESOL Quarterly, 25,* 671-704.

Bachman, L. (2005). Building and supporting a case for test use. *Language Assessment Quarterly, 2,* 1-34.

Bachman, L., & Palmer, A. (1996). *Language testing in practice.* New York: Oxford University Press.

Bailey, K. (1985). Classroom-centered research on language teaching and learning. In M. Celce-Murcia, *Beyond basics: Issues and research in TESOL* (pp. 96-121). Rowley, MA: Newbury House.

Bailey, K. (1990). The use of diary studies in teacher education programs. In Richards & Nunan (1990) (pp. 215-226).

Bailey, K. (1998). *Learning about language assessment: Dilemmas, decisions, and directions.* Boston: Heinle & Heinle.

Bailey, K. (2001). Action research, teacher research, and classroom research in language teaching. In M. Celce-Murcia (Ed.), *Teaching English as a second or foreign language* (3rd ed., pp. 489-499). New York: Heinle & Heinle.

Bailey, K. (2003). Speaking. In D. Nunan (Ed.), *Practical English language teaching* (pp. 47-66). New York: McGraw-Hill Contemporary.

Bailey, K. (2005). *Practical English language teaching: Speaking.* New York: McGraw-Hill.

Bailey, K., Curtis, A., & Nunan, D. (2001). *Pursuing professional development: The self as source.* Boston: Heinle & Heinle.

Bailey, K., & Nunan, D. (1996). *Voices from the language classroom: Qualitative research in second language education.* Cambridge, UK: Cambridge University Press.

Bailey, K., & Savage, L. (Eds.). (1994). *New ways of teaching speaking.* Alexandria, VA: Teachers of English to Speakers of Other Languages.

Bamford, J., & Day, R. (1998). Teaching reading. *Annual Review of Applied Linguistics, 18,* 124–141.

Bardovi-Harlig, K., & Hartford, B. (1997). *Beyond methods: Components of second language teacher education.* New York: McGraw-Hill.

Barnett, M. (1989). *More than meets the eye: Foreign language reading theory in practice.* Englewood Cliffs, NJ: Prentice-Hall.

Bassano, S., & Christison, M. A. (1984). Teacher self-observation. *TESOL Newsletter, 18,* 17–19.

Bax, S. (2003). CALL—Past, present, and future. *System, 31,* 13–28.

Beatty, K. (2003). Computer-assisted language learning. In D. Nunan (Ed.), *Practical English language teaching* (pp. 247–266). New York: McGraw-Hill Contemporary.

Bell, D. (2003). Method and postmethod: Are they really so incompatible? *TESOL Quarterly, 37,* 325–336.

Bell, J., & Burnaby, B. (1984). *A handbook for ESL literacy.* Agincourt, Ontario: Dominie Press.

Benesch, S. (2001). *Critical English for academic purposes.* Mahwah, NJ: Lawrence Erlbaum Associates.

Benson, P. (2001). *Teaching and researching autonomy in language learning.* London: Longman.

Benson, P. (2003). Learner autonomy in the classroom. In D. Nunan (Ed.), *Practical English language teaching* (pp. 289–308). New York: McGraw-Hill Contemporary.

Blackwell, A., & Naber, T. (2006). *Open forum: Academic listening and speaking.* New York: Oxford University Press.

Blake, R. (1998). The role of technology in second language learning. In H. Byrnes (Ed.), *Learning foreign and second languages: Perspectives in research and scholarship.* New York: Modern Language Association.

Bloom, B. (1956). *Taxonomy of educational objectives: Cognitive domain.* New York: David McKay.

Boone, E., Bennett, J., & Motai, L. (1988). *Basics in reading: An introduction to American magazines.* San Francisco: Lateral Communications.

Borg, S. (2003a). Pulp fiction? The research journal and professional development. In T. Murphey (Ed.), *Extending professional contributions* (pp. 39–46). Alexandria, VA: Teachers of English to Speakers of Other Languages.

Borg, S. (2003b). Teacher cognition in language teaching: A review of research on what language teachers think, know, believe, and do. *Language Teaching, 36,* 81–109.

Boswood, T. (1997). *New ways of using computers in language teaching.* Alexandria, VA: Teachers of English to Speakers of Other Languages.

Bowen, J. D. (1972). Contextualizing pronunciation practice in the ESOL classroom. *TESOL Quarterly, 6,* 83–94.

Bowen, J. D., Madsen, H., & Hilferty, A. (1985). *TESOL techniques and procedures.* Rowley, MA: Newbury House.

Braine, G. (1999). *Nonnative educators in English language teaching.* Mahwah, NJ: Lawrence Erlbaum Associates.

Breen, M. (1987). Learner contributions to task design. In C. Candlin & D. Murphy (Eds.), *Language learning tasks* (pp. 23–46). Englewood Cliffs, NJ: Prentice-Hall.

Breen, M., & Candlin, C. (1980). The essentials of a communicative curriculum in language teaching. *Applied Linguistics, 1,* 89–112.

Brinton, D. (2003). Content-based instruction. In D. Nunan (Ed.), *Practical English language teaching* (pp. 199–224). New York: McGraw-Hill Contemporary.

Brinton, D., & Master, P. (1997). *New ways in content-based instruction.* Alexandria, VA: Teachers of English to Speakers of Other Languages.

Brinton, D., & Neuman, R. (1982). *Getting along.* Book 2. Englewood Cliffs, NJ: Prentice-Hall.

Brinton, D., Snow, M.A., & Wesche, M. (1989). *Content-based second language instruction.* Rowley, MA: Newbury House.

Brock, C. (1986). The effects of referential questions on ESL classroom discourse. *TESOL Quarterly, 20,* 47–59.

Brophy, J. (1981). Teacher praise: A functional analysis. *Review of Educational Research, 51,* 5–32.

Brown, G., & Yule, G. (1983). *Teaching the spoken language.* Cambridge, UK: Cambridge University Press.

Brown, H.D. (1970). Categories of spelling difficulty in speakers of English as a first and second language. *Journal of Verbal Learning and Verbal Behavior, 9,* 232–236.

Brown, H.D. (1972). Cognitive pruning and second language acquisition. *Modern Language Journal, 56,* 218–222.

Brown, H. D. (1989). *A practical guide to language learning.* New York: McGraw-Hill.

Brown, H. D. (1991a). *Breaking the language barrier.* Yarmouth, ME: Intercultural Press.

Brown, H.D. (1991b). TESOL at twenty-five: What are the issues? *TESOL Quarterly, 25,* 245–260.

Brown, H. D. (1992). *Vistas: An interactive course in English.* Books 1–4. Englewood Cliffs, NJ: Prentice-Hall Regents.

Brown, H.D. (1993). After method: Toward a principled strategic approach to language teaching. In J. Alatis (Ed.), *Proceedings of the Georgetown University round table on languages and linguistics* (pp. 509–520). Washington, DC: Georgetown University Press.

Brown, H. D. (1999). *New Vistas: An interactive course in English. Getting started,* Books 1 and 2. Upper Saddle River, NJ: Prentice Hall Regents.

Brown, H.D. (2000a). *New Vistas: An interactive course in English.* Book 3. White Plains, NY: Pearson Education.

Brown, H. D. (2000b). *Principles of language learning and teaching* (4th ed.). White Plains, NY: Pearson Education.

Brown, H. D. (2001). *New Vistas: An interactive course in English.* Book 4. White Plains, NY: Pearson Education.

Brown, H. D. (2002a). English language teaching in the "post-methods" era: Towards better diagnosis, treatment, and assessment. In J. Richards & W. Renandya (Eds.), *Methodology in language teaching* (pp. 9–18). Cambridge, UK: Cambridge University Press.

Brown, H. D. (2002b). *Strategies for success: A practical guide to learning English.* White Plains, NY: Pearson Education.

Brown, H. D. (2004). *Language assessment: Principles and classroom practices.* White Plains, NY: Pearson Education.

Brown, H. D. (2007). *Principles of language learning and teaching* (5th ed.). White Plains, NY: Pearson Education.

Brown, H. D., Albarelli-Siegfried, A., Savage, A., & Shafiei, M. (2000). *New vistas.* Books 1–4. White Plains, NY: Pearson Education.

Brown, H. D., Cohen, D., & O'Day, J. (1991). *Challenges: A process approach to academic English.* Englewood Cliffs, NJ: Prentice-Hall Regents.

Brown, J. D. (1991). Do English faculties rate writing samples differently? *TESOL Quarterly, 25,* 587–603.

Brown, J. D. (1992). Classroom-centered language testing. *TESOL Journal, 1,* 12–15.

Brown, J. D. (1995). *The elements of language curriculum: A systematic approach to program development.* Boston: Heinle & Heinle.

Brown, J. D. (2005). *Testing in language programs: A comprehensive guide to English language assessment.* New York: McGraw-Hill.

Brown, J. D., & Hudson, T. (1998). The alternatives in language assessment. *TESOL Quarterly, 32,* 653–675.

Brown, R. (1991). Group work, task difference, and second language acquisition. *Applied Linguistics, 12,* 1–12.

Bruner, J. (1962). *On knowing: Essays for the left hand.* Cambridge, MA: Harvard University Press.

Buck, G. (2001). *Assessing listening.* Cambridge, UK: Cambridge University Press.

Burns, A. (1999). *Collaborative action research for English language teachers.* Cambridge, UK: Cambridge University Press.

Burns, A. (2005). Action research. In E. Hinkel (Ed.), *Handbook of research in second language teaching and learning* (pp. 241–256). Mahwah, NJ: Lawrence Erlbaum Associates.

Bygate, M., Skehan, P., & Swain, M. (Eds.). (2001). *Researching pedagogic tasks: Second language learning, teaching, and testing.* London: Longman.

Byrd, P., & Nelson, G. (2003). *Sustaining professionalism.* Alexandria, VA: Teachers of English to Speakers of Other Languages.

Byrnes, H. (Ed.). (1998). *Learning foreign and second languages: Perspectives in research and scholarship.* New York: Modern Language Association.

Cameron, L. (2003). Challenges for ELT from the expansion in teaching children. *ELT Journal, 57,* 105–112.

Campbell, R. (1978). Notional-functional syllabuses 1978: Part I. In C. H. Blatchford and J. Schachter (Eds.), *On TESOL 78: EFL policies, programs, practices* (pp. 15–19). Washington, DC: Teachers of English to Speakers of Other Languages.

Canagarajah, A. S. (2005). Critical pedagogy in L2 learning and teaching. In E. Hinkel (Ed.), *Handbook of research in second language teaching and learning* (pp. 931–949). Mahwah, NJ: Lawrence Erlbaum Associates.

Canale, M., & Swain, M. (1980). Theoretical bases of communicative approaches to second language teaching and testing. *Applied Linguistics, 1,* 1–47.

Carrell, P., & Eisterhold, J. (1983). Schema theory and ESL reading pedagogy. *TESOL Quarterly, 17,* 553–573.

Carroll, J. (1966). The contributions of psychological theory and educational research to the teaching of foreign languages. In A. Valdman (Ed.), *Trends in language teaching* (pp. 93–106). New York: McGraw-Hill.

Carroll, J., & Sapon, S. (1958). *Modern language aptitude test.* New York: Psychological Corporation.

Casanave, C. (2003). Looking ahead to more socio-politically oriented case study research in L2 writing scholarship (but should it be called "post-process"?). *Journal of Second Language Writing, 12,* 85–102.

Casanave, C. (2004). *Controversies in second language writing.* Ann Arbor: University of Michigan Press.

Cazden, C., & Snow, C. (1990). *English plus: Issues in bilingual education* (Annals of the American Academy of Political and Social Science No. 508). Newbury Park, CA: Sage Publications.

Celce-Murcia, M. (Ed.). (1985). *Beyond basics: Issues and research in TESOL.* Rowley, MA: Newbury House.

Celce-Murcia, M. (1991a). Grammar pedagogy in second and foreign language teaching. *TESOL Quarterly, 25,* 459–480.

Celce-Murcia, M. (Ed.). (1991b). *Teaching English as a second or foreign language* (2nd ed.). New York: Newbury House.

Celce-Murcia, M., Brinton, D., & Goodwin, J. (1996). *Teaching pronunciation: A reference for teachers of English to speakers of other languages.* Cambridge, UK: Cambridge University Press.

Celce-Murcia, M., Dörnyei, Z., & Thurrell, S. (1997). Direct approaches in L2 instruction: A turning point in communicative language teaching? *TESOL Quarterly, 31,* 141–152.

Celce-Murcia, M., & Goodwin, J. (1991). Teaching pronunciation. In M. Celce-Murcia, *Teaching English as a second or foreign language* (2nd ed., pp. 136–153). New York: Newbury House.

Celce-Murcia, M., & Hilles, S. (1988). *Techniques and resources in teaching grammar.* Oxford, UK: Oxford University Press.

Chambers, F. (1997). What do we mean by fluency? *System, 25,* 535–544.

Chamot, A. (2005). Language learning strategy instruction: Current issues and research. *Annual Review of Applied Linguistics, 25,* 112–130.

Chamot, A., & McKeon, D. (1984). *Second language teaching.* Rosslyn, VA: National Clearinghouse for Bilingual Education.

Chamot, A., O'Malley, M., & Kupper, L. (1992). *Building bridges: Content and learning strategies for ESL.* Books 1–3. New York: Heinle & Heinle.

Chapelle, C. (2005). Computer-assisted language learning. In E. Hinkel (Ed.), *Handbook of research in second language teaching and learning* (pp. 743–755). Mahwah, NJ: Lawrence Erlbaum Associates.

Chen, K. (2005). Preferences, styles, behavior: The composing processes of four ESL students. *CATESOL Journal, 17,* 19–37.

Christenbury, L., & Kelly, P. (1983). *Questioning: A path to critical thinking.* Urbana, IL: National Council of Teachers of English.

Christison, M. A. (2003). Learning styles and strategies. In D. Nunan (Ed.), *Practical English language teaching* (pp. 267–288). New York: McGraw-Hill Contemporary.

Christison, M. A. (2005). *Multiple intelligences and language learning.* San Francisco: Alta Book Center Publishers.

Christison, M. A., & Bassano, S. (1984, August). Teacher self-observation. *TESOL Newsletter,* pp. 17–19.

Claire, E. (1988). *ESL teacher's activities kit.* Englewood Cliffs, NJ: Prentice-Hall.

Clark, H., & Clark, E. (1977). *Psychology and language: An introduction to psycholinguistics.* New York: Harcourt Brace Jovanovich.

Clark, J. L. D. (1983). Language testing: Past and current status—directions for the future. *Modern Language Journal, 67,* 431–443.

Clark, J. L. D., & Clifford, R. T. (1988). The FSI/ILR/ACTFL proficiency scales and testing techniques. *Studies in Second Language Acquisition, 10,* 129–147.

Clarke, M. (1990). Some cautionary observations on liberation education. *Language Arts, 67,* 388–398.

Clarke, M. (1994). The dysfunctions of the theory/practice discourse. *TESOL Quarterly, 28,* 9–26.

Clarke, M. (2003). *A place to stand: Essays for educators in troubled times.* Ann Arbor: University of Michigan Press.

Clarke, M., & Silberstein, S. (1977). Toward a realization of psycholinguistic principles for the ESL reading class. *Language Learning, 27,* 135–154.

Coady, J., & Huckin, T. (1997). *Second language vocabulary acquisition: A rationale for pedagogy.* Cambridge, UK: Cambridge University Press.

Coffey, M. (1983). *Fitting in: A functional/notional text for learners of English.* Englewood Cliffs, NJ: Prentice-Hall.

Cohen, A. (1990). *Language learning: Insights for learners, teachers, and researchers.* Rowley, MA: Newbury House.

Cohen, A. (1998). *Strategies in learning and using a second language.* White Plains, NY: Addison-Wesley Longman.

Coleman, A. (1929). *The teaching of modern foreign languages in the United States: A report prepared for the modern language study.* New York: Macmillan.

Connor, U. (1996). *Contrastive rhetoric: Cross-cultural aspects of second language writing.* Cambridge, UK: Cambridge University Press.

Connor, U. (2002). New directions in contrastive rhetoric. *TESOL Quarterly, 36,* 493–510.

Conrad, S. (2005). Corpus linguistics and L2 teaching. In E. Hinkel (Ed.), *Handbook of research in second language teaching and learning* (pp. 393–409). Mahwah, NJ: Lawrence Erlbaum Associates.

Constantino, P., & De Lorenzo, M. (2002). *Developing a professional teaching portfolio.* Boston: Allyn & Bacon.

Cook, V. (1969). The analogy between first and second language learning. *International Review of Applied Linguistics, 7,* 207–216.

Covey, S. (1990). *The seven habits of highly effective people: Powerful lessons in personal change.* New York: Simon & Schuster.

Crandall, J. (1999). Cooperative language learning and affective factors. In J. Arnold (Ed.), *Affect in language learning* (pp. 226–245). Cambridge, UK: Cambridge University Press.

Crookes, G., & Chaudron, C. (1991). Guidelines for classroom language teaching. In M. Celce-Murcia, *Teaching English as a second or foreign language* (2nd ed., pp. 46–66). New York: Newbury House.

Crookes, G., & Schmidt, R. (1991). Motivation: Reopening the research agenda. *Language Learning, 41,* 469–512.

Cross, D. (1991). *A practical handbook of language teaching.* Englewood Cliffs, NJ: Prentice-Hall (Cassell).

Cunningsworth, A. (1995). *Choosing your coursebook.* Oxford, UK: Heinemann.

Curran, C. (1972). *Counseling-learning: A whole person model for education.* New York: Grune & Stratton.

Cziko, G. (1982). Improving the psychometric, criterion-referenced, and practical qualities of integrative language tests. *TESOL Quarterly, 16,* 367–379.

Davidson, F., Hudson, T., & Lynch, B. (1985). Language testing: Operationalization in classroom measurement and L2 research. In M. Celce-Murcia, *Beyond basics: Issues and research in TESOL* (pp. 137–152). Rowley, MA: Newbury House.

Day, R. (Ed.). (1993). *New ways in teaching reading.* Alexandria, VA: Teachers of English to Speakers of Other Languages.

Day, R., & Bamford, J. (1998). *Extensive reading in the second language classroom.* Cambridge, UK: Cambridge University Press.

DeCapua, A., & Wintergerst, A. (2004). *Crossing cultures in the language classroom.* Ann Arbor: University of Michigan Press.

Deci, E. (1975). *Intrinsic motivation.* New York: Plenum Press.

Dervin, F. (2006). Podcasting demystified. *Language Magazine, 5,* 26–29.

Derwing, T., & Munro, M. (2005). Second language accent and pronunciation teaching: A research-based approach. *TESOL Quarterly, 39,* 379–397.

de Szendeffy, J. (2005). *A practical guide to using computers in language teaching.* Ann Arbor: University of Michigan Press.

Devine, J., & Eskey, D. (2004). Literacy as sociocultural practice: Comparing Chinese and Korean readers. *CATESOL Journal, 16,* 81–96.

Dewaele, J.-M. (2004). Slaying the dragon on fanaticism through enlightenment. *Modern Language Journal, 88,* 620–622.

DiPietro, R. (1987). *Strategic interaction: Learning languages through scenarios.* New York: Cambridge University Press.

Doff, A. (1988). *Teach English: A training course for teachers. Teacher's handbook.* Cambridge, UK: Cambridge University Press.

Dole, J., Brown, K., & Trathen, K. (1996). The effects of strategy instruction on the comprehension performance of at-risk students. *Reading Research Quarterly, 31,* 62-88.

Dörnyei, Z. (2001). *Motivational strategies in the language classroom.* Cambridge, UK: Cambridge University Press.

Dörnyei, Z. (2005). *The psychology of the language learner: Individual differences in second language acquisition.* Mahwah, NJ: Lawrence Erlbaum Associates.

Dörnyei, Z., & Csizér, K. (1998). Ten commandments for motivating language learners: Results of an empirical study. *Language Teaching Research, 2,* 203-229.

Dörnyei, Z., & Murphey, T. (2003). *Group dynamics in the language classroom.* Cambridge, UK: Cambridge University Press.

Dörnyei, Z., & Skehan, P. (2003). Individual differences in L2 learning. In C. Doughty & M. Long (Eds.), *The handbook of second language acquisition* (pp. 589-630). Malden, MA: Blackwell Publishing.

Doughty, C. (1991). Second language instruction does make a difference: Evidence from an empirical study of SL relativization. *Studies in Second Language Acquisition, 10,* 245-261.

Doughty, C. (2003). Instructed SLA: Constraints, compensation, and enhancement. In C. J. Doughty & M. H. Long (Eds.), *The handbook of second language acquisition* (pp. 256-310). Malden, MA: Blackwell Publishing.

Doughty, C., & Long, M. (Eds.). (2003). *The handbook of second language acquisition.* Malden, MA: Blackwell Publishing.

Doughty, C., & Pica, T. (1986). 'Information gap' tasks: Do they facilitate second language acquisition? *TESOL Quarterly, 20,* 305-325.

Doughty, C., & Williams, J. (1998). *Focus on form in classroom second language acquisition.* New York: Cambridge University Press.

Douglas, D. (2005). Testing languages for specific purposes. In E. Hinkel (Ed.), *Handbook of research in second language teaching and learning* (pp. 857-868). Mahwah, NJ: Lawrence Erlbaum Associates.

Dunkel, P. (1991). Listening in the native and second/foreign language: Toward an integration of research and practice. *TESOL Quarterly, 25,* 431-457.

Edelsky, C. (1993). Whole language in perspective. *TESOL Quarterly, 27,* 548-550.

Edge, J. (1996). Cross-cultural paradoxes in a profession of values. *TESOL Quarterly, 30,* 9-30.

Edge, J. (Ed.). (2001). *Action research.* Alexandria, VA: Teachers of English to Speakers of Other Languages.

Edge, J. (2003). Imperial troopers and servants of the Lord: A vision of TESOL for the 21st century. *TESOL Quarterly, 37,* 701-709.

Edge, J. (2006, March). *Daring not to evaluate.* Paper presented at TESOL, Tampa, FL.

Edgeworth, F. Y. (1888). The statistics of examinations. *Journal of the Royal Statistical Society, 51,* 599-635.

Egbert, J. (2005). *CALL essentials: Principles and practice in CALL classrooms.* Alexandria, VA: TESOL.

Egbert, J. (Ed.). (2003). *Becoming contributing professionals.* Alexandria, VA: Teachers of English to Speakers of Other Languages.

Ehrman, M. (1990). The role of personality type in adult language learning: An ongoing investigation. In T. Parry & C. Stansfield (Eds.), *Language aptitude reconsidered* (pp. 126–178). New York: Prentice-Hall Regents.

Ehrman, M., & Dörnyei, Z. (1998). *Interpersonal dynamics in second language education: The visible and invisible classroom.* Thousand Oaks, CA: Sage Communications.

Eisenstein, M. (1980). Grammatical explanations in ESL: Teach the student, not the method. *TESL Talk, 11,* 3–11.

Elbow, P. (1973). *Writing Without teachers.* New York: Oxford University Press.

Elley, W. (2001). Literacy in the present world: Realities and possibilities. In L. Verhoeven & C. Snow (Eds.), *Literacy and motivation: Reading engagement in individuals and groups* (pp. 225–242). Mahwah, NJ: Lawrence Erlbaum Associates.

Ellis, G., & Sinclair, B. (1989). *Learning to learn English: A course in learner training.* Cambridge, UK: Cambridge University Press.

Ellis, R. (1997). *SLA research and language teaching.* Oxford, UK: Oxford University Press.

Ellis, R. (2001). Investigating form-focused instruction. *Language Learning, 51* (Suppl. 1), 1–46.

Ellis, R. (2003). *Task-based language teaching and learning.* Oxford, UK: Oxford University Press.

Ellis, R. (2005). Instructed language learning and task-based teaching. In E. Hinkel (Ed.), *Handbook of research in second language teaching and learning* (pp. 713–728). Mahwah, NJ: Lawrence Erlbaum Associates.

Ellis, R. (2006). Current issues in the teaching of grammar: An SLA perspective. *TESOL Quarterly, 40,* 83–107.

Enright, D. (1991). Supporting children's English language development in grade-level and language classrooms. In M. Celce-Murcia (Ed.), *Teaching English as a second or foreign language* (2nd ed., pp. 386–401). New York: Newbury House.

Epstein, J. (1983, December). Intonation. *CATESOL News,* p. 7.

Eskey, D. (2005). Reading in a second language. In E. Hinkel (Ed.), *Handbook of research in second language teaching and learning* (pp. 563–579). Mahwah, NJ: Lawrence Erlbaum Associates.

Eyring, J. (1991). Experiential language learning. In M. Celce-Murcia (Ed.), *Teaching English as a second or foreign language* (2nd ed., pp. 346–359). New York: Newbury House.

Faltis, C. (Ed.). (1995). Alternative assessment. *TESOL Journal, 5.*

Faltis, C., & Hudelson, S. (1994). Learning English as an additional language in K–12 schools. *TESOL Quarterly, 28,* 457–468.

Fantini, A. (1997). *New ways in teaching culture.* Alexandria, VA: Teachers of English to Speakers of Other Languages.

Farhady, H. (1982). Measures of language proficiency from the learner's perspective. *TESOL Quarterly, 16,* 43–59.

Farrell, T. (2002). Lesson planning. In J. Richards & W. Renandya (Eds.), *Methodology in language teaching: An anthology of current practice* (pp. 30–39). Cambridge, UK: Cambridge University Press.

Ferris, D. (1997). The influence of teacher commentary on student revision. *TESOL Quarterly, 31,* 315–339.

Ferris, D., & Hedgcock, J. (2005). *Teaching ESL composition: Purpose, process, and practice* (2nd ed.). Mahwah, NJ: Lawrence Erlbaum Associates.

Field, J. (2005). Intelligibility and the listener: The role of lexical stress. *TESOL Quarterly, 39,* 399–423.

Finocchiaro, M., & Brumfit, C. (1983). *The functional-notional approach: From theory to practice.* New York: Oxford University Press.

Fitzgerald, J. (1994). How literacy emerges: Foreign language implications. *Language Learning Journal, 9,* 32–35.

Flanders, N. (1970). *Analyzing teaching behavior.* Reading, MA: Addison-Wesley.

Flowerdew, J. (Ed.). (1994). *Academic listening: Research perspectives.* Cambridge, UK: Cambridge University Press.

Flowerdew, J., & Miller, L. (2005). *Second language listening: Theory and practice.* Cambridge, UK: Cambridge University Press.

Fotos, S. (1994). Integrating grammar instruction and communicative language use through grammar consciousness-raising tasks. *TESOL Quarterly, 28,* 323–351.

Fotos, S., & Ellis, R. (1991). Communicating about grammar: A task-based approach. *TESOL Quarterly, 25,* 605–628.

Freeman, D. (1998). *Doing teacher research: From inquiry to understanding.* Boston: Heinle & Heinle.

Freeman, D. (2002). The hidden side of the work: Teacher knowledge and learning to teach. *Language Teaching, 35,* 1–13.

Freire, P. (1970). *Pedagogy of the oppressed.* New York: Seabury Press.

Fries, C. (1945). *Teaching and learning English as a foreign language.* Ann Arbor: University of Michigan Press.

Gadd, N. (1998). Point and counterpoint: Towards less humanistic English teaching. *English Language Teaching Journal, 52,* 223–234. [Reply by Jane Arnold, and reply to the reply by Gadd, ibid.]

Gardner, H. (1983). *Frames of mind: The theory of multiple intelligences.* New York: Basic Books.

Gardner, H. (1999). *Intelligence reframed: Multiple intelligences for the 21st century.* New York: Basic Books.

Gardner, H. (2004). *Frames of mind: The theory of multiple intelligences* (2nd ed.). New York: Basic Books.

Gardner, R. (1985). *Social psychology and second language learning.* London: E. Arnold.

Gardner, R., & Lambert, W. (1972). *Attitudes and motivation in second language learning.* Rowley, MA: Newbury House.

Gardner, R., & MacIntyre, P. (1991). An instrumental motivation in language study: Who says it isn't effective? *Studies in Second Language Acquisition, 13,* 57–72.

Gardner, R., & MacIntyre, P. (1993). On the measurement of affective variables in second language learning. *Language Learning, 43,* 157–194.

Gardner, R., & Tremblay, P. (1994). On motivation, research agendas, and theoretical frameworks. *Modern Language Journal, 78,* 359–368.

Garfield, M. (2004, December). *Students' attitudes toward controversial social issues in the ESL classroom*. Paper presented at the MATESOL conference, San Francisco State University, San Francisco.

Garvie, E. (1990). *Story as vehicle: Teaching English to young children*. Clevedon, UK: Multilingual Matters.

Gattegno, C. (1972). *Teaching foreign languages in schools: The silent way* (2nd ed.). New York: Educational Solutions.

Gebhard, J. (2006). *Teaching English as a second or foreign language: A self-development and methodology guide* (2nd ed.) Ann Arbor: University of Michigan Press.

Genesee, F., & Upshur, J. (1996). *Classroom-based evaluation in second language education*. Cambridge, UK: Cambridge University Press.

Gibbons, J. (1985). The silent period: An examination. *Language Learning, 35,* 255–267.

Gilbert, J. (1978). Gadgets: Nonverbal tools for teaching pronunciation. *CATESOL Occasional Papers, 4,* 68–78.

Giroux, H. (2006). *America on the edge: Henry Giroux on politics, culture, and education*. New York: Palgrave Macmillan.

Giroux, H., & McLaren, P. (1989). *Critical pedagogy, the state, and cultural struggle*. Albany: State University of New York Press.

Givner, K. (2004, May). *The use of socially controversial topics in the academic ESL classroom*. Paper presented at the MATESOL conference, San Francisco State University, San Francisco.

Golebiowska, A. (1990). *Getting students to talk: A resource book for teachers*. Englewood Cliffs, NJ: Prentice-Hall Regents.

Goleman, D. (1995). *Emotional intelligence*. New York: Bantam Books.

Goodman, K. (1970). Reading: A psycholinguistic guessing game. In H. Singer & R. B. Ruddell (Eds.), *Theoretical models and processes of reading* (pp. 497–508). Newark, DE: International Reading Association.

Gouin, F. 1880. *L'art d'enseigner et d'étudier les langues*. Paris: Librairie Fischbacher. Translation by H. Swan & V. Bétis (1892), *The art of teaching and studying languages*. London: Philip.

Gower, R., & Walters, S. (1983). *Teaching practice handbook: A reference book for EFL teachers in training*. New York: Heinemann.

Grabe, W. (1991). Current developments in second language reading research. *TESOL Quarterly, 25,* 375–406.

Grabe, W. (Ed.). (1998). *Annual Review of Applied Linguistics*. New York: Cambridge University Press.

Grabe, W. (2004). Research on teaching reading. *Annual Review of Applied Linguistics, 24,* 44–69.

Graves, K. (1996). *Teachers as course developers*. Cambridge, UK: Cambridge University Press.

Graves, K. (2000). *Designing language courses: A guide for teachers*. Cambridge, UK: Cambridge University Press.

Graybill, R., & Shehane, M. (2006, May). *Using global topics in the ESL classroom*. Paper presented at the MATESOL conference, San Francisco State University, San Francisco.

Green, J., & Oxford, R. (1995). A closer look at learning strategies, L2 proficiency, and gender. *TESOL Quarterly, 29,* 261-297.

Hanson-Smith, E. (1997). *Technology in the classroom: Practice and promise in the 21st Century.* Alexandria, VA: Teachers of English to Speakers of Other Languages.

Harmer, J. (2001). *The practice of English language teaching* (3rd ed.). Harlow, UK: Pearson Education Limited.

Haverson, W., & Haynes, J. (1982). *Literacy training for ESL adult learners.* Englewood Cliffs, NJ: Prentice-Hall.

Hedgcock, J. (2002). Toward a socioliterate approach to second language teacher education. *Modern Language Journal, 86,* 299-317.

Hedgcock, J. (2005). Taking stock of research and pedagogy in L2 writing. In E. Hinkel (Ed.), *Handbook of research in second language teaching and learning* (pp. 597-613). Mahwah, NJ: Lawrence Erlbaum Associates.

Hedge, T. (2005). *Writing.* Oxford, UK: Oxford University Press.

Helgesen, M., & Brown, S. (2007). *Practical English language teaching: Listening.* New York: McGraw-Hill.

Hendrick, J., & Butler, M. (1992). *Interaction activities in ESL* (2nd ed.). Ann Arbor: University of Michigan Press.

Hendrickson, J. (1980). Error correction in foreign language teaching: Recent theory, research, and practice. In K. Croft (Ed.), *Readings on English as a second language* (2nd ed., pp. 153-173). Cambridge, MA: Winthrop.

Higgins, C. (2003). "Ownership" of English in the outer circle: An alternative to the NS-NNS dichotomy. *TESOL Quarterly, 37,* 615-644.

Higgs, T., & Clifford, R. (1982). The push toward communication. In T. Higgs (Ed.), *Curriculum, competence, and the foreign language teacher* (pp. 57-79). Lincolnwood, IL: National Textbook Company.

Hinkel, E. (Ed.). (2005). *Handbook of research in second language teaching and learning.* Mahwah, NJ: Lawrence Erlbaum Associates.

Hinkel, E. (2006). Current perspectives on teaching the four skills. *TESOL Quarterly, 40,* 109-131.

Hockman, B., Lee-Fong, K., & Lew, E. (1991, March). Earth saving language. Workshop presented at the convention of Teachers of English to Speakers of Other Languages (TESOL), New York.

Hofstede, G. (1986). Cultural differences in teaching and learning. *International Journal of Intercultural Relations, 10,* 301-320.

Holliday, A. (1994). *Appropriate methodology and social context.* Cambridge, UK: Cambridge University Press.

Howatt, A. (1984). *A history of English language teaching.* Oxford, UK: Oxford University Press.

Hsiao, T.-Y., & Oxford, R. (2002). Comparing theories of language learning strategies: A confirmatory factor analysis. *Modern Language Journal, 86,* 368-383.

Hughes, A. (2003). *Testing for language teachers* (2nd ed.). Cambridge, UK: Cambridge University Press.

Hughes, R. (2002). *Teaching and researching speaking.* London: Pearson Education.

Hulstijn, J. (2001). Intentional and incidental second language vocabulary learning: A reappraisal of elaboration, rehearsal and automaticity. In P. Robinson (Ed.), *Cognition and second language acquisition instruction* (pp. 258–286). Cambridge, UK: Cambridge University Press.

Hunston, S., & Francis, G. (2000). *Pattern grammar: A corpus-driven approach to the lexical grammar of English.* Amsterdam: John Benjamins.

Hunt, J. (1971). Toward a history of intrinsic motivation. In H. Day, D. Berlyne, & D. Hunt (Eds.), *Intrinsic motivation: A new direction in education.* New York: Holt, Rinehart & Winston of Canada.

Igarashi, M. (2004, May). *Using electronic visual feedback to teach pronunciation.* Paper presented at the conference of the MATESOL program, San Francisco State University, San Francisco.

Jacobs, G., & Farrell, T. (2003). Understanding and implementing the communicative language teaching paradigm. *RELC Journal, 34,* 5–30.

Jamieson, J. (2005). Trends in computer-based second language assessment. *Annual Review of Applied Linguistics, 25,* 228–242.

Jensen, L. (2001). Planning lessons. In M. Celce-Murcia (Ed.), *Teaching English as a second or foreign language* (3rd ed., pp. 403–413). Boston: Heinle & Heinle.

Jerald, M., & Clark, R. (1989). *Experiential language teaching techniques.* Brattleboro, VT: Pro Lingua Associates.

Johnson, K. (1999). *Understanding language teaching: Reasoning in action.* New York: Heinle & Heinle.

Johnson, K. (2003). *Designing language teaching tasks.* New York: Palgrave Macmillan.

Johnson, K. (2006). The sociocultural turn and its challenges for second language teacher education. *TESOL Quarterly, 40,* 235–257.

Johnston, B. (2003). *Values in English language teaching.* Mahwah, NJ: Lawrence Erlbaum Associates.

Judd, E. (1987). Teaching English to speakers of other languages: A political act and a moral question. *TESOL Newsletter, 21,* 15–16.

Kachru, B. (1988). Standards, codification, and sociolinguistic realism: The English language in the outer circle. In R. Quirk & H. Widdowson (Eds.), *English in the world: Teaching and learning the language and literatures* (pp. 11–30). Cambridge, UK: Cambridge University Press.

Kachru, B. (1992). World Englishes: Approaches, issues, and resources. *Language Teaching, 25,* 1–14.

Kachru, Y. (2005). Teaching and learning of world Englishes. In E. Hinkel (Ed.), *Handbook of research in second language teaching and learning* (pp. 149–173). Mahwah, NJ: Lawrence Erlbaum Associates.

Kamhi-Stein, L. (2000). Looking to the future of TESOL teacher education: Web-based bulletin board discussions in a methods course. *TESOL Quarterly, 34,* 423–455.

Kamhi-Stein, L. (Ed.). (2004). *Learning and teaching from experience: Perspectives on nonnative English speaking professionals.* Ann Arbor: University of Michigan Press.

Kaplan, R. (1966). Cultural thought patterns in intercultural education. *Language Learning, 16,* 1–20.

Kaplan, R. (2005). Contrastive rhetoric. In E. Hinkel (Ed.), *Handbook of research in second language teaching and learning* (pp. 375-391). Mahwah, NJ: Lawrence Erlbaum Associates.

Keeton, M., & Tate, P. (Eds.). (1978). *New directions for experiential learning.* Columbia, MD: Council for the Advancement of Experiential Learning.

Keirsey, D., & Bates, M. (1984). *Please understand me: Character and temperament types.* Del Mar, CA: Prometheus Nemesis Book Company.

Kelly, L. (1969). *Twenty-five centuries of language teaching.* Rowley, MA: Newbury House Publishers.

Kenning, M.-M. (1990). Computer assisted language learning. *Language Teaching, 23,* 67-76.

Kenworthy, J. (1987). *Teaching English pronunciation.* London: Longman.

Kern, R. (2006). Perspectives on technology in learning and teaching languages. *TESOL Quarterly, 40,* 183-210.

Kinsella, K. (1991, September). Promoting active learning and classroom interaction through effective questioning strategies. Workshop presented at San Francisco State University, San Francisco.

Kinsella, K. (1994). Developing communities of reflective ESL teacher-scholars through peer coaching. *CATESOL Journal, 7,* 31-49.

Kinsella, K. (1995). Understanding and empowering diverse learners in the ESL classroom. In J. Reid (Ed.), *Learning styles in the ESL/EFL classroom* (pp. 170-195). Boston: Heinle & Heinle.

Klippel, F. (1984). *Keep talking: Communicative fluency activities for language teaching.* Cambridge, UK: Cambridge University Press.

Kohn, A. (1990, June 21). Rewards hamper creativity. *San Francisco Chronicle,* pp. B3-B4.

Kohn, A. (2000). *The case against standardized testing.* Westport, CT: Heinemann.

Kohonen, V. (1999). Authentic assessment in affective foreign language education. In J. Arnold (Ed.), *Affect in language learning* (pp. 279-294). Cambridge, UK: Cambridge University Press.

Kramsch, C. (2006). From communicative competence to symbolic competence. *Modern Language Journal, 90,* 249-252.

Krashen, S. (1982). *Principles and practice in second language acquisition.* Oxford, UK: Pergamon Press.

Krashen, S. (1985). *The input hypothesis.* London: Longman.

Krashen, S. (1986). Bilingual education and second language acquisition theory. In California State Department of Education, *Schooling and language: Minority students: A theoretical framework* (pp. 51-79). Sacramento: California State Department of Education.

Krashen, S. (1993). *The power of reading.* Englewood, CO: Libraries Unlimited.

Krashen, S. (1997). *Foreign language education: The easy way.* Culver City, CA: Language Education Associates.

Krashen, S., & Terrell, T. (1983). *The natural approach: Language acquisition in the classroom.* Oxford, UK: Pergamon Press.

Kroll, B. (Ed.). (1990). *Second language writing: Research insights for the classroom*. New York: Cambridge University Press.

Kruse, A. (1987). Vocabulary in context. In M. Long & J. Richards (Eds.), *Methodology in TESOL: A book of readings*. (pp. 312–317). New York: Newbury House.

Kuhn, M., & Stahl, S. (2003). Fluency: A review of development and remedial practices. *Journal of Educational Psychology, 95,* 3–21.

Kumaravadivelu, B. (1994). The postmethod condition: Emerging strategies for second/foreign language teaching. *TESOL Quarterly, 28,* 27–48.

Kumaravadivelu, B. (1995). The author responds . . . [a response to Liu]. *TESOL Quarterly, 29,* 177–180.

Kumaravadivelu, B. (2001). Toward a postmethod pedagogy. *TESOL Quarterly, 35,* 537–560.

Kumaravadivelu, B. (2006a). TESOL methods: Changing tracks, challenging trends. *TESOL Quarterly, 40,* 59–81.

Kumaravadivelu, B. (2006b). *Understanding language teaching: From method to postmethod.* Mahwah, NJ: Lawrence Erlbaum Associates.

Kunnan, A. (2005). Language assessment from a wider context. In E. Hinkel (Ed.), *Handbook of research in second language teaching and learning* (pp. 779–794). Mahwah, NJ: Lawrence Erlbaum Associates.

Kupetz, M. (2003). Having dessert first: Writing book reviews. In J. Egbert (Ed.), *Becoming contributing professionals* (pp. 25–31). Alexandria, VA: Teachers of English to Speakers of Other Languages.

Ladousse, G. (1987). *Role play*. Oxford, UK: Oxford University Press.

Lamendella, J. (1969). On the irrelevance of transformational grammar to second language pedagogy. *Language Learning, 19,* 255–270.

Langi, U. (1984). The natural approach: Approach, design, and procedure. *TESL Reporter, 17,* 11–18.

Larsen-Freeman, D. (1986). *Techniques and principles in language teaching*. New York: Oxford University Press.

Larsen-Freeman, D. (1991). Teaching grammar. In M. Celce-Murcia (Ed.), *Teaching English as a second or foreign language* (2nd ed., pp. 279–296). New York: Newbury House.

Larsen-Freeman, D. (2000). *Techniques and principles in language teaching* (2nd ed.). Oxford, UK: Oxford University Press.

Larsen-Freeman, D. (2003). *Teaching language: From grammar to grammaring*. Boston: Heinle & Heinle.

Larsen-Freeman, D., & Long, M. (1991). *An introduction to second language acquisition research*. London: Longman.

Larson, D., & Smalley, W. (1972). *Becoming bilingual: A guide to language learning*. New Canaan, CT: Practical Anthropology.

Lawrence, G. (1984). *People types and tiger stripes: A practical guide to learning styles*. Gainesville, FL: Center for Applications of Psychological Type.

Lee, J., & VanPatten, B. (2003). *Making communicative language teaching happen* (2nd ed.). New York: McGraw-Hill.

Legutke, M., & Thomas, H. (1991). *Process and experience in the language classroom*. London: Longman.

Leki, I. (1991). Twenty-five years of contrastive rhetoric: Text analysis and writing pedagogies. *TESOL Quarterly, 25,* 123-143.

Lenneberg, E. (1967). *The biological foundations of language.* New York: J. Wiley & Sons.

Leung, C. (2005). Classroom teacher assessment of second language development: Construct as practice. In E. Hinkel (Ed.), *Handbook of research in second language teaching and learning* (pp. 869-888). Mahwah, NJ: Lawrence Erlbaum Associates.

Leung, C., & Lewkowicz, J. (2006). Expanding horizons and unresolved conundrums: Language testing and assessment. *TESOL Quarterly, 40,* 211-234.

Levis, J. (2005). Changing contexts and shifting paradigms in pronunciation teaching. *TESOL Quarterly, 39,* 369-377.

Lewis, Marilyn (Ed.). (1997). *New ways in teaching adults.* Alexandria, VA: Teachers of English to Speakers of Other Languages.

Lewis, Michael (1993). *The lexical approach.* Hove, UK: Language Teaching Publications.

Lewis, M. (1997). *Implementing the lexical approach: Putting theory into practice.* Hove, UK: Language Teaching Publications.

Lewis, M. (2000). *Teaching collocation: Further developments in the lexical approach.* London: Language Teaching Publications.

Lewis, M. (2002). Classroom management. In J. Richards & W. Renandya (Eds.), *Methodology in language teaching: An anthology of current practice* (pp. 40-48). Cambridge, UK: Cambridge University Press.

Linse, C. (2005). *Practical English language teaching: Young learners.* New York: McGraw-Hill.

Littlewood, W. (1981). *Communicative language teaching: An introduction.* Cambridge, UK: Cambridge University Press.

Littlewood, W. (1992). *Teaching oral communication: A methodological framework.* Oxford, UK: Basil Blackwell.

Liu, D. (1995). Comments on B. Kumaravadivelu's "The postmethod condition: Emerging strategies for second/foreign language teaching." *TESOL Quarterly, 29,* 174-177.

LoCastro, V. (2001). Large classes and student learning. *TESOL Quarterly, 35,* 493-496.

Long, M. (1977). Teacher feedback on learner error: Mapping cognitions. In H. D. Brown, C. Yorio, & R. Crymes (Eds.), *Teaching and learning English as a second language: Trends in research and practice* (pp. 278-294). Washington, DC: Teachers of English to Speakers of Other Languages.

Long, M. (1983). Does second language instruction make a difference? A review of research. *TESOL Quarterly, 17,* 359-382.

Long, M. (1985). Input and second language acquisition theory. In S. Gass & C. Madden (Eds.), *Input in second language acquisition* (pp. 377-393). Rowley, MA: Newbury House.

Long, M. (1988). Instructed interlanguage development. In L. M. Beebe (Ed.), *Issues in second language acquisition: Multiple perspectives* (pp. 115-141). New York: Newbury House.

Long, M. (1996). The role of the linguistic environment in second language acquisition. In W. C. Ritchie & T. K. Bhatia (Eds.), *Handbook of second language acquisition* (pp. 413-468). San Diego: Academic Press.

Long, M., & Crookes, G. (1992). Three approaches to task-based syllabus design. *TESOL Quarterly, 26,* 27–56.

Long, M., & Porter, P. (1985). Group work, interlanguage talk, and second language acquisition. *TESOL Quarterly, 19,* 207–228.

Long, M., & Richards, J. (Eds.). (1987). *Methodology in TESOL: A book of readings.* New York: Newbury House.

Long, M., & Sato, C. (1983). Classroom foreigner talk discourse: Forms and functions of teacher questions. In H. W. Seliger & M. H. Long (Eds.), *Classroom oriented research in second language acquisition* (pp. 268–285). Rowley, MA: Newbury House.

Lowe, P., & Stansfield, C. (Eds.). (1988). *Second language proficiency assessment: Current issues.* Englewood Cliffs, NJ: Prentice-Hall Regents.

Lozanov, G. (1979). *Suggestology and outlines of suggestopedy.* New York: Gordon and Breach Science Publishers.

Lund, R. (1990). A taxonomy for teaching second language listening. *Foreign Language Annals, 23,* 105–115.

Lynch, P., & Horton, S. (2002). *Web style guide: Basic design principles for creating web sites* (2nd ed.). New Haven: Yale University Press.

Macedo, D., Dendrinos, B., & Gounari, P. (2003). *The hegemony of English.* Boulder, CO: Paradigm.

MacIntyre, P., Baker, S., Clément, R., & Conrod, S. (2001). Willingness to communicate, social support, and language-learning orientations of immersion students. *Studies in Second Language Acquisition, 23,* 369–388.

MacIntyre, P., Clément, R., Dörnyei, Z., & Noels, K. (1998). Conceptualizing willingness to communicate in a L2: A situational model of L2 confidence. *Modern Language Journal, 82,* 545–562.

Madsen, H. (1983). *Techniques in testing.* New York: Oxford University Press.

Mann, S. (2005). The language teacher's development. *Language Teaching, 38,* 103–118.

Marckwardt, A. (1972). Changing winds and shifting sands. *MST English Quarterly, 21,* 3–11.

Marshall, T. (1989). *The whole world guide to language learning.* Yarmouth, ME: Intercultural Press.

Maslow, A. (1970). *Motivation and personality* (2nd ed.). New York: Harper & Row.

Matsuda, P. (1997). Contrastive rhetoric in context: A dynamic model of L2 writing. *Journal of Second Language Writing, 6,* 45–60.

Matsuda, P. (2003). Process and post-process: A discursive history. *Journal of Second Language Writing, 12,* 65–83.

Matsumoto, D. (2000). *Culture and psychology: People around the world.* Belmont, CA: Wadsworth.

McArthur, T. (2001). World English and world Englishes: Trends, tensions, varieties, and standards. *Language Teaching, 34,* 1–20.

McCarthy, M. (2004). *Touchstone: From corpus to course book.* Cambridge, UK: Cambridge University Press.

McCarthy, M., & O'Keefe, A. (2004). Research in the teaching of speaking. *Annual Review of Applied Linguistics, 24,* 26–43.

McDonald, M. (1989). Oral dialogue journals: Spoken language in a communicative context. *TESL Reporter, 22,* 27–31.

McDonough, J., & McDonough, S, (1997). *Research methods for English language teachers.* New York: St. Martin's Press.

McDonough, K. (2004). Learner-learner interaction during pair and small group activities in a Thai EFL context. *System, 32,* 207–224.

McDonough, K. (2006). Action research and the professional development of graduate teaching assistants. *Modern Language Journal, 90,* 33–47.

McKay, R. (1987). Teaching the information-gathering skills. In M. Long & J. Richards (Eds.), *Methodology in TESOL: A book of readings* (pp. 248–256). New York: Newbury House.

McKay, S. (1985). *Teaching grammar: Form, function, and technique.* New York: Pergamon Press.

McKay, S. (2002). *Teaching English as an international language: Rethinking goals and approaches.* Oxford, UK: Oxford University Press.

McKay, S. (2006). *Researching second language classrooms.* Mahwah, NJ: Lawrence Erlbaum Associates.

McLaren, P. (2005). *Capitalists and conquerors: A critical pedagogy against the empire.* Lanham, MD: Rowman & Littlefield.

McLaughlin, B. (1987). *Theories of second language learning.* London: E. Arnold.

McLaughlin, B. (1990). "Conscious" versus "unconscious" learning. *TESOL Quarterly, 24,* 617–634.

McLaughlin, B., Rossman, T., & McLeod, B. (1983). Second language learning: An information-processing perspective. *Language Learning, 33,* 135–158.

Medgyes, P. (1994). *Non-natives in ELT.* London: Macmillan.

Meek, A. (1991, March). On thinking about teaching: A conversation with Eleanor Duckworth. *Educational Leadership,* p. 34.

Mendelsohn, D. (1998). Teaching listening. *Annual Review of Applied Linguistics, 18,* 81–101.

Mendelsohn, D., & Rubin, J. (Eds.). (1995). *A guide for the teaching of second language listening.* San Diego: Dominie Press.

Mitchell, R., & Myles, F. (1998). *Second language learning theories.* New York: Oxford University Press.

Mitchell, R., & Myles, F. (2004). *Second language learning theories* (2nd ed.). London: Hodder Arnold.

Miyagi, T. (2006, May). *Technology-enhanced collaborative projects and Internet-based instruction.* Paper presented at the conference of the MATESOL program, San Francisco State University, San Francisco.

Moon, J. (2000). *Children learning English.* Oxford, UK: Macmillan Education.

Morley, J. (1991a). Listening comprehension in second/foreign language instruction. In M. Celce-Murcia (Ed.), *Teaching English as a second or foreign language* (2nd ed., pp. 81–106). New York: Newbury House.

Morley, J. (1991b). The pronunciation component in teaching English to speakers of other languages. *TESOL Quarterly, 25,* 481–520.

Moskowitz, G. (1971). Interaction analysis: A new modern language for supervisors. *Foreign Language Annals, 5,* 211–221.

Moskowitz, G. (1976). The classroom interaction of outstanding foreign language teachers. *Foreign Language Annals, 9,* 125–157.

Mueller, M. (1987). Interactive testing: Time to be a test pilot. In W. M. Rivers (Ed.), *Interactive language teaching.* New York: Cambridge University Press.

Mullock, B. (2006). The pedagogical knowledge base of four TESOL teachers. *Modern Language Journal, 90,* 48–66.

Murphey, T. (1995). Tests: Learning through negotiated interaction. *TESOL Journal, 4,* 2–16.

Murphey, T. (Ed.). (2003). *Extending professional contributions.* Alexandria, VA: Teachers of English to Speakers of Other Languages.

Murphey, T., Connolly, M., Churchill, E., McLaughlin, J., Schwartz, S., & Krajka, J. (2005). Creating publishing communities. In T. Murphey (Ed.), *Extending professional contributions* (pp. 105–118). Alexandria, VA: Teachers of English to Speakers of Other Languages.

Murphey, T., & Sato, K. (2005). *Communities of supportive professionals.* Alexandria, VA: Teachers of English to Speakers of Other Languages.

Murphy, J. & Byrd, P. (Eds.). (2001). *Understanding the courses we teach: Local perspectives on English language teaching.* Ann Arbor: University of Michigan Press.

Murphy, J., & Stoller, F. (2001). Sustained content language teaching: An emerging definition. *TESOL Journal, 10,* 3–5.

Murray, D. (2006, March). TESOL's most daring ideas. Paper presented at Teachers of English to Speakers of Other Languages, Tampa, FL.

Nakatani, Y. (2005). The effects of awareness-raising training on oral communication strategy use. *Modern Language Journal, 89,* 76–91.

Nassaji, H. (2002). Schema theory and knowledge-based processes in second language reading comprehension: A need for alternative perspectives. *Language Learning, 52,* 439–481.

Nassaji, H., & Fotos, S. (2004). Current developments in research on the teaching of grammar. *Annual Review of Applied Linguistics, 24,* 126–145.

Nation, I. S. P. (2001). *Learning vocabulary in another language.* Cambridge, UK: Cambridge University Press.

Nation, I. S. P. (2003). Vocabulary. In D. Nunan (Ed.), *Practical English language teaching* (pp. 129–152). New York: McGraw-Hill Contemporary.

Nation, I. S. P. (2005). Teaching and learning vocabulary. In E. Hinkel (Ed.), *Handbook of research in second language teaching and learning* (pp. 581–595). Mahwah, NJ: Lawrence Erlbaum Associates.

Nation, P. (Ed.). (1994). *New ways in teaching vocabulary.* Alexandria, VA: Teachers of English to Speakers of Other Languages.

Nation, P., & Newton, J. (1997). Teaching vocabulary. In J. Coady & T. Huckin (Eds.), *Second language vocabulary acquisition: A rationale for pedagogy* (pp. 238–254). Cambridge, UK: Cambridge University Press.

Nayar, P. (1997). ESL/EFL dichotomy today: Language politics or pragmatics? *TESOL Quarterly, 31,* 9–37.

Nilsen, D., & Nilsen, A. (1971). *Pronunciation contrasts in English.* New York: Regents/Simon & Schuster.

Nolasco, R., & Arthur, L. (1987). *Conversation.* Oxford, UK: Oxford University Press.

Norton, B., & Toohey, K. (Eds.). (2004). *Critical pedagogies and language learning.* Cambridge, UK: Cambridge University Press.

Nunan, D. (1988). *The learner-centered curriculum.* Cambridge, UK: Cambridge University Press.

Nunan, D. (1989a). *Designing tasks for the communicative classroom.* Cambridge, UK: Cambridge University Press.

Nunan, D. (1989b). *Understanding language classrooms: A guide for teacher-initiated action.* Englewood Cliffs, Prentice-Hall.

Nunan, D. (1991a). Communicative tasks and the language curriculum. *TESOL Quarterly, 25,* 279–295.

Nunan, D. (1991b). *Language teaching methodology: A textbook for teachers.* New York: Prentice-Hall.

Nunan, D. (Ed.). (2003). *Practical English language teaching.* New York: McGraw-Hill Contemporary.

Nunan, D. (2004). *Task-based language teaching.* Cambridge, UK: Cambridge University Press.

Nunan, D. (2005). *Practical English language teaching: Grammar.* New York: McGraw-Hill.

Nunan, D. (2006, March). TESOL's most daring ideas. Paper presented at Teachers of English to Speakers of Other Languages, Tampa, FL.

Nunan, D., & Miller, L. (Eds.). (1995). *New ways in teaching listening.* Alexandria, VA: Teachers of English to Speakers of Other Languages.

Nuttall, C. (1996). *Teaching reading skills in a foreign language* (2nd ed.). Oxford, UK: Heinemann.

O'Brien, T. (2004). Writing in a foreign language: Teaching and learning. *Language Teaching, 37,* 1–28.

Oller, J. (1979). *Language tests at school: A pragmatic approach.* London: Longman.

Oller, J. (1983a). Story writing principles and ESL teaching. *TESOL Quarterly, 17,* 39–53.

Oller, J. (Ed.). (1983b). *Issues in language testing research.* Rowley, MA: Newbury House.

Omaggio, A. (1981). *Helping learners succeed: Activities for the foreign language classroom.* Washington, DC: Center for Applied Linguistics.

Omaggio-Hadley, A. (1993). *Teaching language in context* (2nd ed.). Boston: Heinle & Heinle.

O'Malley, J. M., & Valdez-Pierce, L. (1996). *Authentic assessment for English language learners: Practical approaches for teachers.* White Plains, NY: Addison-Wesley.

Ostrander, S., & Schroeder, L. (1979). *Superlearning.* New York: Dell Publishing.

Oxford, R. (1990). *Language learning strategies: What every teacher should know.* New York: Newbury House.

Oxford, R. (1997). Cooperative learning, collaborative learning, & interaction: Three communicative strands in the language classroom. *Modern Language Journal, 81,* 443–456.

Oxford, R., Tomlinson, S., Barcelos, A., Harrington, C., Lavine, R., Saleh, A., et al. (1998). Clashing metaphors about classroom teachers: Toward a systematic typology for the language teaching field. *System, 26,* 3–50.

Paltridge, B. (2004). Academic writing. *Language Teaching, 37,* 87–105.

Park, Y. (2006). Will nonnative-English-speaking teachers ever get a fair chance? *Essential Teacher, 3,* 32–34.

Parks, S., & Raymond, P. (2004). Strategy use by nonnative-English speaking students in an MBA program: Not business as usual! *Modern Language Journal, 88,* 374–389.

Paulston, C., & Bruder, M. (1976). *Teaching English as a second language: Techniques and procedures.* Cambridge, MA: Winthrop.

Pennington, M. (1990). A professional development focus for the language teaching practicum. In J. Richards & D. Nunan (1990) (Eds.), *Second language teacher education* (pp. 132–152). New York: Cambridge University Press.

Pennington, M., & Richards, J. (1986). Pronunciation revisited. *TESOL Quarterly, 20,* 207–225.

Pennycook, A. (1989). The concept of method, interested knowledge, & the politics of language teaching. *TESOL Quarterly, 23,* 589–618.

Pennycook, A. (1994). *The cultural politics of English as an international language.* Harlow, UK: Longman.

Pennycook, A. (Ed.). (1999). Critical approaches to TESOL. *TESOL Quarterly, 33,* 3.

Pennycook, A. (2001). *Critical applied linguistics: A critical introduction.* Mahwah, NJ: Lawrence Erlbaum Associates.

Peterson, P. (1991). A synthesis for interactive listening. In M. Celce-Murcia (Ed.), *Teaching English as a second or foreign language* (2nd ed., pp. 106–122). New York: Newbury House.

Phillips, S. (1993). *Young learners.* Oxford, UK: Oxford University Press.

Phillipson, R. (1992). *Linguistic imperialism.* Oxford, UK: Oxford University Press.

Phillipson, R., & Skutnabb-Kangas, T. (1996). English only worldwide or language ecology? *TESOL Quarterly, 30,* 429–452.

Piaget, J. (1972). *The principles of genetic epistemology.* New York: Basic Books.

Pimsleur, P. (1966). *Pimsleur language aptitude battery.* New York: Harcourt, Brace & World.

Pinter, A. (2006). *Teaching young language learners.* Oxford, UK: Oxford University Press.

Postman, N., & Weingartner, C. (1969). *Teaching as a subversive activity.* New York: Dell Publishing Company.

Prabhu, N. (1990). There is no best method—why? *TESOL Quarterly, 24,* 161–176.

Prator, C., & Celce-Murcia, M. (1979). An outline of language teaching approaches. In M. Celce-Murcia & L. McIntosh (Ed.), *Teaching English as a second or foreign language* (pp. 3–5). New York: Newbury House.

Purgason, K. (1991). Planning lessons and units. In M. Celce-Murcia (Ed.), *Teaching English as a second or foreign language* (2nd ed., pp. 419–431). New York: Newbury House.

Raffini, J. (1996). *150 ways to increase intrinsic motivation in the classroom*. Needham Heights, MA: Allyn & Bacon.

Raimes, A. (1991). Out of the woods: Emerging traditions in the teaching of writing. *TESOL Quarterly, 25,* 407–430.

Raimes, A. (1998). Teaching writing. *Annual Review of Applied Linguistics, 18,* 142–167.

Read, J. (2000). *Assessing vocabulary*. Cambridge, UK: Cambridge University Press.

Read, J. (2004). Research in teaching vocabulary. *Annual Review of Applied Linguistics, 24,* 146–161.

Reid, J. (1993). *Teaching ESL writing*. Englewood Cliffs, NJ: Prentice Hall Regents.

Reid, J. (1994). Responding to students' texts: The myths of appropriation. *TESOL Quarterly, 28,* 273–292.

Reilly, V., & Ward, S. (1997). *Very young learners*. Oxford, UK: Oxford University Press.

Ricento, T., & Hornberger, N. (1996). Unpeeling the onion: Language planning and policy. *TESOL Quarterly, 30,* 401–427.

Richard-Amato, P. (1996). *Making it happen: Interaction in the second language classroom, from theory to practice* (2nd ed.). White Plains, NY: Addison-Wesley.

Richard-Amato, P. (2003). *Making it happen: From interactive to participatory language teaching*. White Plains, NY: Pearson Education.

Richards, J. (1983). Listening comprehension: Approach, design, procedure. *TESOL Quarterly, 17,* 219–239.

Richards, J. (1990). *The language teaching matrix. Cambridge*, UK: Cambridge University Press.

Richards, J. (Ed.). (1993–99). *New ways in TESOL series*. Arlington, VA: Teachers of English to Speakers of Other Languages.

Richards, J. (Ed.). (1998). *Teaching in action: Case studies from second language classrooms*. Alexandria, VA: Teachers of English to Speakers of Other Languages.

Richards, J. (2001). *Curriculum development in language teaching*. Cambridge, UK: Cambridge University Press.

Richards, J. (2002). Theories of teaching in language teaching. In J. Richards & W. Renandya (Eds.), *Methodology in language teaching: An anthology of current practice* (pp. 19–25). Cambridge, UK: Cambridge University Press.

Richards, J., & Farrell, T. (2005). *Professional development for language teachers: Strategies for teacher learning*. Cambridge, UK: Cambridge University Press.

Richards, J., & Nunan, D. (Eds.). (1990). *Second language teacher education*. New York: Cambridge University Press.

Richards, J., & Renandya, W. (Eds.). (2002). *Methodology in language teaching: An anthology of current practice*. Cambridge, UK: Cambridge University Press.

Richards, J., & Rodgers, T. (1982). Method: Approach, design, & procedure. *TESOL Quarterly, 16,* 153–168.

Richards, J., & Rodgers, T. (1986). *Approaches and methods in language teaching.* Cambridge, UK: Cambridge University Press.

Richards, J., & Rodgers, T. (2001). *Approaches and methods in language teaching* (2nd ed.). Cambridge, UK: Cambridge University Press.

Rigg, P. (1991). Whole language in TESOL. *TESOL Quarterly, 25,* 521–542.

Rigg, P., & Enright, D. S. (1982). *Children and ESL: Integrating perspectives.* Washington, DC: Teachers of English to Speakers of Other Languages.

Riley, P. (1988). The ethnography of autonomy. In A. Brookes & P. Grundy (Eds.), *Individualisation and autonomy in language learning* (pp. 12–34). London: British Council.

Ritchie, W., & Bhatia, T. (Eds.). (1996). *Handbook of second language acquisition.* San Diego: Academic Press.

Rivers, W. (1964). *The psychologist and the foreign language teacher.* Chicago: University of Chicago Press.

Rivers, W. (Ed.). (1987). *Interactive language teaching.* New York: Cambridge University Press.

Rivers, W., & Temperley, M. (1978). *A practical guide to the teaching of English as a second or foreign language.* New York: Oxford University Press.

Rixon, S. (1992). English and other languages for younger children: Practice and theory in a rapidly changing world. *Language Teaching, 25,* 73–93.

Robinett, B. (1978). *Teaching English to speakers of other languages: Substance and technique.* Minneapolis: University of Minnesota Press.

Robinson, P. (2005). Aptitude and second language acquisition. *Annual Review of Applied Linguistics, 25,* 46–73.

Rogers, C. (1983). *Freedom to learn for the eighties.* Columbus, OH: C. E. M.

Rost, M. (1991). *Listening in action: Activities for developing listening in language teaching.* Englewood Cliffs, NJ: Prentice-Hall.

Rost, M. (2001). *Teaching and researching listening.* London: Longman.

Rost, M. (2002). *Worldview.* Level 1. White Plains, NY: Pearson Education.

Rost, M. (2005). L2 listening. In E. Hinkel (Ed.), *Handbook of research in second language teaching and learning* (pp. 503–527). Mahwah, NJ: Lawrence Erlbaum Associates.

Rubin, J. (1994). A review of second language listening comprehension research. *Modern Language Journal, 78,* 199–221.

Rubin, J., & Thompson, I. (1994). *How to be a more successful language learner* (2nd ed.). Boston: Heinle & Heinle.

Rumelhart, D. (1977). Toward an interactive model of reading. In S. Dornic (Ed.), *Attention and performance IV* (pp. 722–750). New York: Academic Press.

Sage, H. (1987). *Incorporating literature in ESL instruction.* Englewood Cliffs, NJ: Prentice-Hall.

Sampedro, R., & Hillyard, S. (2004). *Global issues.* Oxford, UK: Oxford University Press.

Sarosy, P., & Sherak, K. (2006). *Lecture ready: Strategies for academic listening, note-taking, and discussion.* New York: Oxford University Press.

Sarwar, Z. (2001). Innovations in large classes in Pakistan. *TESOL Quarterly, 35,* 497–500.

Saslow, J., & Ascher, A. (2006). *Top notch.* Book 2. White Plains, NY: Pearson Education.

Savignon, S. (1982). Dictation as a measure of communicative competence in French as a second language. *Language Learning, 32,* 33–51.

Savignon, S. (1983). *Communicative competence: Theory and classroom practice.* Reading, MA: Addison-Wesley.

Savignon, S. (1991). Communicative language teaching: State of the art. *TESOL Quarterly, 25,* 261–277.

Savignon, S. (2005). Communicative language teaching: Strategies and goals. In E. Hinkel (Ed.), *Handbook of research in second language teaching and learning* (pp. 635–651). Mahwah, NJ: Lawrence Erlbaum Associates.

Savignon, S., & Berns, M. (Eds.). (1984). *Initiatives in communicative language teaching: A book of readings.* Reading, MA: Addison-Wesley.

Schiffler, L. (1992). *Suggestopedic methods and applications.* Philadelphia: Gordon and Breach Science Publishers.

Schinke-Llano, L., & Rauff, R. (Eds.). (1996). *New ways in teaching young children.* Alexandria, VA: Teachers of English to Speakers of Other Languages.

Schleppegrell, M., & Colombi, M. (Eds.). (2002). *Developing advanced literacy in first and second languages: Meaning with power.* Mahwah, NJ: Lawrence Erlbaum Associates.

Schmenk, B. (2005). Globalizing learner autonomy. *TESOL Quarterly, 39,* 107–118.

Scollon, R. (2004). Teaching language and culture as hegemonic practice. *Modern Language Journal, 88,* 271–274.

Scott, W., & Ytreberg, L. (1990). *Teaching English to children.* London: Longman.

Scovel, T. (1979). Review of suggestology and outlines of suggestopedy by Georgi Lozanov. *TESOL Quarterly, 13,* 255–266.

Scovel, T. (2001). *Learning new languages: A guide to second language acquisition.* Boston: Heinle & Heinle.

Setter, J., & Jenkins, J. (2005). Pronunciation. *Language Teaching, 38,* 1–17.

Seymour, S. (2003). Sabbatical projects can make a difference: A tale of curriculum revision. Creating a teaching portfolio. In P. Byrd & G. Nelson (Eds.), *Sustaining professionalism* (pp. 89–96). Alexandria, VA: Teachers of English to Speakers of Other Languages.

Shih, M. (1986). Content-based approaches to teaching academic writing. *TESOL Quarterly 20:* 617–648.

Shoemaker, C. & Shoemaker, F. (1991). *Interactive techniques for the ESL classroom.* New York: Newbury House.

Shohamy, E. (1992). *An introduction to language testing.* Oxford, UK: Oxford University Press.

Shohamy, E. (1997, March). Critical language testing and beyond. Paper presented at the American Association of Applied Linguistics, Orlando, FL.

Shohamy, E. (2001). *The power of tests: A critical perspective on the use of language tests.* Harlow, UK: Pearson Education.

Short, D. (Ed.). (1998). *New ways in teaching English at the secondary level.* Alexandria, VA: Teachers of English to Speakers of Other Languages.

Showers, B. (1985).Teachers coaching teachers. *Educational Leadership, 42,* 43-49.

Silberstein, S., Dobson, B., & Clarke, M. (2002). *Reader's choice* (4th ed.). Ann Arbor: University of Michigan Press.

Silva, T. (1993). Towards an understanding of the distinct nature of L2 writing: The ESL research and its implications. *TESOL Quarterly, 27,* 657-677.

Silva, T., & Brice, C. (2004). Research in teaching writing. *Annual Review of Applied Linguistics, 24,* 70-106.

Silva, T., & Leki, I. (2004). Family matters: The influence of applied linguistics and composition studies on second language writing studies—past, present, and future. *Modern Language Journal, 88,* 1-13.

Singleton, D. (1997). Learning and processing L2 vocabulary. *Language Teaching, 30,* 213-225.

Skehan, P. (1998a). *A cognitive approach to language learning.* Oxford, UK: Oxford University Press.

Skehan, P. (1998b). Task-based instruction. In W. Grabe (Ed.), *Annual review of applied linguistics (1998)* (pp. 268-286). New York: Cambridge University Press.

Skehan, P., & Foster, P. (1997). Task type and task processing conditions as influences on foreign language performance. *Language Teaching Research, 1,* 185-211.

Skehan, P., & Foster, P. (1999). The influence of task structure and processing conditions on narrative retellings. *Language Learning, 49,* 93-120.

Skierso, A. (1991). Textbook selection and adaptation. In M. Celce-Murcia (Ed.), *Teaching English as a second or foreign language* (2nd ed., pp. 432-453). New York: Newbury House.

Skutnabb-Kangas, T., & Phillipson, R. (Eds.). (1994). *Linguistic human rights: Overcoming linguistic determination.* Berlin: Mouton de Gruyter.

Smith, S. (1984). *The theater arts and the teaching of second languages.* Reading, MA: Addison-Wesley.

Snow, D. (2001). *English teaching as Christian mission.* Scottdale, PA: Herald Press.

Snow, M. A. (1998). Trends and issues in content-based instruction. In W. Grabe (Ed.), *Annual review of applied linguistics (1998)* (pp. 243-267). New York: Cambridge University Press.

Snow, M. A., & Brinton, D. (Eds.). (1997). *The content-based classroom: Perspectives on integrating language and content.* New York: Longman.

Sokolik, M. (2003). Writing. In D. Nunan (Ed.), *Practical English language teaching* (pp. 87-108). New York: McGraw-Hill Contemporary.

Spada, N., & Fröhlich, M. (1995). *Communicative orientation of language teaching observation schemes.* Sydney: National Centre for English Teaching and Research, Macquarie University.

Spolsky, B. (1989). *Conditions for second language learning.* Oxford, UK: Oxford University Press.

Spolsky, B. (1997). The ethics of gatekeeping tests: What have we learned in a hundred years? *Language Testing, 14,* 242-247.

Stern, H. H. (1983). *Fundamental concepts of language teaching.* Oxford, UK: Oxford University Press.

Sternberg, R. (1988). *The triarchic mind: A new theory of human intelligence*. New York: Viking Press.

Sternberg, R. (1997). *Successful intelligence: How practical and creative intelligence determine success in life.* New York: Plume.

Stevick, E. (1989). *Success with foreign languages: Seven who achieved it and what worked for them.* New York: Prentice-Hall.

Stoller, F. (2004). Content-based instruction: Perspectives on curriculum planning. *Annual review of applied linguistics, 24,* 261-283.

Swain, M. (1984). Large-scale communicative language testing. In S. Savignon & M. Berns (Eds.), *Initiatives in communicative language teaching: A book of readings* (pp. 185-201). Reading, MA: Addison-Wesley.

Swain, M. (1990). The language of French immersion students: Implications for theory and practice. In J. Alatis (Ed.), *Georgetown University round table on languages and linguistics* (pp. 401-412). Washington, DC: Georgetown University Press.

Tanner, R. (2003). Outside in, inside out: Creating a teaching portfolio. In P. Byrd & G. Nelson (Eds.), *Sustaining professionalism* (pp. 19-25). Alexandria, VA: Teachers of English to Speakers of Other Languages.

Tarone, E. (2005). Speaking in a second language. In E. Hinkel (Ed.), *Handbook of research in second language teaching and learning* (pp. 485-502). Mahwah, NJ: Lawrence Erlbaum Associates.

Taylor, L. (1990). *Teaching and learning vocabulary*. Englewood Cliffs, NJ: Prentice-Hall.

Terrell, T. (1991). The role of grammar instruction in a communicative approach. *Modern Language Journal, 75,* 52-63.

Tollefson, J. (Ed.). (1995). *Power and inequality in language education*. Cambridge, UK: Cambridge University Press.

Underhill, N. (1987). *Testing spoken language: A handbook of oral testing techniques.* Cambridge, UK: Cambridge University Press.

Underwood, M. (1991). *Effective class management*. London: Longman.

Ur, P. (1984). *Teaching listening comprehension*. Cambridge, UK: Cambridge University Press.

Ur, P. (1988). *Grammar practice activities: A practical guide for teachers*. Cambridge, UK: Cambridge University Press.

Ur, P. (1996). *A course in language teaching.* Cambridge, UK: Cambridge University Press.

Valdman, A. (Ed.). (1966). *Trends in language teaching*. New York: McGraw-Hill.

Valdman, A. (Ed.). (1988). The assessment of foreign language oral proficiency. *Studies in Second Language Acquisition,* Special Issue Number 10.

Van Allen, R., & Allen, C. (1967). *Language experience activities*. Boston: Houghton Mifflin.

Vandergrift, L. (2003). Orchestrating strategy use: Toward a model of the skilled second language listener. *Language Learning, 53,* 463-496.

Vandergrift, L. (2004). Listening to learn or learning to listen? *Annual Review of Applied Linguistics, 24,* 3-25.

Vandergrift, L. (2006). Second language listening: Listening ability or language proficiency? *Modern Language Journal, 90,* 6-18.

Van Ek, J., & Alexander, L. (1975). *Threshold level English.* Oxford, UK: Pergamon Press.

Vanett, L., & Jurich, D. (1985, April). The missing link: Connecting journal writing to academic writing. Paper presented at the conference of CATESOL.

Ventriglia, L. (1982). *Conversations with Miguel and Maria: How children learn a second language.* Reading, MA: Addison-Wesley.

Verhoeven, L., & Snow, C. (Eds.). (2001). *Literacy and motivation: Reading engagement in individuals and groups.* Mahwah, NJ: Lawrence Erlbaum Associates.

Vigil, N., & Oller, J. (1976). Rule fossilization: A tentative model. *Language Learning, 26,* 281-295.

Vygotsky, L. (1962). *Thought and language.* Cambridge, MA: MIT Press.

Vygotsky, L. (1978). *Mind in society: The development of higher psychological processes.* Cambridge, MA: Harvard University Press.

Wallace, M. (1998). *Action research for language teachers.* Cambridge, UK: Cambridge University Press.

Wardhaugh, R. (1970). The contrastive analysis hypothesis. *TESOL Quarterly, 4,* 123-130.

Warschauer, M. (1995). *E-mail for English teaching.* Alexandria, VA: Teachers of English to Speakers of Other Languages.

Warschauer, M. (1999). CALL vs. electronic literacy: Reconceiving technology in the language classroom. Retrieved June 20, 2006, from http://www.cilt.org.uk/research/resfor2/warsum1.htm.

Warschauer, M., & Healey, D. (1998). Computers and language learning: An overview. *Language Teaching, 31,* 57-71.

Weaver, S., & Cohen, A. (1997). *Strategies-based instruction: A teacher-training manual.* Minneapolis: University of Minnesota, Center for Advanced Research on Language Acquisition.

Weigle, S. (2002). *Assessing writing.* Cambridge, UK: Cambridge University Press.

Weir, C. (1990). *Communicative language testing.* New York: Prentice Hall.

Wenden, A. (1992). *Learner strategies for learner autonomy.* New York: Prentice Hall.

Wenden, A. (2002). Learner development in language learning. *Applied Linguistics, 23,* 32-55.

Wenden, A., & Rubin, J. (1987). *Learner strategies in language learning.* New York: Prentice Hall International.

Wesche, M. (1983). Communicative testing in a second language. *Modern Language Journal, 67,* 41-55.

White, R. (1995). *New ways in teaching writing.* Alexandria, VA: Teachers of English to Speakers of Other Languages.

Widdowson, H. (1978). *Teaching language as communication.* Oxford, UK: Oxford University Press.

Wilkins, D. (1976). *Notional syllabuses.* London: Oxford University Press.

Williams, E., & Moran, C. (1989). Reading in a foreign language at intermediate and advanced levels with particular reference to English. *Language Teaching, 22,* 217-228.

Williams, J. (2005). Form-focused instruction. In E. Hinkel (Ed.), *Handbook of research in second language teaching and learning* (pp. 671–691). Mahwah, NJ: Lawrence Erlbaum Associates.

Williams, M., & Burden, R. (1997). *Psychology for language teachers: A social constructivist approach*. Cambridge, UK: Cambridge University Press.

Willis, J. (1996). *A framework for task-based learning*. London: Longman.

Wong, R. (1987). *Teaching pronunciation: Focus on English rhythm and intonation*. Englewood Cliffs, NJ: Prentice Hall Regents.

Wright, T. (1987). *Roles of teachers and learners*. Oxford, UK: Oxford University Press.

Wright, T. (1990). Understanding classroom role relationships. In J. Richards & D. Nunan (Eds.), *Second language teacher education* (pp. 82–97). New York: Cambridge University Press.

Yashima, T. (2002). Willingness to communicate in a second language: The Japanese EFL context. *Modern Language Journal, 86*, 54–66.

Young, R., & He, A. W. (1998, March). Talking and testing: Discourse approaches to the assessment of oral proficiency. Colloquium presented at the American Association of Applied Linguistics, Seattle, WA.

Zamel, V. (1982). Writing: The process of discovering meaning. *TESOL Quarterly, 16*, 195–209.

Zimmerman, C. (1997). Historical trends in second language vocabulary instruction. In J. Coady & T. Huckin (Eds.). *Second language vocabulary acquisition: A rationale for pedagogy* (pp. 5–19). Cambridge, UK: Cambridge University Press.

NAME INDEX

Numbers followed by *f*, *t*, or *n* refer to a figure, table, or source note.

SUBJECT INDEX

Multimedia presentation, 205
Multiple Intelligences (MI),
57–58
Music, 27, 28
Myers-Briggs Type Inventory
(MBTI), 265

Native English-speaking
teachers (NESTs), 137, 138
Native language
pronunciation and, 340
subtractive, 139
used in classrooms, 247–248
used in group work,
227–228
Native language effect, 76–77
Natural Approach, 31–32,
36–37, 419
Needs
analysis of, 152–153
hierarchy of, 86–87, 89
objective, 152
subjective, 153
Needs assessment, 152
New Vistas series (Brown), 276
Nonnative English-speaking
teachers (NNESTs), 137–138
Nonverbal communication,
103, 244
Norm-referenced tests, 447, 467
Notional-Functional Syllabus
(NFS), 32–33, 51

Objective needs, 152
Objectives
enabling, 165
explanation of, 155
of lesson plans, 165–166
terminal, 165
Observation
as assessment tool, 477–478
of other teachers, 490,
492–495
Operant conditioning, 66–67
Opinion exchange, 234–235
Oral communication. *See also*
Spoken language
assessment of, 350–353
correcting form and error
problems in, 344–350

microskills and macroskills
of, 327, 328
principles for teaching,
331–339
problems related to,
304–307, 326–327
research on, 322–325
student-initiated, 332
teaching pronunciation of,
339–344
Organizational competence,
420
Orthography, 364, 398
Overhead projection, 199

Pair work, 230–231
Pedagogical tasks, 51
Peer-assessment, 479
Peer coaching, 503
Peer-editing
example using, 409
function of, 407
used with computer-
assisted language
learning, 202
Perceived meaning, 301
Perceptive reading, 385
Performance-based
assessment, 460, 481–482
Peripheral attention, 101, 113n
Personality tests, 265
Personal writing, 402
Pimsleur Language Aptitude
Battery (PLAB), 454
Placement tests, 454
Podcasts, 204
Portfolios
explanation of, 475–476
teaching, 506–507
Postmethod era
communicative language
teaching and, 45–50,
57–58
content-based instruction
and, 55–56
cooperative learning and,
53
dysfunction of theory-
practice dichotomy and,
41–42

enlightened and eclectic
approach and, 42–44
explanation of, 40–41
interactive learning and,
53–54
learner-centered instruction
and, 52–53
task-based language
teaching and, 50–52
whole language education
and, 54–55
Post-secondary education,
142–143
PowerPoint (Microsoft), 205
Practicality, of assessment,
446–447, 480–481
Practice, 42
Pragmatics, 420
Praise, use of, 253
Prereading phase, 375
Prewriting stage, 404
Principles
cognitive, 63–71
linguistic, 75–80
socioaffective, 71–75
Principles of Language
Learning and Teaching
(Brown), 13, 62
Problematizing, 153–155
Problem solving, 234
Procedures
explanation of, 14, 16, 180
for lesson plans, 166
Process writing, 391–393
Product approach, 391–393
Professional conferences,
504–505
Professional writing, 508
Proficiency levels
ACTFL guidelines for,
114–118
explanation of, 110–112
teaching advanced, 127–129
teaching beginning,
112–113, 118–124
teaching grammar and, 422
teaching intermediate,
124–127
Proficiency tests, 453

NOTES

NOTES

NOTES

NOTES

LINCOLN CHRISTIAN UNIVERSITY

418.0071
B8781T
2007

124245

NOTES

3 4711 00212 0550